PERSPECTIVES ON
CONTEMPORARY ISSUES

PERSPECTIVES ON CONTEMPORARY ISSUES

READING ACROSS THE DISCIPLINES

SEVENTH EDITION

KATHERINE ANNE ACKLEY

Professor Emerita, University of Wisconsin at Stevens Point

CENGAGE
Learning®

Australia • Brazil • Japan • Korea • Mexico • Singapore • Spain • United Kingdom • United States

CENGAGE Learning®

Perspectives on Contemporary Issues: Reading across the Disciplines, Seventh Edition
Katherine Anne Ackley

Product Director: Monica Eckman

Product Manager: Kate Derrick

Content Developer: Kathy Sands-Boehmer

Content Coordinator: Danielle Warchol

Product Assistant: Marjorie Cross

Media Developer: Janine Tangney

Senior Marketing Manager: Lydia LeStar

Rights Acquisitions Specialist: Ann Hoffman

Manufacturing Planner: Betsy Donaghey

Art and Design Direction, Production Management, and Composition: PreMediaGlobal

Cover Image: @ Steiner Steiner/Getty

For product information and technology assistance, contact us at **Cengage Learning Customer & Sales Support, 1-800-354-9706**

For permission to use material from this text or product, submit all requests online at **www.cengage.com/permissions**
Further permissions questions can be emailed to **permissionrequest@cengage.com**

Library of Congress Control Number: 2013941843

ISBN-13: 978-1-285-42584-9

ISBN-10: 1-285-42584-7

Cengage Learning
200 First Stamford Place, 4th Floor
Stamford, CT 06902
USA

Cengage Learning is a leading provider of customized learning solutions with office locations around the globe, including Singapore, the United Kingdom, Australia, Mexico, Brazil, and Japan. Locate your local office at: **www.cengage.com/global.**

Cengage Learning products are represented in Canada by Nelson Education, Ltd.

To learn more about Cengage Learning, visit **www.cengage.com.**

Purchase any of our products at your local college store or at our preferred online store **www.cengagebrain.com**

Printed in the United States of America
2 3 4 5 6 7 18 17 16 15 14

For my family

CONTENTS

PREFACE

Perspectives on Contemporary Issues: Reading across the Disciplines, Seventh Edition, presents an approach to thinking, reading, and writing that views learning as the interconnectedness of ideas and disciplinary perspectives. Contemporary issues engage the students, while the readings provide rich material for class discussion and writing topics. The essays by authors from a variety of disciplines and professions focus on individual, national, and global issues. Regardless of their majors, students will enhance their skills through the writing assignments.

The goals of *Perspectives on Contemporary Issues: Reading across the Disciplines* are as follows:

- To sharpen students' thinking skills by presenting them with a variety of perspectives on current issues
- To give students practice in both oral and verbal expression by providing questions for discussion and writing after each selection
- To provide students with a variety of writing assignments representing the kinds of writing they will be asked to do in courses across the curriculum
- To encourage students to view issues and ideas in terms of connections with other people, other disciplines, or other contexts

The questions for discussion and writing encourage critical thinking by asking students to go well beyond simple recall of the readings and to use higher-order skills such as integration, synthesis, or analysis of what they have read. Most of the questions are suitable for work in small groups, as well as for class discussion.

NEW TO THIS EDITION

New Readings. There are thirty-one new readings in this edition, almost all of them published recently. These new readings cover topics of contemporary interest, and their writers sometimes take controversial positions on the issues under discussion. Furthermore, seven of the chapters have been completely revamped, with three of the four readings being replaced with newer ones.

New visuals.   Almost all of the images in the "Responding to Visuals" sections following chapters in Parts 2–5 are new and, for the first time, in color.

Expanded and revised Chapter 2 on the writing process.   Chapter 2 has been heavily revised to cover every stage of the writing process, with a stress on the distinction between revising and editing. The concept of "challenges" focuses on specific aspects of the process, and each challenge is accompanied by advice on meeting the challenge. There are more boxed guidelines and checklists, more exercises, and a new reading in this chapter.

Longer readings.   Quite a number of the new readings are much longer than the ones that they are replacing. Some instructors prefer longer, more detailed readings; others prefer shorter pieces that express an opinion on a topic quickly and pointedly. This seventh edition has tried to strike a balance by providing both long and short readings.

Increased number of paired arguments.   The number of the chapters with pairs of readings that express differing views on the same subject has been increased.

Changes in some of the chapter titles.   To better reflect the focus of the chapter, several of them have been renamed. Chapter 8 is now "Popular Culture," Chapter 16 is now "International Relations," and Chapter 17 is now "Social Media."

READING SELECTIONS

The book has five parts, and the reading selections are organized by four broad disciplinary areas:

- Part Two, Media Studies, Popular Culture, and the Arts (Chapters 8–11), contains chapters with readings on music and video games, media violence, advertising, Hollywood films, television, and the visual arts.
- Part Three, Social and Behavioral Sciences (Chapters 12–16), addresses such matters as education, poverty and homelessness, gender and sex roles, race and ethnicity, and international relations.
- In Part Four, Science and Technology (Chapters 17–18), writers from a variety of disciplines explore such subjects as the relationships among science, technology, and society; social media; environmental issues; and the ethical implications of technology and human genetic experimentation.
- Part Five, Business and Economics (Chapters 19–21), addresses marketing and the American consumer, the workplace, and American business in the global marketplace.

The selections in each chapter encourage students to consider issues from different perspectives because their authors come from a wide range of disciplinary backgrounds and training. Sometimes the writers cross disciplinary lines in their essays. The individual perspectives of the writers may differ markedly from students' own perspectives, thus generating discussion and writing topics.

ACTIVITIES AND ASSIGNMENTS

After each selection,

- Students can make a **Personal Response** to some aspect of the reading.
- Each reading is also followed by several **Questions for Class or Small-Group Discussion**. These questions invite students to consider rhetorical strategies of the piece, think of larger implications, discuss related issues, or make connections between the readings and their own experiences. Many of these questions are appropriate for writing topics as well, and many others will prompt students to discover related topics on which to write.

Toward the end of each chapter, a section called **Perspectives on . . .** provides writing topics based on ideas generated by the collected readings in that chapter. These writing assignments are arranged in two categories:

- **Suggested Writing Topics** are suitable for synthesis, argumentation, and other modes of writing such as the report, the letter, the personal essay, and the comparison and contrast essay.
- **Research Topics** are suitable for development into research papers.

Finally, each chapter in Parts Two through Five concludes with a section called **Responding to Visuals**, which features two photographs or other visual images. These images relate to the thematic focus of the chapter and are accompanied by questions on rhetorical strategies and other relevant matters.

A DEFINITION OF ISSUES

Given the title of this textbook, a definition of *issues* is in order. An issue is usually taken to mean a topic that is controversial, that prompts differences of opinion, or that can be seen from different perspectives. It often raises questions or requires taking a close look at a problem. Although this is not primarily an argument textbook, the inclusion of topics and essays guaranteed to spark controversy is deliberate. Many of the readings will prompt students to take opposing positions. Some of the readings are provocative; others may anger students. Such differences of opinion generate lively class discussions and result in writing opportunities that engage students.

ACKNOWLEDGMENTS

I would like to thank the following reviewers for their helpful suggestions on this new edition:

James Allen, *College of DuPage*

Rebecca Babcock, *University of Texas, Permain Basin*

Dibaker Barua, *Golden West College*

Yvonne Bruce, *John Carroll University*
Elaine Burklow, *Vincennes University*
Michelle Davidson, *University of Toledo*
Anthony Edgington, *University of Toledo*
David Elias, *Eastern Kentucky University*
John Hodgson, *Cameron University*
Caroline Mains, *Palo Alto College*
John Manear, *Seton-La Salle High School*
William Matsen, *North Hennepin Community College*
Thomas Pfister, *Idaho State University*
Charlene Schauffler, *Kent State University;* and
Mitali Wong, *Claflin University*

As always, I thank my husband, Rich, and my family: Heather, Brian, Elizabeth, and Lucas Schilling; Laurel, Gianni, Zack, and Celia Yahi; Jeremy, Jenni, and Che White; Robin Ackley-Fay and Terry Fay; and Jon Ackley.

Many thanks to the following students who gave permission to use material from their course papers: Erin Anderson, Margo Borden, Morris Boyd, Sam Cox, Rita Fleming, Nathan Hayes, Missy Heiman, Linda Kay Jeske, Kelley Kassien, Kari Kolb, Steph Niedermair, Barbara Novak, Shawn Ryan, Lauren Shimulunas, Jodi Simon, Jennifer Sturm, Cory L. Vandertie, and Melinda Vang.

A special thank you to Professor Beate C. Gilliar, Professor of English at Manchester University, North Manchester, Indiana, and the following students in her expository and critical writing course: Samantha Baker, Megan Batten, Shelby Covington, Stephanie Griffith, Brandon Hite, Catherine Lange, David Lloyd, Amy Luthanen, Holly Pawlak, Rebecca Pendergrass, Alison Scholtfeldt, Kristen Wolf, Maria Villafuerta, and Carol Yañez.

I am especially thankful for the gracious willingness of these students to share their written work for use in this textbook: Elizabeth Schilling, Clorinda Tharp, Michael Vawter, and Laurel Yahi.

Finally, I give a special thank you to my editor, Kathy Sands-Boehmer, who has once again been a joy to work with.

PART **ONE**

Writing Critically and Conducting Research

CHAPTER 1

Reading Critically

RHETORICAL ANALYSIS OF A WRITTEN WORK

Although being critical of someone or something expresses a negative or disapproving opinion, **reading critically** has a different meaning. It is the process of making a careful, thoughtful, and thorough consideration of a piece of writing by looking at its different parts, that is, making a **rhetorical analysis** of the work. **Rhetoric** is the study or examination of written or spoken language, particularly the way in which a writer communicates to an **audience; analysis** is the process of taking something that is whole and complex and breaking it into its individual components to better understand it. Thus, a rhetorical analysis is a close examination of not just what a work says but also how it says it. Although you will not be expected to do a formal rhetorical analysis of every piece you read, you will want to read critically, especially when considering the selections in this textbook. You will want to pay attention to various aspects of the piece as you read for two reasons: first, to understand the written work, and second, to assess it. You read for meaning first because, obviously, you must understand what you read before you can examine it. Once you develop a clear understanding of a piece of writing, you have a solid basis for moving beyond comprehension to evaluation.

The process of reading critically involves examining an author's ideas and the evidence the author has supplied in support of those ideas. It means that you try to recognize the difference between reasonable, logical assertions and those that are unreasonable or lack credibility. It requires you to distinguish between fact and opinion; to sort out the evidence an author cites; and to evaluate that evidence in terms of its relevance, accuracy, and importance. Thus, reading critically means that you actively engage in what you read, you analyze it, and you evaluate it. Learning to be a critical reader also helps to make you a better writer. If you pay attention to the ways in which professional writers and scholars use language, structure their essays, and develop their ideas, you will learn some valuable lessons for your own writing.

The following questions to ask about a written work are useful for getting the most from your reading. They provide guidelines for reading that will also be helpful for any kind of writing required in your college courses, especially the one for which you are using this textbook. If you read the assigned selections carefully, you will very likely be fully prepared to write on one of the topics that end each chapter. Certainly, reading critically is a necessity for any of the varieties of writing and strategies discussed in Part One: summary, critique, argument, synthesis, and the research paper.

Questions to Ask about a Written Work

What Does the Title Tell You?   Before you read, consider the title. A title often not only reveals the subject of the piece, but it can also tell you something about the way in which the subject will be treated. It may indicate the position the author takes on the subject or reflect the tone of the piece. (**Tone** refers to the writer's attitude toward the subject and audience, which is conveyed largely through word choice and level of language usage, such as informal or formal, colloquial, or slang.) A number of essays in this textbook have revealing titles. For instance, the title "Why Legalizing Organ Sales Would Help to Save Lives, End Violence" in Chapter 18 clearly indicates the position of its author, Anthony Gregory, on the subject of legalizing the sale of human organs. You cannot tell from the title alone what his arguments are, but you can expect him to argue in favor of legalizing organ sales. Similarly, the title "What Everglades Pythons and Other Invasive Species Are Trying to Tell Us" in Chapter 19 sets up an expectation that the author, Julia Whitty, will explain her rather provocative title about invasive Everglades species. Sometimes authors ask questions in their titles, as several of the readings in this textbook do, for instance, "Sacred Rite or Civil Right?" in Chapter 14. As readers, we assume that the author, Howard Moody, answers the question he poses in his title. There is no indication in that title, however, of how he answers it.

What Do You Know about the Author?   If information about the author is provided, read it. Knowing who the author is, what his or her profession is, and what his or her publications are, for example, gives you an idea of the authority from which the author writes. In magazines, journals, and collections of essays, such as those you will use in many of your college courses, the headnote often tells you about the author. The headnote is the information located between the title and the beginning of the essay, usually highlighted or set off from the body of the essay itself. Here is the headnote for Karen Sternheimer's "Do Video Games Kill?" (Chapter 8):

> *Karen Sternheimer, whose work focuses on youth and popular culture, teaches in the sociology department at the University of Southern California. She is author of* Celebrity Culture and the American Dream: Stardom and Social Mobility *(2011),* It's Not the Media: The Truth about Pop Culture's Influence on Children *(2003);* Kids These Days: Facts and Fictions about Today's Youth *(2006); and* Connecting Popular Culture and Social Problems: Why the Media Is Not the Answer *(2009). Her commentary has been published in several newspapers, and she has appeared on numerous television and radio programs. This article appeared in the Winter 2007 issue of* Contexts, *a quarterly publication of the American Sociological Association.*

The information about Sternheimer's professional interests as an instructor in the sociology department at the University of Southern California, the titles of her books, and the fact that she is invited to write and speak on her research interests all indicate that she is qualified to write on the subject of the relative harm of video games. The place of publication is also important in establishing Sternheimer's credentials as an authority on her subject: journals or periodic publications of professional associations are usually juried (indicating that not everyone who submits an article will be published), and such publications enhance their authors' scholarly reputations. Such qualifications do not guarantee that you will agree with the author's perspectives on a given subject or that you must adopt her position, but they do give clues as to how well informed about her subject the writer might be.

What Is the Purpose?   Good writers have clear purposes in mind as they plan and draft their work. Most nonfiction writing falls into the categories of **persuasive, expository,** and **expressive** writing. These forms of writing are used to achieve different goals, and they adopt different strategies for achieving those goals. In **persuasive writing,** the emphasis is on the reader: the writer's purpose is to convince the reader of the validity of his or her position on an issue and sometimes even to move the reader to action. In **expository writing,** the goal is to inform or present an objective explanation. The emphasis is on ideas, events, or objects themselves, not on how the writer feels about them. Much of the writing in college textbooks is expository, as are newspaper, magazine, and professional journal articles, and nonfiction books. Expository writing can take many forms, including cause–effect analysis, comparison–contrast, definition, and classification. **Expressive writing** emphasizes the writer's feelings and subjective view of the world. The writer's focus is on personal feelings about, or attitude toward, the subject. A journal or diary includes expressive writing. Persuasive, expository, and expressive writing often overlap, but usually a writer has one main purpose. From the opening paragraphs of a written work, you should be able to determine its general purpose or aim. A clearly implied or stated purpose helps the writer shape the writing, and it helps the reader understand and evaluate the work.

Who Is the Intended Audience?   Writers make assumptions about the people they are writing for, including whether their audience will be sympathetic or opposed to their positions, how informed their readers are about the subjects they are writing on, what their education level is, and similar considerations. These assumptions that writers make about their readers directly influence the tone they use; the evidence they select; the way in which they organize and develop their writing; and even their sentence structure, word choice, and diction level. Knowing whom the writer is addressing helps you understand the writer's point of view and explain the choices the writer has made in writing the piece. In writing for college courses, students usually assume a general audience of people like themselves who are reasonably intelligent and interested in what they have to say. However, professional writers or scholars often write for specific audiences, depending on the publications in which their writing appears. Knowing whether an audience is familiar with a subject or whether the audience is specialized or general also governs what kinds of evidence to offer and how much to include. Where the writing is published gives you a good idea of who the audience is. Take, for instance, Karen Sternheimer's "Do Video Games Kill?" (Chapter 8), mentioned earlier. Her piece appeared in a publication of the professional society associated with her area of expertise, sociology. However, *Contexts* is not a professional journal but rather, according to the website of the American Sociological Association (www.asanet.org), "a quarterly magazine that makes cutting-edge social research accessible to general readers. We're the public face of sociology." Knowing this, you can expect the article to be written in accessible language, addressed to an audience familiar with social issues who will need to be presented with convincing or persuasive evidence in support of her thesis.

What Is the Thesis or Main Idea?   The **thesis** states the main idea of the entire essay. Sometimes it is embodied in a single sentence—the thesis statement— and sometimes it is expressed in several sentences. If the main idea is not explicitly stated, it should be clearly implied. Whether the thesis is explicit or implicit, it is a necessary component of a clearly written work. A thesis helps the writer focus the writing and guides the organization and development of key ideas. It also helps to provide direction to the reader by making clear what the point of the essay is, thereby assisting the reader's understanding of the piece.

What Are the Key Ideas and Supporting Evidence or Details?   For this step in your critical reading, you should underline or highlight the major points of the essay. One important tool for an active, critical reader is a pen or pencil. As you read, underline, star, or in some way highlight major points of development. Look for topic sentences of paragraphs. Although the thesis statement answers the question, What is this essay about? the topic sentence answers the question, What is this paragraph about? If a topic sentence is not clearly stated, it should be clearly implied.

What Helpful Marginal Notes Can You Make as You Read?   In the margins, write your response to a passage or make note of words, phrases, or entire passages you think are important to the piece. Make notes about the evidence or details that support major points. If you have a question about something that the author says, write it in the margin for later consideration. If you are not sure of the meaning of a word, circle it and look it up in a dictionary after you have finished reading. Finally, if you are struck by the beauty, logic, or peculiarity of a passage, note marginal comments on that as well.

Can You Summarize What You Have Read in Your Own Words?   This is the point at which you test your understanding of what you have read. Go back now and look at your underlining and notations. Then try to state in your own words what the writing is about and the main points that the writer makes. If you can accurately summarize a piece of writing, then you probably have a good idea of its meaning. Summarizing also helps you recall the piece later, perhaps in class or in small-group discussions. Incidentally, summarizing is also a good strategy for your own study habits. After reading an assignment for any of your courses, try to write or tell someone a summary of your reading. If you cannot express in your own words the major ideas of what you have just read, you should reread. For a more detailed discussion of writing a summary, see Chapter 3.

How Would You Evaluate What You Have Read?   When you are sure that you understand what you have read and can summarize it objectively, you are ready to respond. You can evaluate something in many ways, depending on its purpose. First, consider whether the author achieves the stated or implied purpose and whether the thesis or main idea is thoroughly explained, developed, or argued. Has the writer supplied enough details, examples, or other evidence? If you are evaluating an argument or persuasion essay, is the evidence convincing to you? Does the piece make a logical and reasonable argument? Are you persuaded to the writer's position? What questions do you have about any of the writer's assertions? Do you wish to challenge him or her on any points? If the purpose of the essay is to describe, has the writer conveyed to you the essence of the subject with appropriately vivid language? For any piece of writing, you can assess how well written it is. Is it organized? Is the writing clear to you? Does the introduction give you enough information to get you easily into the essay, and does the conclusion leave you satisfied that the writer has accomplished the purpose for the essay? In Chapter 4, Writing a Critique, you will find a more detailed discussion of how to evaluate a passage or an entire essay.

GUIDELINES FOR READING CRITICALLY

- Consider what the title tells you about the essay.
- Try to learn something about the author.
- Determine the purpose of the writing.
- Determine the audience for whom the piece was written.
- Locate the thesis statement or main idea.
- Locate key ideas and supporting evidence or details.
- Make marginal notes as you read, including not only a summary of key ideas but also your questions about the content.
- Summarize what you have read.
- Evaluate what you have read.

ILLUSTRATION: READING CRITICALLY

A demonstration of how a reader might apply the guidelines for critical reading accompanies the following essay, "What's in a Name? More than You Think," by Joe Saltzman. Read the essay first, noticing words and passages that are underlined and addressed in the marginal comments. Then read the discussion following it and consider the ways in which your own critical reading might differ from the comments there. Would you add anything? What other words or passages would you underline or highlight? What other marginal comments would you make?

WHAT'S IN A NAME?
MORE THAN YOU THINK

JOE SALTZMAN

Academic and professional credentials.

Joe Saltzman is associate mass media editor of USA Today; *associate dean and professor of journalism, University of Southern California Annenberg School for Communication, Los Angeles; and director of the Image of the Journalist in Popular Culture, a project of the Norman Lear Center. He is author of* Frank Capra and the Image of the Journalist in American Film *(2002). Recipient of more than fifty awards, Saltzman produces medical documentaries, acts as a senior investigative producer for* Entertainment Tonight, *and writes articles, reviews, columns, and opinion pieces for hundreds of magazines and newspapers. In this piece, which first appeared in the July 2003 issue of* USA Today Magazine, *Saltzman's use of the phrase "the war in Iraq" refers to the period between the invasion of Iraq by a coalition of American, British, and Australian forces on March 20, 2003, and President George W. Bush's declaration on May 1, 2003, that combat operations in Iraq were over. "The aftermath" is that period immediately following President Bush's declaration.*

His subject.
His thesis—
note word
choice.

Television coverage of the Iraqi war and postwar illustrates once again how American television news is obsessed with show business terminology that at the very least is poor journalism and at its worst corrupts and ignores a basic rule of journalism: fairness and accuracy in all reporting.

With the government's public relations arm pushing hard, phrases to describe the war and postwar stories moved from a fair account of what was going on to an oppressive vocabulary that gave a spin to the coverage. <u>Colorful phrases, sometimes patriotic, sometimes just plain wrong, gave much of the TV news coverage a convenient anti-Iraqi/pro-American stance.</u> Some examples:

<u>"Operation Iraqi Freedom"</u> was used constantly by Fox and MSNBC as a banner for summing up the coverage of the war in the Middle East. Few would dispute that "Operation Iraqi Freedom" <u>sounded noble and gave a heroic and honorable reason for going to war as opposed to the accurate and more evenhanded "The War in Iraq" or "The Iraqi Conflict."</u> Fighting for a country's freedom brings images of the American and French revolutions, of World War II soldiers fighting against Hitler and the Japanese, and of friendly, grateful citizens waving American flags to greet soldiers who had liberated their country. These images neatly fit with a title like "Operation Iraqi Freedom." "The War in Iraq" conjures up destruction and death. It is one thing for the Administration to use favorable phrases to win support for its policies, quite another for the American media to use such phrases in trying to describe what is going on in a Middle East war.

<u>"Coalition forces" sounds as if a worldwide coalition of military force is being used to fight the war.</u> It's certainly the Bush-approved term for the American and British forces fighting in Iraq. News organizations, however, shouldn't use phrases that do not adequately describe the situation. It <u>was American soldiers in Baghdad</u>, not coalition forces, but most of the news media used the phrase "coalition forces" throughout the coverage of the war.

Going into a foreign country to get rid of <u>"weapons of mass destruction"</u> makes sense. As *Time* magazine put it, "they sound so much more <u>fearsome</u> than chemical or biological weapons. A few papers, like *the New York Times,* have been careful to use 'unconventional weapons' or other terms instead."

If you were trying to figure out whether the war in Iraq was justified, see which sentence would convince you: "Operation Iraqi Freedom was underway as coalition forces went into Iraq to discover and destroy weapons of mass destruction"; or "The war in Iraq was underway as American and British forces went into Iraq to discover and destroy unconventional weapons."

<u>"Collateral damage"</u> doesn't sound as horrific as civilian casualties or, even more accurately, civilians who were wounded, maimed, or killed by American bombs and ground fire.

<u>Certain phrases make a difference in our perception of what goes on in our world. Catchphrases that make unpopular</u>

Restates thesis.

1st example: "Operation Iraqi Freedom"— sounds noble and heroic.

2nd example: "coalition forces"—says there was no coalition, just American soldiers.

3rd example: "weapons of mass destruction"— sound fearsome.

Restates main point.

4th example: "collateral damage"— softens the reality.

Reaffirms his position: using catchphrases is demeaning.

Shifts focus to visual images. Says "embedded journalists" give distorted view of war.

Not opposed to embedded reporters, but there should be a broader perspective of what's going on.

Look up definition of "myopic."

Journalists guilty of censorship— kept pictures of POWs and wounded civilians out of media.

Showing "offensive" pictures might balance the picture of war. TV news media need to change approach to reporting war.

events less difficult to accept should not be a part of daily news media coverage. It demeans both the journalist and the viewer.

Many watching the television war coverage were impressed with the pictures sent back by "embedded" journalists traveling with various military units in the field. And many of the images and reports were spectacular, but at what cost? No one would deny that reporters embedded with individual units would be partial to the people around them saving their lives. No one would deny that this kind of coverage simply gives the viewer a glimpse at specific moments in war. No embedded reporter has the chance or the ability to interview the other side during a battle. In many ways, this coverage, while unique in the history of war reporting, gave an even more-distorted view of what was going on in the field than battle reports issued by reporters safely away from the sounds and sights of immediate warfare.

None of this is to say that we shouldn't have reports from embedded reporters. It is one more attempt to figure out what is going on during wartime. It must be put into proper perspective, however. The British broadcasters and the Middle East press did an effective job in showing other sides of the war, other sides that were either not reported by the American news media or given short shrift next to the action-packed, myopic reports from embedded correspondents in the field.

Perhaps even more damaging was the news media's attempt to "censor" unpleasant sights and sounds from the battlefield because they were worried about offending American sensibilities. The most-grievous example was the failure of U.S. news media to show the footage of the American prisoners of war when the entire world was watching what was happening to them. Moreover, other pictures of wounded Iraqi civilians were also missing in much of the American news media coverage. Many viewers turned to other sources for news of the war—newspapers, magazines, the Internet, the BBC, and cable stations showing some of the foreign coverage.

The TV news media never should assume the role of a parent deciding what images and sounds the American people should be allowed to see. While it is true that pictures of wounded Iraqi civilians and abused POWs do not give viewers an accurate and complete picture of the war by themselves, they would have been an important addition to the embedded war coverage of bullets and sand-clouded battles. One wonders what the news media would have shown, however, if an embedded reporter was suddenly blown to bits on camera.

> War is always brutal and the images always horrible and hard to watch. If the American TV news media want to cover modern warfare, they will have to do far more than give us fancy showbiz titles and only the sounds and images that they deem suitable for G-rated TV news.

DISCUSSION OF "WHAT'S IN A NAME? MORE THAN YOU THINK"

Title.   The title tells readers the subject of the article—names and their connotations—but not what kinds of names. The title does suggest that the author is going to be critical of whatever sort of naming he discusses in the paper (names mean "more than you think").

Author.   The information in the headnote suggests that the author seems well qualified to write critically of news reporting. He is a mass media editor of a major news magazine and a professor of journalism. He is active in his discipline, has published a book on the image of journalists in film, and has received numerous awards for his professional work.

Audience.   The headnote also says that "What's in a Name? More than You Think" was first published in *USA Today Magazine,* a publication for a general audience of urban readers who like to get the essentials of news stories quickly. Saltzman likely assumed an audience of educated readers who want analyses of important national and international developments but who do not necessarily have the time to read lengthy articles on those topics. Saltzman therefore writes in a style appropriate to newspapers and news magazines—that is, he avoids informal language such as slang or colloquialisms as well as specialized terms or difficult vocabulary. He uses words and terms that would be familiar to an audience of readers who keep up on America's involvement in Iraq. His word choice and sentence structure are appropriate for educated adults interested in the news.

Purpose and Main Idea.   Saltzman states his subject and main idea in his first sentence: he believes that television coverage of the Iraqi war and postwar is unfair and inaccurate. He elaborates in the second paragraph by suggesting that TV reporters gave in to pressure from the government and adopted "an oppressive vocabulary" to give "spin" to their coverage of the war. We know from the headnote that Saltzman was writing not long after President Bush declared that the coalition invasion of Iraq was over, so his use of present tense is appropriate for reporting what was going on at the time he wrote his piece. [A further comment on verb tenses: when you are writing about another piece of writing, whether fiction or nonfiction, use present tense to discuss what the writer says in the piece.] He uses language that makes his view of such reporting quite clear when he accuses television news of being "obsessed with show business terminology," which "corrupts and ignores" the basic rule of journalism to be fair and accurate in its reporting. It is clear from those opening paragraphs that his purpose is to argue that American television news reporters have been unfair, inaccurate, and demeaning in their reporting of the war in Iraq and its aftermath.

Key Ideas and Supporting Evidence.   Saltzman primarily uses **exemplification** to develop his **argument.** In paragraphs 3–6, he gives examples of the phrases that he finds offensive in American television news reporting, along with his explanation of why their use is bad journalism. He believes that the phrase "Operation Iraqi Freedom," with its associations of patriotism and nobility, is appropriate for the administration, but not for reporters, who are supposed to remain neutral and unbiased. His preferred phrase would be "The War in Iraq." Next he cites the phrase "coalition forces," which suggests a worldwide joining of military forces, when, he asserts, it was only British and American soldiers who were fighting in Baghdad. He goes on to "weapons of mass destruction," a phrase that suggests something quite fearsome, as opposed to a more neutral phrase like "unconventional weapons." His last example is "collateral damage," which he says downplays or helps soften the reality that the phrase refers to "civilian casualties" or "civilians who were wounded, maimed, or killed by American bombs and ground fire" (paragraph 6).

After arguing that the language of American television news reporters is unfair and biased, he goes on to discuss the images that were broadcast on television. He believes that using "'embedded' journalists" gave a narrow, distorted view of the battlefield and that viewers did not get a proper perspective of what was going on in the war. His last example is the "even more damaging" attempts by the media to "'censor' unpleasant sights and sounds from the battlefield" because they did not want to offend "American sensibilities." His point about both embedded journalists and attempts to withhold disturbing images is that reporters give a narrow and distorted perspective of what was happening during the war and what has been going on after it. He argues for a broader picture of the realities of war. Saltzman concludes by asserting that if American television news media want to cover modern warfare, they must drop the "fancy showbiz titles" and stop "censoring" images they believe Americans would find disturbing.

Summary.   In "What's in a Name? More than You Think," Joe Saltzman argues that American television news reporters violate the basic rules of reporting by using language and making choices that give an unfair, inaccurate, and distorted view of the war in Iraq and its aftermath. He gives a number of examples of language to make his point. He cites the phrase "Operation Iraqi Freedom," which stirs up patriotic feelings, more appropriately the business of the government's public relations people than reporters. Saltzman then asserts that "coalition forces" is a misleading and inaccurate phrase because there were only American soldiers in Baghdad, not an alliance of many forces from around the world. His remaining two examples are "weapons of mass destruction," with its connotations of terror, and "collateral damage," which softens the reality of what the term actually denotes. From language, Saltzman moves to the images that were broadcast on television. The use of embedded reporters to cover the war was not a bad idea, he says, but it narrowed the view of the war rather than helped present a broad perspective of what was going on. Worse, he argues, was the decision not to show images of the abuses of prisoners of war and wounded Iraqi citizens. Such a failure amounts to censorship. He concludes by reasserting his major point that American television journalists failed in their coverage of the war in Iraq and the period after the war, and he suggests that they change their ways if they want to report modern warfare accurately and fairly.

Evaluation.   Saltzman's essay is organized sensibly and logically written in clear, straightforward prose. Although the article was published some time ago and the specific events referred to are well in the past, Saltzman's discussion of the ethics and language of journalism is still timely. His use of specific examples and his reasons why they are inappropriate make a convincing case for his argument that American television journalists were inaccurate and unfair in their reporting of the Iraq war. The repetition of "no one would deny" in paragraph 8 lends emphasis to the point he is making about the limited perspective of embedded reporters. Furthermore, the disclaimer in the first sentence of paragraph 9 is his concession, in a way, to readers who may think that he is being overly critical of embedded reporters, and it leads to his repeating—and emphasizing—his opinion. Despite Saltzman's excellent use of examples to support and develop his central idea, he does not go into real depth in his analysis of any of them. It is quite possible that space limitations imposed by the magazine kept him from a fuller discussion. The fact that many of his paragraphs are short—one or two sentences in several cases—may reflect his training in journalism: the physical space of newspaper and in some cases magazine columns require shorter paragraphs.

Saltzman is an accomplished writer who is not afraid to express opinions that may not be popular with the general public, and these opinions raise questions that bear further exploration and thought. His assertion that American television news reporting of war should give a broader picture, showing if possible the perspective of the enemy and the effects of war on the people we are fighting, is fair. On the other hand, is it the place of the press to be critical of the administration or to challenge the decisions of its country's leaders in time of war? Is it not important to keep up morale on the home front as well as on the battlefield? What is gained by a press hostile to or even subversive of its government in a time when patriotism and public support of its military are crucial to the war effort? These are tough questions that both the press and its critics have been struggling with, and Saltzman's essay is a good starting place for an open discussion of the issues he raises.

EXERCISE

Select one reading that interests you from Parts Two through Five. As you read it, apply the guidelines for reading critically, as illustrated earlier. Your instructor may want you to write out your rhetorical analysis or make notes for classroom discussion.

RHETORICAL ANALYSIS OF VISUALS

Rhetorical considerations apply to visual images as well as to written forms of communication. Whether you are critiquing an essay in a book or periodical, a visual art form, or an Internet website, questions of audience, tone, purpose, organization, content, and meaning apply. With visuals, as with written works, you must consider perspective or **point of view, context,** and **connotation.** Connotation—the emotional associations of a thing—is perhaps even more important when viewing visuals than in reading words. Just as words have associations that go beyond the literal term or add layers of meaning to what they denote ("the dictionary definition"), so images have powerful associations. Images often have the ability to express things—emotions, nuances, insights—in a way that words cannot. They can reveal what is difficult to put into words by conveying impressions or depicting in sharp detail what it would take a great many words to describe or explain, including subtleties of meaning that emerge only after thoughtful consideration and careful perusal of the image. Visuals also have the potential to argue a viewpoint or persuade an audience; their authors use strategies to present a viewpoint or make a statement that is similar to those used by authors of written text.

We see images daily in a variety of forms—in photographs, drawings, paintings, pictures, brochures, advertisements, CD album covers, posters, and Internet web pages, and of course on television and in film. Most of these images go unexamined because we see so many images in our lives that we simply do not have time to analyze them all. But when we find it useful to consider an image closely, how do we analyze it? What can we say about it? How can we express in words what an image means or implies? The answer is that analyzing images critically requires skills that are quite similar to those for analyzing a piece of writing critically. Just as writers select details and organize essays to make specific points, so too do artists shooting a scene or painting a picture select details and arrange them in order to convey specific ideas or impressions. Writers and artists alike make judgments that in turn shape how readers or viewers perceive their work.

Analyzing a visual involves doing a close "reading" of the image and asking a series of questions about it. In looking critically at a visual image, you want to consider many aspects of it: What do you see when you first look at it? How do you respond initially? What details does the image highlight? What other details are included and what might have been excluded? How does the positioning of various elements of the image emphasize its meaning? The following list of questions will help you analyze the visual images that are located throughout the textbook in each of the chapters of Parts Two through Five. The answers you get when you ask these questions can give you a greater understanding of the images you are scrutinizing. Most of the visual images reproduced in this textbook are photographs or drawings, so the first set of questions is designed to help you in your analysis of them. However, the questions can easily be adapted to other kinds of images, such as advertisements, newspaper page layouts, and Internet web pages. Furthermore, television, film, music videos, and documentaries also convey messages through images that can be analyzed rhetorically in much the same way as the other forms of visual communication can be.

Questions to Ask about a Visual Image

- **What is your overall immediate impression of the image?** First impressions often linger even after rethinking one's initial response, so what strikes you immediately about an image is particularly important.

- **What detail first catches your attention?** After noting your immediate overall response, consider what detail or details first attract you. Is it the prominence, size, or positioning of the subject? Is it the colors or absence of them? Is it the size, the physical space it occupies? More than likely, the artist wanted you to notice that detail first, and very likely it is an integral part of the "message" or "statement" the image makes.

- **What details emerge after you have studied the image for a while?** Do you detect any pattern in the arrangement of details? If so, how does the arrangement of details function to convey the overall impression?

- **How does the arrangement of objects or people in the picture help draw your attention to the central image, the one you are initially drawn to?** Are some things placed prominently in the center or made larger than others? If so, what is the effect of that arrangement? How does the background function in relation to what is placed in the foreground?

- **If the image is in color, how does the artist use color?** Are the colors selected to represent certain emotions, moods, or other qualities? If it is in black and white, what use does the artist make of the absence of color? Does the artist use degrees of shading and brightness? If so, to what effect?

- **From what perspective does the artist view the subject?** Is it close to or far away from the subject? Is the subject viewed straight-on or from the side? Why do you think the artist selected this particular perspective? How might a shift in perspective alter the view of the subject, not just physically but on the level of meaning as well?

- **What emotions does the image evoke in you?** Why? Which details of the image convey the strongest emotion?

- **Has anything important been left out of the image?** What might have been included, and why do you think it was left out?

- **What is happening in the picture?** Does it tell a story or give a single impression?

- **What does the picture tell you about its subject?** How does it convey that message?

- **If there are people in the image, what can you tell about them?** What details tell you those things? Is it the way they are dressed? Their physical appearance? What are they doing?

- **Does the picture raise any questions?** What would you like to ask about the image, the activity, or the people in it? How would you find the answers to your questions?

EXERCISE

James Schnepf/Getty Images

Figure 1.1 *Man with tattoos on face and chest.*

Ask the relevant questions for analyzing visuals listed earlier as you study the following photograph (Figure 1.1). Then, selecting the details you believe are important, write an analysis of the photograph in either full-length essay or one-paragraph format, depending on what your instructor asks you to do. If your assignment is to write an essay-length analysis, begin with an introductory paragraph that includes a thesis statement or a statement of the main idea of the photograph. This thesis should reflect your understanding of what the photograph means to you—its message, its story, what it suggests symbolically, or whatever ultimately you decide about the photograph. The rest of the paper should draw on details from your answers to the questions as you explain or support your thesis statement. If your assignment is to write a paragraph-length analysis, begin with a sentence that states your understanding of the main idea of the photograph. This is your topic sentence. The rest of the paragraph should supply supporting details from the image that explain or support your topic sentence.

Here are some questions specific to this photograph that you might want to think about as you work through the questions listed earlier:

- Besides showing the tattoo, what effect is achieved by taking the picture looking up from about waist-high?

- Identify the main images in the tattoo. What do the choices that he made to have tattooed on his body suggest to you about the man?

- Do the earrings, nose ring, and stud add anything to your image of the man?

- What does the man's shaved or bald head add to the overall effect?

- Does the man's stance—the way he is standing, the shape of his shoulders, the position of his arms—tell you anything about what he is thinking or how he views himself? Is the man anticipating a challenge? Contemplating something? Feeling secure about himself?

- Comment on the layout of the image, especially the effect of the palm tree fronds behind the man's head.

Questions to Ask about an Advertisement

Advertising is a powerful and pervasive force in our world. Ads have the ability to affect how we think, act, and even feel about ourselves and others. Ads can shape, reflect, or distort both individual perceptions and social values, and they do so by employing some of the classic strategies of argument and persuasion: they have a proposition, they know their audience, they make appeals, they use comparisons and examples, and they particularly want to persuade us to action. In addition to the questions to ask about visual images, the following questions will help you analyze both print and nonprint advertisements:

- **What is the message of the advertisement?** What does it say to potential buyers of the product? That is, what is its argument?

- **Who is the intended audience?** How can you tell?

- **What strategies does the ad use to convey its message?** What appeals—to logic, to emotion, to ethics, or to shared values—does it use? Does it rely primarily on only one appeal, or does it combine them? How do the specific details convey that message?

- **How does the text—the actual words used—convey the message of the advertisement?** How are words arranged or placed in the ad and why are they placed that way? If a nonprint ad, how are the voice-overs or dialogue used to convey the message?

- **How would you describe the style and tone of the advertisement?** How do they help convey the message or sell the product?

EXERCISE

1. Select a print advertisement for analysis. Ask the questions noted in the previous section and write an analysis based on your notes, assessing the effectiveness of the ad in achieving its purpose. Attach the advertisement with your analysis when you hand it in to your instructor.
2. Select two advertisements for the same kind of product (for instance, clothing, toothpaste, or laundry detergent). Apply the questions noted in the previous section and choose the one that you think is more effective at selling or promoting the product. Formulate a thesis sentence that states your preference, and use details from your scrutiny of both of them to support that statement.

Questions to Ask about a Newspaper Page

Newspapers can shape reader response in the choices they make about the layout of text and photographs. Although we like to think that newspapers are unbiased in their reporting of news items, reading just two different newspapers on the same subject reveals that the choices a newspaper makes about a news item have a huge influence on the impressions it leaves on readers. Just the visual effect of a page layout alone tells us many things. What page an article or picture appears on and where on the page it is located represent a judgment on the part of the paper about the importance of the article or image and cannot help but shape how readers respond to it. Consider the following list about photographs and news articles when looking at a newspaper page:

- **Where in the paper is the article or photograph placed?** Front-page placement indicates that the newspaper considers it more important as a news item than placement on the inside pages.

- **How are photographs and news articles positioned on the page?** Items that are placed high on the page or in the center of the page are likely to draw the attention more readily than those placed low or off center.

- **How large are the photographs or the headlines?** Visually, larger photographs or headlines are likely to draw attention and interest more quickly than smaller ones.

- **Are photographs in color or black and white?** Choosing to run a picture in color indicates a value judgment that the paper has made about the interest or newsworthiness of the image.

EXERCISE

1. Select a newspaper page for analysis. Front pages are particularly important in newspapers for attracting reader attention, so perhaps you will want to analyze the front page of the newspaper. Ask the questions listed earlier and write an analysis based on the answers to your questions. What article(s) does the newspaper think more important than others? How are photographs used on the page? Attach the page with your analysis when you hand it in to your instructor.

2. Select two different newspapers covering the same news story and compare their treatment of the story. How do the two newspapers compare and contrast in their handling of the story? Is one more effective than the other in reporting it? Formulate a thesis that reflects your ultimate judgment of the two papers' treatment of the news story and support that thesis with details gathered from your comparison of the two.

RHETORICAL ANALYSIS OF WEBSITES

The Internet provides a seemingly endless variety of sites to visit for every taste and interest. Web pages can function rhetorically to influence visitors to the site in much the same way as other forms of discourse. The very way in which the web page is constructed can work to produce a desired effect, especially if the constructor of the site wishes to persuade an audience, sway opinion, or impose a particular point of view. A rhetorical analysis looks at the ways a site achieves its stated or implied purpose. Because websites vary considerably in their reliability and currency, you will find additional information about evaluating them in Chapter 7. Many of the same questions one asks when evaluating a website apply when doing a rhetorical analysis of it. What follows are some questions to ask as you analyze the rhetorical effectiveness of a website whose goal is to inform, educate, or entertain.

Questions to Ask about a Website

- **Who created the web page?** Is it an individual, an organization, a government agency, an educational institution, or a corporation? Does the text at the site give you information about the author? If not, why do you think that information is not provided? Does the site tell you how to contact the author?

- **What audience does the web page target?** How can you tell? Is the intended audience stated or implied? Does it make assumptions about values, beliefs, age, sex, race, national origin, education, or socioeconomic background of its target audience?

- **What is the purpose of the website?** Does the web page want to inform, entertain, sell, argue a position, or persuade people to change their minds or to take action? If it has more than one purpose, what combination of purposes does it have? Is the implied purpose the same as the stated purpose? Does the text state one purpose while word choice, graphics, and page layout suggest or imply another? For instance, a political candidate's website might state that it has no intention of bringing up an opponent's past wrongdoings, while the very fact of stating that there are past wrongdoings to bring up casts doubt on the character of the opponent.

- **What rhetorical appeals does the written text make?** Does the text of the website make an appeal to logic or reason? Does it appeal to emotions? If emotions, which ones does it appeal to—pity, fear, joy, anger, sympathy?

- **How would you evaluate the content?** Does the website cover the topic thoroughly? Does it use language that you understand? Does it offer links and, if so, how many links? Are the links still active? What is the quality of the links?

- **What use does the site make of color?** How does the background color choice affect the mood and tone of the page? Is it a vibrant color or a sober one? Does it intrude on the text or enhance it?

- **What do you observe of the page layout?** Is there space between items on the page or are things cramped together? How does the use of space on the page affect your overall impression of the page and your ability to read it?

- **What gets loaded first when you go to the web page? Where is that material positioned?** What is loaded later or positioned low on the page?

Sometimes certain components of a web page are purposely programmed to load first in order to further emphasize the purpose of the site.

- **Are graphics on the web page static or active?** Is the print used for the text large, small, or a mix of both? If a mix, what does larger print emphasize that smaller print doesn't? What font is used? Are bold print, italics, or underlining used, and if so, to what effect? Is there a banner? What purpose does the banner serve?

- **If photographs or other images are used, what is their function?** Do they illustrate or help explain something, give information, or serve to decorate the page?

- **Does the web page make use of contrasts of light and dark?** If so, what is the effect of those contrasts?

EXERCISE

Locate two websites on the same topic and compare and contrast their rhetorical effectiveness by applying the relevant questions listed earlier. After deciding which one you think is more effective, write an analysis in which your thesis states which site you prefer. Use details from your perusal of both of them as proof or evidence to support your thesis statement.

Forums on the Web

In addition to websites that people go to for information, entertainment, or news, the Internet has available a number of forums for people to participate in, such as chat rooms, newsgroups, discussion lists (listservs), blogs, and social networking sites. Although most websites are fairly dynamic in that they are (or should be) regularly updated, forums typically change throughout the day. Popular forums such as **listservs, blogs,** and **social networking sites** are capable of influencing people's views or the way they think about the topics being discussed at the sites; they even have the potential to actually bring about changes because of the high degree of involvement that they have generated among visitors to their sites. Another distinguishing characteristic of such sites is that people are invited to participate in an ongoing, ever-changing discussion. People who become members of these sites have an opportunity to be not just passive readers but also active writers.

Listservs.   Listservs are e-mail–based discussion groups linked to specific topics. Listservs function as forums for the exchange of ideas, where members can debate, discuss, post news items, seek or give advice, and share in a community of people who have in common their interest in the topic of the listserv. Although listservs have official websites where people can subscribe, read the rules for posting, and locate archived postings, among other things, the real activity takes place through e-mail. Members can elect to receive messages either individually as they are posted or in digests that are sent daily, or whenever a specific number of messages have posted. Members are usually required to follow certain standards, primarily those related to conduct and appropriate content, and often the listserv has a moderator who monitors the content of messages to make sure that posts do not violate those rules. Listservs typically archive messages by date, subject of message, and/or author, and these archives can be viewed by nonmembers as well as members. They vary widely in membership numbers, from just a few people to thousands. Because listservs attract people with at least the subject of the listserv in common, they can create a strong sense of community among subscribers. Although listservs are good for reading what many people have to say on various subjects related to the primary topic of the discussion group, postings are, in general, unedited and may not be completely reliable. On the other hand, a posting that seems wrongheaded or erroneous is likely to be corrected or at least commented on by other members of the group.

Blogs.   The term *blog* (web log) describes an activity that people had been doing long before the term was coined: maintaining a website where they record personal thoughts and provide links to other sites. Many of them are essentially personal pages that bloggers (owners of the sites) update daily. They provide a forum for the bloggers themselves to argue, explain, comment on, vent frustrations, air opinions, or just gossip, while visitors to the site can express their own opinions or make observations. Membership is not required; anyone can read and respond to anyone's blog. In addition to online journals, blogs can be news summaries, collections of bits and pieces from other websites, and valuable resources for instant access to the latest news. Thus blogs have been described as a cross between an online diary and a cybermagazine, but one of the key characteristics of the most successful or popular blogs is that they are constantly updated. Although just a few years ago there were only a small number of blogs, today there are millions of them. Many blogs are run by professionals like educators, reporters, researchers, scientists, and political candidates, with visits to the sites numbering in the thousands and in a few cases millions, but the vast majority are run by individuals who see them as chatty, stream-of-consciousness journals and whose readership is very limited.

A few blogs have attracted so many readers that they have achieved or exceeded the kind of readership that large newspapers enjoy. Because of the sheer number of readers and their ability to communicate instantly with other bloggers around the world, a few blogs have been responsible for bringing to light events or issues that mainstream media have ignored by focusing public attention on a current issue. Blogs with the most impact on public affairs appear to be those with large numbers of daily visitors, and they tend to have the most influence in politics. Blogs have certain common features, including making it convenient for people to post or respond to the blog owner, posting messages in reverse chronological order for others to read, and providing links to other blogs and websites. However, blogs differ greatly in the quality and reliability of the information at the site. Blogs by definition are logs or journals and as such are often unedited, not-very-well-thought-out musings on a variety of topics. Be very careful when choosing blogs to follow and even more careful in accepting as truth what you read on a blog. You can apply the same questions to blogs that you would use for analyzing other websites rhetorically, but keep in mind the special nature of blogs and how their unrestricted, constantly changing content is very likely slanted or biased to fit the viewpoint of the blogger.

Social Networking Websites.   There are many online services dedicated to establishing networks among people. Some are fairly limited to certain groups of people, such as those graduating from a particular high school or college or those belonging to certain ethnic, religious, or even family groups. Two worldwide, all-encompassing, and well-established services are Facebook and Twitter. Facebook users can register personal information, communicate with friends and colleagues, post pictures, and establish networks with people all over the world. Twitter is similar in purpose to Facebook but is a micro-blogging site that limits messages to 140 characters. Twitter emerged as a significant service when users began posting what was happening at moments of key social and political unrest or upheaval. As with all websites with countless users of all political, social, economic, and ethnic backgrounds, postings can be extremely biased and inaccurate.

EXERCISE

Select one of the following:
1. Locate two listservs on topics that interest you and read a few days' worth of posts. How do they compare and contrast? What is your impression of the sense of community among the members? What sorts of posts do people send? Do they stay on topic? Do the listservs have moderators? If you were going to join a listserv, which one would you prefer?
2. Locate several blogs on a topic that interests you—baseball, water skiing, crime prevention, politics, a hobby, your major—and assess their rhetorical effectiveness, using the guidelines discussed.
3. Follow a thread or two on a social networking service and assess the sorts of postings people make. How would you characterize the sense of community among the posters? How would you rate the quality of the comments? What conclusions can you draw about the usefulness or purpose of the service?

CHAPTER 2

The Writing Process

Writing for any purpose involves a progression of stages that begins with determining your purpose, then finding what you want to say, developing a strategy for organizing your thoughts, writing a rough draft, revising, editing, and, last, proofreading the final copy. All writers, not just college students, benefit from treating a written endeavor as a process. Even professional writers plan, draft, revise, and edit before turning in their work. This chapter discusses the challenges that writers face in the writing process, suggests ways to meet those challenges, and provides guidelines for revising and editing their paper. The guidelines presented here assume that you are writing for a college class and that your instructor has given you at least a general or broad subject area to write about with a specified purpose. Often instructors give students a number of choices, but they still outline their expectations for the assignment.

The writing process can be frustrating because it is made up of many components. The key to writing well is to take those components in turn, focusing on each stage rather than worrying about producing a perfect end product right from the beginning of the assignment. It takes time to discover how you are going to approach an assignment, what you have to say about your topic, and how you are going to organize your ideas into a clear, coherent whole. Good writers know that writing often involves false starts, wrong turns, and dead ends; but they also know that giving the writing assignment thought and taking time to prewrite, plan, draft, and revise will produce a sense of satisfaction when they hand in their finished paper to the instructor.

CHALLENGES IN THE PREWRITING STAGE

Prewriting is the first stage of any writing project and includes everything you do before you write your first draft. At this stage, you want to think about the best approach to your subject. You want to determine your purpose, identify your audience, and explore ideas. Whether your instructor has given you a specific assignment or you are to select your own from a variety of possibilities, you need to spend time thinking about the assignment, identifying what you already know about it, discovering what you need to know, and narrowing your focus from a general subject to a specific topic. The practices used in prewriting usually spill over into other stages of the writing process as well. Through drafting, revising, editing, and producing the finished product, you are thinking about your topic, discovering new strategies or information, and determining how best to organize, develop, and polish your piece.

Challenge: Determining a Purpose.
A paper without a purpose wanders aimlessly, making the writing task difficult. As a result, the paper is vague and fails to engage reader interest.

Meeting the Challenge. Make sure that you understand the requirements of the assignment and spend time thinking about how best to satisfy those requirements. As mentioned in Chapter 1, most writing can be classified as one of several types: argumentative, expository, or expressive. These types take many forms and have differing purposes. Are you to argue a position, persuade an audience to take action, explain a phenomenon, analyze an event, conclude something, or describe or narrate an experience? Are you to write a summary or a critique? Perhaps you are to examine the ideas of several people on a specific topic, arrive at your own conclusions, and then incorporate the comments of those people into your own argument or explanation. It is crucial that you know what you hope to accomplish with the piece of writing at the beginning of each written assignment. Knowing your purpose puts you on the right track for the other stages of the process.

Challenge: Identifying Your Audience.
Even with a clear understanding of purpose, you may not achieve your goal if you do not know the audience you are to address in the assignment.

Meeting the Challenge. Often the nature of a writing assignment will help determine your audience. For college work, your audience may be your instructor alone, but more often it includes your writing group, your classmates, or an audience whom you identify specifically for the assignment. Ask yourself whether you are writing to a group of peers, to an older or younger audience, to those in authority, or to the general public. Each audience requires a different approach to your subject if you are to achieve your purpose. For instance, if you are to argue a position on a controversial topic, it makes a difference whether you write to people who agree with you or to those who disagree with you. Your argument is likely to be more effective if you write to an audience who needs to be convinced because such an audience requires strong proof or persuasive evidence. If your purpose is to explain, illustrate, or analyze, your audience is likely to be informed in general, but not have a deep understanding of your subject. Unless instructed otherwise, assume an intelligent audience of nonspecialists who are interested in learning more about the topic of your paper. Imagining this audience will keep you from having to define or explain every term or concept and will give you room for interesting, informative, and/or intriguing material about the topic. Whether your instructor tells you what audience to write for or leaves the selection of an audience up to you, knowing whom you are writing to or for will help you determine details you need to include in your paper.

Challenge: Generating Ideas and Discovering Your Topic.   Students sometimes are stumped right at the beginning of the writing process because they believe they have nothing to say. This early challenge requires an investment of time that will make the drafting process go much more smoothly later on.

Meeting the Challenge. After establishing your purpose and audience, turn your thoughts next to the task of coming up with ideas or details that you can use in your paper. A number of useful exercises will help you discover what you know about your subject, generate ideas for your paper, and open up ways for you to narrow your subject to a workable topic. Keep in mind the distinction between **subject** and **topic**: subject is the general area of investigation or thought, whereas topic is one narrow aspect of that subject. These exercises will help you come up with ideas for your topic:

- **Brainstorming or free writing.** This act involves simply writing without stopping for a set time, noting everything that occurs to you as you think about your subject. Time yourself for five or ten minutes while you write on a blank sheet of paper or your computer everything that occurs to you about your broad subject in an effort to narrow to a workable topic. When your time is up, read through everything that you have written. Look for ideas that you think are promising for your assignment, and if you need to explore them further, brainstorm or freewrite on those, or try one of the other exercises for generating ideas.

- **Asking questions.** A good way to find out more about your subject is to simply ask questions about it. The most obvious questions are those that journalists routinely use: Who? What? When? Where? Why? How? Depending on your initial broad subject area, any of the following may help you come up with ideas for your paper: Who is affected? Who is responsible? What does it mean? When did it happen or take place? How is it done? Why does it matter? How does it work? What are its components? What happened? Where did it happen? Why did it happen? As you can tell, not every question is relevant for a subject, but asking some of them about your subject when appropriate alerts you to areas that you may need to explore and helps anticipate the kinds of questions readers may have when reading your paper.

- **Making lists.** List everything you know or are curious about for the subject you are working on. Listing is similar to brainstorming but involves just making a simple list of ideas, thoughts, or information related to your subject. Sometimes seeing ideas, concepts, or key words in a list leads to further development of those things.

- **Clustering around a central idea.** Clustering involves placing a key word or central idea in the center of your page and writing related words, phrases, or ideas around this central idea. As you move out from the central point by creating related ideas, you may see patterns emerge or recognize ways to develop your topic.

- **Talking to others.** Discussing your subject with other people can be enormously helpful, whether it be friends, classmates, or your instructor. Often discussing a subject out loud with someone else helps you clarify thoughts or discover new ideas or approaches.

- **Researching.** Reading about or researching your subject will give you information, details, or arguments that you can use in your writing assignment. If you use the Internet to locate information, be cautious about which sources you accept. Keeping in mind the guidelines in Chapter 1 on evaluating Internet sources, choose your search engine from among the best known or most used; they are likely to be the most reliable.

If you use any of these techniques—brainstorming/freewriting, asking questions, listing, clustering, talking to others, researching your area of interest—you should be able to come up with narrow aspects of the general subject from which you can select what you want to write about. If one technique does not work, try another, and keep at it until you are satisfied with the topic you have generated.

Challenge: Adopting an Appropriate Tone.   Conveying the wrong tone, or attitude toward subject and audience, suggests to your readers that you are not comfortable with your purpose, topic, or nature of your audience or that you are unsure of yourself as a writer.

Meeting the Challenge. Adopt a suitable tone to your purpose and audience and that accurately conveys your attitude toward your subject. Tone is conveyed through word choice, diction, and even the way you structure sentences. It reflects your attitude toward your subject and your view of yourself as writer. Thus, you want to use language that reflects your confidence as a writer and that successfully achieves your purpose. Again the questions of why you are writing, what you hope to achieve, and to whom you are writing are important. You want to be authoritative but not overly artificial and stilted, nor do you want to be too informal. Before writing your first draft, you should be aware of the tone you will take in your paper. Even if your audience is your peers, you would not write in an assignment the way you might talk to them if you were chatting informally outside class. Likewise, if you attempt a very formal tone that seems unfamiliar to you, the result is likely to be stiff and unnatural. Because tone is linked to purpose and audience, when you have those clearly in mind, you will have a better idea of the tone you should adopt.

CHALLENGES IN THE DRAFTING STAGE

Having determined your purpose, audience, topic, and tone, you are ready to write. The first draft represents your unpolished initial effort to create the entire essay, to put all of your ideas about your topic into an organized, coherent whole. Your drafting process often begins with fashioning a working title that best reflects what you plan to do in the paper and writing a paragraph that introduces your topic by providing a context or background for it and that leads to a **thesis statement.** This is followed by the **body of your paper,** the paragraphs between your introductory and concluding paragraphs, where you will want to construct fully developed paragraphs, each of which is focused on one specific topic—often stated in a **topic sentence**— that is related to your thesis. Finally, you will bring your paper to an end by writing an appropriate **conclusion.**

Challenge: Drafting a Working Title.   The title is the first thing that your readers see, so a weak or misleading title does not make a good first impression.

Meeting the Challenge. In the draft stage, do your best to come up with a working title, one that best reflects what you think you are going to do in your paper. You will almost surely change your title as your paper goes through various drafts, and you may even want to wait until you have written a draft or two before you create your title. However, many writers find it helpful to have a title in mind as one more aid in focusing the direction of the paper. Titles serve a useful purpose. For example, if you knew nothing but the title of Kevin Fagan's "Homeless, Mike Dick Was 51, Looked 66" (Chapter 13), you would have a fairly good idea of what his article is about. On the other hand, a colorful title may serve to capture or reflect what the paper is about, but in an intriguing way. Thus, Will Wright's title "Dream Machines" (Chapter 8) does not tell readers what his topic is, but it is enticing. As it happens, Wright never uses the phrase "dream machines" in his article, but the content of his piece very clearly indicates what he means by his title.

Challenge: Writing an Introduction.   After reading your title, your audience reads the first paragraph of your paper: introduction. If this introductory paragraph does not adequately set the stage for the rest of the paper, you might lose your readers right at the beginning.

Meeting the Challenge.   Draft an introduction that presents your topic and prepares for the rest of the paper. Writing instructors often advise students to begin with a general statement that serves to intrigue readers or catch their attention. That general sentence leads to more specific sentences, which in turn lead to an even more specific one, the thesis statement. The first paragraph not only introduces readers to the specific focus of the paper but also sets the tone, prepares readers for what is to follow, and engages their interest. As with your title, you may not be satisfied with your introduction in the first draft or two. You may not know exactly how to introduce your paper until you have organized your thoughts and written at least one complete draft. Do not get frustrated if you cannot think of a good introduction as you begin the draft stage. Because of its importance, you will want a working introduction, but most likely your finished version of the introduction will come only after you are fully satisfied with the body of your paper.

An example of an effective introduction is the opening paragraph of Chris Gould's "Batman: The Unexpected Cultural Revolution" (Chapter 10):

> Fifty-five years ago, in 1966, one of the more unusual experiments in American popular culture took place. Producer William Dozier took an almighty gamble by introducing *Batman* to the TV screen via America's ABC network. The caped crime-fighter originally created by Bob Kane had certainly built up a fan base in DC Comics since 1939, but he had never been portrayed the way Dozier presented him. Dispensing with every aspect of the Dark Knight's dark comic book existence, Dozier offered America a laughably gentle Batman who even winced at the bad language used by criminals, such were his outrageously high moral standards. The *Batman* TV show thus became a depiction of pop art utopia, where bright colors forever defeated darkness, where creativity forever defeated logic, and where Good forever triumphed over Evil.

Gould's paragraph is a model of how to introduce one's subject, provide background information, entice readers, and set the stage for what the paper will do. His opening sentences tell readers the specific subject of his paper, whereas his thesis implicitly promises that he will discuss the 1960s *Batman* television series as a "pop art utopia" and give examples of the show's depiction of "bright colors" defeating darkness, of "creativity forever defeat[ing] logic," and of "Good forever triumph[ing] over Evil." Thus Gould's thesis is essentially an outline of what the paper seeks to do.

Challenge: Avoiding Unclear or Weak Focus.   If your essay does not have a clearly recognizable central purpose that is strong or complex enough to warrant a full exploration in your paper, readers will be lost.

Meeting the Challenge. You can sharpen, clarify, or strengthen your focus with a relevant introduction and clear thesis or statement of purpose. Throughout the essay, keep your central purpose in mind and include only material that relates to that purpose. Not every kind of writing requires a thesis, but most do, especially the kinds of writing that you will do for your college courses. Not every thesis needs to be stated explicitly, either, but there must almost always be some clearly implied central point to your writing. For instance, the introduction and thesis in John J. Savant's argumentative essay "Imagining the Immigrant: Why Legality Must Give Way to Humanity" (Chapter 15) establishes the focus of the paper and sets up an expectation about the rest of the essay. Clarifying the focus early on works for both the writer in the process of drafting the essay and readers of the final version:

> Great detectives, we are told, are able to think like criminals. Similarly, effective therapists learn to enter into the fantasies of their patients. These behaviors are a function of that supreme and godlike faculty we call imagination. Unlike daydream or fancy—a centrifugal spinning away from reality, the mind on holiday—imagination is centripetal, a disciplined contemplation of reality

that takes us beneath appearances and into the essence of what we contemplate. Imagination, therefore, can lead to moral clarification. In issues where law and morality seem to clash, as in the current debate over undocumented immigrants, imagination (which speaks to both heart and mind) can lead to right action.

Savant begins with two general statements that he then explains in sentence three are examples of imagination. In sentence four, he both defines and contrasts daydream or fancy with imagination, which leads to sentence five, a declaration that "imagination leads to moral clarification." This statement, then, takes readers to his thesis, which introduces the subject of undocumented immigrants as a specific example of the "clash" between law and morality and his position on that issue. Readers now expect that Savant will examine both legal and moral aspects of the undocumented immigrant issue and argue in favor of using imagination—"both heart and mind"—over application of the law.

Challenge: Developing a Strategy for Organizing Your Paper.   In the same way that an essay without a clear purpose leaves readers confused, so does a paper that is not organized in a logical or sensible way.

Meeting the Challenge. The key questions of how you will organize your essay and what strategies you will use to develop and support your thesis assume primary importance as you begin to draft the body of your paper. Here again, a strong thesis statement will be invaluable in helping you plan your essay. After all, if it serves to direct readers of your paper, it must beforehand direct you as writer of the paper. As noted earlier in the comments on "Batman: The Unexpected Cultural Revolution" (Chapter 10), Chris Gould's introduction and thesis set the stage for what he does in the rest of his paper. Similarly, in "Imagining the Immigrant: Why Legality Must Give Way to Humanity," John J. Savant's thesis sets up an expectation of the areas that he will address in the essay. In both examples, each writer's thesis names aspects that serve as a guideline or bare-bones sketch of what he will discuss in the rest of the paper.

Although your thesis is in a sense a directional statement for the paper's organization and development, more considerations come into play in planning the body of the paper. Using the thesis as your guide, write down the major points that you want to make in support or explanation of that thesis. For each major point, make a list of minor points or supporting examples or illustrations that you will use to make that point. Ask yourself if the major points are in a logical order or if they need to be shifted about to make them logical. Consider whether every major point does indeed support, illustrate, or in some way relate to your overarching purpose or thesis. If not, discard the irrelevant ones and look for more directly relevant points. Your chief concern when considering how to organize your paper is always directly connected to whether the points you make support or illustrate your position or in same way advance the development of your paper.

Writers use many different **rhetorical modes** or patterns to organize and develop their ideas, depending on their purposes, whether those are persuasive, expository, or expressive purposes. Whatever a writer's purpose, some fairly standard models can help to organize written work. These include **argumentation/ persuasion, narration, description,** or expository modes such as **cause-effect analysis, classification-division, comparison/contrast,** and **definition.** These various ways of organizing and developing ideas are almost never used in isolation. Seldom will you find a piece of writing that does not combine two or more of these strategies, and they are all equally useful, depending on your purpose for writing, the audience you are writing to, and the context you are writing in. You will notice as you read the essays in this textbook that all of the writers employ a variety of strategies to achieve their purpose.

Challenge: Drafting the Body of Your Paper. No matter how strong your title and introduction, the success of your writing efforts lies largely in how well you explain, defend, or develop your central point in the body of your paper.

Meeting the Challenge. The body of your paper should consist of a number of paragraphs that relate directly to your thesis. A successful writer ensures that each paragraph in the body contains key ideas, supporting evidence, detailed explanation, or other information that directly advances the purpose of the paper.

A **typical paragraph** in the body of the paper focuses on one topic related to the thesis of the paper; has a topic sentence that expresses that single topic; contains perhaps seven to ten supporting sentences; and has a concluding sentence that leads to the next paragraph:

- **Topic sentence.** Each of the paragraphs in the body of the paper should have a topic sentence. Remember that the thesis statement answers the question "What is this essay about?" In the same way, the topic sentence answers the question "What is this paragraph about?" As with a thesis, if your topic sentence is not clearly stated, it should be clearly implied.

- **Supporting sentences.** Sentences in the paragraph should have a logical organization, should support only the topic of that paragraph, and should lead clearly and smoothly from one to another. They are used to support the topic sentence, that is, to explain it, illustrate it, amplify or expand on it. Paragraphs contain details related to and supportive of the focus of the paragraph and include a mix of both general and specific or detailed statements.

- **Concluding sentence(s).** The final sentence or sentences summarize the connections between the sentences and bring the paragraph to closure. Sometimes the final sentence points to the subject of the next paragraph.

EXERCISE

A useful and fun exercise is to put the sentences of a scrambled paragraph back into their correct order. Such an exercise demonstrates that sentences within well-constructed paragraphs have an apparent and sensible order. Unscramble the following paragraph, a student's brief narrative of a poignant moment, by putting its sentences in their logical order:

1. As high school graduates preparing to go off to different colleges in the fall, we both felt uncertain about what the future held.
2. Matt motioned to the smaller boy, with red Kool-aid stains extending beyond the corners of his lips, reached out with the ball, and said: "Go deep."
3. The two children whose ball it was seemed intimidated by our older age and size, expecting us to kick it back hard or, worse, keep it for ourselves.
4. It wasn't a smile of joy but rather a bittersweet one, prompted by childhood memories of our boyhood time playing ball and the prospect now of adulthood.
5. The ball bounced off the grass, spinning end over end, and skidded off the weathered blacktop into Matt's hands.
6. Instead, Matt and I looked at each other and smiled.

Compare your results with your classmates or group and discuss the clues that led to your solution. How did you know which was the first sentence? What words helped determine which sentences follow one another? How did you know which sentence came last in the paragraph? [Here is the sequence of sentences as the paragraph was originally written: 5-3-6-4-1-2.]

Challenge: Providing Transition.   Transition is the linking or connecting of ideas or statements. If you do not use words that show the connection between ideas, clauses, sentences, and paragraphs, your writing will seem to be a series of disconnected statements.

Meeting the Challenge. As demonstrated in the preceding scrambled paragraph exercise, providing effective transition helps the reader follow what you are saying. Whether at the sentence, paragraph, or whole-essay level, you need to make connections clear to your readers. In any kind of writing, you want to try to be as coherent as possible; you will go a long way toward achieving that goal when you provide clear markers to help your readers follow the development of your paper and see connections between ideas and points. We have many tools with which to link or show the connection between thoughts and ideas.

- **Repeating key words, using pronouns to refer to nouns, and using transitional words** all help achieve clarity or coherence. The following are just a few examples of the many words we have to make transitions clear:
  - **To show addition:** furthermore, in addition, also, again, too, as well as, another
  - **To show consequence:** therefore, as a result, because, consequently, thus, then, hence, so that, for this reason, because

- **To show contrast:** on the other hand, however, in contrast, instead, conversely, on the contrary, but, yet, compared to
- **To show similarity:** likewise, similarly, in the same way, moreover, analogous to
- **To illustrate:** for example, such as, in particular, to illustrate, for instance, for one thing, to explain, namely, that is, in this case
- **To show time relationship:** later, earlier, afterward, before, next, eventually, at length, before long, meanwhile, subsequently
- **To make a concession:** although, even though, still, of course, while it may be true, in spite of, at any rate
- **To emphasize:** importantly, unquestionably, without a doubt, of prime importance, certainly, undeniably
- **To summarize:** in brief, in summary, in essence, in other words, to conclude, generally, in any event, on the whole, as I have shown

Challenge: Distinguishing among Levels of Generality.   A paper that stays only at the general level usually lacks substance; not providing enough detail or specificity will likely weaken your overall effect.

Meeting the Challenge. One feature of a fully developed paper is the use of exemplification, details or illustrations. Whenever you make a general statement, make sure the following sentences provide specifics about that general statement. When you feel that you have not said enough to convincingly or fully develop or explain your central idea, ask yourself where you can add examples or illustrations. Examples and illustrations are crucial to writing, no matter what the primary purpose is. Without them, writing stays at the general or abstract level and leaves readers only vaguely understanding what the writer means. They make meaning clear and help make writing more interesting, livelier, and more engaging than an essay without details. Examples may be brief and numerous or extended and limited in number, and they may take the form of narratives. They do not have to begin with the words *for example* or *to illustrate* nor ostentatiously announce that an example is coming. Most of the readings in this textbook contain examples of one kind or another to both illustrate and argue their theses. It would be difficult to find an effective piece of writing that does not use examples of some sort.

An example of effective use of details to illustrate meaning appears in the entire first paragraph of Andrew Keen's "Sharing Is a Trap" (Chapter 17):

> Panic about privacy has often been triggered by technology. When Gutenberg invented his printing press, authors of the day feared having their thoughts and identities recorded permanently and distributed widely. The first serious discussion of a legal right to privacy in the US came in 1890, with the invention of the Kodak camera and the rise of the penny press. Telephones, miniature microphones, video cameras and RFID chips all triggered much fretting. It should come as no surprise, then, that the internet would provoke warnings that privacy is dead, but those alarms will likely lead to more regulation of privacy than ever. We need protection of our privacy and we're getting it.

Keen's opening sentence is a generality and the next sentences are specific examples to illustrate what that general statement means. How might the impact or effectiveness of the paragraph change if you remove sentences two, three, and four?

Challenge: Drafting Your Concluding Paragraph.   Without a concluding paragraph, readers are left with a feeling that you have not finished whatever points you have been making.

Meeting the Challenge. Write a final paragraph that brings the paper to a satisfying end. For a long paper, such as a research project, your conclusion may take more than one final paragraph, but no matter its length, a paper should have a conclusion. You may not be ready to write your conclusion when you write the first draft of your paper because the conclusion should come logically from all that has gone before. Sometimes you need to write several drafts before you can write your conclusion. When you are ready to write it, you have many approaches to choose from. Sometimes writers simply restate their introductions, but try to be more imaginative. You don't have to restate major points, as they should be clear in readers' minds, but referring to them or highlighting them lends emphasis to what you have written and stresses its significance. Try to leave your readers with something to think about: stress the importance of what you have written, suggest a course of action, or point to questions raised by your paper that need further study or exploration. You might refer back to your introduction by mentioning a detail or image from it, or end with an amusing anecdote or humorous or striking comment. No matter what strategy you choose for concluding your paper, readers should feel that they have come to a satisfactory end.

Here is the conclusion to Chris Gould's "Batman, the Unexpected Cultural Revolution," whose introduction you will recall from above. Whereas the introduction effectively sets forth his subject, the 1960s *Batman* television program, and tells readers what he plans to do in the essay, now his conclusion summarizes the essence of his paper and raises an interesting point that resulted from the way that the series depicted Batman:

> *Batman* set out to challenge the established wisdom over how television programs should be produced, but the approach actually sowed the seeds of its own destruction. TV's regular stars were so impressed that they queued up in droves to take part in the project. Sammy Davis Jr., Liberace, Joan Collins, and Zsa Zsa Gabor were just some of the names who either guest starred or cameoed. Scripts and viewing figures suddenly became dependent on the guest star, and the show's quality suffered immensely. Despite this, the show made an immense impact on American popular culture in a relatively short time. It challenged people to aspire to a world where right and wrong were easily distinguishable. And it spawned a vast counter-revolution in future representations of Batman, with movie directors from the 1980s to the present obsessed with returning the character to his darker, more sinister, past.

Gould's concluding paragraph makes reference to the points that he has made about the TV show, summarizes quickly his conclusion about the causes of its demise, and ends with a statement about its long-term influence on depictions of the classic comic book hero that followed. It is a fitting end to the essay.

REVISING YOUR PAPER GLOBALLY

After you have written a draft of your paper, set it aside for a while—a few hours, overnight, a day or two if you have the time—and then return to it to closely reexamine and revise what you have written. Revision is a crucial step in the writing process, for it is here that you turn your draft into a polished piece of writing. The word *revision* means to look again or revisit, and that is what you do at this stage: examine the substance of your paper with a critical eye, looking for ways to improve what you have written. While you might have done some rewriting when drafting your paper, the really serious work comes during revision. This section suggests approaches to revising your paper. Your first concern when revising is to consider whole-essay or "global" matters, so reread your entire paper to begin the revision process. Don't worry at this time about whether you have made grammatical errors or whether every word is spelled correctly. These are matters that you will address after you have worked on larger issues. In the global revision stage, you may find yourself deleting or moving entire sections of what you wrote in the draft stage until you are satisfied with the focus, organization, and development of your essay.

Revision addresses the issues of purpose, audience, organization, and content, which include the development of ideas, and both the introduction and conclusion of your essay. Apply the same questions to your own writing that you ask when evaluating the writing of others, as detailed in Chapter 1 on critical reading. Writers use many techniques to make the revision process meaningful. You truly want to revise, not simply rewrite, your paper, so leave some time between drafts to give yourself a fresh perspective on what you have written. Obviously that means not starting any writing project at the last minute. You will find that it works to your advantage to begin writing as soon as possible after getting an assignment. The more time you have to draft and revise, the more satisfied you are likely to be with your final effort. When revising, try reading your paper out loud and listening to how it sounds, or read it to someone else to get feedback from an objective audience. Revise passages that sound awkward or seem to lead nowhere; move things around if the paper seems disorganized; and look for ways to improve the development of every point you make. Include entire paragraphs in the revision process. Make sure that every paragraph is itself fully explained and that each paragraph directly relates to your central purpose. Consider how well your introduction truly focuses on your paper and whether your concluding paragraph gives a sense of closure to the paper.

Of prime importance is the question of whether all components of your paper are directly related to your thesis. Remember that your thesis indicates the central idea of your paper, suggests the direction you will take with that idea, states your position on a topic, or asks a question that you will answer in the course of your paper. After you have read through your arguments or supporting examples or illustrations, ask yourself if you have left any important points out. Are there places where readers might argue with or take exception to what you have written and, if so, how would you respond? Consider addressing those matters in your paper, anticipating reader responses. For instance, if the purpose of the essay is to describe, have you conveyed the essence of the thing with appropriately vivid words? If your purpose is to argue or persuade, is your evidence convincing? Is the argument logical and reasonable? Have you avoided fallacies in the logic of your argument? Ask yourself if the essay has a clear plan or organizing principle and if your final paragraph brings your paper to a satisfactory conclusion.

GUIDELINES: A CHECKLIST FOR REVISING GLOBALLY

- Does your introduction focus on the main point or thesis of the paper? Does it state your purpose clearly? Does it create interest or otherwise pique reader curiosity?
- Is your audience clearly defined and do you consistently write to that audience throughout the paper?
- Have you chosen an appropriate tone for your topic? Is that tone consistent throughout the paper?
- Is the essay organized logically?
- Do paragraphs have clearly stated or implied topic sentences? Are they developed in a coherent, logical way?
- Have you provided transition from thought to thought or point to point?
- Does your paper distinguish among levels of generality within paragraphs and within the essay as a whole?
- Do any passages need to be clarified?
- Does anything you have written need to be shifted to somewhere else in the paper or deleted entirely?
- Does your final paragraph bring your paper to a satisfactory end?

ILLUSTRATION: REVISING GLOBALLY

The following example illustrates how the revision process works. The draft of Elizabeth's first two paragraphs of her research paper, "Then and Now in China: Comparing Revolutionary with Modern Ballet" (Chapter 7), appears first, followed by the revisions that she made on it, and then the revised version, with sources in correct MLA format.

FIRST DRAFT:

China has a long history of forcing women into subservient roles, viewing them as second-class citizens. Historically, the male dominated culture expected women to serve men, often as slaves or concubines. The plight of a Chinese woman was once controlled first by her father and then by her husband, with whom her father had arranged the relationship. Typically, artistic endeavors, including operas, ballets, writings, and art, perpetuated these traditional roles of women, keeping them in their submissive places through the creation of compliant female characters who rarely challenged their male counterparts. The ballet especially created a canvas for developing cultural expectations and citizens of all socio-economic levels valued and continue even today to cherish Chinese ballet. Over time, interactions with Western culture have influenced the way Chinese society sees women, and modernization of women's roles has occurred. Yet, artists seem unhurried to incorporate these modern roles to the stage. This slowness, however, may be intentional, as artists work to influence their audiences. At the height of the spread of Communism, China entered an organized political period called the Cultural Revolution, a time when the government was heavy handed in influencing culture and focused on imposing Mao's ideals into the State. Since the 1960s, the West has had a variety of influences on Chinese culture, but not in all genres. Despite changes in Chinese society since the Cultural Revolution, modern Chinese ballet continues to reflect the traditional attributes of female characters and to rely on revolutionary plots.

After the Great Leap Forward in the 1950s, Mao Zedong's power and popularity began to dissipate because of his failure at modernizing the economic system of China. Mao feared that the new leaders would take the State in the wrong direction; as a result, he instigated the Cultural Revolution to exert that his power over the State and citizens still remained strong (Trueman). As detailed in Patricia Ebrey's *Sourcebook of Chinese Civilization*, "The aim of the Cultural Revolution was to attack the Four Olds—old ideas, old culture, old customs, and old habits—in order to bring the areas of education, art and literature in line with Communist ideology (Ebrey). To align society with his philosophy, Mao completely overhauled the Chinese culture. The Communist regime deemed non-supporters of Mao's views and the values of the State as an "enemy of the party and people" (Ebrey). In order to avoid persecution or arrest, Chinese citizens complied with the government's mandates. Ultimately, the Cultural Revolution especially affected the arts; in fact, for a period of time there was absolutely no music in China. Eventually, Mao's wife, Jiang Qing, fostered the production of eight "Model Operas" that applied the acceptable revolutionary themes, performed continuously with mandatory attendance (Ebrey). Different than preceding eras, the Cultural Revolution has had a significant, long-lasting effect on the Chinese society, especially on the arts, and yet, even though the regime's policies ended long ago, modern Chinese ballets still rely on the strong elements found in the "Model Eight" (Mittler). Nowhere is this more evident than in the ties between the late 1950s ballet *The White-Haired Girl* and the 1990s ballet *Raise the Red Lantern*.

DRAFT WITH REVISIONS NOTED:

Elizabeth's next sentence states essentially the same thing, so she deleted the unnecessary words.

This sentence is irrelevant.

The sentence is wordy and redundant as written; deleting unnecessary words and changing "through the creation of" to "creating" tightens the sentence and reduces clutter.

China has a long history of ~~forcing women into subservient roles,~~ viewing ~~them~~ women as second-class citizens. Historically, the male dominated culture expected women to serve men, often as slaves or concubines. ~~The plight of a Chinese woman was once controlled first by her father and then by her husband, with whom her father had arranged the relationship.~~ Typically, artistic endeavors, including operas, ballets, writings, and art, perpetuated these traditional roles of women, ~~keeping them in their submissive places through the creation of~~ creating compliant female characters who rarely challenged their male counterparts. The ballet, still valued and cherished by Chinese citizens of all socio-economic levels, especially created a canvas for developing cultural expectations., ~~and citizens of all socio-economic levels valued and continue even today to cherish Chinese ballet. Over time, interactions with Western culture have influenced the way Chinese society sees women, and modernization of women's roles has occurred. Yet, artists seem unhurried to incorporate these modern roles to the stage. This slowness, however, may be intentional, as artists work to influence their audiences. At the height of the spread of Communism, China entered an organized political period called the Cultural Revolution, a time when the government was heavy handed in influencing culture and focused on imposing Mao's ideals into the State. Since the 1960s, the West has had a variety of influences on Chinese culture, but not in all genres.~~ Though interactions with Western culture since the 1960s have helped modernize the way that Chinese society views women and their roles, artists seem unhurried to incorporate these changes to the stage. Despite changes in Chinese society since the Cultural Revolution, modern Chinese ballet continues to reflect the traditional attributes of female characters and to rely on revolutionary plots.

> *Elizabeth noticed that she could write a more effective sentence and provide variety by shifting words about.*

> *Elizabeth removed irrelevant or unnecessary details, combined essential ideas, and narrowed her focus.*

> *This is a general statement of her central idea. Her specific form of proof or support is stated at the end of the 2nd paragraph.*

After the Great Leap Forward in the 1950s, Mao Zedong's power and popularity began to dissipate ~~because of his failure at modernizing the economic system of China~~. Because Mao feared that the new leaders would take the State in the wrong direction; ~~as a result,~~, he instigated the Cultural Revolution ~~exert that his power over the State and citizens still remained strong~~ to maintain his influence over the State and its citizens (Trueman). As ~~detailed in~~ Patricia Ebrey~~'s~~ explains in *Sourcebook of Chinese Civilization*," The aim of the Cultural Revolution was to attack the Four Olds—old ideas, old culture, old customs, and old habits—in order to bring the areas of education, art and literature in line with Communist ideology" (Ebrey). To align society with his philosophy, Mao completely overhauled the Chinese culture. The Communist regime deemed non-supporters of Mao's views and the values of the State as ~~an "enemy~~ [enemies] of the party and people" (Ebrey). In order to avoid persecution or arrest, Chinese citizens complied

> *Not relevant to her central point.*

> *The original wording was clumsy.*
> *The introduction to the quotation seemed awkward. This revision makes the transition into the quotation smoother.*
> *Elizabeth changed the singular word in the quotation to the plural, which she puts in brackets to indicate that it is her word. The plural noun now agrees with what it refers to, "non-supporters."*

with the government's mandates. Ultimately, the Cultural Revolution ~~especially~~ affected the arts so strongly that ~~in fact,~~ for a period of time there was absolutely no music in China. Eventually, Mao's wife, Jiang Qing, fostered the production of eight "Model Operas" that applied the acceptable revolutionary themes~~;~~ and were performed continuously with mandatory attendance (Ebrey). ~~Different than preceding eras, the Cultural Revolution has had a significant, long-lasting effect on the Chinese society, especially on the arts, and yet, e~~Even though *the regime's policies* ended long ago, modern Chinese ballets still rely on ~~the~~ strong elements ~~found in~~ of the "Model Eight" (Mittler). Nowhere is this more evident than in the ties between the late 1950s ballet *The White-Haired Girl* and the 1990s ballet *Raise the Red Lantern*.

Wordy and not directly relevant.

This sentence states explicitly how she will support her more general central idea at the end of the first paragraph.

REVISED VERSION:

China has a long history of viewing women as second-class citizens. Historically, the male dominated culture expected women to serve men, often as slaves or concubines. Typically, artistic endeavors, including opera, ballet, creative writing, and art, perpetuated these traditional roles of women, creating compliant female characters who rarely challenged their male counterparts. The ballet, still valued and cherished by Chinese citizens of all socio-economic levels, especially created a canvas for developing cultural expectations. Though interactions with Western culture since the 1960s have helped modernize the way that Chinese society views women and their roles, artists seem unhurried to incorporate these changes to the stage. Despite changes within Chinese society since the Cultural Revolution, modern Chinese ballet continues to reflect the traditional attributes of female characters and to rely on revolutionary plots.

After the Great Leap Forward in the 1950s, Mao Zedong's power and popularity began to dissipate. Because Mao feared that the new leaders would take the State in the wrong direction, he instigated the Cultural Revolution to maintain his influence over the State and its citizens (Trueman). As Patricia Ebrey explains in *Sourcebook of Chinese Civilization*, "The aim of the Cultural Revolution was to attack the Four Olds—old ideas, old culture, old customs, and old habits—in order to bring the areas of education, art and literature in line with Communist ideology" (Ebrey). To align society with his philosophy, Mao completely overhauled the Chinese culture. The Communist regime deemed non-supporters of Mao's views and the values of the State as "[enemies] of the party and people" (Ebrey). In order to avoid persecution or arrest, Chinese citizens complied with the government's mandates. Ultimately, the Cultural Revolution affected the arts so strongly that for a period of time there was absolutely no music in China. Eventually, Mao's wife, Jiang Qing, fostered the production of eight "Model Operas" that applied the acceptable revolutionary themes and were performed continuously with mandatory attendance (Ebrey). Even though the regime's policies ended long ago, modern Chinese ballets still rely on strong elements of the "Model Eight" (Mittler). Nowhere is this more evident than in the ties between the late 1950s ballet *The White-Haired Girl* and the 1990s ballet *Raise the Red Lantern*.

WORKS CITED

Ebrey, Patricia. "A Visual Sourcebook of Chinese Civilization: Cultural Revolution." *Education Division of the National Endowment for the Humanities*. Web. 14 Nov. 2014.

Mittler, Barbara. "Eight Stage Works for 800 Million People: The Great Proletarian Cultural Revolution in Music—A View from Revolutionary Opera." *The Opera Quarterly* 26.2-3 (2010): 377-401. Print.

Trueman, Chris. "The Cultural Revolution." *History Learning Site*. Web. 7 Nov. 2014.

The revised version of Elizabeth's opening paragraphs eliminates wordiness and unnecessary information and combines components of some sentences for better effect. As you will see when you read her research paper in chapter 7, these paragraphs comprise her introduction, and her thesis comes at the end of her second paragraph.

REVISING FOR STYLE AND CLARITY

Besides being focused, organized, and developed well, your paper will be more successful if it is written in an engaging style. **Style** in writing refers to your overall written effect and is characterized by such things as word choice, tone, and sentence structure or **syntax** (the arrangement of words or phrases to create sentences). **Throughout the revision process, whether globally or at the individual sentence level, look for clumsy, wordy, ineffective, or unclear passages**. If you find that you have written several very short simple sentences in a row, for instance, try combining them. Look for ways to vary sentence structure and length to avoid monotony or choppiness, and select words and details for greatest effect and interest. Use language that is appropriate for your topic and idiomatic, avoiding slang and clichés. Structure sentences to their best advantage, as Elizabeth has done in the revision example earlier. Consider ways to reword what you have written so that it more accurately reflects what you mean. Watch out for some fairly common pitfalls in sentence construction, such as wordiness, misplaced modifiers, **passive voice for active voice,** and faulty parallelism.

ILLUSTRATION: REVISING FOR STYLE AND CLARITY

In her expository writing class, Professor Gilliar assigned students to write a cover letter for a job application. She then selected passages from the students' work and asked them to edit the passages and explain how the reworked versions are more effective than the original. Here are examples of the process that the students went through in doing this exercise.

1. ORIGINAL SENTENCE: Not only through my passion but also through my experience conducting research and interviews, I plan to make a difference in the outreach of a news organization.

    Revised Version 1:
    With my strong passion for improving the lives of others and my savvy approach to conducting research and interviews, I will thoroughly inform my readers and move them to action.

    Rationale for rewrite:
    The first sentence is too vague with phrases like "my experience" and "make a difference." In addition, the first sentence doesn't explain what "my passion" really is or what the "outreach of a news organization" aims to do. So the revised sentence states what the passion is for and better explains the experience of conducting research and interviews. Rather than stating "the outreach of a news organization," I stated my aims of writing for a newspaper: inform readers and move them to action. Moreover, I said "I will" rather than "I plan" because it's more decisive and shows that this is something I'm going to do no matter what.

2. ORIGINAL PASSAGE: I have had a lot of fine experiences while at school that prepared me for the challenges at your competitive company. There are many ways that allow me to apply the multiple skills and expertise I have to offer.

    Revised Version 1:
    As a college student, I have conducted rigorous research and conveyed my findings in understandable, concise reports. My savvy approach to research, coupled with my excellent interpersonal skills, makes me an excellent candidate for your company.

Rationale for rewrite:

This revised version is much more specific and clearly indicates the experience I have learned at school. It touches upon the skills rather than simply saying "I have skills."

Revised Version 2:

As a college student, I researched the difference in symptoms of patients with latent tuberculosis compared to the symptoms of patients with active tuberculosis in the laboratory, collected all of my data in a research report that was published in a local science journal, and presented my findings at a Science Seminar that was attended by a large number of fellow science students, faculty, and staff members. Through this experience, I gained several skills including collecting and recording data in the laboratory, organizing the data in a professional format that led to acceptance by a local journal, and professional communication skills through my presentation of my findings. All of these skills make me a top candidate for the position you are offering.

Rationale for rewrite:

This rewrite explains specifically what my experience at college was and what skills were gained from these experiences that would make me a better candidate.

3. ORIGINAL SENTENCE: My natural ability and passion for writing can only be rivaled by my desire to write.

Revised Version 1:

I possess a natural ability to write, evidenced by my winning an English Department award for the best essay in my writing class, which is complemented by my desire to write.

Rationale for rewrite:

Ability and passion are fine qualities, but evidence to support such claims gives the sentence weight. A "desire" for writing is also important, so I chose to keep that word and stated that the "natural ability" is complemented by the "desire" to write, thus making me highly marketable by showing both stamina and ability.

Revised Version 2:

Writing is a natural ability, a passion, and a desire of mine. I constantly jot down notes, write in my journal, or make lists of ideas and prompts.

Rationale for rewrite:

The rivalry between "natural ability and passion" and the "desire to write" is not one of compelling logic. It is more powerful to put these factors together to work as a team of a love for writing.

Revised Version 3:

My natural ability and passion for writing allow me to produce effective, professional work of the kind that your prestigious company values.

Rationale for rewrite:

This version shows how my writing would help the organization. It is written more gracefully than the previous version, and it is easier to understand what I mean.

EXERCISE

Imagine that you are applying for your dream job and want to explain in your cover letter why you would be a good choice. Compose a paragraph for this hypothetical job application. Select one or two sentences that you think would make you stand out from the other applicants and revise the sentence(s). For each revised version, write an analysis of why the revision is an improvement over the previous draft. Do this until you are satisfied that your final version is the best that you can write. Spend time reflecting on how your selection evolved from being acceptable to being outstanding. Be prepared to share your work with your classmates or hand it in to your instructor.

ILLUSTRATION: REVISING AT THE SENTENCE LEVEL

As noted earlier, revision at the sentence level focuses on style, clarity, or effectiveness. The following examples illustrate just a few of the writing problems that you might discover in a careful rereading of your draft. They represent some of the most typical sentence-level challenges.

1. **Revising to avoid wordiness and passive construction:** My first day on campus was one of learning my way around.

   Revised: I spent my first day on campus learning my way around.

   Rationale: The revised sentence avoids the passive construction and reduces the wordiness that of "my first day . . . was one of" causes.

2. **Revising to avoid dangling modifiers:**

   a. Standing straight and breathing hard, my mother's face appeared in the aisle.

      Revised: My mother, standing straight and breathing hard, appeared in the aisle.

      Rationale: The revision shifts the modifying phrase "standing straight and breathing hard" to apply to "mother," not just to her face.

   b. Entering the classroom late, a pop quiz had already been collected.

      Revised: Entering the classroom late, I learned that a pop quiz had already been collected.

      Rationale: In the original, the "dangling" modifier does not clearly modify anything in the sentence, whereas the revision clarifies who entered the classroom.

3. **Revising to avoid awkward construction:** That really hit home to me, the fact that other people were having the same experiences of shyness as me when it came to meeting people for the first time.

   Revised: I realized that others were just as shy as I when meeting new people.

   Rationale: The revision removes unnecessary words and makes the meaning straightforward rather than getting lost among the excess words.

4. **Revising to make equal sentence parts parallel:**

   a. He is polite, gracious, considerate and has high standards.

      Revised: He is not only polite, gracious, and considerate, but he also has high standards.

   b. Classes are limited and not a big variety.

      Revised: Classes are limited and lack variety.

   c. We worked on his reading skills, interaction with others, or I simply read to him.

      Revised: We worked on his reading skills and interaction with others; sometimes I simply read to him.

      Rationale: In each of the original sentences, different parts of speech are linked. The revisions avoid that error by linking nouns with nouns and verbs with verbs.

GUIDELINES: A CHECKLIST FOR REVISING FOR STYLE AND CLARITY

- Have you used colorful, engaging, and/or lively language?
- Have you constructed sentences that are varied in structure and length?
- Have you avoided slang and clichés?
- Have you avoided wordiness?
- Are verbs active rather than passive?
- Have you avoided shifts in verb tense?
- Are equal sentence parts parallel and modifiers correctly placed?
- Can you combine short sentences into longer, more complex ones to avoid a choppy effect?
- Have you written with clarity and grace, to the best of your ability?

ILLUSTRATION OF A WRITING STRATEGY: PARALLELISM FOR EFFECT

For an analysis of how one particular strategy in writing can have a powerful effect, read the following essay by Richard Lederer, in which he explains how President Kennedy's use of parallelism makes his inaugural speech one of the most memorable in history.

A STYLISH INAUGURATION SPEECH

RICHARD LEDERER

Richard Lederer is the author of more than 40 books about language, history, and humor, including his best-selling Anguished English *series and his current books,* The Gift of Age, A Tribute to Teachers, American Trivia, *and* Amazing Words. *He has been profiled in magazines as diverse as* The New Yorker, People, *and the* National Inquirer *and was founding co-host of "A Way with Words" on Public Radio. This piece was most recently published in the January 2011 issue of the online magazine* The Vocabula Review. *According to its website,* The Vocabula Review *"battles nonstandard, careless English and embraces clear, expressive English. We hope we can encourage our readers to do as much."*

Fifty years ago, on January 20, 1961, thousands of visitors converged on Washington, D.C., for the inauguration of our 35th president, John Fitzgerald Kennedy. A blizzard had struck the eastern seaboard that day. The streets of the capital were clogged with snow and stranded automobiles, but the inaugural ceremony went on, and a new president delivered one of the most memorable addresses in American history.

What makes President Kennedy's speech so unforgettable is its striking use of parallel structure—the repetition of grammatical forms to emphasize similar ideas. Let's look at four brief excerpts from that famous inaugural address that exemplify the president's powerful use of parallelism. Examine each section with an ear and eye toward incorporating parallel structure and other uses of balanced prose into your own speaking and writing styles.

The address begins with this clarion-call sentence: "We observe today not a victory of party but a celebration of freedom," immediately followed by the tandem participial phrases "symbolizing an end as well as a beginning, signifying renewal as well as change." The echoic sounds of *symbolizing* and *signifying* enhance the parallel "as well as" prepositional phrases.

Two paragraphs later, Kennedy proclaims:

> *Let the word go forth from this time and place, to friend and foe alike, that the torch has been passed to a new generation of Americans, born in this century, tempered by war, disciplined by a hard and bitter peace, proud of our ancient heritage, and unwilling to permit the slow undoing of those human rights to which this nation has always been committed and to which we are committed today at home and around the world.*

Reprinted with permission from *The Vocabula Review,* January 2011, vol. 13, no. 1.

Let every nation know, whether it wishes us well or ill, that we shall pay any price, bear any burden, meet any hardship, support any friend, oppose any foe to assure the survival and success of liberty.

Here the new president gathers momentum with two prepositional phrases, "From this time and place, to friend and foe alike," and then launches into five adjective phrases—"born . . . , tempered . . . , disciplined . . . , proud . . . , and unwilling . . . ." And the first four of these adjectives are modified by parallel prepositional phrases. The 81-word sentence ends with parallel adjective clauses—"to which this nation is committed and to which we are committed today"—and prepositional phrases—"at home and around the world." In the next sentence, after a brief parallelism of two balanced adjectives, "whether it wishes us well or ill," Kennedy employs five parallel verb-direct object constructions—"pay any price, bear any burden, meet any hardship, support any friend, oppose any foe." The alliteration of *pay/price, bear/burden,* and *friend/foe* is capped by *survival/success.*

Toward the end of his inaugural address, Kennedy declares: "So let us begin anew, remembering on both sides that civility is not a sign of weakness, and sincerity is always subject to proof. Let us never negotiate out of fear, but let us never fear to negotiate." Following the balanced noun clauses—"that civility is not a sign of weakness, and sincerity is always subject to proof," Kennedy utters the memorable "Let us never negotiate out of fear, but let us never fear to negotiate." Here the powerful "Let us . . ." clauses are marked by chiasmus, a rhetorical term that describes the effective transposition of key words—in this case *negotiate* and *fear.*

Near the conclusion of his address, Kennedy again employs chiasmus to craft what is probably his most enduring statement: "And so, my fellow Americans, ask not what your country can do for you; ask what you can do for your country. My fellow citizens of the world, ask not what America will do for you, but what together we can do for the freedom of man." In this ringing passage, each sentence begins with a direct address—"my fellow Americans" and "my fellow citizens of the world"—and the two chiasmi—"country . . . you" and "you . . . country"—work their magic with four parallel noun clauses—"what your country can do . . . , what you can do . . . , what America will do. . . , what we can do . . . ."

I do not contend that President Kennedy's oration is so unforgettable solely because of its parallel structure. But would we remember his message as vividly if he had said, "You shouldn't worry about the things you can get from your country. Instead consider how you can contribute to America?"

EXERCISE

Applying the strategy that Richard Lederer uses in his rhetorical analysis of President Kennedy's *Inaugural Address,* write an analysis of President Abraham Lincoln's November 19, 1863, *Gettysburg Address,* reprinted next. The speech was delivered at the dedication of the Soldiers' National Cemetery in Gettysburg, Pennsylvania. Although there are at least five drafts of the address, this is the one that appears on the Lincoln Memorial in Washington, D.C. Alternatively, select another memorable speech, which you can find at www.americanrhetoric.com, and do a rhetorical analysis of it.

THE GETTYSBURG ADDRESS

ABRAHAM LINCOLN

Four score and seven years ago our fathers brought forth on this continent a new nation, conceived in liberty, and dedicated to the proposition that all men are created equal.

Now we are engaged in a great civil war, testing whether that nation, or any nation, so conceived and so dedicated, can long endure. We are met on a great battlefield of that war. We have come to dedicate a portion of that field, as a final resting place for those who here gave their lives that that nation might live. It is altogether fitting and proper that we should do this.

But, in a larger sense, we cannot dedicate, we cannot consecrate, we cannot hallow this ground. The brave men, living and dead, who struggled here, have consecrated it, far above our poor power to add or detract. The world will little note nor long remember what we say here, but it can never forget what they did here. It is for us the living, rather, to be dedicated here to the unfinished work which they who fought here have thus far so nobly advanced. It is rather for us to be here dedicated to the great task remaining before us—that from these honored dead we take increased devotion to that cause for which they gave the last full measure of devotion—that we here highly resolve that these dead shall not have died in vain—that this nation, under God, shall have a new birth of freedom—and that government of the people, by the people, for the people, shall not perish from the earth.

EDITING YOUR PAPER

While sentence-level revision aims to increase the clarity and effectiveness of your work, sentence-level editing focuses on grammar, mechanics, and punctuation. **Grammar** refers to such things as avoiding sentence fragments and run-on or fused sentences; subject-verb and pronoun-antecedent agreement; correct use of case for nouns and pronouns; and using adjectives and adverbs correctly, **Mechanics** refers to spelling words correctly, including correct hyphenation; correct use of italics; and use of capital letters, numbers, and abbreviations. **Punctuation** involves using correctly such things as commas, colons, semicolons, apostrophes, and quotation marks. Although the most important aspect of your writing is your content—what you say, how well you say it, and how well you present it—you also want to pay attention to these matters, especially if you know that you have problems in certain areas. If you have trouble with writing sentence fragments or run-ons, get confused about apostrophe or comma use, or misspell the same words all the time, make a conscious effort to look for those trouble spots. Errors at this level distract your reader from what you are saying, and too many such errors weaken your effectiveness as a writer.

GUIDELINES: A CHECKLIST FOR EDITING YOUR PAPER

- Are your words spelled correctly?
- Are sentences complete?
- Have you avoided fragments and run-on sentences?
- Are sentences punctuated according to standard conventions; that is, are commas, colons, semicolons, and apostrophes used correctly?
- Do pronouns and antecedents agree?
- Do subjects and verbs agree?
- Have you used pronouns in the correct case, that is, subjective pronouns like "I," "he," "we," and "they" used in subject positions and "me," "him/her," "us," and "them" used in object positions?

ILLUSTRATION: EDITING FOR ERRORS IN GRAMMAR AND PUNCTUATION

Misspelling: There opening hours show that **their** willing to devote **alot** of time to **acomodating** customer needs.

Edited: Their opening hours show that **they're** willing to devote **a lot** of time to **accommodating** customer needs.

Fragment: In college, it's nothing to have a class of 150 to 200 **students. Whereas** in high school, my classes never had more than 30 students.

Edited: In college, it's nothing to have a class of 150 to 200 **students, whereas** in high school, my classes never had more than 30 students.

Comma splice: When making drives, one group of hunters stays in one **area, another** group walks through a nearby area and tries to make the deer move toward the group that is standing.

Edited: When making drives, one group of hunters stays in one **area; another** group walks through a nearby area and tries to make the deer move toward the group that is standing.

Run-on or fused sentence: There were no cars zooming or people **talking the only** sound came from the forest creatures.

Edited: There were no cars zooming or people **talking. The only** sound came from the forest creatures.

Misuse of semicolon: Basic communication has only two people **involved; the** sender and the receiver.

Edited: Basic communication has only two people **involved: the** sender and the receiver.

Pronoun-antecedent disagreement: A student who wants to improve **their grade** can ask for a tutor at the writing lab.

Edited: A student who wants to improve **his or her grade** can ask for a tutor at the writing lab. OR, **Students who want** to improve **their grade** can ask for a tutor at the writing lab.

Subject-verb disagreement: The **number** of violent crimes in my old neighborhood **have gone** done dramatically in the last decade.

Edited: The **number** of violent crimes in my old neighborhood **has gone** done dramatically in the last decade.

Incorrect pronoun case: Both **Steve and myself** loved hunting.

Edited: Both **Steve and I** loved hunting.

Incorrect apostrophe use: My **parent's** have been married for 30 years.

Edited: My **parents** have been married for 30 years.

PROOFREADING

Leave time to proofread your final version and make any last-minute corrections, preferably on the word processor, but if necessary, written neatly in ink. At this final stage, you are looking for careless or previously undiscovered errors that you can fix easily. You might discover a misspelled word or a comma in the wrong place, or you might notice that you have left a word out. If you have given yourself time to write several drafts, edit, and revise, the proofreading stage should just be a final check of work well done.

CHAPTER 3

Writing a Summary

Students often must write both informal exercises and formal papers based on readings in their textbooks. In writing assignments for the course using this textbook, for instance, you will find frequent use for information or ideas discussed in the readings. For formal writing assignments, you may be instructed to choose among the writing topics that end each chapter in Parts Two through Five, or you may be asked to suggest your own topic for a paper on a reading or readings. You may choose to argue in favor of or against a position another author takes; you may use information from one or more of the readings to write an essay suggested by a particular chapter; you may decide to compare and contrast two or more essays in a chapter or explain various perspectives on an issue. At some point, you may want to use some of the readings from this or another textbook in combination with other print and Internet resources in a research paper.

This chapter and the next three introduce several specific types of assignments that you may be asked to write and provide guidelines for writing them. This chapter focuses on the summary, Chapter 4 on writing a critique, Chapter 5 on writing an argument, and Chapter 6 on writing a synthesis with documentation. In all of these assignments, you may be called on to paraphrase, quote, and document material on which you are writing. The guidelines for paraphrasing, quoting, and documenting sources are explained in Chapter 6. All illustrations of handling source material follow MLA (Modern Language Association) documentation style. If your instructor prefers that you use APA (American Psychological Society) documentation style, see Chapter 7 for guidelines.

WRITING A SUMMARY

Summarizing produces an objective restatement of a written passage in your own words, in a much shorter version than the original. The purpose of a **summary,** sometimes called a **précis,** is to highlight both the central idea or ideas and the major points of a work. A summary does not attempt to restate the entire reading. You might summarize an entire book in the space of a paragraph or perhaps even a sentence, although you will not do full justice to a lengthy work that way.

Many writing assignments call for summarizing. Your instructor may ask you to write a summary of an essay, or a passage from one, to gauge your understanding. Such an assignment may be informal, something that you write in class as a quiz or an ungraded journal entry, or you may be assigned a formal summary, a longer piece that you write out of class in detail and with care. Many kinds of writing include summaries as part of the development of their main ideas. For instance, if you are asked to report on an individual or group research project for a science class, you will probably summarize your purpose, methodology, data, and conclusions. If you write an argumentative paper, you may need to summarize either opposing viewpoints or your own supporting evidence. A research paper often includes summaries of information from source materials, and the research process itself necessitates summarizing portions of what you read. Reviews of books or articles almost always include summaries of the works under discussion, and essay questions on an examination often require summaries of information or data. Across the curriculum, no matter what course you are taking, you will probably be asked to summarize.

Summaries serve useful purposes. Professors summarize as they lecture in order to convey information in a condensed way when a detailed review would take far too much time. Textbook chapters often present summaries of chapter contents as part of chapter introductions (as in Parts Two through Five of this textbook). In this textbook, some of the questions for small-group and class discussion following the readings ask you to summarize major points or portions of readings in order to facilitate your understanding of the text. That process, in turn, enhances the quality of your classroom experience and develops your abilities to follow the discussion intelligently and to make useful contributions to the discussion yourself. Your instructor may ask you to write a summary of a piece you have read as a formal assignment. Summarizing is also an excellent strategy to enhance your own study habits. After reading an assignment for any of your courses, try to write a summary of the reading. If you cannot put into your own words the major ideas of what you have just read, you may need to go back and reread the material.

Outside the classroom and the academic environment, summaries routinely give brief introductions, overviews, and conclusions of subjects at hand. In business, industry, law, medicine, scientific research, government, or any other field, both managers and workers often need quick summaries to familiarize themselves with the high points or essence of information. Knowing how to summarize accurately is a useful skill in both your academic writing and your profession or job.

A Summary Is Not a Substitute for Analysis.   Do not mistakenly assume that putting another person's words into your own words is an analysis. Instead, **a summary is a brief, concise, objective restatement of the important elements of a piece of writing of any length,** from a paragraph to an entire book. A summary may be brief, as in a one-paragraph abstract that precedes a report or long paper and gives a very short overview of it, or it may be several paragraphs or even pages in length, depending on the length of the writing or writings being summarized. You may summarize as an informal exercise for your own purposes or as a formal assignment that you hand in to your instructor for evaluation.

Abstract.   An abstract, like all summaries, is a condensed, objective restatement of the essential points of a text. Its distinguishing characteristic is its brevity. Abstracts are usually quite short, perhaps 100 to 200 words, whereas summaries may be much longer, depending on the length of what is being summarized. As with all summaries, an abstract helps readers determine quickly whether an article or a book will be of interest or use. It can also serve as a brief guide to the key points before reading an article or as an aid in recalling the contents of the piece after reading it. You will almost always find an abstract before the beginning of a research paper or an article in the sciences. Following this is the abstract that precedes a research paper by Laurel Yahi titled "Effects of His Mother's Death on Joseph's Social and Emotional Development." This abstract provides a broad overview of her paper, including her major points and conclusions. In her paper, she discusses or develops each of these components at length, providing examples and supporting evidence where necessary. In 161 words, the abstract condenses a paper of more than 2,000 words to its most essential points. You can see how an abstract, like summaries of other lengths, is useful for getting a quick overview of a report or an essay.

Effects of His Mother's Death on Joseph's Social and Emotional Development

Laurel Yahi

Abstract

Four-year-old Joseph suddenly lost his mother two years ago. I have observed Joseph in my home daycare for 50 hours a week since his mother's death. With ample opportunity to observe him in this natural setting, I set about determining whether his mother's death might have long-term effects on Joseph's social and emotional development. At play, when working alone, at lunch time, and nap time, Joseph's cognitive abilities, vocabulary skills, willingness to listen to and obey adults, and social interaction skills appear normal for his age. He is well liked by the other children in the daycare. His progress, determination to learn, and intellectual growth all reflect a natural resiliency that lets him grow and mature without serious developmental problems. With a strong support system and a loving family, he should be able to grow into a healthy adult with no lasting negative effects on his ability to form relationships and participate fully in social settings, and enjoy good emotional health.

Formal and Informal Summaries.   Informal summaries are primarily for personal use and are usually not handed in for evaluation by an instructor. Formal summaries are those that others will read and are sometimes graded assignments. In either case, the process for writing a summary is virtually the same. For an example of an informal summary that would help a student prepare for a class discussion or recall key elements of an article, see the summary of Joe Saltzman's "What's in a Name? More than You Think," located in the discussion that follows that reading in Chapter 1. An example of a formal summary follows Charles Krauthammer's "The Moon We Left Behind," later in this chapter. The summaries of both Saltzman's and Krauthammer's articles underscore the need for a close, critical reading of the text to fairly represent what a writer says.

Although the process is the same for both an assignment that you will hand in to your instructor and a summary for your own use, a formal summary requires the kind of care that you give to longer writing assignments. The following directions will help you prepare and draft your formal summary:

Prewriting

1. Begin by carefully reading the work. Make a mental note of its thesis or main idea, but do not write anything in the margins yet. If you try to highlight for a summary on your first reading, you might end up underlining or noting too many things. Wait until you have read the entire selection through once before writing anything.

2. After your first reading, write in your own words the thesis or central idea as you understand it. Then go back to the article, locate the thesis or main idea, underline it, and compare it with the sentence you wrote. If your sentence differs from the sentence(s) you underlined, rephrase your own sentence.

3. Next, read the article again, this time looking for major points of development or illustration of the thesis. As you reread, make marginal notes and underline, circle, or in some way mark the key supporting points or major ideas in the development of the thesis.

4. After you have finished reading, look at your notes and state in one sentence, in your own words, the thesis and each major point. Do not include details or minor supporting evidence unless leaving them out would misrepresent or unfairly represent what you are summarizing. If the writing you are summarizing comes to any important conclusions, note them as well in one sentence in your own words.

5. If you are still unclear about which are major and which are minor points, give the piece another reading. The more you read it, the better you understand its purpose, method of development, and major points.

Writing Your Summary

1. In your opening sentence, state the author's full name, the title of the work, and the thesis or main idea. Write in complete sentences, whether your summary is 100 words or 500 words long.

2. Use the author's last name when referring to what he or she says in the article or when quoting the author directly.

3. Use attributive tags throughout; that is, use words and phrases that attribute or point to your source. Such tags serve the purpose of reminding your readers who you are quoting or summarizing. They may take the form of the author's last name or pronouns referring to the author, credentials of the author, published source of the material, or other information that

identifies the author (for example, "Krauthammer, in a recent article from the *New York Times,* observes that" or "he argues").

4. Do not use the exact words of the author unless you use quotation marks around those words. The summary must use your own wording. Use direct quotations sparingly, and only for a significant word, phrase, or sentence, and make sure that anything you put in quotation marks uses the exact wording of the article.

5. Use present tense to describe or explain what the author has written ("Krauthammer explains" or "Krauthammer concludes").

6. Provide clear transitions from point to point, just as you would in a longer assignment, and write in clear, coherent language.

7. Edit what you have written before turning it in to your instructor.

The key to summarizing accurately is knowing what is important and therefore must be included, and what is secondary and therefore should be omitted. Here you see the usefulness of the guidelines for critical reading. When you read critically, you identify the main idea or thesis of the selection, and you highlight or in some way mark major points. A summary must include the main idea of what you are summarizing, and it should include major points, and only major points. Thus, if you learn to read critically, you can write a summary.

GUIDELINES FOR WRITING A SUMMARY

- On your first reading, mentally note the thesis or central idea of the work or passage you are summarizing without writing anything down.
- After your first reading, write down your understanding of the thesis, locate the thesis in the work, underline it, check what you have written against it, and adjust your own sentence if necessary.
- Now reread the work, noting key points, either in the margin, by highlighting, or on a separate piece of paper.
- When you have finished your second reading, once again write in your own words a one-sentence summary of the thesis or central idea. Use the author's name and title of the reading in that sentence.
- Write in your own words a one-sentence summary of each major point the author has used to develop, illustrate, or support the thesis or central idea. State only essential details related to each major point.
- Do not include minor points unless you believe their omission would give an unfair representation of what you are summarizing.
- Where appropriate, write in your own words a one-sentence summary of any conclusion from the piece.
- Use attributive tags throughout your summary.
- Keep your summary short, succinct, and focused on the central idea and major points of the piece you are summarizing.
- Edit for grammar, punctuation, and spelling before handing in your assignment.

ILLUSTRATION: MAKING MARGINAL NOTES AND SUMMARIZING

Charles Krauthammer's opinion piece "The Moon We Left Behind" is reprinted here along with examples of marginal notes that would help prepare a written formal summary of it. The notes highlight the central idea and major points of the selection. A sample summary of the essay follows it.

THE MOON WE LEFT BEHIND

CHARLES KRAUTHAMMER

Charles Krauthammer, contributing editor to the New Republic *and* Time *magazine, writes a weekly syndicated column for the* Washington Post. *A political scientist, psychiatrist, journalist, and speech writer, Krauthammer won a Pulitzer Prize in 1987 for his commentary on politics and society and was the 2004 winner of the first $250,000 Bradley Prize, awarded to individuals of extraordinary talent who have made contributions of excellence in their field. He is author of the book* Cutting Edges: Making Sense of the Eighties *(1985). This essay appeared in the July 17, 2009, issue of the* Washington Post.

Opening quotation leads to his central point: dismay that we have stopped exploring the moon. Introduction ends with thesis.

Michael Crichton once wrote that if you told a physicist in 1899 that within a hundred years humankind would, among other wonders (nukes, commercial airlines), "travel to the moon, and then lose interest . . . the physicist would almost certainly pronounce you mad." In 2000, I quoted these lines expressing Crichton's incredulity at America's abandonment of the moon. It is now 2009 and the moon recedes ever further.

Next week marks the 40th anniversary of the first moon landing. We say we will return in 2020. But that promise was made by a previous president, and this president has defined himself as the antimatter to George Bush. Moreover, for all of Barack Obama's Kennedyesque qualities, he has expressed none of Kennedy's enthusiasm for human space exploration.

Does not believe we will return to moon in 2020 as promised.

So with the Apollo moon program long gone, and with Constellation, its supposed successor, still little more than a hope, we remain in retreat from space. Astonishing. After

Astonished by "retreat" from the space program.

Note loaded words: "magnificent bird" now a "truck" for "hauling." Is dismissive of "tinkertoy" space station.

Look up references to Spruce Goose and Concorde.

Says that we'll never fix problems on Earth, so no need to wait to go back to moon.

Look up "Manhattan Project."

Says that we have enough money to return to moon.

Says we must explore the moon for its "immense possibilities."

countless millennia of gazing and dreaming, we finally got off the ground at Kitty Hawk in 1903. Within 66 years, a nanosecond in human history, we'd landed on the moon. Then five more landings, 10 more moonwalkers and, in the decades since, nothing.

To be more precise: almost 40 years spent in low Earth orbit studying, well, zero-G nausea and sundry cosmic mysteries. We've done it with the most beautiful, intricate, complicated—and ultimately, hopelessly impractical—machine ever built by man: the space shuttle. We turned this magnificent bird into a truck for hauling goods and people to a tinkertoy we call the international space station, itself created in a fit of post–Cold War internationalist absentmindedness as a place where people of differing nationality can sing "Kumbaya" while weightless.

The shuttle is now too dangerous, too fragile and too expensive. Seven more flights and then it is retired, going—like the Spruce Goose and the Concorde—into the Museum of Things Too Beautiful and Complicated to Survive.

America's manned space program is in shambles. Fourteen months from today, for the first time since 1962, the United States will be incapable not just of sending a man to the moon but of sending anyone into Earth orbit. We'll be totally grounded. We'll have to beg a ride from the Russians or perhaps even the Chinese.

So what, you say? Don't we have problems here on Earth? Oh, please. Poverty and disease and social ills will always be with us. If we'd waited for them to be rectified before venturing out, we'd still be living in caves.

Yes, we have a financial crisis No one's asking for a crash Manhattan Project. All we need is sufficient funding from the hundreds of billions being showered from Washington—"stimulus" monies that, unlike Eisenhower's interstate highway system or Kennedy's Apollo program, will leave behind not a trace on our country or our consciousness—to build Constellation and get us back to Earth orbit and the moon a half-century after the original landing.

Why do it? It's not for practicality. We didn't go to the moon to spin off cooling suits and freeze-dried fruit. Any technological return is a bonus, not a reason. We go for the wonder and glory of it. Or, to put it less grandly, for its immense possibilities. We choose to do such things, said JFK, "not because they are easy, but because they are hard." And when you do such magnificently hard things—send sailing a Ferdinand Magellan or a Neil Armstrong—you open new human possibility in ways utterly unpredictable.

Blue Planet icon of environmentalism came from trip to moon.

The greatest example? Who could have predicted that the moon voyages would create the most potent impetus to—and symbol of—environmental consciousness here on Earth: Earthrise, the now iconic Blue Planet photograph brought back by Apollo 8?

Ironically, that new consciousness about the uniqueness and fragility of Earth focused contemporary imagination away from space and back to Earth. We are now deep into that hyper-terrestrial phase, the age of iPod and Facebook, of social networking and eco-consciousness.

Urges readers to look at the moon—a "nightly rebuke" for retreating from it.

But look up from your BlackBerry one night. That is the moon. On it are exactly 12 sets of human footprints—untouched, unchanged, abandoned. For the first time in history, the moon is not just a mystery and a muse, but a nightly rebuke. A vigorous young president once summoned us to this new frontier, calling the voyage "the most hazardous and dangerous and greatest adventure on which man has ever embarked." And so we did it. We came. We saw. Then we retreated.

How could we?

SAMPLE SUMMARY

Summary: "The Moon We Left Behind"

CHARLES KRAUTHAMMER

In his recent *New York Times* column "The Moon We Left Behind," Charles Krauthammer laments the decision by the United States to further postpone exploration of the moon for at least another decade. Declaring that he finds this decision "astonishing," Krauthammer extols the beauty of the space shuttle and bemoans its use as a delivery truck to the international space station. Describing the manned space program as being in "shambles" and dismissing the argument that we need to pay more attention to problems on Earth, Krauthammer answers the question "Why do it?" by affirming that undertaking difficult journeys has wonderfully unpredictable, glorious results. The moon, he writes, serves as "a nightly rebuke" for our retreat from lunar exploration.

EXERCISE

Select one reading that interests you in Parts Two through Five. Read it, take notes, and write a brief summary of it. Your instructor may want you to hand in your work or use it as part of a class or small-group discussion on summarizing effectively.

CHAPTER 4

Writing a Critique

THE CONNECTION BETWEEN READING CRITICALLY AND WRITING A CRITIQUE

Recall the guidelines for reading critically outlined in Chapter 1. The final step is to evaluate what you have read. **A critique is the written form of an evaluation of a passage or an entire work.** Reading critically is the biggest aid to writing a critique; applying the guidelines for reading critically is a crucial part of preparing to write a critique. You will need to understand not only the purpose of the piece and its central idea but also the writer's main points. Reading critically enriches your understanding of a work and its components, enabling you to focus your critique. So the first step in writing a critique is to read critically and, in the process, to determine your opinion of the piece.

Apply the guidelines detailed in Chapter 1, but especially look for the following: thesis and purpose of the writing, who the likely intended audience is, key ideas or supporting evidence for the thesis, the author's use of language, how well the piece is organized, and how successfully the piece has achieved its stated or implied goal. You may need to read the piece several times before you are clear on your own viewpoint and therefore prepared to write.

WRITING A CRITIQUE

When you write a critique, your goal is to make a formal analysis of and response to a piece of writing, whether a selected passage or an entire essay. Your purpose encompasses both explaining and evaluating a piece of writing. **A critique differs from a summary, which is an objective restatement in your own words of the original material. When you summarize, you leave out your personal or subjective viewpoint. In a critique, you begin objectively but then add your own subjective response to the work.** The components of your critique paper are as follows: introduction, summary, analysis, personal response, and conclusion. Before you begin to draft your critique, you will need to think about each of these components. Prewriting exercises are excellent preparation for the draft stage.

Prewriting

Determine Your Position.   To convince an audience that your analysis and response are reasonable or valid, you must convey your views confidently. Thus, before you even begin writing your critique, you must have a clear idea of your own viewpoint on the work. A firm conviction of your own position will help persuade an audience that your critique is sensible and fair.

How do you arrive at your position? You do so by carefully reading and rereading the piece that you are to critique, by thinking seriously about what the piece says and how it says it, and by assessing how persuaded you are as a reader by what the author has said. This stage in the writing process is crucial for helping you formulate and make concrete the points you want to make in the formal assignment.

As with other kinds of writing, any number of tools for generating writing ideas can be used to help you arrive at your position when writing a critique. The following suggestions are variations on those mentioned in Chapter 2, but here they are worded specifically to help you discover your response to a piece of writing that you are to critique.

- **Freewriting.** As soon as you have read the work, write for five to ten minutes on any impressions of any aspect of the piece that occur to you. Write down everything that comes to mind, no matter how jumbled. When your time is up, select a phrase or word that seems important to your purpose, no matter how vague it is, and write a sentence with the phrase or word in it. Put that sentence at the top of another blank piece of paper and repeat the process of writing for another five or ten minutes without thinking very deeply or long about what you are writing. If you do this several times, you should end up with a fairly good idea of the position you want to take in the analysis/assessment part of your paper. If you find that you cannot write very much, go back and reread the piece. It may be that you missed some important points on your first read-through and that a second or even a third reading will greatly clarify your position or view on the work.

- **Summarizing.** A summary of the piece is the first main part of your critique, but the act of summarizing can be a key part of your prewriting efforts. If you get stuck on generating ideas by brainstorming, perhaps you do not completely understand the work. This may be the writer's fault, and that criticism may become a part of your critique, but assuming that the piece itself is clearly written, it may be helpful for you to put in your own words what the author says. Doing that may help you discover the position you will take in your critique of the piece.

- **Listing.** Another way to discover your viewpoint is to simply list terms or phrases describing your response to the piece you are critiquing. Then study your list and group related ideas together. Do you see a pattern? Does one dominant viewpoint emerge from these groupings? If so, write a statement reflecting that pattern or viewpoint. That should give you a sense of your position when it comes to writing your assessment of and response to the work.

- **Asking questions.** Asking questions is a very useful tool for generating ideas, perhaps most useful when thinking about and drafting your response to a piece of writing. The discussion on analysis that follows suggests a number of useful points to consider when assessing the success of a writer's argument, language, evidence, and logic. Turning them into questions in the prewriting stage can help you arrive at your overall response to the work and to discover your own position in relation to that of the writer whose work you are critiquing. Because the response section of a critique expresses your personal, subjective reaction to the work, you will want to ask yourself these questions:

  - Do you agree with the writer's position on the subject? Why or why not?
  - What reasons can you give for supporting or disagreeing with the writer?
  - Are you convinced by the writer's logic, evidence, and language? Why or why not?
  - If you are not convinced, can you give other evidence to counter the arguments or evidence of the writer?

You need not go into great detail in the response section of your paper, but you do need to explain your reasons for your response. **Give careful thought, then, not only to *what* you think of the piece of writing but also to *why* you think that way.** What specific elements of the work influence your reaction to the work? As with freewriting, summarizing, and listing, write out your questions and answers, either on paper or on your computer. Review what you have written and consider whether you have left anything unasked or unanswered.

GUIDELINES FOR WRITING A CRITIQUE: PREPARATION AND PREWRITING

- First read the text carefully, applying the guidelines for reading critically (Chapter 1).
- Brainstorm, summarize, list, and/or ask questions.
- Determine the main points, the chief purpose, and the intended audience.
- Identify arguments that support or develop the main point.
- Locate evidence used to support the arguments.
- Determine any underlying biases or unexamined assumptions.

Drafting Your Critique

When you are satisfied with your prewriting activities and feel that you have generated enough ideas to write your critique confidently, you are ready to write your first draft. As with all writing assignments, you will likely write several drafts of a paper before you reach the final version.

COMPONENTS OF A CRITIQUE

The following section lists the components of a formal critique and gives directions for writing each of those components. In general, a written critique includes these components: (1) an introduction; (2) an objective, concise summary of the work or passage; (3) an objective analysis of the author's presentation; (4) a subjective response detailing your opinion of the author's views; and (5) a conclusion.

1. Introduction.   The first paragraph of your critique should name the author and title of the work that you are critiquing. Do not neglect this information, as it immediately tells readers the subject of your critique. Then give a very brief overview of the piece in two to four sentences. Your intent in the introduction is not to summarize the piece but to tell readers its purpose. Generally, stating the thesis or central idea of the piece along with a highlight or two and/or its major conclusion(s) will be enough to convey its essence and provide background for the rest of your paper. Finally, your introduction should state your own thesis. In one sentence, indicate your assessment of the passage or work that you examined. Your thesis statement should be worded to reveal your position to readers before they begin reading the body of your paper.

2. Summary.   The first section in the body of your critique should offer an objective summary of the piece. This summary states the original author's purpose and includes key ideas and major points. Where appropriate, include direct quotations that are particularly important to the development of the piece, but quote sparingly: the summary should be largely in your own words. Use direct quotations only when your own words would not do justice to the original. Do not write anything evaluative or subjective at this point. Your purpose here is to give a fair and accurate summary of the intent and main points of the work you are analyzing.

3. Analysis.   Once you have summarized the work by stating its purpose and key points, begin to analyze the work. Your goal is to examine how well the author has achieved the purpose and to consider the validity or significance of the author's information. Do not try to look at every point the author makes; rather, limit your focus to several important aspects of the piece. Remain as objective as possible in this section, saving your personal opinion of the author's position for the response section of your critique. Different purposes for writing—persuasive, expository, and expressive—require application of different criteria to judge a writer's success in achieving the intended purpose. In general, however, certain considerations help in the assessment of any piece of writing. **Questions about validity, accuracy, significance, and fairness help you evaluate any author's success or failure.**

Assess Persuasive Writing. Recall that in Chapter 2 argumentative writing is defined as a mode of persuasion in which the goal is either to convince readers of the validity of the writer's position (argument) or move readers to accept the author's view and perhaps even act on it (persuasion). This means that the writer must supply evidence or proof to support his or her position in such a way as to convince readers that the position is valid, whether they agree with the position. If the purpose is to persuade, the supporting evidence or proof must be so convincing that readers adopt the position themselves. Chapter 5 is devoted to a fuller discussion of writing an argument, so you may want to look at that chapter. In any event, when assessing the success of another writer's argument, you should gauge how well that writer has used the standard strategies for argumentation. Furthermore, pay attention to the writer's use of language. Finally, assess the validity of the argument by examining the evidence the writer presents to support his or her position and the logic of his or her conclusions.

Look Closely at a Writer's Language. In particular, make sure that the writer defines any words or terms that may be unclear, abstract, or ambiguous. Ask yourself whether the writer's language seems intended to intimidate or confuse readers or whether the writer attempts to manipulate readers by relying on emotionally loaded words. Does the writer make sarcastic remarks or personal attacks? Ultimately, examine a writer's evidence to evaluate credibility and fairness. Good writers do not rely on manipulative language, unclear terms, or loaded or sarcastic words to achieve their purposes.

Examine a Writer's Use of Appeals. Appeals are persuasive strategies that support claims or assertion or that respond to opposing arguments. They call upon logic, ethical considerations, or emotion to convince. An appeal to reason or logic uses statistics, facts, credible authority, expert testimony, or verifiable evidence to support claims in a reasoned, nonemotional way. Karen Sternheimer in "Do Video Games Kill?" (Chapter 8) relies on statistics to counter the claim that there is a causal relation between video games and the impulse to commit murder. Ethical appeals call upon shared values or beliefs to sway readers or motivate them to act. Jeff Corwin in "The Sixth Extinction" (Chapter 19) calls upon shared beliefs and the common good to urge individuals to become socially responsible for ultimately ensuring the future of mankind by taking care of all living creatures on Earth, not just humans. Emotional appeals use heavily charged language to evoke feelings of pity, awe, sympathy, or shock, for instance, rather than intellectual responses not tied to the feelings. Joe Saltzman in "What's in a Name?" (Chapter 1) discusses ways that reporters can sway emotions by the words they choose to describe the war in Iraq, whereas Jean Kilbourne in "Jesus Is a Brand of Jeans" (Chapter 9) looks at some of the ways in which advertisers use loaded words and images to manipulate people to buy their products. A balance of these three kinds of appeals makes the best arguments. As you examine a writing for the appeals used, determine how balanced they are. If a writer relies heavily on one kind of appeal to the exclusion of the others, especially if the main appeal is to emotion, the argument is probably weak.

Evaluate a Writer's Evidence. A writer should support any generalizations or claims with ample, relevant evidence. As a critical reader, consider the kinds of evidence used and the value or significance of that evidence. Evidence may take many forms, including hard fact, personal observation, surveys, experiments, and even personal experience. In evaluating evidence, ask how well the writer provides a context or explanation for the evidence used. Consider whether the writer establishes the significance of the evidence and how it is relevant to the thesis or central point. For instance, factual evidence may be supplied in the form of statistics, facts, examples, or appeals to authorities. Statistics can be manipulated to conform to the needs of the person using them, so make sure that they are based on a large and representative sample; the method of gathering the statistics yields accurate results; and the statistics come from reliable sources. Look closely at statements of facts as well; they should give accurate, complete, and trustworthy information. Examples are specific instances or illustrations that reveal a whole type, and they should give believable, relevant, reliable, and representative support for an author's thesis. Finally, authorities are people who have the training or experience needed to make trustworthy and reliable observations on matters relating to their areas of expertise. In completing a critique, make sure, as far as possible, that the piece under study appeals to believable and credible authorities.

Judge a Writer's Logic. Argumentative or persuasive writing must portray a logical, reasonable, and accurate reasoning process supplemented by relevant, sensible supporting proofs. You will be in a good position to evaluate a writer's reasoning process if you are mindful of any pitfalls that undermine the success of the argument. Evaluating the writer's logic is part of the process of critiquing a work. *For a discussion and examples of common flaws or fallacies, see the section on assessing evidence in Chapter 5.*

WRITING A CRITIQUE: QUESTIONS FOR ANALYSIS AND EVALUATION

- Has the author clearly stated or implied a thesis, main idea, or position?
- Has the author written to a clearly identifiable audience?
- What rhetorical strategies in the development and organization of the essay does the writer use? Is the development appropriate to the purpose?
- Is the essay logically and clearly organized?
- If the writing is an argument, does the author use verifiable facts or convincing evidence?
- If the essay seeks to explain, define, describe, or accomplish some other purpose, has the writer supplied enough details to clearly achieve the stated or implied purpose?
- Are language and word choice accurate, imaginative, correct, and/or appropriate?
- Does the text leave any unanswered questions?

4. Response.   In this part of your critique, express your own position relative to that of the writer of the piece and give reasons why you believe as you do. You may find yourself in total agreement or absolutely opposed to the author's position, or you may place yourself somewhere in between. You may agree with some points the author makes but disagree with others. No matter what position you take, you must state your viewpoint clearly and provide reasons for your position. These reasons may be closely linked to your assessment of key elements of the paper, as laid out in your assessment section, or they may spring from ideas that you generated in your prewriting activities.

5. Conclusion.   The final paragraph of your critique should reiterate in several sentences your overall assessment of the piece, the conclusions you have drawn from your analysis, and your personal response to the work. This section is not the place to introduce new material; rather, it is an opportunity to provide an overall summary of your paper. You want your readers to feel that you have given them a thorough and thoughtful analysis of the work under consideration and that you have brought your comments to a satisfying close.

GUIDELINES FOR WRITING A CRITIQUE

- **Begin with an introduction.** The introduction familiarizes readers with the work under discussion, provides a context for the piece, and states your thesis. State the author's name and the title of the piece.
- **Summarize main points.** The summary tells readers what major points the writer makes to support his or her position.
- **Analyze how well the writer has achieved the purpose of the piece.** The analysis tells readers what aspects of the work you have examined. In general, assess the overall presentation of evidence, judging its validity, accuracy, significance, and fairness.
- **Explain your response to the piece.** The response section tells readers your personal viewpoint by explaining the extent to which you agree or disagree with the author and why.
- **Conclude with your observations of the overall effectiveness** of the piece and your personal views on the subject. The conclusion summarizes for readers the results of your analysis and your overall judgment of the piece.

HANDLING SOURCE MATERIAL

Verb Tenses, Quoting, Paraphrasing, and Citing Sources.   As you draft your critique, keep in mind the following notes about verb tense and handling source material:

- **Verb tense.** Whenever you write about or refer to another person's work, use the present tense: "Lane Wallace *argues* . . ." or "Wallace *asserts* that. . . ." Use the past tense only to refer to something that happened before the time span of the essay: "**Wallace** offers a "cautionary tale" by relating the experiment that Bell Telephone made in 1952 to expand their managers' education . . ." (par. 7).

- **Handling quotations and paraphrases.** When writing a critique, you will often want to quote a passage directly or paraphrase it. In either case, you must cite the source where the original appears and use **attributive tags (words that identify the source)** to give credit to the source. Full details about handling source material appear in Chapter 6, with further examples in Chapter 7, but here are examples from the sample critique, that follows "Liberal Arts and the Bottom Line."

Celia quotes part of a sentence in this way:

In paragraph 2, still referring to Friedman's statement, Wallace refers to the bottom line as "the almighty measure of success" and then flippantly mocks that viewpoint with informal language.

In this example, Celia attributes the material to Wallace, uses quotation marks around words that she has taken directly from the source, and gives the paragraph number where the material appears for ease in locating it. Note that Celia uses the author's name (or a pronoun when the antecedent is clear) throughout the paper whenever she refers to her work. At the first mention of her name, Celia uses her full name; thereafter, she uses just her last name.

Here Celia paraphrases (puts in her own words) some of Wallace's main points:

Wallace offers a "cautionary tale" by relating the experiment that Bell Telephone made in 1952 to expand their managers' education and thereby better equip them to make sound business decisions (par. 7).

The words *cautionary tale* are Wallace's, so Celia uses quotation marks around them. The rest of the sentence paraphrases what Wallace says in her article.

In this example, Celia quotes a passage that is in quotation marks in the article:

Wallace begins her essay with a reference to economist Milton Friedman's often quoted observation that " 'the business of business is business'" (par. 1).

The single mark within the double indicates that the material is in quotation marks in the original.

Here Celia quotes material but leaves a word out to make her sentence grammatically correct:

In contrast, she says, the liberal arts student learns to be "a good global citizen, . . . balancing the numbers with more intangible metrics of success" (par. 14).

The **three spaced periods (ellipsis points)** indicate where the word appears in the original.

Here Celia adds an explanatory phrase, using brackets to indicate that the addition is hers:

Even her use of quotation marks indicates her viewpoint when she writes of the current interest in solving "the growing number of 'wicked' problems confronting [business executives]" (par. 4).

The words *business executives* do not occur in this passage from paragraph 4, so Celia replaced the word *them* with the bracketed information. Note also that "wicked" is in quotation marks in the original, hence the single quotation marks around it.

One of your primary obligations in any writing that incorporates the words or ideas of other authors is fairness to those you borrow from. Along with that is the obligation to be as clear and accurate as possible for your readers. Quoting and paraphrasing your sources and using attributive tags help you realize those obligations.

Citing Source Material

You have several options for citing source material, depending on the assignment. If the assignment is for everyone in the class to critique the same reading in your textbook and that reading is your only source, your instructor may tell you that it is not necessary to give a page number or to construct a separate "Work Cited" entry at the end of your paper. You must always name the author and title of the work you are critiquing in your opening paragraph, so that information is clearly stated from the beginning. It is quite useful for you to identify which paragraph your paraphrase or quotation is taken from, however, especially if the assignment is to critique a reading in this textbook, as paragraphs are numbered.

Even if everyone is critiquing the same reading, your instructor may want you to cite the source anyhow, just to get in the habit of citing sources. You will certainly want to cite your source if the assignment is to choose any reading in this textbook to critique and students are all doing different readings. In the case of the Lane Wallace reading that follows, and if your paper uses only that source, this is how you would cite it:

```
                          WORK CITED
         Wallace, Lane. "Liberal Arts and the Bottom
             Line." Perspectives on Contemporary
             Issues: Reading across the Curriculum.
             7th ed. Ed. Katherine Anne Ackley. Bos-
             ton: Wadsworth/Cengage, 2015. 67-69.
             Print.
```

The heading "Work Cited" is singular because there is only one source named. This format identifies the specific reading, beginning with the author, last name first, followed by the title of the reading. Next comes the name of the book in which the article appears. Note the punctuation between each component of the citation. The edition number follows the textbook, and that is followed by the name of the editor. The abbreviation "Ed." that precedes her name indicates that she is the editor. Place of publication, shortened title of publisher, and year of publication follow. The inclusive page numbers identify specifically which pages in the book the article is on, and the word *print* distinguishes the source from an electronic one.

If you supplement your critique with readings from other sources, then you will need to create a Works Cited list, with the word *Works* made plural because more than one source is listed. The list is alphabetical. Here is a hypothetical Works Cited list that includes the Wallace reading and additional sources:

WORKS CITED

Davis, Wes. "The 'Learning Knights' of Bell
    Telephone." *Nytimes.com*. 15 June 2010.
    Web. 12 Oct. 2014.

Neem, Johann. "The Liberal Arts, Economic
    Value, and Leisure." *Insidehighered.
    com*. 23 Oct. 2012. Web. 12 Oct. 2014.

Wallace, Lane. "Liberal Arts and the Bottom
    Line." *Perspectives on Contemporary
    Issues: Reading across the Curriculum*.
    7th ed. Ed. Katherine Anne Ackley. Boston:
    Wadsworth/Cengage, 2014. 67-69. Print.

GUIDELINES: HANDLING SOURCE MATERIAL IN A CRITIQUE

- Use present tense when referring to what the writer says in the work.
- Use past tense only to refer to events that happened before the article was written.
- When quoting directly, use exact words and cite the source of material.
- Use attributive tags, such as *the author says, comments, points out, observes, argues,* or similar words and phrases.
- When quoting directly, use brackets to enclose anything that you have added and ellipses to indicate where you have omitted words.
- When paraphrasing, use your own words and cite the source of material.
- The first time you mention the author, use his or her full name. Thereafter, use last name only. Never use first name only to refer to an author.
- If you use more than one source in your critique, alphabetize the sources in a separate list labeled "Works Cited" at the end of your paper.
- If you use one source, list it as a "Work Cited" or, if everyone is critiquing the same reading and your instructor agrees, omit that page.

EXERCISE

Read Lane Wallace's "Liberal Arts and the Bottom Line" and the sample critique that follows it. Prepare for class discussion by considering how you would critique the piece and how your response to the piece compares to that of the writer.

LIBERAL ARTS AND THE BOTTOM LINE

LANE WALLACE

Lane Wallace, columnist for The Atlantic *and editor for* Flying
Magazine, has written six books for NASA on flight and space explo-
ration. She has also worked as a writer and producer on a number of
television and video projects. Her latest book, Unforgettable *(2009),*
is a collection of some of her best adventure tales. She is an honorary
member of the United States Air Force Society of Wild Weasels and
won a 2006 Telly Award for her work on a documentary of the ex-
perimental aircraft X-31 crash, Breaking the Chain. *This piece was*
published in The Atlantic *on July 4, 2010.*

The popularity of the late economist Milton Friedman's philosophy among business people has never surprised me much. After all, telling business people that "the
business of business is business" is rather like telling people that eating dessert is
actually good for you. It tells your audience what they want to believe, and relieves
their guilt feelings about doing what they want to do anyway. No need to worry
about pesky issues like employee welfare, environmental impact (unless required),
or improving the social fabric of the community. No need to weigh the intangible
costs to others of moving a business overseas, closing a factory for a quick profit, or
paving roads through the Amazon to extract and export the oil.

By concentrating on the bottom line as the almighty measure of success,
Friedman's philosophy also tends to focus employees on numbers as a measure of their
own success. That focus, of course, encourages employees to work harder to increase
those numbers. Which, in turn—surprise, surprise!—improves the company's bottom
line even more. It's an incredibly convenient system that offers the appeal of neat and
clean boundaries, and maximum profit for the company. Really . . . what's not to like?

What's not to like, of course, is an uneasy feeling that sets in, periodically, that
perhaps the world isn't as neat as Friedman's economic model suggests. That by focusing exclusively on their own bottom lines, businesses can do extraordinary harm. (See:
recent economic meltdown and the BP oil disaster in the Gulf of Mexico.)

4   As a result of some of those recent disasters, as well as increasingly complex
global markets and a growing belief that today's business executives need what
investment icon Charlie Munger calls a "latticework of frameworks" to solve the
growing number of "wicked" problems confronting them, a movement has begun
to change what business students learn. At undergraduate and graduate business
schools across the country—including Wharton, Harvard, Stanford, Yale and a
host of other big names—curricula are being changed to include a greater focus
on multi-disciplinary approaches, ethics, critical and integrative thinking, and
even, in some cases, history and literature.

Roger Martin, the dean of the Rotman School of Management at the University of Toronto, has said openly that he's trying to create the first "liberal arts MBA." And when I asked David Garvin, a professor at the Harvard Business School and co-author of the recently published *Re-thinking the MBA: Business Education at a Crossroads* what he thought about that, he answered, "Is business education becoming more like the liberal arts? If the question is, 'are we trying to teach more about how to be a well-rounded human being who happens to be practicing business,' the answer is absolutely, 'yes.'"

On one level, these changes are an effort to assuage society's concerns about bloodthirsty and uncaring business executives bringing down economies or risking the destruction of an entire coastline in the name of profit. But on another level, they reflect a growing belief that the kind of complex, critical thinking and ability to look at problems in larger contexts and from multiple points of view that a liberal arts education instills (at least in theory) actually leads to better decision-making skills in business executives.

It's a viewpoint I actually endorse. Quite enthusiastically, as a matter of fact. But I recently came across a bit of history (in a *New York Times* article) [Davis, Wes. "The 'Learning Knights' of Bell Telephone." *New York Times* 16 June 2010: A31.] that offered a bit of a cautionary tale on this front—at least in terms of businesses buying into the goal of making managers more well-rounded human beings.

8   In 1952, the president of Bell Telephone of Pennsylvania apparently became concerned that his managers, most of whom had purely technical backgrounds, did not have the broader knowledge they required to make superior business decisions. "A well-trained man knows how to answer questions," the Bell executives were reported as reasoning. "But a well-educated man knows what questions are worth asking."

Bell paired up with the University of Pennsylvania to offer a 10-month immersion course in the Humanities and Liberal Arts for up-and-coming Bell managers. The managers studied history and architecture. They read classics like James Joyce's *Ulysses* and poetry by Ezra Pound. They toured art museums and attended orchestral concerts. They argued philosophy from multiple points of view.

At the end of the 10 months, the managers were reading far more than they had before—if, in fact (as the article's author pointed out), they'd even *read* before. They were far more curious about the world around them. And in the polarized world of the early 1950s, at the height of McCarthyism, the Bell managers now "tended to see more than one side to any given argument." As hoped, they were far more equipped to make better and more thoughtful decisions, and to figure out what questions were worth asking.

By all appearances, the program was a rousing success, as well as a ringing endorsement of the benefits of a liberal arts education. There was, however, an unexpected twist in the program's impact on the Bell managers. After learning about how much more there was in life than business, one of the questions they apparently decided was worth asking was, "why am I working so darn hard?" As the article put it, "while executives came out of the program more confident and more intellectually engaged, they were also less interested in putting the company's bottom line ahead of their commitments to their families and communities."

12   Within a few years, Bell had discontinued the program.

It's an interesting and—when you think about it—completely reasonable outcome. Aside from developing the ability to think critically and approach subjects from multiple perspectives and disciplines, the idea of a liberal arts education is to develop—as Professor Gavin said—a more well-rounded person. And being a workaholic is antithetical to a well-rounded person's psyche.

The current movement to make business students "more well-rounded human beings who happen to practice business" will almost assuredly create managers who think more about long-term consequences, impact on external audiences, being a good global citizen, and balancing the numbers with more intangible metrics of success. They may also be far more agile and creative thinkers who find successful middle ground between entrenched or polarized camps, generate more innovative solutions to sticky problems, and devise ingenious ways to responsibly benefit both their companies and the communities they serve.

But these more well-rounded managers may also go home earlier, or choose options—for themselves or for their companies—that put some other value above maximizing profit for the company or its shareholders. [As] Adam and Eve discovered, a little knowledge can be a very dangerous thing.

16   The question will be, somewhere down the line, what businesses or shareholders think of all that. For all the lip service we pay to wanting more well-rounded managers and responsible corporations, are we prepared to back that when it's our own income, stock or profit that's affected by those more balanced and responsible decisions? Or will we gravitate once more to Friedman's far less conflicted philosophy that—whatever else can be said about it—conveniently aligns the numbers-oriented thinking and motivation of managers with the best interests of their employers?

(SAMPLE CRITIQUE

Mitchell 1

Celia Mitchell

Dr. Jones

English 150:2

15 Oct. 2014

A Critique of "Liberal Arts and the

Bottom Line"

In her essay "Liberal Arts and the

Bottom Line," Lane Wallace discusses a

Title states specifically what is critiqued.

Title and author named, with author's full name used.

Mitchell 2

recent movement in higher education to try to create well-rounded business majors by requiring them to take liberal arts courses. The idea, Wallace says, is to broaden business students' focus from the "bottom line" to the larger world perspective fostered by courses in ethics, critical thinking, humanities, and the arts. Although she believes that liberal arts courses can help create such a perspective, she wonders if this recent trend will be accepted wholeheartedly. She poses a question: which do we—employers, employees, investors, society at large—value more, the bottom line or a more fulfilling life? Wallace suggests that ultimately we are more interested in the bottom line. While she makes some intriguing comments, her treatment of the subject relies on manipulative language and remains fairly shallow throughout.

Wallace begins her essay with a reference to the popularity of economist Milton Friedman's often-quoted comment that "'the business of business is business.'" The quotation serves as a springboard to the main focus of her essay, the efforts of some business schools to change the training of business students away from a narrow perspective by requiring them to take liberal arts courses.

This is the second mention of the author's name, so Celia uses last name only.

The introduction summarizes briefly what the article is about and states as a thesis Celia's assessment of the article.

The effects of focusing solely on the
bottom line, Wallace notes, can be seriously harmful, as exemplified by the BP
oil spill and the "recent economic meltdown" (par. 3). It also produces workers
with narrow world views and an inability to entertain multiple perspectives in
decision making or to think critically
(par. 14). She praises the recent trend
of business schools' incorporating liberal
arts courses into their curricula in order
to produce well-rounded managers and executives who can be "good global citizen[s]"
and who can think creatively and responsibly (par. 15).

This paragraph summarizes Wallace's essay in part. The summary continues in the next paragraph.

However, Wallace offers a "cautionary tale" by relating the experiment that
Bell Telephone made in 1952 to expand
their managers' education and thereby
better equip them to make sound business
decisions (par. 7). Managers took such
courses as art, history, and literature;
they engaged in cultural activities like
going to art museums and concerts. As a
result, the managers did indeed become
"well-rounded," but they also began to
value other things more highly than their
job with Bell Telephone. In the end, Bell
Telephone dropped the program. Wallace
implies that the same thing might happen
if the new business curricula actually

Mitchell 4

succeed in broadening future managers'
and executives' world views. While we
as "businesses or shareholders" might
pay "lip service" to the idea of turning managers into well-rounded people,
if it becomes a question of "our own
income, stock or profit that's affected,"
she wonders if we will prefer that those
business people pay more attention to the
bottom line (par. 16). This is the question that her essay builds toward and the
answer that she implies.

Note that Celia remains neutral in her summary of the main points of Wallace's essay.

        Wallace writes to a general audience
of presumably educated people, as readers of *The Atlantic* are likely to be, but
her word choice and tone are manipulative
from the beginning. She borders on the
sarcastic at times. She selects words that
reveal her own position on the issue even
before she openly states that position.
For instance, her first paragraph sar-
castically refers to businesses endorsing
Milton Friedman's view and disregarding
"pesky issues" like the environment, the
welfare of their workers, and the impact
of moving factories overseas. These issues
are not just "pesky," and she knows it. In
paragraph 2,
still referring to Friedman's statement,
she refers to the bottom line as "the
almighty measure of success" and then

Here Celia begins her analysis of the essay, focusing first on Wallace's word choice and tone.

Celia uses examples from the essay to illustrate her critique.

Mitchell 5

flippantly mocks that viewpoint with
informal language: "surprise, surprise!"
and "what's not to like?" Even her use of
quotation marks indicates her viewpoint
when she writes of the current interest in
solving "the growing number of 'wicked'
problems confronting [business execu-
tives]" (paragraph 4). Her references to
society's concerns about business executives being "bloodthirsty and uncaring"
lend weight to those allegations, whether
they are true or not, as does her suggestion that, when businesses focus on their
bottom lines to the exclusion of everything else, they "can do extraordinary
harm" (paragraph 3).

Now Celia states what she believes is a fault in Wallace's reasoning.

Furthermore, Wallace is guilty of
a kind of narrow vision of her own. She
views the distinction between business and
liberal arts as a black and white issue,
whereby the business student learns to
be a "workaholic," focusing only on the
needs of business, more specifically its
bottom line (par. 13). In contrast, she
says, the liberal arts student learns to
be "a good global citizen, . . . balancing the numbers with more intangible metrics of success" (par. 14). She implies
quite strongly that business majors cannot be well-rounded and that the business
curriculum is narrow and limiting. At the

same time, she states that liberal arts majors are capable of complex thinking and have the ability to consider multiple perspectives, abilities that make them better decision makers than those who take only business courses. She does mention at one point that it is "at least in theory" that the liberal arts trains people to think critically, thus allowing for the possibility that not all liberal arts students learn to take in multiple perspectives and think critically, but the phrase is an aside and has no real place in her argument.

While Wallace raises some interesting points related to this issue and her use of the Bell Telephone experiment gives her warning some weight that it might not otherwise have, she is unfair to business majors and ends with a question that needs much more discussion. Overall, her lightweight tone and language choices undermine her position. Furthermore, in not allowing for the possibility that business students can become well-rounded citizens or that liberal arts students might focus too narrowly on their careers, she is guilty of hasty generalizations that weaken her overall effect. Surely there is much more to this issue than Wallace has indicated in her article.

The conclusion summarizes Celia's own view of the Wallace essay, including what she sees as its strengths and weaknesses.

WORK CITED

Wallace, Lane. "Liberal Arts and the Bottom
    Line." *Perspectives on Contemporary
    Issues: Reading across the Curriculum.*
    7th ed. Ed. Katherine Anne Ackley.
    Boston: Cengage, 2015. 67-69. Print.

EXERCISE

Select a reading that interests you in Parts Two through Five. Read it, take notes, and write a critique of it. Your instructor may want you to hand in your work or use it as part of a class or small-group discussion on summarizing effectively.

CHAPTER 5

Writing an Argument

Much of the writing that you do for your college classes is argumentation. It may not be called that formally, but any writing exercise that asks you to state a position and defend it with evidence that is true or reasonable is a form of argument. Whenever you state your opinion or make an assertion and back it with proof, you are making an argument. As you can see, just about any writing that has a thesis or implicit central idea that requires evidence or proof is a form of argument. Whether you provide evidence to explain, illustrate what you know, inform, prove a point, or persuade, if you take a position on a subject and support or develop it with evidence to demonstrate that it is valid or sound, you are making an argument.

Oftentimes students are specifically assigned the rhetorical mode of argumentation, a reasoning process that seeks to provide evidence or proof that a proposition is valid or true. **An argument sets forth a claim in the form of a thesis statement, refutes the arguments of the opposition—sometimes giving in or conceding to certain points—and presents a coherent, organized set of reasons why the claim is reasonable. To demonstrate that your position is logical or right, you must offer reasons why you believe that way in order to convince your audience.** An argument may have several goals or purposes, either singly or in combination, such as to show relationships between things (**causal argument**), to explain or define something (**definition argument**), to evaluate something or support a position on it (**evaluative argument**), to inform (**informative argument**), or to sway an audience to change a position or take action on something (**persuasive argument**). Argumentation is a useful tool for developing critical thinking because doing it well requires close analysis of your own ideas as well as those of others. Writing an argument involves the same general procedure as that detailed in Chapter 2 on the writing process: prewriting or planning, drafting, revising, and editing.

NARROWING YOUR FOCUS AND DISCOVERING YOUR POSITION

All arguments begin with a position, claim, or proposition that is debatable and that has opposing viewpoints. Statements of fact are not debatable; abstract generalizations are too vague. If your position is not debatable, there is no argument. Furthermore, in an argument, your goal is to convince those opposed to your position or who are skeptical of it that yours is valid or true. You might even want to persuade your audience to abandon their position and adopt yours or go beyond that and perform some action. Your first step, then, is to select a controversial subject or issue in which you have a strong interest. That begins the process that will ultimately lead you to the position that you want to argue.

A good starting point for discovering a topic to argue is to make a list of controversial issues currently in the news or being discussed and debated publicly or among your friends or family. *Remember that this is only a starting point.* These general topics are far too broad for a short paper, but they give you a beginning from which to start narrowing your focus. From your list, select the subjects that interest you most or that you feel strongly about and develop a series of questions that you might ask about them. This process of considering a variety of views when contemplating a topic you would like to argue helps you solidify your position. For instance, you might ask the following: Should bilingual education be offered in public schools? Should the Electoral College be abolished? Is affirmative action a fair policy? Should gay couples be allowed to marry? Although such questions seldom have absolutely right or wrong answers, it is useful to frame your position by saying (or implying), "Yes, bilingual education should be offered in public schools," or, "No, affirmative action is not a fair policy." But making up your mind about how you feel about an issue is only the beginning. You must also convince others that your position is logical, reasonable, or valid. You do that by providing strong evidence or reasons to support your position and by anticipating and addressing the arguments of those who do not agree with you.

The following list of potentially controversial subjects may give you an idea of the kinds of general topics that can be narrowed for an argumentative paper. To this list, add others that appeal to you as potential topics for an argument. Then, select those subjects that you have the strongest interest in or hold opinions about and, taking each in turn, spend some time writing down questions that come to mind about that subject, issues related to it that you are aware of, and/or what your preliminary position on the subject is: What is the controversy? Who is affected by it? Why is it controversial? What is the context or situation? What is your position on that controversy? Why do you believe as you do? What evidence or proof do you have to support your position? What do those opposed to your position argue?

At this stage, you are simply **brainstorming or freewriting** to see what you know about certain self-selected subjects that you would be comfortable with developing into an argument paper. When you have finished, examine the results of your brainstorming session and narrow your list to the one or two that you have the most to say about or feel most strongly about. Brainstorm further on those issues by framing questions about the subject or trying to identify the problem associated with it. Keep in mind that you not only want to find an issue or issues that you have a strong interest in, but you must also consider the implications of the position you take on that issue. How will you convince your audience that your position is reasonable or logical? How can you best defend your position? How can you best meet the arguments of those opposed to you?

You are looking for a topic that poses a question or problem you believe that you know the answer or solution to. This is your position. Once you know your position, you are ready to commit time to thinking about and researching the best evidence or proof to support your position.

POSSIBLE SUBJECTS FOR ARGUMENTATION

Adolescents tried as adults	English-only movement	National security
Advertising images	The environment	Nuclear energy
Affirmative action	Free agency in sports	Nuclear proliferation
Airline security	Gender issues	Nuclear waste
Animal rights	Gender roles	Ozone layer depletion
Bilingual education	Genetic engineering	Pay inequity
Censorship	Global warming	Regulating toxic emissions
Civil rights	Gun control/gun rights	Same-sex marriages
College—is it for everyone?	Home schooling	Space exploration
Compensation for organ donors	Human cloning	Special-interest groups
Controversial speaker on campus	Illegal aliens	Sports violence
Cyber bullying	Immigration	Steroids and athletes
Cyber stalking	Intellectual freedom	Stereotypes in mass media
Drunken driving or DUI punishment	Intellectual property rights	Sweatshops
Electoral College	Internet: government control	Terrorism in America
Eliminating the grading system		
Embryo or stem-cell research		

Examples of Narrowing a Focus

1. Suppose you are interested in the subject of downloading copyrighted music from the Internet without paying for it, currently illegal but still being done all over the world. Some people argue that this act violates intellectual property rights. Should those who download music from the Internet be charged with a crime? Should those who wish to download music from the Internet have to pay for that service? People will disagree on how these questions should be answered; thus, they are legitimate subjects for argumentation. Suppose you believe that, no, downloading music from the Internet should not be regarded as a criminal act. What other questions does that position lead to, then? Should downloading music be free and open to anyone who wants to do it? If so, what is the fairest way to treat artists whose copyrighted music is being downloaded from the Internet? Do they not have the right to profit from the use of their music?

2. Consider the suggestion that the grading system at the college level be abolished. You might wonder: Should the grading system be abolished? Who would benefit from abolishing the grading system? Why should the grading system be abolished? Why should the grading system not be abolished? What would replace the grading system were it abolished? How would abolishing the grading system affect students and instructors? Would it change the dynamics of the learning process?

3. Imagine that the office in charge of programming at your campus wants to bring a controversial person for its speaker series. Suppose you are a student at a private faith-based liberal arts college and the speaker is an avowed atheist, or suppose you are a state-funded liberal arts university and the speaker is a religious-right fundamentalist. Who would support bringing this speaker to campus? Who would oppose it? What reasons might both those in favor of and against bringing the speaker to campus give to support their positions? Are there contexts or situations where it might be appropriate and others where it would not? Which side would you support in such a controversy?

4. Erin was intrigued by an essay that she read on advertising images of women, so she began the process of discovering her position on that topic by thinking about the very general subject "advertising images." Here are the questions she asked and the thoughts that she jotted down:
   - Do advertising images affect behavior?
   - Isn't it the purpose of an ad to influence behavior?
   - So what if advertisements do affect behavior? What's the harm?
   - Such power might influence behavior the wrong way.
   - What is the wrong way? Affects self-esteem. Makes people feel inadequate. Reduces women to objects.
   - What about men? Ads affect them too.
   - Some ads set up unrealistic, even impossible-to-attain, images of men and women. Young or old, male or female.

- Ads present false images of relationships between men and women. Ads focus a lot on sex and on attacking people's vulnerabilities.
- Who bears responsibility? Advertisers. They need to consider the effects of their ads.
- What should they do? Modify images that attack and weaken self-esteem.
- Topic: advertisers' responsibility for their ads.

Her questions, answers, and ideas may look rambling, but they ultimately led her to her topic, which she refined by focusing specifically on ads featuring women that have the potential to affect self-esteem and body image.

5. In her introductory women's studies and sociology classes, Rita became interested in the status of women in the workforce. She learned about federal legislation that made it illegal to discriminate in the workplace on the basis of sex, among other things. She also knew that when her mother and grandmother were growing up, the women's movement had done much to address inequities in women's lives. So she was surprised by some of the facts that she learned in her classes about women's work force participation and earnings. On the other hand, Rita had often heard people comment that women have now achieved equity, even arguing that there was no longer job discrimination or discrepancies between what men and women earn for the same work. Furthermore, several class-action sex-discrimination lawsuits brought by female employees against large corporations had been in the news recently, with the corporations hotly denying any form of sex discrimination. Therefore, when her English instructor assigned an argumentative paper using source materials, Rita decided to research this controversial subject.

   Rita's question was, Have women really achieved equality in the workplace? Her reading in this area led her to the conclusion that, no, despite everything that has been done to make women equal to men in employment, they have not yet achieved that goal. Although she found that there are differences not only in earnings but also in rates of promotion and representation at higher, managerial ranks, she decided to focus her paper on just the issue of the wage gap. The proposition she formulated for her paper is the following: Despite decades of struggling for women's equality in the workplace, the wage gap between men and women remains unacceptably wide. Rita's paper is located at the end of this chapter.

GUIDELINES FOR NARROWING YOUR FOCUS AND DISCOVERING YOUR POSITION

- Jot down a controversial or arguable subject that you have a strong interest in or about which you have an opinion.
- Ask questions about that subject from as many angles as you can think of.
- Write down ideas that occur to you as you ask questions.

- Repeat the brainstorming process by asking more questions and writing more thoughts as they occur. At this stage you are working toward a defensible position on a fairly narrow topic.
- Consider how you might defend your position, how you would counter the arguments against it, and what evidence you might need.
- Begin the process of thinking about, researching, and writing your paper on that narrow topic.

STRUCTURING AN ARGUMENT

Structuring an argument is similar to structuring most other kinds of writing. Recall that in Chapter 2, the typical essay has certain components: a title, an opening paragraph that introduces the topic by providing a context or background for it and that leads to a **thesis statement;** fully developed paragraphs in the body of the paper that advance, support, illustrate, or otherwise relate to the thesis; and a **conclusion.** Effective arguments follow that pattern, with some additions or variations. In formal argumentation, these parts of your essay might be labeled differently, but they are essentially the same. For instance, a thesis might be called a proposition or position statement, but it is still the central idea of the paper. Development might be referred to as offering supporting proof by refuting the opposition, making concessions where necessary, and offering evidence in a logical, well-reasoned way.

What follows are various components of a well-organized and well-developed argument. The discussion in general assumes a traditional, formal Aristotelian mode of argument, with the goal of proving one's proposition or thesis while countering or refuting the opposition, but there are other approaches that use different lines of reasoning. Two of the most prominent are the informal approach of Toulmin and Rogers. The Toulmin approach, like the Aristotelian, views argument as oppositional, with a goal to proving one's position; the Rogerian, on the other hand, uses conflict-resolution based on compromise, a goal that searches for common ground or mutual agreement rather than refuting the opposition. These three approaches are discussed in more detail in the section labeled "Strategies for Arguing Effectively," under the heading "Follow a Logical Line of Reasoning."

Introduction.   The opening of your argument lays the groundwork for the rest of the paper by establishing the tone you will take, providing any clarification or preliminary information necessary and/or giving a statement of your own qualifications for asserting a position on the topic. Here is an opportunity to provide a context for your argument, establish your initial credibility, and connect with your audience. Credibility is the level of trustworthiness your audience perceives in you. If you can convey an impression that you are credible early in your paper, your audience may be more willing to think of you as reliable or trustworthy and therefore be more receptive to your argument. Otherwise, they may dismiss your evidence, question your motive, or simply refuse to accept what you are saying.

Context.   When explaining background or situation, you establish a context within which your audience is to consider your argument. Establishing tone is part of the context. You might provide a striking quotation, cite statistics, or define the problem or controversy in terms that everyone agrees on. Brad Zembic's opening in "Print Media and the Rabbit Hole" (Chapter 9) provides a context for his argument that the print media are more deceptive than ever by describing an advertisement for a recent film version of *Alice in Wonderland* that superimposed an image of Johnny Depp as the Mad Hatter over the front page of *The Los Angeles Times,* in effect using the newspaper as a billboard. Zembic needed to establish this context immediately in order to explain both the title and the reason for the essay. When an issue is particularly controversial, writers may not be able to establish sympathy with readers. Nevertheless, some sort of context or reason for writing needs to be established early in the essay. We see this in Anthony Gregory's "Why Legalizing Organ Sales Would Help Save Lives, End Violence" (Chapter18) Gregory takes a usually unpopular position on the issue of legalizing live organ donations by countering some of the moral and ethical objections to doing so. The issue of voluntary, compensated organ sales, particularly of kidneys, has been debated for years, rather heatedly at times. Gregory has to couch his argument in non-offensive and conciliatory tones in order to avoid offending readers from the start.

Credibility.   Any number of strategies help to establish credibility in an argument. Beginning with your introduction and continuing throughout your argument, demonstrating to your readers that you are fully informed, reasonable, and fair establishes credibility and makes your audience more receptive to your position. Using trustworthy outside sources to support, explain, defend, or back general statements demonstrates that your position is based on more than just your personal opinion. To show that others, perhaps professionals with more experience than you, have done research or hold similar views reflects well on your own credibility. Furthermore, citing sources or statistics shows that you have done your homework, that you are so familiar with or knowledgeable about your subject, and that you know what others have to say about it. These things go toward establishing your credibility as a writer. Using hard data such as facts or statistics also helps, as does acknowledging and countering viewpoints opposed to yours.

Statement of the Case.   As clearly as possible in your opening paragraph(s), provide a rationale or need for what you are arguing. Provide a context for the argument, give relevant background material, or explain why you believe as you do. Establishing need helps to convey your credibility by showing that you are knowledgeable about your subject. It is also a good strategy for connecting with your audience. In stating the case for the argument, you might explain that it is worth upholding or endorsing because it has some bearing on the lives of readers or the common good of a community or society. You may also want to indicate the degree to which a particular issue or policy is controversial. Take, for instance, Michael Crichton's opening in "Patenting Life" (Chapter 18): "You, or someone you love, may die because of a gene patent that should never have been granted in the first place. Sound far-fetched? Unfortunately, it's only too real." His next sentences elaborate on that opening, but the compelling first few sentences strongly suggest a need to look at the issue of gene patents.

Proposition.   The proposition is an assertion or claim about the issue. It is virtually the same as a thesis or position statement and should be stated clearly near the beginning of the essay. Jean Kilbourne, in her essay "Jesus Is a Brand of Jeans" (Chapter 9), states her proposition after opening with examples of advertisements that lead to her assertion: "Ads have long promised us a better relationship via a product: *buy this and you will be loved.* But more recently they have gone beyond that proposition to promise us a relationship with the product itself: *buy this and it will love you.* The product is not so much the means to an end, as the end itself." In most arguments, as Kilbourne does in hers, you must make your position clear very early and then devote the rest of your paper to providing supporting evidence, details, or facts to "prove" that your position is a logical or reasonable one. The strength of your argument will come from your skill at refuting or challenging opposing claims or viewpoints; giving in or conceding on some points; and then presenting your own claims, evidence, or other details that support your position.

Refutation of Opposing Arguments.   It is not enough to find facts or evidence that argue your own position and therefore prove its validity; you must also realize that those opposed to your position will have their own facts or evidence. You must try to project what you think others may say or even try to put yourself into their position. An excellent strategy for argumentation, therefore, is to first look at the claims of others and challenge or dispute them. One of the chief strengths of a good argument is its ability to counter evidence produced by the opposing side. In fact, you must imagine more than one opposing side. Rarely is an issue represented by just two equal and opposing arguments. Often it is represented by multiple viewpoints. Obviously you cannot present every aspect and every position of an issue, but you must demonstrate that you are aware of the major viewpoints on your subject and that the position you have taken is a reasonable one. The preparatory step of anticipating or imagining the opposing position(s) will be a huge help in developing your own argument. Ask yourself what you think will be the strategy of those opposed to your position and how you can best address that opposition and counter it with your own logical reasoning. Ignoring an opposing opinion is a major fault in argumentation because it suggests that you have not explored enough aspects of the topic to warrant the position you are taking. For more on refutation, see the section on anticipating the opposition in the section on strategies for effective argumentation later.

Concessions to Opposing Arguments.   Often, some of what those opposed to your position argue is valid or irrefutable. A very effective, necessary, and wise strategy is to make concessions to the opposition. It helps establish your reliability as a fair-minded person. The act of acknowledging limitations or exceptions to your own argument and accepting them actually strengthens your argument. It indicates your commitment to your position despite its flaws, or suggests that, even flawed, your position is stronger than the positions of those opposed to it. It is best to make these concessions or acknowledgments early in your paper rather than later. For more on making concessions, see the section on conceding to the opposition in the section on strategies for effective argumentation.

Development of Your Argument.   In this stage of the process, you present evidence or proof to persuade your audience of the validity of your position. The argument will be most effective if it is organized with the least convincing or least important point first, building to its strongest point. This pattern lends emphasis to the most important points and engages readers in the unfolding process of the argument as the writer moves through increasingly compelling proofs. A successful argument also gives evidence of some sort for every important point. Evidence may include statistics, observations or testimony of experts, personal narratives, or other supporting proof. A writer needs to convince readers by taking them from some initial position on an issue to the writer's position, which readers will share if the argument succeeds. The only way to do this is to provide evidence that convinces readers that the position is a right or valid one.

Conclusion.   In the closing paragraph(s) of your paper, you have a final opportunity to convince your audience that the evidence you have presented in the body of your paper successfully demonstrates why your proposition is valid. You may want to summarize your strongest arguments or restate your position. You may want to suggest action, solutions, or resolutions to the conflict. This final part of your paper must leave your audience with a feeling that you have presented them with all the essential information they need to know to make an intelligent assessment of your success at defending your position and possibly persuading them to believe as you do.

GUIDELINES: BASIC STRUCTURE OF AN ARGUMENT

- **Introduction**—Familiarizes audience with subject, provides background or context, conveys credibility, and establishes tone.
- **Statement of the case**—Provides rationale or need for the argument.
- **Proposition**—Asserts a position or claim that will be supported, demonstrated, or proved in the course of the paper.
- **Refutation of opposing arguments**—Mentions and counters potential evidence or objections of opposing arguments.
- **Concession**—Acknowledges validity of some opposing arguments or evidence.
- **Development of the argument**—Offers convincing, creditable, evidence in support of proposition.
- **Conclusion**—Brings paper to a satisfactory end.

STRATEGIES FOR ARGUING EFFECTIVELY

Whereas the previous section outlines the essential structure of an argument, the following comments will also help you write an effective argument.

Know Your Audience.   A consideration of who your audience is will help you anticipate the arguments of those opposed to you. Many instructors tell students to imagine an audience who disagrees with them. After all, there really is no argument if you address an audience of people who believe exactly as you do. Knowing your audience will help you figure out what strategies you must use to make your position convincing. Imagine that you are addressing an audience who is either indifferent to or opposed to your position. This will help direct the shape of your argument because such an audience will require solid evidence or persuasive illustrations to sway its opinion.

Establish an Appropriate Tone.   Tone refers to the writer's attitude toward his or her subject. As a writer of argument, you want your audience to take you seriously; weigh what you have to say in defense of your position; and, ideally, not only agree that your reasoning is sound but also agree with your position. Therefore, try to keep your tone sincere, engaging, and balanced. You do not want to take a hostile, sarcastic, or antagonistic tone because then you risk alienating your audience. If you are too light, flippant, or humorous, your audience might believe you to be insincere or not truly interested in your topic.

Anticipate the Arguments of the Opposition.   As mentioned earlier, one key aspect of argumentation is refuting arguments of those who hold opposing opinions. How do you anticipate what those opposed to your position believe? Perhaps you are already familiar with opposing positions from your own observations or discussions with others, but a good step in your preparation is to look for articles or books that express an opinion or a position that you do not share. Read the arguments, determine the authors' positions, and note the evidence they produce to support their positions. How can you refute them? What evidence of your own contradicts them and supports your own position? Sometimes students find themselves being convinced by the arguments of others and switch their positions. Do not worry if that happens to you. In fact, it will probably aid you in your own argument because you are already familiar with the reasoning of that position and can use the new evidence that persuaded you to find fault with your old position.

Keep in mind that this strategy of refuting an opposing argument does not always require disproving the point. You may also question its credibility, challenge the point, identify faulty logic, or otherwise cast doubt on it. Take care when challenging the opposition that you are on solid ground and can back up your own claims with proof. To attack a point by simply declaring it wrongheaded or insubstantial without having your own solid evidence is to considerably weaken your argument. So look for any of the following ways to challenge the opposition:

- **Question the validity of data or evidence: Are statistics accurate?** What is the source of data? Does the opposition skew or slant data to fit its own needs?

- **Question authority: What are the credentials of authorities cited in arguments?** Do their credentials qualify them to have informed opinions on the topic? Do they have questionable motives?

- **Challenge the logic of the opposition: What fallacies do you find?** What flaws in the reasoning process are there?

Make Concessions.   Sometimes it is necessary to concede a point to the opposition—that is, to acknowledge that the opposition has made a reasonable assertion. Making a concession or two is inevitable in arguments of complex issues. Conceding to the opposition is actually a good strategy as long as you follow such a concession with even stronger evidence that your position is the reasonable one. You agree that the opposition makes a good point, but you follow that agreement with an even more persuasive point.

Follow a Logical Line of Reasoning.

Aristotelian Logic. Formal, classic argumentation typically follows one of two common lines of reasoning, **deductive** and **inductive** reasoning. In deductive reasoning, you move from a general principle, or shared premise, to a conclusion about a specific instance. Premises are assumptions that people share, and the conclusion will be implied in the premises or assumptions. The traditional form of deductive reasoning is the **syllogism,** which has two premises and a conclusion. A **premise** is defined as an assumption or a proposition on which an argument is based or from which a conclusion is drawn. The premises are often referred to as major and minor, with the major premise being the general truth and the minor premise a specific instance. The classic syllogism, offered by Aristotle (384–322 BCE), a Greek mathematician and logician, is the following:

Major premise: All men are mortal.
Minor premise: Socrates is a man.
Conclusion: Socrates is mortal.

This simple example of syllogism indicates the basic formula: A is B. C is B. Therefore A is C. Arguments are described as valid when the premises lead logically to the conclusion. If they do not, the argument is invalid. Similarly, an argument is said to be sound if the argument is valid and leads to the conclusion; it is unsound if the argument is valid but does not lead to the conclusion or if the conclusion is valid but the argument is not. Here is another example:

Major premise: Driving while drunk is illegal.
Minor premise: Joe was drunk when he drove home from the party.
Conclusion: Joe committed a crime.

In contrast, inductive reasoning moves from a number of specific instances to a general principle. Rather than begin with a shared assumption or generalization, you must provide sufficient data or evidence that the generalization is warranted. Your intent is to show the general pattern by presenting relevant specific instances as evidence. To avoid being accused of overgeneralizing or making a hasty generalization, you must provide enough data, examples, or specific instances to ensure that your audience is satisfied with your conclusion. In contrast to deductive reasoning, which rests on certainties (shared or commonly acknowledged truths), inductive reasoning relies on probability (the likelihood that something is true).

Example.

Observation one: Students entering the classroom have wet hair and damp clothes.

Observation two: Students typically come from outside the building to class.

Conclusion: It must be raining outside.

With induction, you must be very careful that your data do indeed warrant your conclusion. For instance, consider the following example of **hasty generalization:**

Observation one: The daily high temperatures for the last several days have been unusually high.

Observation two: I don't remember it ever being this hot during the summer.

Conclusion: We must be experiencing global warming.

Obviously there is not enough evidence in either of the observations to establish that global warming accounts for the recent high temperatures.

Although formal argumentation is useful when arguing in abstract or ideal disciplines, such as mathematics, it is less effective in complex, real-world situations—that is, the kinds of arguments in which you are likely to be engaged. Aristotle himself realized that syllogistic reasoning, which deals in absolutes, was not suited to all arguments and that many arguments depended on an informal logic of probabilities or uncertainties. His study of this system of reasoning was known as **rhetoric,** which he defined as "the faculty of discovering in any particular case all of the available means of persuasion." Formal syllogistic logic typically leads to one correct and incontrovertible conclusion, while informal or rhetorical logic allows for probable or possible conclusions. As in syllogistic logic, the reasoning process must be rational and practical.

The Toulmin Model of Reasoning. A model of informal argumentation, or practical reasoning, is that described by Stephen Toulmin, a twentieth-century philosopher, mathematician, and physicist. This method is not as constrictive as formal syllogistic reasoning because it allows for probable causes and reasonable evidence. With this method, an argument is broken down into its individual parts and examined: each stage of the argument leads to the next. Toulmin defined argumentation as a process or logical progression from **data** or **grounds** (evidence or reasons that support a claim) to the **claim** (the proposition, a debatable or controversial assertion, drawn from the data or grounds) based on the **warrant** (the underlying assumption). The *claim* is the point your paper is making, your thesis or arguable position statement. *Data* or *grounds* constitute your proof and demonstrate how you know the claim is true or the basis of your claim. *Warrants* are the underlying assumptions or inferences that are taken for granted and that connect the claim to the data. They are typically unstated or implied and can be based on any of several types of appeals: logic, ethics, emotion, and/or shared values.

This view of argumentation as a logical progression has similarities to formal argumentation but does not rely on inductive or deductive reasoning that leads inevitably to one true conclusion. Rather, it relies on establishing the relationship between data and the claim by offering evidence that supports the warrant and leads to the best possible, the most probable, or the most likely conclusion. In such reasoning, the argument often attempts to defuse opposing arguments with the use of **qualifiers** such as *some, many, most, usually, probably, possibly, might,* or *could.* Qualifiers indicate awareness that the claim is not absolute but reasonable in the specific instance. This step reveals how sure you are of your claim.

The argument should also recognize any **conditions of rebuttal**—that is, exceptions to the rule. Rebuttals address potential opposing arguments, usually by showing flaws in logic or weakness of supporting evidence. An argument will also, if necessary, make **concessions** or acknowledgments that certain opposing arguments cannot be refuted. Often **backing**—additional justification or support for the warrant—is supplied as a secondary argument to justify the warrant. To succeed, an argument following the Toulmin model depends heavily on the strength of its warrants or assumptions, which in turn means having a full awareness of any exceptions, qualifications, or possible reservations.

Rogerian Argument. Based on the work of the American psychologist Carl R. Rogers, this approach adopts the stance of listening to arguments opposed to your own with an open mind, making concessions, and attempting to find a common ground. Thus it attempts to compromise rather than assume confrontational or adversarial opposition. The Rogerian approach is well suited to subjects that are particularly explosive or controversial, when the writer knows that the audience will be hostile or hold opinions and beliefs different from her own. This approach to argumentation differs from both the Aristotelian and Toulmin methods by focusing on conflict resolution, with both sides finding aspects of the issue that they can agree on. An argumentative essay using the Rogerian method will usually begin with a statement of common beliefs or goals and then proceed in the body of the paper to give as reasonable an explanation of the writer's position as possible without being overtly defensive or aggressive. The conclusion will present a position that encompasses the concessions the writer has made.

Use Appeals Effectively.   An appeal is a rhetorical strategy whose object is to persuade. Appeals go beyond fact or logic to engage the audience's sympathy, sense of authority or higher power, or reason. Aristotle maintained that effective persuasion is achieved by a balanced use of three appeals to an audience: *logos* **(logic)**, *ethos* **(ethics)**, and *pathos* **(emotion)** related to the words *pathetic, sympathy,* and *empathy.* Other appeals may be used, such as shared values. In the Toulmin method, appeals support warrants. The appeal to ethos is a strong characteristic of Rogerian argumentation, with its emphasis on finding a common ground and its genuine attempts to understand opposing arguments and resolve conflicts. But a good argument does not rest solely on any one appeal. Thus, a good argument will use sound reasoning or apply inductive or deductive reasoning **(logic)**, it will call upon recognized authority or establish the credibility of its sources **(ethics)**, and it will reach audience members on an affecting, disturbing, touching, or other poignant level **(emotion)**. An argument may also make appeals to the audience on the basis of shared values, such as human dignity, free speech, and fairness.

Logical appeals offer clear, reasonable, well-substantiated proofs, including such things as data, statistics, case studies, or authoritative testimony or evidence, and they acknowledge and refute the claims of the opposition. We see such a logical appeal in Julia Whitty's "What Everglades Pythons and Other Invasive Species Are Trying to Tell Us" (Chapter 19) when she cites statistics to support her point about the widespread invasion of deadly species in many parts of the world.

Ethical appeals are often made in the introduction and conclusion because they are not based on statistics or hard data. Rather, they take advantage of the beliefs or values held by the audience and often help establish context. In "The Sixth Extinction," an essay about the potential for half of the Earth's species to disappear by the end of the century (Chapter 19), Jeff Corwin cites the work of scientists around the world who are helping to reverse the trend, and then he concludes with an ethical appeal: "These committed scientists bring great generosity and devotion to their respective efforts to stop the sixth extinction. But if we don't all rise to the cause and join them in action, they cannot succeed. The hour is near, but it's not too late." Corwin calls on the shared interests and values of his audience to take action to help prevent global disaster.

Emotional appeals can be quite effective but must not be overdone, certainly not to the exclusion of logical appeals. Anna Quindlen in "Our Tired, Our Poor, Our Kids" (Chapter 13) makes a strong emotional appeal in her opening paragraph with a striking and startling description: "Six people live here, in a room the size of the master bedroom in a modern suburban house. . . . One woman, five children. The baby was born in a shelter." Her opening touches readers on an emotional level and sets the tone for what she argues in the rest of her article.

Use Analogy.   An analogy is a comparison of two things in order to show their similarities. Often the comparison is of a difficult or unfamiliar concept to a simpler or more familiar one, an excellent way to advance your argument. As a strategy in argumentation, you want to make the point that if the situation in the example is true or valid, it will be true or valid in the situation you are arguing. Paul Johnson in "American Idealism and Realpolitik" (Chapter 16) uses an extended analogy when he compares the concept of life without America's taking responsibility for enforcing law abroad to "the bestial existence described in Thomas Hobbes' great work,

Leviathan." You must choose your comparisons wisely and avoid making false comparisons: if the argument is weak for your example, it will be weak for the argument you are making.

Assess the Evidence.

Reading critically is important in argumentation. You can build your own argument by trying to keep an open mind when analyzing the arguments of those opposed to your position as you read in search of evidence to support your position. What questions should you ask when analyzing the positions of those opposed to you? Consider the following: What is the author's purpose? How well does he or she achieve that purpose? What evidence does the writer give in support of that purpose? How does the author know the evidence is true? What is the argument based on? Has the writer omitted or ignored important evidence? Does the author's argument lead to a logical conclusion? Sometimes something that seems to be logical or reasonable turns out to be false. Are you convinced that the author's sources are trustworthy? What sort of language does the writer use? Is it clear and fair? Does the writer use words that are heavily charged or "loaded" and therefore likely to play on emotions rather than appeal to reason? Does the writer make any of the common fallacies (errors of reasoning) associated with attempts to be logical and fair?

Avoid Common Rhetorical Fallacies.

Part of your strategy in writing a good argument is to evaluate your own reasoning process as well as that of other writers, especially those whose works you may use in support of your own argument. A fallacy is a flaw or an error in reasoning that makes an argument invalid or, at best, weak. Look for these **common flaws** or **fallacies** in your own writing or in that of any writing you analyze:

- *Ad hominem* **arguments.** This Latin term means "against the man" or "toward the person" and applies to arguments that attack the character of the arguer rather than the argument itself. *Ad hominem* arguments often occur in politics, for instance, when opponents of a candidate refer to personal characteristics or aspects of the candidate's private life as evidence of his or her unsuitability to hold office. **Examples:** Arguing that because someone has been in prison, you shouldn't believe anything she says is an *ad hominem* attack. Arguing that a candidate would not make a good senator because he is a single parent or that a candidate would not be effective as mayor because she is homosexual ignores the more important questions of qualifications for the office, the candidate's stand on issues relevant to the position, the candidate's experience in political office, and similar substantive considerations.

- **Circular reasoning or begging the question.** This error makes a claim that simply rephrases another claim in other words. It assumes as proof the very claim it is meant to support. **Examples:** This sort of logic occurs in statements such as "We do it because that's the way we've always done it," which assumes the validity of a particular way of doing things without questioning or examining its importance or relevance. Other examples are stating that your candidate is the best person for an office because she is better than the other candidates, or a parent replying "because I said so" when a child asks why he or she must do something.

- **Either–or reasoning.** If a writer admits only two sides to an issue and asserts that his or her is the only possible correct one, the writer has probably not given full thought to the subject or is unaware of the complexity of the issue. Most arguable topics are probably complex, and few are limited to either one or another right viewpoint. Be wary of a writer who argues that there is only one valid position to take on an issue. **Example:** Arguing that if a fellow citizen does not support your country's involvement in war as you do, he or she is not patriotic. The implication is that "either you are for your country or you are against it, and the right way is my way."

- **Emotionally charged language.** Writers may rely on language guaranteed to appeal to their audiences on an emotional level rather than an intellectual level. This appeal can be effective when used sparingly, but it becomes a fault in logic when the argument is based entirely on such language. Arguments on ethical or moral issues such as abortion or capital punishment lend themselves to emotional appeals, but arguments on just about any subject may be charged with emotion. This fallacy can appeal to any number of emotions, such as fear, pity, hatred, sympathy, or compassion. Emotionally charged language also includes **loaded words,** those whose meanings or emotional associations vary from person to person or group to group, and **slanted words,** those whose connotations (suggestive meaning as opposed to actual meaning) are selected for their emotional association. **Examples:** Evoking images of dirty homeless children in rags living on dangerous streets and eating scraps of garbage when arguing for increased funds for child services is an appeal to the emotions. Abstract words, such as *democracy, freedom, justice,* or *loyalty,* are usually loaded. Words may be slanted to convey a good association, such as those used in advertisements—cool, refreshing, or smooth—or to convey a bad association—sweltering, noisy, or stuffy. **In argumentative writing, loaded or slanted language becomes problematic when it is used to deceive or manipulate.**

- **False analogy.** A writer may falsely claim that, because something resembles something else in one way, it resembles it in all ways. This warning does not deny that analogy has a place in argument. It can be an extremely useful technique by emphasizing a comparison that furthers an argument, especially for a difficult point. Explaining a difficult concept in terms of a simpler, more familiar one can give helpful support to readers. However, make sure that the analogy is true and holds up under close scrutiny. **Examples:** Arguing that antiabortionists cannot favor the death penalty because they view abortion as murder is a false analogy. A controversial analogy that is sometimes used is the comparison of America's internment of American citizens of Japanese descent during World War II to Hitler's concentration camps. On some levels the comparison is justified: people in the U.S. internment camps were held against their will in confined areas guarded by armed soldiers, they often lost all of their property, and some were even killed in the camps. On the other hand, they were not starved to death, exterminated, or used as subjects of medical experiments. The analogy is useful for making a point about the unfair treatment of American citizens during wartime, but many would argue that the analogy breaks down on some very important points.

- **Faulty appeal to authority.** Stating that a claim is true because an authority says it is true may be faulty if the authority is not an expert in the area being discussed, the subject is especially controversial with much disagreement over it, or the expert is biased. Such false appeals often appear in advertisement, as when an actor who portrays a lawyer on television appears in an ad for a real-life law firm. Similarly, actors who portray doctors on medical television shows are often used in health and beauty products to present an appearance of authority. The underlying assumption seems to be that audience members will equate the fictional lawyer's or doctor's words with those of an actual lawyer or physician.

- **Hasty generalization.** A writer makes a hasty generalization if he or she draws a broad conclusion on the basis of very little evidence. Such a writer probably has not explored enough evidence and has jumped too quickly to conclusions. **Examples:** Assuming that all politicians are corrupt because of the bad behavior of one is an example of making a hasty generalization. Assuming that all rock musicians use hard drugs before performances because of the highly publicized behavior of one or two musicians is an example of faulty generalization.

- **Oversimplification.** In oversimplification, the arguer offers a solution that is too simple for the problem or issue being argued. This fault in logic overlooks the complexity of an issue. **Examples:** Arguing that the problem of homelessness could be solved by giving jobs to homeless people overlooks the complexity of the issue. Such a suggestion does not take into account matters such as drug or alcohol dependency that sometimes accompanies life on the streets or a range of other problems faced by people who have lost their homes and learned to live outdoors. Arguing that the crime rate will go down if we just outlaw handguns overlooks such important considerations as crimes committed with weapons other than handguns and the likely probability that the criminal underworld would continue to have access to guns, illegal or not.

- *Non sequitur.* This Latin term, meaning "does not follow," refers to inferences or conclusions that do not follow logically from available evidence. *Non sequiturs* also occur when a person making an argument suddenly shifts course and brings up an entirely new point. **Examples:** The following demonstrates a *non sequitur*: "My friend Joan broke her arm during a gymnastics team practice after school. After-school activities are dangerous and should be banned." Reminding a child who will not eat his or her food of all the starving children in the world is a line of reasoning that does not follow. If the child eats his or her food, will that lessen the starvation of other children? If the child does not eat the food, can the food itself somehow aid those starving children?

- *Post hoc, ergo propter hoc* **reasoning.** This Latin term means "after this, therefore because of this." It applies to reasoning that assumes that Y happened to X simply because it came after X. **Example:** Accusing a rock group of causing the suicide of a fan because the fan listened to the group's music just before committing suicide is an example of such reasoning. Although the music might be a small factor, other factors are more likely to account for the suicide, such as a failed love relationship, feelings of low self-worth, or personal despair for a variety of reasons.

- **Red herring.** A red herring diverts the audience's attention from the main issue at hand to an irrelevant issue. The fallacy is to discuss an issue or a topic as if it were the real issue when it is not. Writers of mystery fiction often use red herrings to distract readers from identifying the stories' criminals. That is part of the fun of reading a mystery. But an argumentative writer who tries to use red herrings probably does not have enough relevant supporting evidence or does not recognize the irrelevance of the evidence. **Examples:** Arguing against the death penalty on the grounds that innocent people have been executed avoids the issue of why the death penalty is wrong. Citing the execution of innocent people is a red herring. Similarly, calling attention to the suffering of a victim's family when arguing for the death penalty shifts focus away from the relevant reasons for capital punishment.

- **Stereotyping.** Another form of generalization is stereotyping—that is, falsely applying the traits of a few individuals to their entire group or falsely drawing a conclusion about a group on the basis of the behavior or actions of a few in that group. Stereotyping is also oversimplification because it ignores the complexity of humans by reducing them to a few narrow characteristics. Stereotyping produces a false image or impression of a large number of people who have a certain thing in common—most frequently race, ethnicity, gender, or sexual preference—but also such widely differing things as occupation, hair color, speech habits, or educational level.

Examples: Any assertion about an entire group of people on the basis of a few in that group is stereotyping. Arguing that women are not suited for combat because women are weaker than men is a stereotype based on the fact that the average woman is weaker than the average man. Not all women are weaker than men.

GUIDELINES: STRATEGIES FOR CONSTRUCTING A CONVINCING ARGUMENT

- **Know your audience.** Whether identified by your instructor or left up to you, imagine an audience opposed to your position. This helps you understand what evidence you need to make your argument convincing.
- **Establish appropriate tone.** Your attitude toward your subject is important in making your argument convincing. Using the appropriate tone strengthens your argument.
- **Anticipate the arguments of those opposed to you.** Anticipating and countering others' arguments strengthens your own position.
- **Make concessions where necessary.** Acknowledging truths in the arguments of others reveals that you are aware of those truths but are still committed to your own position. Follow such concessions with your own even stronger evidence, proof, or support.
- **Follow a logical line of reasoning.** Whether formal or informal, inductive or deductive, or some other method recommended by your instructor, your argument must be reasonable and sound.
- **Use appeals effectively.** Appeals to logic, ethics, emotions, or shared values all help develop your argument. Be cautious when appealing to emotions; such appeals are all right in small measure, but your main appeals should be to logic and/or ethics.
- **Assess the evidence.** Examine carefully the evidence you use for your argument. Weak or flawed evidence weakens your own argument.
- **Look for flaws in your own and others' reasoning process.** Avoid fallacies or errors in reasoning in your own writing and examine the arguments of others for such flaws.

SAMPLE ARGUMENT

On the following pages you will find Rita Fleming's argumentative paper annotated with marginal comments on her strategies. In addition to noting Rita's argumentative strategies, pay attention to the ways in which she uses sources to bolster her argument. **Note that she follows MLA style guidelines for handling source material as outlined in Chapters 6 and 7.**

Fleming 1

Rita Fleming

English 102-2

Professor White

21 Oct. 2014

Women in the Workforce: Still
Not Equal

Nearly seventy-two million American
women, over half of those over the age of
16, are in the civilian labor force, and
over half of those women work full time,
year round (WB). Many people have the perception that women's large presence in the
workforce in combination with federal laws
that prohibit job discrimination means
that women enjoy equality with men in the
workplace. However, recent class-action
sex-discrimination suits brought by women
workers against large corporations suggest
that millions of women feel discriminated
against in the workplace. Furthermore, a look
at labor statistics compiled by the federal
government, such as those from the U.S.
Census Bureau and the Department of Labor,
reveals that women on average are still paid
significantly less than men. Despite decades of struggling for women's equality in
the workplace, the wage gap between men and
women remains unacceptably wide.

Some argue that workplace inequity
has disappeared as a result of federal
legislation that makes discrimination

Rita begins with background information and establishes importance of the issue by appealing to the common good.

Her proposition states clearly what her position is.

Rita acknowledges the opposition and makes concessions.

Fleming 2

in employment illegal. It is true that
efforts to correct disparities between
men's and women's wages have a long history. Executive Orders have been legislated
to fight discrimination in employment,
beginning in 1961 with President John F.
Kennedy's Executive Order 10925 creating a
President's Committee on Equal Employment
Opportunity prohibiting discrimination on
the basis of sex, race, religious belief,
or national origin. The Equal Pay Act of
1963 prohibits paying women less than men
working in the same establishment and performing the same jobs, and Title VII of the
1964 Civil Rights Act prohibits job discrimination on the basis of not only race,
color, religion, and national origin but
also sex. It is also true that when the
Equal Pay Act was signed, women working
full-time, year round made only 59 cents
on average for every dollar a man made and
that the figure had increased to 82 cents
by 2010 (BLS), and has hovered around that
figure since. Yes, women have made gains
over the past decades, but is 82 cents
for every dollar a man makes acceptable?
If women are truly equal to men in this
society, why are their average earnings not
equal?

Having made concessions, she reaffirms her position.

Fleming 3

According to the United States Census
Bureau findings in 2010, the national
median income of men working full-time,
year-round, was $49,453.00, while the
median income for women working full-time,
year round was $38,052.00. This makes the
ratio of women's earnings to men's 77%
(DeNavus-Walt, Proctor and Smith). While
this exact ratio varies state by state,
the gap between women's and men's earnings
exist in every state. <u>There are many reasons for this inequity.</u> One reason is that
most women work in service and clerical
jobs, including such occupations as secretaries, teachers, cashiers, and nurses.
For instance, in 2011, 91.1% of registered
nurses and 81.8% of elementary and middle
school teachers were women (WB). In 2011
97.0% of preschool and kindergarten teachers, 95.1% of dental hygienists, and 97.9%
of secretaries were women (BLS). Women also
tend to work at jobs that pay less than the
jobs that men typically work at. Eitzen and
Zinn point out that, as the economy shifted
in recent times from being manufacturing-
based to being more service oriented, a
dual labor market emerged. In a dual labor
market, there are two main types of jobs,
primary and secondary. Primary jobs are
usually stable, full-time jobs with high
wages, good benefits, and the opportunity

Rita offers explanations for the inequity by citing data supporting her position.

to move up the promotion ladder, whereas
secondary jobs are the opposite. Secondary occupations are unstable, normally part
time, with few benefits and little opportunity for advancement (218). Unfortunately,
large corporations have been eliminating
many primary jobs and creating new, secondary jobs to take their places, and it is
mostly women who are hired to fill these
secondary positions.

Rita continues to explain, backing assertions with supporting proof.

The term "occupational segregation"
is used to describe the phenomenon of women
workers being clustered in secondary or
low-paying jobs (Andersen and Collins 238).
This segregation is particularly startling
when you consider such statistics as the
following: "Since 1980, women have taken
80 percent of the new jobs created in the
economy, but the overall degree of gender segregation has not changed much since
1900" (Andersen and Collins 236). Fully 60%
of women workers are in clerical and service occupations, while only 30% are managers and professionals "Women"). According
to research drawn from Bureau of Labor
statistics, "Women continue to be highly
overrepresented in clerical, service, and
health-related occupations, while men tend
to be overrepresented in craft, operator,
and laborer jobs" ("Women"). Women are simply not crossing over into traditionally

Fleming 5

male-dominated occupations at a very high
rate. This does not mean that women do not
have opportunities or are not educated. It
could mean, however, that the workplace is
still plagued by old, outdated stereotypes
about gender-based occupations.

Another explanation for the wage gap
is that women earn less because of the differences in years of experience on the job.
Collectively, women earn less because they
haven't worked as many years as men have
in certain professions (Robinson 183-84).
Women often drop out of the job market to
have their families, for instance, while
men stay at their jobs when they have families. Yet another reason for the wage gap,
offered by Borgna Brunner, is that older
women may be working largely in jobs that
are "still subject to the attitudes and
conditions of the past." Brunner points
out: "In contrast, the rates for young
women coming of age in the 1990s reflect
women's social and legal advances. In
1997, for example, women under 25 working full-time earned 92.1% of men's sala-
ries compared to older women (25-54), who
earned 74.4% of what men made." This is
great news for young women but a dismal
reality for the significantly large number
of working women who fall into the 25-54
age group.

*As she offers
more reasons
to account for
the wage gap,
Rita reinforces
her position
that the gap is
unacceptable.*

Rita notes that the wage gap cannot be fully explained.

Reasons to account for the persistence of a wage gap are many, but sometimes there is no explanation at all.
Analysts have tried to determine why, as
the U.S. Census Bureau figures reveal,
men of every race or ethnicity earn more
than women at every educational level
(Julian and Kominski) Surprisingly, the
wage gap is greater than one might expect
at the professional level: female professionals (doctors, lawyers, dentists)
make substantially less than what male
professionals make. Female physicians
and surgeons aged 35-54, for instance,
earned 69% of what male physicians and
surgeons made (WB). How can such a wage
gap be explained? The reality is that
"there is a substantial gap in median
earnings between men and women that is
unexplained, even after controlling for
work experience . . . education, and
occupation" (BLS). Given this statement,
one has to ask if the most obvious reason
of all to explain why women are paid less
than men for the same or equal work is
simply discrimination. What can be done
to correct the wage differential between
men's and women's earnings?

Rita suggests an explanation for the seemingly inexplicable.

Rita suggests actions to address the problem she has substantiated in her paper.

Laws have failed to produce ideal
results, but they have done much to further women's chances in the workplace and

Fleming 7

they give women legal recourse when they
feel that discrimination has taken place.
Therefore, better vigilance and stricter
enforcement of existing laws should help
in the battle for equal wages. Young women
should be encouraged to train for primary
jobs, while those who work in secondary
jobs should lobby their legislators or form
support groups to work for better wages and
benefits. Working women can join or support the efforts of such organizations as
9to5, the National Association of Working
Women. Women's position in the workforce
has gradually improved over time, but given
the statistics revealing gross differences
between their wages and those of men, much
remains to be done.

WORKS CITED

Andersen, Margaret L., and Patricia Hill
    Collins, eds. *Race, Class and Gender:
    An Anthology*. 8th ed. Boston: Cengage,
    2010. Print.

Brunner, Borgna. "The Wage Gap: A History
    of Pay Inequity and the Equal Pay Act."
    Infoplease. March 2005. PDFfile.

DeNavus-Walt, Carmen, Bernadette D. Proc-
    tor, and Jessica C. Smith. U.S. Census
    Bureau, Current Population Reports,
    P60-243. *Income, Poverty, and Health
    Insurance Coverage in the United*

Fleming 8

States: *2011*. Washington, D.C.: U. S.
Government Printing Office, 2012. Web.
14 October 2014.

Eitzen, Stanley D., and Maxine Baca Zinn.
Social Problems. 12th ed. Upper Saddle
River, NJ: Prentice Hall, 2010. Print.

Julian, Tiffany, and Robert Kominski. *Edu-
cation and Synthetic Work-Life Earnings
Estimates*. United States Census Bureau.
September 2011. Web. 13 Oct. 2014.

"101 Facts on the Status of Working Women."
Business and Professional Women October
2007. Web. 12 October 2014.

Robinson, Derek. "Differences in Occupational Earnings by Sex." In *Women,
Gender, and Work*. Ed. Martha Fetherolf
Loutfi. Geneva: International Labor Office, 2001. Print.

United States. Department of Labor Bureau
of Labor Statistics (BLS). *Women in the
Labor Force: A Databook (2011 Edition)*.
Dec. 2011. Web. 12 Oct. 2014.

United States. Department of Labor Women's
Bureau (WB). *Women in the Labor Force
2010*. Jan. 2011. Web. 12 Oct. 2014.

"Women in Male-Dominated Industries and
Occupations in U.S. and Canada." *Catalyst*. 17 April 2012. Web. 12 Oct. 2014.

Read the following essay and analyze its effectiveness as an argument by considering the strategies that the authors use. Write out your analysis to hand in to your instructor, or take notes in preparation for class discussion. Here are some points to consider:

1. On the basis of information about the authors provided in the headnote, how well suited do you think they are to write on the subject of this essay?
2. Describe the tone adopted by the authors. What audience are the authors writing to?
3. Where do the authors state their thesis or proposition?
4. What appeals do the authors rely on? How credible or convincing do you consider those appeals? Explain your answer.
5. What evidence do the authors supply to support their argument? Do you find the evidence persuasive?
6. How well do the authors anticipate opposing opinions? Do the authors make any concessions to opposing opinions?
7. Are the authors guilty of any flaws in their reasoning?
8. Are you convinced by the authors' argument? Why or why not?

THE MYTH OF MEAN GIRLS

MIKE MALES AND MEDA-CHESNEY LIND

Mike Males, senior researcher at the Center on Juvenile and Criminal Justice, is author of The Scapegoat Generation: America's War on Adolescents *(1996);* Framing Youth: Ten Myths About the Next Generation *(1998);* Smoked: Why Joe Camel Is Still Smiling *(1999);* Juvenile Injustice: America's "Youth Violence" Hoax *(2000); and* Kids & Guns: How Politicians, Experts, and the Press Fabricate Fear of Youth *(2001). Meda-Chesney Lind, a professor of women's studies at the University of Hawaii, Manoa, is the author of* Girls, Delinquency and Juvenile Justice *(1997) and* The Female Offender: Girls, Women and Crime *(2010). She co-edited* Female Gangs in America: Essays on Girls, Gangs and Gender *(1999);* Invisible Punishment: The Collateral Consequences of Mass Imprisonment *(2003);* Girls, Women, and Crime: Selected Reading *(2003);* Beyond Bad Girls: Gender, Violence, and Hype *(2007); and* Fighting for Girls: New Perspectives on Gender and Violence *(2010). This essay first appeared on the Op-Ed page of the New York Times on April 2, 2010.*

If nine South Hadley, Mass., high school students—seven of them girls—are proved to have criminally bullied another girl who then committed suicide, as prosecutors have charged, they deserve serious legal and community condemnation.

However, many of the news reports and inflamed commentaries have gone beyond expressing outrage at the teenagers involved and instead invoked such cases as evidence of a modern epidemic of "mean girls" that adults simply fail to comprehend. Elizabeth Scheibel, the district attorney in the South Hadley case, declined to charge school officials who she said were aware of the bullying because of their "lack of understanding of harassment associated with teen dating relationships." A *People* magazine article headlined "Mean Girls" suggested that a similar case two years ago raised "troubling questions" about "teen violence" and "cyberspace wars." Again and again, we hear of girls hitting, brawling and harassing.

But this panic is a hoax. We have examined every major index of crime on which the authorities rely. None show a recent increase in girls' violence; in fact, every reliable measure shows that violence by girls has been plummeting for years. Major offenses like murder and robbery by girls are at their lowest levels in four decades. Fights, weapons possession, assaults and violent injuries by and toward girls have been plunging for at least a decade.

4   The Federal Bureau of Investigation's Uniform Crime Reports, based on reports from more than 10,000 police agencies, is the most reliable source on arrests by sex and age. From 1995 to 2008, according to the F.B.I., girls' arrest rates for violent offenses fell by 32 percent, including declines of 27 percent for aggravated assault, 43 percent for robbery and 63 percent for murder. Rates of murder by girls are at their lowest levels in at least 40 years.

The National Crime Victimization Survey, a detailed annual survey of more than 40,000 Americans by the Department of Justice's Bureau of Justice Statistics, is considered the most reliable measure of crime because it includes offenses not reported to the police. From 1993 through 2007, the survey reported significant declines in rates of victimization of girls, including all violent crime (down 57 percent), serious and misdemeanor assaults (down 53 percent), robbery (down 83 percent) and sex offenses (down 67 percent).

Public health agencies like the National Center for Health Statistics confirm huge declines in murder and violent assaults of girls. For example, as the number of females ages 10 to 19 increased by 3.4 million, murders of girls fell from 598 in 1990 to 376 in 2006. Rates of murders of and by adolescent girls are now at their lowest levels since 1968—48 percent below rates in 1990 and 45 percent lower than in 1975.

The Bureau of Justice Statistics' Intimate Partner Violence in the United States survey, its annual Indicators of School Crime and Safety, the University of Michigan's Monitoring the Future survey and the Centers for Disease Control's Youth Risk Behavior Surveillance all measure girls' violent offending and victimization. Virtually without exception, these surveys show major drops in fights and other violence, particularly relationship violence, involving girls over the last 15 to 20 years. These surveys also indicate that girls are no more likely to report being in fights, being threatened or injured with a weapon, or violently victimizing others today than in the first surveys in the 1970s.

8   These striking improvements in girls' personal safety, including from rape and relationship violence, directly contradict recent news reports that girls suffer increasing danger from violence by their female and male peers alike.

There is only one measure that would in any way indicate that girls' violence has risen, and it is both dubious and outdated. F.B.I. reports show assault arrests of girls under age 18 increased from 6,300 in 1981 to a peak of 16,800 in 1995, then dropped sharply, to 13,300 in 2008. So, at best, claims that girls' violence is rising apply to girls of 15 to 25 years ago, not today.

Even by this measure, it's not girls who have gotten more violent faster—it's middle-aged men and women, the age groups of the many authors and commentators disparaging girls. Among women ages 35 to 54, F.B.I. reports show, felony assault arrests rocketed from 7,100 in 1981 to 28,800 in 2008. Assault arrests among middle-aged men also more than doubled, reaching 100,500 in 2008. In Northampton, the county seat a few miles from South Hadley, domestic violence calls to police more than tripled in the last four years to nearly 400 in 2009. Why, then, don't we see frenzied news reports on "Mean Middle-Agers"?

What's more, the Department of Justice's Office of Juvenile Justice and Delinquency Prevention concluded that girls' supposed "violent crime increase" in the '80s and '90s resulted from new laws and policies mandating arrests for domestic violence and minor youth offenses "that in past years may have been classified as status offenses (e.g., incorrigibility)" but "can now result in an assault arrest." Thus, the Justice Department found, increased numbers of arrests "are not always related to actual increases in crime."

12   This mythical wave of girls' violence and meanness is, in the end, contradicted by reams of evidence from almost every available and reliable source. Yet news media and myriad experts, seemingly eager to sensationalize every "crisis" among young people, have aroused unwarranted worry in the public and policy arenas. The unfortunate result is more punitive treatment of girls, including arrests and incarceration for lesser offenses like minor assaults that were treated informally in the past, as well as alarmist calls for restrictions on their Internet use.

Why, in an era when slandering a group of people based on the misdeeds of a few has rightly become taboo, does it remain acceptable to use isolated incidents to berate modern teenagers, particularly girls, as "mean" and "violent" and "bullies"? That is, why are we bullying girls?

CHAPTER 6

Writing a Synthesis and Documenting Sources

A synthesis draws conclusions from, makes observations on, or shows connections between two or more sources. In writing a synthesis, you attempt to make sense of the ideas of those sources by extracting information relevant to your purpose. The ability to synthesize is an important skill, for people are continuously bombarded with a dizzying variety of information and opinions that need sorting out and assessment. To understand your own thinking on a subject, it is always useful to know what others have to say about it. You can see the importance of reading and thinking critically when synthesizing the ideas of others. The sources for a synthesis may be essays, books, editorials, lectures, movies, group discussions, or any of the myriad forms of communication that inform academic and personal lives. At minimum, in a synthesis you will be required to reflect on the ideas of two writers, assess them, make connections between them, and arrive at your own conclusions based on your analysis. Often you will work with more than two sources; certainly you will do so in a research paper.

Your purpose for writing a synthesis will be determined by the nature of your assignment, although syntheses are most commonly used to either explain or argue. Perhaps you want to explain how something works or show the causes or effects of a particular event. You may argue a particular point, using the arguments of others as supporting evidence or as subjects for disagreement in your own argument. You may want to compare or contrast the positions of other writers for stating your own opinion on the subject. When you write a research paper, you must certainly synthesize the ideas and words of others. Whether your synthesis paper is a report or an argument, you must sort through and make sense of what your sources say. Sometimes you will want to read many sources to find out what a number of people have to say about a particular subject in order to discover your own position on it.

Synthesis, then, involves not only understanding what others have to say on a given subject but also making connections between them, analyzing their arguments or examples, and/or drawing conclusions from them. You routinely employ these processes in both your everyday life and in your courses whenever you consider the words, ideas, or opinions of two or more people or writers on a topic. Each chapter in Parts Two through Five ends with a list of suggestions for writing. Many of the topics require that you synthesize material in the readings of that chapter. These topics ask you to argue, to compare and contrast, to explore reasons, to explain something, to describe, or to report on something, using at least two of the essays in the chapter.

In all cases, no matter what your purpose for writing the synthesis, you will need to state your own central idea or **thesis** early in your paper. In preparation for writing your essay, you will complete a very helpful step if you locate the central idea or thesis of each of the works under analysis and summarize their main points. The summary is itself a kind of synthesis, in that you locate the key ideas in an essay, state them in your own words, and then put them back together again in a shortened form. This process helps you understand what the authors believe and why they believe it. Furthermore, your own readers benefit from a summary of the central idea or chief points of the articles you are assessing. As you write your essay, you will not only be explaining your own view, opinion, or position, but you will also be using the ideas or words of the authors whose works you are synthesizing. These will have to be documented, using the appropriate formatting for documenting sources illustrated in this chapter. See the box "Guidelines for Writing a Synthesis" for step-by-step directions on writing your synthesis.

GUIDELINES FOR WRITING A SYNTHESIS

- **Determine your purpose for writing by asking yourself what you want to do in your essay.** Without a clear purpose, your synthesis will be a loosely organized jumble of words. Although your purpose is often governed by the way in which the assignment is worded, make sure you understand exactly what you intend to do.
- **Consider how best to accomplish your purpose.** Will you argue, explain, compare and contrast, illustrate, show causes and effects, describe, or narrate? How will you use your sources to accomplish your purpose?
- **Read each source carefully and understand its central purpose and major points.** If you are unclear about the meaning of an essay, reread it carefully, noting passages that give you trouble. Discuss these passages with a classmate or with your instructor if you still lack a clear understanding.
- **Write a one-sentence statement of the central idea or thesis and a brief summary of each source you will use in your paper.** This process will help clarify your understanding of your sources and assist you in formulating your own central idea. These statements or summaries can then be incorporated appropriately into your synthesis.
- **Write a one-sentence statement of your own thesis or central purpose for writing the synthesis.** This statement should be a complete sentence, usually in the first paragraph of your essay. The thesis statement helps you focus your thoughts as you plan your essay by limiting the nature and scope of what you intend to accomplish. It is also a crucial aid to your readers, because it is essentially a succinct summary of what you intend to do.
- **Develop or illustrate your thesis by incorporating the ideas of your sources into the body of your paper, either by paraphrasing or by directly quoting.** Part of your purpose in writing a synthesis is to demonstrate familiarity with your sources and to draw on them in your own essay. This goal requires that you make reference to key ideas of the sources.
- **Document your sources.** Keep in mind the guidelines for documenting all borrowed material.

CITING AND DOCUMENTING SOURCES USING MLA STYLE

Although Chapter 7 on the research paper addresses in detail the matter of citing and documenting a variety of sources, you will need some guidelines for handling sources when writing a synthesis paper. No matter what your purpose or pattern of development, if you draw on the writing of someone else, you must be fair to the author of the material you borrow. Whether paraphrasing an author's words or quoting them exactly as they appear in the original text, whenever you use the ideas or words of another, you must give credit to your source. In academic writing, credit is given by naming the author of the borrowed material; its title; the place and date of publication or location where it appears; and the page number or numbers where the information is located, if the work is paginated.

The rest of this chapter introduces some basic skills needed to incorporate the words and ideas of others into your own written work. **Because the chapter focuses on how to draw material on two or more sources in a collection such as this or a similar text book, the examples will largely be from print sources that are paginated. For other kinds of sources, see Chapter 7.** The discussion begins with guidelines for documenting sources, goes on to provide examples of paraphrasing and quoting, illustrates some useful tools for handling and integrating source materials, and ends with directions for documenting sources from collections of essays, such as this textbook. The guidelines used in this chapter follow MLA (Modern Language Association) documentation style. (*Note:* If your instructor prefers that you use APA style or gives you a choice of styles, refer to guidelines for APA documentation style that appear in Chapter 7.) MLA style is used primarily in the humanities disciplines, such as English and philosophy, whereas other disciplines have their own guidelines. If you learn the skills necessary for paraphrasing, quoting, and documenting the material located in this textbook or in any collection of readings, you will be prepared to incorporate library and Internet resources, as well as other materials, into long, complex research papers. For more discussion of MLA style, with sample works-cited entries for a broad range of both print and nonprint sources, including the Internet, see Chapter 7.

IN-TEXT CITATIONS AND LIST OF WORKS CITED

The MLA style of documentation requires that you give a brief reference to the source of any borrowed material in a parenthetical note that follows the material. This parenthetical note contains only the last name of the authority and the page number or numbers on which the material appears, or only the page number or numbers if you mention the author's name in the text. This in-text citation refers to specific information or ideas from a source for which you give complete bibliographic information at the end of the paper in the works-cited list. With the name of the author (or title, if no author's name) given in the paper itself, your readers can quickly locate full details of your source by looking at the alphabetical list of all the works that you drew upon in your paper.

The parenthetical citation is placed within the sentence, after the quotation or paraphrase, and before the period. If punctuation appears at the end of the words you are quoting, ignore a comma, period, or semicolon but include a question mark or exclamation mark. In all cases, the period for your sentence follows the parenthetical citation.

The name or title that appears in the parenthetical citation in your text corresponds to an entry in the works-cited list at the end of your paper. This list is labeled "Works Cited." Individual entries in this list contain complete bibliographic information about the location of the works you reference, including the full name of the author (if known), the complete title, the place of publication, and the date of publication (if known).

Treat World Wide Web and other electronic sources as you do printed works. This means name the author, if known, or the title if no author is named. If you use a source with no page numbers, such as a website or a film, you cannot give a page number in the parenthetical citation.

Illustration: In-Text Citations and Works-Cited Entries.   The following examples show formats for citing sources in the text of your paper. The works-cited formats for many of the references are included here. You can find more examples in Chapter 7.

- **Book or article with one author.** Name of the author followed by the page number:

   (Booth 367)

   Source as it appears on the list of works cited:
   Booth, William. "One Nation, Indivisible: Is It History?" *Perspectives on Contemporary Issues: Readings across the Disciplines.* 6th ed. Ed. Katherine Anne Ackley. Boston: Wadsworth/Cengage Learning, 2009. 366–371. Print.

- **Book or article with two or three authors.** Last names of authors followed by the page number:

   (Pojman and Pojman 110), (Newton, Dillingham, and Choly 24)

   Sources as they appear on the list of works cited:
   Pojman, Paul, and Louis P. Pojman. *Environmental Ethics.* Boston: Wadsworth, 2011. Print.

   Newton, Lisa H., Catherine K. Dillingham, and Joanne H. Choly. *Watersheds 4: Ten Cases in Environmental Ethics.* Boston: Wadsworth, 2005. Print.

- **Book or article with more than three authors.** Name just the first author followed by "et al." (Latin for "and others") and then the page number:

   (Mitchell et al. 29)

Source as it appears on the list of works cited:
   Mitchell, James, Jane Smith, Julia Simmons, and Al Young. *Herbal Supplements: Benefits and Dangers.* Los Angeles: Global Health Press, 2014. Print.

Comment

When there are two or more authors, reproduce the names in the order in which they appear on the title page. If they are not listed alphabetically, do not change their order.

- **Article or other publication with no author named.** Give a short title followed by the page number, if available:

   ("New Year's Resolutions" 1), ("44 Ways")

   Sources as they appear on the list of works cited:
   "New Year's Resolutions." *Columbia City Post and Mail* [Indiana] 2 Jan. 2014: 11. Print.

   "44 Ways to Kick-Start Your New Year." *Success.Com. Success Media,* 30 Nov. 2014. Web. 12 Dec. 2014.

- **If you cite two anonymous articles beginning with the same word,** use the full title of each to distinguish one from the other:

   ("Classrooms without Walls" 45), ("Classrooms in the 21st Century" 96)

   Sources as they appear in the list of works cited:
   "Classrooms without Walls." *21 Century Teacher* Oct. 2014: 44–49. Print.

   "Classrooms in the 21st Century." *Journal of Teacher Education* Sept./ Oct. 2014: 94–98. Print.

- **Two works by the same author.** Give the author's name followed by a comma, a short title and the page number:

   (Heilbrun, *Hamlet's Mother* 123), (Heilbrun, *Writing a Woman's Life* 35)

   Sources as they appear in the list of works cited:
   Heilbrun, Carolyn. *Hamlet's Mother and Other Women.* 2nd ed. New York: Columbia UP, 2002. Print.

   —. *Writing a Woman's Life.* New York: Norton, 2008. Print.

Comment

Three hyphens followed by a period indicate that the author's name is identical to that in the preceding entry. The entries themselves are alphabetized by the first letter of the titles of the works.

- **An Internet work.** Use author's last name or short title:

  (Fletcher)

  Source as it appears on the list of works cited:
  Fletcher, Dan. "Say No More: The Banned Words of 2010." *Time.com.*
  Time Magazine, 02 Jan. 2010. Web. 21 Sept. 2014.

- **An article from an electronic database.** Use author's last name and page number:

  (Harvey and Delfabbro 4)

  Source as it appears on the list of works cited:
  Harvey, J., and P. H. Delfabbro. "Psychological Resilience in Disadvantaged
  Youth." *Australian Psychologist* 39.1 (Mar. 2004): 3–13. Academic Search
  Premier. Web. 12 Nov. 2014.

GUIDELINES FOR DOCUMENTING SOURCES

- Provide a context for your paraphrase or quotation by naming the author or the title of the work, or by using attributive tags, such as *observes, comments, points out,* or *argues*.
- Provide a citation every time you paraphrase or quote directly from a source.
- Give the citation in parentheses following the quotation or paraphrase.
- In the parentheses, give the author's last name and the page number or numbers from which you took the words or ideas, if available. Do not put any punctuation between the author's last name and the page number.
- If you name the author as you introduce the words or ideas, the parentheses will include only the page number or numbers. If source is from the Internet with no page numbers and you name the author in your text, no parentheses are needed.
- At the end of your paper, provide an alphabetical list of the authors you quoted or paraphrased and give complete bibliographic information, including not only author and title but also where you found the material. This element is the Works-Cited page.

PARAPHRASING

Paraphrasing is similar to summarizing in that you restate in your own words something someone else has written, but a paraphrase restates everything in the passage rather than highlighting just the key points. Summaries give useful presentations of the major points or ideas of long passages or entire works, whereas paraphrases are most useful in clarifying or emphasizing the main points of short passages.

To paraphrase, express the ideas of the author in your own words, being careful not to use exact phrases or key words of the original. Read your source carefully, more than once if necessary, and then write down what you understand the source to say. It will help if you put the source aside or do not look at it when restating the material in your own words. Then you won't be tempted to use the exact words of the original. Another approach is to jot down a few notes while you are reading and then, without looking at the original source, use your notes to write what you recall of the passage. After you have finished paraphrasing a section, compare what you have written to make sure it is fair to the original and does not use exact words. Paraphrases are sometimes as long as the original passages, but usually they are shorter. The purpose of paraphrasing is to convey the essence of a sentence or passage in an accurate, fair manner and without the distraction of quotation marks. If your paraphrase repeats the exact words of the original, then you are quoting, and you must put quotation marks around those words. **A paper will be more interesting and more readable if you paraphrase more often than you quote.** Think of your own response when you read something that contains quotations. Perhaps, like many readers, you will read with interest a paraphrase or short quotation, but you may skip over or skim quickly long passages set off by quotation marks. Readers generally are more interested in the ideas of the author than in his or her skill at quoting other authors.

GUIDELINES FOR PARAPHRASING

- Read the passage carefully, perhaps taking a few notes, and then try to recall without looking at it what the essential ideas are.
- Restate in your own words the important ideas or essence of a passage.
- Do not look at your source when paraphrasing. This will help you avoid using the exact words. Do not repeat more than two or three exact words of any part of the original, unless you enclose them in quotation marks. If you must repeat a phrase, clause, or sentence exactly as it appears in the original, put quotation marks around those words. Give the source of the paraphrased information either in your text or in parentheses immediately after the paraphrase.
- Check that you have paraphrased fairly and accurately by comparing your paraphrase to the original words.
- In your paper, use attributive tags or the author's name when paraphrasing.
- Try to paraphrase rather than quote as often as possible, saving direct quotations for truly remarkable language, startling or unusual information, or otherwise original or crucial wording.

Illustration: Paraphrasing.   This section provides examples of paraphrases using selected passages from the sources indicated.

1. **Source:** Isaacson, Walter. *Einstein: His Life and Universe.* New York: Simon, 2007. Print.

> **Original** (page 54): Among the many surprising things about the life of Albert Einstein was the trouble he had getting an academic job. Indeed, it would be an astonishing nine years after his graduation from the Zurich Polytechnic in 1900—and four years after the miracle year in which he not only upended physics but also finally got a doctoral dissertation accepted—before he would be offered a job as a junior professor.

Paraphrase: In his biography of Albert Einstein, Walter Isaacson notes the rather surprising fact that Einstein not only had trouble finding a teaching job after college graduation, but it took nine years to do so (54).

Comment

Even when you put the material into your own words, you must cite the source and give a page number where the paraphrased material is located. Use attributive words or tags ("In his biography of Albert Einstein, Walter Isaacson notes ...").

2. **Source:** Gibbs, Nancy. "The End of Helicopter Parents." *Time* 30 Nov. 2009: 52–57. Print.

Original (page 54): The insanity crept up on us slowly; we just wanted what was best for our kids. We bought macrobiotic cupcakes and hypoallergenic socks, hired tutors to correct a 5-year-old's "pencil-holding deficiency," hooked up broadband connections in the treehouse but took down the swing set after the second skinned knee. We hovered over every school, playground and practice field—"helicopter parents," teachers christened us, a phenomenon that spread to parents of all ages, races, and religions.

Paraphrase: In a cover story for *Time* magazine, Nancy Gibbs discusses the trend that has developed among parents to do everything they can think of to protect and provide for their children. Teachers have coined the term "helicopter parents" to describe the moms and dads who stay close to their children, "hover[ing]" over them in their efforts to protect them (54).

Comment

When it is clear that you are paraphrasing from the same source in two or more consecutive sentences *and* you have named the author or source in the first sentence, you need give only one parenthetical citation at the end of the series of sentences. Note also that key terms from the original are placed in quotation marks to indicate that they are not the student's own words.

3. **Source:** Camarota, Steven A. *The High Cost of Cheap Labor: Illegal Immigration and the Federal Budget*. Center for Immigration Studies. August 2004. Web. 12 Oct. 2014.

Original: Our findings show that many of the preconceived notions about the fiscal impact of illegal households turn out to be inaccurate. In terms of welfare use, receipt of cash assistance programs tends to be very low, while Medicaid use, though significant, is still less than for other households. Only use of food assistance programs is significantly higher than that of the rest of the population. Also, contrary to the perceptions that illegal aliens don't pay payroll taxes, we estimate that more than half of illegals work "on the books." On average, illegal households pay more than $4,200 a year in all forms of federal taxes. Unfortunately, they impose costs of $6,950 per household.

Paraphrase: According to a 2004 study by the Center for Immigration Studies of the impact of illegal immigration on the federal budget, many of the notions about illegal immigrants are incorrect. Although they do receive more food aid than the general population, they receive less welfare and Medicaid benefits. Furthermore, most illegal immigrants pay federal taxes (Camarota).

Comment

For Internet or other electronic sources without pagination, many instructors recommend that you repeat the author's name in parentheses after all paraphrases and direct quotations, even if the name is already included in the text.

QUOTING

When you want to include the words of another writer, but it is not appropriate to either paraphrase or summarize, you will want to quote. Quoting requires that you repeat the exact words of another, placing quotation marks before and after the material being quoted. **A crucial guideline requires that you copy the words exactly as they appear in the original text.** To omit words or approximate the original within quotation marks is sloppy or careless handling of your source material.

Be selective in the material you choose to quote directly, however. You should usually paraphrase the words of another, restating them in your own language, rather than relying on exactly copying the words. How do you know when to quote rather than paraphrase? You should quote only words, phrases, or sentences that are particularly striking or that must be reproduced exactly because you cannot convey them in your own words without weakening their effect or changing their intent. Quote passages or parts of passages that are original, dramatically worded, or in some way essential to your paper. Otherwise, rely on paraphrasing to refer to the ideas of others. In either case, document your source by identifying the original source and the location of your information within that source.

GUIDELINES FOR QUOTING

- Be selective: Quote directly only words, phrases, or sentences that are particularly striking or original, or whose meaning would be lost in a paraphrase.
- Quote directly passages that are so succinct that paraphrasing them would be more complicated or take more words than a direct quotation would require.
- Enclose the exact words you are quoting between quotation marks.
- Do not change any word of the original unless you indicate with brackets, ellipses, or other conventions that you have done so.
- Provide the source of your quoted material either in your text or in parentheses following the material.

Illustration: Quoting.   This section provides examples of quotations using selected passages from an article called "Mad for Dickens" by Joshua Hammer. The source for all examples in this section is the following:

Hammer, Joshua. "Mad for Dickens." *Smithsonian* February 2012: 70–78. Print.

1. **Original** (page 72): Dickens burst onto the London literary scene at age 23, and as the world celebrates his 200th birthday on February 7, "The Inimitable," as he called himself, is still going strong.

   Quotation: In an article about writer Charles Dickens' 200th birthday, Joshua Hammer observes that Dickens was only 23 when he "burst onto the London literary scene" (72).

Comments

- Place double quotation marks before and after words taken directly from the original.
- When the quoted material is an integral part of your sentence, especially when preceded by the word *that*, do not capitalize the first letter of the first word.
- Where possible, name the author whose ideas or words you are quoting or paraphrasing.
- Providing information on the source material helps provide a context for the quoted and paraphrased material.
- In parentheses after the quotation, give the page number in the source where the quotation is located (hence the phrase "parenthetical citation"). This example contains only the page number because the author's name is mentioned in the text. If the text had not given the author's name, it would be included in the parenthetical citation.

2. **Original** (page 74): The Dickens family was forced to move frequently to avoid debt collectors and, in 1824, was engulfed by the catastrophe that has entered Dickens lore: John was arrested for nonpayment of debts and jailed at Marshalsea in London.

   Quotation: Hammer comments that "the Dickens family was forced to move frequently to avoid debt collectors and, in 1824, . . . [Dickens' father] John was arrested for nonpayment of debts" (75).

Comments

- When a quotation preceded by *that* forms an integral part of your sentence, do not capitalize the first word in the quotation, even when it is capitalized in the original.
- Use the ellipsis (three spaced periods) to indicate the omission of text from the original.
- Use brackets to enclose explanatory material not given in the quotation itself.

3. **Original** (page 72): The word "Dickensian" permeates our lexicon, used to evoke everything from urban squalor to bureaucratic heartlessness and rags-to-riches reversals.

   Quotation: In discussing the influence of Dickens two centuries after his birth, Hammer notes: "The word 'Dickensian' permeates our lexicon from urban squalor to bureaucratic heartlessness ..." (73).

Comments

- If your direct quotation is preceded by introductory text and a colon or comma, capitalize the first letter of the first word of the quotation.
- If you quote something that appears in quotation marks in the original source, use single marks within the double quotes.
- If your quotation appears to be a complete sentence but the actual sentence continues in the original, you must use the ellipsis at the end of your quotation to indicate that.
- If an ellipsis comes at the end of a quotation, the closing quotation mark follows the third period, with no space between the period and quotation mark. The parenthetical citation follows as usual.

Combination of Paraphrase and Direct Quotation. The following example illustrates how one can combine paraphrasing and quoting for a balanced handling of source material.

4. **Original** (page 75): With his father incarcerated, Charles, a bright and industrious student, was forced to leave school at around age 11 and take a job gluing labels on bottles at a London bootblacking factory. "It was a terrible, terrible humiliation," Tomalin told me, a trauma that would haunt Dickens for the rest of his life.

   Paraphrase and Quotation: The young Charles had to leave school and work in a factory when his father was sent to jail, an experience that Hammer describes as "a trauma that would haunt Dickens for the rest of his life" (75).

More Examples of Correctly Handled Direct Quotations.

5. Jack Santino in "Rock and Roll as Music; Rock and Roll as Culture" maintains that "such things as suicide, drugs, sex, and violence *are* teenage concerns" and that, "while artists have a responsibility not to glamorize them, that does not mean these themes should not be explored" (196).

6. In "Rock and Roll as Music; Rock and Roll as Culture," Jack Santino observes: "Furthermore, such things as suicide, drugs, sex, and violence *are* teenage concerns. While artists have a responsibility not to glamorize them, that does not mean these themes should not be explored" (196).

Comments

- Notice the difference between examples 5 and 6. The first integrates the quoted material into the sentence with the word *that,* so the first words in each of the quoted passages do not require a capital first letter.
- In the second example, the quotation is introduced and set off as a separate sentence, so the first word after the quotation mark begins with a capital letter.

INTEGRATING SOURCE MATERIALS INTO YOUR PAPER

When quoting or paraphrasing material, pay special attention to your treatment of source materials. Authors have developed many ways of skillfully integrating the words and ideas of other people with their own words. Your paper should not read as if you simply cut out the words of someone else and pasted them in your paper. You can achieve smooth integration of source materials into your text if you keep the following suggestions in mind:

- **Mention the cited author's name in the text of your paper to signal the beginning of a paraphrase or quotation.** The first time you mention the name, give both first and last names. After the first mention, give only the last name:

  Joshua Hammer notes that Dickens referred to himself as "The Inimitable" (72). **Hammer** explains that Dickens' meteoric rise to fame came at quite a young age for a writer, describing him as "newly famous [and] upperly mobile" (75).

- **Mention the source if no author is named.** This practice gives credit to the source while providing an introduction to the borrowed material:

  A *U.S. News & World Report* article notes that, although no genes determine what occupation one will go into, groups of genes produce certain tendencies—risk-taking, for instance—that might predispose one to select a particular kind of work ("How Genes Shape Personality" 64).

CAUTION—AVOID DROPPED QUOTATIONS

Never incorporate a quotation without in some way introducing or commenting on it. A quotation that is not introduced or followed by some concluding comment, referred to as a "dropped" quotation, detracts from the smooth flow of your paper.

- **Give citations for all borrowed material.** State the authority's name, use quotation marks as appropriate, give the source and page number in a parenthetical citation, give some sort of general information, and/or use a pronoun to refer to the authority mentioned in the previous sentence. **Do not rely on one parenthetical citation at the end of several sentences or an entire paragraph:**

> **Regna Lee Wood** has also researched the use of phonics in teaching children to read. **She** believes that the horrible failure of our schools began years ago. Wood notes that "it all began in 1929 and 1930 when hundreds of primary teachers, guided by college reading professors, stopped teaching beginners to read by "matching sounds with letters that spell sounds" (52). **She** adds that since 1950, when most reading teachers switched to teaching children to sight words rather than sound them by syllable, "fifty million children with poor sight memories have reached the fourth grade still unable to read" (52).

- **Vary introductory phrases and clauses.** Avoid excessive reliance on such standard introductory clauses as "Smith says," or "Jones writes." For instance, vary your verbs and/or provide explanatory information about sources, as in the following examples:

  > Michael Liu notes the following:
  >
  > Professor Xavier argues this point convincingly:
  >
  > According to Dr. Carroll, chief of staff at a major health center:
  >
  > As Marcia Smith points out,

- **The first mention of an authority in your text (as opposed to the parenthetical citation) should include the author's first name as well as last name.** The second and subsequent references should give the last name only (never the first name alone).

  > **First use of author's name in your paper: Susan Jaspers** correctly observes that . . .
  >
  > **Second and subsequent mentions of that author: Jaspers** contends elsewhere that . . .

- **Combine quotations and paraphrases.** A combination provides a smoother style than quoting directly all of the time:

  > W. H. Hanson's 2008 survey of college students reveals that today's generation of young people differs from those he surveyed in 2003. Hanson discovered that today's college students "are living through a period of profound demographic, economic, global, and technological change." Since these students of the first decade of the 21st century see themselves living in a "deeply troubled nation," they have only guarded optimism about the future (32–33).

- **For long quotations (more than four typed lines), set the quoted material off from the text (referred to as a block quotation).** Write your introduction to the quotation, generally followed by a colon. Then begin a new line indented ten spaces from the left margin, and type the quotation, double spaced as usual.

- **Do not add quotation marks for block quotations indented and set off from the text. If quotation marks appear in the original, use double quotation marks, not single.** If you quote a single paragraph or part of one, do not indent the first line any more than the rest of the quotation.

- **For block quotations, place the parenthetical citation after the final punctuation of the quotation.** See the following example of a block quotation:

  > In her article exploring the kind of workforce required by a high-tech economy, Joanne Jacobs suggests that many of today's high school graduates lack crucial skills necessary for jobs in the rapidly growing technical and computer industries. For instance, a number of corporations agreed on the following prerequisites for telecommunications jobs:
  >
  > - Technical reading skills (familiarity with circuit diagrams, online documentation, and specialized reference materials).
  > - Advanced mathematical skills (understanding of binary, octal, and hexadecimal number systems as well as mathematical logic systems).
  > - Design knowledge (ability to use computer-aided design to produce drawings). (39–40)

USING ELLIPSIS POINTS, SQUARE BRACKETS, SINGLE QUOTATION MARKS, AND "QTD. IN"

This section offers some additional guidelines on the mechanics of handling source materials and incorporating them into your paper.

Ellipsis Points

- **If you want to omit original words, phrases, or sentences from your quotation of source material, use ellipsis points to indicate the omission.** Ellipsis points consist of three spaced periods, with spaces before, between, and after the periods. In quotations, ellipses are most frequently used within sentences, almost never at the beginning, but sometimes at the end. In every case, the quoted material must form a grammatically complete sentence, either by itself or in combination with your own words.

  Original: The momentous occurrences of an era—from war and economics to politics and inventions—give meaning to lives of the individuals who live through them.

  Quotation with an ellipsis in the middle: Arthur Levine argues, "The momentous occurrences of an era . . . give meaning to lives of the individuals who live through them" (26).

- **Use ellipsis marks at the end of a quotation only if you have not used some words from the end of the final sentence quoted.** In that case, include four periods. When the ellipsis coincides with the end of your own sentence, use four periods with no space either before the first or after the last.

  Quotation with an ellipsis at the end: You know the old saying, "Eat, drink, and be merry. . . ."

- **If a parenthetical reference follows the ellipsis at the end of your sentence, use a space before each period and place the sentence period after the final parenthesis:**

  > According to recent studies, "Statistics show that Chinese women's status has improved . . ." (*Chinese Women* 46).

- **Ellipsis points are not necessary** if you are quoting a fragment of a sentence, that is, a few words or a subordinate clause, because context will clearly indicate the omission of some of the original sentence.

  > Sociobiologists add that social and nurturing experiences can "intensify, diminish, or modify" personality traits (Wood and Wood 272).

Square Brackets

The MLA Handbook for Writers of Research Papers, 7th ed., says that "unless indicated in brackets or parentheses . . . , changes must not be made in the spelling, capitalization, or interior punctuation of the source" (3.7.1). Although you should look for ways to integrate source material into your text that avoid overuse of square brackets, the following guidelines apply when changing source material is unavoidable.

- **If you want to change a word or phrase to conform to your own sentence or add words to make your sentence grammatically correct, use square brackets to indicate the change.** The square brackets enclose only the changed portion of the original.

  > **Original:** They were additional casualties of our time of plague, demoralized reminders that although this country holds only two percent of the world's population, it consumes 65 percent of the world's supply of hard drugs.
  >
  > **Quotation:** According to Pete Hamill in his essay "Crack and the Box," America "holds only two percent of the world's population, [yet] it consumes 65 percent of the world's supply of hard drugs" (267).
  >
  > **Original:** In a miasma of Walt Disney images, Bambi burning, and Snow White asleep, the most memorable is "Cinderella."
  >
  > **Quotation:** Louise Bernikow recalls spending Saturday afternoons at the theatre when she was growing up "in a miasma of Walt Disney images, . . . the most memorable [of which] is 'Cinderella'" (17).

Comment

This example illustrates the use not only of square brackets but also of ellipsis points and single and double quotation marks.

- **Use square brackets if you add some explanatory information or editorial comment.**

Original: Then, magically, the fairy godmother appears. She comes from nowhere, summoned, we suppose, by Cinderella's wishes.

Quotation: Louise Bernikow points out that "she [the fairy godmother] comes from nowhere, summoned . . . by Cinderella's wishes" (19).

- **If the passage you quote already contains an ellipsis, place square brackets around your own ellipsis.** The brackets tell readers that the ellipsis without brackets is in the original and that the ellipsis in brackets is your addition. MLA notes that, alternatively, you can add an explanatory note in parentheses after the quotation, if you prefer.

    Source: Du Maurier, Daphne. "Don't Look Now." *Don't Look Now: Stories.* Ed. Patrick Mc Grath. New York: New York Review Books, 2008. 3–58. Print.

    Original (page 10): She seemed normal, herself again. She wasn't trembling. And if this sudden belief was going to keep her happy he couldn't possibly begrudge it. But . . . but . . . he wished, all the same, it hadn't happened. There was something uncanny about thought-reading, about telepathy.

    Quotation with an added ellipsis: The husband in "Don't Look Now" is disturbed after an encounter that his wife has just described: "He couldn't possibly begrudge it. But . . . but . . . he wished, all the same, it hadn't happened. There was something uncanny about [. . .] telepathy" (Du Maurier 10).

    Alternative handling of added ellipsis: The husband in "Don't Look Now" is disturbed after an encounter that his wife has just described: "He couldn't possibly begrudge it. But . . . but . . . he wished, all the same, it hadn't happened. There was something uncanny about . . . telepathy" (Du Maurier 10; 1st ellipsis in orig.).

- **The Latin word *sic* (meaning "thus") in square brackets indicates that an error occurs in the original source of a passage you are quoting.** Because you are not at liberty to change words when quoting word for word, reproduce the error but use [*sic*] to indicate that the error is not yours.

    Original: Thrills have less to do with speed then changes in speed.

    Quotation: Dahl makes this observation: "Thrills have less to do with speed then [*sic*] changes in speed" (18).

Single Quotation Marks

- **If you quote text that itself appears in quotation marks in the original, use single marks within the double that enclose your own quotation.**

    Original: This set me pondering the obvious question: "How can it be so hard for kids to find something to do when there's never been such a range of stimulating entertainment available to them?"

    Quotation: Dahl is led to ask this question: " 'How can it be so hard for kids to find something to do when there's never been such a range of stimulating entertainment available to them?' " (18–19).

Qtd. in.

- **If you quote or paraphrase material that is quoted in an indirect source, use the abbreviation "qtd." with the word "in."** An indirect source is a second-hand one that quotes or paraphrases another's words, unlike a primary source, which is the writer's own work. In college research papers, you want to use primary sources as often as possible, but you are likely to have occasion to use secondary sources as well. Use "qtd. in" whenever you quote or paraphrase the published account of someone else's words or ideas. The works-cited list will include not the original source of the material you quoted or paraphrased but rather the indirect source, the one where you found the material. You will likely be using the single quotation marks within the double because you are quoting what someone else has quoted.

  Original: Printed in bold letters at the entrance of the show is a startling claim by Degas' fellow painter Auguste Renoir: "If Degas had died at 50, he would have been remembered as an excellent painter, no more; it is after his 50th year that his work broadened out and that he really becomes Degas."

  Quotation: Impressionist painter Auguste Renoir observed of Degas: "'If Degas had died at 50, he would have been remembered as an excellent painter, no more; it is after his 50th year that his work broadened out and that he really becomes Degas'" (qtd. in Benfey).

GUIDELINES FOR INTEGRATING SOURCE MATERIALS INTO YOUR PAPER

- Avoid "dropped" quotations by introducing all direct quotations.
- Use the author's name, where appropriate, to signal the beginning of a paraphrase or quotation.
- Use attributive tags, short identifying words, phrases, or clauses that identify source and introduce borrowed material.
- Cite sources for all borrowed material, either as attributive tags or parenthetically after the quotation or paraphrase.
- Name a source title, if the source does not list an author's name.
- Vary the way you introduce source material.
- Try combining direct quotations and paraphrases in the same sentence.
- Become familiar with appropriate uses of ellipsis points, brackets, single quotation marks, and "qtd. in."

DOCUMENTING SOURCES IN A COLLECTION OF ESSAYS

You have been reading about and looking at examples of one important component of source documentation: in-text citations. The other component is the alphabetical list, appearing on a separate page at the end of your paper, of all the works that you quoted from or paraphrased. This is the list of works cited. Each entry in the list begins with the author's name—last name first—followed by the title of the article, book, or other source and information about its place and date of publication. The author's name (or title of the work, if it is published anonymously) in the text's parenthetical citation refers to one item in this list at the end of the paper.

You will find more discussion of documenting sources in Chapter 7, but the brief treatment here gives useful guidelines for short papers using materials reprinted in a collection of essays, such as this textbook. Although the examples in this section illustrate how to document materials reprinted in this textbook, the guidelines apply to any collection of essays. Because much of *Perspectives on Contemporary Issues* is a collection of other people's works, not the editor's, you will probably not have occasion to use the words or ideas of Ackley herself. However, because you are not reading the essays in their original source, you must indicate that you have read them in her book.

Citing One Source in a Collection.   Suppose your paper quotes or paraphrases a statement from a reading in the seventh edition of *Perspectives on Contemporary Issues,* Donna Beegle's "All Kids Should Take 'Poverty 101.'" After you write either the exact words of Beegle or paraphrase her words, open a parenthesis, write the author's last name and the page number where you read the words with no punctuation between them, and then close the parenthesis (Beegle 345-347). Do not write the word *page* or *pages* nor insert a comma between the author's name and the number of the page. If Beegle's piece is the only one you use in your paper, write "Work Cited" (note the singular form of "Work") at the end of your paper and enter complete bibliographic information for the article:

> WORK CITED
>
> Beegle, Donna. "All Kids Should Take
>   'Poverty 101.'" *Perspectives on
>   Contemporary Issues: Readings across
>   the Disciplines.* 7th ed. Ed. Katherine
>   Anne Ackley. Boston: Wadsworth Cengage,
>   2015. 345-347. Print.

Citing Two or More Sources in a Collection.   If you draw material from two or more works in a collection, MLA style recommends that you create an entry for the collection and then cross-reference each work to that collection. That is, you need not repeat the full information for the collection with the citation for each essay. Instead, list the collection by the editor's name, giving full bibliographic information. Then list separately each article you use by author and title, but after each essay title, give only the collection editor's name and the inclusive page numbers of the essay.

For example, suppose you write a paper on the power of words and images to affect behavior. In your essay, you use information from several essays in the seventh edition of this textbook. Here is how your Works Cited page might look:

WORKS CITED

Ackley, Katherine Anne, ed. *Perspectives on Contemporary Issues: Readings
across the Disciplines.* 7th ed. Boston:
Wadsworth Cengage 2015. Print.

Beegle, Donna. "All Kids Should Take 'Poverty 101.'" Ackley 345-347.

Friedman, Thomas. "Pass the Books. Hold the
Oil." Ackley 325-328.

Ravitch, Diane. "Critical Thinking? You
Need Knowledge." Ackley 321-323.

STUDENT PAPER DEMONSTRATING SYNTHESIS WITH IN-TEXT CITATIONS USING MLA STYLE

Following is a student paper that synthesizes material from several works in one collection and follows MLA guidelines for paraphrasing and quoting. Michael Vawter, in "More than Just a Place" uses sources from a collection of essays, stories, and poems on the subject of the environment. His assignment in a literature and environment course was to explain a key theme or main point that several of the writers had in common. His paper may be used as a model for papers that you are asked to write using readings from this or any other textbook, or from a similar collection of works, such as the one that Michael uses. The marginal comments call attention to various strategies of writing an effective synthesis.

Comments

- MLA formatting guidelines for papers call for the author's last name to appear in the running head before the page number, even on the first page.
- Note also that the student's name, class, instructor's name, and date appear on the left-hand side above the title of the paper.
- MLA style recommends using the day/month/year format for the date. Double-space between all lines of your paper, including between the date and your title and between your title and the first line of your paper.

- A works-cited list appears on a separate page at the end. The works-cited list gives full bibliographic information for the collection and cross-references the individual works to the collection.
- Works are listed alphabetically and each citation conforms in punctuation and spacing to the MLA style of documentation
- For more on using MLA style in writing that uses sources, including guidelines for formatting the works-cited list, see Chapter 7.

Vawter 1

Michael Vawter

Prof. Weaver

FYS 101

13 Feb 2014

More than Just a Place

The opening paragraph introduces readers to the subject of the paper.

Science tells us that we are the product of two fundamental forces, our genetic code and our environment. These two factors have not only propelled our evolution as a species, but they have also given us our sense of personality, culture, and identity. While our genetic code is fixed, our cultural and physical environments can be fluid and ever changing. Feeling rooted or closely connected to the environment can be extremely beneficial for the development of personal and cultural wellness. To have this sort of connection with one's environment, one must develop a strong sense of place and an identity that is grounded in location. We see the importance of place and its transcendence beyond just a physi-

Michael's thesis sets the direction of the paper.

cal location in the works of four writers as they reflect on their environments.

Vawter 2

Michael begins with a quotation and discussion of the importance of being "placed."

Scott Russell Sanders writes in *Staying Put* that one needs an adequate measuring stick to experience the world at large. He argues that a person can never fully appreciate any environment—or any aspect of nature for that matter—without having an environment of his or her own to compare it to: "How can you value other places if you do not have one of your own? If you are not yourself placed, then you wander the world like a sightseer, a collector of sensations, with no gauge for measuring what you see" (114). How can a person adequately understand the significance of any place he or she happens to spend time in without a reference point in the form of a home environment with which to identify?

The source of the quotation is named in the text, so just a page number is needed in the parentheses following the quotation

This paragraph continues the discussion of Sanders' view on rootedness and valuing one's environment.

Elsewhere, in his essay "Buckeye," Sanders argues that each of us has a responsibility to adopt our local environment and to care for it. He refers to the words of another writer, Simone Weil, who wrote: "'Let us love the country of here below. . . . It is this country that God has given us to love. He has willed that it should be difficult yet possible to love it'" (293). Sanders suggests here that the important thing is not caring for the environment at large, but rather caring for the specific chunk of it within which one

Michael quotes Sanders quoting Weil, so her words are in single marks within double. He has omitted some words, as the ellipses indicate.

Vawter 3

lives. He argues that we are intrinsically
tied to the environment that we inhabit,
and that just as we cannot effectively enjoy nature by disassociating from our homes
and haphazardly attempting to take all of
it in at once, we cannot effectively protect nature by aiming to protect all of it
instead of just concerning ourselves with
our own areas. One's home, for Sanders, is
more than just a place.

Michael makes the transition to his discussion of another writer.

Sanders is not alone in his belief
that nature—our environment—has a profoundly direct impact on our personal identities. Wendell Berry, in his poem "Stay
Home," claims nature itself as his most
beloved home and reveals the impact that
nature has had on the shaping of his identity. He feels grounded and rooted whenever
he is in the wild and derives pleasure from
that profound sense of rootedness:

When quoting more than three lines of a verse, set them off from the text and begin each line on a new line.

> I will be standing in the woods
> where the old trees
> move only with the wind
> and then with gravity.
> In the stillness of the trees
> I am at home. (8-13)

He seems to derive pleasure and fulfillment from being out in the woods, but
this is not his focus. His emphasis is on
his feeling at home—on the fact that these
pleasurable experiences he derives from

Vawter 4

being in the woods are not just exciting, but are also grounding and definitive.

At the same time, Berry recognizes that other people have different homes and that they derive different sorts of identities based on those different homes. He seems to suggest that this is okay. As long as he can remain rooted to his own conception of "home," others can feel free to root themselves differently: "I am at home. Don't come with me. / You stay home too" (6-7; 13-14). The repetition of these lines at the conclusion of each stanza reinforces this view. Berry does not argue that everyone should find "home" by seeking to experience nature the way that he does. He seems to suggest that the important thing is to find your unique environment and unique source of grounding and to maintain them.

The impact of environment on rootedness is observable not only in the context of personal identity, but also in the context of cultural identity. In her essay "Touching the Earth," bell hooks argues that the African American people developed a unique cultural identity while enslaved in the South, and that this identity was tied at a fundamental level to their plantation environment and to the Southern land itself. When slavery in the U.S. was

When quoting fewer than four lines of poetry, integrate them into the text and use a slash with spaces before and after to indicate line separation.

Michael provides transition as he moves from paragraph to paragraph.

Writer bell hooks does not capitalize her name, so references to her name should be lowercased.

finally abolished and African Americans
began migrating northward in search of new
opportunities, many of them lost a certain
element of their identity. Observing that
many African Americans realized this and
began travelling back to their homelands in
the South, hooks writes: "Generations of
black folks who migrated north . . . returned down home in search of a spiritual
nourishment, a healing, that was fundamentally connected to reaffirming one's connection to nature" (172). The process of
northward migration uprooted the African
American people from their environment,
which had a negative effect on their general wellness. Unfortunately, it also seems
to have had a far-reaching effect on their
general confidence as a race, as hooks
writes: "Learning contempt for blackness,
[African American] southerners transplanted
in the north suffered both culture shock
and soul loss" (172). With their cultural confidence in shambles, the African
American people who were scattered across
the North began to be affected by the racist attitudes present in their surrounding environment. They began internalizing
the lies perpetuated by those Northerners
who didn't believe that African Americans
were a competent race, and this in turn had
a profoundly negative effect on American

Vawter 6

society as a whole. Uprooting oneself from
a "home" environment and moving into a more
hostile one is clearly a very dangerous
pursuit.

The past environments of one's ancestors may even be a factor in rootedness
and in cultural identity. In his poem "The
Negro Speaks of Rivers," Langston Hughes
suggests that his identity has been shaped
not only by his own environment but also
by the environments that played a role in
his ethnic heritage. He defines himself not
only in the context of his own environment,
but also in the context of the environments
of his African ancestors: "I bathed in the
Euphrates when dawns were young. / I built
my hut near the Congo and it lulled me to
sleep. / I looked upon the Nile and raised
the pyramids above it" (4-6). Hughes himself never slept in huts by the Congo or
built pyramids by the Nile, but he considers himself to be a product of that environment nonetheless. His message here seems
to be that a "rooted" person should be cog-
nizant not only of his or her current environment but also of the environments that
rooted their ancestors.

Hughes is far more than just cogni-
zant of these extended roots, however. He
insists that the Congo and the Nile have
had a deep impact on him, though he has
perhaps never seen them. He writes, "I've

Vawter 7

known rivers: / Ancient, dusky rivers. /
My soul has grown deep like the rivers"
(8-10). He recognizes that his ancestors
were, in many ways, the direct product of
interaction with these formidable rivers,
and that this environmental impact has been
passed down to him through stories, traditions, and possibly even genetic traits.
His way of life as well as his way of
thinking may have been directly influenced
by his ancestors' relationship with rivers.

Michael's conclusion brings his paper to a close by summarizing what he has gained from reading selected works of four writers on the importance of feeling connected to a place.

Home is more than a place. Home is
not simply a building that one regularly
inhabits, a town that one was born in, or a
park that one enjoys walking through. Those
buildings, towns and parks do directly influence us, however, and can even become a
part of us; in fact, they *should* become a
part of us. While at times it may be necessary to uproot oneself and move to a new
environment—such as in the example of the
northward migration of African Americans
after their liberation—this uprooting can
be a difficult and even painful process. In
the fast pace of modern society, it can be
easy for one to lose connection with the
immediate environment and with one's true
home. This type of disconnect should not
be taken lightly. In order to firmly root
oneself and obtain a profound and lasting
sense of personal and cultural identity,
one must have a home.

Vawter 8

Michael's list
of works cited
includes four
selections from
an anthology as
well as two works
by the same
author. The three
hyphens indicate
that the name is
identical to that
in the preceding
entry; the entries
themselves
are listed
alphabetically by
the first letter of
the title. Do not
change the three
hyphens to a
long dash.

Works Cited

Anderson, Lorraine, Scott P. Slovic, and
    John P. O'Grady, eds. *Literature and*
    the Environment: A Reader on Nature
    and Culture. New York: Longman, 1999.
    Print.

Berry, Wendell. "Stay Home." Anderson,
    Slovic, and O'Grady 222-23.

hooks, bell. "Touching the Earth."
    Anderson, Slovic, and O'Grady 169-73.

Hughes, Langston. "The Negro Speaks of
    Rivers." Anderson, Slovic, and O'Grady
    168-69.

Sanders, Scott Russell. "Buckeye."
    Anderson, Slovic, and O'Grady 290-95.

---. *Staying Put: Making a Home in a*
    Restless World. Boston: Beacon, 1991.

CHAPTER 7

Writing a Research Paper

When you are asked to write a paper using sources, no matter what course it is for, your goal is the same: to support skillfully a carefully formulated thesis with documented evidence. Writing such a paper can seem both overwhelming and exciting, especially if you have never written one before. This chapter presents a brief overview of the key steps in locating a topic you want to spend time with, researching it, and writing a paper incorporating the sources you have used. Keep in mind the discussion in Chapter 6 on paraphrasing, quoting, and documenting sources. A research paper is likely to be much longer than a writing assignment generated from readings in this book, but otherwise little difference separates the processes of using materials from this textbook and using materials from other sources in terms of accuracy and fairness to your sources. Furthermore, the process of writing a research paper is not much different from that of writing any other paper, as explained in Chapter 2. To do your best work, you will go through the prewriting, drafting, revising, editing, and proofreading stages.

DEFINING YOUR PURPOSE

Your instructor will tell you whether your purpose in the research paper is to argue, explain, analyze, or come to some conclusion about something. Many instructors prefer that students write argumentative papers. In that case, you will make a judgment about your topic based on what you find in your research. Recall the discussion in Chapter 5 on writing an argument. The same guidelines apply whether you are writing a researched argument or one without sources. You will begin your research with an idea of what your position is, then research your subject extensively, arrive at an informed opinion, and finally defend that position by presenting evidence that seems valid (that is, logical and convincing) to you. If you want to go a step further and convince your audience to adopt your position or to act on suggestions you propose, then your purpose is persuasion. The subjects for argumentative papers are virtually unlimited, but they often include controversial issues, such as those addressed in this textbook, topics on which people hold widely varying opinions.

On the other hand, some instructors direct students to explain or analyze something in their research papers. An informative paper does not necessarily address a controversial subject. If you are to write an explanatory paper, you will gather information about your topic and present it in such a way that your reader fully understands it. You will explain, describe, illustrate, or narrate something in full detail, such as what a black hole is, how photosynthesis works, the circumstances surrounding a historical event, and significant events in the life of a famous person.

Audience.   Having a clear sense of your audience will direct your research and help you write your paper. If you are writing an argument, the most useful audience to address is one that is opposed to your position or, at best, uncertain about where they stand on the issue. A good argument seeks to persuade or convince an audience, so anticipating readers who are not already convinced will help sharpen your argument. If your purpose is to explain, illustrate, or analyze, your audience is likely to be informed in general about the particular subject of your paper, but not in great depth. Unless instructed otherwise, assume an intelligent audience of nonspecialists who are interested in learning more about the topic of your paper. Imagining this audience will keep you from having to define or explain every term or concept and give you room for interesting, informative, and/or intriguing material about the topic.

FINDING A TOPIC

Once you know your purpose and audience, the next step in writing a research paper is to find a subject that you will be comfortable working with for many weeks and then narrow it to a specific topic. Some instructors assign topics, but most leave the choice to students. The freedom to choose your own research paper topic can be intimidating because so much depends on selecting the right topic. You want a topic that not only holds your interest but that also offers you an opportunity to investigate it in depth.

The process of discovering or locating what you will write about involves first determining the broad subject you are particularly interested in pursuing. Once you have settled on the subject, you will need to narrow it to one specific aspect of that subject. For many research paper assignments, that topic will have to be arguable, one that requires you to investigate from several angles and arrive at and defend your own position. This position will be worded in the form of a hypothesis or thesis, stated most often as a declarative statement but sometimes as a question. Settling on your final topic takes time, so do some serious thinking about this important step as soon as the paper is assigned. You will be reshaping, narrowing, and refining your topic for much of the research process, so you do not want to switch subjects halfway through.

Any or all of the suggestions for generating ideas in the prewriting stage that are discussed in Chapter 2 would be useful when trying to discover a topic for your research paper. Brainstorming, making lists, clustering, even researching in a preliminary way and talking with others can be of use. Asking questions, thinking about your personal interests or personal opinion, considering commonly held opinions, and thinking about controversial topics can all be quite helpful in the process of narrowing down to a research topic that you are interested in pursuing.

Asking Questions.   One of the best ways to approach the research project is to ask questions about a subject that interests you and that seems worth investigating. As you read through the suggestions for locating a topic that follow, think in terms of questions that you might ask about the initial subjects you come up with. Try to think in terms of questions that can be answered in a research paper as opposed to a short essay. As you narrow your field of potential topics, look for those about which you can ask questions whose answers are neither too broad nor too narrow. You want the topic that you ultimately select to be challenging enough that your paper will be interesting to you as well as to your audience. Avoid topics about which questions are unanswerable or highly speculative. Your goal in the research process will be to arrive at an answer, insofar as that is possible, to your question.

Any of the topics listed as possible subjects of argumentation in Chapter 5 are appropriate for researched writing. Here are examples of questions that one might ask about various argumentative subjects when trying to generate ideas for a research paper:

- Under what conditions, if any, is censorship justifiable?
- Should research into human cloning continue?
- Do advertising images of women set up impossible standards of femininity?
- What is the appropriate punishment for steroid use in athletes?
- Which plays a more prominent role in determining behavior, genes, or environment?
- What role does phonics education play in the teaching of reading?
- How dangerous is secondhand smoke?
- Should cities be allowed to ban smoking in public places such as bars, restaurants, and private clubs?
- Should sex education be taught by parents or by schools?
- Was King Arthur a real person?
- What is the best strategy for combating terrorism?
- Are restrictions on freedom of speech necessary in time of war?

- How far should Homeland Security go to protect Americans from terrorists?

- Is there still a "glass ceiling" for women in the workforce?

- Should the government provide child day care for all workers?

- Does watching too much television have a harmful effect on preschool children?

- What factors affect academic success in females versus males?

- Should the Electoral College be abolished?

- Does America need an official language?

- Is hormone replacement therapy a safe choice for women?

- Do women do better academically in all-female schools?

- Should prostitution be legalized?

- Should there be a formal apology from the government for slavery?

- Should there be reparations for slavery, as there has been for Japanese interned in camps during WWII?

- Should grades be abolished?

- Should the HPV vaccination be mandatory?

- What should be done about illegal immigrants in the United States?

Generating Topics from Personal Interest.   One way to find a topic for your research paper is to begin with subjects you already know well, are interested in, or think you would like to improve your knowledge of. Begin by writing down such things as hobbies, sports, issues in your major, contemporary social issues, or topics in classes you are taking. Consider topics that attracted your interest in high school or in previous college classes; any reading you have already done on subjects that appeal to you; or the kinds of things that capture your attention when you watch television news, read news magazines or newspapers, or select nonfiction books for leisure-time reading.

Generating Topics from Personal Opinions.   Virtually any topic can be turned into an argument, but opinions are always subject to debate. Therefore, one way to generate a research paper topic is to begin with your own strongly held opinions.

Caution: Avoid a topic that is based entirely on opinion. Evaluative statements are especially good for argumentative papers because they are likely to have differing opinions. Once you say that something is the best, the most significant, the most important, or the greatest, for instance, you have put yourself in the position of defending that statement. You will have to establish your criteria for making your judgment and defend your choice against what others might think. Here are some ideas for this particular approach:

- The most influential person in the twenty-first century (or in America; in the world; in a particular field such as education, government, politics, arts, entertainment, or the like)

- The most significant battle in the Civil War (or World War I or World War II)

- The greatest basketball (or football, tennis, soccer, baseball) player (either now playing or of all time)

- The greatest or worst president

- The best movie, book, or album of all time

- The business or industry with the greatest impact on American life in the last decade (or last twenty years, last fifty years, or last century)

Because your conclusion on any of these or similar topics is your opinion, you need to establish criteria for your conclusion, clearly describe the process you used to make it, and explain the logical basis for that process.

Generating Topics from Opinions Based on Stereotypes. Another possibility for a research paper topic is to take an opinion (though not necessarily one that you share) based on stereotyped assumptions about a group or class of people, and explore the validity of that belief. Your goal is to determine whether the opinion is a valid, partially valid, or invalid position. Even if you cannot arrive at a definitive evaluation of the validity of the statement, you can still present the evidence you find and explain why your research does not reach a conclusion. Here are examples of beliefs that some people may have:

- Watching violence on television produces violent behavior.
- Men naturally perform mechanical tasks better than women do.
- Women naturally perform better at nurturing children than men do.
- Young people do not have much hope for a bright future.
- Women are more emotional than men.
- People stay on welfare because they are too lazy to work.
- Homeless people could get off the streets if they really tried.

When determining the validity of a commonly held opinion or belief, your research focuses on gathering evidence without bias. Although you may want to interview people about their opinions on a particular belief, the basis of your conclusion must rest on clearly reliable evidence.

Generating Topics from Controversy.   Yet another way to discover a topic you find intriguing enough to commit many hours of time to is to think of controversial issues that always generate heated debate. These topics may be frequently discussed in newspapers, news magazines, and on television news programs and talk shows. They may be issues on which candidates for public office, from local county board members to state and federal officials, are pressed to take stands. Here are some examples of controversial statements:

- Affirmative action laws are unfair to white males and should be repealed.

- Media coverage of celebrity trials should be banned.

- Birth parents should always have a legal right to take back children they have given up for adoption.

- Children whose parents are on welfare should be placed in state-run orphanages.

- Women should be barred from participating in combat duty.

- Graphic violence in the movies (or in video games or MTV videos) poses a serious threat to the nation's moral values.

- The federal government should stop funding projects in the arts and the humanities.

- The federal government should provide unlimited funds to support research to find a cure for AIDS.

- Children who commit murder should be tried as adults no matter what their age.

- Illegal aliens should be forced to return to their country of origin.

Narrowing Your Subject to a Specific Topic.   Most research paper assignments are short enough that you simply must narrow your focus to avoid a too shallow or too hopelessly general treatment of your topic. Keep in mind the distinction between **subject** and **topic**: subject is the general area under investigation, whereas topic is the narrow aspect of that subject that you are investigating. For example, Jack the Ripper is a subject, but entire books have been written on the notorious 1888 murders in the Whitechapel area of London. A suitable topic on the subject would be to explore the controversy surrounding the alleged links of the Duke of Clarence with the murders, taking a position in favor of the theory most plausible to you.

One way to get a sense of how a general topic can be narrowed is to look at the table of contents of a book on a subject that interests you. Notice the chapter headings, which are themselves subtopics of the broad subject. Chapters themselves are often further subdivided. You want to find a topic that is narrow enough that you can fully explore it without leaving unanswered questions, yet broad enough that you can say enough about it in a reasonably long paper.

To narrow your subject to a topic, take a general subject and go through the brainstorming process again, this time listing everything that comes to your mind about that particular subject. What subtopics does your subject have? What questions can you ask about your general subject? How might you narrow your focus on that subject? Ultimately, you want to generate an idea that gives focus to your preliminary library search.

FORMING A PRELIMINARY THESIS AND A WORKING BIBLIOGRAPHY

No matter what your purpose or who your audience is, you will have one central idea, most often articulated early in the paper in the form of a single thesis statement. You will take a position on your topic and defend or illustrate it convincingly with evidence from your source materials.

When you believe that you have narrowed your topic sufficiently, you are ready to form your preliminary thesis. This is the position that you believe you want to take on your topic, based on your early thinking about and narrowing down of a subject. Your preliminary or working thesis can be in the form of either a question or a statement. In much the same way as your final thesis gives direction and focus to your paper, your preliminary thesis gives you direction and focus in the research process. As you review potential sources and read about your topic, you may find yourself changing your preliminary thesis for any number of reasons. Perhaps your topic is too narrow or too new and you simply cannot find enough sources with which to write a fair and balanced research paper. Or you may discover that your topic is too broad to cover in a research paper and that you need to narrow your focus even more.

A common reason for changing a preliminary thesis is that, once you actually start reading sources, you discover that you want to change your initial position. You may discover that you were wrong in your assumption or opinion about your topic and that you are persuaded to change your position. Part of the pleasure in researching a topic is discovering new ideas or information, so it makes sense that your early views on your topic may shift as you learn more about it. More than likely, your final thesis will differ in some way from your preliminary thesis.

With your preliminary thesis in mind, you are ready to start the actual research process. First, you need to locate potential sources. A working bibliography is a list of the sources you **might** use in your research paper, those that look particularly promising during a preliminary search. At this point, you will not have had time to read or even carefully skim all potential sources, let alone imagine how they fit together to support your working thesis. Your goal is to find the sources that bear most directly on your topic and select from them the most useful ones to read carefully, taking notes as you read. One obvious place to start looking for sources is the library; another source is the Internet.

FINDING SOURCES

The Library.   Your library has a good number of valuable resources to help you in your search for materials on your research topic. Although the Internet has made searching for reference materials easy and quick, libraries house books, periodicals, and other materials that you can hold, leaf through, check out, and read. Furthermore, many libraries have special collections on specific subjects and offer access to online databases that they subscribe to. Increasingly, libraries are working to connect their own digital resources stored in databases to Internet search engines. In the meantime, do not overlook the potential for excellent sources available on your own campus or through your university library's online catalog. Your library may have print copies of sources that you cannot find on the Internet.

Online Catalog. Begin your library search for sources on your general subject or topic (if you have sufficiently narrowed your focus) by reviewing the online catalog for titles of potential sources. In this searching stage, you probably will not know titles of works or authors, so you will begin by looking under subject headings for titles that seem relevant to your research subject. One advantage of using your library is that you can physically examine a book, flip through its table of contents, check its index, read the author's credentials, and skim some of the text. If it seems to suit your purpose, you can check it out and take it home with you.

Electronic Databases. Most libraries provide access to electronic indexes or databases and often have CD-ROMs or DVD-ROMS that have full-text copies of periodical articles or bibliographies of books and periodical articles related to particular subject areas. CD- and DVD-ROMs have a disadvantage that the Internet does not have in that, once they are produced, they cannot be updated. Still, they can be very useful for locating articles for research.

The Internet.   To find Internet materials, you can use any of a number of equally good search engines available on the web. Search engines collect many sites in their databanks; they return sites that match the keywords you type to begin your search. Search engines get their information in one of two major ways, either by crawler-based technology or by human-powered directories, but increasingly they use a combination of both. Crawler-based search engines gather their information automatically by "crawling" or sending "spiders" out to the web, searching the contents of other systems and creating a database of the results. Human-powered directories depend on humans for the listings you get in response to a search; they manually approve material for inclusion in a database.

Be very careful when searching for sources on the Internet: keep in mind the guidelines in Chapter 1 on evaluating Internet sources. Begin by choosing your search engine from among the best known or most used; they are likely to be the most reliable. Commercially backed search engines are usually well maintained and frequently upgraded, thus ensuring reliable results.

Other Sources.   Do not overlook other excellent sources of information, such as personal interviews, surveys, lectures, taped television programs, films, documentaries, and government publications. For example, if you research the human genome project, you will likely find a number of books, periodical articles, and government documents on the subject. A search of the web will turn up hundreds of thousands of site matches. You could easily become overwhelmed by the mass of materials available on your subject. Your task is to select the sources that seem most relevant to your project and to narrow your research topic as quickly as possible to avoid wasting time gathering materials you ultimately cannot use. To clarify and focus your own approach to the subject, you may want to interview a biology professor for information about the scientific aspects of the project and a philosophy professor for an opinion on its ethical implications. In addition to such interviews, you may use material from a lecture, a television documentary, a film, or your own survey.

The Difference between Primary and Secondary Sources.   "Primary" refers to original sources, actual data, or firsthand witnesses, such as interviews, surveys, speeches, diaries, letters, unpublished manuscripts, photographs, memoirs or autobiographies, published material written at the time of the event such as newspaper articles, and similar items. They are actual recorded accounts or documentary evidence of events. "Secondary" refers to sources like books and articles that discuss, explain, or interpret events or that are seen secondhand. They are written or recorded after the fact and represent processed information: interpretations of or commentary on events.

For instance, student Sam Cox read primary sources for his paper "Proving Their Loyalty During World War I: German Americans Confronted with Anti-German Fervor and Suspicion." (See introduction and conclusion to his paper later in this chapter.) Sam was interested in the subject of the loyalty of German-Americans living in the United States during WWI. To find out about it, he read numerous newspaper accounts of and by German-Americans as reported in two newspapers and written in both German and English. To help him come to his conclusion that German-Americans were loyal to America at the time that America was at war with Germany, Sam read dozens of both primary and secondary sources. These are listed together in his Works-Cited page at the end of his paper. A selection of his sources appear later in this chapter, as do his opening paragraphs.

Reporting the Results of a Survey Using Tables and Graphs.   Surveys are another good primary source. For instance, in a group-written paper, four students were interested in the question of the influence of gender on academic success on their college campus. They prepared a survey that they distributed to classmates. Their paper reports the results of their findings based on 103 surveys and includes four charts and graphs that represent these findings. One of these is reproduced in the guidelines for putting all of the parts of a paper together later in this chapter. You can also find examples in Chapter 23 in Benjamin Powell's article, "In Defense of 'Sweatshops.'"

GUIDELINES FOR DEVELOPING A WORKING BIBLIOGRAPHY

- List sources that sound promising for your research, recording titles and locations as you discover them.
- If the source is a library book, record the title, author, and call number.
- If the source is an article from your library, write the title of the piece, the name of its author, the title of the magazine or journal where it appears, the date of the issue, and the inclusive pages numbers. You will need all this information to find the article.
- For other sources in the library, such as videotapes, audiotapes, government documents, or pamphlets, write down as much information as you can find to help locate them. Write the location of any source, such as a special collection, government document, stack, and periodical.
- For an Internet site, record the URL (Uniform Resource Locator) or bookmark it on your computer. Record the title; the author, if known; the name of the site; the name of its creator, if available; and the date the site was created, if available. If you use the source in your paper, you will add the date that you accessed the material in the works-cited entry, so include that as well.
- You may want to retrieve the full text files of Internet sites that seem promising, as you discover them, to ensure their availability when you are ready to begin reading and taking notes.

CREATING A PRELIMINARY BIBLIOGRAPHY

Once you complete a list of sources to investigate, you need to evaluate them as potential references for your research paper. If you discover that you cannot use a source, cross it off your list or delete it from your bookmarked sites. When you find a source that definitely looks promising for your research topic, make sure that you have recorded all pertinent bibliographic information, preferably in the form in which it will appear on your Works-Cited page. The section in this chapter entitled "Documenting Sources" lists appropriate formats for various kinds of sources. Note the following sample work-cited formats for some common types of sources:

Book with One Author.

```
Pollock, Jocelyn M. Ethical Dilemmas and
    Decisions in Criminal Justice. Boston:
    Wadsworth, 2013. Print.
```

Journal Article with One Author.

> Moon, Kristen. "On a Temporary Basis:
> Immigration, Labor Unions, and the
> American Entertainment Industry, 1880s-
> 1930s." *Journal of American History* 99
> (Dec. 2012): 771-72. Print.

Journal Article with Two Authors.

> Cusimano, Michael, and Judith Kwok. "Skiers,
> Snowboarders, and Safety Helmets."
> *JAMA* 303.7 (2010): 661-62. Print.

Journal Article with No Author Named.

> "Class Action Suits in the Workplace Are on
> the Rise." *HR Focus* April 2012: 84-85.
> Print.

Newspaper Article with Author Named.

> Fagan, Kevin. "Homeless, Mike Dick Was 51,
> Looked 66." *San Francisco Chronicle* 2
> Mar. 2008: G1+. Print.

Newspaper Article, Online.

> Wilford, John Noble. "Malaria Most Likely
> Killed King Tut, Scientists Say." *New
> York Times*. New York Times, 16 Feb.
> 2010. Web. 12 Oct. 2014.

Magazine Article with Author Named.

> Hammer, Joshua. "Mad for Dickens." *Smithso-*
>   *nian* February 2012: 70-78. Print.

Magazine Article with Author Named, Online.

> McCabe. Janice. "Gender Bias in
>   Children's Books." *Medical News*
>   *Today*. MediLexicon, Intl., 4 May.
>   2011. Web. 11 Nov. 2014.

Magazine Article with No Author Named.

> "Mercury Rising." *National Geographic* Dec.
>   2012: 35. Print.

Chapter from a Collection of Essays.

> Smiley, Jane. "You Can Never Have Too
>   Many." *The Barbie Chronicles: A Living*
>   *Doll Turns Forty*. Ed. Yona Zeldis
>   McDonough. New York: Touchstone/Simon,
>   1999. 189-92. Print.

Government Document.

> United States. Cong. House. Committee on
>   Education and the Workforce. *Education*
>   *Reforms: Hearing before the Early*
>   *Childhood, Elementary and Secondary*
>   *Education Subcommittee*. 112th Cong.,
>   1st sess. 21 Sept 2011: 112-30. Print.

Internet Website.

> "Women in Male-Dominated Industries and
> Occupations in U.S. and Canada." *Cata-*
> *lyst* 17 April 2012. Web. 21 Sept. 2014.

A Translation.

> Witten, Johann. "Letters to Christoph
> Witten, 3 December 1914, 5 December
> 1915, 9 September 1919, 18 September
> 1920." *News from the Land of Freedom:*
> *German Immigrants Write Home.* Trans.
> Susan Vogel. Eds. Walter Kamphoefner,
> Wolfgang Helbich, and Ulrike Sommer.
> Ithaca, NY: Cornell UP, 1991. 278-83.
> Print.

Following the formatting guidelines for the Works-Cited page will save time later in the process when you put your paper in its final form. As you record information in the proper format, alphabetize your list, placing new items in the appropriate alphabetical position. Then, when you need to assemble the Works-Cited page, just move the list to the file where you store your paper (or keep the list in the same file). As you evaluate sources to determine whether they are appropriate for your paper, delete those that you decide not to pursue further. Here is how a list of the works on the previous sample bibliography entries would look in a computer file:

> WORKS CITED
>
> "Class Action Suits in the Workplace Are on
> the Rise." *HR Focus* April 2012: 84-85.
> Print.
> Cusimano, Michael, and Judith Kwok. "Ski-
> ers, Snowboarders, and Safety Helmets."
> *JAMA* 303.7 (2010): 661-62. Print.

Fagan, Kevin. "Homeless, Mike Dick Was 51,
    Looked 66." *San Francisco Chronicle* 2
    Mar. 2008: G1+. Print.

Hammer, Joshua. "Mad for Dickens." *Smithso-
    nian* February 2012: 70-78. Print.

McCabe. Janice. "Gender Bias in Children's
    Books." *Medical News Today*. MediLexicon,
    Intl., 4 May. 2011. Web. 11 Nov.
    2014.

"Mercury Rising." *National Geographic* Dec.
    2012: 35.

Moon, Kristen. "On a Temporary Basis: Immi-
    gration, Labor Unions, and the American
    Entertainment Industry, 1880s-1930s."
    Journal of American History 99 (Dec.
    2012): 771-72. Print.

Pollock, Jocelyn M. *Ethical Dilemmas and
    Decisions in Criminal Justice*. Boston:
    Wadsworth, 2013. Print.

Smiley, Jane. "You Can Never Have Too
    Many." *The Barbie Chronicles: A Living
    Doll Turns Forty*. Ed. Yona Zeldis
    McDonough. New York: Touchstone/Simon,
    1999. 189-92. Print.

United States. Cong. House. Committee on
    Education and the Workforce. *Education
    Reforms: Hearing before the Early
    Childhood, Elementary and Secondary
    Education Subcommittee*. 112th Cong.,
    1st sess. 21 Sept 2011: 112-30. Print.

Wilford, John Noble. "Malaria Most Likely
    Killed King Tut, Scientists Say." *New
    York Times*. New York Times, 16 Feb.
    2010. Web. 12 Oct. 2014.

Witten, Johann. "Letters to Christoph
Witten, 3 December 1914, 5 December
1915, 9 September 1919, 18 September
1920." *News from the Land of Freedom:
German Immigrants Write Home.* Trans. Susan
Vogel. Eds. Walter Kamphoefner, Wolfgang
Helbich, and Ulrike Sommer. Ithaca, NY:
Cornell UP, 1991. 278-83. Print.

"Women in Male-Dominated Industries and
Occupations in U.S. and Canada."
Catalyst. 17 April 2012. Web. 21 Sept.
2014.

EVALUATING PRINT SOURCES

Before you begin taking notes from any source, carefully assess its reliability. Ideally, your research should rely on unbiased, current, well-documented sources written by people with the authority to discuss the subject. However, you are likely to find a great number of sources that are written from particular perspectives that are out of date or incomplete, that are written by people with no authority whatsoever, or that do not document their own sources. Part of your job as a researcher is to try to discover these aspects of your sources, to reject those that are completely unreliable, and to use caution with sources when you lack complete confidence in them. Although you may never know for sure how much to trust a particular source, you can check certain things to help in your assessment.

Check for Bias.   Try to find out whether the author, publication, organization, or person being interviewed is known to give fair coverage. People, organizations, and publications often promote particular perspectives, which you should recognize and take into account. You need not reject sources outright if you know they take particular positions on subjects, especially controversial issues. However, your own paper should be as unbiased as possible, which requires acknowledgment of the known biases of your sources.

Check the Date of Publication.   In general, an increasingly recent publication or update of a website provides an increasingly reliable source. For many subjects, current information is crucial to accurate analysis. If you are researching issues such as global warming, morality at high governmental levels, or controversial treatments for AIDS victims, for instance, you need the most recent available information. However, if you are examining a historical matter, such as the question of Richard III's guilt in his two young cousins' deaths or whether King Arthur of Britain is an entirely mythical figure, you can rely in part on older materials. You still want to look for the latest theories, information, or opinions on any subject you research, though.

Check the Author's Credentials.   Find out whether the author has sufficient education, experience, or expertise to write or speak about your subject. You can do this in a number of ways. Any book usually gives information about an author, from a sentence or two to several paragraphs, either on the dust jacket or at the beginning or end of the book. This information reveals the author's professional status, other books he or she has published, and similar information that helps to establish his or her authority. You can also look up an author in sources like *Contemporary Authors, Current Biography,* and *Who's Who.* Other checks on an author's reliability might review what professionals in other sources say about his or her or note how often his or her name shows up on reference lists or bibliographies on your subject.

Check the Reliability of Your Source.   In evaluating a book, determine whether the publishing house is a respectable one. For a magazine, find out whether it is published by a particular interest group. Evaluation of a book could include reading some representative reviews to see how it was received when first published. Both the *Book Review Digest* and *Book Review Index* will help you locate reviews.

Check the Thoroughness of Research and Documentation of Sources.   If your source purports to be scholarly, well informed, or otherwise reliable, check to see how the evidence was gathered. Determine whether the source reports original research or other people's work and what facts or data support its conclusions. Look for references either at the end of chapters or in a separate section at the end of a book. Almost all journal articles and scholarly books document sources, whereas few magazine articles and personal accounts do. Also, consider how statistics and other data are used. Statistics are notoriously easy to manipulate, so check how the author uses them and confirm his or her fair interpretation.

EVALUATING INTERNET SOURCES

As with print sources, you must take care to evaluate any material you locate on the Internet before you use it in your paper. The Internet may pose more difficulty because its resources may offer fewer clues than a book or journal article might give. However, searching the Internet will turn up many useful sources, such as scholarly projects, reference databases, text files of books, articles in periodicals, and professional sites. You must use your judgment when selecting sources for your research paper. Remember that anyone with some knowledge of the Internet can create a website, so be very cautious about accepting the authority of anything you find on the Internet. In general, personal sites are probably not as reliable as professional sites and those of scholarly projects. Reference databases can be extremely useful tools for locating source materials.

You must apply the same sort of skills that you bring to critical reading when looking at an Internet website, particularly when searching for materials for a class assignment. You must ask a number of questions about the site before accepting and using materials that you locate on the Internet. Some key areas to consider are the authority or credentials of the person or persons responsible for the site, the scope, accuracy, timeliness, and nature of the information at the site, and the presentation of the information at the site. Here is a list of questions that will help you evaluate Internet websites:

- **What do you know about the author of the site?** Is the author of the website qualified to give information on the subject? Does the site give information about the author's qualifications? Are the author's credentials, such as academic affiliation, professional association, or publications, easily verified? Because anyone can create a web page, you want to determine whether the author of the website you are looking at is qualified to give the information you are seeking.

- **Is the material on the website presented objectively, or do biases or prejudices reveal themselves?** The language used may be a clue, but probably the best way to discover a particular bias is to look at a great many sites (and other sources) on the same topic. When you understand the complexity of your topic and the variety of viewpoints on it, you should be able to determine whether a site is objective or subjective.

- **Is the information reliable?** Can you verify it? How does it compare with information you have learned from other sources? How well does the website compare with other sites on the same topic? Does the site offer unique information, or does it repeat information that you can find at other sites?

- **How thoroughly does the website cover its topic?** Does it provide links to other sites for additional information? Does the site have links to related topics, and do those links work?

- **How accurate is the information?** This may be difficult to assess when you first begin your research, but the more you read about your topic and examine a variety of sources, the better able you will be to evaluate information accuracy.

- **When was the site last updated?** Is the information at the site current?

- **What is your impression of the visual effect of the site?** Are the graphics helpful or distracting, clear or confusing? Are words spelled correctly? Is the page organized well?

GUIDELINES: QUESTIONS TO ASK WHEN EVALUATING SOURCES

- Is the publication or site known to be fair, or does it have a bias or slant?
- Does the source seem one-sided, or does it try to cover all perspectives on an issue?
- Is the information current or outdated?
- Does the authority have respectable credentials?
- How reliable is the source?
- How thoroughly does the source cover its subject?
- Does the source offer adequate documentation for its information?
- If the source relies on research data, how was evidence gathered? Are statistics used fairly, or are they misrepresented?

TAKING NOTES

When you find an article, book, pamphlet, website, or other source you believe will be important or informative in your research, take notes from that source. There are several kinds of notes that you will take:

Summary.   A summary produces an objective restatement of a written passage in your own words. A summary is much shorter than the original work. Because its purpose is to highlight the central idea or ideas and major points of a work, make summary notes to record general ideas or main points of a large piece of writing—perhaps several pages, a chapter, or an entire article.

Paraphrase.   A paraphrase is a restatement of the words of someone else in your own words. Use paraphrasing when you want to use another writer's ideas but not the exact words, or to explain difficult material more clearly. Your own version of someone else's words must be almost entirely your own words. When incorporating paraphrased material into your research paper, you must be clear about when the paraphrased material begins and ends.

Direct Quotation.   A direct quotation is a record of the exact words of someone else. You will want to quote directly when the words are unique, colorful, or so well stated that you cannot fairly or accurately paraphrase them. Use direct quotations when you do not want to misrepresent what an author says or when the author makes a statement that you wish to stress or comment on. You may want to quote directly in order to analyze or discuss a particular passage. Use direct quotations sparingly and integrate them smoothly into your paper. Too many direct quotations in your paper will interrupt the flow of your own words.

Recording Source and Page Numbers.   Note taking is crucial to the success of your paper. You must take accurate and careful notes, reproducing an author's words exactly as they appear if you quote, completely restating the author's words if you paraphrase, and accurately capturing the essence of the material if you summarize. In any case, you will give a citation in your paper, so **you must record the source and page number for any notes.**

> ## CAUTION
>
> When taking notes, some students are tempted to write every detail as it appears in the original, thinking that they will paraphrase the material at some later time. They must then spend valuable time later rephrasing material when they should be concentrating on writing their papers, or else they take the easier route and use the direct quotations. The result may be a paper that is too full of direct quotations and lacking in effective paraphrases. Remember that you should quote directly only language that is particularly well expressed or material that you do not feel you can adequately restate in your own words. Your final paper should have far more paraphrases than direct quotations.

Where you record your notes does not matter, as long as you develop an efficient system. The important consideration is the accuracy and fairness of your notes. Traditionally, researchers used 4 × 6 inch cards because they are large enough to record ideas, summaries, quotations, or major points. When the note-taking part of the research ends, the researcher can shuffle the cards about, arranging them in the order that makes sense for the research paper. Some people like the note card system and work well with it, but most now prefer to use a computer as a more convenient way to record and store notes.

A computer can be very helpful for organizing and sorting notes. Most programs allow you to arrange your notes in numerical order. However, make sure to develop a filing system for your notes. If your program lets you create folders, you can keep your notes from different sources under specific headings, each with its own subheadings.

Place the subject heading at the beginning of your notes, and put the page number at the end. *Make sure that your notes clearly identify sources for all information.*

GUIDELINES FOR TAKING NOTES

- **Write both the author's last name and the page number from which the information is taken.** That is all the information you need, as long as you have a bibliography card or file for the source that lists complete bibliographic information.
- **Use subject headings as you take notes.** This labeling system will help you sort and arrange your notes when you write your paper.
- **Record only one idea or several small, related ones in each note.** This practice will help you organize your notes when you begin writing.
- **Place quotation marks before and after the material taken directly from a source.**
- **Don't rely on memory to determine whether words are identical to the original or paraphrased.**
- **Use notes to summarize.** A note may refer to an entire passage, an article, or a book, without giving specific details. Make a note to remind you that the information is a summary.
- **Use notes to record original ideas that occur to you while you are reading.** Make sure you identify your own ideas.

HANDLING SOURCE MATERIAL

Handling source material fairly, accurately, and smoothly is one of your main tasks in writing a successful research paper. More than likely, your instructor will evaluate your research project not only on how successfully you argue, explain, examine, or illustrate your topic but also on how skillfully you handle source materials. This means that you must take great care not only when you take notes but also when you transfer those notes into your paper. Always keep in mind—as you are taking notes, when drafting your paper, and when writing its final version—that you must acknowledge the source for all borrowed material. Any information that you take from a source must be properly attributed to its author or, if no author, to its title. At the same time, you must not simply drop material into your text but be mindful of providing smooth integration of your source material into your own text. After all, the text is your work: the thesis of the paper, the overall organization and development, transitions from point to point, general observations, and the conclusions are all yours. Your source materials serve to support, illustrate, develop, or exemplify your own words. Source materials must not interrupt the flow of your words or call attention to themselves. They are an important and integral part of your own paper.

Chapter 6 has detailed directions and summary guidelines for both paraphrasing source material and quoting directly. Chapter 6 also discusses some common tools for handling source material: ellipsis points, brackets, single quotation marks, and "qtd. in." Sample research papers located later in this chapter also give examples of the correct handling of source material. The following guidelines highlight important points of the discussion of summarizing, paraphrasing, and quoting discussed in Chapter 6.

GUIDELINES FOR HANDLING SOURCE MATERIAL

- **Introduce or provide a context for quoted material.** "Dropped" quotations occur when you fail to integrate quotations smoothly into your text. The abrupt dropping of a quotation disrupts the flow of your text.

- **Name your authority or, when no author is named, use the title of the source.** Provide this information either in the text itself or in the parenthetical citation. Rely on standard phrases such as "one writer claims," "according to one expert," and the like to introduce quotations or paraphrases.

- **Use both first and last names of author at the first mention in your text.** After that, use just the last name. Always use last name only in parenthetical citations (unless you have sources by two authors with the same last name).

- **Acknowledge source material when you first begin paraphrasing.** Make sure you give some kind of signal to your reader when you begin paraphrasing borrowed material. This is particularly important if you paraphrase more than one sentence from a source. Otherwise, your reader will not know how far back the citation applies.

- **Quote sparingly.** Quote directly only those passages that are vividly or memorably phrased, so that you could not do justice to them by rewording them; those that require exact wording for accuracy; or those that need the authority of your source to lend credibility to what you are saying.
- **Intermingle source material with our own words.** Avoid a "cut-and-paste" approach to the research process. Remember that source materials serve primarily to support your generalizations. Never run two quotations together without some comment or transitional remark from you.
- **Make sure that direct quotations are exact.** Do not change words unless you use brackets or ellipses to indicate changes. Otherwise, be exact. For instance, if your source says "$2 million," do not write "two million dollars."
- **Make sure that paraphrases are truly your own words.** Do not inadvertently commit plagiarism by failing to paraphrase fairly.

AVOIDING PLAGIARISM

Giving proper credit to your sources is a crucial component of the research process. It is also one of the trickiest aspects of the process because it requires absolute accuracy in note taking. Many students have been disheartened by low grades on papers that took weeks to prepare, because they were careless or inaccurate in handling and documenting source materials.

Simply defined, **plagiarism** is borrowing another person's words without giving proper credit. The worst form of plagiarism is deliberately using the words or important ideas of someone else without giving any credit to that source. Handing in a paper someone else has written or copying someone else's paper and pretending it is yours are the most blatant and inexcusable forms of plagiarism, crimes that on some campuses carry penalties like automatic failure in the course or even immediate expulsion from school. Most student plagiarism is not deliberate, but rather results from carelessness either in the research process, when notes are taken, or in the writing process, when notes are incorporated into the student's own text. Even this unintentional plagiarism can result in a failing grade, however, especially if it appears repeatedly in a paper.

Keep the following standards in mind when you take notes on your source materials and when you write your research paper:

- **You commit plagiarism if you use the exact words or ideas of another writer without putting quotation marks around the words or citing a source.** The reader of your paper assumes that words without quotation marks or a source citation are your own words. To use the words of another without proper documentation suggests that you are trying to pass the words off as your own without giving credit to the writer.

- **You commit plagiarism if you use the exact words of another writer without putting quotation marks around those words, even if the paper cites the source of the material.** Readers assume that words followed by a parenthetical citation are paraphrased from the original—that is, that they are your own words and that the general idea was expressed by the author of the source material. Be especially carefully when you copy and paste from an Internet site: always use quotation marks around such material to remind yourself that they are the exact words.

- **You commit plagiarism if you paraphrase by changing only a few words of the original or by using the identical sentence structure of the original, with or without a source.** Again, readers assume that words without quotation marks followed by a parenthetical citation are your own words, not those of someone else. In a paraphrase, the *idea* is that of another; the *words* are your own.

- **You inaccurately handle source material when you use quotation marks around words that are not exactly as they appear in the original.** Readers assume that all words within quotation marks are identical to the original.

Obviously, accuracy and fairness in note taking are essential standards. Exercise care when you read your source materials and again when you transfer your notes to your final paper.

ILLUSTRATION: PLAGIARISM, INACCURATE DOCUMENTATION, AND CORRECT HANDLING OF SOURCE MATERIAL

The passage that follows is from an opinion column by Anna Quindlen. Complete bibliographic information follows, as it would appear on your bibliography list and on the Works-Cited page of a research paper:

Quindlen, Anna. "A Teachable Moment."
    Newsweek 27 April 2009: 64. Print.

Here is the passage:

Several years ago a psychologist named Laurie Miller Brotman spearheaded a study of young children that yielded stunning results. The kids were from poor and troubled families, the preschool-age siblings of older children who were already acquainted with the criminal-justice system. Brotman's team tested levels of cortisol, a hormone that usually spikes when human beings are under stress. On average, these kids had flattened cortisol in stressful situations; so do many who have been maltreated or have behavior problems.

So far, so bad. But here's what happened to half the children in this study: their parents were enrolled in a program that helped them learn the kind of child rearing that Dr. Spock made popular. Consistent discipline without corporal punishment. Positive reinforcement for good behavior. Even how to get down on the floor and play.

And their kids' cortisol levels changed. Or, as the study itself says in science-speak, "family-based intervention affects the stress response in preschoolers at high risk." By the time those same kids were 11, both boys and girls were less aggressive, and the girls less obese, than the kids in a control group. Having their parents learn the basics of good child rearing had actually shifted the biology of these kids, so that it became similar to that of "normally developing, low-risk children."

Now look at each of these sentences from a hypothetical research paper using information from the Quindlen article. The commentary that follows identifies plagiarism, inaccurate handling of the original source material, or correct handling of source material:

1. Having their parents learn the basics of good child rearing actually shifted the biology of kids from poor and troubled families, the preschool-age siblings of older children who were already acquainted with the criminal-justice system.

   [This is **plagiarism**: Quotation marks are needed around words identical to the original, and a source must be cited.

   Correct: "Having their parents learn the basics of good child rearing," Quindlen notes, "actually shifted the biology" of kids "from poor and troubled families, the preschool-age siblings of older children who were already acquainted with the criminal-justice system" (64).]

2. The results of the study are impressive: having their parents learn the basics of good child rearing actually shifted the biology of kids (Quindlen 64).

   [This is **plagiarism**: Quotation marks are needed around words taken directly from the original.

   Correct: The results of the study are impressive: "Having their parents learn the basics of good child rearing actually shifted the biology of kids" (Quindlen 64).]

3. Parents were taught the approach to child-rearing that Dr. Spock made popular, consistent discipline without corporal punishment and positive reinforcement for being good (Quindlen 64).

   [This is **plagiarism**: Original words are changed only slightly and the original sentence structure is retained.

   Correct: Parents were taught Dr. Spock's approach to child-rearing: "Consistent discipline without corporal punishment . . . [and] [p]ositive reinforcement for good behavior" (Quindlen 64).]

4. Quindlen cites the study's conclusion that "family-based intervention affects the stress response in preschoolers at high risk" (64).

   [This is **inaccurate documentation**: Single quotation marks are needed within the double marks to indicate that quotation marks are in the original.

   Correct: Quindlen cites the study's conclusion that " 'family-based intervention affects the stress response in preschoolers at high risk' " (64).]

5. Dr. Spock's child-rearing advice includes telling parents "how to play with their children on the floor" (Quindlen 64).

   [This is **inaccurate documentation**: Material included within quotation marks must be identical to the way it is worded in the original.

   Correct: Dr. Spock's child-rearing advice includes telling parents "how to get down on the floor and play" with their children (Quindlen 64).]

6. Writer Anna Quindlen notes the results of a recent study on the effects of good parenting on children's well-being. The study suggests that when parents of children who have been in trouble with the law are taught nonviolent forms of punishment and other positive parenting skills, the effects on their children are profound. The study concluded that "the basics of good child rearing had actually shifted the biology of these kids" (64).

[This is **correct**: The text acknowledges the author, and the general idea of the article is adequately summarized. Quotation marks enclose material taken directly from the original.]

Students are sometimes frustrated by these guidelines governing note taking and plagiarism, arguing that virtually everything in the final paper will be in quotation marks or followed by citations. But keep in mind that your final paper is a synthesis of information you have discovered in your research with your own thoughts on your topic, thoughts that naturally undergo modification, expansion, and/or revision as you read and think about your topic.

Probably half of the paper will be your own words. These words will usually include all of the introductory and concluding paragraphs, all topic sentences and transitional sentences within and between paragraphs, and all introductions to direct quotations. Furthermore, you need give no citation for statements of general or common knowledge, such as facts about well-known historical or current events. If you keep running across the same information in all of your sources, you can assume it is general knowledge.

GUIDELINES FOR AVOIDING PLAGIARISM

- **For direct quotations, write the words exactly as they appear in the original.** Put quotation marks before and after the words. Do not change anything.
- **For paraphrased material, restate the original thought in your own words, using your own writing style.** Do not use the exact sentence pattern of the original, and do not simply rearrange words. You have to retain the central idea of the paraphrased material, but do so in your own words.
- **When using borrowed material in your paper, whether direct quotations or paraphrases, acknowledge the source by naming the author or work as you introduce the material.** Doing so not only tells your reader that you are using borrowed material but also often provides a clear transition from your own words and ideas to the borrowed material that illustrates or expands on your ideas.
- Provide a parenthetical, in-text citation for any borrowed material. Give the author's last name if it is not mentioned in the text of the paper, followed by page number(s). If the source material is anonymous, use a shortened version of the title in place of a name.
- **Assemble all sources cited in your paper in an alphabetical list at the end of the paper.** This is your list of works cited, containing only those works actually used in the paper.

DOCUMENTING SOURCES

Follow the Appropriate Style Guidelines. The examples of documentation and sample research papers that appear in this chapter all follow MLA (Modern Language Association) documentation style. That style governs because this textbook is often used in English courses, and English is located within the discipline of the humanities. However, your instructor may permit you to choose the style appropriate to the major field you intend to study. A section later in this chapter provides guidelines for writing a research paper using APA (American Psychological Association) style. That style is probably as commonly used as MLA in undergraduate course papers. In addition to MLA and APA, other frequently used documentation styles are CBE (Council of Biology Editors) and CMS (Chicago Manual of Style). Following this summary of the chief differences among those four styles, the chapter lists stylebooks that give additional guidelines.

Style Guides. To find full details on a particular documentation style, consult the following style guides:

MLA
Modern Language Association of America. *MLA Handbook for Writers of Research Papers.* 7th ed. New York: MLA, 2009.

APA
American Psychological Association. *Publication Manual of the American Psychological Association.* 6th ed. Washington: APA, 2010.

CBE
CBE Style Manual Committee. *Scientific Style and Format: The CBE Manual for Authors, Editors, and Publishers.* 7th ed. Reston, VA: Council of Science Editors, 2006.

CMS
Turabian Kate L. *Student's Guide to Writing College Papers.* 4th ed. Rev. by Gregory G. Colomb, Joseph M. Williams, and Chicago UP Editorial Staff. Chicago: U of Chicago P, 2010.

University of Chicago Press Staff. *The Chicago Manual of Style.* 16th ed. Chicago: U of Chicago P, 2010.

SUMMARY OF DIFFERENCES AMONG DOCUMENTATION STYLES

- **MLA:** Used by writers in the many areas of the humanities (English, foreign languages, history, and philosophy); requires parenthetical in-text citations of author and page number that refer to an alphabetical list of works cited at the end of the paper.
- **APA:** Used by writers in the behavioral and social sciences (education, psychology, and sociology); requires parenthetical in-text citations of author and date of publication that refer to an alphabetical list of references at the end of the paper.

- **CBE:** Used by writers in technical fields and the sciences (engineering, biology, physics, geography, chemistry, computer science, and mathematics); requires either a name–year format or a citation–sequence format. The name–year format places the author's last name and the year of publication in parentheses, referring to an alphabetical list of references at the end of the paper.

- **CMS:** Used by some areas of the humanities, notably history, art, music, and theatre; requires a superscript number (e.g., 1) for each citation, all of which are numbered sequentially throughout the paper; no number is repeated. Numbers correspond either to footnotes at the bottoms of pages or a list of notes at the end of the paper. The first note gives complete information about the source, with shortened information for each subsequent reference to that source. A bibliography follows the notes, giving the same information, except for the page number, as in the first citation of each source. The information is also punctuated and arranged differently from the note copy.

Internet Citation Guides.   Many research resources, including guides for citing such sources, are available on the Internet. Your university librarian may have created a website where you will find the names of sites that give directions for citing electronic sources. Because Internet sites constantly change, URLs are not provided in the following list. You can locate the website by searching for the name. The ease of changing and updating Internet sites often means that they may have more current information than print guides offer. If you doubt the reliability and currency of a website, consult with your instructor about the advisability of using the site. Here are a few reliable sites that provide guidelines and models for finding and documenting sources. Many university libraries offer such services online:

- *How to Cite Primary Sources,* Library of Congress. Explains how to cite primary sources available online, such as films, music, maps, photographs, and texts. Covers MLA and Chicago styles.

- *How to Cite Electronic Sources*, Indiana University. Covers MLA and APA.

- *MLA Style,* Modern Language Association of America. Includes list of frequently asked questions about MLA style.

- *MLA Formatting and Style Guide*, Purdue University's Online Writing Lab (OWL). Covers both MLA and APA styles.

- *Research Guide to Documentation Online by Diana Hacker.* Covers MLA, APA, and Chicago styles.

- *Style Sheet for Citing Resources (Print & Electronic).* UC–Berkeley Library. Provides examples and rules for MLA, APA, Chicago, and Turabian.

PARENTHETICAL DOCUMENTATION—CITING SOURCES IN THE TEXT

Recall from the discussion in Chapter 6 on documenting sources with in-text citations and the discussion in this chapter on taking notes that a crucial task of the researcher is to identify accurately sources for all borrowed material. This section expands the discussion from Chapter 6 with illustrations of treatments for several types of sources. It also includes guidelines for creating a list of works cited that incorporates a variety of sources, including electronic sources. These examples follow MLA guidelines as they appear in the *MLA Handbook for Writers of Research Papers*, seventh edition.

Parenthetical, In-Text Citations

Remember that you must name your source for any borrowed material. The parenthetical citation must give enough information to identify the source by directing your reader to the alphabetized list of works cited at the end of your paper. The citation should also give the page number or numbers, if available, on which the material appears.

Author–Page Format

MLA guidelines call for the author–page format when acknowledging borrowed material in the text of your paper. You must name the author (or source, if no author is named) and give a page number or numbers where the borrowed material appears in the source. The author's name or title that you give in your text directs readers to the correct entry in the works-cited list, so the reference must correspond to its entry on that list. Here are some examples:

Book or Article with One Author.   Author's last name and page number, without punctuation.
    (Smith 67)

Book or Article with Two or Three Authors.   Both or all three authors' last names followed by the page number.
    (Barrett and Rowe 78)   (Fletcher, Miller, and Caplan 78)

Note: Reproduce the names in the order in which they appear on the title page. If they are not listed alphabetically, do not change their order.

Book or Article with More Than Three Authors.   First author's last name followed by et al. and page number.
    (Leitch et al. 29)

Article or Other Publication with No Author Named.   Short title followed by page number.
    ("Teaching" 10)

Note: When citing any source in a parenthetical reference in your text that appears on your works-cited list, use the full title if short or a shortened version. When using a shortened version, begin with the word by which the source is alphabetized.

Two Anonymous Articles Beginning with the Same Word.   Use the full title of each to distinguish one from the other.
("Classrooms without Walls" 45)   ("Classrooms in the 21st Century" 96)

Two Works by the Same Author.   Author's name followed by a comma, a short title, and the page number.
(Heilbrun, *Hamlet's Mother* 123)   (Heilbrun, *Writing a Woman's Life* 35)

Works by People with the Same Last Name.   First and last names of author and page number.
(Che White 16)

Sources as they appear on the list of works cited:

White, Che. "The Groundbreaking Musical *Rent*." *Review of Contemporary Theatre* 1.1 (2014): 12–16. Print.

White, Jeremy. *Card Games You Never Knew Existed.* Chicago: Leisure Games, 2014. Print.

Exceptions to Author–Page Format Such as a Lecture or Television Program.   Many papers must accommodate some exceptions to the basic author–page parenthetical citation. For instance, for nonprint sources such as an Internet website, a lecture, a telephone conversation, a television documentary, or a recording, name the source in parentheses after the material without giving a page number:

("U.S. Technology in Iran")

Source as it appears on the list of works cited:

"U.S. Technology in Iran." Narr. Lesley Stahl. *Sixty Minutes*. CBS. WPTA, Fort Wayne, 21 Feb. 2014. Television.

Citing an Entire Work.   You may want to refer to an entire work rather than just part of it. In that case, name the work and the author in the text of your paper, without a parenthetical citation:

Sir Arthur Conan Doyle's *Hound of the Baskervilles* features Watson to a much greater degree than do the earlier Holmes stories.

MLA suggests that this approach might be appropriate for web publications with no pagination, television broadcast, movies, and similar works.

Citing Volume and Page Number of a Multivolume Work.   If you refer to material from more than one volume of a multivolume work, state the volume number, followed by a colon, and then the page number. Do not use the words or abbreviations for *volume* or *page*. The two numbers separated by a colon explicitly

indicate volume and page. Your works-cited entry will state the number of volumes in the work.

> Edgar Johnson's critical biography of Charles Dickens concludes with a rousing tribute to the author's creative imagination: "The world he [Dickens] created shines with undying life, and the hearts of men still vibrate to his indignant anger, his love, his tears, his glorious laughter, and his triumphant faith in the dignity of man" (2: 1158).

Source as it appears on the list of works cited:

> Johnson, Edgar. *Charles Dickens: His Tragedy and Triumph.* 2 vols. New York: Simon, 1952.

If you draw material from just one volume of a multivolume work, your works-cited entry states which volume, and your in-text citation gives only the page number:

> The works of Charles Dickens fervently proclaim "his triumphant faith in the dignity of man" (Johnson 1158).

Source as it appears on the list of works cited:

> Johnson, Edgar. *Charles Dickens: His Tragedy and Triumph.* Vol. 2. New York: Simon, 1952.

Citing a Work by a Corporate Author or Government Agency.

Cite the author's or agency's name, followed by a page reference, just as you would for a book or periodical article. However, if the title of the corporate author is long, put it in the body of the text to avoid an extensive parenthetical reference:

> Testifying before a subcommittee of the U.S. House Committee on Public Works and Transportation, a representative of the Environmental Protection Agency argued that pollution from second-hand smoke within buildings is a widespread and dangerous threat (173–74).

Citing Internet Sources.

According to the MLA guidelines, works on the World Wide Web are cited just like printed works when citing sources in your text, that is, with author's name or short title if there is no author listed. A special consideration with web documents is that they generally do not have fixed page numbers or any kind of section numbering. If your source lacks numbering, there your parenthetical citation will give the author's last name if known, for example, (Plonsky), or the title if the original gives no author's name, for example, ("Psychology with Style"). If an author incorporates page numbers, section numbers, or paragraph numbers, you may cite the relevant numbers. Give the appropriate abbreviation before the numbers: (Plonsky, pars. 5–6). (*Pars.* is the abbreviation for *paragraphs.*) For a document on the World Wide Web, the page numbers of a printout should normally not be cited, because the pagination may vary in different printouts.

Remember that the purpose of the parenthetical citation is to indicate the location of the quotation or paraphrase in the referenced work and to point to the referenced work in the list of works cited. The entry that begins the reference in the works-cited list (i.e., author's last name or title of work) is the same entry that should also appear in the parenthetical reference or in the body of the text.

GUIDELINES FOR PARENTHETICAL DOCUMENTATION

- **Name the source for all borrowed material**, including both direct quotations and paraphrases, either in your text or in parentheses following the borrowed material.
- **Give the citation in parentheses at the end of the sentence** containing the quotation or paraphrase.
- **In the parentheses, state the author's last name and the page number** or numbers from which you took the words or ideas, with no punctuation between the name and the page number.
- **When citing Internet or other sources such as television broadcasts, movies, or lectures that have no page numbers, use the author's last name in parentheses.** If you mention the author's name in your text, it is helpful to repeat it in the parenthetical citation as well, to indicate where the borrowed material ends, though MLA style does not require it.
- **For smooth transition to borrowed material, name the author or source as you introduce the words or ideas.** In that case, the parentheses will include only the page number or numbers.
- **At the first mention of an author in your text, use the author's full name.** Thereafter, use the last name only.
- **Create a page titled "Works Cited" at the end of your paper** that lists all sources quoted or paraphrased in the paper. Do not include any works that you consulted but did not directly use in your paper.

CREATING A WORKS-CITED PAGE USING MLA STYLE

The Works-Cited page of a research report lists in alphabetical order all the sources you cite in your paper. It comes at the end of your paper, beginning on a separate page.

Include an entry for every work quoted from, paraphrased, summarized, or otherwise alluded to in your paper. *Do not include on your list of works cited any sources you read but did not use in the paper.* You may want to include a list of useful works that informed your understanding of the topic but that you did not quote or paraphrase from in your final paper; to do so, create a separate page entitled "Works Consulted."

GENERAL GUIDELINES FOR CREATING A LIST OF WORKS CITED

- **Begin your list of cited works on a new page after the conclusion of your paper.**
- **Center the title "Works Cited" one inch from the top of the page.**
- **Continue the page numbers of the text, with a separate number for each of the Works-Cited pages.**
- **Alphabetize the list of sources.**
- **Begin the first line of each entry flush with the left margin. Indent the second and subsequent lines within each entry five spaces.**

- **Begin with the author's last name, followed by a comma and then the first name. For a source with two or more authors, invert only the first name. List the other name or names in normal order.**
- **Italicize the titles of books, journals, magazines, newspapers, and websites**. Do not use quotation marks.
- **Double-space within and between all entries.**
- **Place a period at the end of each entire entry.**

The remainder of this section gives guidelines for creating works-cited entries for books, periodicals, and electronic sources, supplemented by models for miscellaneous types of entries. The numbers on this list correspond to the numbered illustrations in each section (books, periodicals, electronic sources, miscellaneous) in the following pages:

Print Sources.

1. Book with a single author
2. Collection or anthology
3. Article in a collection or an anthology
4. Book by two or three authors or editors
5. Book by more than three authors or editors
6. Two works by the same author
7. Reprint of a book
8. Preface, foreword, introduction, or afterword to a book
9. Edition of a book
10. Multivolume work
11. Article in a journal with continuous pagination
12. Article in a journal with separate pagination
13. Article in a weekly or biweekly magazine
14. Article in a monthly or bimonthly magazine
15. Article in a quarterly magazine
16. Magazine article with no author
17. Newspaper article
18. Periodical article that does not appear on consecutive pages

Creating a Works-Cited List for Electronic Sources.

19. Scholarly project
20. Professional site
21. Article in a reference database
22. Online article

Online Sources of Full-Text Articles.

23. Article with author named, scholarly journal
24. Article in magazine
25. Article with no author named
26. Article in magazine from personally subscribed service

Miscellaneous Electronic Sources.

27. Posting to a discussion group
28. E-mail message
29. Government document

Works-Cited Formats for Sources Other Than Books, Periodicals, and Electronic Sources.

30. Congressional record
31. Government publication
32. Lecture
33. Letter
34. PDF file
35. Personal interview
36. Telephone interview
37. Pamphlet
38. Television or radio program
39. Sound recording
40. Article in a reference book

Books in a Work-Cited List.   Citations for books have several main parts: author's name, title of book, and publication information, including place of publication, publisher, and date the book was published. Often a book has more than one author or an editor, and often books are collections of a number of essays with individual authors. The following section provides guidelines for documenting the most common kinds of books that you are likely to come across in your research.

GUIDELINES FOR CITING BOOKS ON THE WORKS-CITED LIST

- **Begin with the author's last name, followed by a comma, and then the first name, followed by a period.** For a source with two or more authors, invert the first author's name with a comma before and after the first name, then write the word *and* and put the other author's name in normal order.
- **Italicize the title of the book.**
- **State the city of publication, the publisher, and the date the book was published: City: Publisher, date**. Note that only the city name is given unless it is unclear which city it is. For cities like Boston, New York, Los Angeles, and London, for instance, you would not need to add state or country. For a city like

Athens, it is necessary to add the state to avoid ambiguity: Athens, OH. Use the same state abbreviation system as for zip codes.

- **Separate each item in an entry by a period: Author. Title. Publication information and date.** Note that each period is followed by one space. MLA guidelines recommend using only one space after a concluding punctuation mark unless your instructor requests that you use two.
- **For essays in collections, begin by listing the author of the essay, then the title within quotation marks, the book it appears in, the editor's name, and publication information for the book.** Put the inclusive page numbers of the essay at the end of the entry.
- **Shorten publishers' names and drop such words as *Inc.*, *Co.*, and *Press*.** Abbreviate *University* and *Press* for university presses, as "U of Wisconsin P" for University of Wisconsin Press or "Oxford UP" for Oxford University Press.
- **State the medium of publication (Print).**

1. Book with a Single Author

> Author's name. *Title of Book*. City of publication: Publisher, date of publication. Print.
>
> Cummings, Claire Hope. *Uncertain Peril: Genetic Engineering and the Future of Seeds*. Boston: Beacon, 2008. Print.

2. Collection or Anthology

Use this format when you cite the ideas of the editor(s) or when you refer to the entire collection. Name the editor, followed by the abbreviation "ed." Treat the rest of the entry as you would for a book.

> Editor's name, ed. *Title of Collection*. City of publication: Publisher, date of publication. Print.
>
> Taylor, Helen, ed. *The Daphne Du Maurier Companion*. London: Virago, 2007. Print.

For two or more editors, list the first editor's name in inverted order, followed by a comma, the word *and*, and the second editor's name in normal order.

> Pellotta, Tom, and Heidi Pitlar, eds. *The Best American Short Stories*. New York: Mariner/Houghton Mifflin, 2012. 212–35. Print.

3. Article in a Collection or an Anthology

Use this format when you cite an article in a collection or anthology. Name the author, the title of the article, the title of the collection, the editor or coeditors of the collection, publication information, and the **inclusive page numbers** of the entire article. Follow this format:

> Author's name. "Title of Article." *Title of Collection*. The abbreviation "Ed." Editor's name in normal order. City of publication: Name of publisher, date of publication. Inclusive page numbers on which the article appears. Print.

> Munford, Rebecca. "Spectres of Authorship: Daphne du Maurier's Gothic Legacy." *The Daphne Du Maurier Companion.* Ed. Helen Taylor. London: Virago, 2007. 68–74. Print.

If the edition has two or more editors, use the abbreviation "Eds." followed by both editors' names:

> Saunders, George. "The Tenth of December." *The Best American Short Stories.* Eds. Tom Pellotta and Heidi Pitlar. New York: Mariner/Houghton Mifflin, 2012. 212–35. Print.

4. **Book by Two or Three Authors or Editors**

List the names of the authors in the same order as they are listed on the title page, even if they are not in alphabetical order.

> First author's name in inverted order, and second author's name in normal order. *Name of Book.* City of publication: Publisher, date of publication. Print.
>
> Vaughn, Brian K., and Fiona Staples. *Saga.* Berkeley, CA: Image Comics, 2012. Print.
>
> Brandon, Lee, and Kelly Brandon, eds. *Sentences, Paragraphs, and Beyond: With Integrated Readings.* Boston: Wadsworth, 2013. Print.

5. **Book by More Than Three Authors or Editors**

List the names of the authors in the same order as they are listed on the title page, even if they are not in alphabetical order. MLA style gives you the option of listing all of the authors or editors or just the first one, followed by *et al.* ("and others").

> Leitch, Vincent B., William E. Cain, Laurie Finke, Barbara Johnson, John McGowan, T. Denean Sharpley-Whiting, and Jeffrey T. Williams, eds. *The Norton Anthology of Theory and Criticism.* 2nd ed. New York: Norton, 2010. Print.

OR

> Leitch, Vincent B., et al., eds. *The Norton Anthology of Theory and Criticism.* 2nd ed. New York: Norton, 2010. Print.

6. **Two Works by the Same Author**

List the books in alphabetical order by title. For the second and subsequent books by the same author, type three hyphens followed by a period in place of the name.

> Chabon, Michael. *Summerland.* New York: Hyperion, 2011. Print.
> ———. *Telegraph Avenue: A Novel.* New York: Harper, 2012. Print.

7. **Reprint of a Book**

Follow the same format as for books, but add the date of the first publication after the title.

> Author's name. *Title of Book.* First date of publication. City of publi-
> cation of this edition: Publisher, date of publication. Print.
>
> Symons, Julian. *Bloody Murder: From the Detective Story to the Crime
> Novel: A History.* 1972. 1985. London: Pan Macmillan, 1992.
> Print.

If a different publisher produced earlier editions, you have the option of
naming the place of publication and publisher for the other editions as well
as for the current one.

> Symons, Julian. *Bloody Murder: From the Detective Story to the Crime
> Novel: A History.* London: Faber, 1972. London: Viking, 1985.
> London: Pan Macmillan, 1992. Print.

8. Preface, Foreword, Introduction, or Afterword to a Book

If you use material *only* from the preface, foreword, introduction, or
afterword of a book, your works-cited entry begins with the name of the
person who wrote the selection you use, not necessarily with the author
of the book (though sometimes they are the same person). You will need
to indicate what part of the book you cite (preface, foreword, introduction, or afterword), then name the book and author and give complete
bibliographic information. Finally, give the inclusive page numbers of
the preface, foreword, introduction, or afterword. Follow this model:

> Author of introduction. Introduction. *Title of Book.* By author's name
> in normal order. Place of publication: Publisher, date of publica-
> tion. Inclusive page numbers on which the introduction appears.
> Print.
>
> Green, Richard Lancelyn. Introduction. *The Adventures of Sherlock
> Holmes.* By Arthur Conan Doyle. 1892. Oxford: Oxford UP,
> 1993. xi–xxxv. Print.

9. Edition of a Book

Use this format for a book prepared for publication by someone other than
the author if you refer primarily to the text itself:

> Doyle, Arthur Conan. *The Adventures of Sherlock Holmes.* Ed. Richard
> Lancelyn Green. Oxford: Oxford UP, 1994. Print.

If you refer primarily to the work of the editor, for instance, material from
the introduction or notes to the text, begin with the editor's name:

> Green, Richard Lancelyn, ed. *The Adventures of Sherlock Holmes.* By
> Arthur Conan Doyle. 1892. Oxford: Oxford UP, 1993. Print.

10. Multivolume Work

If you draw material from two or more volumes of a work, cite the total
number of volumes in the entire work. When you refer to the work in the

text of your paper, your parenthetical reference gives the volume number and page number.

> Johnson, Edgar. *Charles Dickens: His Tragedy and Triumph*. 2 vols. New York: Simon, 1952. Print.

If you refer to only one volume of a multivolume work, state the number of that volume in the works-cited entry. Your parenthetical in-text citation supplies page number only, not volume and page.

> Johnson, Edgar. *Charles Dickens: His Tragedy and Triumph*. Vol. 2. New York: Simon, 1952. Print.

Periodicals in a Works-Cited List.   Periodicals are magazines or journals that are published frequently and at fixed intervals. Distinguish between journals and magazines by considering audience, subject matter, and frequency of publication. Journals are fairly specialized, usually written for people in a specific profession, and more technical and research oriented than magazines; they generally appear much less frequently than magazines, perhaps bimonthly or four times a year. Magazines, on the other hand, are intended for general audiences, are not heavily research-oriented, and usually appear in monthly or even weekly editions. As with books, works-cited entries for periodicals have three main divisions: the author's name, the title of the article, and publication information, including the name of the periodical, the date the article was published, and the inclusive page numbers on which it appears.

GUIDELINES FOR CREATING WORKS-CITED ENTRIES FOR PERIODICALS

- **Place the author's name first, in inverted order, followed by a period.**
- **If the article is published anonymously, begin the entry with the title.** For placing the entries in alphabetical order on the list, ignore *The, A, And,* and numbers at the beginnings of titles.
- **State the title of the article, enclosing it in quotation marks, ending with a period.**
- **State the name of the periodical, italicized, followed by no punctuation.**
- **State series number, volume number, and/or issue number, if relevant.**
- **State the date of publication. For publications with a specific day and month named, use this format: day month year.** For scholarly journals, include volume number and issue number, if given, and enclose the date in parentheses. Abbreviate the names of all months except May, June, and July.
- **Follow the date with a colon and the inclusive page numbers of the article. Put a period after the page numbers.**
- **Do not use the abbreviations "p." or "pp." for pages.**
- **State the medium of the publication (Print) followed by a period.**

11. **Article in a Journal with Continuous Pagination**
Use this format for journals that continue pagination throughout the year.

> Author's name. "Title of Article." *Name of Periodical* volume number. issue number (date): inclusive page numbers of article. Print.
> Allen, Paul. "Dickens in Composition Classrooms." *College English* 92.4 (Mar. 2011): 325–33. Print.

12. **Article in a Journal with Separate Pagination**
Use this format for journals that begin each issue with page 1. Give the issue number as well as the volume number.

> Author's name. "Title of Article." *Name of Periodical* volume number. issue number (date): inclusive page numbers of article. Print.
> Nevens, Kate. "The Youth are Revolting." *Harvard International Review* 34.2 (Fall 2012): 32–35. Print.

13. **Article in a Weekly or Biweekly Magazine**

> Author's name. "Title of Article." *Name of Magazine* complete date, beginning with the day and abbreviating the month, page number(s). Print.
> Beech, Hanna. "The Cult of Apple in China." *Time* 2 July 2012: 44–49. Print.

Note: If the article is not printed on consecutive pages, give just the first page followed by a plus sign, with no space between, as in this example:

> Meacham, Jon. "The American Dream: A Biography." *Time* 2 July 2012: 26+. Print.

14. **Article in a Monthly or Bimonthly Magazine**

> Author's name. "Title of Article." *Name of Magazine* date, including month and year: page number(s). Print.
> Samuels, David. "Wild Things." *Harper's* June 2012: 28–42. Print.

15. **Article in a Quarterly Magazine**

> Fletcher, John C., Franklin G. Miller, and Arthur L. Caplan. "Facing Up to Bioethical Decisions." *Issues in Science and Technology* Fall 2012: 75–80. Print.

16. **Magazine Article with No Author**

> "Title of Article." *Name of Magazine* date, including month and year: page number(s). Print.
> "Findings." *Harper's* June 2012: 80. Print.

17. **Newspaper Article**
Supply the following, in this order:
a) author's name, if known;
b) article title;

c) name of the newspaper, italicized;

d) city where the newspaper is published, if not included in its name, in brackets after the name;

e) the date, beginning with the day, abbreviating the month, and the year, followed by a colon;

f) page number(s) where the article appears. If the newspaper has more than one section and each section is paginated separately, give both section and page number. If you gather material from a special edition of the newspaper, indicate that fact, as well.

> Author last name, first name. "Title of article." *Name of newspaper* date: page number. Print.
> Kingsolver, Barbara. "A Pure, High Note of Anguish." *Los Angeles Times* 23 Sept. 2001: M1. Print.

18. Periodical Article That Does Not Appear on Consecutive Pages

Give only the first page number, followed by a plus sign:

> Nye, Joseph S. Jr. "The Decline of America's Soft Power." *Foreign Affairs* May–June 2004: 16+. Print.

Creating a Works-Cited List for Electronic Sources.   As with other types of sources you cite in your research paper, your works-cited entries for electronic sources should provide enough information that your reader can locate them. These sources pose a particular problem that books, periodicals, and other print media do not: they change frequently, are updated, move to new sites, or are even removed from the Internet. References to electronic works require slightly more and certainly different information than print sources require. Supply as much of the following information as is available, in this order:

a) author's name;

b) title of the work;

c) title of the site;

d) publisher or sponsor of the site; N. p. if not available;

e) date the site was created or updated;

f) the medium of publication (web); and

g) date that you accessed the material.

See the guidelines that follow for additional details. Keep in mind that electronic sources are not uniform in the amount of information they provide. A site may not incorporate page numbers, an author's name, reference markers such as paragraph or page breaks, or other conventional print references. You can supply only the information that is available at any particular site. Use common sense: include as much information as you have available to you.

GUIDELINES FOR CREATING A WORKS-CITED LIST FOR ELECTRONIC SOURCES

- Name the author, editor, narrator, or compiler, if known, last name first, followed by a period.
- State the title of the work, if part of a larger work, in quotation marks. If independent, italicize it. Follow with a period.
- State the title of the site, italicized, followed by a period.
- If a scholarly project or database, name the editor, if known.
- Supply any identifying information, such as version, volume, or issue number.
- For a posting to a newsgroup, discussion group, or forum, give the date of the posting.
- For a periodical article that also appears in print form, include page numbers if provided or the abbreviation *n. pag.* if no pagination is provided.
- For a posting to a discussion list or forum, give the name of the list or forum.
- Supply the name of any institution or organization sponsoring or associated with the site, followed by a comma.
- State the date of publication, followed by a period. If no date is given, use *n.d.*
- State the medium of publication (web), followed by a period.
- State the date you visited the site, followed by a period.

19. **Scholarly Project**

> *Virtual London: Monuments and Dust.* Co-directors Michael Levenson, David Trotter, and Anthony Wohl. U of Virginia. 4 Sept. 2012. Web. 12 Nov. 2014.

20. **Professional Site**

> *The Camelot Project.* Eds. Alan Lupack and Barbara Tepa Lupack. 3 Sept. 2012. U of Rochester. Web. 4 Dec. 2014.

21. **Article in a Reference Database**

> "Susan Brownell Anthony." *The Columbia Encyclopedia*, 6th ed. Columbia UP. 2003. Web. 12 Apr. 2014.

22. **Online Article**

> Benfey, Christopher. "The Alibi of Ambiguity." *The New Republic* 7 June 2012. N. pag. Web. 14 Nov. 2014.

Online Sources of Full-Text Articles. Examples 23–26 illustrate citations from online services offering full-text articles, such as EBSCO, Gale, InfoTrac College Edition, Proquest, and Periodicals Abstract. The format remains essentially the same as for other electronic sources:

a) name of author (if given);

b) title of article;

c) title of journal or magazine; volume and issue number if a journal;

d) date of publication;

e) page number(s) if given or *n. pag.* (for no pagination);

f) name of the service, such as EBSCO, InfoTrac College Edition, or LexisNexis Academic;

g) Medium of publication (web); and

h) date that you read the material.

23. **Article with Author Named, Scholarly Journal**

> Taylor, Susan Lee. "Music Piracy: Differences in the Ethical Perceptions of Business Majors and Music Business Majors." *Journal of Education for Business* 79.5 (May–June 2004): 306. InfoTrac College Edition. Web. 14 Nov 2014.

24. **Article in Magazine**

> Murphy, Victoria. "The Enemy Strikes Back." *Forbes* 24 Nov. 2003: 218. LexisNexis Academic. Web. 6 Nov. 2014.

25. **Article with No Author Named**

> "Yelling 'Fire.'" *New Republic* 3 April 2000: 9. EBSCO. Web. 12 Oct 2014.

26. **Article in Magazine from Personally Subscribed Service**

If you access an article through a service that you subscribe to, such as America Online, give the information as usual, followed by the name of the service, the date you accessed it, and the keyword you used to retrieve the source.

> Kalb, Claudia. "The Life in a Cell; Stem-Cell Researchers Find Fresh Hope for Curing Deadly Diseases—Along with New Controversies." *Newsweek International* 28 June 2004: 50. Web. 12 Oct. 2014.

Miscellaneous Electronic Sources.

27. **Posting to a Discussion Group**

> Walton, Hilary. "New Pym Biography." Online posting. 2 Feb. 2008. Pym-1. Web. 3 Feb. 2014.

28. **E-Mail Message**

> Konrad, Lucas. "Antique Fire Trucks." Message to the author. 11 Nov. 2014. E-mail.

29. **Government Document**

> United States. Dept. of Labor. Bureau of Labor Statistics. *Occupational Outlook Handbook, 2010–2011.* Web. 12 Oct. 2014.

Works-Cited Formats for Sources Other Than Books, Periodicals, and Electronic Sources.

30. Congressional Record

> United States. Senate. *Children's Health Care Quality Act.* 111th Cong., 1st sess. S225. Washington: GPO, 2010. Print.
>
> United States. House. Committee on Energy and Commerce. *E-Rate 2.0 Act of 2010.* 111th Cong. 2nd sess. H. R. 4619. Washington: GPO, 2010. Print.

31. Government Publication

> United States. Dept. of Justice. *A Guide to Disability Rights.* Washington, DC: DOJ, Sept. 2010. Print.

32. Lecture

> Schilling, Brian. "The Role of First Responders in Medical Emergencies." Careers Club. Manchester High School, North Manchester. 22 Dec. 2014. Lecture.

33. Letter

> White, Jeremy. Letter to the author. 1 Oct. 2014. MS.

Note that *MS* represents a work prepared by hand. For machine-generated work, use *TS*, for typescript.

34. PDF file

> Brunner, Borgna. "The Wage Gap: A History of Pay Inequity and the Equal Pay Act." *Infoplease* March 2005. PDF file.

35. Personal Interview

> Yahi, Mourad. Personal interview. 10 Nov. 2014.

36. Telephone Interview

> Yahi, Laurel. Telephone interview. 12 Jan. 2014.

37. Pamphlet

> Tweddle, Dominic. *The Coppergate Helmet.* York, UK: Cultural Resource Management, 1984.

38. Television or Radio Broadcast

> "U.S. Technology in Iran." Narr. Lesley Stahl. *Sixty Minutes.* CBS. WPTA, Fort Wayne, 21 Feb. 2014. Television.
>
> *Morning Edition.* WERN. Madison, WI, 12 Nov. 2014. Radio.
>
> "Lights Out." *ER.* NBC. 23 Sept. 1999. DVD.

39. **Sound Recording**

   List first the aspect of the recording you want to emphasize: composer, conductor, or performer. Give that name first, then the title of the recording or selection, the manufacturer, the year of issue (write *n.d.* if no date appears on the package or disc), and the medium (compact disc, audiotape, audiocassette). Do not enclose the name of the medium in italics or quotation marks.

   > Uchida, Mitsuko, pianist. *Piano Sonatas in D,* KV. 284, *Sonata in B flat,* KV. 570, and *Rondo in D,* KV. 485. By Wolfgang Amadeus Mozart. Philips, 1986. CD.

40. **Article in a Reference Book**

   Treat an entry in an encyclopedia or dictionary as you would an article in a collection, but do not cite the book's editor. If the article is signed, begin with the author's name, followed by the title of the entry; otherwise, begin with the title. For familiar reference books such as standard encyclopedias and dictionaries that are frequently updated and reissued, you need not give publication information. Just list the edition (if stated) and year of publication.

   > Watkins, Calvert. "Indo-Europe and the Indo-Europeans." *American Heritage Dictionary of the English Language.* 3rd ed. 1991. Print.

   When citing less familiar books, give full publication information.

   > Rose-Bond, Sherry, and Scott Bond. "Sherlockiana." *Encyclopedia Mysteriosa: A Comprehensive Guide to the Art of Detection in Print, Film, Radio, and Television.* Ed. William L. DeAndrea. New York: Prentice, 1994. 327–330. Print.

Sample Works-Cited Pages.   Here is an alphabetized list of sources drawn from the examples on the previous pages, using a hypothetical student's last name.

White 15

WORKS CITED

Benfey, Christopher. "The Alibi of Ambiguity." *The New Republic* 7 June 2012. N. pag. Web. 14 Nov. 2014.

Cummings, Claire Hope. *Uncertain Peril: Genetic Engineering and the Future of Seeds.* Boston: Beacon, 2008. Print.

"Findings." *Harper's* June 2012: 80. Print.

Kingsolver, Barbara. "A Pure, High Note of Anguish." *Los Angeles Times* 23 Sept. 2001: M1. Print.

White 16

Meacham, Jon. "The American Dream: A

Biography." *Time* 2 July 2012: 26+. Print.

Murphy, Victoria. "The Enemy Strikes Back."

Forbes 24 Nov. 2003: 218. LexisNexis

Academic. Web. 6 Nov. 2014.

Nevens, Kate. "The Youth Are Revolting."

Harvard International Review 34.2 (Fall

2012): 32-35. Print.

Nye, Joseph S. Jr. "The Decline of

America's Soft Power" *Foreign Affairs*

May-June 2004: 16+. Print.

Samuels, David. "Wild Things." *Harper's* June

2012: 28-42. Print.

Saunders, George. "The Tenth of December."

The Best American Short Stories. Eds.

Tom Pellotta and Heidi Pitlar. New

York: Mariner/Houghton Mifflin, 2012.

212-35. Print.

United States. Dept. of Justice. *A Guide to

Disability Rights*. Washington, DC: DOJ,

Sept. 2010. Print.

"U.S. Technology in Iran." Narr. Lesley

Stahl. *Sixty Minutes*. CBS. WPTA, Fort

Wayne, 21 Feb. 2014. Television.

ASSEMBLING THE PARTS OF A RESEARCH PAPER

In general, putting a research paper together is not so different from writing any other kind of paper. Following the guidelines explained in Chapter 2 on the writing process, you will have the same components in a longer paper with sources as you do in a shorter one. You will have an introduction, though it is likely to be longer than in other writing assignments. You must have a thesis statement or clearly evident central idea. Your paper as a whole and individual paragraphs within it must be organized and fully developed. Sentences must be crafted grammatically and imaginatively, and your language should be idiomatic, colorful, and clear. You must provide transitions between points within paragraphs and from paragraph to paragraph throughout the paper, and you must have a conclusion that brings the paper to a satisfactory finish. Of course, a major difference between the research paper and other papers you will write for your college classes is that research papers incorporate the works of others. Thus, you will have in-text citations for all references to your sources and a work-cited list of all sources referenced in your paper. Your instructor may also ask you to include an outline of your paper.

The following sections will take you through the process of putting together your final paper. They address the following components:

- First page of paper without a separate title page
- Title page
- First page of a paper with a separate title page
- Pagination and spacing
- Tables, figures, and illustrations
- Outline page
- Introductory paragraph and body of the paper
- Conclusion
- Works Cited page
- The complete research paper

First Page of a Research Paper without a Separate Title Page.   MLA guidelines state that a research paper does not need a separate title page. Follow these guidelines:

- Type your last name and the number 1 in the upper right-hand corner, one-half inch from the top of the page, flush with the right margin.
- Place your name, your instructor's name, the course title and section, and the date in the upper left-hand corner, one inch from the top of the paper and flush with the left margin.
- Double-space between each line.
- Double-space below the date and center your title.
- Do not italicize your title, enclose it in quotation marks, capitalize every letter, or place a period after it.
- Capitalize the first letter of every important word in the title.
- Double-space again and begin the body of your paper.

```
                                                    Hayes 1

         Nate Hayes

         Professor White

         English 102-8

         15 April 2014

                 A Positive Alternative to Cloning

                 Since Dr. Ian Wilmut's successful clon-

         ing of a sheep in 1996, the debate over how
```

```
                                              Hayes 2
         far medical science should be allowed to go
         has grown increasingly heated. Some people
         are completely opposed to any kind of experi-
         mentation that involves genetic manipulation
         or the development of procedures that some
         consider should be reserved only for God.
```

Title Page.   Although MLA style does not require a separate title page, many instructors ask for it. If your instructor requires a title page, follow these guidelines:

- Center your title about one-third to halfway down the page.
- Do not italicize your title, enclose it in quotation marks, capitalize every letter, or place a period after it.
- Capitalize the first letter of every important word in the title.
- Underneath the title, about halfway down the page, write your name, centered on the line.
- Drop farther down the page and center on separate lines, double spaced, your instructor's name; the course name, number, and section; and the date.

```
         Arthur of Camelot: The Once and Future King
                            by
                       Shawn Ryan




                     Professor Zackary
                     English 102-21
                     1 May 2014
```

First Page of a Research Paper with a Separate Title Page.   If your instructor requires a separate title page, follow these guidelines for the first text page of your paper:

- Type your last name and the number 1 in the upper right-hand corner, one-half inch from the top of the page, flush with the right margin.
- Drop down two inches from the top of the page and center your title, exactly as it appears on your title page.
- Do not italicize your title, enclose it in quotation marks, capitalize every letter, or place a period after it.
- Capitalize the first letter of every important word in the title.
- Double-space and begin the body of your paper.

```
                                        Ryan 1
            Arthur of Camelot: The Once and Future King
                North and west the wind blew beneath the
            morning sun, over endless miles of rolling
            grass and far scattered thickets . . . [and]
            Dragonmount, where the dragon had died, and
            with him, some said, the Age of Legend—
            where prophecy said he would be born again.
            (Jordan 13)
```

Pagination and Spacing.   The entire paper should be double-spaced, with each page numbered in the upper right-hand corner, one-half inch from the top and flush with the right margin. MLA style requires that pagination begin with page 1 and recommends that you include your last name before the page number.

Tables, Figures, and Illustrations.   Place tables, figures, and illustrations close to the parts of the paper that they relate to.

Table.   A table is labeled *Table*, given an Arabic number, and captioned. This information is capitalized as you would a title, placed above the table, and typed flush with the left-hand margin on separate lines. Place the name of the source and any additional comments directly below the table, as illustrated here:

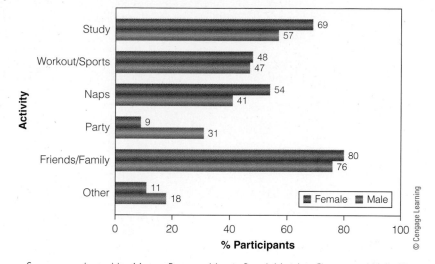

Source: Survey conducted by Margo Borgen, Morris Boyd, Maicha Chang, and Kelly Kassien, University of Wisconsin–Stevens Point, May 2008.

Figures and Illustrations.   Visual images such as photographs, charts, maps, and line drawings are labeled *Figure* (usually abbreviated *Fig.*), assigned an Arabic number, and given a title or caption. A label and title or caption are positioned ***below the illustration and have the same margins as the text.*** The following illustrates correct handling of a visual image:

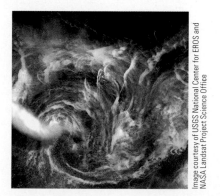

Fig. 1. Whirlpool in the Air: a spinning formation of ice, clouds, and low-lying fog off the eastern coast of Greenland.

Outline Page.   If your instructor requires a formal outline, place it immediately after the title page. Your instructor will tell you how detailed your outline should be, but follow these basic directions in most cases:

- Begin your outline with the thesis statement of your paper.

- Double-space between all lines of the outline.

- If your instructor requires a topic outline, use only short phrases or key words. If your instructor requires a sentence outline, write complete sentences.

- Use uppercase roman numerals (I, II, III) for each major division of your outline and capital letters (A, B, C) for each subdivision under each major division.

- If you find it necessary to further subdivide, use Arabic numerals (1, 2, 3) under capital letters and lowercase letters (a, b, c) under Arabic numerals.

- Number the outline page(s) with lowercase roman numerals (i, ii, iii, iv) placed in the upper right-hand corner, one-half inch from the top of the page and flush with the right margin. Include your last name.

- End with a statement summarizing your conclusion.

Here is a sample topic outline page from a student paper.

```
                                              Ryan i

                      Outline
Thesis: An examination of some of the re-
search on Arthurian legend suggests that
the evidence supports the theory that a man
like Arthur did exist.
    I. The birth of Arthur
       A.  The legend
       B.  Evidence of Tintagel
   II. The places and people most important
       to Arthur
       A.  Camelot
       B.  Glastonbury Abbey
       C.  Lancelot and Perceval
```

```
                                                 Ryan ii

    III. Arthur's impact on society
         A.  His image
         B.  The difference between the man
             and the legend
    Conclusion: Arthur's existence as a man is
    indeterminable, but Arthur's presence in
    the minds and hearts of people everywhere
    gives credence to his existence as a leader
    of nations.
```

Introductory Paragraphs and Body of the Paper. As for any other kind of writing assignment, begin with an introduction that provides background information that clearly portrays the topic of your paper or the direction your argument will take, or that in some way sets the stage for what follows. State your thesis or central idea early in the paper. If your topic is controversial, explain the nature of the controversy. Once you have introduced your topic sufficiently, begin developing your argument. Here are the opening paragraphs from Sam Cox's paper "Proving Their Loyalty During World War I: German-Americans Confronted with Anti-German Fervor and Suspicion."

```
                                                 Cox 1

    Sam Cox
    Professor Heather Stewart
    Humanities 310-01
    12 April 2014
     Proving Their Loyalty During World War I:
    German-Americans Confronted with Anti-German
              Fervor and Suspicion
        In May 1915, a Milwaukee Abendpost
    editorial voiced the unsettling feelings
```

Cox 2

that German-Americans were experiencing in
the early months of the First World War
and that would intensify as the war dragged
on. Supportive of the Fatherland in the
European conflict, German-Americans found
themselves at odds with an English-speaking
majority and Anglo-oriented government.
After the United States entered the war
on the side of the Triple Entente, many
German-Americans were faced with the ago-
nizing choice of whom to support. A review
of the *Indianapolis Telegraph und Tribüne*
and the *Indianapolis Spottvogel* leads
to the conclusion that German-Americans
unwaveringly supported their new homeland
in the war in nearly all instances.

     Nevertheless, the loyalty and
trustworthiness of German-Americans was
questioned by many in the public. The government implemented certain measures intended to track the activity of the German
population in the United States and censor
their publications. German culture came
under popular and official attack throughout the country as German-Americans experienced intense pressure to Americanize.
German-Americans responded by trying to
prove their loyalty to the United States.
They participated in Liberty Loan war bond
drives and discontinued the use of the
German language. As a result, the influence
of Germans on American life faded after
World War I. German-Americans were forced

Coax 3

to decide whether their loyalties lay
with Germany, the land of their heritage,
or with the United States, their adopted
homeland and enemy of Germany. Finding
their loyalty questioned all around them,
German-Americans sacrificed their culture,
language, and unique identity in the face
of overwhelming pressure to become true
Americans and prove their dedication to
their new homeland.

Conclusion.   Recall from Chapter 2 that the conclusion brings the paper to a satisfying end, no matter what its length. Whether the assignment is a 500-word essay or a 5,000-word research paper, readers should not be left with unanswered questions and should have a sense that the writer has fully explained, argued, developed, or illustrated the central idea or thesis. A good conclusion forcefully reiterates the introduction, reinforces the writer's connection with the audience, looks to the future, reemphasizes the central argument, or suggests a course of action. Here is the conclusion to Sam Cox's paper. Notice how his conclusion reinforces points made in the opening paragraphs above but does so without repeating them word for word.

Cox 14

German-Americans bore an unfounded attack on their language and culture during
World War I. Efforts to wipe out their language, their cultural establishments, their
newspapers, and their ethnic identity were so
powerful in that era of suspicion, threats,
and violence, that most German-Americans

Cox 15

succumbed to the unyielding pressure. They
changed the names of clubs, shut down newspapers, bought Liberty Bonds, and stopped
speaking German. Done willingly but often
reluctantly, these actions demonstrated
their loyalty to their new homeland during the time when their loyalty was demanded
most. Despite their deep affection for their
old Fatherland and the knowledge that they
were surrendering much of their cultural
identity, German-Americans wanted to prove
that they were steadfast patriots of their
new homeland of freedom and prosperity.

Works-Cited Page.   Here is the page listing works cited in Sam Cox's paper "Proving Their Loyalty During World War I: German-Americans Confronted with Anti-German Fervor and Suspicion," which uses both primary and secondary sources.

Cox 16

WORKS CITED

"The Alarm against Spies." *The Literary
Digest* 21 July 1917: 13-14. Print.
"Am Dienstag kommen die deutschen Zeitungen
unter den Arm des Censors." *Indianapolis
Spottvogel* 14 October 1917: 1. Print.

Coax 17

Brocke, Frank. " 'We Had to Be so Careful'
    A Farmer's Recollections of Anti-German
    Sentiment in World War I." *History
    Matters: The U.S. Survey Course on the
    Web*. 31 March 2006. Web. 30 Oct. 2010.
"A Call to German Americans to 'Organize.' "
    The Literary Digest 50 9 January 1915:
    42-43. Print.
"Deutsche Kundgebung in New York." *Indianap-
    olis Spottvogel* 9 August 1914: 4. Print.
"German-American Loyalty." *The Literary
    Digest 50* 29 May 1915: 1262-64. Print.
Heinrichs, Rudolf. "A Family Letter." *Atlan-
    tic Monthly* 120 (1917): 739-45. Print.
"Der Kampf für Erhaltung der persönlichen
    Freiheit ist der Kampf der Deutschen in
    Amerika." *Indianapolis Spottvogel* 16
    August 1914: 17. Print.
"Malicious Anti-German Attacks." *Indianapo-
    lis Spottvogel* 16 August 1914: 9. Print.
Ramsey, Paul. "The War against German-
    American Culture: The Removal of German
    Language Instruction from the Indianapo-
    lis Schools, 1917-1919." *Indiana Magazine
    of History* 95.4 (2002): 285-303. Print.
Witten, Johann. Letters to Christoph Witten.
    3 December 1914, 5 December 1915,
    9 September 1919, 18 September 1920.
    Trans. Susan Vogel. *News from the Land of
    Freedom: German Immigrants Write Home*.
    Eds. Walter Kamphoefner, Wolfgang Helbich,
    and Ulrike Sommer. Ithaca: Cornell Uni-
    versity Press, 1991. 278-83. Print.

STUDENT RESEARCH PAPER USING MLA STYLE

The following student research paper implements MLA style guidelines for incorporating and documenting source material as explained in Chapters 6 and 7. Marginal notes point out various components of the research paper.

Schilling 1

Elizabeth Schilling

Music and Politics in China

Dr. Cheng

17 November 2014

Then and Now:

Comparing Revolutionary and Modern Ballet

China has a long history of viewing
women as second-class citizens. Historically, the male dominated culture expected
women to serve men, often as slaves or
concubines. Typically, artistic endeavors,
including opera, ballet, creative writing, and art, perpetuated these traditional
roles of women, creating compliant female
characters who rarely challenged their male
counterparts. The ballet, still valued and
cherished by Chinese citizens of all socio-
economic levels, especially created a canvas for developing cultural expectations.
Though interactions with Western culture
since the 1960s have helped modernize the
way that Chinese society views women and
their roles, artists seem unhurried to
incorporate these changes to the stage.
Despite changes within Chinese society
since the Cultural Revolution, modern

Schilling 2

Elizabeth's opening paragraph gives background information as a context for her central idea, stated in the last sentence.

Chinese ballet continues to reflect the traditional attributes of female characters and to rely on revolutionary plots.

After the Great Leap Forward in the 1950s, Mao Zedong's power and popularity began to dissipate because of his failure to modernize the economic system of China. Because Mao feared that the new leaders would take the State in the wrong direction, he instigated the Cultural Revolution to maintain his influence over the State and its citizens (Trueman). As Patricia Ebrey explains in *Sourcebook of Chinese Civilization*, "The aim of the Cultural Revolution was to attack the Four Olds—old ideas, old culture, old customs, and old habits—in order to bring the areas of education, art and literature in line with Communist ideology" (Ebrey). To align society with his philosophy, Mao completely overhauled the Chinese culture. The Communist regime deemed non-supporters of Mao's views and the values of the State as "[enemies] of the party and people" (Ebrey). In order to avoid persecution or arrest, Chinese citizens complied with the government's mandates. Ultimately, the Cultural Revolution affected the arts so strongly that for a period of time there was absolutely no music in China. Eventually, Mao's wife,

Although the source is named in her text, Elizabeth repeats the author's name in the parenthetical citation. There are no page numbers for her web source.

Schilling 3

Jiang Qing, fostered the production of eight "Model Operas" that applied the acceptable revolutionary themes and were performed continuously with mandatory attendance (Ebrey). Even though Mao's policies ended long ago, modern Chinese ballets still rely on strong elements of the "Model Eight" (Mittler). Nowhere is this more evident than in the ties between the late 1950s ballet *The White-Haired Girl* and the 1990s ballet *Raise the Red Lantern*.

A basic similarity between *The White-Haired Girl* and *Raise the Red Lantern* can be seen in the progression of the protagonist in each ballet. J. Norman Wilkinson explains this common thread by noting that *The White-Haired Girl* revolves around the story of a young girl, His-erh, who is forced to work for a landlord who treats her brutally and eventually sells her into prostitution. Though the audience believes that she has died, they later discover that she has actually escaped to the wilderness. Because she has no food and little sunlight, her hair turns white, so other characters think that she is haunting the area. Eventually, some army men find her, one of whom is her former lover. Together they bring justice to the landlord, and she fights so that others can

Elizabeth's second paragraph continues to give background information but narrows the focus.

This sentence specifies how she will support her more general statement at the end of paragraph one.

The author is named at the beginning of a series of sentences paraphrasing the source, ending with a direct quotation.

Schilling 4

earn the rights that she has attained
(169-72).

   Raise the Red Lantern, adapted from
the movie in 1991, is also about a young
girl, Songlian. The ballet version begins
with her moving into her master's home. As
a concubine she has difficulties adjusting, struggling the first time that she is
called to the dominating man's bedroom and
feeling jealous of the other "top" mis-
tresses. During her time there, she has a
secret affair with her former lover. An en-
vious fellow concubine sees them and tells
their master; as a result, all three people
are executed. Before they die, though, the
two concubines forgive each other (*Raise
the Red Lantern*).

   While they take place during different time periods, the two ballets share
a similar theme. Each portrays the story
of a woman owned by a man, one as a serv-
ant, the other as a mistress. To better the
status of their families, both are placed
in miserable and emotionally devastating positions. As strong women, both rebel
against conforming to what is expected of
them; they fight oppression from beginning
to end. Although Songlian's master kills
her and His-erh defeats her master, both
women are eager for a true, free love with
the man they have selected, not an arranged

The source is a film version of the ballet that Elizabeth summarizes.

All of this paragraph is in Elizabeth's own words, so no source is cited.

relationship. The real difference between
the two female characters lies in the fact
that Songlian does not get the chance to
escape with her lover before she is caught
and sentenced to death, while His-erh escapes and eventually lives to find her
"true love" again and bring revenge upon
her master.

Even though decades have passed since
the first of the "Model Eight" operas was
performed, modern ballets reflect similar
themes, explicitly demonstrating the lasting impact of the Cultural Revolution on
the arts. *The White-Haired Girl*, one of the
most respected pieces of the revolutionary era, played continuously for decades in
a variety of formats. First performed as
a ballet in 1958, composers modified the
piece many times into appropriate revolutionary versions, removing a pregnancy as a
result of rape and adding militant features
(Wilkinson 171). In a similar manner, *Raise
the Red Lantern* has undergone modification:
Songlian is killed by her master in an ending that would never have appeared during
the Cultural Revolution because it is not
ideal for the "hero."

A main revolutionary aspect in *The
White-Haired Girl* is its direct military
features, fully embodying all the pomp and
circumstance of a militant regime. "It is

*Elizabeth
continues to
give supporting
evidence to prove
her thesis.*

Schilling 6

Elizabeth varies her handling of a direct quotation by attributing the source after the quotation.

on this high and militant note that the ballet ends," Wilkinson notes (172). During the Cultural Revolution this ending would have had a strong effect on the Chinese citizens. According to Elizabeth Urban in her undergraduate thesis, *The White-Haired Girl* is considered one of the eight-model works because of its strong revolutionary themes (18). These themes encompass ideas from Mao's Yen'an Forum speech:

Quotations longer than four lines are set off from the text.

> There is absolutely no such thing in the world as love or hatred without reason or cause. As for the so-called love of human-ity, there has been no such all-inclusive love since humanity was divided into classes. . . . There will be genuine love of hu-manity—after classes are elimi-nated all over the world. Classes have split society into many an-tagonistic groupings; there will be love of all humanity when classes are eliminated, but not now. We cannot love enemies, we cannot love social evils; our aim is to destroy them. (Wang)

There are no page numbers for a class lecture, so repeating the source's name is helpful, especially after a long quotation set off from the text.

One sees the application of Mao's words in *The White-Haired Girl*: His-erh and her land-lord come from opposite ends of the societal spectrum and she is his property. Placed in this subservient and demeaning role, she can neither love him nor respect him, and yet it is her duty to serve him, sacrificing her own feelings. This theme also applies to the more recent ballet *Raise the Red Lantern* in which the protagonist, Songlian, finds herself in a similar submissive role as a mistress. The presence of revolutionary themes in both of these ballets demonstrates that, despite their differences, modern audiences desire and approve of revolutionary themes, perhaps because of the sense of security that tradition provides.

Each of the female characters strongly represents the masses, as well. In *The White-Haired Girl*, His-erh embodies the peasants as she rebels against the ruling social class. Similarly, as Paul Coughlin explains, Songlian of *Raise the Red Lantern* represents the inhibited masses, as a woman owned by a man; when she continually tries to rebel, she is further repressed and eventually killed (129). This contemporary ballet portrays revolutionary themes, fully representing the oppressed. The revolutionary theme runs deep in both of these popular ballets, illustrating the strong relationship between the two.

One can see that there are many similarities between the roles of the female characters in the two ballets. The

Schilling 8

protagonists are both young women who make
sacrifices for their families and must leave
what they know to live with a man who treats
them badly. According to Richard King, "The
story [*The White-Haired Girl*] is not structured around her (His-erh), but around the
ownership of her" (194). This statement could
easily apply to the main character of *Raise
the Red Lantern*. The strongest tie between
the two heroines is their representation of
the masses and the ways in which they demonstrate bravery. Even though the two ballets
are from different time periods, their
female central characters continue to serve
as role models for Chinese women.

While the Cultural Revolution ended
decades ago, it certainly had a lasting
effect on the themes, plots and traits of
the female characters of modern Chinese
compositions no matter what their genre.
Two prominent ballets, from time periods
thirty years apart, fully demonstrate this
heavy-handed influence. By recognizing the
similarities and differences in character
traits and noticing trends in revolutionary
themes, one can see that *The White-Haired
Girl* and *Raise the Red Lantern* are quite
similar. With strong female characters, the
ballets present Chinese audiences with the
very models of the perfect Chinese woman
that they desired.

Elizabeth supplies explanatory information in brackets.

Elizabeth's conclusion summarizes the main points of her paper.

Schilling 9

WORKS CITED

Ebrey, Patricia. "A Visual Sourcebook
    of Chinese Civilization: Cultural
    Revolution." *Education Division of the
    National Endowment for the Humanities*.
    Web. 14 Nov. 2014.

Coughlin, Paul. "Iron Fists and Broken
    Spirits: Raise the Red Lantern as
    Allegory." *Screen Education* 36 (Spring
    2004): 125-31. Print.

King, Richard, ed. *Art in Turmoil: the
    Chinese Cultural Revolution, 1966-76*.
    Vancouver: UBC Press, 2010. Print.

Mittler, Barbara. "Eight Stage Works
    for 800 Million People: The Great
    Proletarian Cultural Revolution in
    Music—A View from Revolutionary Opera."
    The Opera Quarterly 26.2-3 (2010):
    377-401. Print.

Raise the Red Lantern Ballet drama. Dir.
    Zhang Yimou. National Project to the
    Distillation of the Stage Arts. DVD.

Trueman, Chris. "The Cultural Revolution."
    History Learning Site. Web. 7 Nov.
    2014.

Urban, Elizabeth C. "The Evolution of
    Revolution: The Dilemma of Censorship
    and Fifth Generation Filmmakers." Hon-
    ors College thesis 88. Pace University,
    2010. *Digital Commons.pace*. Web. 25
    Sept. 2014.

Schilling 10

Wang, Rujie. "Lecture Notes: 'The White
    Haired Girl.' " Chinese 220, Fall 2011.
    The College of Wooster, Wooster, OH.
    Web. 6 Nov. 2014.

Wilkinson, J. Norman. " 'The White-Haired
    Girl': From 'Yangko' to Revolution-
    ary Modern Ballet." *Educational Thea-
    tre Journal* 26 (1974): 164-74. Web. 27
    Sept. 2014.

WRITING A RESEARCH PAPER USING APA STYLE

The documentation style of the American Psychological Association (APA), also referred to as the *author–date system,* is used widely in the behavioral and social sciences. Its style differs from that of the Modern Language Association (MLA), used primarily in the humanities, in some significant ways. APA style cites sources in parenthetical notes in the sentences to which they refer, as does MLA style, but the contents of the notes differ. In the APA system, the year of publication is given in the parenthetical note, and page numbers are given only for quotations, not for paraphrases. Finally, sources are listed at the end of the paper on a page called *References* rather than *Works Cited,* and formatting for that page is quite different from formatting in MLA style. This section gives general guidelines for both parenthetical citations and composing a references page using APA style. The guidelines are accompanied by sample pages from a student research paper using APA documentation style. For complete guidelines on APA Style, consult the following book:

American Psychological Association. *Publication Manual of the American Psychological Association.* 6th ed. Washington: APA, 2010.

For the latest updates on APA Style, go to the official website of the American Psychological Association, located at www.apastyle.org.

PARENTHETICAL CITATIONS USING APA STYLE

Quotations.

- Include the author's last name, a comma, the year the work was published, another comma, and the page number, preceded by the abbreviation *"p."* or *"pp."*:

  > Many experts agree that "it is much easier and more comfortable to teach as one learned" (Chall, 2009, p. 21).

- If the source has two authors, name them both, and separate their names with an ampersand (&):

  > President Truman and his advisors were aware that the use of the bomb was no longer required to prevent an invasion of Japan by the Soviets (Alperovitz & Messer, 1991).

- Omit from the parenthetical citation any information given in the text:

  > Samuel E. Wood and Ellen R. Green Wood (2003a) note that sociobiologists believe that social and nurturing experiences can "intensify, diminish, or modify" personality traits (p. 272).

- If the author's name is given in the text, follow it with the year of publication in parentheses:

  > Nancy Paulu (1988) believes that children who are taught phonics "get off to a better start" than those who are not taught phonics (p. 51).

- For works with three to five authors, name all of the authors the first time you refer to the work, but give only the last name of the first author followed by "et al." in subsequent citations. For a work with six or more authors, give only the first author's last name, followed by "et al." for all citations, including the first.

- If the author's name is repeated in the same paragraph, it is not necessary to repeat the year. However, if the author is cited in another paragraph, give the year of the work again.

- For summaries and paraphrases, give author and year, but not the page number where the information appears:

  > Minnesota scientists have concluded that this data shows that genes are more influential than nurture on most personality traits (Bazell, 2007).

- If the source names no author, cite a short form of the title:

The twins were both born with musical abilities, but their unique experiences determined whether they acted on this ability ("How Genes Shape Personality," 2007).

Note: The first letter of each word in the short title is capitalized, but in the references list, only the first letter of the first word is capitalized.

- If you use two or more sources by the same author and they were published in the same year, add lowercase letters to refer to their order on the references page:

    Wood and Wood (2003a) observe that . . .
    Other authorities (Wood & Wood, 2003b) agree, pointing out that . . .

- If one of your sources quotes or refers to another, and you want to use the second source in your paper, use the words "cited in," followed by the source you read and the year the source was published. If you quote directly, give the page number of the source you read on which the quotation appeared:

    Gerald McClearn, a psychologist and twin researcher at Pennsylvania State University, explained personality development realistically when he said: " 'A gene can produce a nudge in one direction or another, but it does not directly control behavior. It doesn't take away a person's free will' " (cited in "How Genes Shape Personality," 2007, p. 62).

- To cite electronic material, indicate the page, chapter, figure, table, or equation at the appropriate point in the text. Give page number(s) for quotations, if available. If the source does not provide page numbers, use paragraph number if available, preceded by the paragraph symbol or the abbreviation para. If neither page number or paragraph number is visible, cite the heading and the number of the paragraph so that the reader can locate the material at the website:

    (Merriwether, 2004, p. 27)
    (Johnson, 2009, para. 3)
    (Shaw, 2003, conclusion section, para. 1)

Abstract.   Papers written in APA style often have an abstract, which succinctly summarizes its important points, instead of an outline. Here is the abstract of the paper by a group of students who surveyed classmates on various study and leisure-time patterns to discover whether biological sex has an influence on academic achievement:

```
EFFECT OF BIOLOGICAL SEX ON GRADES                2

                    Abstract

        Can differences in academic achieve-

   ment be explained on the basis of biologi-

   cal sex? We hypothesized that sex is not

   the dominating factor influencing the suc-

   cess of University of Wisconsin-Stevens
```

EFFECT OF BIOLOGICAL SEX ON GRADES   3

Point (UWSP) students. We conducted a survey of 108 college students, investigating
their pastimes, study habits, work sched-
ules and housing status in addition to
their grade point averages (GPA). The data
showed a small difference in GPAs with
respect to sex, but not large enough for
sex alone to be the deciding factor. Our
hypothesis that sex alone does not account
for academic success was proved. We found
that other factors, such as length of time
spent studying, the number of hours of work
per week, and time spent partying, all play
significant roles as well.

APA-STYLE REFERENCES LIST

- Bibliographic entries for all works cited in a paper are listed in alphabetical order on a page entitled *References*.
- After the first line of each entry, use a hanging indentation of five spaces.
- Give the last names and only the initials of the first and middle names of authors.
- The year of publication, in parentheses, follows the author's name.
- For a book, capitalize only proper nouns and the first word of the title and subtitle; italicize the title.
- If a book is edited, place the abbreviation "Ed." or "Eds." in parentheses after the name(s) of the editor(s).
- If a citation names two or more authors, each name is reversed and an ampersand (&), not the word *and,* is placed before the last name.
- For an article, book chapter title, or title of an essay in a collection, capitalize as for a book title and do not use quotation marks or italicize.

- Capitalize the first letters of all important words in the name of the periodical and italicize it.

- Use the abbreviations "p." and "pp." for inclusive page numbers of articles in newspapers, but not in magazines and journals. If volume number is given for a periodical, place it after the name of the periodical and italicize it. If an issue number is also given, place it in parentheses after the volume number, but do not italicize it:

    Hamby, A. L. (2001, Spring). An American Democrat: A reevaluation of the personality of Harry S. Truman. *Political Science Quarterly, 106*, 33–55.

    Stephenson, F. (2012, Aug.). The phonics revival. *Florida Trend, 45* (4), 10–24.

- If two or more works by the same author appear on the references list, put them in chronological order. Repeat the author's name each time, followed by the date in parentheses.

- If you cite two works of one author published in the same year, alphabetize them by title, and give each entry a lowercase letter: (1996a), (1996b).

- Words like "university" and "press" are spelled out, not abbreviated.

Below is the reference list for the group project of four students who used a survey for their primary source and supplemented with several secondary sources retrieved from the Internet.

EFFECT OF BIOLOGICAL SEX ON GRADES   15
                           References
    Burke, P. (1989, June). Gender identity,
        sex, and school performance. *Social
        Psychology Quarterly*. Retrieved from
        http://www.jstor.org/pss/2786915
    Duckworth, A. L., & Seligman, M. E. P.
        (2006, February). Self-discipline
        gives girls the edge: Gender in self-
        discipline, grades and achievement test
        scores. *Journal of Education Psychol-
        ogy*. Retrieved from *www.sas.upenn.*

EFFECT OF BIOLOGICAL SEX ON GRADES   16

        edu/~duckwort/images/GenderDifferences-
        Feb2006.pdf

    Pajares, F. (2002). Gender and perceived
        self-efficacy in self-regulated learn-
        ing. *Theory into Practice.* Retrieved
        from http://www.jstor.org/pss/1477463

Wang, Y., Arboldea, A., Shelly II, M. C., &
        Whalen, D. F. (2004). The influence of
        residence hall community on academic suc-
        cess of male and female undergraduate
        students. *Journal of College & University*
        Student Housing, 33 (1), 16-22.

SAMPLE PAGES FROM A STUDENT RESEARCH PAPER USING APA STYLE, WITH TITLE PAGE, ABSTRACT, BODY OF PAPER, AND REFERENCES

Here are sample pages, with marginal comments, of a student research paper illustrating in-text citations using APA style. The first several pages of the paper are given, along with the concluding paragraph and list of references.

Indicate what your running head is by writing the words "Running head" followed by a colon and title of article.

All pages are numbered, beginning with the first or cover page.

Drop halfway down the page, center the information, and write your title on one line, name on the next, and academic affiliation on the third line.

Running Head: USING READERS' THEATER TO DEVELOP
FLUENCY IN STUDENTS WITH LEARNING DISABILITIES   1

      Using Readers' Theater to Develop
      Fluency in Students with Learning
             Disabilities

          Clorinda Tharp
        Manchester University

USING READERS' THEATER TO DEVELOP FLUENCY
IN STUDENTS WITH LEARNING DISABILITIES   2

Abstract

Successful readers must master reading
fluency, which includes accuracy, automaticity,
and prosody. The repeated reading strategy,
sometimes used to help develop fluency
in young children, lacks motivation for students to reread a text several times. Readers'
theater, however, combines the repeated reading strategy with an authentic performance,
which research suggests is an excellent strategy for developing fluency for all types of
learners, including those with disabilities.
Research shows that performing motivates students to read more and promotes success. All
ages and levels of readers can benefit from
the use of readers' theater because teachers
and students can alter the scripts to meet the
needs of each student. Motivation, however,
has ultimately made readers' theater the most
successful at improving students' fluency.

Keywords: readers' theater, fluency,
repeated reading, motivation, disabilities

Following the cover page, write your abstract. Include running head and page number.

Keywords highlight essential components of the paper and give readers important clues about the content of the paper.

USING READERS' THEATER TO DEVELOP FLUENCY
IN STUDENTS WITH LEARNING DISABILITIES   3

Using Readers' Theater to Develop Fluency
in Students with Learning Disabilities

Characterized by the ability to read
quickly and accurately, good readers must
master reading fluency. When good readers

Running head, in caps, appears on all pages. Repeat title, upper and lower cased, at the beginning of your paper, even though the running head is on the page.

USING READERS' THEATER TO DEVELOP FLUENCY
IN STUDENTS WITH LEARNING DISABILITIES   4

Clorinda's opening paragraphs provide background information to give a context for her research.

pick up books, their fluency allows them to
read with accuracy, automaticity, and prosody, ultimately leading to better comprehension of the text. For quite awhile, teachers
have recognized the importance of fluency,
characterized by reading quickly and accurately, but unfortunately, they often ignore
the importance of prosody. Prosody refers to
the expression and phrasing one uses while
reading orally or silently. A student with
a disability may assume that good readers merely read quickly, thus he or she may
compete with others in the class to finish
reading a book first. However, this strategy
lacks the other key component of fluency,
prosody. If a student lacks the ability to
incorporate expression in his or her reading, then he or she may not fully comprehend
the text. Additionally, a student with a
disability may not even try to improve his
or her fluency and reading skills due to a
lack of motivation and repeated failure.

Clorinda's thesis.

Fortunately, readers' theater provides an
excellent strategy for developing fluency
for all types of learners, including those
with disabilities, because it incorporates
repeated reading and motivates students.

The structure of the repeated reading strategy helps develop reading fluency
because students read the same text several
times to improve word recognition, speed,
comprehension, and accuracy, but students

USING READERS' THEATER TO DEVELOP FLUENCY
IN STUDENTS WITH LEARNING DISABILITIES   5

lack the motivation to repeatedly read the
same text (Corcoran, 2005, p. 106). In their
article "Using Readers Theatre to Foster
Fluency in Struggling Readers: A Twist on
the Repeated Reading Strategy," Tyler and
Chard (2000) also suggest that repeated
reading increases fluency and comprehension
when reading new text (p. 165). Essentially,
repeated reading equals practice which just
like in other disciplines helps develop
skills. Samuels, the originator of the repeated reading method in 1979, suggests that
musicians that repeatedly practice a piece
of music obtain more skills; therefore students, who repeatedly read a passage become
more fluent at reading that passage and
those skills transfer to new passages as
well (Graves, Juel, Graves, & Dewitz, 2011,
p. 227). Obviously, research suggests that
the repeated reading strategy increased fluency but lacks the motivation component that
students need to fully utilize the strategy.
Unfortunately, not all students are motivated to read the same text over and over
again. Some students get bored or do not
understand the purpose of repeated reading
and therefore do not benefit fully from the
strategy. Research suggests that "some [stu-
dents] find the notion of reading the same
text over and over absurd, regardless of
the teacher's explanations" (Tyler & Chard,
2000, p. 165). Motivation, therefore, would

With 3, 4, or 5 authors, give all surnames the first time the reference is cited. Thereafter, give only the first author's surname followed by et al.

USING READERS' THEATER TO DEVELOP FLUENCY
IN STUDENTS WITH LEARNING DISABILITIES   6

make the strategy more successful at increasing fluency. However, reading programs
need strategies such as repeated reading to
promote fluency due to fluency's importance
in reading; the key lies in finding the element of motivation in repeated readings.

* * * * *

Clorinda's conclusion summarizes the results of her research.

     In order to develop the fluency of
all types of learners, including those with
disabilities, teachers must use a combination of the repeated reading strategy along
with an authentic performance. Research
shows that performing a script motivates
students to read more and promotes success.
When students are successful, they perform
the act of reading more readily and consequently improve their skills. Reading fluency increases readers' success which also
helps develop other essential skills such as
comprehension. Primary to upper elementary
can benefit from the use of readers' theater
because the scripts can be altered to meet
the needs of each student. Differentiating
the script helps meet the needs of all types
and levels of learners. The motivation component of readers' theater has allowed it
to successfully improve students' fluency.
Research has shown that readers' theater has
effectively motivated struggling readers
which have lead them to be more successful
readers. Consequently, students can continue
to improve their literacy skills in a positive and successful manner.

*Running head
and page number
appear on the
references page.*

USING READERS' THEATER TO DEVELOP FLUENCY
IN STUDENTS WITH LEARNING DISABILITIES   PAGE 7

References

Clark, R., Morrison, T. G., & Wilcox, B.
    (2009). Readers' theater: A process
    of developing fourth-graders' reading
    fluency. *Reading Psychology, 30*(4),
    359-385.

Corcoran, C. A. (2005). A study of the ef-
    fects of readers' theater on second and
    third grade special education students'
    fluency growth. *Reading Improvement,
    42*(2), 105-111.

Garrett, T. D., & O'Connor, D. (2010).
    Readers' theater: "Hold on, let's read
    it again." *Teaching Exceptional Chil-
    dren, 43*(1), 6-13.

Graves, M. F., Juel, C., Graves, B.B.,
    Dewitz, P. (2011). *Teaching reading in
    the 21st century: Motivating all learn-
    ers.* Boston, MA: Pearson.

Tyler, B., & Chard, D. J. (2000). Using
    readers theatre to foster fluency in
    struggling readers: A twist on the
    repeated reading strategy. *Reading &
    Writing Quarterly, 16*(2), 163.

Young, C., & Rasinski, T. (2009). Imple-
    menting readers theatre as an approach
    to classroom fluency instruction.
    Reading Teacher, 63(1), 4-13.

PART **TWO**

Popular Culture, Media Studies, and the Arts

CHAPTER 8

Popular Culture

The field of popular culture studies encompasses a wide range of subjects, including some that overlap with the subjects of other chapters in this book. Popular culture includes television programming, newspaper reporting, music, best-selling novels, and movies. Sports, politics, fashions, and fads are also aspects of popular culture. The focus of popular culture studies is on the choices that people make when searching for entertainment and how various components of popular culture affect behavior and influence attitudes and beliefs. Those who study popular culture are interested in why a particular game, movie, book, television, show, or song becomes wildly popular and how such popularity changes or influences people.

A strong and pervasive component of popular culture is video games, whether played on handheld electronic devices, on phones, in arcades, or on one's television. Critics of video games question whether they have any "redeeming social value," a question that applies particularly to games involving high-body-count killings by assault weapons and other powerful guns. With vivid graphics and sound effects, such games seem to their critics to condone violence and condition their players to be unfeeling or insensitive to real violence.

The first reading in this chapter is by Will Wright, a pioneer in the game field who began creating videogames over thirty years ago. His Sims series is one of the most popular games ever created. As you might expect, he is a strong champion of videogames, for reasons that he explains in "Dream Machines." In contrast to those who see games as negative, even harmful aspects of popular culture, Wright sees them as beneficial. Whether you are a gamer or not, assess the persuasiveness of his argument. Are you convinced that games have the potential to be all that Wright claims they will become?

For an intriguing commentary on the effects of playing violent video games on young people in this chapter, read Karen Sternheimer's "Do Video Games Kill?" An academic whose article was published in a sociological periodical, Sternheimer argues that blaming youth violence on video games is unfair and inaccurate. Citing newspaper articles and studies done following some high-profile school shootings in the late 1990s, she argues that much more than playing violent video games is to blame for the deviant behavior of a few white middle-class males who murdered their classmates.

Although video games are a very recent development in popular culture, evidence suggests that music has been an integral part of humans' lives from their earliest existence. Song and instrumental music have spoken to, soothed, excited, and otherwise influenced humans of virtually all cultures and time periods in a seemingly endless variety of styles, subject matter, and methods of delivery. Each new musician, composer, or singer hopes to create a style uniquely his or her own, often acknowledging the influence of a previous form or artist. Sometimes a wholly new form of musical expression is created, from which generations of musicians and music lovers in turn take their inspiration.

Among the most controversial forms of contemporary music are certain types of rock, hip-hop, and gangsta rap. Their lyrics generate heated debate, with defenders of the music just as convinced of their legitimacy as their detractors are that such lyrics are abusive and even dangerous. Like violent video games, sexually explicit and violently graphic music lyrics come under frequent and vocal attack from those who believe they have devastating effects on certain groups of people. Cathleen McLune asserts in "Hip-Hop's Betrayal of Black Women" that "women too are raised in this environment of poverty and violence but have yet to produce the same negative and hateful representation of black men that male rappers are capable of making against women." As you read her essay, think about your reaction to and understanding of hip-hop and gangsta rap music. Are you sympathetic to her view?

The chapter ends with a look at another pop culture phenomenon, the popularity, especially among young adult readers, of dystopian fiction. Dystopian fiction depicts a world characterized by widespread devastation, whether by famine, totalitarian rule, mass extinction, or other forms of evil that have broken the culture. Those dystopian works whose target audiences are young readers often feature children or young adults as protagonists trying to survive in a world that seems uninhabitable or intolerable. Phillip Reeve, an author of books for young adults, reflects on the general tenor of dystopian fiction being written today. In "The Worst Is Yet to Come," he laments that it is so grim and hopeless, suggesting that, while it is true that "[young adult] authors should try to reflect the fears about the future that young readers feel," authors "also have a duty to challenge the prevailing pessimism of mainstream society." See if you agree with him that there should be utopian novels written to counterbalance dystopian fiction.

DREAM MACHINES
WILL WRIGHT

Will Wright has created more than a dozen games, beginning with SimCity *in 1989, but he is perhaps best known for* The Sims *(2000). Wright was awarded a lifetime achievement award by Game Developers Choice in 2001. His latest software game,* Spore, *is based on the model of evolution and scientific advancement. This article first appeared in* Wired *Magazine, in April 2006.*

The human imagination is an amazing thing. As children, we spend much of our time in imaginary worlds, substituting toys and make-believe for the real surroundings that we are just beginning to explore and understand. As we play, we learn. And as we grow, our play gets more complicated. We add rules and goals. The result is something we call games.

Now an entire generation has grown up with a different set of games than any before it and it plays these games in different ways. Just watch kids with a new videogame. The last thing they do is read the manual. Instead, they pick up the controller and start mashing buttons to see what happens. This isn't a random process; it's the essence of the scientific method. Through trial and error, players build a model of the underlying game based on empirical evidence collected through play. As the players refine this model, they begin to master the game world. It's a rapid cycle of hypothesis, experiment, and analysis. And it's a fundamentally different take on problem-solving than the linear, read-the-manual-first approach of their parents.

In an era of structured education and standardized testing, this generational difference might not yet be evident. But the gamers' mindset—the fact that they are learning in a totally new way—means they'll treat the world as a place for creation, not consumption. This is the true impact videogames will have on our culture.

4   Society, however, notices only the negative. Most people on the far side of the generational divide—elders—look at games and see a list of ills (they're violent, addictive, childish, worthless). Some of these labels may be deserved. But the positive aspects of gaming—creativity, community, self-esteem, problem-solving—are somehow less visible to nongamers.

I think part of this stems from the fact that watching someone play a game is a different experience than actually holding the controller and playing it yourself. Vastly different. Imagine that all you knew about movies was gleaned through observing the audience in a theater—but that you had never watched a film. You would conclude that movies induce lethargy and junk-food binges. That may be true, but you're missing the big picture.

So it's time to reconsider games, to recognize what's different about them and how they benefit—not denigrate—culture. Consider, for instance, their "possibility space": Games usually start at a well-defined state (the setup in chess, for instance) and end when a specific state is reached (the king is checkmated). Players navigate this possibility space by their choices and actions; every player's path is unique.

Games cultivate—and exploit—possibility space better than any other medium. In linear storytelling, we can only imagine the possibility space that surrounds the narrative: What if Luke had joined the Dark Side? What if Neo isn't the One? In interactive media, we can explore it.

8   Like the toys of our youth, modern videogames rely on the player's active involvement. We're invited to create and interact with elaborately simulated worlds, characters, and story lines. Games aren't just fantasy worlds to explore; they actually amplify our powers of imagination.

Think of it this way: Most technologies can be seen as an enhancement of some part of our bodies (car/legs, house/skin, TV/senses). From the start, computers have been understood as an extension of the human brain; the first computers were referred to as mechanical brains and analytical engines. We saw their primary value as automated number crunchers that far exceeded our own meager abilities.

But the Internet has morphed what we used to think of as a fancy calculator into a fancy telephone with email, chat groups, IM, and blogs. It turns out that we don't use computers to enhance our math skills—we use them to expand our people skills.

The same transformation is happening in games. Early computer games were little toy worlds with primitive graphics and simple problems. It was up to the player's imagination to turn the tiny blobs on the screen into, say, people or tanks. As computer graphics advanced, game designers showed some Hollywood envy: They added elaborate cutscenes, epic plots, and, of course, increasingly detailed graphics. They bought into the idea that world building and storytelling are best left to professionals, and they pushed out the player. But in their rapture over computer processing, games designers forgot that there's a second processor at work: the player's imagination.

12   Now, rather than go Hollywood, some game designers are deploying that second processor to break down the wall between producers and consumers. By moving away from the idea that media is something developed by the few (movie and TV studios, book publishers, game companies) and consumed in a one-size-fits-all form, we open up a world of possibilities. Instead of leaving player creativity at the door, we are inviting it back to help build, design, and populate our digital worlds.

More games now include features that let players invent some aspect of their virtual world, from characters to cars. And more games entice players to become creative partners in world building, letting them mod its overall look and feel. The online communities that form around these imaginative activities are some of the most vibrant on the Web. For these players, games are not just entertainment but a vehicle for self-expression.

Games have the potential to subsume almost all other forms of entertainment media. They can tell us stories, offer us music, give us challenges, allow us to communicate and interact with others, encourage us to make things, connect us to new communities, and let us play. Unlike most other forms of media, games are inherently malleable. Player mods are just the first step down this path.

Soon games will start to build simple models of us, the players. They will learn what we like to do, what we're good at, what interests and challenges us. They will observe us. They will record the decisions we make, consider how we solve problems, and evaluate how skilled we are in various circumstances. Over time, these games will become able to modify themselves to better "fit" each individual. They will adjust their difficulty on the fly, bring in new content, and create story lines. Much of this original material will be created by other players, and the system will move it to those it determines will enjoy it most.

16   Games are evolving to entertain, educate, and engage us individually. These personalized games will reflect who we are and what we enjoy, much as our choice of books and music does now. They will allow us to express ourselves, meet others, and create things that we can only dimly imagine. They will enable us to share and combine these creations, to build vast playgrounds. And more than ever, games will be a visible, external amplification of the human imagination.

PERSONAL RESPONSE

Comment on your own experience with game-playing. If you are a player, explain its appeal; if you are not a player, explain why you think it does not appeal to you.

QUESTIONS FOR CLASS OR SMALL-GROUP DISCUSSION

1. Wright comments that society, especially "elders," sees only the negative effects of videogames (paragraph 4). What are those negative effects? Can you account for this view that videogames have a negative effect on the culture? In your experience, is Wright correct that "elders" view videogames negatively?

2. State in your own words what you understand Wright to mean when he says that "it's time to reconsider games, to recognize . . . how they benefit—not denigrate—culture" (paragraph 6).

3. Explain what you understand Wright to mean by the phrase "possibility space" (paragraph 7).

4. Analyze Wright's argument. How effective do you find it? What evidence or supporting proof does he supply? Does he concede anything to those opposed to his position? Where does he use analogy? Do you think that his argument would convince those who see videogames only negatively?

DO VIDEO GAMES KILL?

KAREN STERNHEIMER

Karen Sternheimer, whose work focuses on youth and popular culture, teaches in the sociology department at the University of Southern California and is the author of Celebrity Culture and the American Dream: Stardom and Social Mobility *(2011),* Connecting Popular Culture and Social Problems: Why the Media Is Not the Answer *(2009),* Kids These Days: Facts and Fictions about Today's Youth *(2006), and* It's Not the Media: The Truth about Pop Culture's Influence on Children *(2003). Her commentary has been published in several newspapers, and she has appeared on numerous television and radio programs. This article appeared in the Winter 2007 issue of* Contexts, *a quarterly publication of the American Sociological Association.*

As soon as it was released in 1993, a video game called *Doom* became a target for critics. Not the first, but certainly one of the most popular first-person shooter games, *Doom* galvanized fears that such games would teach kids to kill. In the years after its release, *Doom* helped video gaming grow into a multibillion-dollar industry, surpassing Hollywood box-office revenues and further fanning public anxieties.

Then came the school shootings in Paducah, Kentucky; Springfield, Oregon; and Littleton, Colorado. In all three cases, press accounts emphasized that the shooters loved *Doom*, making it appear that the critics' predictions about video games were coming true.

But in the ten years following *Doom*'s release, homicide arrest rates fell by 77 percent among juveniles. School shootings remain extremely rare; even during the 1990s, when fears of school violence were high, students had less than a 7 in 10 million chance of being killed at school.

4   During that time, video games became a major part of many young people's lives, few of whom will ever become violent, let alone kill. So why is the video game explanation so popular?

Contemporary Folk Devils

In 2000 the FBI issued a report on school rampage shootings, finding that their rarity prohibits the construction of a useful profile of a "typical" shooter. In the absence of a simple explanation, the public symbolically linked these rare and complex events to the shooters' alleged interest in video games, finding in them a catchall explanation for what seemed unexplainable—the white, middle-class school shooter. However, the concern about video games is out of proportion to their actual threat.

Politicians and other moral crusaders frequently create "folk devils," individuals or groups defined as evil and immoral. Folk devils allow us to channel our blame and

Sternheimer, Karen. "Do Video Games Kill?" From *CONTEXTS*, Winter 2007, Vol. 6, No. 1, pp. 13–17. Reprinted by permission of Sage Publications, Inc fear, offering a clear course of action to remedy what many believe to be a growing problem. Video games, those who play them, and those who create them have become contemporary folk devils because they seem to pose a threat to children.

Such games have come to represent a variety of social anxieties: about youth violence, new computer technology, and the apparent decline in the ability of adults to control what young people do and know. Panics about youth and popular culture have emerged with the appearance of many new technologies. Over the past century, politicians have complained that cars, radio, movies, rock music, and even comic books caused youth immorality and crime, calling for control and sometimes censorship.

8   Acting on concerns like these, politicians often engage in battles characterized as between good and evil. The unlikely team of Senators Joseph Lieberman, Sam Brownback, Hillary Rodham Clinton, and Rick Santorum introduced a bill in March 2005 that called for $90 million to fund studies on media effects. Lieberman commented, "America is a media-rich society, but despite the flood of information, we still lack perhaps the most important piece of information— what effect are media having on our children?" Regardless of whether any legislation passes, the senators position themselves as protecting children and benefit from the moral panic they help to create.

Constructing Culpability

Politicians are not the only ones who blame video games. Since 1997, 199 newspaper articles have focused on video games as a central explanation for the Paducah, Springfield, and Littleton shootings. This helped to create a groundswell of fear that schools were no longer safe and that rampage shootings could happen wherever there were video games. The shootings legitimated existing concerns about the new medium and about young people in general. Headlines such as "Virtual Realities Spur School Massacres" (*Denver Post*, July 27, 1999), "Days of Doom" (*Pittsburgh Post-Gazette*, May 14, 1999), "Bloodlust Video Games Put Kids in the Crosshairs" (*Denver Post*, May 30, 1999), and "All Those Who Deny Any Linkage between Violence in Entertainment and Violence in Real Life, Think Again" (*New York Times*, April 26, 1999) insist that video games are the culprit.

These headlines all appeared immediately after the Littleton shooting, which had the highest death toll and inspired most (176) of the news stories alleging a video game connection.

Across the country, the press attributed much of the blame to video games specifically, and to Hollywood more generally. The *Pittsburgh Post-Gazette* article "Days of Doom" noted that "eighteen people have now died at the hands of avid *Doom* players." The *New York Times* article noted above began, "By producing increasingly violent media, the entertainment industry has for decades engaged in a lucrative dance with the devil," evoking imagery of a fight against evil. It went on to construct video games as a central link: "The two boys apparently responsible for the massacre in Littleton, Colo., last week were, among many other things, accomplished players of the ultraviolent video game *Doom*. And Michael Carneal, the 14-year-old boy who opened fire on a prayer group in a Paducah, Ky., school foyer in 1997, was also known to be a video-game expert."

12   Just as many stories insisted that video games deserved at least partial blame, editorial pages around the country made the connection as well:

> President Bill Clinton is right. He said this shooting was no isolated incident, that Kinkel and other teens accused of killing teachers and fellow students reflect a changing culture of violence on television and in movies and video games. (*Cleveland Plain Dealer,* May 30, 1998)
>
> The campaign to make Hollywood more responsible . . . should proceed full speed ahead. (*Boston Herald*, April 9, 2000)
>
> Make no mistake, Hollywood is contributing to a culture that feeds on and breeds violence. . . . When entertainment companies craft the most shocking video games and movies they can, peddle their virulent wares to an impressionable audience with abandon, then shrug off responsibility for our culture of violence, they deserve censure. (*St. Louis Post-Dispatch*, April 12, 2000)

The video game connection took precedence in all these news reports. Some stories mentioned other explanations, such as the shooters' social rejection, feelings of alienation at school, and depression, but these were treated mostly as minor factors compared with video games. Reporters gave these other reasons far less attention than violent video games, and frequently discussed them at the end of the articles.

The news reports typically introduce experts early in the stories who support the video game explanation. David Grossman, a former army lieutenant described as a professor of "killology," has claimed that video games are "murder simulators" and serve as an equivalent to military training. Among the 199 newspaper articles published, 17 of them mentioned or quoted Grossman. Additionally, an attorney who has filed several lawsuits against video game producers wrote an article for the *Denver Post* insisting that the games are to blame. By contrast, only seven articles identified sociologists as experts. Writers routinely presented alternative explanations as rebuttals but rarely explored them in depth.

Reporting on Research

By focusing so heavily on video games, news reports downplay the broader social contexts. While a handful of articles note the roles that guns, poverty, families, and the organization of schools may play in youth violence in general, when reporters mention research to explain the shooters' behavior, the vast majority of studies cited concern media effects, suggesting that video games are a central cause.

16   Since the early days of radio and movies, investigators have searched for possible effects—typically negative—that different media may have on audiences, especially children. Such research became more intense following the rise in violent crime in the United States between the 1960s and early 1990s, focusing primarily on television. Several hundred studies asked whether exposure to media violence predicts involvement in actual violence.

Although often accepted as true—one scholar has gone so far as to call the findings about the effects of media violence on behavior a "law"—this body of research has been highly controversial. One such study fostered claims that television had led to more than 10,000 murders in the United States and Canada during the 20th century. This and many other media-effects studies rely on correlation analysis, often finding small but sometimes statistically significant links between exposure to media violence and aggressive behavior.

But such studies do not demonstrate that media violence causes aggressive behavior, only that the two phenomena exist together. Excluding a host of other factors (such as the growing unrest during the civil rights and antiwar movements, and the disappearance of jobs in central cities) may make it seem that a direct link exists between the introduction of television and homicides. In all likelihood any connection is incidental.

It is equally likely that more aggressive people seek out violent entertainment. Aggression includes a broad range of emotions and behaviors, and is not always synonymous with violence. Measures of aggression in media-effects research have varied widely, from observing play between children and inanimate objects to counting the number of speeding tickets a person received. Psychologist Jonathan Freedman reviewed every media-violence study published in English and concluded that "the majority of studies produced evidence that is inconsistent or even contradicts" the claim that exposure to media violence causes real violence.

20   Recently, video games have become a focus of research. Reviews of this growing literature have also been mixed. A 2001 meta-analysis in *Psychological Science* concluded that video games "will increase aggressive behavior," while a similar review published that same year in a different journal found that "it is not possible to determine whether video game violence affects aggressive behavior." A 2005 review found evidence that playing video games improves spatial skills and reaction times, but not that the games increase aggression.

The authors of the *Psychological Science* article advocate the strong-effects hypothesis. Two of their studies were widely reported on in 2000, the year after the Columbine High School shootings, with scant critical analysis. But their research was based on college undergraduates, not troubled teens, and it measured aggression in part by subjects' speed in reading "aggressive" words on a computer screen or blasting opponents with sound after playing a violent video game. These measures do not approximate the conditions the school shooters experienced, nor do they offer much insight as to why they, and not the millions of other players, decided to acquire actual weapons and shoot real people.

Occasionally reporters include challenges like this in stories containing media-effects claims, but news coverage usually refers to this body of research as clear, consistent, and conclusive. "The evidence, say those who study violence in culture, is unassailable: Hundreds of studies in recent decades have revealed a direct correlation between exposure to media violence—now including video games—and increased aggression," said the *New York Times* (April 26, 1999). The *Boston Herald* quoted a clinical psychologist who said, "Studies have already shown that watching television shows with aggressive or violent content makes children more aggressive" (July 30, 2000). The psychologist noted that video game research is newer, but predicted that "in a few years, studies will show that video games increase a child's aggression even more than violent TV shows." News reports do not always use academic sources to assess the conclusiveness of media effects research. A *Pittsburgh Post-Gazette* story included a quote by an attorney, who claimed, "Research on this has been well-established" (May 14, 1999).

It is no accident that media-effects research and individual explanations dominate press attempts to explain the behavior of the school shooters. Although many politicians are happy to take up the cause against video games, popular culture itself suggests an apolitical explanation of violence and discourages a broader examination of structural factors. Focusing on extremely rare and perhaps unpredictable outbursts of violence by young people discourages the public from looking closely at more typical forms of violence against young people, which is usually perpetrated by adults.

24   The biggest problem with media-effects research is that it attempts to decontextualize violence. Poverty, neighborhood instability, unemployment, and even family violence fall by the wayside in most of these studies. Ironically, even mental illness tends to be overlooked in this psychologically oriented research. Young people are seen as passive media consumers, uniquely and uniformly vulnerable to media messages.

Missing Media Studies

News reports of the shootings that focus on video games ignore other research on the meanings that audiences make from media culture. This may be because its qualitative findings are difficult to turn into simple quotations or sound bites. Yet in seeking better understanding of the role of video games in the lives of the shooters and young people more generally, media scholars could have added much to the public debate.

For instance, one study found that British working-class boys boast about how many horror films they have seen as they construct their sense of masculinity by appearing too tough to be scared. Another study examined how younger boys talk about movies and television as a way to manage their anxieties and insecurities regarding their emerging sense of masculinity. Such studies illustrate why violent video games may appeal to many young males.

Media scholars have also examined how and why adults construct concerns about young people and popular culture. One such study concluded that some adults use their condemnation of media as a way to produce cultural distinctions that position them above those who enjoy popular culture. Other researchers have found that people who believe their political knowledge is superior to that of others are more likely to presume that media violence would strongly influence others. They have also found that respondents who enjoy television violence are less likely to believe it has a negative effect.

28   Just as it is too simplistic to assert that video game violence makes players more prone to violence, news coverage alone, however dramatic or repetitive, cannot create consensus among the public that video games cause youth violence. Finger-wagging politicians and other moralizers often alienate as many members

of the public as they convert. In an ironic twist, they might even feed the antiauthoritarian appeal that may draw players of all ages to the games.

The lack of consensus does not indicate the absence of a moral panic, but reveals contradictory feelings toward the target group. The intense focus on video games as potential creators of violent killers reflects the hostility that some feel toward popular culture and young people themselves. After adult rampage shootings in the workplace (which happen more often than school shootings), reporters seldom mention whether the shooters played video games. Nor is an entire generation portrayed as potential killers.

Ambivalence about Juvenile Justice

The concern in the late 1990s about video games coincided with a growing ambivalence about the juvenile justice system and young offenders. Fears about juvenile "super-predators," fanned by former Florida Representative Bill McCollom's 1996 warning that we should "brace ourselves" against the coming storm of young killers, made the school shootings appear inevitable. McCollom and other politicians characterized young people as a "new breed," uniquely dangerous and amoral.

These fears were produced partially by the rise in crime during the late 1980s and early 1990s, but also by the so-called echo boom that produced a large generation of teens during the late 1990s. Demographic theories of crime led policymakers to fear that the rise in the number of teen males would bring a parallel rise in crime. In response, virtually every state changed its juvenile justice laws during the decade. They increased penalties, imposed mandatory minimum sentences, blended jurisdiction with criminal courts, and made it easier to transfer juvenile cases to adult criminal courts.

32   So before the first shot was fired in Paducah, politicians warned the public to be on the lookout for killer kids. Rather than being seen as tragic anomalies, these high-profile incidents appeared to support scholarly warnings that all kids posed an increasing threat. Even though juvenile (and adult) crime was in sharp decline by the late nineties, the intense media coverage contributed to the appearance of a new trend.

Blaming video games meant that the shooters were set aside from other violent youth, frequently poor males of color, at whom our get-tough legislation has been targeted. According to the National Center for Juvenile Justice, African-American youth are involved in the juvenile justice system more than twice as often as whites. The video game explanation constructs the white, middle-class shooters as victims of the power of video games, rather than fully culpable criminals. When boys from "good" neighborhoods are violent, they seem to be harbingers of a "new breed" of youth, created by video games rather than by their social circumstances. White, middle-class killers retain their status as children easily influenced by a game, victims of an allegedly dangerous product. African-American boys, apparently, are simply dangerous.

While the news media certainly asked what role the shooters' parents may have played, the press tended to tread lightly on them, particularly the Kinkels of Springfield, Oregon, who were their son's first murder victims. Their middle-class, suburban, or rural environments were given little scrutiny. The white school shoot-ers did more than take the lives of their classmates; their whiteness and middle-class status threatened the idea of the innocence and safety of suburban America.

In an attempt to hold more than just the shooters responsible, the victims' families filed lawsuits against film producers, Internet sites, and video game makers. Around the same time, Congress made it more difficult to sue gun manufacturers for damages. To date, no court has found entertainment producers liable for caus-ing young people to commit acts of violence. In response to a lawsuit following the Paducah shootings, a Kentucky circuit judge ruled that "we are loath to hold that ideas and images can constitute the tools for a criminal act," and that product liabil-ity law did not apply because the product did not injure its consumer. The lawsuit was dismissed, as were subsequent suits filed after the other high-profile shootings.

Game Over?

36   Questions about the power of media and the future of the juvenile justice system persist. In March 2005, the U.S. Supreme Court ruled that juvenile executions were unconstitutional. This ruling represents an about-face in the 25-year trend toward toughening penalties for young offenders. While many human rights and children's advocates praised this decision, it was sharply criticized by those who believe that the juvenile justice system is already too lenient. Likewise, critics continue to target video games, as their graphics and plot capabilities grow more complex and at times more disturbing. Meanwhile, youth crime rates continue to decline. If we want to understand why young people, particularly in middle-class or otherwise stable environments, become homicidal, we need to look beyond the games they play. While all forms of media merit critical analysis, so do the suppos-edly "good" neighborhoods and families that occasionally produce young killers.

Recommended Resources

Burns, Ronald, and Charles Crawford. "School Shootings, the Media, and Public Fear: Ingredients for a Moral Panic." *Crime, Law, and Social Change* 32 (1999): 147–68. *Examines fears about school shootings in the 1990s, paying special attention to the disproportional response compared to the actual threat.*

Freedman , Jonathan L. *Media Violence and Its Effect on Aggression: Assessing the Scientific Evidence.* Toronto: U of Toronto P, 2002. *A thorough analysis of media-effects research, with a critique of methods and interpretation of results.*

Goode, Erich, and Nachman Ben-Yehuda. *Moral Panics: The Social Construction of Deviance.* 2nd ed. Malden, MA: Wiley-Blackwell, 2009. *A primer on moral panics, with basic definitions as well as several seminal case studies.*

40   Springhall, John. *Youth, Popular Culture and Moral Panics: Penny Gaffs to Gangsta-Rap, 1830–1996.* New York: St. Martin's, 1998. *A history of fears about young people and media.*

Franklin E. Zimring. *American Youth Violence.* Oxford: Oxford U P, 1998. *A comprehensive look at trends in youth crime, juvenile justice, and political discourse about youth violence.*

PERSONAL RESPONSE

What is your opinion of violent video games? Are they harmless fun, or do you believe that they may have some effect on behavior? What is your experience with playing such games or watching others play them?

QUESTIONS FOR CLASS OR SMALL-GROUP DISCUSSION

1. Explain in your own words what you understand Sternheimer to mean by the term "folk devils." She suggests that "video games, those who play them, and those who create them have become contemporary folk devils" (paragraph 4). Can you give examples of other such "folk devils?"

2. What criticisms of media-effects research does Sternheimer make? What do you think of her rationale for those criticisms?

3. Discuss the factors besides video games that may account for aggressive behavior in teenagers, according to Sternheimer.

4. What point does Sternheimer make about poor males of color who get in trouble with the law vs. white middle-class males who kill? Do your own observations confirm or contradict her viewpoint?

5. Analyze the structure of Sternheimer's argument. What is her thesis? Where does she make concessions? What evidence does she supply? How convinced are you by her evidence?

HIP-HOP'S BETRAYAL OF BLACK WOMEN

JENNIFER MCLUNE

Jennifer McLune is a librarian, activist, and writer living in Washington, D.C. This piece appeared in Z Magazine Online in the July/August 2006 issue. According to its mission statement, Z Magazine is "dedicated to resisting injustice, defending against repression, and creating liberty. It sees the racial, gender, class, and political dimensions of personal life as fundamental to understanding and improving contemporary circumstances; and it aims to assist activist efforts for a better future." You can view Z at www.zcommunications.org/zmag.

Kevin Powell in "Notes of a Hip Hop Head" writes, "Indeed, like rock and roll, hip-hop sometimes makes you think we men don't like women much at all, except to objectify them as trophy pieces or, as contemporary vernacular mandates, as baby mommas, chickenheads, or bitches.

"But just as it was unfair to demonize men of color in the 1960s solely as wild-eyed radicals when what they wanted, amidst their fury, was a little freedom

Z MAGAZINE ONLINE July/August 2006. Reprinted by permission.

and a little power, today it is wrong to categorically dismiss hip-hop without taking into serious consideration the socioeconomic conditions (and the many record labels that eagerly exploit and benefit from the ignorance of many of these young artists) that have led to the current state of affairs. Or, to paraphrase the late Tupac Shakur, we were given this world, we did not make it."

Powell's "socioeconomic" explanation for the sexism in hip-hop is a way to silence feminist critiques of the culture. It is to make an understanding of the misogynistic objectification of black women in hip-hop so elusive that we can't grasp it long enough to wring the neck of its power over us. His argument completely ignores the fact that women, too, are raised in this environment of poverty and violence, but have yet to produce the same negative and hateful representation of black men that male rappers are capable of making against women.

4   Powell's understanding also lends itself to elitist assumption that somehow poverty breeds sexism, or at least should excuse it. Yet we all know that wealthy white boys can create the same hateful and violent music as poor black boys. As long as the boys can agree that their common enemy is female and that their power resides in their penis, women must not hesitate to name the war they have declared on us.

Hip-hop owes its success to the ideology of woman-hating. It creates, perpetuates, and reaps the rewards of objectification. Sexism and homophobia saturate hip-hop culture and any deviation from these forms of bigotry is made marginal to its most dominant and lucrative expressions. Few artists dare to embody equality and respect between the sexes through their music. Those who do have to fight to be heard above the dominant chorus of misogyny.

The most well known artists who represent an underground and conscious force in hip-hop—like Common, The Roots, Talib Kweli, and others—remain inconsistent, apologetic, and even eager to join the mainstream player's club. Even though fans like me support them because of their moments of decency toward women, they often want to remain on the fence by either playing down their consciousness or by offering props to misogynistic rappers. Most so-called conscious artists appear to care more about their own acceptance by mainstream artists than wanting to make positive changes in the culture.

The Roots, for example, have backed Jay-Z on both his *Unplugged* release and Fade to Black tours. They've publicly declared their admiration for him and have signed on to his new "indie" hip-hop imprint Def Jam Left to produce their next album. Yet Jay-Z is one of the most notoriously sexist and materialistic rappers of his generation.

8   Hip-hop artists like Talib Kweli and Common market themselves as conscious alternatives, yet they remain passive in the face of unrelenting woman-hating bravado from mainstream artists. They are willing to lament in abstract terms the state of hip-hop, but refuse to name names—unless it's to reassure their mainstream brethren that they have nothing but love for their music.

Talib Kweli has been praised for his song "Black Girl Pain," but clearly he's clueless to how painful it is for a black girl to hear his boy Jay-Z rap, "I pimp hard on a trick, look Fuck if your leg broke bitch, hop up on your good foot."

The misogyny in hip-hop is also given a pass because some of its participants are women. But female hip-hop artists remain marginalized within the industry and culture—except when they are trotted out to defend hip-hop against feminist criticism. But the truth is, all kinds of patriarchal institutions, organizations, and movements have women in their ranks in search of power and meaning. The token presence of individual women changes nothing if women as a group are still scapegoated and degraded.

Unlike men, women in hip-hop don't speak in a collective voice in defense of themselves. The pressure on women to be hyper-feminine and hyper-sexual for the pleasure of men, and the constant threat of being called a bitch, a ho—or worse, a dyke—as a result of being strong, honest, and self-possessed, are real within hip-hop culture and the black community at large. Unless women agree to compromise their truth, self-respect, and unity with other women and instead play dutiful daughter to the phallus that represents hip-hop culture, they will be either targeted, slandered, or ignored altogether. As a result, female rappers are often just as male-identified, violent, materialistic, and ignorant as their male peers.

12   Hip-hop artist Eve, who describes herself as "a pit bull in a skirt," makes an appearance in the Sporty Thieves video for "Pigeons," one of the most hateful misogynistic anthems in hip-hop. Her appearance displays her unity not with the women branded "pigeons," but with the men who label them. This is a heartbreaking example of how hip-hop encourages men to act collectively in the interest of male privilege while dividing women into opposing camps of good and bad or worthy and unworthy of respect.

Lip-service protest against sexism in hip-hop culture is a sly form of public relations to ensure that nobody's money, power, or respect is ever really threatened. Real respect and equality might interfere with hip-hop's commercial appeal. We are asked to dialogue about and ultimately celebrate our "progress"—always predicated on a few rappers and moguls getting rich. Angry young black women are expected to be satisfied with a mere mention that some hip-hop music is sexist and that this sexism of a few rappers is actually, as Powell calls it, "the ghetto blues, urban folk art, a cry out for help." My questions then are: "Whose blues? Whose art? Why won't anybody help the women who are raped in endless rotation by the gaze of the hip-hop camera?"

They expect us to deal with hip-hop's pervasive woman-hating simply by alluding to it, essentially excusing and even celebrating its misogyny, its arrogance, its ignorance. What this angry black woman wants to hear from the apologists is that black women are black people too. That any attack on the women in our community is an attack on us all and that we will no longer be duped by genocidal tendencies in black-face. I want to hear these apologists declare that any black man who makes music perpetuating the hatred of women will be named, shunned, and destroyed, financially and socially, like the traitor of our community he is. That until hip-hop does right by black women, everything hip-hop ever does will fail.

If we accept Powell's explanation for why hip-hop is the way it is—which amounts to an argument for why we should continue to consume and celebrate it—then ultimately we are accepting ourselves as victims who know only how to imitate our victimization while absolving the handful of black folk who benefit from its tragic results. I choose to challenge hip-hop by refusing to reward its commercial aspirations with my money and my attention.

16   I'm tired of the ridiculous excuses and justifications for the unjustifiable pillaring of black women and girls in hip-hop. Are black women the guilty parties behind black men's experience of racism and poverty? Are black women acceptable scapegoats when black men suffer oppression? If black women experience double the oppression as both blacks and women in a racist, patriarchal culture, it is our anger at men and white folks that needs to be heard.

The black men who make excuses for the ideology of woman-hating in hip-hop remind me of those who, a generation ago, supported the attacks on black female writers who went public about the reality of patriarchy in our community. The fact that these black female writers did not create incest, domestic violence, rape, and other patriarchal conditions in the black community did not shield them from being skewered by black men who had their feelings hurt by the exposure of their male privilege and domination of black women. Black women's literature and activism that challenges sexism is often attacked by black men (and many male-identified women) who abhor domination when they are on the losing end, but want to protect it when they think it offers them a good deal.

Black women writers and activists were called traitors for refusing to be silent about the misogynistic order of things and yet women-hating rappers are made heroes by the so-called masses. To be sure, hip-hop is not about keeping it real. Hip-hop lies about the ugly reality that black women were condemned for revealing. Hip-hop is a manipulative narrative that sells because it gets men hard. It is a narrative in which, as a Wu Tang Clan video shows, black women are presented as dancing cave "chicks" in bikinis who get clubbed over the head; or where gang rapes are put to a phat beat; or where working class black women are compared to shit-eating birds.

As a black woman who views sexism as just as much the enemy of my people as racism, I can't buy the apologies and excuses for hip-hop. I will not accept the notion that my sisters deserve to be degraded and humiliated because of the frustrations of black men—all while we suppress our own frustrations, angers, and fears in an effort to be sexy and accommodating. Although Kevin Powell blames the negatives in hip-hop on everything but hip-hop culture itself, he ultimately concludes, "What hip-hop has spawned is a way of winning on our own terms, of us making something out of nothing."

20   If the terms for winning are the objectification of black women and girls, I wonder if any females were at the table when the deal went down. Did we agree to be dehumanized, vilified, made invisible? Rather than pretending to explain away the sexism of hip-hop culture, why doesn't Powell just come clean—in the end it doesn't matter how women are treated. Sexism is the winning ticket to mainstream acceptability and Powell, like Russell Simmons and others, knows this. It's obvious that if these are the winning terms for our creativity, black women are ultimately the losers. And that's exactly how these self-proclaimed players, thugs, and hip-hop intellectuals want us—on our backs and pledging allegiance to the hip-hop nation.

If we were to condemn woman-hating as an enemy of our community, hip-hop would be forced to look at itself and change radically and consistently. Then it would no longer be marketable in the way that these hip-hop intellectuals celebrate. As things stand, it's all about the Benjamins on every level of the culture and black women are being thugged and rubbed all the way to the bank.

PERSONAL RESPONSE

Write in response to McLune's statement in paragraph 5 that "[h]ip-hop owes its success to the ideology of woman hating."

QUESTIONS FOR CLASS OR SMALL-GROUP DISCUSSION

1. How well do you think that McLune explains her title? In what ways is hip-hop a betrayal of black women, according to her?

2. Explain in your own words McLune's argument against Kevin Powell's explanation for the "misogynistic objectification of black women in hip-hop" (paragraph 3).

3. McLune writes: "Few artists dare to embody equality and respect between the sexes through their music" (paragraph 5). What do you think of her assessment of those few artists she names who "represent an underground and conscious force in hip-hop" (paragraph 6)? Can you name similar artists who resist using sexist and homophobic lyrics?

4. To what extent do you agree with McLune's comments on female hip-hop artists (paragraphs 10–12)?

5. Discuss your opinion of what McLune calls for apologists of black hip-hop music and the artists themselves to do.

THE WORST IS YET TO COME

PHILIP REEVE

Philip Reeve is a British author and illustrator of many novels for children and young adults, including Scrivener's Moon *(2011),* Fever Crumb *(2009),* Larklight *(2006), and* Mortal Engines *(2001), which won the Nestlé Smarties Book Prize and was short-listed for the Whitbread Award. This article was first published in* School Library Journal, *August 1, 2011.*

Tomorrow isn't what it used to be. The latest trend in young adult fiction features visions of the future, and most of them are pretty grim. In Suzanne Collins's *The Hunger Games* (Scholastic, 2008), the teenagers of a fractured future U.S.A. are

Reprinted by permission from *School Library Journal*, August 1, 2011.

pitted against one another in televised battles to the death. In Paolo Bacigalupi's *Ship Breaker* (Little, Brown, 2010), the oil has run out and child laborers dismantle obsolete supertankers on the beaches of the Gulf Coast. Moira Young's striking debut, Blood *Red Road* (S & S/Margaret K. McElderry Bks., 2011), pits its young heroine against the perils of a post-catastrophe world, while Jo Treggiari's *Ashes, Ashes* (Scholastic, 2011) vividly describes a flooded, quake-prone Manhattan depopulated by deadly plagues. I mention those four in particular because I happen to have read them, and know them to be very good, but there are many more YA dystopias already published or forthcoming. What is it about these grim futures that young readers find so appealing?

Dystopias, of course, are nothing new. Ever since H. G. Wells's Martians trashed London back in 1898, science fiction has delighted in showing us our world in ruins. There was no YA genre as such when I was a young adult, but I grew up reading grim tales of life after the bomb by such authors as Robert C. O'Brien and Russell Hoban, or in the totalitarian states of George Orwell's *1984* and Ray Bradbury's *Fahrenheit 451*, while John Wyndham and J. G. Ballard provided eerie visions of futures blighted by everything from killer shrubs and melting ice caps to runaway crystallization. With influences like those, it's little wonder that some of the worlds I've imagined in my own novels have strong dystopian elements.

The attraction of such stories for teenage readers is clear. Stuck in those awkward years between childhood and full adulthood, bridling against the authority of parents and high school teachers, they can draw a bleak satisfaction from imagining adult society reduced to smoking rubble. They are also, perhaps, becoming aware of the deep injustices in the wider world, which dystopian fiction often reflects. I know that some people find it distasteful when an author simply relocates to North America or Western Europe the sorts of poverty and oppression that are all too common elsewhere (scrap yards like the one in *Ship Breaker* already exist in India, for instance). But by visiting such woes on teenagers like themselves, these stories may make it easier for young readers to think about them, and to imagine what it might be like to live in a police state or a shantytown.

4   Or maybe it's just cool to mentally recast yourself as a rebel against some future tyranny. There's a strong element of wish fulfillment in dystopian fiction. When you're a teenager, the prospect of having to leave home and make your own way in society can seem such an alarming one that it's perversely comforting to picture that society swept away. Treggiari's *Ashes, Ashes* is a powerful expression of this fantasy: its heroine, Lucy Holloway, has always considered herself plain, clumsy, and "not good at anything"; she's unnoticed by her teachers and unpopular with her classmates—but she has the last laugh when all the jocks and prom queens are wiped out by mutant smallpox, leaving her to live by her wits in the ruins of Central Park.

In the end, despite some well-depicted self-doubt, Lucy proves more than capable of looking after herself. That's something she has in common with the protagonists of most of the recent dystopian novels. Each features a strong hero or heroine who survives by intelligence, resourcefulness, and good old-fashioned pluck. There's no room here for Ballard's apathetic heroes who listlessly come to accept their transformed worlds, nor for doomed rebels like Orwell's Winston Smith or Huxley's Savage. The *Hunger Games*'s Katniss Everdeen would never be persuaded to love Big Brother; she'd be far more likely to lead a rebellion and overthrow him. The others might not go that far, but they'd certainly escape from Room 101 and light out for 1984's equivalent of the Territory. I'm sure that it's this, as much as the post-apocalyptic backgrounds, that explains the success of these books. The settings may be nihilistic, but the message that an individual can make a difference and that courage and ingenuity can triumph even in the most dreadful circumstances, is anything but.

And yet my brief tour of contemporary dystopias has left me feeling slightly uneasy. I mean no criticism of any particular book, but when viewed as a genre "YA Dystopian" seems to be lacking something.

A sense of humor, for instance. The end of the world is just no fun anymore. The dystopian stories that I encountered as a young teenager were often grim, but at the same time, there were many that took their lead from Dr. Strangelove, the funniest and most potent movie of the Cold War, and treated the threat of thermonuclear Armageddon as pure black comedy. Douglas Adams's *The Hitch-hiker's Guide to the Galaxy* isn't usually classified as dystopian, but it starts with the demolition of the Earth and the death of almost the whole human race, and still manages to be wildly funny. That element of satire and graveyard humor seems largely absent from the current crop of dystopias. Where's the modern, YA equivalent of Kurt Vonnegut? The apocalypse, we seem to be teaching young readers, is something that you have to take seriously. . . .

8   More worrying still is the absence of any counterbalance. Half of the science-fiction stories that I read in my teens seemed to predict terrible ends for us all, but the other half concerned themselves with bright, shining futures in which human beings would spread out among the stars, having overcome such trifling problems as poverty, war, and racial prejudice. As far as I'm aware, no one in the YA field is writing things like that anymore: if they are, their books have yet to achieve the same high profile as the dystopias. It's as if optimism has become so hopelessly quaint that we can no longer allow ourselves even to imagine a better future.

YA authors didn't invent this profound pessimism, of course: predictions of catastrophe pervade modern Western culture. Politicians and the media thrive on a culture of fear, and love to make our flesh creep by inflating remote threats like terrorism or swine flu to apocalyptic proportions. The environmental movement has gloomy sci-fi scenarios of its own to peddle and seems increasingly intolerant of any suggestion that progress is good, or that science might provide us with ways to ease the world's ills. I frequently meet young people nowadays who have been led to believe that human beings are inherently wasteful and stupid, and (chillingly) that there are Far Too Many Of Us. It's hardly surprising that, when they picture the future, they tend to see themselves snacking on refried schnauzer in a tar-paper shack.

Yet the world in which we now live is actually far closer to the hi-tech futures that the optimists of the 1950s and '60s envisioned than to any of the blighted wastelands that the doomsayers predicted. It's true that many of science fiction's sunnier visions seem naive today: racism and war persist; spindle-shaped rocket ships can't carry us to Mars, and I still haven't got the jet pack and flying car that I remember being promised. Yet in many ways, our society is kinder and safer, and some of today's technologies are far more impressive than flying cars. Some of this may have come about precisely because the children of earlier generations were excited by fictional visions of a brighter future and ended up as the scientists and social reformers, innovative engineers and hi-tech entrepreneurs who helped to make it happen. What sort of future awaits a society whose young people are taught that there's nothing to look forward to but decline and disaster, and that decline and disaster may be all that they deserve?

It's entirely natural that YA authors should try to reflect the fears about the future that young readers feel, but I'm coming to think that we also have a duty to challenge the prevailing pessimism of mainstream culture. Dystopian fiction, while appearing to offer a radical criticism of modern society, is often deeply conservative. Portraying our civilization as doomed, it looks to the past for answers—to the rugged individualism of the frontier spirit, or a meek retreat to preindustrial ways of life. I'm happy to celebrate and recommend the excellent dystopian novels that I mentioned above, and I'm certain that there are many others every bit as fine, but I think what we could really use right now are a few utopian novels to set beside them.

PERSONAL RESPONSE

Write in response to Reeve's observation in paragraph 9 that young people today are pessimistic about their future. Do you agree with him? Why or why not?

QUESTIONS FOR CLASS OR SMALL-GROUP DISCUSSION

1. In paragraph 1, Reeve asks: "What is it about these grim futures that young readers find so appealing?" How does he answer that question? To what extent do you agree with him?

2. What is it that Reeve feels is missing from today's young adult dystopian fiction? What faults does he find with it?

3. Explain whether you accept Reeve's assertion in paragraph 11 that authors "have a duty to challenge the prevailing pessimism of mainstream culture." Are you convinced by his argument that dystopian fiction does a disservice to young people and that writers need to produce utopian fiction as a counterbalance?

4. If you have read or seen film versions of any of the novels that Reeve mentions in his essay, use them as examples to support an analysis of Reeve's central idea. Whether you have read or seen such works, assess the argument that Reeve makes. Does he have a clear thesis? Are his examples convincing? Is the essay well organized?

PERSPECTIVES ON POPULAR CULTURE
Suggested Writing Topics

1. Argue your position on Will Wright's statement in "Dream Machines" that "games are not just entertainment but a vehicle for self-expression."

2. Will Wright in "Dream Machines" wrote in 2006 that "soon games will start to build simple models of us, the players. . . . Over time, these games will become able to modify themselves to better 'fit' each individual." Using the example of a specific video game (or more than one, if you like), argue whether you believe that games today have achieved that goal.

3. Argue in support of or against the statement in Will Wright's "Dream Machines" that video games "benefit . . . culture."

4. Rock, hip-hop, rap, and other musical groups have long been able to whip a crowd into an almost hysterical frenzy during their performances. If you have ever seen or experienced such a phenomenon, describe what happened and explore why you think music has that kind of control over people's emotions.

5. Refute or support this statement in Jennifer McLune's "Hip-Hop's Betrayal of Black Women": "Sexism and homophobia saturate hip-hop culture and any deviation from these forms of bigotry is made marginal to its most dominant and lucrative expressions" (paragraph 5). Use examples from song lyrics to support your position.

6. If you are familiar with the dystopian fiction that Philip Reeve discusses in "The Worst Is Yet to Come," explain whether you agree with him by using examples from works you have read.

7. Write a detailed analysis of a dystopian novel or film such as the ones mentioned in Philip Reeve's "The Worst Is Yet to Come." Do not simply give a plot summary but concentrate on using details from the work to support a central idea or thesis that takes a position on the world view or view of the future portrayed in the work.

8. Do a detailed analysis of a hip-hop, rap, or other song that you are familiar with. What images does it portray? What message, if any, does it send? How do the lyrics work to make the song artistically good?

9. Analyze the lyrics of a song that you believe to be socially responsible or that comments on a current social issue.

10. Analyze your involvement with a video game that you find particularly compelling.

11. Argue for or against extending the First Amendment's guarantee of freedom of speech to include violent or offensive lyrics in hip-hop, rock, or other forms of music. Consider how far you think First Amendment's protection of free speech should be allowed to go.

12. Drawing on any of the readings in this chapter, argue in support of or against the statement that music or video games influence violent behavior in individuals.

Research Topics

1. Argue in support of or against the view that rock or hip-hop music is violent or that it is a menace to society. Research the development of hip-hop or gangsta rap music, taking into consideration Jennifer McLune's "Hip-Hop's Betrayal of Black Women."

2. Research the subject of the influence of violent video games on behavior, drawing on Karen Sternheimer's "Do Video Games Kill?" Note the list of resources that she mentions at the end of her article.

3. Use an approach similar to that of Karen Sternheimer in "Do Video Games Kill?" to analyze newspaper coverage of a school shooting, such as the student massacre at Virginia Tech in April 2007 or the Sandy Hook Elementary murders in 2012.

4. Research the phenomenon of the physiological and/or psychological effects of music. Look not only for information about scientific research on the subject but also for comments or criticisms of people skeptical of such research. Weigh the evidence and arrive at your own opinion on the subject.

5. Research a particular musician, musical group, or entertainer from an earlier decade, such as the 1950s, 1960s, 1970s, 1980s, or 1990s. Find out the performer's history, the audience he or she appealed to, what distinguished him or her from others, and what his or her influence seems to have been on popular culture. Formulate your own assessment of the entertainer's significance and make that your thesis or central idea.

6. Research a particular kind of music, such as hip-hop, rap, "grunge," alternative, blues, jazz, or salsa, for the purpose of identifying its chief characteristics, the way it differs from and is influenced by other kinds of music, and its artistic merit or social significance. Include opposing viewpoints and argue your own position on its merits or significance.

7. Examine allegations of racism, sexism, and/or homophobia leveled against a particular video game, song, musician, or group, and draw your own conclusions about the fairness, appropriateness, and/or accuracy of those allegations.

8. Research the latest studies and opinion pieces on the cultural impact of dystopian fiction and draw your own conclusions about their influence on young readers of such works.

9. Research the history of a popular handheld video game, taking into consideration marketing strategy, target audience, responses of users, and/or longevity of the game.

10. Research the latest studies and opinion pieces on the cultural impact of video games, and draw your own conclusions about their importance in shaping culture.

RESPONDING TO VISUALS

Barry Downard/Ikon Images/Getty Images

Hungry wolves circling urban lobby.

1. Describe the mood created by this image. What details convey that mood?
2. What is the effect of having the perspective from right behind a close-up of the nearest wolf? What would change if the perspective were from inside the lobby looking out or from some distance away, looking at the entire scene?
3. How might the image be representative of the nature of dystopian fiction?

RESPONDING TO VISUALS

Young girl with handheld device.

1. What details of this image suggest that the child is using her imagination?
2. How does the image combine a traditional concept of "imagination" with a modern one?
3. How would the effect of the image change were the girl photographed with the butterfly wings only? How might the effect of the image change were she holding the electronic device but not wearing the wings?

Media Studies

Because of the pervasiveness of the media in American culture, critics, researchers, and others assume that it affects people in both obvious and subtle ways. Analysts are interested in how newspapers, magazines, film, television, video games, interactive computer programs, music, or the Internet influence behavior, habits, thought, and opinions. There are myriad ways that this wide range of media can influence people of all ages. For example, students of media studies may examine the effects of advertising on people's self-image, how they perceive others, what they choose to buy at the market, or which fast food restaurant to eat at. They may be interested in how certain video games, television programs, or comic books influence the behavior of children. Any research on the general topic "media studies" will lead you to dozens of directions that you can go in looking at the ways in which media influence people.

Although the subjects of the other chapters in Part Two are also "media," those chapters look at issues relating to specific media; this chapter considers broader issues relating to "the media" as a whole or several kinds of media, particularly print media. Media analysts often serve as watchdogs against threats to freedom of speech and thought. They concern themselves with social issues such as media violence, censorship in the media, biased reporting, discrimination in programming, the ways that advertising manipulates people, and the ways in which the media shape social and political discourse. They analyze the power of the media and the power behind the media.

A look at the goals and purposes of university media studies programs gives an idea of what is involved in "media studies." Such programs examine the social, cultural, political, ethical, aesthetic, legal, and economic effects of the media and are interested in the variety of contexts in which the media have influence in those areas. They cite in their rationales for their programs the proliferation of media, the interconnectedness of media on a global level, and the pervasiveness of media in our lives. Furthermore, large numbers of groups, agencies, and organizations identify themselves as "media watchers" and many are media activists. You will find both conservative and liberal, extremists and moderates on such a list. As discussed in Chapter 8 on popular culture, one particular subject that media analysts have long been interested in is violence in the media and its influence on people, especially young people. The first reading in this chapter, Henry Jenkins' "A Pedagogical Response to the Aurora Shootings: 10 Critical Questions about Fictional Representations of Violence," offers a thorough and thoughtful approach to examining fictional representations of violence, especially those that are frequently blamed when horrific events such as school shootings or other mass murders occur. His piece was published following a mass shooting in 2012 in an Aurora, Colorado, theatre at the premier showing of *The Dark Knight Rises,* though it was originally written in response to shootings at Virginia Tech in 2007. Although Jenkins' article is addressed to teachers (hence the word *pedagogical*), it is completely accessible to students to help assess the role of violence in fiction, especially in literature or film. A useful class exercise would be to select a violent novel, television show, or movie and, working in small groups, take one or two each of Jenkins' ten questions and do a class analysis of the work. Whether you work individually, in groups, or as a class, after reading this piece, you may find yourself thinking about violent fiction in popular culture with a new or different perspective.

The other three readings in this chapter focus on subjects related to print media, from the power of journalists to shape the news to decisions made by editors to the power wielded by advertisements. Media watchers know that which news stories are reported and how they are reported—what gets emphasized and what gets left out—can shape or destroy someone's reputation or bring an issue to the public's attention. Peter H. Gibbon's "The End of Admiration: The Media and the Loss of Heroes" focuses on the subject of the role that journalists play in building or destroying the reputations of public figures. He suggests that journalists, by encouraging cynicism and celebrity worship, discourage hero worship and idealism. He believes that, with the media's central bias toward bad news, journalists have made it difficult, if not impossible, for Americans to have heroes. Consider his words carefully as you read his essay. Is he on target with his critique, or does he overgeneralize or ignore positive examples to prove his point? Can you supply examples to either support or refute his argument?

Next, Brad Zembic in "Print Media and the Rabbit Hole" addresses a form of product placement that he finds annoying, if not unethical, the practice of some newspapers and magazines of passing off advertisements as editorial content. This practice, Zembic contends, is yet another reason why, according to him, the press has lost "credibility and respect." He believes that the blurring of ads and editorial content leads to reader distrust and even a kind of cynicism if readers want to "separate information from manipulation." As you read his explanation of why he is upset, consider whether you agree with him. Do you side with newspaper and magazine editors as well as advertisers themselves, or with readers like Zembic who find the practice deceptive?

Another issue of concern to media analysts is the way in which many ads imply the promise that consumer goods will give people intangibles that they crave, such as love, affection, status, or respect. Jean Kilbourne in "Jesus Is a Brand of Jeans" argues that ads promise far more than the product being advertised can give. She goes so far as to assert that "advertising creates a world view that is based upon cynicism, dissatisfaction, and craving." Ads, she maintains, are not evil but they "are often destructive." Is she overstating the power of advertising to shape people's desires and even to brainwash them? As you read her examples and assess her argument, see if you can think of other examples to either support or refute what she claims.

A PEDAGOGICAL RESPONSE TO THE AURORA SHOOTINGS: 10 CRITICAL QUESTIONS ABOUT FICTIONAL REPRESENTATIONS OF VIOLENCE

Henry Jenkins

Henry Jenkins is Provost's Professor of Communication, Journalism, and Cinematic Arts at the University of Southern California. Among his publications are dozens of periodical articles and twelve books on various aspects of the media and popular culture, beginning in 1992 with What Made Pistachio Nuts? Early Sound Comedy and the Vaudeville Aesthetic *and* Textual Poachers: Television Fans and Participatory Culture. *Among his other books are* Classical Hollywood Comedy *(1994), coedited with Kristine Brunovska Karnick;* From Barbie to Mortal Kombat: Gender and Computer Games *(1998), coedited with Justine Cassell;* Hop on Pop: The Politics and Pleasures of Popular Culture *(2003), coedited with Tara McPherson and Jane Shattuc;* Rethinking Media Change: The Aesthetics of Transition *(2003), coedited with David Thorburn;* Convergence Culture: Where Old and New Media Collide *(2006);* Fans, Bloggers and Gamers: Exploring Participatory Culture *(2006); and* Reading in a Participatory Culture *(2012). His weblog address is www.henryjenkins.org. This article was first published on his website on July 22, 2012.*

The horrifying and tragic news of the shooting in Aurora, Colorado this weekend requires some degree of reflection on our parts. As someone who found himself very much involved in the national debates surrounding the Columbine Shootings in the late 1990s, there is a terrible sense of deja vu: we all know all too well the twists and turns the national debate will take and the dangers of what happens when "moral panic" spins hopelessly out of control.

Today, I wanted to share some pedagogical materials which I developed through the New Media Literacies Project in the aftermath of the Virginia Tech shootings, where, once again, anxieties about popular culture substituted for serious reflections on the many root causes of violence in American culture.

To be extra clear, I do not think media is where this debate should be focused. The conversation needs to be centered on the root causes of violence and the need to develop a much stronger infrastructure around mental health issues in this country. But, media violence issues are often used as a distraction from serious conversations about public policies in the aftermath of such incidents. If we are going to be discussing "media violence," we need to do so with sufficient nuance to have a meaningful discussion, and ideally, we need to do so in a way which moves us from thinking about simplistic models of "media effects" towards a focus on the meanings of representations of violence as understood in the context of the work as a whole. See my essay on "The War Between Effects and Meanings" in *Fans, Bloggers, and Gamers*, for an explanation of this distinction.

4   First, I wanted to share a passage from a statement about violence I wrote for teachers, which expresses something I was unable to meaningfully communicate via Twitter in an online exchange yesterday:

> Why is violence so persistent in our popular culture? Because violence has been persistent across storytelling media of all kinds. A thorough account of violence in media would include: fairy tales such as Hansel and Gretel, oral epics such as Homer's *Iliad*, the staged violence of Shakespeare's plays, paintings of the Rape of the Sabine Women, and stained glass window representations of saints being pumped full of arrows, or, for that matter, talk show conversations about the causes of school shootings. Violence is fundamental to these various media because aggression and conflict are core aspects of human experience. We need our art to provide some moral order, to help us sort through our feelings, to provoke us to move beyond easy answers and to ask hard questions.
>
> Our current framing of media violence assumes that it most often attracts us, that it inspires imitation, whereas throughout much of human history, representations of violence were seen as morally instructive, as making it less likely that we are going to transgress against various social prohibitions. When we read the lives of saints, for example, we are invited to identify with the one suffering the violence and not the one committing it. Violence was thought to provoke empathy, which was good for the soul. Violence was thought to make moral lessons more memorable.

Moral reformers rarely take aim at mundane and banal representations of violence, though formulaic violence is pervasive in our
culture. Almost always, they go after works that are acclaimed elsewhere as art—the works of Martin Scorsese or Quentin Tarantino,
say—precisely because these works manage to get under their skin.
For some of us, this provocation gets us thinking more deeply about
the moral consequences of violence, whereas others condemn the
works themselves, unable to process the idea that such a work might
provoke us to reflect about the violence that it represents. The study
of literature offers a remarkable opportunity to engage young people
in conversations about such issues, expanding the range of stories
about violence which they encounter, introducing them to works that
encourage reflection about the human consequences of revenge and
aggression, and broadening the range of meanings they attach to such
representations.

In order to encourage such reflections in the classroom, I developed a set of
basic questions we should ask about any representation of violence. I was struck
re-reading this today that I had already written here about the role of violence
in the Batman saga, though this came out prior to the *Dark Knight* films by
Christopher Nolan.

Ten Critical Questions to Ask about Fictional Representations of Violence

1. What basic conflicts are being enacted through the violence?

    Literary critics have long identified the core conflicts that shape much
    of the world's literature: Human vs. Human, Human vs. Nature, Human vs.
    Self, and sometimes Human vs. Machine. Such conflicts spark drama. Any of
    these conflicts can erupt in violence—directly against other people, against
    the natural world, or against ourselves.

    You might ask which of these forms of conflict are most visible in con-
    temporary video games, on television, or in the cinema and why some forms
    of conflict appear more often in these media than others. For example, video
    game designers have historically found it difficult to depict characters' in-
    ternalized conflict (human vs. self), in part because contest or combat are
    central building blocks of most games.

2. Do the characters make conscious choices to engage in acts of violence? How
    do they try, through language or action, to explain and justify those choices?

    In the real world, an act of violence may erupt in a split second: one mo-
    ment, people we care about are alive; the next, they are dead. The violence
    may be random: there is no real reason why these victims were singled out
    over others; they were in the wrong place at the wrong time. Yet, works of fic-
    tion often focus our attention on moments when characters make decisions,
    often based on aspects of their personalities which they little recognize or
    control, and those choices may have repercussions that echo across the work
    as a whole.

8

The events could take a different shape, though the shape of a plot can give depicted events a sense of inevitability. Some forms of tragedy, for example, rely on the notion that characters are unable to escape their fates, no matter what choices they make, or that the final acts of violence and destruction flow logically from some "tragic flaw." In trying to make sense of a fictional representation of violence, you want to seek out moments where the characters make choices that ultimately lead towards acts of aggression or destruction. Often, authors provide those characters with rationalizations for their choices, offering some clues through their words, thoughts, or actions about why they do what they do.

At such moments, the work also often offers us alternatives to violence, other choices the characters could have made, though such choices may remain implicit rather than being explicitly stated. Different works and different genres may see these alternatives to violence as more or less plausible, attractive, or rational. So, if you are being chased by a mad man waving a chain saw in a horror film, engaging him in a conversation may not be a rational, plausible, or attractive alternative. Genre fiction constructs contexts where the protagonist has no choice but to resort to violence, though what separates heroes from villains may be their relative comfort in deploying violence to serve their own interests. In many American movies, the hero is reluctant to turn towards violence, seeing it as a last resort. By contrast, the villain may deploy violence in situations where she has other alternatives, suggesting cruelty or indifference.

In dealing with violence in video games, then, you may want to ask what options are available to the player for dealing with a certain situation. In some games, there may be no options other than violence, and the game itself may spend very little time offering the character a rationalization for such actions. It is fight or flight, kill or be killed. Many games are simply digital versions of the classic shooting galleries: the game space is designed as an arena where players can shoot it out with other players or with computer-controlled characters. In other games, there may be options that allow the protagonist to avoid violence, but they may not be emotionally satisfying; they may put the player at a significant disadvantage; they may be hard to execute. So, helping students to interpret the options available to characters in a literary fiction may help them to reflect more consciously on the more limited choices available to them as gamers.

3.   What are the consequences of the violence depicted in the work?

12   Many popular stories don't pay sufficient attention to the consequences of violence. Rambo may slaughter hundreds and yet, much as in a video game, the bodies simply disappear. We get no sense of the human costs involved in combat on such a scale. Many medieval epics consisted primarily of hack and slash battle sequences; yet, periodically, the action would stop, and the bard would enumerate the names of the dead on both sides, acknowledging that these warriors paid a price even if their actions help to establish the nation state or restore order to the kingdom. Gonzala Frasca has argued that video

games inherently trivialize violence because they operate in a world where the player can simply reboot and start over if their character dies.

In contrast, westerns follow a basic formula: the protagonist (most often male) would resort to violence to battle other aggressive forces that threaten his community; his heroic actions would restore justice and order, but the hero could not live within the order he had helped to create and would be forced to ride off into the sunset at the end of the story. Susan Sontag has written about "the Imagination of Disaster," suggesting that films about apocalyptic events often create a rough moral order in which characters are rewarded or punished based on the values they display under extreme circumstances.

4.   What power relationships, real or symbolic, does the violence suggest?

In many cases, storytellers deploy violence as a means of embodying power. We should not be surprised by this tendency given the way sociologists have characterized rape as the deployment of male power against women or lynching as the enactment of white power against blacks. Historically, wars have been seen as a way of resolving conflicts between nations through the exercise of power, while trial by combat was a means of deploying power to resolve individual conflicts and disagreements.

Media representations of violence can give viewers a seductive sense of empowerment as they watch characters who are hopelessly out-numbered triumph or they watch segments of the population who seem disempowered in the real world deploy violence to right past wrongs. Some have argued that young people play violent video games, in part, as a means of compensating for a sense of disempowerment they may feel at school.

16   Conversely, stories may encourage our sense of outrage when we see powerful groups or individuals abusing their power, whether in the form of bullies degrading their victims or nations suppressing their citizens. This abuse of power by powerful forces may prepare us for some counter-balancing exercise of power, setting up the basic moral oppositions upon which a story depends.

A key challenge will be to identify the different forms of power at play within the narrative and to map the relations between them. Which characters are in the most powerful positions and what are their sources of power? Which characters are abusing their power? What sources of power are ascribed to characters who might initially seem powerless, and to what degree is violence depicted as a means of empowerment?

5.   How graphic is the depiction of violence?

One of the limits of the study on violence in American cartoons released by the American Academy of Pediatrics is that it counts "violent acts" without considering differing degrees of stylization. In fact, children at a pretty young age—certainly by the time they reach elementary school—are capable of making at least crude distinctions between more or less realistic representations of violence. They can be fooled by media which offers ambiguous cues, but they generally read media that seems realistic very differently from media that seems cartoonish or larger than life. For that reason, they are often more emotionally disturbed by documentaries that depict predators and prey, war, or crime, than they are by the hyperbolic representations we most often are talking about when we refer to media violence.

While most of us have very limited vocabularies for discussing these different degrees of explicitness, such implicit distinctions shape the ways we respond to representations of violence within fictions. We each know what we can tolerate and tend to avoid modes of representation we find too intense or disturbing. Most ratings systems distinguish between cartoonish and realistic forms of violence. We need to guard against the assumption, however, that the more graphic forms of violence are necessarily "sick" or inappropriate. More stylized forms can make it much easier to ignore the gravity of real world violence through a process of sanitization. In some cases, more graphic depictions of violence shatter that complacency and can force us to confront the human costs of violence.

20   Literary critics have long made a distinction between showing and telling. We might extend this distinction to think about media representations of violence. An artist may ask us to directly confront the act of violence, or she may ask us to deal with its repercussions, having a character describe an event which occurred before the opening of the narrative or which took place off stage. Some very famous examples of media violence—such as the torture sequences in *Reservoir Dogs* or *Pulp Fiction*—pull the camera away at the moments of peak intensity, counting on the viewer's imagination to fill in what happens, often based on cues from the soundtrack, or in the case of *Pulp Fiction*, the splattering of blood from off-camera.

6.   What function does the violence serve in the narrative?

Critics often complain about "gratuitous violence." The phrase has been used so often that we can lose touch with what it means. According to the dictionary, "gratuitous" means "being without apparent reason, cause, or justification." So, before we can decide if an element in a fictional work is gratuitous, we have to look more closely at why it is present (its motivation) and what purposes it serves (its function).

Keep in mind that we are not talking here about why the character performs the violent act but rather why the artist includes it in the work. An artwork might depict senseless killings, as occur at certain moments in *No Country for Old Men* where the killer is slaughtering people seemingly at random. This doesn't necessarily mean that the violence is "gratuitous" since in this case, the violence sets the action of the story into motion, and the work is very interested in how other characters react to the threat posed by this senseless violence. There is artistic motivation for including the violence, even if the directors, the Coen Brothers, are uninterested in the killer's psychological motives.

An element in a work of fiction may be motivated on several different levels: it may be motivated realistically, in the sense that a story about contemporary urban street gangs might be expected to depict violence as part of their real world experience; it might be motivated generically, in the sense that people going to see a horror movie expect to see a certain amount of gore and bloody mayhem; it may be motivated thematically, in the sense that an act of violence may force characters to take the measure of their own values and ethical commitments; it may be motivated symbolically, in the sense that a character dreams about performing violence and those dreams offer us a window into his or her thinking process. In each case, the violence has a different motivation, even though the actions depicted may be relatively similar.

24   By the same token, we might ask what functions an act of violence plays in the work. One way to answer that question is to imagine how the work would be different if this element were not included. Would the story have the same shape? Would the characters behave in the same way? Would the work have the same emotional impact? Some acts of violence motivate the actions of the story; some bring about a resolution in the core conflict; still others mark particular steps in the trajectory of the plot; and in some rare cases, the violent acts may indeed be gratuitous, in that their exclusion would change little or nothing in our experience of the work.

But keep in mind that the violence which disturbs us the most on first viewing is not necessarily gratuitous and is often violence which has ramifications throughout the rest of the story. Describing a scene as "gratuitous" is easy, especially when it shortcuts the process of engaging more critically with the structure and messages of the work in question.

7. What perspective(s) does the work offer us towards the character engaging in violence?

Media theorists have spent a great deal of time trying to determine what we mean when we say we identify with a character in a fictional work. At the most basic level, it means we recognize the character; we distinguish the fictional figure from others depicted in the same work. From there, we may mean that the work devotes a great deal of time and space to depicting the actions of this particular character. Typically, the more time we spend with a character, the more likely we are to see the world from her point of view. Yet, this is not always the case. We may be asked to observe and judge characters, especially if their actions and the values they embody fall outside of the stated perspective of the work. We may grow close to a character only to be pushed away again when the character takes an action we find reprehensible and unjustifiable.

There is a distinction to be drawn here between the structuring of narrative point of view and the structuring of moral judgments on the character. Part of what helps us to negotiate between the two is the degree to which we are given access to the thoughts and feelings of the character (and in the case of an audio-visual work, the degree to which we see the world from his or her optical point of view).

28   Consider, for example, the use of first person camera in a work like *Jaws* where scenes are sometimes shot from the perspective of the shark as it swims through the water approaching its human prey. At such moments, we feel fear and dread for the human victims, not sympathy for the sharks.

Filmmakers quickly learned to manipulate this first person camera, some-times duplicating the same camera movement, tricking us into thinking the monster is approaching, and then, demonstrating this to be a false alarm. So, it is possible to follow characters but not get inside their head, and it is pos-sible to have access to characters' thoughts and still not share their moral perspective.

And indeed, all of these relationships may shift in the course of reading a book as we may feel the character's actions are justified up until a certain point and then cross an implicit line where they become monstrous. Homer shares Ulysses's point of view throughout much of the *Odyssey*, but we still are inclined to pull back from him at a certain point as he brings bloody ven-geance upon Penelope's suitors in the final moments of the epic.

We might think about a common device in television melodrama where we've seen a scene of conflict between two characters who believe they are alone and then at the end, the camera pulls back to show the reaction of a previously undisclosed third-party figure who has been watching or over-hearing the action. Such moments invite us to reassess what we've just seen from another vantage point.

In video games, the category of "first person shooters" has been espe-cially controversial with critics concerned about the implications of players taking on the optical point of view of a character performing acts of violence; often, critics argue, the player doesn't just watch a violent act but is actively encouraged to participate. Gamers will sometimes refer to their characters in the third person ("he") and sometimes in the first person ("I"), pronoun slip-pages that suggest some confusions brought about by the intense identifica-tion players sometimes feel towards their avatars.

32   Yet, even here, we need to be careful to distinguish between following pattern, optical point of view, and moral attitude. In games, we typically remain attached to a single character whom we control, and thus we have a very strong following pattern. In first person shooters, we see the action through the optical point of view of that character, though we may feel no less connected to the characters we control in a third person game (where we see the full body of the character from an external perspective). The Second Person video game confounds our normal expectations about optical point of view, inviting us to see the action from an unfamiliar perspective, and thus it may shake up our typical ways of making sense of the action.

Those who have spent time watching players play and interviewing them about their game experiences find that in fact, identification works in complex ways, since the player is almost always thinking tactically about the choices that will allow her to beat the game. Winning often involves stepping outside a simple emotional or moral connection with an individual character. Players are encouraged to think of the game as a system, not unlike taking a more omniscient perspective in reading a work of fiction, even as other aspects of the game's formal structure may encourage them to feel a close alignment with a particular character whose actions are shaped by their own decisions.

Game designer Will Wright (*The Sims, Sim City*) has argued that games may have a unique ability to make players experience guilt for the choices their characters have made in the course of the action. When we watch a film or read a novel, we always reserve the ability to pull back from a character we may otherwise admire and express anger over choices he or she has made or to direct that anger towards the author who is reflecting a world view we find repugnant. Yet, in a game, because players are making choices, however limited the options provided by the designer, they feel some degree of culpability. And a game designer has the ability to force them to reflect back on those choices and thus to have an experience of guilt.

8. What roles (aggressor, victim, other) does the protagonist play in the depiction of violence?

Many of the media texts which have been most controversial are works which bring the viewer into the head of the aggressor—from the gangster films of the 1930s through contemporary films like *Natural Born Killers* and *American Psycho*, television series like *Dexter* and *The Sopranos*, and games like *Grand Theft Auto*. All of these works are accused of glamorizing crime.

As we've already discussed, we need to distinguish between following pattern, optical and psychological point of view, and moral alignment. Many of these works bring us closer to such figures precisely so that we can feel a greater sense of horror over their anti-social behavior. Consider, for example, *Sweeney Todd*, which depicts a murderous barber and his partner, a baker, who turns the bodies of his victims into meat pies she sells to her customers. We read the story from their perspective and we are even encouraged to laugh at their painful and heartless puns about the potential value of different people as sources for human meat. Yet, our strong identification with these characters allows us to feel greater horror and sorrow over the final consequences of their actions.

At the other end of spectrum, literary scholar James Cain describes how a whole genre of literary works arose in the Middle Ages around representations of saints as victims:

> The persecutions of early Christians gave rise to an extraordinary collection of tales commemorating the supernatural endurance of victims who willingly suffered heinous atrocities and ultimately gave their lives bearing witness to their faith. From accounts of the stoning of the first martyr, St. Stephen, to the broiling of St. Lawrence on an open grill, the strapping of St. Catherine to a mechanical wheel of torture, the gouging-out of St. Lucy's eyeballs, the slitting-open of St. Cecilia's throat, the slicing-off of St. Agatha's breasts, the feeding of St. Perpetua and St. Felicitas to the lions, the piercing of St. Sebastian with a barrage of arrows—the graphic brutality undoubtedly exceeds even the most violent images in media today. . . . The strong emotional responses these images conjured up in their observers were deliberately designed to produce lasting impressions in people's memories and imaginations, to enable further reflection.

Far from being corrupting, representations of violence are seen as a source of moral instruction, in part because of our enormous sense of empathy for the saints' ability to endure suffering.

Most American popular culture negotiates between the two extremes. In the case of superheroes, for example, their origin stories often include moments of victimization and loss, as when young Bruce Wayne watches his mother and father get killed before deciding to devote his life to battling crime as the Batman, or when Peter Parker learns that "with great power comes great responsibility" the hard way when his lack of responsibility results in the death of his beloved uncle. In the world of the superheroes, the villains are also often victims of acts of violence, as when the Joker's face (and psyche) are scarred by being pushed into a vat of acid. The superhero genre tends to suggest that we have a choice how we respond to trauma and loss. For some, we emerge stronger and more ethically committed, while for others, we are devastated and bitter, turning towards anti-social actions and self-destruction.

40 A work like David Cronenberg's *A History of Violence* is particularly complex, since we learn more and more about the character's past as we move more deeply into the narrative and since the protagonist moves from bystander to victim and then reverses things, taking his battle to the gangsters, and along the way, becomes increasingly sadistic in his use of violence. Cronenberg wants to have the viewer rethinking and reassessing the meaning of violence in almost every scene of the film.

The filmmaker Jean Renoir famously said, "Every character has his reason." His point was that if we shift point of view, we can read the aggressor as victim or vice versa. Few people see themselves as cruel; most find ways to justify and rationalize acts of even the rawest aggression. And a literary work may invite us to see the same action from several different perspectives, shifting our identifications and empathy in the process. Even when the artist doesn't fill in these other perspectives, critics and spectators can step back from a scene, put themselves in the heads of the various characters, and imagine what the world might look like from their point of view. Consider the novel and stage play, *Wicked*, which rereads *The Wizard of Oz* from the vantage point of the Wicked Witch and portrays Dorothy as a mean spirited trespasser who has murdered the witch's sister.

9. What moral frame (pro-social, antisocial, ambiguous) does the work place around the depicted violence?

Some fictions focus on violence as the performance of duty. The police, for example, are authorized to use certain sanctioned forms of violence in the pursuit of criminals and in the name of maintaining law and order. Some of these—for example, the television series *The Shield*—find great drama in exploring cops who "cross the line," seeing brutality or unnecessary use of force as a symptom of a police force no longer accountable to its public.

Similarly, much fiction centers on themes of war, with works either endorsing or criticizing military actions as forms of violence in the service of the state and of the public. There is a long tradition of national epics, going back to classical times, which depict the struggles to establish or defend the nation with violence often linked to patriotic themes and values. In the American tradition, this function was once performed by the western, which depicts the process by which "savagery" gave way to "civilization," though more recent westerns have sometimes explored the slaughter of the Indians from a more critical perspective as a form of racial cleansing.

44

So, even within genres that depict the use of force in pro-social or patriotic terms, there are opportunities for raising questions about the nature and value of violence as a tool for bringing about order and stability.

On the other hand, many stories depict violence as anti-social, focusing on criminals, gangsters, or terrorists, who operate outside the law and in opposition to the state or the community. The cultural critic Robert Warshow discusses the very different representations of "men with guns" found in the western, the gangster film, and the war movie, suggesting that all three genres have strong moral codes which explain when it is justifiable to use force and depicting what happens to characters who transgress those norms. The westerner cannot live in the community he has helped to create through his use of force; the gangster (see *Scarface* for example) frequently is destroyed by the violence he has abused to meet his personal desires and ambitions; and the hero returns home at the end of the war, albeit often psychologically transformed by the violence he has experienced.

Just as fictions that seem to depict the pro-social use of violence may contain critiques of the abuse of power by the police or the horrors of war, fictions which depict the anti-social use of violence may include strong critiques of the gangster lifestyle. Robin Woods has famously summed up the basic formula of the horror films as "normality is threatened by monstrosity." In such a formula, there are three important terms to consider—what constitutes normality, what constitutes the monstrous, and what relationship is being posited between the two. Some horror films are highly moralistic, seeking to destroy anything which falls outside of narrow norms; others use the monster as the means of criticizing and questioning the limits of normality.

In many works, there is a core ambiguity about the nature of the violence being depicted. We may be asked to identify with several characters who have different moral codes and thus who see their actions in different terms. Our judgments may shift in the course of the narrative. The characters may understand their actions as pro-social even as the author invites us to read them as antisocial. Or the work may be saying that there's no simple distinction to be drawn between different forms of violence: it's all equally destructive. We might even imagine a truly nihilistic work in which all violence is justified. It isn't that we want students to fit works into simple either/or categories here. Rather, asking this question can force them towards a more complex understanding of the moral judgments the work is making—as opposed to simply those being made by the characters—about the value of the violence to society.

10. What tone does the work take towards the represented violence?

48   We've already seen the importance of distinguishing between the forms of violence being depicted in a work and the position the work takes on those actions. We've seen that identification with a protagonist is fragile and shifting across a work, so that we may sometimes feel a strong emotional bond with a character for much of the story and yet still feel estranged from her when the author reveals some darker side of her personality.

A work may depict the pro-social use of violence and either endorse or criticize the Establishment being depicted. A work may depict anti-social forms of violence in ways which are conservative in their perspective on those groups who use force outside legal contexts. Or a work may depict forms of violence that are hard to classify in those terms and thus invite readers to struggle with that ambiguity.

Similarly, we need to consider the range of different emotional responses a work may evoke through its use of violent images. Some fictions about violence, such as the action sequences in an Indiana Jones movie, may thrill us with exciting, larger than life heroics. Some, such as *Saving Private Ryan* or *Glory*, may appeal to our sense of national pride towards the brave men who gave their lives defending their country. Some, such as the scene in *Old Yeller* where the boy is forced to shoot his dog, may generate enormous empathy as we feel sorry for the characters who are forced to deploy or suffer violence against their will. Some, such as depictions of human suffering around the world, may seek to shock us into greater social consciousness and civic action. Some, such as slapstick comedy, may encourage us to laugh at highly stylized depictions of physical aggression. And still others, such as *Saw* or *Nightmare on Elm Street*, may provoke a sense of horror or disgust as we put ourselves through a series of intense emotional shocks in the name of entertainment.

We cannot understand what representations of violence mean, then, without paying attention to issues of tone. Popular texts tend to create broadly recognizable and easily legible signs of tone, though many of the works of filmmakers like Tarantino or Scorsese generate controversy because they adopt a much more complex and multivalent tone than we expect from other texts in the same genre. We might compare Tarantino or Scorsese to certain writers—William Faulkner or Flannery O'Connor come to mind— who also seek complicated or contradictory emotional reactions to grotesque and violent elements in their narratives.

PERSONAL RESPONSE

Jenkins refers to "'moral panic'" (paragraph 1) and a short time later, in the quoted passage in paragraph 4, to "moral reformers" and "the moral consequences of violence." To what degree have you considered the moral issues attached to fictional representations of violence? Are there moral consequences to such depictions, or is Jenkins exaggerating or overreacting?

QUESTIONS FOR CLASS OR SMALL-GROUP DISCUSSION

1. In paragraph 3, Jenkins writes: "To be extra clear, I do not think media is where this debate should be focused." How well do you think he supports that statement? To what extent do you agree with him on this point?

2. In question 6, Jenkins addresses the issue of gratuitous violence. Explain in your own words what he says about that and then comment on whether you agree with him.

3. In question 7, Jenkins discusses the matter of identifying with a character in a fictional work. Can you give an example from your own reading or viewing to illustrate what he means by "identifying" with a fictional character?

4. In question 8, Jenkins seems to be defending various media depicting violence—film, television, and games—against the charge that they glamorize violence. State in your own words what Jenkins' rationale for his defense is and to what extent you agree with his position on this point.

5. Select any question not already discussed and state in your own words what you understand Jenkins to mean by it. Give examples, if possible, from your own experience to support or refute his point,

THE END OF ADMIRATION: THE MEDIA AND THE LOSS OF HEROES

Peter H. Gibbon

Peter H. Gibbon is a senior Research Fellow at Boston University's School of Education. He has done extensive research on the educational systems of Japan, China, and Germany and is coauthor, with Peter J. Gomes, of A Call to Heroism: Renewing America's Vision of Greatness *(2002), about the disappearance of public heroes in American society. His articles have appeared in magazines such as* Newsweek *and* Time *and in a number of newspapers, including the New York Times, Los Angeles Times, Philadelphia Inquirer, and Washington Post. He has also made guest appearances on many television and radio programs and travels the country talking to both general audiences and students about heroism. This piece, based on a talk he delivered at a seminar on the history of journalism hosted by Hillsdale College, appeared in the May 1999 issue of* Imprimis.

I travel around the country talking to Americans about the loss of public heroes. I point out that New York City's Hall of Fame for Great Americans attracts only a few thousand visitors each year, while Cleveland's Rock and Roll Hall of Fame draws over one million.

Reprinted by permission from Imprimis, a publication of Hillsdale College.

I describe a 25-foot stained glass window in the Cathedral of St. John the Divine—dedicated in the 1920s to four athletes who exemplified good character and sportsmanship—and I offer a quick list of titles of contemporary books on sports: *Shark Attack,* on the short and bitter career of college coaches; *Meat on the Hoof,* about the mercenary world of professional football; *Personal Fouls,* on the mistreatment of college athletes; *The Courts of Babylon,* on the venality of the women's professional tennis circuit; and *Public Heroes, Private Felons,* on college athletes who break the law.

I contrast two westerns: *High Noon,* which won four Academy Awards in 1959, and *Unforgiven,* which was voted "Best Picture" in 1992. The hero of *High Noon,* Will Kane, is a U.S. marshal. The hero of *Unforgiven,* Will Munny, is a reformed killer and alcoholic reduced to pig farming.

4   I mention that our best-selling postage stamps feature Elvis Presley and Marilyn Monroe and that our most popular TV show was, until it left the air recently, *Seinfeld.*

I remind my audiences that Thomas Jefferson is now thought of as the president with the slave mistress and Mozart as the careless genius who liked to talk dirty.

I add that a recent biography of Mother Teresa is titled *The Missionary Position.*

I offer some reasons for the disappearance of public heroes. Athletes have given up on being team players and role models. Popular culture is often irreverent, sometimes deviant. Revisionist historians present an unforgiving, skewed picture of the past. Biographers are increasingly hostile toward their subjects. Social scientists stridently assert that human beings are not autonomous but are conditioned by genes and environment.

8   Hovering in the background are secularism, which suggests that human beings are self-sufficient and do not need God, and modernism—a complex artistic and literary movement that repudiates structure, form, and conventional values.

Finally, in an age of instant communication, in which there is little time for reflection, accuracy, balance or integrity—the media creates the impression that sleaze is everywhere, that nothing is sacred, that no one is noble, and that there are no heroes.

Nothing to Admire

Radio, television, and computers offer news with such speed that newspaper and magazine circulation has plummeted, and readers have smaller vocabularies. I recently wrote an op-ed piece syndicated in several newspapers. My title, "*Nil Admirari,*" which means "nothing to admire," came from the Roman lyric poet Horace.

None of the newspapers used the title, and one editor reminded me that newspaper stories are now aimed at a sixth-grade reading level.

12   In the Age of Information, the image reigns. There are 81 television sets for every 100 Americans. In the typical household, the television is on six hours a day. Television has become our chief source of local and national news, and broadcast

journalists have become more prominent and more powerful than columnists. There used to be three channels. Now, there are over one hundred. When we weary of television channels, we can turn to countless radio stations, videotapes, and web pages.

This explosion of information means we now have a vast menu of choices that allows us to be transported to many different worlds and provides us with educational opportunities undreamed of thirty years ago. It also means that we spend more time in front of television and computer screens and less time reading to our children. It is no wonder that our children have shorter attention spans and smaller vocabularies.

A Wired World

Along with this vast menu of choices is the absence of gatekeepers. As parents, we need to realize that there are dangers that come with too many choices and too few guides. We need to remind ourselves that their well-being depends not only on nutrition, sunlight, and exercise; on friendship, work, and love; but also on *how they see the world*. Subtly and powerfully, the media helps shape their world view.

The media has a liberal bias, but its *central* bias is toward bad news. Accidents, crimes, conflict, and scandal are interesting. Normality is boring. The prevalence of bad news and the power of the image encourage children—and us—to overestimate the chance of an accident, the risk of disease, the rate of violence, the frequency of marital infidelity. The average policeman, for example, never fires a gun in action, and most Americans are monogamous.

16   In a wired world with no restraint, the media can misinform us. It can also make us suspicious, fearful, and cynical. It can lead us to lose faith in our nation, repudiate our past, question our leaders, and cease to believe in progress.

We know the worst about everyone instantly. Over and over again, we see clips of George Bush vomiting, Dan Quayle misspelling "potato," Gerald Ford tripping.

No longer do we want our child to grow up and become president. We harbor dark suspicions about the personal conduct of scoutmasters, priests, and coaches. We think army sergeants harass their subordinates. We have trouble calling any public figure a hero. A wired world becomes a world without heroes, a world of *nil admirari*, with no one to admire.

Americans tell pollsters the country is in moral and spiritual decline. In the midst of peace and prosperity, with equality increasing and health improving, we are sour. With our military powerful and our culture ascendant, pessimism prevails.

Crusaders or Rogues?

20 Should we blame journalists? It is certainly tempting. Just as we blame teachers for the poor performance of students, so we can blame reporters for the nation's malaise.

But just as teachers are not responsible for poverty and disintegrating families, journalists are not responsible for satellites, fiber optic cables, transistors, and microprocessors—the inventions that make possible instant information. Journalists did not cause the sexual revolution. They did not invent celebrity worship or gossip. Nor did they create leaders who misbehave and let us down.

At the same time, in the world of *nil admirari,* journalists are not innocent, and they know it. Roger Rosenblatt, a veteran of the *Washington Post, Time, Life,* and the *New York Times Magazine,* says, "My trade of journalism is sodden these days with practitioners who seem incapable of admiring others or anything." In his memoir, former presidential press secretary and ABC News senior editor Pierre Salinger writes, "No reporter can be famous unless they have brought someone down." And *New Yorker* writer Adam Gopnik comments, "The reporter used to gain status by dining with his subjects; now he gains status by dining on them."

Journalists can also be greedy. Eager for money, some reporters accept handsome speaking fees from organizations they are supposed to be covering. Some are dishonest, making up quotations, even inventing stories. No longer content with anonymity, many reporters seek celebrity, roaming the talk shows and becoming masters of the sound bite. They write autobiographies and give interviews to other journalists.

24   Just as our president is enamored of Hollywood, so are our journalists. Larry King recently spent a full hour interviewing singer Madonna. *Sixty Minutes* devoted much of a show to "bad boy" actor Sean Penn. Actors, supermodels, and musicians are no longer just entertainers. They are treated like philosopher–kings, telling us how to live. In a recent interview, actress Sharon Stone, star of *Basic Instinct,* advises parents to make condoms available to their teenagers.

Aggressive and anxious for ratings, television news shows feature hosts and guests who come armed with hardened opinions. Many are quick to judge and prone to offer easy solutions for complex problems. "Talking heads" argue, yell, interrupt, and rarely make concessions.

But in the world of *nil admirari,* journalists are now reviled more often than revered. In the 1980s, muckraker Steven Brill skewered lawyers. In his new magazine, *Brill's Content,* he lambastes journalists. In *Right in the Old Gazoo,* former Wyoming Senator Alan Simpson accuses journalists of becoming "lazy, complacent, sloppy, self-serving, self-aggrandizing, cynical and arrogant beyond belief." In *Breaking the News,* writer James Fallows comments that while movies once portrayed journalists as crusaders, they are now portrayed as rogues "more loathsome than . . . lawyers, politicians, and business moguls."

How much of this is new?

28   Since the founding of America, reporters have been harsh critics of public figures. George Washington did not like reading in pamphlets that the essence of his education had been "gambling, reveling, horse racing and horse whipping." Thomas Jefferson did not relish the label "effeminate." Abraham Lincoln did not appreciate being portrayed by cartoonists as a baboon.

Throughout our history, reporters have also received harsh criticism. Just after the Civil War, abolitionist Harriet Beecher Stowe claimed the press had become so vicious that no respectable American man would ever again run for president. In 1870, the British critic and poet Matthew Arnold toured America and concluded, "If one were searching for the best means . . . to kill in a whole nation . . . the feeling for what is elevated, one could not do better than take the American newspaper." At the turn of the century, novelist Henry James condemned what he called the "impudence [and] the shamelessness of the newspaper and the interviewer." In the early decades of the 20th century, "yellow journalism," "muckraking," and "debunking" became household words to describe newspaper stories that exaggerated and distorted events to make them more sensational.

Nor is the media's fascination with celebrities new. When silent screen idol Rudolph Valentino and educational reformer Charles William Eliot died within a day of each other in 1926, high-minded Americans complained that the press devoted too many columns to a celebrity and too few to a hero of education. Between 1925 and 1947, millions of Americans listened to Walter Winchell's radio program, *The Lucky Strike Hour* and read his column in the *New York Mirror*. Winchell hung out at the Stork Club, collecting gossip about celebrities and politicians from tipsters. He urged all newspaper offices to post these words on their walls: "Talk of virtue and your readers will become bored. Hint of gossip and you will secure perfect attention."

In short, media critics have always called reporters cynical. Reporters have always collected gossip and featured celebrities. And high-minded Americans have always warned that journalists could lower the nation's moral tone.

An Empire of Information

32 From the outset, thoughtful critics conceded that journalists had an obligation to inform and expose. But those same critics were afraid that reporters would eliminate privacy and slander leaders; that by repeating gossip and emphasizing crime and corruption, newspapers would coarsen citizens; and that journalists would become more influential than ministers, novelists, professors, and politicians. They were right.

Journalists *have* become more powerful than ministers, novelists, professors, and politicians. They preside over an empire of information unimaginable to our ancestors—an empire that reaches small villages in India and can change governments in China; an empire characterized by staggering choice, variety, and technological sophistication.

An empire of information ruled by the modern media *has* eliminated privacy. With recorders and cameras, reporters freely enter dugouts, locker rooms, board rooms, hotel rooms. There are neither secrets nor taboos. Some listen in on private telephone conversations and sift through garbage for incriminating documents.

Early critics were also right to worry that journalists could contribute to a decline in taste and judgment, could destroy the feeling for the elevated, could eliminate appetite for the admirable. The empire they have created is slick, quick, hard-hitting, entertaining, and inescapable. It makes us more knowledgeable, but it also leaves us overwhelmed, convinced that the world is a sleazy place, and mistrustful of authority and institutions. It all but extinguishes our belief in heroism.

Hope for the Future

36   Are there reasons to be hopeful about the future of America and the future of the media? I believe there are. Intent on exposing our faults, we forget what we do well. America is much better and healthier than the country portrayed in the media and in pessimistic opinion polls. The American people are basically hardworking, idealistic, compassionate, and religious.

American journalism is still biased, but it is slowly becoming more balanced. We have the *Washington Times* as well as the *Washington Post, U.S. News & World Report* as well as *Newsweek, National Review* as well as the *Nation,* the *Wall Street Journal* as well as the *New York Times.* We have prominent conservative and liberal commentators.

In the late 1990s, newspaper and television journalists have become more self-critical. Some recognize the need to become less cynical, less greedy, less celebrity oriented, less combative; and a few recognize the need to report the normal and the good rather than only the sensational and the deviant.

Reporters, editors, and publishers are influential, but they are not all-powerful. In America, the consumer is king. We choose our sources of information just as we purchase cars and potato chips. When CNN interrupted its coverage of the Lorena Bobbitt trial to report on the Chernobyl nuclear disaster, the number of angry callers caused the network's switchboard to crash. Reporters could be more courageous and less concerned with profits, but American citizens could be more high-minded.

40   In the Age of Information, journalists and citizens face the same challenges. We need to study the past so as not to become arrogant, to remember the good so as not to become cynical, and to recognize America's strengths so as not to dwell on her weaknesses. We need to be honest and realistic without losing our capacity for admiration—and to be able to embrace complexity without losing our faith in the heroic.

PERSONAL RESPONSE

Gibbon states that "we have trouble calling any public figure a hero" (paragraph 16). Are there public figures whom you admire as heroes, and if so, what makes them heroic? If you cannot think of any public hero whom you would regard as a hero, explore reasons why this is so.

QUESTIONS FOR CLASS OR SMALL-GROUP DISCUSSION

1. Assess the effectiveness of the series of contrasts that Gibbon makes in the first six paragraphs. Then discuss the explanations he gives to account for them in the next several paragraphs. Do you accept his explanations? Are there any that you would challenge?

2. Gibbon alleges that journalists can be greedy and dishonest, seeking celebrity status for themselves (paragraphs 24 and 25). To what extent do you agree with Gibbon? Can you give examples of journalists who either support or refute his claims?

3. In paragraph 34, Gibbon briefly summarizes both positive and negative views of journalists over time, with emphasis on the negative. He concludes that those who feared the worst "were right." To what extent do you agree with Gibbon that the worst fears of critics of journalists have been realized?

4. Explain whether you agree with Gibbon in this passage from paragraph 37: "The empire they created is slick, quick, hard-hitting, entertaining, and inescapable. It makes us more knowledgeable, but it also leaves us overwhelmed, convinced that the world is a sleazy place, and mistrustful of authority and institutions. It all but extinguishes our belief in heroism"? Do you think that he is wrong or unfair in any part of this passage?

PRINT MEDIA AND THE RABBIT HOLE

Brad Zembic

Brad Zembic lives in Vancouver, British Columbia. This article appeared in the Analysis/Commentary/Research issue of Media Ethics Magazine, *Spring 2010, with the subtitle "You'd be as mad as a hatter to believe the printed word is beyond reproach."*

Without going into statistics, it seems very clear to me that the press cannot tolerate much further loss of credibility and respect. The *Los Angeles Times* recently[1] raised the ire of its readers and journalists who objected to its front page being used as a wrap-around—a commercial billboard. It sported a full-color headshot of Johnny Depp in his role as the Mad Hatter in Disney's new interpretation of *Alice in Wonderland*. The newspaper went to some length to ensure readers didn't merely flip the page in search of news; the photo was superimposed on old and fake editorial content— which gave time for Depp's maniacal image to become etched onto readers' unconscious things-to-do list. It appears to me there's more deception in print media these days than in a Shakespearean play, and trusted publications are in danger of becoming "shoppers" or "flyers" in drag.

Reprinted from *Media Ethics Magazine*, Spring 2010 by permission of the author.

Advertising has its place. Companies need to peddle their wares. But I like to have the choice of whether or not I want to be sold to. I'd like to pick up a newspaper or magazine feeling confident that what I'm reading is trustworthy news or information that isn't bundled with a marketing scheme. The line between ad and editorial is being blurred to the point that the choice to block out advertising is being taken from us, right before our eyes.

Another example: I was sitting in my favorite mom-and-pop café recently, uncurled my morning paper, turned to the Homes Section to read anything about—well, buying a home. A few pages into the section was a two-page spread focusing on a new condo development. The article touted the development's avant-garde design as a feather in the hat of the architect and developer and boasted that each apartment had been outfitted with state-of-the-art appliances. The story read like an advertisement. But it had a by-line, and its format didn't appear different from other stories in the paper. I nearly coughed up my muffin at the thought that I had, perhaps, been tricked into reading a ventriloquized sales pitch. In a matter of seconds I went from confusion to anger. I don't think this was the kind of reaction that the developer wanted.

4 Kelly McBride, an ethics group leader at the Poynter Institute, a prominent American journalism organization, seems equally annoyed at the dubious practice of publications using staff or contributing writers to pen advertisements in order to give us the impression they are editorial matter. In Maria Aspan's *New York Times* article "A Magazine Interview or an Ad? Read the Fine Print,"[2] McBride complained that "As a member of the audience, how do I know where [a writer's] loyalties are when I see his byline on something else?"

As my coffee sat idle, losing much of its mellowness to my fractious state-of-mind, I wondered if other news features in my daily paper were advertisements in disguise. I questioned if perhaps I should be more cautious about what I read—or believe. I thought about how often I may have been duped into buying products, or at least into thinking that a newspaper or magazine endorses them. I even scanned a few articles for signs of product placement.

Of course, there are at least two sides to every story, and the debate on how clean the separation between ad and editorial ought to be is no exception. According to Advertorial.org, a company that produces what are known as advertorials—advertisements that read like editorial matter—such news and feature-mimicking ads are not the wolves in sheep's clothing many critics make them out to be. Advertorials "inform your prospective buyers, while at the same time [promoting] your product," they claim on their Web site.[3] They make people aware of what's on the market; they educate people, as editorials and similar content often do. As Deborah Carr of Writing Services comments, they also have "more credibility with the readership than an advertisement."[4]

And why wouldn't media use any means available to draw us into an ad? It's the advertising dollar that's paying for most of the protein-rich editorial material—news commentary, features, opinion—that muscles-up our flabby intellects and keeps us aware and in touch with the world. Think about all the journalists, editors, proofreaders and printers that need to earn a living. And paper and ink certainly aren't cheap. Mix shrinking advertising budgets with free online editions, blend in a readership that, because of being constantly bombarded with ads, regards advertising as noise, and what's a publication to do but to dream up more imaginative—and occasionally sneaky—ways to help businesses get their messages across?

8   In the case of advertorials, it is the readers' relationship to a publication that advertisers want to cash in on. But it's a case of the goose and the golden egg. What happens when readers lose their trust that a respected publication is giving them the straight goods? How far will high-quality magazines and newspapers go to stay in the black? The pressure on publications to attract ad revenue is so great that concerned professional bodies such as the American and the Canadian Society of Magazine Editors have created a set of guidelines on how magazines ought to behave concerning ads. These include recommendations that ad layout, design and typeface be markedly different from news stories, feature articles and editorials, and that if ads too closely resemble the other kinds of content they should be clearly labelled as advertisements. According to CSME, "The integrity and long term viability of magazines depends on a clear distinction between editorial and advertising, or both lose credibility, eventually, so too will the magazine."[5]

But do guidelines work? Not according to T. Cameron and Kuen Hee Ju-Pak whose research, published in the *Newspaper Research Journal*,[6] suggests that newspapers in the U. S. using advertorials "do not fully comply with purported editorial standards." Their study indicates that "newspapers do more to signal the commercial nature of advertorials than was found using the same content analytical methods in magazine studies." One might assume from Cameron and Ju-Pak's findings that newspapers are more ethical about ads than magazines. This doesn't seem to have been the case with the *Los Angeles Times* whose *Alice in Wonderland* ad doesn't come near meeting CSME's guideline that "the front cover and spine [of magazines] are editorial space" and that "companies and products should appear on covers only in an editorial context and not in a way that suggests advertisement."[7]

With so much craftiness in advertising these days, it usually takes a discerning eye and a small dose of cynicism to separate information from manipulation. The Los Angeles Times attempt described at the start of this article was blatant, and used what traditionally has been "editorial space." Print media has its head in a rabbit hole, however, if it thinks readers are going to be more forgiving than the Red Queen after they've being hornswoggled into reading an ad. Next time you settle into a newspaper or magazine story check if there's any fine print. It's always been a "reader beware" world, but the bar is being raised, and you'd be as mad as a hatter to believe that the printed word is beyond reproach.

References

1. http://www.reuters.com/article/idUSTRE6250BL20100306
2. http://www.nytimes.com/2006/07/03/ business/media/03premiere.html
3. http://www.advertorial.org/faq.html
4. http://www.deborahcarr.ca/advertorial.htm
5. http://www.canadianeditors.com/News/article/sid=2.htm
6. Glen T. Cameron and Kuen-Hee Ju-Pak, "Information Pollution? Labeling and Format of Advertorials," *Newspaper Research Journal* 21:2 (Winter 2000).
7. http://kellyawards.net/asme/asme guidelines/guidelines.aspx

PERSONAL RESPONSE

Are you bothered when, while reading a magazine or newspaper, you come across something that appears to be an article but is instead an advertisement? Do you think you have been "duped into buying products" (paragraph 5) by such a practice?

QUESTIONS FOR CLASS OR SMALL-GROUP DISCUSSION

1. Explain the title. Where do you find references to it in the article?
2. State in your own words what Zembic's complaint is. Where have you seen the practices that he complains about?
3. Assess the strength of Zembic's argument. How logical is his reasoning? Does he make a creditable case for his position? How well does he make use of example?
4. Where does Zembic make concessions to those opposed to his position? How well do you think he handles potential arguments of those opposed to him?

JESUS IS A BRAND OF JEANS

JEAN KILBOURNE

Jean Kilbourne is a social theorist who has lectured for many years on advertising images of women and on alcohol and liquor advertisements. A widely published writer and speaker who has twice been named Lecturer of the Year by the National Association of Campus Activities, she is perhaps best known for her award-winning documentaries on advertising images, Killing Us Softly, Slim Hopes, *and*

Pack of Lies. *She is author of* Can't Buy My Love: How Advertising Changes the Way We Think and Feel *(2000) (hard cover title:* Deadly Persuasion: Why Women and Girls Must Fight the Addictive Power of Advertising). *Her latest book, coauthored with Diane E. Levin, is* So Sexy So Soon: The New Sexualized Childhood and What Parents Can Do to Protect Their Kids *(2009). This piece was first published in* New Internationalist Magazine *in 2006. You can find additional resources and other information at Kilbourne's website: www.jeankilbourne.com.*

A recent ad for Thule car-rack systems features a child in the backseat of a car, seatbelt on. Next to the child, assorted sporting gear is carefully strapped into a child's car seat. The headline says: "We Know What Matters to You." In case one misses the point, further copy adds: "Your gear is a priority."

Another ad features an attractive young couple in bed. The man is on top of the woman, presumably making love to her. However, her face is completely covered by a magazine, open to a double-page photo of a car. The man is gazing passionately at the car. The copy reads, "The ultimate attraction."

These ads are meant to be funny. Taken individually, I suppose they might seem amusing or, at worst, tasteless. As someone who has studied ads for a long time, however, I see them as part of a pattern: just two of many ads that state or imply that products are more important than people. Ads have long promised us a better relationship via a product: *buy this and you will be loved.* But more recently they have gone beyond that proposition to promise us a relationship with the product itself: *buy this and it will love you.* The product is not so much the means to an end, as the end itself.

4   After all, it is easier to love a product than a person. Relationships with human beings are messy, unpredictable, sometimes dangerous. "When was the last time you felt this comfortable in a relationship?" asks an ad for shoes. Our shoes never ask us to wash the dishes or tell us we're getting fat. Even more important, products don't betray us. "You can love it without getting your heart broken," proclaims a car ad. One certainly can't say that about loving a human being, as love without vulnerability is impossible.

We are surrounded by hundreds, thousands of messages every day that link our deepest emotions to products, that objectify people and trivialize our most heartfelt moments and relationships. Every emotion is used to sell us something. Our wish to protect our children is leveraged to make us buy an expensive car. A long marriage simply provides the occasion for a diamond necklace. A painful reunion between a father and his estranged daughter is dramatized to sell us a phone system. Everything in the world—nature, animals, people—is just so much stuff to be consumed or to be used to sell us something.

The problem with advertising isn't that it creates artificial needs, but that it exploits our very real and human desires. Advertising promotes a bankrupt concept of *relationship.* Most of us yearn for committed relationships that will last. We are not stupid: we know that buying a certain brand of cereal won't bring us one inch closer to that goal. But we are surrounded by advertising that yokes our needs with products and promises us that *things* will deliver what in fact they never can. In the world of advertising, lovers are things and things are lovers.

It may be that there is no other way to depict relationships when the ultimate goal is to sell products. But this apparently bottomless consumerism not only depletes the world's resources, it also depletes our inner resources. It leads inevitably to narcissism and solipsism. It becomes difficult to imagine a way of relating that isn't objectifying and exploitative.

Tuned In

8   Most people feel that advertising is not something to take seriously. Other aspects of the media are serious—the violent films, the trashy talk shows, the bowdlerization of the news. But not advertising! Although much more attention has been paid to the cultural impact of advertising in recent years than ever before, just about everyone still feels personally exempt from its influence. What I hear more than anything else at my lectures is: "I don't pay attention to ads... I just tune them out . . . they have no effect on me." I hear this most from people wearing clothes emblazoned with logos. In truth, we are all influenced. There is no way to tune out this much information, especially when it is designed to break through the "tuning out" process. As advertising critic Sut Jhally put it: "To not be influenced by advertising would be to live outside of culture. No human being lives outside of culture."

Much of advertising's power comes from this belief that it does not affect us. As Joseph Goebbels said: "This is the secret of propaganda: those who are to be persuaded by it should be completely immersed in the ideas of the propaganda, without ever noticing that they are being immersed in it." Because we think advertising is trivial, we are less on guard, less critical, than we might otherwise be. While we're laughing, sometimes sneering, the commercial does its work.

Taken individually, ads are silly, sometimes funny, certainly nothing to worry about. But cumulatively they create a climate of cynicism that is poisonous to relationships. Ad after ad portrays our real lives as dull and ordinary, commitment to human beings as something to be avoided. Because of the pervasiveness of this kind of message, we learn from childhood that it is far safer to make a commitment to a product than to a person, far easier to be loyal to a brand. Many end up feeling romantic about material objects yet deeply cynical about other human beings.

Unnatural Passions

We know by now that advertising often turns people into objects. Women's bodies—and men's bodies too these days—are dismembered, packaged and used to sell everything from chainsaws to chewing gum, champagne to shampoo. Self-image is deeply affected. The self-esteem of girls plummets as they reach adolescence partly because they cannot possibly escape the message that their bodies are objects, and imperfect objects at that. Boys learn that masculinity requires a kind of ruthlessness, even brutality.

12   Advertising encourages us not only to objectify each other but to feel passion for products rather than our partners. This is especially dangerous when the products are potentially addictive, because addicts do feel they are in a relationship with their substances. I once heard an alcoholic joke that Jack Daniels was her most constant lover. When I was a smoker, I felt that my cigarettes were my friends. Advertising reinforces these beliefs, so we are twice seduced—by the ads and by the substances themselves.

The addict is the ideal consumer. Ten per cent of drinkers consume over sixty per cent of all the alcohol sold. Most of them are alcoholics or people in desperate trouble—but they are also the alcohol industry's very best customers. Advertisers spend enormous amounts of money on psychological research and understand addiction well. They use this knowledge to target children (because if you hook them early they are yours for life), to encourage all people to consume more, in spite of often dangerous consequences for all of us, and to create a climate of denial in which all kinds of addictions flourish. This they do with full intent, as we see so clearly in the "secret documents" of the tobacco industry that have been made public in recent years.

The consumer culture encourages us not only to buy more but to seek our identity and fulfillment through what we buy, to express our individuality through our "choices" of products. Advertising corrupts relationships and then offers us products, both as solace and as substitutes for the intimate human connection we all long for and need.

In the world of advertising, lovers grow cold, spouses grow old, children grow up and away—but possessions stay with us and never change. Seeking the outcomes of a healthy relationship through products cannot work. Sometimes it leads us into addiction. But at best the possessions can never deliver the promised goods. They can't make us happy or loved or less alone or safe. If we believe they can, we are doomed to disappointment. No matter how much we love them, they will never love us back.

16   Some argue that advertising simply reflects societal values rather than affecting them. Far from being a passive mirror of society, however, advertising is a pervasive medium of influence and persuasion. Its influence is cumulative, often subtle and primarily unconscious. A former editor-in-chief of *Advertising Age*, the leading advertising publication in North America, once claimed: "Only eight per cent of an ad's message is received by the conscious mind. The rest is worked and re-worked deep within, in the recesses of the brain."

Advertising performs much the same function in industrial society as myth did in ancient societies. It is both a creator and perpetuator of the dominant values of the culture, the social norms by which most people govern their behavior. At the very least, advertising helps to create a climate in which certain values flourish and others are not reflected at all.

Advertising is not only our physical environment; it is increasingly our spiritual environment as well. By definition, however, it is only interested in materialistic values. When spiritual values show up in ads, it is only in order to sell us something. Eternity is a perfume by Calvin Klein. Infiniti is an automobile, and Hydra Zen a moisturizer. Jesus is a brand of jeans.

Sometimes the allusion is more subtle, as in the countless alcohol ads featuring the bottle surrounded by a halo of light. Indeed products such as jewelry shining in a store window are often displayed as if they were sacred objects. Advertising co-opts our sacred symbols in order to evoke an immediate emotional response. Media critic Neil Postman referred to this as "cultural rape."

20   It is commonplace to observe that consumerism has become the religion of our time (with advertising its holy text), but the criticism usually stops short of what is at the heart of the comparison. Both advertising and religion share a belief in transformation, but most religions believe that this requires sacrifice. In the world of advertising, enlightenment is achieved instantly by purchasing material goods. An ad for a watch says, "It's not your handbag. It's not your neighborhood. It's not your boyfriend. It's your watch that tells most about who you are." Of course, this cheapens authentic spirituality and transcendence. This junk food for the soul leaves us hungry, empty, malnourished.

Substitute Stories

Human beings used to be influenced primarily by the stories of our particular tribe or community, not by stories that are mass-produced and market-driven. As George Gerbner, one of the world's most respected researchers on the influence of the media, said: "For the first time in human history, most of the stories about people, life and values are told not by parents, schools, churches, or others in the community who have something to tell, but by a group of distant conglomerates that have something to sell."

Although it is virtually impossible to measure the influence of advertising on a culture, we can learn something by looking at cultures only recently exposed to it. In 1980 the Gwich'in tribe of Alaska got television, and therefore massive advertising, for the first time. Satellite dishes, video games and VCRs were not far behind. Before this, the Gwich'in lived much the way their ancestors had for generations. Within 10 years, the young members of the tribe were so drawn by television they no longer had time to learn ancient hunting methods, their parents' language or their oral history. Legends told around campfires could not compete with Beverly Hills 90210. Beaded moccasins gave way to Nike sneakers, and "tundra tea" to Folger's instant coffee.

As multinational chains replace local character, we end up in a world in which everyone is Gapped and Starbucked. Shopping malls kill vibrant downtown centers locally and create a universe of uniformity internationally. We end up in a world ruled by, in John Maynard Keynes's phrase, the values of the casino. On this deeper level, rampant commercialism undermines our physical and psychological health, our environment and our civic life, and creates a toxic society.

24   Advertising creates a world view that is based upon cynicism, dissatisfaction and craving. Advertisers aren't evil. They are just doing their job, which is to sell a product; but the consequences, usually unintended, are often destructive. In the history of the world there has never been a propaganda effort to match that of advertising in the past 50 years. More thought, more effort, more money goes into advertising than has gone into any other campaign to change social

consciousness. The story that advertising tells is that the way to be happy, to find satisfaction—and the path to political freedom, as well—is through the consumption of material objects. And the major motivating force for social change throughout the world today is this belief that happiness comes from the market.

PERSONAL RESPONSE

Kilbourne says that, despite what people think, advertising affects us all. To what extent do you feel yourself affected by advertising? If you have you ever purchased a product solely because of its advertisement, explain that experience.

QUESTIONS FOR CLASS OR SMALL-GROUP DISCUSSION

1. State in your own words the issues that Kilbourne is most concerned about in this article. Do you agree with her?
2. Explain the title. How does it connect with Kilbourne's central idea? Where does she use the reference in the title to support one of her arguments?
3. What do you think of the examples that Kilbourne uses to support her argument? For instance, how effective do you find her example of the Gwich'in tribe in paragraph 22?
4. What do you understand Kilbourne to mean when she writes, "The addict is the ideal consumer" (paragraph 13)?

PERSPECTIVES ON MEDIA STUDIES
Suggested Writing Topics

1. Select one or two questions from Henry Jenkins' "A Pedagogical Response to the Aurora Shootings: 10 Critical Questions about Fictional Representations of Violence" and apply them to a fictional work depicting violence.
2. Select a statement or a passage in Henry Jenkins' "A Pedagogical Response to the Aurora Shootings: 10 Critical Questions about Fictional Representations of Violence" that interests, intrigues, or angers you and write a detailed explanation of your response.
3. Select a story, novel, or film that you have read and analyze it in terms of what Henry Jenkins says in question 6 in "A Pedagogical Response to the Aurora Shootings: 10 Critical Questions about Fictional Representations of Violence" about the function that violence serves in the narrative.
4. Imagine that you are preparing to give a talk to a group of children about the possible dangers of exposure to media violence. Write an essay with that group as your audience and include details, facts, or references to studies that you think would make an impression on them.

5. With Peter H. Gibbon's "The End of Admiration: The Media and the Loss of Heroes" in mind, argue either in support of or against the statement that America no longer has heroes.

6. Define the word *hero* and use a person you admire to illustrate the meaning of the word.

7. Listen to two radio talk shows or television programs, one liberal and one conservative, and compare the two. What subjects do they discuss? How do their approaches differ? Do you find yourself persuaded by one over the other? Why?

8. Select a news item in the headlines this week and follow the media's coverage of it, mixing media if possible. For instance, you could track the story as reported on an Internet site, on a national news program, and in a newspaper, or as it is handled by several different Internet sites, television programs, or newspapers. What conclusions can you draw about the media's handling of the story? Do you detect any bias in reporting it?

9. Advertisers contend that they do not create problems, but simply reflect the values of society. Explain your position on the subject of how much responsibility advertisers should bear for the images they produce in their advertisements.

10. Survey a selection of magazine or television advertisements and apply the kind of analysis that Jean Kilbourne does in "Jesus Is a Brand of Jeans." Explain what you find and whether your conclusions agree with or differ from hers. Do certain advertising "exploits our very real and human desires" (paragraph 7)?

11. Jean Kilbourne in "Jesus Is a Brand of Jeans" writes that advertising "encourages us not only to objectify each other but to feel passion for products rather than our partners" (paragraph 12). Give examples of ads that would support this statement.

12. Write a paper in response to the central argument of any of the essays in this chapter. For instance, Brad Zembic in "Print Media and the Rabbit Hole" expresses great annoyance at the intrusiveness of advertisements into his life, particularly "advertorials," or advertisements passing themselves off as editorial content. What position do you take on that subject"? Is any space fair game for advertisements, or should there be limits?

Research Topics

1. Using Henry Jenkins' "A Pedagogical Response to the Aurora Shootings: 10 Critical Questions about Fictional Representations of Violence" as a basis for your research, and supplementing it with other sources, write an analysis of a work of fiction such as a novel, film, or game that has been criticized for glorifying violence.

2. Research the subject of advertising ethics by locating articles and books representing the opinions of both those who are critical of advertisements and those who defend them. Argue your own position on the subject, supporting it with relevant source materials.

3. Using Brad Zembic's article "Print Media and the Rabbit Hole" as a starting point, research the subject of "advertorials." Locate sources mentioned in his article or find your own online or in the library. Develop a position on the issue and defend that position with supporting evidence from your research.

4. Research the subject of product placement in the media by locating the controversy over its practice, who uses it and where, and audience or reader response. Determine your own position on the practice and support it with evidence from your reading and viewing.

5. Research images of a specific group in advertising. For instance, you could focus on images of women of men, or of minorities and locate additional research and opposing viewpoints. Or, instead of images, consider researching the topic of advertisements that encourage destructive behavior or advertisements aimed at children.

6. Take as your starting point any of the general statements that Jean Kilbourne makes in "Jesus Is a Brand of Jeans" about the message of advertisements, especially the promises they seem to make. Locate sources, do some preliminary reading, and narrow your focus on one aspect of the broader topic. For instance, in paragraph 5 she writes that ads "link our deepest emotions to products, . . . objectify people and trivialize our most heartfelt moments and relationships." Elsewhere, in paragraph 11, she states that advertisements deeply affect self-image. Kilbourne makes many such statements. Select one as a starting point for your research. Does your research support or refute the generalization?

7. Research the subject of the cultural impact of advertising.

8. Research the question of whether allegations that the media have a liberal bias are true. Is it simply a perception, or can such bias, if it exists, be documented?

9. Select a news story that got a great deal of media coverage and research how it was reported in a variety of media sources. Compare the handling of the news item by the different sources. What conclusions can you draw on whether there is bias in reporting the story?

10. Explain your perspective on some aspect of media studies, taking into account the views expressed by any of the writers in this chapter. Focus on a specific issue about which you have formed an opinion after reading their views, refer to the other writers as a way of providing the context for your own essay, supplement those readings with additional research, and then explain in detail your own position.

RESPONDING TO VISUALS

Warren Miller/The New Yorker Collection/www.cartoonbank.com

"I like it. It's dumb without trying to be clever." Executive with cigar exclaims while looking at advertising mockups.

1. What are the implications of this cartoon about consumers?
2. What aspects of advertising and consumers does the cartoon make fun of?
3. What does the cartoon imply about the role of advertisements?

RESPONDING TO VISUALS

Alberto Ruggieri//Illustration Works/Corbis

Effect of TV advertising on children

1. Why does the figure coming out of the screen have a smile on his face and his hand over the child's eyes?
2. What sorts of things is the figure casting behind him? What do they represent?
3. What commentary does the image make on the effects of television advertising on children?

CHAPTER 10

Film and Television

Film studies programs at campuses across the nation share similar characteristics: they are almost always interdisciplinary in approach, offering courses relating to the arts, humanities, and social studies. These courses look at the history, criticism, theory, and sociocultural impacts of cinema and other moving image media. Similarly, television studies programs, though more often incorporated into media studies or popular culture programs, offer courses that look at television programming critically and across a wide range of disciplines such as political science, sociology, psychology, and the humanities. Film and television overlap considerably and are often studied in the same media studies or popular culture programs. Makers of Hollywood films, television shows, and other products of the entertainment industry hope to tap into or even create trends that will have widespread appeal and thus result in huge profits. Because of its high visibility, ready availability, and ease of access to all age groups, the entertainment industry has always been closely scrutinized and subject to attack by its critics. Popular Hollywood films and television programs are particularly prime targets for both criticism and praise. Hollywood watchdogs and film critics pay attention not only to the craft of film production but also to the content of films. Indeed, the current film ratings system evolved in response to alarm at young viewers' exposure not only to scenes of graphic sex and violence but also to intensely frightening scenes. In recent years, many people have been sharply critical of films and television programs for what they see as irresponsible depiction of shocking images, excessive violence, and unnecessarily graphic sex. Defenders have been just as heated in their responses.

Television has been the target of suspicion, attack, and ridicule from the time it was invented. Though it is probably hard to believe now, when it was first invented, people thought "the tube" would never replace the radio, especially when its early live-only broadcasts included inevitable comical errors. Once the problems were resolved and television broadcasting became increasingly sophisticated in both technology and programming, television became an established medium. Television programs now number in the thousands, with cable access and computer-controlled satellite dishes bringing a dizzying array of viewing choices into people's homes. Households have two or three (or more) televisions and DVR and DVD players. It is commonplace to download television programs on computers and handheld electronic devices as well. With the seemingly endless demand for television shows from viewers, network producers and local station managers are always looking for programs that will attract viewers and draw sponsors.

The first reading in this chapter, Chris Gould's, "Batman, the Unexpected Cultural Revolution," takes an historical approach to television criticism by examining the cultural aspects of the enormously popular American television show *Batman*, which ran from 1966 to 1968. Such an approach is useful for understanding the cultural and social norms of the past as reflected on the small screen. Such an approach is also useful for commenting on current culture by comparison. Gould deftly points out the many cultural, political, and technological conditions that the television show's writers satirized and by implication criticized. *Batman*, he concludes, was "a classic encapsulation of an American pop art phenomenon." It would be interesting to compare this 1966 series with the comic book series that preceded it or with the many film representations of Batman that followed. As Gould's title indicates, the 1966 television series stands out as an unexpected example of a "cultural revolution" that he describes in the text as "pop art utopia."

Another area of television programming that researchers have begun to investigate is reality shows. These programs follow real people over time behaving in unscripted situations, such as surviving on a faraway and exotic island, selecting a potential mate from a group of twenty-five hopefuls, having a new home built for them, or competing to be the top singer or dancer in the nation. At least a couple of dozen such shows air during the regular television season and even more in the summer. The concept is not new: in the 1950s, for instance, *Queen for a Day* was an early variation, where contestants were selected to tell their sad stories and the winner was the one who garnered the loudest audience applause. But the proliferation of such programs is a twenty-first-century phenomenon. In "Getting Real with Reality TV," Cynthia M. Frisby discusses research that helps explain why audiences view such television programs. After defining the social comparison theory developed in the 1950s, Frisby explains the results of a survey that she and others conducted to determine how that theory applies to reality-show viewers. As you read her article, think about your own viewing habits, particularly if you watch reality television shows.

The other two articles in this chapter discuss the subject of films. In "Creating Reel Change," Donovan Jacobs is interested in the positive effects of certain television and Hollywood films, especially documentaries, that deal with important social issues and that hope to influence audiences to take action in the interest of whatever cause the film is about. In contrast to so many critics of Hollywood films who believe that they promote antisocial behavior, Jacobs focuses on films that provide examples of pro-social behavior. As you read his article, see whether you have viewed any of the films he mentions, and if so, consider whether you responded in the way that companies who produce such films and documentaries hope viewers will respond.

Finally, Sady Doyle looks at the wild popularity among teen and preteen girls of the *Twilight* series of films and novels. The subtitle of her article reveals her position: "The unwarranted backlash against fans of the world's most popular vampire-romance series." If you have been accustomed to dismissing teenage girls as silly and overly romantic, consider whether this article makes you rethink your attitude.

BATMAN, THE UNEXPECTED CULTURAL REVOLUTION

CHRIS GOULD

Chris Gould describes himself on his website as having been "born in Europe, preserved in Japan, and thriving on the riches of numerous cultures." He has published many articles on such topics as football, sumo wrestling, travel, and political satire. He is author of Batman at 45: A Milestone Tribute to Pow, Bam and Zap! *(2011) and the e-books* Aristotle: Politics, Ethics, and Desirability *(2011) and* My First Date with Sumo *(2012). This article was first published in* Magazine Americana *in January 2011.*

Fifty-five years ago, in 1966, one of the more unusual experiments in American popular culture took place. Producer William Dozier took an almighty gamble by introducing *Batman* to the TV screen via America's ABC network. The caped crime-fighter originally created by Bob Kane had certainly built up a fan base in DC Comics since 1939, but he had never been portrayed the way Dozier presented him. Dispensing with every aspect of the Dark Knight's dark comic book existence, Dozier offered America a laughably gentle Batman who even winced at the bad language used by criminals, such were his outrageously high moral standards. The *Batman* TV show thus became a depiction of pop art utopia, where bright colors forever defeated darkness, where creativity forever defeated logic, and where Good forever triumphed over Evil.

The actor chosen to play Dozier's Batman, a rather dashing six-foot-two inch Adam West, accepted the role because, in his own words, he found the script "excruciatingly funny." Indeed, the dead pan delivery of ridiculous lines, revolutionary for its time, made *Batman* a comedy classic. Only on this show could a criminal be described as a "pompous, waddling master of a million criminal umbrellas" in the normal flow of conversation. Equally hilarious was the irony behind some of the lines as illustrated by the absurd situation when Batman enters a library. While wearing a cape, a bat logo, pants outside his trousers and a bat-shaped mask with eyebrows inexplicably carved into it, he says to a librarian: "Have you seen any unusual looking people around here?" She replies, in all earnestness: "No, but then I see so many people during the course of the day."

While the characters of Batman and teenage sidekick Robin were amusingly gentle, the villains were amusingly insane. The Riddler, expertly played by impressionist Frank Gorshin, was depicted as a complete maniac, forever shouting his plans to the rooftops and squealing with crazed laughter. The Joker, played by Latin legend Cesar Romero, also laughed crazily, sported outrageous hair, and had white facial paint daubed over his moustache (which he apparently refused to shave for the role). A nod to girl power was made in the form of Catwoman, a highly sexualized villainess with skin-tight leathers who urged a henchman to "tickle my pussy feathers." Although she was clearly referring to nearby flowers of that name, it is astonishing that such a line would escape the censors' wrath!

4   Extra villains without a comic-book past were created especially for the TV show, the most memorable being Victor Buono's King Tut, an obese, goatee-bearded Yale University professor who started believing he was an ancient King of the Nile every time he was struck on the head. Another impressive character was the Bookworm, played by Roddy MacDowell, whose writing career had failed because of his lack of originality but who was capable of devising all manner of crimes from books he had read. Bookworm's episodes, aired during national reading week, were actually designed to highlight the importance of reading to the show's younger viewers. It was one of many "good upbringing" messages included in *Batman*, with the superhero himself often stressing the importance of fresh fruit, education, and safe driving.

Part of *Batman*'s charm was that it drew unmistakably clear distinctions between Right and Wrong. The forces of Law and Order were simply whiter than white, with Batman even explaining to Robin that the reason they consistently escaped the villains' traps was that their "hearts were pure." They were joined by the equally pure-hearted Police Commissioner Gordon and the slightly dim-witted Chief O'Hara, two figures who would never even fiddle with an expenses claim. The villains, on the other hand, despite wearing colorful costumes and appearing cuddlier than their comic book counterparts, were portrayed as unspeakably evil and selfish, only ever thinking about crimes to commit. Good always defeats Evil in the end, though, usually via a daft fight scene with large words splurged over the screen, trumpet sounds to mark every punch, and a brilliant atonal musical score put together by Nelson Riddle. The fact that Batman's alter-ego, Bruce Wayne, is a millionaire whereas the villains scrape together an existence in abandoned warehouses with malnourished henchmen is the starkest illustration that crime doesn't pay.

Batman was far more than just an adventure story. It took itself seriously as a social commentator and certainly pulled no pow!-style punches when analyzing popular trends of the day. The electoral system suffered an almighty bashing when arch villain the Penguin ran for Mayor of Gotham City, in an episode aired during the 1966 mid-terms. "I should have been a politician years ago!" croaks the umbrella-wielding, cigar smoking Penguin—expertly played by Burgess Meredith. "I can use all my dirty, slurpiest tricks, and now they're legal!" Symbolizing everything the public love to hate about politicians, Penguin also tells a campaign rally that voters love "bands and girls and balloons and hoopla! But remember: no politics! Issues confuse people." In this episode, police and local politicians decide that the only way to defeat Penguin's highly slick PR campaign is to offer Batman as a rival mayoral candidate. Batman's subsequent election win, while hailed as a triumph for clean politics over skulduggery, may in fact be taken as a further slight against an electorate willing to vote in a man whose face they have never seen!

It is, in some ways, a miracle that the show became a pop art phenomenon. After all, much of the script suggests that the writers were incredibly dismissive of the young social movements taking place around them, coming as they did from an older generation. Pop art itself certainly takes a pounding in the episode which sees super criminal Joker perfectly cast in the role of pop artist, winning a competition by painting nothing on his canvas and then declaring a smashed table to be his latest masterpiece. The writers' disdain is expressed further when Joker teaches a pop art master class, in which it is impossible to tell what the sculptures resemble. Bruce Wayne, who has entered the class, assesses Joker's art as "about the level of a three year old."

8   The hippie movement also comes in for criticism, with the young people in question portrayed as ignorant and naïve. A flower-power criminal named Louis the Lilac, played by Milton Berle, was created to illustrate this point, expressing the belief that hippies could be easily controlled and manipulated to serve his own nefarious ends. The movement was also scorned when 65-year-old Alan Napier, who plays Batman's butler Alfred, disguised himself as "the world's oldest hippie." The writers were equally mocking in their treatment of beach surfers, portraying them as clueless youths whose every conversation included surfing terms as "down cold!" and "reverse it!" The contemptuous treatment is extended when a 69-year-old Commissioner Gordon dresses up in beach shorts to go undercover, and explains to a similarly-clad Chief O'Hara that "most true surfers are known as Duke, Skip, Rabbit or Buzzy." The resultant comedy, though, which sees Batman also don beach shorts over his bat suit to defeat Joker in a surfing contest, is highly enjoyable.

Joker, incidentally, only gained his surfing knowhow by stealing it from champion Skip Parker via "a Surfing Experience and Ability Transferometer." The proliferation of such zany devices not only illustrates the script writers' scant regard for scientific fact but represents a biting commentary on the fears and anxieties surrounding technology. The Batcave illustrates that when technology is placed in the right hands it is an overwhelming force for good, especially when fighting crime. The villains, meanwhile, illustrate that when technology falls into the wrong hands havoc can be wreaked. Nuclear energy also comes under the spotlight, hailed as a wonderful source of power for the Batmobile but having its danger exposed when it claims the life of villainess Jill St John.

Largely because of the sheer speed at which episodes needed to be turned around, the *Batman* concept completely ran out of steam and the show was cancelled in March 1968. The final episode thus took the form of a tirade from bitter Batman producers against the executives who pulled the plug. Producers Dozier and Howie Horwitz both appeared in cameos, the latter explaining to a masseuse that he became rich by "never hiring method actors and always ignoring network executives." Caring no more for quality, Dozier and Horowitz set themselves a simple goal for the finale: to include every single Batman cliché imaginable, even ridiculing their own overused plot-devices. It is doubtful if a show has ever been so self-deprecating but the result was certainly positive: a classic encapsulation of an American pop art phenomenon. Most memorable is the mockery of Batman's ability to produce any tool imaginable from his utility belt. When asked by Commissioner Gordon: "How could you open a safe to which you did not know the combination in three seconds flat?" the caped crusader coolly replies: "With my Three-Second-Flat Bat-vault Combination Unscrambler, Commissioner."

Batman set out to challenge the established wisdom over how television programs should be produced, but the approach actually sowed the seeds of its own destruction. TV's regular stars were so impressed that they queued up in droves to take part in the project. Sammy Davis Jr., Liberace, Joan Collins, and Zsa Zsa Gabor were just some of the names who either guest starred or cameoed. Scripts and viewing figures suddenly became dependent on the guest star, and the show's quality suffered immensely. Despite this, the show made an immense impact on American popular culture in a relatively short time. It challenged people to aspire to a world where right and wrong were easily distinguishable. And it spawned a vast counter-revolution in future representations of Batman, with movie directors from the 1980s to the present obsessed with returning the character to his darker, more sinister, past.

PERSONAL RESPONSE

If you are a fan of Batman in any of his representations—in comic books or on film or on television—explain his appeal. If not, explain why you think you are not drawn to the character.

QUESTIONS FOR CLASS AND SMALL-GROUP DISCUSSION

1. State in your own words why, according to Gould, the 1960s television show *Batman* was an "unexpected cultural revolution" (title).

2. Gould says that Batman "took itself seriously as a social commentator" (paragraph 6). What aspects of popular culture and society did the show mock? Can you give examples of recent television shows or films that try to make social commentary through its plot lines?

3. Gould says that the *Batman* series was "a pop art phenomenon" (paragraph 7) that "made an immense impact on American popular culture" (paragraph 11). State in your own words what you understand Gould to mean and give examples of current pop art phenomena.

4. Why, according to Gould, did the series end? Do you think that a television series such as the 1960s *Batman* show could survive on television today? Why or why not?

GETTING REAL WITH REALITY TV

CYNTHIA M. FRISBY

Cynthia M. Frisby is associate professor of advertising at the University of Missouri School of Journalism, Columbia, and coeditor of Journalism Across Cultures *(2003). Her research interests include identifying the sources of American viewers' fascination with reality TV and the effects of idealized images on perceptions of body esteem among African American women. This essay appeared in the September 2004 issue of* USA Today *magazine.*

Every year, television networks vie to create cutting edge programming. New shows promise more drama, suspense, and laughter while pushing the envelope of what is morally and socially acceptable, funny, thrilling, and, of course, entertaining. Fitting all these criteria—at least according to the soaring ratings—is reality based television.

Reality TV is a genre of programming in which the everyday routines of "real life" people (as opposed to fictional characters played by actors) are followed closely by the cameras. Viewers cannot seem to help but become involved in the captivating plotlines and day-to-day drama depicted daily on their screens. Apparently, people simply take pleasure in watching other people's lives while those under scrutiny enjoy being on television enough to go on for free.

There are three major categories within the reality genre: game shows (e.g., "Survivor"), dating shows (e.g., "The Bachelor"), and talent shows (e.g., "American Idol"). While reality programming breeds fiercely during the regular season, in summer there is an even greater glut since such programs are cheap to produce and, if they fail to draw ratings, they quickly can be flushed away and replaced with something else.

4   It is becoming increasingly difficult to avoid contact with reality TV these days. In offices, hair salons, health clubs, restaurants, and bars, the general public is discussing what happened on television the night before—and it is not the world news they are dissecting. Rather, the hot topic may be what happened on "The Apprentice." Then again, it might be a "did-you-see" conversation concerning "The Bachelor" or "For Love or Money."

Shows such as "The Apprentice," "Survivor," "Fear Factor," "The Amazing Race," "American Idol," "American Girl," "Big Brother," "Extreme Makeover" "Temptation Island," "Cheaters," "The Simple Life," "Queer Eye for the Straight Guy," "The Bachelor," and "The Bachelorette" have reached out and grabbed today's American television viewer. During the 2003–04 season, 10 reality shows ranked among the top 25 prime-time programs in the audience-composition index for adults 18–49 with incomes of $75,000 or more. Nielsen ratings indicate that more than 18,000,000 viewers have been captivated by television programs that take ordinary people and place them in situations that have them competing in ongoing contests while being filmed 24 hours a day. What is it about these shows that attracts millions of loyal viewers week after week? Is it blatant voyeurism, or can their success be explained as a harmless desire for entertainment?

From "Survivor" to "Elimidate" to "Average Joe," to "Joe Millionaire," it seems that reality TV succeeds because it plays off of real-life concerns— looking for love, competing to win a job or big prize, or becoming a millionaire— situations (or dreams) that most people can relate to. However, as these shows become more pervasive, their grip on "reality" seems to be growing more tenuous.

"It's refreshing to see everyday people getting some of the spotlight, rather than just seeing movie stars all the time," maintains CBS News associate Presley Weir. According to CBS, the same element of being human that encourages people to gossip about the lives of their friends, family, and even total strangers is what fosters an audience for reality television. Much like a car crash on the side of the freeway, glimpses into the interior workings of other human beings is often shocking, yet impossible to turn away from. It was this theory that produced MTV's "The Real World," often referred to as "the forerunner of reality television shows." Seven strangers are selected to live together, and viewers watch to find out what happens when individuals with different backgrounds and points of view are left in close quarters.

Media Gratification

8   Researchers frequently refer to at least six gratifications of media use: information (also known as surveillance or "knowledge"), escape, passing time, entertainment, social viewing/status enhancement, and relaxation. Although the names or labels for these gratifications may change, various studies confirm

that they hold up in and across all situations. So what type of gratifications do viewers receive from reality TV?

Actually, individuals compare themselves with others for a variety of reasons, including to: determine relative standing on an issue or related ability; emulate behaviors; determine norms; lift spirits or feel better about life and personal situations; and evaluate emotions, personality, and self-worth.

Those made with others who are superior to or better off than oneself are referred to as upward comparisons. Individuals engaging in upward comparison may learn from others, be inspired by their examples, and become highly motivated to achieve similar goals. Upward comparisons, research suggests, are invoked when a person is motivated to change or overcome difficulties. Self-improvement is the main effect of an upward comparison because the targets serve as role models, teaching and motivating individuals to achieve or overcome similar problems.

On the other hand, when a social comparison involves a target who is inferior, incompetent, or less fortunate, it is referred to as a downward comparison. Its basic principle is that people feel better about their own situation and enhance their subjective well-being when they make comparisons with others who are worse off. Supposedly, downward comparisons help individuals cope with personal problems by allowing them to see themselves and their difficulties in a more positive light by realizing there are others who face more difficult circumstances.

12   A social comparison does not mean that the individual has to give careful, elaborate, conscious thought about the comparison, but implies that there has to be, to some degree, an attempt to identify or look for similarities or differences between the other and self on some particular dimension. There are theorists who might argue that, for a comparison to be considered a comparison, the individual must be aware of the comparison and come into direct contact with the other person. However, psychologists have discovered that social comparisons do not require conscious or direct personal contact because fictional characters illustrated in the media can represent meaningful standards of comparison.

Data on social comparisons and media use suggest that everyday encounters with media images may provide viewers with information that encourages them to engage in an automatic, spontaneous social comparison. This ultimately affects mood and other aspects of subjective well-being. People just might not be able to articulate consciously the comparison process or consciously register its effects (i.e., self-enhancement, self-improvement, etc.).

Reality TV allows audiences to laugh, cry, and live vicariously through so-called everyday, ordinary people who have opportunities to experience things that, until the moment they are broadcast, most individuals only dream about. Viewers may tune into these shows: because they contain elements the audience would like to experience themselves; to laugh at the mistakes of others and/or celebrate successes; or to feel better about themselves because they are at least not as "bad as the people on television."

Exposure to tragic events or bad news invites social comparison among viewers. It is believed that reality audiences may be encouraged to compare and contrast their own situation with those of the reality show stars, and that this comparison process eventually could produce a form of self-satisfaction.

16   In real-life, everyday situations, it would be extremely difficult to avoid making some type of comparison. Frequently, people may compare themselves with others in their immediate environment or in the mass media in order to judge their own personal worth.

We contacted 110 people and asked them to complete a uses and gratifications survey on reality television with two goals in mind: to demonstrate that social comparisons may be elicited by certain television content and to explore if viewers use reality television's content and images as a source for social comparison.

Of the respondents, 78.2% reported being regular viewers of reality television programs. A list of 37 reality shows was presented to the participants. They were asked to check those that they watch on a regular basis, and indicate on a scale of 1–5—number 1 signifying "liked a lot" and number five meaning "extreme dislike"—whether they liked or disliked each of the 37 programs. This paper-and-pencil test also asked respondents to identify the extent to which they considered themselves a "regular viewer of reality television." For purposes of conceptualization, a regular viewer was defined as "one who watches the show every week, and/or records episodes to avoid missing weekly broadcasts."

Data was obtained on other television viewing preferences by asking respondents to indicate how regularly they watch programs like news magazines, talk shows, reality programs, daytime serials, and other offerings and to identify the gratifications obtained from watching reality television.

20   To better understand the cognitive responses made when exposed to media content, a content analysis of the thoughts generated while watching reality TV was conducted. The researcher coded any and all thoughts that contained expressions of, or alluded to, social comparisons that participants "appeared to have" made spontaneously.

Participants were told that they later would see a segment of reality TV and encouraged to view that segment as if they were watching the program at home. While viewing the segment, participants were asked to record all their thoughts, and were given ample space to do so.

Data show that, of all the responses made concerning reality programming, most expressed some type of comparison between themselves and the reality show's stars. We conducted a content analysis of the thoughts and responses provided by the participants and found that, for the most part, men and women, as well as regular viewers and nonviewers, did not differ in terms of how they responded to people on reality shows.

We then compared mood ratings obtained prior to viewing the reality show with those from immediately following exposure to the program. Analysis clearly indicated that regular viewers and nonviewers alike experienced a significant mood enhancement after exposure to reality television.

Captivating Audiences

24 We know that reality television can captivate millions of viewers at any given time on any given day. Research has begun to document how people engage in automatic, spontaneous social comparisons when confronted by certain media images, particularly those of reality TV. We also know that one major effect of exposure to reality television is to feel better about one's own life circumstances, abilities, and talents. Reality TV also serves as a much-needed distraction from the ongoing parade of tragic world events. It allows viewers an outlet by watching others overcome hardships, escape danger, live in a rainforest, land a dream job, learn to survive in Corporate America, and yes, even find love.

Whether the aim is money, love, becoming a rock star, creative expression, or just a chance to be seen on TV, the effect on audiences is the same. People like knowing that there are others who are going through the same life experiences that they are and often make the same mistakes. Despite the shifting desires of society and the fickleness of television audiences, the human need to compare and relate has provided a market for this genre.

So, while viewers realize they are not America's Next Top Model, may not have a chance at becoming the next American Idol, or even an All American Girl, they do enjoy the fact that, through a vicarious social comparison process, they can fall in love, win $1,000,000, or get the office snitch fired.

PERSONAL RESPONSE

Do you watch any reality television shows? If so, explain their appeal. If not, explain why they do not appeal to you.

QUESTIONS FOR CLASS OR SMALL-GROUP DISCUSSION

1. What functions do the opening paragraphs serve? What is Frisby's thesis? How well organized and developed do you find her essay?

2. Explain in your own words what the social comparison theory is (paragraph 9) and how it applies in general to viewers of reality television programs, according to Frisby.

3. How do the terms "upward comparison" (paragraph 11) and "downward comparison" specifically apply to viewers who watch reality television shows, according to Frisby?

4. Summarize the results of the uses and gratifications survey (paragraph 18) that Frisby and colleagues conducted. Do you think that Frisby's observations accurately describe the people you know who view reality television programs?

CREATING REEL CHANGE

DONOVAN JACOBS

Donovan Jacobs, a story development consultant based in Los Angeles, has been script consultant for many motion picture production companies and television networks, including Warner Brothers, ABC, and Touchstone Pictures. A graduate of the prestigious Warner Bros. Writers Workshop for television, he specializes in the development of family movies for television. Jacobs also writes grants for nonprofit organizations and serves as story editor and researcher in the television documentary world. He contributed a chapter to a book by Act One: Training for Hollywood called Behind the Screen: Hollywood Insiders on Faith, Film and Culture *(2005). This piece was written for the November 2006 issue of* Sojourners.

Movie and television directors, producers, and writers interested in saying something of substance to their audiences have often been confronted with a quote generally attributed to former studio head Jack Warner: "If you want to send a message, call Western Union." Despite this adage's implication that films and TV programs should avoid the political and stick to entertaining (and make their studios and networks gobs of money), a number of movies and TV shows over the years have dealt with vital issues and encouraged pro-social behavior.

Now—whether because of, or in response to, opportunities offered by newer media such as the Internet and cable television—a variety of untraditional film and documentary makers seek to do more than portray positive action on the screen. These companies and artists want to motivate their audiences to get better informed on their issues, volunteer to help the subjects of the movie or program, and even advocate for legislation that offers protection to victims and tries to right the wrongs portrayed.

Probably the most publicized of these filmmakers is former eBay president Jeff Skoll, who through his company Participant Productions has committed an estimated $100 million to co-financing and producing a slate of theatrical releases. These movies include *An Inconvenient Truth*, Al Gore's documentary on global warming released earlier this year, and the current *Fast Food Nation*, about a marketing expert's odyssey to discover how his hamburger chain really makes its meat.

4 Participant's distinctiveness thus far hasn't been marked in Hollywood's traditional measures of achievement (four of the company's movies were nominated for Oscars in 2005 but have had mixed success at the box office). Rather, its chief innovation is creation of Internet-based campaigns for each film that allow viewers to join with established organizations to both make personal changes and call for social action in response to the movie's themes.

It's difficult to measure the success of these campaigns. Participant's October 2005 release of *North Country* (about a pioneering female coal miner harassed by male co-workers) was timed to allow audiences to support the National Organization for Women and other feminist groups in efforts to renew the federal Violence Against Women Act (VAWA). North Country only grossed $18 million, meaning about 2 million people saw it in theaters. But if even a small percentage of that number demanded approval of the act, the film may have contributed to the bill's passage in January 2006.

The TV industry has long been criticized for shying away from socially significant topics. But in recent years, the rise of cable television has allowed newer networks to present programs on controversial and vital issues of interest to their targeted audiences.

MTV, which has a reputation for offensive and sexually explicit programs, has also aired documentaries (many starring music and entertainment celebrities) intended to inform and inspire its teen and young adult audiences regarding issues—including discrimination and sexual health—that often escape mainstream media attention. Last summer, MTV announced plans for a special to feature hip-hop star Jay-Z and his efforts to raise awareness of the lack of safe drinking water in several countries during his September international concert tour. MTV's Web site will offer ways for viewers to contribute to building "Play-Pumps," playground carousels that pump fresh water as kids spin them.

8   Lifetime Television has gained solid ratings with its heavily female viewership for a series of issue-based movies and miniseries, including *A Girl Like Me: The Gwen Araujo Story*, about a Latina mother who first opposes then supports her son's determination to live as a woman. Premiering last June, the movie was followed by public service announcements offering suggestions for encouraging tolerance and ending discrimination against transgender persons.

Lifetime's public affairs office has emerged as a lobbying force in Washington, D.C., credited by Rep. Carolyn Maloney with assisting in the passage of legislation involving women's issues such as quick DNA testing of rape kits and video voyeurism (the latter the subject of a 2004 Lifetime movie).

Many of the most vibrant movies and documentaries committed to advocacy come from less prominent filmmakers who use technologies such as DVDs and Web sites not only to inform supporters, but to distribute their work to much wider audiences than otherwise possible. Brave New Films, a Los Angeles-based company run by veteran television producer Robert Greenwald, has focused on creating documentaries (such as last year's *Wal-Mart: The High Cost of Low Price*) that premiere in theaters and then are shown in public DVD screenings with discussion sessions after the film.

The company's current release, *Iraq for Sale: The War Profiteers*, deals with corporations, including Halliburton and Blackwater, that collect billions in taxpayer funds while allegedly delivering shoddy services that endanger U.S. troops and Iraqi citizens. Brave New Films arranged screenings of the movie for thousands of groups in July, devoting each day of a particular week to different audiences and the causes supported by co-sponsoring groups. The timing of these screenings shortly before the 2006 elections was no accident: One of the moviemakers' goals was to aid "get out the vote" drives across the country.

12   The filmmakers also hope to generate support for two proposed bills. One would form a congressional investigative entity to root out corruption and expose wrongdoers, modeled after the World War II-era "Truman Committee." The other legislation is the Honest Leadership and Accountability in Contracting Act of 2006, which defines and demands stiff penalties for war profiteering.

The Social Action goals of the three 20-something filmmakers behind the DVD documentary *Invisible Children* are equally ambitious. After graduating from film school, Jason Russell convinced childhood friends Bobby Bailey and Laren Poole to travel with him to Africa in 2003 to make a movie. The trio stumbled upon the story of thousands of children in northern Uganda, many of them orphans in refugee camps, who must hide in the countryside and in basements each night to avoid abduction by the Lord's Resistance Army, a rebel force that turns its victims into child soldiers and maims or kills those who resist.

Invisible Children seems amateurish and silly in spots, but the film's irreverence may make its heavy subject matter more appealing to the thousands of groups (mainly high school and college students) who have attended screenings around the United States. The movie's Web site features stories of young people inspired by the documentary to raise thousands of dollars to fund educational programs set up by the filmmakers in Uganda. This school year, more than 600 Ugandan teenagers will have their schooling paid for by American student fundraisers and the sale of native bracelets through the Web site. Natalia Angelo, a spokesperson for the filmmakers, told *Sojourners* that one of the most gratifying aspects of the movie's success has been the opportunity to spotlight stories of altruism and sacrifice by teens and young adults, which counters the prevailing myth of the supposed selfishness and materialism of American youth.

The short movies available through the New York-based Media That Matters Film Festival may seem small in scope, but they still convey a strong sense of urgency regarding the subjects they explore. The 16 documentaries and fictional films in the festival are first screened on the Internet and then made available on DVD each fall to educators across the country, along with teachers' guides that can be downloaded from the festival Web site.

16   Internet links and information in the guides provide sources of detailed information and opportunities for volunteerism and advocacy relating to the movies' broad range of themes. The festival is also affiliated with MediaRights, an organization that helps non-profits and advocacy groups learn to use documentaries to reach out to potential supporters and create change.

One of the shorts in the festival is *In the Morning,* a prizewinning fictional movie based on the true story of an honor killing in Turkey, where a rape victim was murdered by her brother to prevent her from bringing further "shame" on the family. Filmmaker Danielle Lurie stresses that honor killings, which occur primarily in the Middle East, are not linked to Islam—the basis for the killings is tribal. Lurie hopes the movie—which, thanks to the Internet, can be seen in Turkey and throughout the world—might help persuade the young boys often chosen by their fathers to commit the murders (because they tend to get shorter sentences) to not kill their sisters.

Lurie might be echoing everyone from a Hollywood producer like Jeff Skoll to her fellow young filmmakers when she says, "I would be naive to say that any single film on its own could make a difference, but my hope is that a movie, along with other films and educational tools, could create enough awareness that those in positions of power could effect change." Increasingly, it looks like these and other movies are placing the audience in those positions of power.

PERSONAL RESPONSE

Write about a film that has made a difference to you, perhaps one that made you aware of a problem you did not know about before or that moved you to act or think differently.

QUESTIONS FOR CLASS OR SMALL-GROUP DISCUSSION

1. What, according to Jacobs, have nontraditional films and documentaries done to "promote pro-social behavior" (paragraph 2)?

2. How convincing do you find Jacobs' examples and his explanations of how they support his thesis?

3. Discuss the range of topics covered by the films that Jacobs mentions. If you have seen any of them, what did you think of them? If you haven't seen any of them, which might you be interested in viewing, based on Jacobs' comments about them?

4. Discuss additional topics that you think would make good subjects for the kinds of films that Jacobs is writing about.

GIRLS JUST WANNA HAVE FANGS: THE UNWARRANTED BACKLASH AGAINST FANS OF THE WORLD'S MOST POPULAR VAMPIRE-ROMANCE

SADY DOYLE

Sady Doyle is a writer living in New York. Her articles have appeared in online editions of The American Prospect *and London's* Guardian, *as well as other publications. She blogs at Tigerbeatdown. com. This article was posted on November 19, 2009, at the online site www.Prospect.org and published in the November 2009 print issue of* The American Prospect.

When *New Moon*, the second film adaptation of Stephenie Meyer's four-part *Twilight* series, opens in theaters this month, those who see it will not be getting great art. The faults of Meyer's immensely popular teen vampire-romance novels have been endlessly, and publicly, rehashed: the retrograde gender roles, the plodding plotlines, the super-heated goofiness of Meyer's prose. I can confirm for you that these faults are real!

Yet I could not stop reading the series. The books—all about sexy teen vampire Edward Cullen, his sexy teen werewolf rival Jacob Black, and their joint quest to stalk, control, and condescend their way into the ever-turgid affections of sexy teen (human) narrator Bella Swan—are slow, repetitive, and often unintentionally hilarious. ("If I hadn't seen him undressed, I would have sworn there was nothing more beautiful than Edward in his khakis." Wait. Hold up. The vampire is wearing khakis?)

Twilight isn't a literary masterpiece and doesn't need to be. There is, I would argue, a place for fantasies like these—specifically, a place in the lives of adolescent girls, who often find actual teenage boys more intimidating than the fictional vampire variety, and for whom imaginary worlds (where no one has to grow up, where danger is the prelude to a rescue, where boys have no hidden agendas aside from loving you forever) can be a shelter from the terrors of puberty. The books are silly—and have been roundly critiqued by feminists—but they speak to a legitimate need.

4   Meyer's commitment to satisfying that need hasn't gone unrewarded. In the first quarter of 2009, *Twilight* novels composed 16 percent of all book sales—four out of every 25 books sold were part of the series. The final installment, *Breaking Dawn*, sold 1.3 million copies on the day of its release in August 2008.

And then there are the movies. The first, *Twilight*, made $70.6 million on its opening weekend last November and set the record for biggest opening weekend for a film by a female director. The soundtrack sold 2.2 million copies. The follow-up film, *New Moon*, began selling out screenings more than two months ago, and its soundtrack is expected to be one of the top-selling albums of 2009, even though it's composed mostly of songs by indie artists.

Twilight is more than a teen dream. It's a massive cultural force. Yet the very girliness that has made it such a success has resulted in its being marginalized and mocked. Of course, you won't find many critics lining up to defend Dan Brown or Tom Clancy, either; mass-market success rarely coincides with literary acclaim. But male escapist fantasies—which, as anyone who has seen *Die Hard* or read those Tom Clancy novels can confirm, are not unilaterally sophisticated, complex, or forward-thinking—tend to be greeted with shrugs, not sneers. The *Twilight* backlash is vehement, and it is just as much about the fans as it is about the books. Specifically, it's about the fact that those fans are young women.

Twilight fans (sometimes known as "Twi-Hards") are derided and dismissed, sometimes even by outlets that capitalize on their support. MTV News crowned "Twilighters" its Woman of the Year in 2008, but referred to them as "shrieking and borderline-stalker female fans." You can count on that word—shrieking—to appear in most articles about *Twilight* readers, from *New York* magazine's Vulture blog ("Teenage girls shrieking . . . before the opening credits even begin") to *Time* magazine ("Shrieking fangirls [outdoing] hooting fanboys . . . in number, ardor, and decibel level") to *The Onion*'s A.V. Club ("Squealing hordes of (mostly) teenage, female fans") to *The New York Times* ("Squeals! The 'Twilight Saga: New Moon' Teaser Trailer Is Here!"). Yes, Twi-Hards can be loud. But is it really necessary to describe them all by the pitch of their voices? It propagates the stereotype of teen girls as hysterical, empty-headed, and ridiculous.

8   Self-described geeks and horror fans are especially upset at how the series introduces the conventions of the romance novel—that most stereotypically feminine, most scorned of literary forms—into their far more highbrow and culturally relevant monster stories. At the 2009 Comic-Con, *Twilight* fans were protested and said to be "ruining" the event. Fans of *Star Wars*, *Star Trek*, *X-Men*, and *Harry Potter* are seen as dorks at worst, participants in era-defining cultural phenomena at best. Not so for *Twilight* fans. What sets *Twilight* apart from Marvel comics? The answer is fairly obvious, and it's not—as geeks and feminists might hope—the quality of the books or movies. It's the number of boys in the fan base.

Compare Meyer to J. K. Rowling. The *Harry Potter* author had her detractors, too. In a 2000 *Wall Street Journal* article, Harold Bloom turned up his nose at the *Harry Potter* series, calling the books "not well written" and an example of cultural "dumbing-down." The headline: "Can 35 Million Book Buyers Be Wrong? Yes." In 1999, *The New York Times* seemed bewildered by the popularity of *Harry Potter* and noted, in a hilariously late-'90s turn of phrase, that "the books have become the literary equivalent of Furby stuffed animals." Yet *Potter* fans were never mocked as much as *Twilight* fans are, and respect for the series grew along with its readership. The final three books in the series were given full-length considerations in the *Times* by that most respected of book reviewers, Michiko Kakutani. "J. K. Rowling's monumental, spellbinding epic, 10 years in the making, is deeply rooted in traditional literature," reads her review of the final *Potter* novel, published in 2007.

There's little doubt that Rowling's success stemmed from her talent. But she also benefited from escaping the girly ghetto to which *Twilight* has been confined. Her publishers, famously, asked her to bill herself as J. K. rather than Joanne so as not to alienate male readers, and her books focused on a male hero and included lots of boy-friendly elements such as sports and warfare. She won a male readership, and with it, praise for the "universality" of her work.

Meyer, meanwhile, decided to forgo a pen name in favor of Stephenie, and *Twilight* is largely narrated by a girl. The books don't strive to draw in straight, male readers: There's little action, lots of emotion, and much lavish description of Edward Cullen's beauty. The vampire heartthrob isn't exactly macho. He's smooth-skinned, delicate-featured, and his body even sparkles. Edward abstains from sex and human blood, turning down several opportunities to enjoy both, and talks about his feelings frequently. To be blunt, he's not much of a man by sexist standards. In less-civilized regions of the Internet, the words "gay," "faggot," and "pussy" are thrown around liberally in discussions of the series, and of Edward.

12   Is it any wonder that there are so few visible male *Twilight* fans? Although boys' lack of interest in the series is used to argue against its "universality," the fact is that boys who do like it may be legitimately scared to say so. The vitriol aimed at the series is often about policing gender and punishing girliness—and boys who dare to enjoy something so blatantly non-masculine would almost certainly find themselves harshly judged.

Yet, if the numbers are any indication, you don't need male fans to dominate the marketplace. In this decade, teen girls have backed the success of Taylor Swift (who ranks above every artist on the pop charts except for Michael Jackson), Miley Cyrus (responsible for multiple best-selling albums, a television series, a concert film, a movie, and various merchandise including a best-selling book), and the blockbuster movie franchise *High School Musical*. In the 1990s, teenage girls were responsible for the runaway success of Justin Timberlake, Britney Spears, and *Titanic*, the top-grossing movie of all time. A fan base of teen girls launched Madonna's multi-decade career. And there was that 1960s boy band—the one with all the catchy, cheery pop songs and the cute, nonthreatening members who made girls squeal. I believe they called themselves The Beatles.

Teen girls have the power to shape the market because they don't have financial responsibilities, tend to be passionate about their interests, and share those interests socially. If a girl likes something, she's liable to recommend it to her friends; a shared enthusiasm for Edward, or the Jonas Brothers, or anything else, becomes part of their bond. Marketers prize teenage girls, even as the media scoff at them.

If you want to matter, though, apparently you need boys. The third film adaptation of the *Twilight* series, *Eclipse*, will be helmed by horror director David Slade, who has made such movies as *Hard Candy* and *Thirty Days of Night*. Even though it will not hit theaters until June 2010, it is already being touted as "darker," more action-packed, and more "guy friendly." Because the popularity of the *Twilight* formula guarantees *Eclipse* will be a box-office smash, the decision to consciously appeal to boys seems more like a grab at credibility than at profit. Romance-loving Twi-Hards be damned! Who cares about disappointing a huge, passionate, lucrative fan base if they're all a bunch of *girls*?

16   As *Twilight* demonstrates, not everything girls like is good art—or, for that matter, good feminism. Still, the *Twilight* backlash should matter to feminists, even if the series makes them shudder. If we admit that girls are powerful consumers, then we admit that they have the ability to shape the culture. Once we do that, we might actually start listening to them. And I suspect a lot of contemporary girls have more to talk about than Edward Cullen.

PERSONAL RESPONSE

If you have read the books and/or seen the films that Doyle discusses, explain your response to them. If you haven't read the books or seen the films, explain whether you are intrigued by them after reading this article.

QUESTIONS FOR CLASS OR SMALL-GROUP DISCUSSION

1. Why do you think Doyle begins her essays by pointing out the faults and weaknesses of the *Twilight* series? Do you consider it an effective strategy in her argument?

2. Summarize Doyle's argument. What evidence does she provide to support her position? Are you convinced that the backlash against fans of the *Twilight* series is "unwarranted" (subtitle)?

3. According to Doyle, what is the difference between teenage girls' escapist fantasies and the escapist fantasies of males? Do you agree with her on this point?

4. In your own words, state the differences that Doyle sees between two successful female writers of popular series, Stephenie Meyer and J. K. Rowling. Can you add anything to her comparison? Are there any points on which you disagree with Doyle?

PERSPECTIVES ON FILM AND TELEVISION

Suggested Writing Topics

1. Argue for or against Sady Doyle's position that the backlash against "Twi-Hards" is "unwarranted" in "Girls Just Wanna Have Fangs: The Unwarranted Backlash Against Fans of the World's Most Popular Vampire-Romance."

2. Like advertisers, producers of television shows argue that they do not create problems but simply reflect the values of society. Explain your position on the subject of how much responsibility television producers should bear for the images portrayed in their programs.

3. Write an analysis of a popular television show or film. Your analysis can be either positive or negative, depending on your feelings about it. You may criticize it as ridiculous, boring, or poorly acted, for instance, or you may praise a brilliant, hilarious, or wonderfully acted one.

4. Chris Gould in "Batman, the Unexpected Cultural Revolution," refers to the 1960s *Batman* series as "a depiction of pop art utopia." In Chapter 8, writer Philip Reeve in "The Worst Is Yet to Come" calls for more utopian fiction to counterbalance the dark dystopian fiction being written today. Argue for or against the proposition that we need more utopian works like the *Batman* series or other fictional representations of utopia in popular culture.

5. Explore the positive and negative aspects of a particular type of television programming, such as situation comedies, medical dramas, or soap operas. Use several programs of the type as examples.

6. Assess the quality of today's films by using examples of a film or films you have seen recently. Consider, for instance, evaluating the values endorsed by the film(s).

7. Write a position paper on the topic of sexually explicit and graphically violent Hollywood films by selecting one film for close analysis. You may want to mention two or three other examples to support your position.

8. Explore the effects on you, either positive or negative, of a movie or television program that you saw when you were growing up.

9. If you are a fan of reality shows on television, choose one that you particularly like and explain why it appeals to you. If you do not like reality shows, pick one that you particularly dislike and explain why you do not like it.

10. Examine portrayals of any of the following in several television programs: the American family, women, men, a particular ethnic group, or a particular age group.

11. Write a letter to the president of one of the major television networks in which you express your views on the nature and quality of its programming for children.

12. Write a letter to either or both the sponsors and the producer of a television program you find particularly violent, mindless, or vulgar, explaining your complaint and what you would like to see changed. Or, write a letter to the sponsors or producer of a television program you find intellectually stimulating, educational, or informative, praising the program and pointing out its best features.

Research Topics

1. Research the critical responses to the *Twilight* series of books or films and compare them with the critical responses to the Harry Potter series of books or films. As part of your research, read books or view films in both series and formulate a position on how the two compare.

2. Chris Gould in "Batman, the Unexpected Cultural Revolution" states that the 1960s television series *Batman* "spawned a vast counter-revolution in future representations of Batman" (paragraph 11). Research representations of Batman since the 1960s to demonstrate or counter Gould's assertion.

3. Select a particular genre of film, such as comedy, western, romance, fantasy, or action, and research observations of various film historians, film critics, and/or other film commentators about the films in that genre. This is a broad topic, so be sure to narrow your focus early on. One approach is to assess the historical development of the genre and its current state. As you do your preliminary reading, look for a controversial issue on which to focus your research. Then draw your own conclusions after you thoroughly research your subject.

4. Select a particular type of television program, such as reality TV, news program, talk show, children's entertainment, drama, or situation comedy, and research what critics say about such programming currently and historically. Is there a program that represents the best of the type? The worst of the type?

5. Film or television critics and commentators sometimes use the term *golden age* to refer to a period in the past when a particular type of film or program reached its peak of excellence. Select a medium—film or television—and a genre—comedy, drama, or another of your choice—and research what characterizes "golden age" for the type and which program(s) or film(s) represent the type. If possible, view representative programs or films and include your responses to them in your research paper.

6. Much has been written about certain images in films or on television, such as the portrayal of women, of minorities, and of class issues. Select a particular image or theme to research for its representation in films or on television. Choose a specific period (films/programs from this year or last year, or films/programs from a previous decade, for instance) and narrow your focus as much as possible. This task will become more manageable once you begin searching for sources and discover the nature of articles, books, and other materials on the general subject.

7. Research a recent film that generated controversy, or view any of the films mentioned in Donovan Jacobs's "Creating Reel Change." View the film and read what critics and other authorities on the subject of film have to say about this particular one.

8. Research the Television Violence Act. Find out what it is and what critics, behaviorists, and media experts say about its potential effectiveness. Then explain your own opinion of the effectiveness of such an act.

9. In 1961, Newton N. Minow coined the term *vast wasteland* for what he saw as television's empty content and anti-intellectualism. Argue either that television remains a vast wasteland or that the phrase is unfair to television today. Base your position on research into the views of experts or others who have published opinions on the subject. Include the results of studies or any other relevant data you find.

RESPONDING TO VISUALS

Dave Hogan/Getty Images

Enthusiastic fans of *Breaking Dawn* show their excitement at the movie premiere in London.

1. What do the looks on the fans' faces tell you about their attitude toward the film and its characters?
2. How do the signs the fans are holding contribute to the overall image?
3. How do the details of this photograph support the comments that Sady Doyle makes about the fans of the *Twilight* series in her essay "Girls Just Wanna Have Fangs"?

RESPONDING TO VISUALS

In search of America's laziest man

1. What do the man's clothing and the fact that he's asleep say about him as a television viewer?
2. How does the image of the man relate to the words coming from the television program?
3. What comment on reality television shows does this cartoon make?

CHAPTER 11

The Arts

Humans have always used a variety of creative ways in which to express themselves imaginatively through such forms as storytelling, drawing, painting, sculpture, and music. Researchers have discovered paintings in prehistoric caves that provide evidence of the earliest humans' compulsion to tell stories or depict significant aspects of their lives through pictures. Literature has long been regarded as a significant art form. Indeed, some would claim that imaginative writing, whether it be a short story, a novel, a play, a poem, or some other form of creative expression, is just as crucial to the nurturing of the human soul as are visual arts and music.

Today some would argue that video games, websites, and other digital forms are the latest developments in mankind's quest to express itself aesthetically. The question of whether video games are art has been taken seriously in the twenty-first century, as evidenced by the many articles and books on the subject. An exhibition called "The Art of Video Games" in 2012 at the Smithsonian American Art Museum in Washington, D.C., certainly gave renewed impetus to the discussions, sometimes quite serious, sometimes frivolous, about the merits of video games as art. Indeed, a well-known film critic, Roger Ebert, weighed in on the subject and participated in a number of debates and forums about the legitimacy of games as an art form. The controversy was sparked by Ebert's remarks in 2005 about the film version of the game *Doom*, which ultimately led him to declare that games are not art because they do not and cannot explore what it means to be human as other art forms do. The discussion, heated at times, has continued to the present time, as evidenced by Rich Stanton's article "Who Framed Roger Ebert?" Although Stanton begins with a discussion of video games as art, he expands his focus to the general question of what art is, raising the classic issue of the distinction between "mass culture" and "high art." If you are a gamer, you will likely be interested and perhaps surprised by what he has to say about games as art. If you are not a gamer, you may nonetheless be intrigued by how he distinguishes what "art" is from what it is not.

The next two essays provide two sides of an argument over whether the plays of William Shakespeare should be revised for modern times. First, *Washington Post* theatre critic Peter Marks in "What's Wrong with the Old Bard, Pard?" laments the "meddling" frequently done these days with Shakespeare's plays by setting them in locations and times far from their original settings. He calls for a "more conscientious" tailoring of the plays to their original contexts and for more "common sense." In opposition, the artistic director of the Shakespeare Theatre Company, Michael Kahn, defends modern interpretations of the plays. Suggesting that the " 'traditional' vs. 'non-traditional' " argument has long been over, he gently rebukes Marks for his article and insists that "an artist's or theater's approach to art is a continually evolving process." As you read the two pieces, see which writer you agree with. Do you think it fair to update 400-year-old plays to more contemporary times and places, or is it better to leave them as originally written?

Many strong supporters of the arts believe that society would be lost without them. Such is the underlying assumption of Morris Dickstein's "How Song, Dance and Movies Bailed Us Out of the Depression." Demonstrating the role of artistic enterprises in shoring up the spirits of a desperate nation throughout the Great Depression, Dickstein argues that the creative arts may be called upon to do exactly the same thing in the current economic slump.

The subject of art and artists is so vast that these few readings serve only to indicate the breadth and depth of possible related topics and issues. Despite the persistence of art throughout time, the role of the artist in society and the relative value of art often are frequently debated topics. Tastes change and differ from generation to generation and individual to individual, as do values and beliefs about what is important to sustain and nurture a society and the standards by which people judge the merits of works of art. Determining what makes an artwork "good" or "bad" is often a subjective response to the art rather than a conscious application of objective standards. Do you have trouble determining whether a new movie, painting, or song is a good or bad one? How do you judge such works? As you consider the points made by the writers in this section, also think about the kinds of creative art that appeal to you, including what imaginative writing you like to read and perhaps write yourself. Think about the role that all of these forms of expression play in humans' lives: How might their absence affect humanity? Do you think your life would be impoverished without art, music, and literature? Why or why not?

WHO FRAMED ROGER EBERT?

RICH STANTON

Rich Stanton has been writing for Eurogamer since 2011, and also contributes to places like Edge, Nintendo Gamer, *and* PC Gamer. *He lives in Bath, England. This article was first published at EuroGamer.net 18 January, 2012.*

Are video games art? What's your reaction to that question? For me it's always a weary groan of resignation, followed by skipping the rest of the article. Perhaps that's arrogance, because for a sizeable chunk of the gaming audience it is a very big deal indeed, and a topic that won't go away. When there's a flashpoint, such as a couple of articles by the film critic Roger Ebert, no one could miss the storm. But whether games are art is not a question that needs answering, and these pieces are a useful tool for explaining why.

I'm not going to spend this article arguing with Ebert, but it's worth briefly reminding ourselves of what was said and done. The first salvo came after a review of the execrable movie version of *Doom*. In response to a comment from a reader, Ebert said "As long as there is a great movie unseen or a great book unread, I will continue to be unable to find the time to play video games."

Pretty cranky stuff, but each to their own. By March 2010 Kelee Santiago of thatgamecompany was delivering a talk at Ted in direct response to Ebert: "Stop the Debate: Video games are art, so what's next?" Santiago showed Waco Resurrection, Braid, and Flower while offering reasons for why games like these should be considered as art.

4   Ebert's most flammable statements came in his reply to this talk: "Perhaps it is foolish of me to say "never," because never, as Rick Wakeman informs us, is a long, long time. Let me just say that no video gamer now living will survive long enough to experience the medium as an art form."

And by the way, when games get close to "art" they cease to be games: "Santiago might cite a[n] immersive game without points or rules, but I would say then it ceases to be a game and becomes a representation of a story, a novel, a play, dance, a film. Those are things you cannot win; you can only experience them." At this point it should be clear that Ebert doesn't know anything about games and is pretty much making up points or rules as he goes along.

His final piece was in July 2010: "Okay, kids, play on my lawn." "There are many, many things I believe many members of our society don't "get," but I don't think they're too old or too young to "get" them, only differently evolved." If you don't get the things Ebert does, you're "differently evolved". Despite that, "I had to be prepared to agree that gamers can have an experience that, for them, is Art. I don't know what they can learn about another human being that way, no matter how much they learn about Human Nature."

Reprinted from Euorogamer.net, January 18, 2012, by permission of the author.

The idea that "art" now depends on learning about another human being is tossed in to keep games out, but the concept is not precise—it's another arbitrary line in the sand, another hoop to jump through after which there will be another. The argument is circular, resting on assumptions about shared values and the existence of art with a capital A that seem positively quaint. It's bunk—Ebert doesn't know about games, which is fine, and there this should have ended.

8   Instead, everyone had a reaction: the *Guardian* was the coolest head in the crowd; *Cracked* took it head-on; and every popular specialist site from 1Up to Gamasutra addressed it in their own style. There are many hundreds more examples; Twitter at the time was swamped with it, and a quick google found a blog about it from as recently as last month. Nearly every response includes examples of games that the authors believe deserve recognition as art.

Responses to Ebert were *everywhere*. People found the topic irresistible—Ebert's two blog posts have around 6,600 comments total at the time of writing. Perhaps the fullest was Professor Brian Moriarty's talk at GDC 2011 "An Apology for Roger Ebert." It's an interesting and witty take, and fully aware of how swampy an issue "art" is—but despite this, falls into a nasty trap extremely common among the responses. It does down games. Moriarty's talk posits that games may one day be art, but that there are no games yet that fit the bill. His reasoning comes down to a distinction between mass culture (what games are now) and high art (what they may one day achieve)—in this talk, the terms are "Kitsch" and "Sublime Art":

> Kitsch is fundamentally standard, and when standards change, it becomes first irrelevant, then corny, and finally the subject of nostalgia. Sublime art is either always relevant, or not at all. It is never the subject of nostalgia, but often the subject of discovery.

These definitions make so many assumptions they mean nothing. Whose and what standards? Who defines relevance, and in relation to whom? Trends are different everywhere, they come and go and no single creator or medium is independent of them. You may as well say "sublime art is either always here, or there."

This is what high art versus mass culture always comes down to, an indefinable quality that the former possesses which is discernible only to a few. This mystical knowledge confers an unquestioned authority, and is "profound", "transcendent", "sacred" and other such absolutes. In Moriarty's case, "Sublime art is the still evocation of the inexpressible." Or to put it another way—I don't know much about art, but I know what I like.

12   None of this should be news in the 21st century—the idea of art as something that can be defined objectively began to crumble almost 100 years ago when Marcel Duchamp exhibited a urinal titled "Fountain". My favorite example of this is an exhibition held in 1958 by Yves Klein where the Parisian gallery was left entirely empty. Not because I like the idea of attending, but because it's fun watching defenders of art fit it into their schema—clearly, Klein's exhibition is a special type of nothing.

I'm not here to bash modern art—I love all this stuff. But it's important to distinguish our appreciation of any work from a term that is meaningless. Art is a word that denotes exclusivity, but in the current day its meaning can only ever be inclusive. What is art? Art is what any single person considers to be art. There is no such thing as an objective definition, because all that anyone can ever truly know of something is their own experience. When the only possible judgments are subjective, a belief in the existence of a category of things that are "art" is absurd.

Yet the term still has power. The history of art when we're talking of literature or music or painting is an invented one—those works deemed by this or that critic to be worthy of exalted status. The canon in any medium is the product of remarkably few minds. I think this is why games writers were drawn to Ebert's remarks. It is often a navel-gazing profession, and one whose practitioners agonize over the question of their own importance.

People want to feel special, like their impressions and understanding of a work somehow mean more. Not only does this make the traditionally weighty topic of art appealing, but as a subject it binds criticism into a reassuring loop of self-aggrandizement. The only reason Ebert's remarks acquired any traction whatsoever is because he is seen as an embodiment of taste—a Real Critic who knows about Real Art.

16   But writers aren't the only culprits here. That old fox Ebert saw our glowing weak spot a mile off. "Why aren't gamers content to play their games and simply enjoy themselves? They have my blessing, not that they care. Do they require validation? In defending their gaming against parents, spouses, children, partners, co-workers or other critics, do they want to be able to look up from the screen and explain, "I'm studying a great form of art?" Then let them say it, if it makes them happy."

This is it. In arguing for "games as art" we betray a desire for approval—for the wise words and nodding head of an arbiter. Everyone knows several people, young and old, who don't get games and regard them as children's amusements. I know many more than that. So the thought of describing them as art is comforting, it's authoritative, and a salve to the nagging feeling you're wasting your time. Don Quixote tilts at the windmills, and the windmills tilt back. No one breaks the spell.

We're at the forefront of the only medium in history in which the defining characteristic is interactivity. Is that not enough? I never feel like I'm wasting my time playing a game. Roger Ebert doesn't play videogames and doesn't know anything about them—so why did his argument become a focal point, taken seriously enough to be the subject of so many talks, comments, and even articles like this? The fact is that *we* framed Roger Ebert, contextualizing his words with a jabber of conferences, blogs, and click-throughs. Yet the problem was never his opinion, or indeed any other ad hominem attack on video games.

The problem is that in engaging with the question we put art on a pedestal—and "art" just doesn't exist. It's a confidence trick, a way of putting things down. No critic can quite pin art down, but plenty will assure you it is a very grand thing, and they have the refined sensibilities to identify it. Who is the greater fool? The next time someone questions games, remember Yves Klein and his exhibition of thin air. There's never been a more perfect image of art, and just how empty defining it is.

PERSONAL RESPONSE

How do you answer Stanton's opening question, "Are videogames art"?

QUESTIONS FOR CLASS AND SMALL-GROUP DISCUSSION

1. What does Stanton mean by his title? What answer does he give to the question posed by the title?

2. Explain your understanding of the distinction between "mass culture" and "high art" (paragraph 9) or "Kitsch" and "Sublime art" (paragraph 10).

3. Summarize the controversy over the definition of art. What is Stanton's position on the subject? Do you agree with him?

4. Stanton says that "the term [art] still has power" (paragraph 15). What do you think he means by that? Do you agree with him?

WHAT'S WRONG WITH THE OLD BARD, PARD?

PETER MARKS

Peter Marks has been theater critic for the Washington Post *since 2002 and writes reviews and features on topics related to Washington and other theaters. This column appeared in the* Washington Post *on July 1, 2012.*

Members of the theatergoing jury: I come before you today to speak in favor of men in tights.

It is the fashion in these meddling times—now perhaps more than ever—to put the doublets in mothballs and tie up Shakespeare in the threads of ponderous context. Only cursory consideration seems to be given in Washington or Baltimore, London or New York to whether it makes sense to dress Petruchio in chaps or Macbeth's witches in the aprons of abattoir workers. To transport Lear to the heath of *Waiting for Godot* or *Shylock* to a tenement on the Lower East Side. To decide that Messina is not on Sicily but a stone's throw from Havana, or that the Rome of "Julius Caesar" was actually meant to be the Baghdad of Saddam Hussein.

Yes, somehow, a consensus has been reached that William Shakespeare was not a playwright but a time-travel agent, one whose points of geographic and temporal reference were meant as mere suggestions. A milestone of sorts was achieved this season at Washington's Tony Award-winning Shakespeare Theatre Company, where all three of its Shakespeare productions—*Much Ado about Nothing*, *The Two Gentlemen of Verona* and current *The Merry Wives of Windsor*—have been set, with wildly varying degrees of success, in the century between 1915 and now.

4   The city's other influential outlet for Shakespeare, the Folger Theatre, has proved just as seducible by directors lugging in their conceptual baggage. A rootin', tootin' *The Taming of the Shrew*, set in the Old West, just finished a run in its Capitol Hill playhouse, where one would have been forgiven for wondering why angry Kate didn't use her trusty gun, or how Padua wound up being a suburb of Tombstone. The scouting for unique environments in which to speak in iambic pentameter goes on apace in other major cities: Witness the arch and overpraised new *As You Like It* in New York's Central Park, set in the wilderness of mid-19th-century America, with banjo-picking exiles from the court—in this case, a fort like those eternally under attack in vintage cowboy-and-Indian flicks.

The fussing with the cosmetics of Shakespeare has become so routine that it is a shock to more devoted patrons of the Bard when any of his plays are performed these days in both the time and place the author intended them. Has a belief taken hold that only by placing Shakespeare's characters in elaborate disguise can a contemporary theatergoer view them as relevant? The compulsive tinkering yields distressing side effects. Distracted audiences can not only lose touch with the pleasure of listening to Shakespeare's language but also may become less able to distinguish clearly the worthier attempts at innovation.

The application, for instance, of anachronism to enlarge a theme can be a very useful tool, one that director Rebecca Bayla Taichman employed to fine effect in her abstracted updating of *The Taming of the Shrew* at Shakespeare Theatre in 2007. The difference here was in a director, challenging *Shrew*'s antiquated view of women, who carefully chose a dim sum of modern references that helped us see where attitudes have (or haven't) evolved since Shakespeare's time. In the cases of Shakespeare's broader comedies, where the expectation expands for some degree of absurdity, the demand for rigorous logic recedes. This is partly why director Michael Kahn's psychedelic Beatles-inspired *Love's Labor's Lost* in 2006 proved so easy to digest—and like.

Certainly, the exuberant elasticity of Shakespeare's brain, and the sometimes fantastic landscapes he conjured, for places he'd never been—the enchanted island of *The Tempest*; the Alexandria of *Antony and Cleopatra*—justifiably electrify the creative impulses of directors and designers. I have no desire to curb the fertile dreamers of the theater. Sometimes a play fairly seamlessly accommodates a temporal transfer, as director Stephen Rayne accomplishes in his *Merry Wives*, by retaining the evocative English milieu of Windsor and simply pushing the era forward to World War I. And for the purposes of introducing the youngest to Shakespeare, some artful analogizing is useful, as the playwright Ken Ludwig has demonstrated, in adapting Shakespeare for high school drama clubs.

8   What I pine for, though, is for dreaming to be tailored a bit more conscientiously to the contours of the plays—and common sense.

How far from sense the ideas can veer was illustrated in Shakespeare Theatre Company's recent transposition of *Much Ado about Nothing* to a hacienda in 1930s Cuba. Director Ethan McSweeny's overly specific reinterpretation not only compelled an audience into a contrived cultural framework but also committed the clumsy error of translating characters' names into what some perceived as ethnic stereotypes. The low characters Hugh Oatcake and George Seacoal became Juan Huevos and Jose Frijoles. After protests were raised, many of them by Latino artists, the production sensibly reverted to the original Shakespearean names.

As in Aaron Posner's Wild West *Shrew* at Folger, it erred by hewing so faithfully to a concept that it was drained of an ineffable essence of authenticity.

My sneaking suspicion is that the mania for transporting a Rosalind or a Richard III to a newfangled forest or kingdom may sometimes be an anxious reflex, a product of a general unease in contemporary theater over the rigors of speaking the verse and fully illuminating character. What better way to take some of the pressure off a cast's uneven vocal skills than to plop actors into realms in which the flatness of speech more easily echoes that of our own?

12   Some of the problems of transposition can be mitigated by actors of elite skill; Ian Merrill Peakes, whose range at Folger has encompassed both Iago and Henry VIII, comes to mind as an interpreter of Shakespeare who transcends concept; there is an invisibility to his technique—and a confidence with the language—that allows him to be absorbed into any scenario. For me, though, the ultimate in high-concept Shakespeare is a stripping away of all concept, epitomized by director Trevor Nunn's extraordinary *Macbeth* with Judi Dench and Ian McKellen, way back in 1976. I've never again felt the minds of Elizabethan villains opened so nakedly before me.

Perhaps it's the perpetual yearning for Shakespeare with that kind of sizzling immediacy that fuels my impatience with the intrusive global bunting that's draped over his plays. And maybe that's why my recent visit to Staunton, Va.'s American Shakespeare Center, where the staging is crisp and unvarnished, felt like such a tonic. In any event, I'm not holding my breath for a wholesale shift to bare-bones stagings and simpler dramatic virtues. The next time Verona looks like Vegas, or Viola pulls up in a Volvo, I'll merely chalk it up to the same old, same old.

PERSONAL RESPONSE

To what extent do you agree that updates to character, setting, and time period in productions of works by writers such as Shakespeare are necessary and/or right in order to appeal to today's audiences?

QUESTIONS FOR CLASS OR SMALL-GROUP DISCUSSION

1. What does Marks mean by his opening sentence: "Members of the theater-going jury: I come before you today to speak in favor of men in tights."
2. What is Marks' complaint? Does he want all of Shakespeare's plays produced today as they were originally written?
3. Where does Marks make concessions in his argument?
4. What does Marks mean when he states that Shakespeare was "a time-travel agent" (paragraph 3)? How would you characterize the tone of this article? Where else does Marks use language that conveys his tone?

SHAKESPEARE MEETS THE 21st CENTURY

Michael Kahn

Michael Kahn has been the artistic director of the Shakespeare Theatre Company in Washington, D.C. since 1986. He has been nominated for and won many awards for his work, including a Tony nomination, a Saturday Review *award, a Macarther award, and many Helen Hayes awards, along with numerous others.*

I confess I experienced a slight case of reverse culture shock upon reading *Post* theater critic Peter Marks's recent article on contextualizing Shakespeare ["What's Wrong with the Old Bard, Pard?" Arts, July 1]. I had just spent a stimulating week in London seeing a collection of classical plays produced in a diversity of styles. The houses were packed with enthusiastic audiences, and it seemed to me that the old argument of "traditional" vs. "nontraditional" interpretations had long ago faded away.

In a sense, all productions of Shakespeare are interpretations: We do not know the performance style of Shakespeare's actors, so succeeding generations have adapted their performance to the dominant acting style of the day. In the past several decades, there has been a major shift from the beautifully voiced rhetorical approach, best exemplified by John Gielgud, to attempts to create a more conversational tone that still respects the rhyme and meter. We have no idea how Burbage looked, but the heavily operatic makeup as worn by the Laurence Oliviers and Michael Redgraves (de rigueur for the mid-20th century classical plays) has been replaced by little to none. Even though scholars disagree on what Elizabethan actors' pronunciation sounded like, the assumption that U.S. actors must adopt an upper-class English accent to be "classical" has undergone a significant revision (as has the British actor).

Reprinted from *The Washington Post,* August 3, 2012, by permission of the author.

Shakespeare's theater was itself based on a creative process of "interpretation." The playwright borrowed his stories from Ovid, Plutarch and Holinshed and set them in ancient Greece, ancient Rome, Sicily, France, and in the 12th to 16th centuries without an attempt at historicity: basic setting, Elizabethan clothes (Cleopatra in a farthingale, King John in "pumpkin pants"). Imagine the immediacy of audiences coming to the Globe or the Rose, without years of accumulated theatrical traditions or cultural baggage, encountering extraordinary characters, incidents and ideas. Kings, queens and peasants— dressed exactly as themselves, in modern dress, speaking in their accents. How very electric the connection between audience and player must have been!

4   I believe all theater artists who approach these plays envy that encounter and explore strategies to re-create that experience in their own time. Some do it by erecting a historical space; others through the investigation of new theater practices that help connect modern audiences, raised on film and TV, to the material or that encourage audiences that perhaps have seen a particular play many times to look and hear it afresh.

The aesthetics of today's directors come from a variety of influences and information: film, visual arts, psychology, sociology and new theater techniques but also iconic and resonant historical periods—the Weimar Republic, Freud's Vienna, Stalinist, Prohibition, Victorian, etc. Their overwhelming desire is to illuminate the play they have chosen and to see it live onstage.

I have been influenced by many things: Kabuki, Brecht, Strehler, Zeffirelli, Brook, Fassbinder, Orson Welles, Bergman's late staging of *Hamlet* and by a continually growing understanding of how to close-read a play.

I am grateful that, years ago, Joseph Papp of the Public Theater asked me to direct *Measure for Measure* based on my production of an avant-garde play he'd seen off-off-off Broadway. It was important for me to create a decadent and specifically urban environment in which to explore the complex issues investigated in this often-ambitious text. I asked designer Ming Cho Lee to build a brick wall with something that looked like fire escapes to blot out the overwhelming sylvan beauty of Central Park. Papp hated it and wanted it changed, but it was too late. The production worked; the audience got it and so did the critics. It won a bunch of prizes, I began a career and Joe apologized. I felt passionately about the play and its resonance for New York at the time.

8   I am so grateful to be able to bring work like this to Washington and to work with inventive, intelligent and courageous directors who are equally passionate about plays that are more than four centuries old. I am also grateful to the audiences who go along with us . . . most of the time.

An artist's or a theater's approach to art is a continually evolving process. As Marks said in his review of our all-male (and admittedly not completely successful) production of *Romeo and Juliet*, the "gender-restricted gambit is an estimable reminder of how many routes can be traveled with Shakespeare—and how many more this company needs to explore."

PERSONAL RESPONSE

Discuss your experience with Shakespeare's works: have you read plays or sonnets, acted in a Shakespearean play, or seen a production, either on stage or on film, of a play?

QUESTIONS FOR CLASS OR SMALL-GROUP DISCUSSION

1. What does Kahn think of Peter Marks' article "What's Wrong with the Bard, Pard"?
2. What argument does Kahn make in reply to Marks? What evidence does he use to support his argument?
3. What does Kahn have to say about today's theater directors? Does this strengthen or weaken his argument?
4. What do you understand Kahn to mean when he writes that "an artist's or a theater's approach to art is a continually evolving process" (paragraph 9)? Do you agree with him?

HOW SONG, DANCE AND MOVIES BAILED US OUT OF THE DEPRESSION

MORRIS DICKSTEIN

Morris Dickstein is Distinguished Professor of English at the Gradu-ate Center of the City University of New York and senior fellow of the Center for the Humanities, which he founded in 1993 and directed for seven years. He is author of the following books: Gates of Eden: American Culture in the Sixties *(1977, 1997);* Double Agent: The Critic and Society *(1992);* Leopards in the Temple: The Trans-formation of American Fiction, 1945–1970 *(2002); and* Dancing in the Dark: A Cultural History of the Great Depression *(2009). This article appeared in the April 1, 2009, issue of* the Los Angeles Times.

Many were surprised that the final stimulus legislation signed by President Obama preserved a $50-million increase in arts funding that had been the sub-ject of a heated battle in Congress. Though it amounted to only a tiny fraction of the measure's total cost, it had become the target of conservatives, many of whom consider the arts frivolous, elitist and, frankly, left-wing. They showed their disdain in February when they pushed for—and passed—a Senate amendment ruling out stimulus funds for museums, arts centers and theaters.

From the *Los Angeles Times*, April 1, 2009. Reprinted by permission of the author.

That shortsighted decision was reversed at the last moment, after supporters made a good case that the arts are often the linchpin of downtown neighborhoods, creating jobs and providing many other economic benefits: stimulating business, promoting urban renewal and attracting tourists.

But was that really the point? Is that really why we need the arts? These days, it seems that every discussion of the economic situation includes the obligatory comparison to the prolonged crisis of the 1930s, yet what the Depression and the New Deal actually showed is that the value of the arts goes well beyond job creation and economic stimulus.

4   Studies of the 1930s have shown how the economic meltdown was accompanied by psychological depression: loss of morale, a sense of despair, grave fears for the future. Going to the movies or listening to the radio could not solve these problems, but they could ease them in the same way that President Franklin D. Roosevelt's intimate fireside chats boosted morale and restored confidence.

The most durable cliché about the arts in the 1930s is that despite the surge of social consciousness among writers, photographers and painters (some of it supported by federal dollars), the arts offered Depression audiences little more than fluffy escapism, which was just what they needed.

But that's not the whole story. It's certainly a paradox that dire economic times produced such a fizzy, buoyant popular culture. From the warring couples of screwball comedy and the magical dancing of Fred Astaire and Ginger Rogers to the sophisticated music and lyrics of Cole Porter, Rodgers and Hart, and the Gershwins, the '30s generated mass entertainment legendary for its wit, elegance and style. This culture had its roots in the devil-may-care world of the 1920s, but it took on new meaning as the Depression deepened.

The engine of the arts in the '30s was not escapism, as we sometimes imagine, but speed, energy and movement at a time of economic stagnation and social malaise. When Warner Bros.—which avoided bankruptcy with its lively and topical gangster films, backstage musicals and Depression melodramas—promised a "New Deal in Entertainment," it was offering the cultural equivalent of the New Deal, a psychological stimulus package that might energize a shaken public.

8   With his roots in the ethnic slums, the gangster was a dynamic figure who somehow mastered his own fate even as he trampled on other people's lives. Busby Berkeley's showgirls were at the center of glittering fables of success and failure, wondrous changes in fortunes that resonated for '30s audiences. Against all odds, the performers came together into a working community; so did the stricken victims in topical melodramas right up through "The Grapes of Wrath," who discovered that they were helpless on their own but had a chance if they banded together and helped one another.

If we look at the arts as a life-giving form of social therapy, many other fads and fashions of the 1930s fall into place. The thrust of the culture, like the aims of the New Deal, was to get the country moving again. At cross-purposes in conversation, Astaire and Rogers seem perfectly ill-matched. Endlessly bickering with each other, they can agree on nothing. But once they dance, a swirling poetry of movement takes over.

The public also loved comedies about the very rich. Everyone could feel superior to their silliness, the weightlessness of their lives, yet live vicariously through their energy, irresponsibility and freedom, the snap of their delicious dialogue. Meanwhile, musical standards created a seductive dreamland, somewhere "over the rainbow," a better world where cloudy skies and rainy days somehow promised "pennies from heaven."

The propulsive swing music of the big bands, produced by performers and band leaders such as Duke Ellington, Artie Shaw and Benny Goodman, brought jazz to a mass audience for the first time—jazz to dance to, not simply to listen to. It filled the airwaves, ballrooms, nightclubs, even concert halls.

12   The visual equivalent of swing music was Art Deco. Gifted designers such as Raymond Loewy, Donald Deskey, Walter Dorwin Teague and Norman Bel Geddes stimulated consumption by putting a fluid sense of movement into everything from locomotives to table radios, projecting the consumer into a streamlined future otherwise hard to imagine. This culminated in the design of the 1939 New York World's Fair, with its flowing crowds and futuristic visions of "The World of Tomorrow."

Today's economic and cultural climate is still a long way from the Depression, which was already in its fourth year when FDR kicked off the New Deal. A quarter of the workforce was unemployed. The stock market had crashed, and the banking system had failed. Yet there are eerie resemblances, especially in the crisis of confidence that froze credit markets and blasted consumer spending almost overnight in mid-September of last year.

There is little sign so far of how the arts will respond to the damage done to our confidence and morale this time around. But movie-going has already increased by almost 16% this year. We know from the 1930s that the stimulating effect of art and entertainment comes not only in the jobs produced but in the emotional links with the public that absorbs this work and takes it to heart.

The arts can be a lifeline as well as a pleasant diversion, a source of optimism and energy as well as peerless insight, especially when so many people are stymied or perplexed by the unexpected changes in their world. As our troubles worsen, as stress morphs into anxiety and depression, we may desperately need the mixture of the real and the fantastic, the sober and the silly, that only the arts can bring us.

PERSONAL RESPONSE

How important are the arts to you? Which arts interest you most?

QUESTIONS FOR CLASS OR SMALL-GROUP DISCUSSION

1. State in your own words "How Song, Dance and Movies Bailed Us Out of the Depression" (title), according to Dickstein.

2. Dickstein reminds readers of a commonly held view of the arts during the Depression as "fluffy escapism" (paragraph 5). What argument does he make against that viewpoint? Are you convinced by his examples?

3. What is the New Deal (paragraph 3) that Dickstein refers to throughout his essay? What does he compare to the New Deal? Do you find the analogy effective?

4. Identify the following from paragraph 6: Fred Astaire and Ginger Rogers, Cole Porter, Rodgers and Hart, the Gershwins. Explain the reference to "Busby Berkeley's showgirls" (paragraph 8). Who are Duke Ellington, Artie Shaw, and Benny Goodman (paragraph 11)? What is Art Deco (paragraph 12)?

PERSPECTIVES ON THE ARTS

Suggested Writing Topics

1. Write in response to either Peter Marks' "What's Wrong with the Bard, Pard?" or Michael Kahn's "Shakespeare Meets the 21st Century."

2. Argue in support of or against Michael Kahn's statement in "Shakespeare Meets the 21st Century" that "an artist's or a theater's approach to art is a continually evolving process."

3. Explore the subject of how artists benefit society. Would society lose its soul without artists, as some critics suggest? How would society—or you personally—change without art?

4. Explain the importance of music and dance to society, or explain what it means to you personally. Can you envision your life without them?

5. If you have found that a particular form of creative art is a way to express yourself or use your imagination, explain what that art is and how it enables you to find self-expression.

6. One of the oldest forms of art is personal decoration. The body is still being used as a surface for symbolic expression by some young people, who use such techniques as branding, piercing, and tattooing. Defend or attack these practices by considering their relative artistic or creative merits.

7. Argue your position on the question of whether video games are art.

8. Defend the central place of art in education.

9. Drawing on at least two of the selections in this chapter, explain your viewpoint on the importance of art. Be sure to defend your position by supplying evidence not only from the essays but also from your own observations.

10. Who do you think are today's most creative people? You might highlight a particular group of people (artists, musicians) or a particular person. Give supporting evidence to substantiate your viewpoint.

11. Define *excellence* in relation to a specific art form (for instance, a painting, a novel, a poem, a dance, a song, or a film) by stating the criteria you use for judging that abstract quality and by giving examples you believe best illustrate it.

12. Select a work of art in any medium—painting, music, graphic literature, the theatre, dance, literature—and analyze its importance as a work of art, including what it means to you personally.

13. Answer the question: In what ways do the arts—music, art, drama, literature—contribute to the culture of a people? What is the value of art?

14. Explore the question of what makes some art live for all time and other art disappear. What makes a "timeless" work of art? Select a particular painting as an example and explain, in as much detail as possible, why you believe as you do.

15. Explain what you think is gained by a culture's interest in and support of the arts and what you think would be lost without it. As an alternative, argue that nothing is gained by a culture's art and that little or nothing would be lost without it. Make sure you explain why you feel as you do on this subject.

Research Topics

1. Research the subject of traditional versus nontraditional productions of Shakespeare's plays, starting with the two articles in this chapter that represent opposing views on the subject. Find out what other directors and critics have to say on the subject and form your own opinion based on your research.

2. Select an issue or a question related to the broad subject of the role of the artist in society to research and then argue your position on that issue. For instance, what is the role of the arts in today's culture? Do we need the arts? How do we define art?

3. In recent years, some people have been highly critical of what they see as obscenity or immorality in contemporary art. Some time ago, the works of Robert Mapplethorpe, for instance, were the object of such widespread, heated public debate that the National Endowment for the Arts was threatened with funding cuts because of similar projects it had supported with grants. Research the issue of censorship in the arts, and write an opinion paper on the subject. Consider: Does society have a moral obligation to limit what people can say, do, or use in their art, or do First Amendment rights extend to any subject or medium an artist wants to use?

4. The discoveries of prehistoric cave drawings that are fairly sophisticated in technique and meaning have led some art historians to suggest that art did not necessarily develop progressively, as has been commonly believed. Research this topic by reading about some of the prehistoric cave drawings that have been discovered and the theories of art historians about their importance. Then weigh the evidence and arrive at your own opinion about the nature and purpose of prehistoric art or its place in the historical development of art.

5. Research the role of the arts in strengthening students' abilities in other subject areas.

6. Research the contributions to art of a well-known artist or performer. Although you will want to provide a brief biographical sketch, your paper should focus on assessing the particular way(s) the artist had an effect on not only his or her own specialty but also "the arts" in general.

7. Research the history of a particular dance form.

8. Morris Dickstein in "How Song, Dance and Movies Bailed Us Out of the Depression" makes reference to many artists popular during the period of the Great Depression and the years following it. Research either an art form or a particular person or group mentioned in his article on the role it/they played in helping people cope with the Depression. You may want to use his book *Dancing in the Dark: A Cultural History of the Great Depression* as one of your sources, or use it as a way to discover what interests you most about the role of the arts in that period.

9. Research the subject of video games as art, selecting one specific aspect of what can be a very broad subject. For instance, locate information about art exhibitions featuring video games and see what the curators of the exhibitions as well as reviews by art critics. Read articles by scholars in professional journals, articles by art critics in popular periodicals, and books on the subject. Consider taking as a starting point the articles surrounding the controversy over Roger Ebert's declaration that video games are not and never will be "art," as discussed in Rich Stanton's "Who Framed Roger Ebert?" Consider whether games have any cultural or societal value and where the boundary is between a game as art rather than sheer entertainment—or can it be both?

RESPONDING TO VISUALS

SAUL LOEB/AFP/GettyImages

A woman tours a retrospective of US pop artist Roy Lichtenstein, including his 1963 canvas, "Whaam!" at the National Gallery of Art in Washington, D.C.

1. What story does the Lichtenstein painting tell?
2. What aspects of the image make it "pop art" rather than "art"? Comment on whether you think that the work of pop artists such as Lichtenstein should be exhibited in art galleries such as the National Gallery of Art in Washington.
3. Comment on the perspective from which the photograph is taken, the positioning of the woman looking at the canvas, and the use of light and dark. How would the image change if the woman were not in it?

RESPONDING TO VISUALS

1876 drawing, Romeo and Juliet   A modern-day Romeo and Juliet

1. What details make the one image specifically twenty-first century, or at least modern, and the other nineteenth century, or clearly an older time.

2. Comment on the contrast between the modern representation of the balcony scene in *Romeo and Juliet* and the nineteenth-century artist's interpretation of the play. If you have read the play, which image more closely represents your mental picture of the balcony scene? If neither image does, explain why not.

3. To what extent do you agree that updates to the works of historical writers such as Shakespeare are necessary and/or right?

PART THREE

Social and Behavioral Sciences

CHAPTER 12

Education

Education is a complex and crucially important subject. Without education, people face obstacles to participating fully in society. Because of its importance, education is also the subject of controversy. People are divided on issues such as what materials and activities are appropriate for the classroom, what methods of delivering material work best, how much homework ought to be required of students, and what skills and knowledge students must demonstrate to go on to subsequent educational levels. Periodically, philosophies of education change, curricula are restructured, classrooms are transformed, and instructors learn new approaches to teaching their subject matter. As a student who has gone through many years of education, beginning in the primary grades, you are uniquely positioned to comment on this subject. You have been immersed in education and are presumably currently enrolled in at least one class, the course for which you are using this textbook. In the essays in this chapter, writers express their strong opinions on the subject of education and criticize certain aspects of the educational system in America, so you are likely to find yourself either nodding your head in agreement or shaking your head in disagreement with what they say.

In the first essay in this chapter, Judy Blume recounts her experiences with banned books as a child and her sometimes painful experience of having her own books banned, attacked, censored, and vilified. In "Censorship: A Personal View," which is her introduction to a collection of stories by writers who have been censored, Blume explains how she "found [her]self at the eye of a storm." She also asks the question, "What is censorship?" You might think that there is an obvious definition, but she maintains that if you ask a dozen people, you will get a dozen different definitions. So as you read her essay, ask yourself what you consider censorship to be. You also may be interested to note, if you have read any of the titles that she mentions, which have been banned from the classroom or school libraries. What sorts of things were banned or censored when you were in school?

Following Blume's thoughts on censorship and what to do about it is a *Boston Globe* opinion column by Diane Ravitch on the subject of what she describes as a skill-centered fad in K–12 education. In "Critical Thinking? You Need Knowledge," Ravitch explains why she is critical of the "21st-Century Skills" initiative in public schools. As you read her piece, consider how you would define an intelligent person. What skills and knowledge must a truly educated student have?

Next is an excerpt from Mike Rose's book *Why School?* in which he narrates an encounter with a slightly brain-damaged student in a community college basic skills program. As you read about Anthony's achievements, can you think of students you have known who might be similarly challenged and motivated? What does the example of Anthony add to your understanding of the importance of education?

Finally, Thomas L. Friedman in "Pass the Books. Hold the Oil" explains why his favorite country, aside from the United States, is Taiwan. His explanation has to do with the value that the country and others like it place on education. Referring to studies that show correlations between a country's lack of resources in relation to how well its high school students do on certain standardized tests, he makes some observations about the importance of education, of knowledge, and of nurturing citizens' skills. You may be surprised to read the results of the studies he mentions and the recommendations he makes for a country's future well-being.

As you read these selections, think about your own education, the courses you have taken, your classroom activities, the teachers who have taught you, and your own reading habits. Where do you agree with the authors, and where do you disagree? Are your experiences similar to or different from what they describe? What is your own philosophy of education? How important do you believe education is to your well-being and sense of self? How important is reading to you?

CENSORSHIP: A PERSONAL VIEW

JUDY BLUME

Judy Blume's novels have sold over 80 million copies and have been translated into over thirty languages worldwide. Hers are also among the most frequently banned or challenged books in America because of

Reprinted with the permission of Simon & Schuster Books for Young Readers, an imprint of Simon & Schuster Children's Publishing Division from *Places I Never Meant to be* by Judy Blume. Copyright © 1999 Judy Blume.

her frank treatment of issues relating to children and young adults.
Among her more than two dozen novels are Are You There, God?
It's Me, Margaret *(1970);* It's Not the End of the World *(1972);*
Tales of a Fourth Grade Nothing *(1974);* Forever *(1975);* Wifey
(1978); Summer Sisters *(1998); and* Double Fudge *(2002). Blume*
is founder of the charitable and educational foundation The Kids Fund.
Because of her experiences with censorship, she edited Places I Never
Meant to Be: Original Stories by Censored Writers *(1999),*
a collection of short stories by authors who have been censored or banned.
The introduction to that collection is reprinted here.

When I was growing up I'd heard that if a movie or book was "Banned in Boston" everybody wanted to see it or read it right away. My older brother, for example, went to see such a movie—*The Outlaw,* starring Jane Russell—and I wasn't supposed to tell my mother. I begged him to share what he saw, but he wouldn't. I was intensely curious about the adult world and hated the secrets my parents, and now my brother, kept from me.

A few years later, when I was in fifth grade, my mother was reading a novel called *A Rage to Live,* by John O'Hara, and for the first time (and, as it turned out, the only time) in my life, she told me I was never to look at that book, at least not until I was *much* older. Once I knew my mother didn't want me to read it, I figured it must be really interesting!

So, you can imagine how surprised and delighted I was when, as a junior in high school, I found John O'Hara's name on my reading list. Not a specific title by John O'Hara, but *any* title. I didn't waste a minute. I went down to the public library in Elizabeth, New Jersey, that afternoon—a place where I'd spent so many happy hours as a young child, I'd pasted a card pocket on the inside back cover of each book I owned—and looked for *A Rage to Live.* But I couldn't find it. When I asked, the librarian told me *that* book was *restricted.* It was kept in a locked closet, and I couldn't take it out without written permission from my parents.

4   Aside from my mother's one moment of fear, neither of my parents had ever told me what I could or could not read. They encouraged me to read widely. There were no "Young Adult" novels then. Serious books about teenagers were published as adult novels. It was my mother who handed me *To Kill a Mockingbird* and Anne Frank's *Diary of a Young Girl* when they were first published.

By the time I was twelve I was browsing in the bookshelves flanking the fireplace in our living room where, in my quest to make sense of the world, I discovered J.D. Salinger's *The Catcher in the Rye,* fell in love with the romantic tragedies of Thomas Hardy and the Brontë sisters, and over-identified with "Marjorie Morningstar."

But at the Elizabeth Public Library the librarian didn't care. "Get permission in writing," she told me. When I realized she was not going to let me check out *A Rage to Live,* I was angry. I felt betrayed and held her responsible. It never occurred to me that it might not have been her choice.

At home I complained to my family, and that evening my aunt, the principal of an elementary school, brought me her copy of *A Rage to Live.* I stayed up half the night reading the forbidden book. Yes, it was sexy, but the characters and their story were what kept me turning the pages. Finally, my curiosity (about that book, anyway) was satisfied. Instead of leading me astray, as my mother must have feared, it led me to read everything else I could find by the author.

8   All of which brings me to the question *What is censorship?* If you ask a dozen people you'll get twelve different answers. When I actually looked up the word in *The Concise Columbia Encyclopedia* I found this definition: "[The] official restriction of any expression believed to threaten the political, social, or moral order." My thesaurus lists the following words that can be used in place of *ban* (as in book banning): *Forbid. Prohibit. Restrict.* But what do these words mean to writers and the stories they choose to tell? And what do they mean to readers and the books they choose to read?

I began to write when I was in my mid-twenties. By then I was married with two small children and desperately in need of creative work. I wrote *Are You There God? It's Me, Margaret* right out of my own experiences and feelings when I was in sixth grade. Controversy wasn't on my mind. I wanted only to write what I knew to be true. I wanted to write the best, the most honest books I could, the kinds of books I would have liked to read when I was younger. If someone had told me then I would become one of the most banned writers in America, I'd have laughed.

When *Margaret* was published in 1970 I gave three copies to my children's elementary school but the books never reached the shelves. The male principal decided on his own that they were inappropriate for elementary school readers because of the discussion of menstruation (never mind how many fifth- and sixth-grade girls already had their periods). Then one night the phone rang and a woman asked if I was the one who had written that book. When I replied that I was, she called me a communist and hung up. I never did figure out if she equated communism with menstruation or religion.

In that decade I wrote thirteen other books: eleven for young readers, one for teenagers, and one for adults. My publishers were protective of me during those years and didn't necessarily share negative comments about my work. They believed if I didn't know some individuals were upset by my books, I wouldn't be intimidated.

12   Of course, they couldn't keep the occasional anecdote from reaching me: the mother who admitted she'd cut two pages out of *Then Again, Maybe I Won't* rather than allow her almost thirteen-year-old son to read about wet dreams. Or the young librarian who'd been instructed by her male principal to keep *Deenie* off the shelf because in the book, Deenie masturbates. "It would be different if it were about a boy," he'd told her. "That would be normal."

The stories go on and on but really, I wasn't that concerned. There was no organized effort to ban my books or any other books, none that I knew of, anyway. The seventies were a good decade for writers and readers. Many of us came of age during those years, writing from our hearts and guts, finding editors and publishers who believed in us, who willingly took risks to help us find our audience. We were free to write about real kids in the real world. Kids with feelings and emotions, kids with real families, kids like we once were. And young readers gobbled up our books, hungry for characters with whom they could identify, including my own daughter and son, who had become avid readers. No mother could have been more proud to see the tradition of family reading passed on to the next generation.

Then, almost overnight, following the presidential election of 1980, the censors crawled out of the woodwork, organized and determined. Not only would they decide what *their* children could read but what *all* children could read. It was the beginning of the decade that wouldn't go away, that still won't go away almost twenty years later. Suddenly books were seen as dangerous to young minds. Thinking was seen as dangerous, unless those thoughts were approved by groups like the Moral Majority, who believed with certainty they knew what was best for everyone.

So now we had individual parents running into schools, waving books, demanding their removal—books they hadn't read except for certain passages. Most often their objections had to do with language, sexuality, and something called "lack of moral tone."

16   Those who were most active in trying to ban books came from the "religious right" but the impulse to censor spread like a contagious disease. Other parents, confused and uncertain, were happy to jump on the bandwagon. Book banning satisfied their need to feel in control of their children's lives. Those who censored were easily frightened. They were afraid of exposing their children to ideas different from their own. Afraid to answer children's questions or talk with them about sensitive subjects. And they were suspicious. They believed if kids liked a book, it must be dangerous.

Too few schools had policies in place enabling them to deal with challenged materials. So what happened? The domino effect. School administrators sent down the word: Anything that could be seen as controversial had to go. Often books were quietly removed from school libraries and classrooms or, if seen as potential troublemakers, were never purchased in the first place. These decisions were based not on what was best for the students, but what would not offend the censors.

I found myself at the center of the storm. My books were being challenged daily, often placed on *restricted* shelves (shades of Elizabeth, New Jersey, in 1955) and sometimes removed. A friend was handed a pamphlet outside a supermarket urging parents to rid their schools and libraries of Judy Blume books. Never once did the pamphlet suggest the books actually be read. Of course I wasn't the only target. Across the country, the Sex Police and the Language Police were thumbing through books at record speed, looking for illustrations, words or phrases that, taken out of context, could be used as evidence against them.

Puberty became a dirty word, as if children who didn't read about it wouldn't know about it, and if they didn't know about it, it would never happen.

20   The Moral Tone Brigade attacked *Blubber* (a story of victimization in the classroom) with a vengeance because, as they saw it, in this book evil goes unpunished. As if kids need to be hit over the head, as if they don't get it without having the message spelled out for them.

I had letters from angry parents accusing me of ruining Christmas because of a chapter in *Superfudge* called "Santa Who?" Some sent lists showing me how easily I could have substituted one word for another: meanie for bitch; darn for damn; nasty for ass. More words taken out of context. A teacher wrote to say she blacked out offending words and passages with a felt-tip marker. Perhaps most shocking of all was a letter from a nine-year-old addressed to *Jew*dy Blume telling me I had no right to write about Jewish angels in *Starring Sally J. Freedman as Herself.*

My worst moment came when I was working with my editor on the manuscript of *Tiger Eyes* (the story of a fifteen-year-old girl, Davey, whose beloved father dies suddenly and violently). When we came to the scene in which Davey allows herself to *feel* again after months of numbness following her father's death, I saw that a few lines alluding to masturbation had been circled. My editor put down his pencil and faced me. "We want this book to reach as many readers as possible, don't we?" he asked.

I felt my face grow hot, my stomach clench. This was the same editor who had worked with me on *Are You There God? It's Me, Margaret; Then Again, Maybe I Won't; Deenie; Blubber; Forever*—always encouraging, always supportive. The scene was psychologically sound, he assured me, and delicately handled. But it also spelled trouble. I got the message. If you leave in those lines, the censors will come after this book. Librarians and teachers won't buy it. Book clubs won't take it. Everyone is too scared. The political climate has changed.

24   I tried to make a case for why that brief moment in Davey's life was important. He asked me *how* important? Important enough to keep the book from reaching its audience? I willed myself not to give in to the tears of frustration and disappointment I felt coming. I thought about the ways a writer brings a character to life on the page, the same way an artist brings a face to life on canvas—through a series of brush strokes, each detail adding to the others, until we see the essence of the person. I floundered, uncertain. Ultimately, not strong enough or brave enough to defy the editor I trusted and respected, I caved in and took out those lines. I still remember how alone I felt at that moment.

What effect does this climate have on a writer? *Chilling.* It's easy to become discouraged, to second-guess everything you write. There seemed to be no one to stand up to the censors. No group as organized as they were; none I knew of, anyway. I've never forgiven myself for caving in to editorial pressure based on fear, for playing into the hands of the censors. I knew then it was all over for me unless I took a stand. So I began to speak out about my experiences. And once I did, I found that I wasn't as alone as I'd thought.

My life changed when I learned about the National Coalition Against Censorship (NCAC) and met Leanne Katz, the tiny dynamo who was its first and longtime director. Leanne's intelligence, her wit, her strong commitment to the First Amendment and helping those who were out on a limb trying to defend it, made her my hero. Every day she worked with the teachers, librarians, parents and students caught in the cross fire. Many put themselves and their jobs on the line fighting for what they believed in.

In Panama City, Florida, junior high school teacher Gloria Pipkin's award-winning English program was targeted by the censors for using Young Adult literature that was *depressing, vulgar and immoral,* specifically *I Am the Cheese,* by Robert Cormier, and *About David,* by Susan Beth Pfeffer.

28   A year later, when a new book selection policy was introduced forbidding vulgar, obscene and sexually related materials, the school superintendent zealously applied it to remove more than sixty-five books, many of them classics, from the curriculum and classroom libraries. They included *To Kill a Mockingbird, The Red Badge of Courage, The Great Gatsby, Wuthering Heights,* and *Of Mice and Men.* Also banned were Shakespeare's *Hamlet, King Lear, The Merchant of Venice,* and *Twelfth Night.*

Gloria Pipkin fought a five-year battle, jeopardizing her job and personal safety (she and the reporter covering the story received death threats) to help reinstate the books. Eventually, the professional isolation as well as the watered-down curriculum led her to resign. She remains without a teaching position.

Claudia Johnson, Florida State University professor and parent, also defended classic books by Aristophanes and Chaucer against a censor who condemned them for promoting "women's lib and pornography." She went on to fight other battles—in defense of John Steinbeck's *Of Mice and Men,* and a student performance of Lorraine Hansberry's *A Raisin in the Sun.*

English teacher Cecilia Lacks was fired by a high school in St. Louis for permitting her creative writing students to express themselves in the language they heard and used outside of school every day. In the court case that followed, many of her students testified on their teacher's behalf. Though she won her case, the decision was eventually reversed and at this time Lacks is still without a job.

32   Colorado English teacher Alfred Wilder was fired for teaching a classic film about fascism, Bernardo Bertolucci's *1900.*

And in Rib Lake, Wisconsin, guidance counselor Mike Dishnow was fired for writing critically of the Board of Education's decision to ban my book *Forever* from the junior high school library. Ultimately he won a court settlement, but by then his life had been turned upside down.

And these are just a few examples.

This obsession with banning books continues as we approach the year 2000. Today it is not only Sex, Swear Words and Lack of Moral Tone—it is Evil, which, according to the censors, can be found lurking everywhere. Stories about Halloween, witches, and devils are . . . [all] suspect for promoting Satanism. *Romeo and Juliet* is under fire for promoting suicide; Madeleine L'Engle's *A Wrinkle in Time,* for promoting New Age-ism. If the censors had their way it would be good-bye to Shakespeare as well as science fiction. There's not an *ism* you can think of that's not bringing some book to the battlefield.

36   What I worry about most is the loss to young people. If no one speaks out for them, if they don't speak out for themselves, all they'll get for required reading will be the most bland books available. And instead of finding the

information they need at the library, instead of finding the novels that illuminate life, they will find only those materials to which nobody could possibly object.

Some people would like to rate books in schools and libraries the way they rate movies: G, PG, R, X, or even more explicitly. But according to whose standards would the books be rated? I don't know about you but I don't want anyone rating my books or the books my children or grandchildren choose to read. We can make our own decisions, thank you. Be wary of the censors' code words—*family friendly; family values; excellence in education.* As if the rest of us don't want excellence in education, as if we don't have our own family values, as if libraries haven't always been family-friendly places!

And the demands are not all coming from the religious right. No . . . the urge to decide not only what's right for their kids but for all kids has caught on with others across the political spectrum. Each year *Huckleberry Finn* is challenged and sometimes removed from the classroom because, to some, its language, which includes racial epithets, is offensive. Better to acknowledge the language, bring it out in the open, and discuss why the book remains important than to ban it. Teachers and parents can talk with their students and children about any book considered controversial.

I gave a friend's child one of my favorite picture books, James Marshall's *The Stupids Step Out,* and was amazed when she said, "I'm sorry, but we can't accept that book. My children are not permitted to use that word. Ever. It should be changed to 'The Sillies Step Out.'" I may not agree, but I have to respect this woman's right to keep that book from her child as long as she isn't trying to keep it from other people's children. Still, I can't help lamenting the lack of humor in her decision. *The Stupids Step Out* is a very funny book. Instead of banning it from her home, I wish she could have used it as an opportunity to talk with her child about why she felt the way she did, about why she never wanted to hear her child call anyone stupid. Even very young children can understand. So many adults are exhausting themselves worrying about other people corrupting their children with books, they're turning kids off to reading instead of turning them on.

40   In this age of censorship I mourn the loss of books that will never be written, I mourn the voices that will be silenced—writers' voices, teachers' voices, students' voices—and all because of fear. How many have resorted to self-censorship? How many are saying to themselves, "Nope . . . can't write about that. Can't teach that book. Can't have that book in our collection. Can't let my student write that editorial in the school paper."

PERSONAL RESPONSE

Describe an experience that you have had with being forbidden to read, watch, or listen to something because it was considered inappropriate. How did it make you feel? What was it like to finally read, watch, or listen to it?

QUESTIONS FOR CLASS OR SMALL-GROUP DISCUSSION

1. Blume asks "What is censorship?"(paragraph 8) and observes that it has different meanings to different people. How do you define "censorship"? Give examples to illustrate your definition.

2. Explain in your own words why Blume's books have been challenged or censored.

3. Discuss your own experience in junior and senior high school with banned or challenged books. Were your librarians and teachers free to choose any books they wanted for the library or classroom? If not, what books were not allowed?

4. Under what circumstances do you think it justifiable to forbid children or young adults to read something?

5. If you have read any of the novels that Blume mentions as having been challenged, banned, or censored, what did you think of them? What parts of the books do you think drew the attention of censors? Do you agree that the books should be withheld from children or young adults?

CRITICAL THINKING? YOU NEED KNOWLEDGE

DIANE RAVITCH

Diane Ravitch is a research professor of education at New York University and cochair of Common Core. She has published numerous articles and books, including The Language Police: How Pressure Groups Restrict What Students Learn *(2003);* The English Reader: What Every Literate Person Needs to Know *(edited with Michael Ravitch) (2006);* Edspeak: A Glossary of Education Terms, Phrases, Buzz Words, and Jargon *(2007); and* The Death and Life of the Great American School System: How Testing and Choice Are Undermining Education *(2010). In addition, she has edited fourteen books and published over 500 articles and reviews for both scholarly and popular publications. This article was published in the* Boston Globe *on September 15, 2009.*

The latest fad to sweep K–12 education is called "21st-Century Skills." States—including Massachusetts—are adding them to their learning standards, with the expectation that students will master skills such as cooperative learning and critical thinking and therefore be better able to compete for jobs in the global economy. Inevitably, putting a priority on skills pushes other subjects, including history, literature, and the arts, to the margins. But skill-centered, knowledge-free education has never worked.

From *The Boston Globe,* September 15, 2009. Reprinted with permission of the author.

The same ideas proposed today by the 21st-Century Skills movement were iterated and reiterated by pedagogues across the 20th century. In 1911, the dean of the education school at Stanford called on his fellow educators to abandon their antiquated academic ideals and adapt education to the real life and real needs of students.

In 1916, a federal government report scoffed at academic education as lacking relevance. The report's author said black children should "learn to do by doing," which he considered to be the modern, scientific approach to education.

4   Just a couple of years later, "the project method" took the education world by storm. Instead of a sequential curriculum laid out in advance, the program urged that boys and girls engage in hands-on projects of their own choosing, ideally working cooperatively in a group. It required activity, not docility, and awakened student motivation. It's remarkably similar to the model advocated by 21st-century skills enthusiasts.

The list goes on: students built, measured, and figured things out while solving real-life problems, like how to build a playhouse, pet park, or a puppet theater, as part of the 1920s and 1930s "Activity Movement." From the "Life Adjustment Movement" of the 1950s to "Outcome-Based Education" in the 1980s, one "innovation" after another devalued academic subject matter while making schooling relevant, hands-on, and attuned to the real interests and needs of young people.

To be sure, there has been resistance. In Roslyn, Long Island, in the 1930s, parents were incensed because their children couldn't read but spent an entire day baking nut bread. The Roslyn superintendent assured them that baking was an excellent way to learn mathematics.

None of these initiatives survived. They did have impact, however: They inserted into American education a deeply ingrained suspicion of academic studies and subject matter. For the past century, our schools of education have obsessed over critical-thinking skills, projects, cooperative learning, experiential learning, and so on. But they have paid precious little attention to the disciplinary knowledge that young people need to make sense of the world.

8   For over a century we have numbed the brains of teachers with endless blather about process and abstract thinking skills. We have taught them about graphic organizers and Venn diagrams and accountable talk, data-based decision-making, rubrics, and leveled libraries.

But we have ignored what matters most. We have neglected to teach them that one cannot think critically without quite a lot of knowledge to think about. Thinking critically involves comparing and contrasting and synthesizing what one has learned. And a great deal of knowledge is necessary before one can begin to reflect on its meaning and look for alternative explanations.

Proponents of 21st-Century Skills might wish it was otherwise, but we do not restart the world anew with each generation. We stand on the shoulders of those who have gone before us. What matters most in the use of our brains is our capacity to make generalizations, to see beyond our own immediate experience. The intelligent person, the one who truly is a practitioner of critical thinking, has the capacity to understand the lessons of history, to grasp the inner logic of science and mathematics, and to realize the meaning of philosophical debates by studying them.

Through literature, for example, we have the opportunity to see the world through the eyes of another person, to walk in his shoes, to experience life as it was lived in another century and another culture, to live vicariously beyond the bounds of our own time and family and place.

12 Until we teach both teachers and students to value knowledge and to love learning, we cannot expect them to use their minds well.

PERSONAL RESPONSE QUESTION

Comment on your own high school education. Do you recall any particular approach to learning that teachers had in common? If so, what was it? If not, how would you characterize your teachers' educational philosophy? How well do you believe that your high school education prepared you for college?

QUESTIONS FOR CLASS OR SMALL-GROUP DISCUSSION

1. Summarize in your own words the approaches to teaching that Ravitch complains about.

2. What rhetorical purpose is served by Ravitch's review of twentieth-century educational movements?

3. What is that Ravitch feels is missing in the current educational movement? Do you agree with her?

4. Explain in your own words Ravitch's definition of an intelligent person. What, if anything, would you add to her definition?

EXCERPT FROM WHY SCHOOL? A STUDENT IN A COMMUNITY COLLEGE BASIC SKILLS PROGRAM

MIKE ROSE

Mike Rose, a professor of Social Research Methodology at UCLA, has a special interest in educational programs for economically impoverished or underprepared students. He has written extensively on language, literacy, and the teaching of writing. His books include The Mind at Work: Valuing the Intelligence of the American Worker *(2004);* Lives on the Boundary *(2005);* An Open Language: Selecting Writing on Literacy, Learning, and Opportunity *(2005);*

and Writer's Block: The Cognitive Dimension *(2009). Rose*
posted this excerpt from his book Why School? *(2009) at his blog on*
October 12, 2009.

Food wrappers and sheets of newspaper were blowing in the wet wind across the empty campus. It was late in the day, getting dark fast, and every once in a while I'd look outside the library—which was pretty empty too—and imagine the drizzly walk to the car, parked far away.

Anthony was sitting by me, and I was helping him read a flyer on the dangers of cocaine. He wanted to give it to his daughter. Anthony was enrolled in a basic skills program, one of several special programs at this urban community college. Anthony was in his late-thirties, had some degree of brain damage from a childhood injury, worked custodial jobs most of his life. He could barely read or write, but was an informed, articulate guy, listening to FM radio current affairs shows while he worked, watching public television at home. He had educated himself through the sources available to him, compensating for the damage done.

The librarian was about to go off shift, so we gathered up our things—Anthony carried a big backpack—and headed past her desk to the exit. The wind pushed back on the door as I pushed forward, and I remember thinking how dreary the place was, dark and cold. At that moment I wanted so much to be home.

4   Just then a man in a coat and tie came up quickly behind us. "Hey man," he said to Anthony, "you look good. You lose some weight?" Anthony beamed, said that he had dropped a few pounds and that things were going o.k. The guy gave Anthony a cupping slap on the shoulder, then pulled his coat up and walked head down across the campus.

"Who was that?" I asked, ducking with Anthony back inside the entryway to the library. He was one of the deans, Anthony said, but, well, he was once his parole officer, too. He's seen Anthony come a long way. Anthony pulled on the straps of his backpack, settling the weight more evenly across his shoulders. "I like being here," he said in his soft, clear voice. "I know it can't happen by osmosis. But this is where it's at."

I've thought about this moment off and on for twenty years. I couldn't wait to get home, and Anthony was right at home. Fresh from reading something for his daughter, feeling the clasp on his shoulder of both his past and his future, for Anthony a new life was emerging on the threshold of a chilly night on a deserted campus.

These few minutes remind me of how humbling work with human beings can be. How we'll always miss things. How easily we get distracted—my own memories of cold urban landscapes overwhelmed the moment.

8   But I also hold onto this experience with Anthony for it contains so many lessons about development, about resilience and learning, about the power of hope and a second chance. It reminds us too of the importance of staying close to the ground, of finding out what people are thinking, of trying our best—flawed though it will be—to understand the world as they see it … and to be ready to

revise our understanding. This often means taking another line of sight on what seems familiar, seeing things in a new light.

And if we linger with Anthony a while longer, either in the doorway or back inside at a library table, we might get the chance to reflect on the basic question of what school is for, the purpose of education. What brought Anthony back to the classroom after all those years? To help his economic prospects, certainly. Anthony wanted to trade in his mop and pail for decent pay and a few benefits. But we also get a glimpse as to why else he's here. To be able to better guide his daughter. To be more proficient in reading about the events swirling around him—to add reading along with radio and television to his means of examining the world. To create a new life for himself, nurture this emerging sense of who he can become.

PERSONAL RESPONSE QUESTION

Write for a few minutes on your reasons for going to college.

QUESTIONS FOR CLASS OR SMALL-GROUP DISCUSSION

1. State in your own words the point or central purpose of this piece.
2. Comment on the rhetorical effectiveness of Rose's use of one extended example to achieve his purpose.
3. Rose says that his experience with Anthony contains "so many lessons" (paragraph 8). What do you understand those lessons to be, and how does Anthony illustrate them?
4. In the concluding paragraph, Rose suggests that the experience with Anthony raises "the basic question of what school is for, the purpose of education." Discuss how Rose answers the question of what school is for and whether you agree with him. Would you add other reasons to those that Rose names?

PASS THE BOOKS. HOLD THE OIL

THOMAS L. FRIEDMAN

Thomas L. Friedman has written for the New York Times *since 1981. In 1995, he became the paper's foreign affairs columnist. Friedman was awarded the 1983 Pulitzer Prize for international reporting (from Lebanon) and the 1988 Pulitzer Prize for international reporting (from Israel). In 2002, he won the Pulitzer Prize for commentary. His book* From Beirut to Jerusalem *(1989) won the National*

Book Award for nonfiction in 1989. The Lexus and the Olive Tree: Understanding Globalization *(2000) won the 2000 Overseas Press Club award for best nonfiction book on foreign policy and has been published in twenty languages. He is also author of* Longitudes and Attitudes: Exploring the World after September 11 *(2002);* The World Is Flat: A Brief History of the Twenty-First Century *(2005);* Hot, Flat, and Crowded: Why We Need a Green Revolution—and How It Can Renew America *(2008); and* That Used to Be Us: How America Fell Behind in the World We Invented and How We Can Come Back *(2012). This piece was written for the opinion page of the March 11, 2012, issue of the* New York Times.

EVERY so often someone asks me: "What's your favorite country, other than your own?"

I've always had the same answer: Taiwan. "Taiwan? Why Taiwan?" people ask.

Very simple: Because Taiwan is a barren rock in a typhoon-laden sea with no natural resources to live off of—it even has to import sand and gravel from China for construction—yet it has the fourth-largest financial reserves in the world. Because rather than digging in the ground and mining whatever comes up, Taiwan has mined its 23 million people, their talent, energy and intelligence—men and women. I always tell my friends in Taiwan: "You're the luckiest people in the world. How did you get so lucky? You have no oil, no iron ore, no forests, no diamonds, no gold, just a few small deposits of coal and natural gas—and because of that you developed the habits and culture of honing your people's skills, which turns out to be the most valuable and only truly renewable resource in the world today. *How did you get so lucky?*"

4   That, at least, was my gut instinct. But now we have proof.

A team from the Organization for Economic Cooperation and Development, or O.E.C.D., has just come out with a fascinating little study mapping the correlation between performance on the Program for International Student Assessment, or PISA, exam—which every two years tests math, science and reading comprehension skills of 15-year-olds in 65 countries—and the total earnings on natural resources as a percentage of G.D.P. for each participating country. In short, how well do your high school kids do on math compared with how much oil you pump or how many diamonds you dig?

The results indicated that there was a "a significant negative relationship between the money countries extract from national resources and the knowledge and skills of their high school population," said Andreas Schleicher, who oversees the PISA exams for the O.E.C.D. "This is a global pattern that holds across 65 countries that took part in the latest PISA assessment." Oil and PISA don't mix. (See the data map at http://www.oecd.org/dataoecd/43/9/49881940.pdf)

As the Bible notes, added Schleicher, "Moses arduously led the Jews for 40 years through the desert—just to bring them to the only country in the Middle East that had no oil. But Moses may have gotten it right, after all. Today, Israel has one of the most innovative economies, and its population enjoys a standard of living most of the oil-rich countries in the region are not able to offer."

8   So hold the oil, and pass the books. According to Schleicher, in the latest PISA results, students in Singapore, Finland, South Korea, Hong Kong and Japan stand out as having high PISA scores and few natural resources, while Qatar and Kazakhstan stand out as having the highest oil rents and the lowest PISA scores. (Saudi Arabia, Kuwait, Oman, Algeria, Bahrain, Iran and Syria stood out the same way in a similar 2007 Trends in International Mathematics and Science Study, or Timss, test, while, interestingly, students from Lebanon, Jordan and Turkey—also Middle East states with few natural resources—scored better.) Also lagging in recent PISA scores, though, were students in many of the resource-rich countries of Latin America, like Brazil, Mexico and Argentina. Africa was not tested. Canada, Australia and Norway, also countries with high levels of natural resources, still score well on PISA, in large part, argues Schleicher, because all three countries have established deliberate policies of saving and investing these resource rents, and not just consuming them.

Add it all up and the numbers say that if you really want to know how a country is going to do in the 21st century, don't count its oil reserves or gold mines, count its highly effective teachers, involved parents and committed students. "Today's learning outcomes at school," says Schleicher, "are a powerful predictor for the wealth and social outcomes that countries will reap in the long run."

Economists have long known about "Dutch disease," which happens when a country becomes so dependent on exporting natural resources that its currency soars in value and, as a result, its domestic manufacturing gets crushed as cheap imports flood in and exports become too expensive. What the PISA team is revealing is a related disease: societies that get addicted to their natural resources seem to develop parents and young people who lose some of the instincts, habits and incentives for doing homework and honing skills.

By, contrast, says Schleicher, "in countries with little in the way of natural resources—Finland, Singapore or Japan—education has strong outcomes and a high status, at least in part because the public at large has understood that the country must live by its knowledge and skills and that these depend on the quality of education. ... Every parent and child in these countries knows that skills will decide the life chances of the child and nothing else is going to rescue them, so they build a whole culture and education system around it."

12   Or as my Indian-American friend K. R. Sridhar, the founder of the Silicon Valley fuel-cell company Bloom Energy, likes to say, "When you don't have resources, you become resourceful."

That's why the foreign countries with the most companies listed on the Nasdaq are Israel, China/Hong Kong, Taiwan, India, South Korea and Singapore—none of which can live off natural resources.

But there is an important message for the industrialized world in this study, too. In these difficult economic times, it is tempting to buttress our own standards of living today by incurring even greater financial liabilities for the future. To be sure, there is a role for stimulus in a prolonged recession, but "the only sustainable way is to grow our way out by giving more people the knowledge and skills to compete, collaborate and connect in a way that drives our countries forward," argues Schleicher.

In sum, says Schleicher, "knowledge and skills have become the global currency of 21st-century economies, but there is no central bank that prints this currency. Everyone has to decide on their own how much they will print." Sure, it's great to have oil, gas and diamonds; they can buy jobs. But they'll weaken your society in the long run unless they're used to build schools and a culture of lifelong learning. "The thing that will keep you moving forward," says Schleicher, is always "what you bring to the table yourself."

PERSONAL RESPONSE

What does getting an education mean to you? Write about whether you have the support of your family, community, and/or society in getting an education.

QUESTIONS FOR CLASS AND SMALL-GROUP DISCUSSION

1. Friedman mentions "honing skills" in paragraphs 3 and 10. What skills do you think he is referring to?

2. Friedman says that there is an important message in the studies that he refers to. What do you understand that message to be? Do you agree with him?

3. Friedman mentions "the habits and culture of honing young people's skills" (paragraph 3 and "instincts, habits, and incentives" in paragraph 10. What do you think he means by those terms. What habits, skills, and incentives would a nation need to cultivate in order to thrive?

4. Friedman quotes Andreas Schleicher as saying that "'knowledge and skills have become the global currency of 21-st century economies'" (paragraph 15). *Knowledge* and *skills* are abstract terms. What concrete examples would illustrate what both Schleicher and Friedman mean?

PERSPECTIVES ON EDUCATION

Suggested Writing Topics

1. With Judy Blume's "Censorship: A Personal View" in mind, define "censorship," using your own experience with a banned, censored, forbidden, or challenged book.

2. Read one or more of the books that Judy Blume mentions in "Censorship: A Personal View" and write an essay explaining why you think it was challenged, censored, or banned and whether you agree that it should have been.

3. Explain what you see as the role of parents in children's education.

4. Define education, using specific examples to illustrate general or abstract statements. You may want to focus specifically on high school education, as you experienced it, or higher education, which you are currently experiencing.

5. Distinguish among the words *education*, *knowledge*, and *wisdom*. How are they similar? How are they different? Would a standardized test measure any of them?

6. With Diane Ravitch's "Critical Thinking? You Need Knowledge" in mind, define an "intelligent person." You may want to include specific instances of someone you know who exemplifies that term for you.

7. Explain whether you think Diane Ravitch ("Critical Thinking? You Need Knowledge") would consider Anthony of Mike Rose's excerpt from *Why School?* "an intelligent person."

8. Argue in support of or against this statement from Thomas L. Friedman's "Pass the Books. Hold the Oil": "It's great to have oil, gas, and diamonds; they can buy jobs. But they'll weaken your society in the long run unless they're used to build schools and a culture of lifelong learning" (paragraph 15).

9. Thomas L. Friedman in "Pass the Books. Hold the Oil" stresses the importance of cultivating good homework habits and getting an education. Write a personal essay on your study and homework habits, including how you feel about education and what you hope to achieve with it.

10. Write a paper about a book that had a profound effect on you. Explain briefly what the book is and what it is about, but focus on aspects of it that affected you. Perhaps it moved you emotionally as no other book has or it directed you on a specific path in life.

11. Write about a teacher who made an impression and had a significant effect on you. What made that teacher so important to you? Try to explain not only physical characteristics but, more importantly, personality features and admirable qualities. If a particular incident was especially significant in your relationship, narrate what happened.

12. Some people argue that not everyone deserves to go to college and that admitting average or mediocre students into colleges has debased American higher education. Argue in support of or against that position.

13. Imagine that the number of students admitted to college directly after high school has been limited to the upper 33 percent of all graduating seniors and that you do not meet the requirements for admission to college. Under special circumstances, students who fall below the 33 percent mark may be admitted. In a letter to the admissions officer at the college of your choice, argue that you should be admitted despite your class ranking and give reasons why you would make a good student.

Research Topics

1. Research the subject of governmental plans to measure learning in institutions of higher education by using a standardized test, and argue your position on the subject.

2. Research opinions for and against requiring students to write an essay as part of their qualifications for a degree, as some universities now do. Arrive at your own viewpoint based on your research, and argue your position.

3. Read one of the books that Judy Blume mentions in "Censorship: A Personal View," and research the controversy surrounding it. Explain the arguments both for and against banning or censoring the book, and then argue your own position.

4. Research the tracking systems used in many schools. Find opinions supporting and opposing such systems, consider their advantages and disadvantages, and arrive at your own conclusion based on your reading.

5. Spend some time searching the Internet or going through your library's catalog of books and periodicals on the subject of education. You will find a very large number of subtopics under that broad heading. Select a seemingly controversial subtopic that interests you. Keep searching until you have narrowed your focus to one specific aspect of the subject that is suitable for your research project.

6. Research the conflict of traditional versus revisionist curriculum. Consider interviewing educators as part of your research. Read periodical articles from the last several years on political correctness, defenses for or against the canon, or related topics.

7. Research the subject of the role of television or of the Internet in relationship to the reading habits of Americans.

8. Research the 21st-Century Skills movement. Define it, explain its purpose, and assess its usefulness in producing truly educated students.

9. Expand on Thomas L. Friedman's "Pass the Books. Hold the Oil" by locating the studies that he refers to, or similar, more recent ones. Read what experts say on the subject and then either support or refute Friedman's assertion that "honing your people's skills" is more important to a nation than having an abundance of resources.

RESPONDING TO VISUALS

Chris Ryan/OJO Images/Getty Images

Bored college students in class.

1. What do you think the photographer hopes to convey with this picture?
2. Although the caption describes the photograph as that of bored students, what other emotions do the facial expressions of the students suggest? What does their body language reveal about how they view this particular classroom experience?
3. Why do you think the teacher is not shown in the photograph? What course do you think the students are taking, or does it not matter? What circumstances might account for a scene such as the one photographed here?

RESPONDING TO VISUALS

altrendo images/Getty Images

Portrait of a blindfolded young woman reading a book.

1. Analyze the composition of this image. For instance, what is the effect of making the blindfold black and the book the woman is reading red? Would the effect be different if the colors were reversed? What might be lost if the image was a close-up of just the woman and the book she is reading, excluding the stacks of books that she is resting her arms on? Comment on other details that you notice about the image.

2. How effective do you think this image is as a comment on censorship in general and book censorship in particular? Do you think that making a comment on censorship is the only message of this image, or are there other ways of interpreting it?

3. Do you think books should be banned for school-aged children? If so, who should make the decision about which books to ban: parents, the administration, or teachers? What if one group believes a book should be banned while another defends it as literature and finds it acceptable?

CHAPTER 13

Poverty and Homelessness

Once largely ignored, the issues of poverty, homelessness, and welfare have prompted heated discussion in recent years. At the community level, social workers and staff members at shelters for the homeless and impoverished struggle to meet the needs of desperate people, while at the state and federal levels, legislators argue over whether to cut welfare funding. The numbers of people in poverty, especially women and children, continue to rise. Many families whose incomes provide just enough for basic necessities, such as shelter and food, are only a paycheck or two away from living on the streets. Worse, a growing number of the nation's poor actually work full time. Compounding the difficulty of these issues are certain attitudes toward or stereotyped beliefs about people on welfare or living on the streets. Charges of laziness and fraud are often leveled at welfare recipients, despite studies that demonstrate that the vast majority of people on welfare want to work and live independent lives.

    The essays in this chapter examine some of the issues associated with poverty and homelessness. First, Anna Quindlen in "Our Tired, Our Poor, Our Kids" looks at the plight of homeless mothers and children in America. She points out some of the effects of homelessness on children, emphasizes the importance of affordable housing, and touches on the effects of welfare reform on homelessness. Although her essay was first published in 2001, the problems facing homeless women and children that she details have not changed significantly since then. Indeed, according to the president of the Children's Defense Fund, Marian Wright Edelman, as of 2012 "there are 16.4 million poor children in rich America, 7.4 million living in extreme poverty. A majority of public school students and more than three out of four Black and Hispanic children, who will be a majority of our child population by 2019, are unable to read or compute at grade level in the fourth or eighth grade and will be unprepared to succeed in our increasingly competitive global economy" (www.childrensdefense.org). These sobering statistics reinforces Quindlen's image of poor and homeless children.

In contrast to Quindlen's focus on children is Kevin Fagan's piece on an older population of people living on the street. "Homeless, Mike Dick Was 51, Looked 66" takes a close look at a man who is representative of "old folks who have no business living in the gutter," as Fagan describes them. The dire picture he draws in his piece, written in 2008, again remains relatively unchanged, with slight decreases in numbers. According to a 2012 report on the state of homelessness in America, issued by the National Alliance to End Homelessness, during the period from 2009 to 2011:

- The nation's homeless population decreased 1 percent, or by about 7,000 people; it went from 643,067 in 2009 to 636,017 in 2011. There were a decreased number of people experiencing homelessness in most of the subpopulations examined in this report: families, individuals in families, chronic, and individuals. The only increase was among those unsheltered.

- The national rate of homelessness was 21 homeless people per 10,000 people in the general population. The rate for veterans was 31 homeless veterans per 10,000 veterans in the general population.

- Chronic homelessness decreased by 3 percent from 110,911 in 2009 to 107,148 in 2011. The chronically homeless population has decreased by 13 percent since 2007. The decrease is associated with an increase in the number of permanent supportive housing beds from 188,636 in 2007 to 266,968 in 2011. Permanent supportive housing ends chronic homelessness.

- A majority of homeless people counted were in emergency shelters or transitional housing programs, but nearly four in ten were unsheltered, living on the streets, or in cars, abandoned buildings, or other places not intended for human habitation.

- The unsheltered population increased by 2 percent from 239,759 in 2009 to 243,701 in 2011, the only subpopulation to increase.

- The number of individuals in homeless families decreased by 1 percent nationally, but increased by 20 percent or more in eleven states.

Next, Barbara Ehrenreich addresses the subject of the newly poor versus the working poor. She compares the situations of middle-class, white-collar workers who have suffered in a slumped economy with those of people whose blue-collar jobs pay only enough for them to just manage to scrape by. Following up on some of the people she interviewed for her book *Nickel and Dimed*, Ehrenreich highlights the special problems faced by low-wage earners in a weak economy.

Finally, in "All Kids Should Take 'Poverty 101,'" Donna Beegle writes movingly of her own experience with generational poverty and the things that go with that—lack of education, sometimes illiteracy, and lack of skills. As creator of a consulting firm that conducts workshops called "Poverty 101," she explains what people, including those who are impoverished, need to learn about poverty. You may be surprised to learn that there are several kinds of poverty: generational, working-class (addressed in Ehrenreich's essay), immigrant, and situational. Beegle argues that only when people understand the conditions that create poverty will they—and those experiencing it—be able to begin to help the impoverished. This is the goal of "Poverty 101." As you read these essays, think about your own attitudes toward welfare, homelessness, and poverty. These are tough social problems that just about every society must face, but especially so in countries with large urban areas and great gaps between the rich and the poor. Do the Quindlen and Fagan essays in any way reinforce or change your attitudes about these issues? Are you moved by Ehrenreich's description of the desperately uncertain lives of the working poor? Does Beegle expand your understanding of the issue?

OUR TIRED, OUR POOR, OUR KIDS

ANNA QUINDLEN

Anna Quindlen is a novelist, social critic, and journalist who began her career at the New York Post *and then became deputy metropolitan editor of the* New York Times. *In 1986, she began her syndicated column "Life in the Thirties" and a few years later "Public and Private," for which she won a Pulitzer Prize in 1992. She contributed to* Newsweek's *prestigious back-page column, "The Last Word," every other week until she retired in 2009. Her columns are collected in* Living Out Loud *(1988);* Thinking Out Loud *(1992); and* Loud and Clear *(2004). She has written the following novels:* Object Lessons *(1991);* One True Thing *(1994);* Black and Blue *(1998);* Blessings *(2003);* Being Perfect *(2004);* Every Last One: A Novel *(2010). Among her nonfiction books are* How Reading Changed My Life *(1998);* A Short Guide to a Happy Life *(2000);* Imagining London: A Tour of the World's Greatest Fictional City *(2004); and* Rise and Shine (2006). *This essay appeared in the March 12, 2001, issue of* Newsweek.

Six people live here, in a room the size of the master bedroom in a modest suburban house. Trundles, bunk beds, dressers side by side stacked with toys, clothes, boxes, in tidy claustrophobic clutter. One woman, five children. The baby was born in a shelter. The older kids can't wait to get out of this one. Everyone gets up at 6 a.m., the little ones to go to day care, the others to school. Their mother goes out to look for an apartment when she's not going to drug-treatment meetings. "For what they pay for me to stay in a shelter I could have lived in the Hamptons," Sharanda says.

Here is the parallel universe that has flourished while the more fortunate were rewarding themselves for the stock split with SUVs and home additions. There is a boom market in homelessness. But these are not the men on the streets of San Francisco holding out cardboard signs to the tourists. They are children, hundreds of thousands of them, twice as likely to repeat a grade or be hospitalized and four times as likely to go hungry as the kids with a roof over their heads. Twenty years ago New York City provided emergency shelter for just under a thousand families a day; last month it had to find spaces for 10,000 children on a given night. Not since the Great Depression have this many babies, toddlers and kids had no place like home.

Three mothers sit in the living room of a temporary residence called Casa Rita in the Bronx and speak of this in the argot of poverty. "The landlord don't call back when they hear you got EARP," says Rosie, EARP being the Emergency Assistance Rehousing Program. "You get priority for Section 8 if you're in a shelter," says Edna, which means federal housing programs will put you higher on the list. Edna has four kids, three in foster care; she arrived at Casa Rita, she says, "with two bags and a baby." Rosie has three; they share a bathroom down the hall with two other families. Sharanda's five range in age from 13 to just over a year. Her eldest was put in the wrong grade when he changed schools. "He's humiliated, living here," his mother says.

4   All three women are anxious to move on, although they appreciate this place, where they can get shelter, get sober and keep their kids at the same time. They remember the Emergency Assistance Unit, the city office that is the gateway to the system, where hundreds of families sit every day surrounded by their bags, where children sleep on benches until they are shuffled off dull-eyed for one night in a shelter or a motel, only to return as supplicants again the next day.

In another world middle-class Americans have embraced new-home starts, the stock market and the Gap. But in the world of these displaced families, problems ignored or fumbled or unforeseen during this great period of prosperity have dovetailed into an enormous subculture of children who think that only rich people have their own bedrooms. Twenty years ago, when the story of the homeless in America became a staple of news reporting, the solution was presented as a simple one: affordable housing. That's still true, now more than ever. Two years ago the National Low Income Housing Coalition calculated that the hourly income necessary to afford the average two-bedroom apartment was around $12. That's more than twice the minimum wage.

The result is that in many cities police officers and teachers cannot afford to live where they work, that in Las Vegas old motels provide housing for casino employees, that in shelters now there is a contingent of working poor who get up off their cots and go off to their jobs. The result is that if you are evicted for falling behind on your rent, if there is a bureaucratic foul-up in your welfare check or the factory in which you work shuts down, the chances of finding another place to live are very small indeed. You're one understanding relative, one paycheck, one second chance from the street. And so are your kids.

So-called welfare reform, which emphasizes cutbacks and make-work, has played a part in all this. A study done in San Diego in 1998 found that a third of homeless families had recently had benefits terminated or reduced, and that most said that was how they had wound up on the street. Drugs, alcohol and domestic abuse also land mothers with kids in the shelter system or lead them to hand their children over to relatives or foster homes. Today the average homeless woman is younger than ever before, may have been in foster care or in shelters herself and so considers a chaotic childhood the norm. Many never finished high school, and have never held a job.

8   Ralph Nunez, who runs the organization Homes for the Homeless, says that all this calls for new attitudes. "People don't like to hear it, but shelters are going to be the low-income housing of the future," he says. "So how do we enrich the experience and use the system to provide job training and education?" Bonnie Stone of Women in Need, which has eight other residences along with Casa Rita, says, "We're pouring everything we've got into the nine months most of them are here—nutrition, treatment, budgeting. By the time they leave, they have a subsidized apartment, day care and, hopefully, some life skills they didn't have before."

But these organizations are rafts in a rising river of need that has roared through this country without most of us ever even knowing. So now you know. There are hundreds of thousands of little nomads in America, sleeping in the back of cars, on floors in welfare offices or in shelters five to a room. What would it mean, to spend your childhood drifting from one strange bed to another, waking in the morning to try to figure out where you'd landed today, without those things that confer security and happiness: a familiar picture on the wall, a certain slant of light through a curtained window? "Give me your tired, your poor," it says on the base of the Statue of Liberty, to welcome foreigners. Oh, but they are already here, the small refugees from the ruin of the American dream, even if you cannot see them.

PERSONAL RESPONSE

What image of the homeless did you have before reading this essay? Has your understanding of them changed in any way now that you have read it? If so, in what way has it changed? If not, explain why.

QUESTIONS FOR CLASS OR SMALL-GROUP DISCUSSION

1. Were you surprised by this statement: "Not since the Great Depression have this many babies, toddlers and kids had no place like home" (paragraph 2)? What do you think Quindlen hopes to achieve by the reference to the Great Depression?

2. Explain why, according to Quindlen, there are so many homeless women and children in America. What is the effect of homelessness on children? Are you persuaded of the seriousness of the problem?

3. What does Quindlen mean by the term *working poor* (paragraph 6)?

4. Quindlen uses the term so-called to describe welfare reform (paragraph 7). Why do you think she does that? What fault does she find with welfare reform? Do you agree with her?

HOMELESS, MIKE DICK WAS 51, LOOKED 66

Kevin Fagan

Kevin Fagan, a San Francisco Chronicle *staff writer, and photographer Brant Ward covered homelessness for* The Chronicle *locally and nationally from 2003 to 2006. They spent many nights outside with street people in San Francisco. For their "Shame of the City" series, in 2004, Fagan won an Excellence in Urban Journalism award and Brant the Robert F. Kennedy journalism prize. In 2005 together they were given the James Aronson award for social justice journalism. This follow-up article on one of the men they followed during that period was published in the* San Francisco Chronicle *on March 2, 2008.*

Mike Dick looked like a thousand other old homeless guys—a lump of blankets, jacket and jeans so grimy-gray from the street you couldn't tell what color they used to be. And when Chronicle photographer Brant Ward and I strolled up to his doorway in downtown San Francisco two years ago for a chat, his response was the typical old-homeless-guy response.

A blank stare.

So Brant pulled out a cigarette. Mike allowed the hint of a smile, baring his only two teeth. He lit up and took a drag.

"Cold f-ing day, ain't it?" he eventually let out. Then he coughed violently. Which was no surprise, considering he had emphysema, bronchitis, a congestive heart condition and high blood pressure. Not to mention a cold.

4   But on the street, a cigarette is a luxury nobody refuses, especially if it isn't a scrounged butt. Besides, the crack habit he had was worse. As were the 22 years of horrific wear and tear Mike bore on his beanpole of a body from shivering under

Reprinted by permission from *The San Francisco Chronicle*, March 2, 2008.

wet blankets on sidewalks and getting the tar kicked out of him fairly frequently. His right eye wandered from one of those kicks, and his forehead bore a ragged hole where doctors sliced out a cue-ball-size tumor. Battered, sad and hopeless-looking—that was Mike.

There are more like him on the street every day—old folks who have no business living in the gutter. And even if they're rescued, it's often way too late.

Brant and I knew Mike back during our years as the only newspaper team in the United States covering homelessness full time—him the photographer, me the word man. Mike was 51 when we met him, but that was really what counselors would call a "street 66"—meaning his years of homelessness made him look and function 15 years older than he was. He shuffled more than walked, had a bushy gray beard to his chest, and the worry lines in his face looked carved. Brant and I marveled that he was still alive, as we did when we met so many other "streets 66s," "street 70s," or even "street 80s."

Our worries, it turned out, were well-placed. Mike died Dec. 29.

8   The irony is that by then, he had been scooped off the street by city homelessness counselors and given a roof—the Coast Hotel, a supportive housing complex. There, residents live rent-free while on-site counselors help them wrestle the demons that put them on the street. Mike had been at the Coast for 15 months, probably the happiest period of his life, and if fate had been more benevolent, he would have passed many years there getting his act together.

But homeless decay doesn't leave your bones just because you leave the sidewalk.

He died sitting in the hotel's television lounge. His battered heart just finally gave out, and he looked so peaceful in the chair that his pals thought he was sleeping until one noticed his face was unusually pale two hours after his death.

I think what happened to Mike is that he finally relaxed the tensely clenched defense mechanisms he held in all those years, physically and mentally, to keep himself alive through thrashings, hunger and freezing cold. Once he got a safe, permanent roof and natural vulnerability was allowed to settle in, his body just allowed itself to surrender to death.

12   We're going to see more Mikes dying—in and out of housing—before we see fewer.

That's because Mike, and most of the old homeless folks you see panhandling or snoring outside, hit the streets back in the 1980s during what experts call the "big boom" of homelessness. Now, all these years later, they are simply aging toward a premature death—right where they sit, stand and sleep.

UCSF Assistant Professor Judy Hahn in 2006 led what is believed to be the most significant study of older homeless people in the United States, and she found that the median age of street people in San Francisco was 50—compared with 37 in 1990. They all had far more problems with emphysema and other ailments than non-homeless people their age, "the rates of disease you would expect in a much older population," Hahn said. She says the median age will go up every year.

Mike never knew what was coming.

16   "I feel better than ever," Mike told me last summer when I bought him a cup of coffee in the Tenderloin. "I never thought I'd get to really move inside, but I guess it was finally my time."

Clapton's Saddest Songs

Mike's gentleness that charmed me and Brant on the street, his fervor for reading Tom Clancy novels and listening to Eric Clapton's saddest songs—all characteristics invisible to those who would walk by him with revulsion—were even more vivid than before. But his lingering cough and the very way he stood, like a reed ready to fall over, told me he was either fooling himself or too happy to acknowledge how broken he was.

Mike wasn't even the worst off of the older street folks whom Brant and I have known. Our homeless beat included dozens of them known, like hoboes, by one-name handles: Georgia. Rhonda. Grimes. Peg. Red. And lots of Mikes and Mamas.

Several died before they could get inside. Others who did manage to find a roof are, like Mike, no longer with us—most notably Jill May, who last spring was beaten and set on fire by thugs.

20   They all had addiction and other hobbles in common—but one commonality stood out: Almost every one grew up poor and abused, and though they made stabs at normal life, they never had a chance.

In Mike's case, his mother died a month after giving birth to him, and his father was a drunk. Mike left his home in Idaho at 14 and wandered through janitor jobs and youth homes before hitting the gutter in 1984.

Odd Jobs, of Short Duration

His demons were drugs and booze, and although he held odd jobs now and then as an adult—florist's aide was the pinnacle—they never lasted long. By the time we met Mike, he was scraping up $4 a day by recycling from trash cans.

In a rich country where *actors* can make millions of dollars pretending, on a movie screen, to be poor like Mike and then go home to one of their mansions at night, we can do better. San Francisco, like many cities, has made sincere efforts to get old homeless folks into housing—but the city can't fund enough of it alone. Huge cuts to federal housing and poverty programs over the past two decades have not been replaced with anything effective.

24   This is a problem that's not going away. The nation needs to commit, emotionally and economically, to saving these older folks. It's too late for Mike—but not for the hundreds of thousands like him.

PERSONAL RESPONSE

What is your emotional response to the life of Mike Dick? Do you feel sympathetic toward him? Is your attitude toward him different from or similar to the attitude you had toward the homeless living on the street before reading this article? Explain your answer.

QUESTIONS FOR CLASS OR SMALL-GROUP DISCUSSION

1. What is the rhetorical effect of focusing on one specific person, as Fagan has done here, rather than on older homeless people in general?
2. What do you think that Fagan hoped to achieve by writing about Mike Dick? Does he have a stated or an implied purpose?
3. What conclusions can you draw about the backgrounds of older homeless people and/or the reasons why they end up on the streets? What do they have in common?
4. What actions does Fagan call for to address the problem of homelessness? Can you suggest other solutions besides those he names?

TOO POOR TO MAKE THE NEWS

BARBARA EHRENREICH

Barbara Ehrenreich's articles appear in a variety of popular magazines and newspapers, including Time, *the* Progressive, *and the* New York Times. *Her books include the following:* Hearts of Men: American Dreams and the Flight from Commitment *(1984);* Blood Rites: Origins and History of the Passions of War *(1997);* Fear of Falling: The Inner Life of the Middle Class *(2000);* Nickel and Dimed: On (Not) Getting By in America *(2001);* Bait and Switch: The (Futile) Pursuit of the American Dream *(2006);* Dancing in the Streets: A History of Collective Joy *(2007);* This Land Is Their Land: Reports from a Divided Nation *(2008); and* Bright-Sided: How the Relentless Promotion of Positive Thinking Has Undermined America *(2009). This article was first published in the June 15, 2009, issue of the* New York Times.

The human side of the recession, in the new media genre that's been called "recession porn," is the story of an incremental descent from excess to frugality, from ease to austerity. The super-rich give up their personal jets; the upper middle class cut back on private Pilates classes; the merely middle class forgo vacations and evenings at Applebee's. In some accounts, the recession is even described as the "great leveler," smudging the dizzying levels of inequality that characterized the last couple of decades and squeezing everyone into a single great class, the Nouveau Poor, in which we will all drive tiny fuel-efficient cars and grow tomatoes on our porches.

But the outlook is not so cozy when we look at the effects of the recession on a group generally omitted from all the vivid narratives of downward mobility—the already poor, the estimated 20 percent to 30 percent of the population who struggle to get by in the best of times. This demographic, the working poor, have already been living in an economic depression of their own. From their point of view "the economy," as a shared condition, is a fiction.

This spring, I tracked down a couple of the people I had met while working on my 2001 book, "Nickel and Dimed," in which I worked in low-wage jobs like waitressing and housecleaning, and I found them no more gripped by the recession than by "American Idol"; things were pretty much "same old." The woman I called Melissa in the book was still working at Wal-Mart, though in nine years, her wages had risen to $10 an hour from $7. "Caroline," who is increasingly disabled by diabetes and heart disease, now lives with a grown son and subsists on occasional cleaning and catering jobs. We chatted about grandchildren and church, without any mention of exceptional hardship.

4   As with Denise Smith, whom I recently met through the Virginia Organizing Project and whose bachelor's degree in history qualifies her for seasonal $10-an-hour work at a tourist site, the recession is largely an abstraction. "We were poor," Ms. Smith told me cheerfully, "and we're still poor."

But then, at least if you inhabit a large, multiclass extended family like my own, there comes that e-mail message with the subject line "Need your help," and you realize that bad is often just the stage before worse. The note was from one of my nephews, and it reported that his mother-in-law, Peg, was, like several million other Americans, about to lose her home to foreclosure.

It was the back story that got to me: Peg, who is 55 and lives in rural Missouri, had been working three part-time jobs to support her disabled daughter and two grandchildren, who had moved in with her. Then, last winter, she had a heart attack, missed work and fell behind in her mortgage payments. If I couldn't help, all four would have to move into the cramped apartment in Minneapolis already occupied by my nephew and his wife.

Only after I'd sent the money did I learn that the mortgage was not a subprime one and the home was not a house but a dilapidated single-wide trailer that, as a "used vehicle," commands a 12-percent mortgage interest rate. You could argue, without any shortage of compassion, that "Low-Wage Worker Loses Job, Home" is nobody's idea of news.

8   In late May I traveled to Los Angeles—where the real unemployment rate, including underemployed people and those who have given up on looking for a job, is estimated at 20 percent—to meet with a half-dozen community organizers. They are members of a profession, derided last summer by Sarah Palin, that helps low-income people renegotiate mortgages, deal with eviction when their landlords are foreclosed and, when necessary, organize to confront landlords and bosses. The question I put to this rainbow group was: "Has the recession made a significant difference in the low-income communities where you work, or are things pretty much the same?" My informants—from Koreatown, South Central, Maywood, Artesia and the area around Skid Row—took pains to explain that things were already bad before the recession, and in ways that are disconnected from the larger economy. One of them told me, for example, that the boom of the '90s and early 2000s had been "basically devastating" for the urban poor. Rents skyrocketed; public housing disappeared to make way for gentrification.

But yes, the recession has made things palpably worse, largely because of job losses. With no paychecks coming in, people fall behind on their rent and, since there can be as long as a six-year wait for federal housing subsidies, they often have no alternative but to move in with relatives. "People are calling me all the time," said Preeti Sharma of the South Asian Network. "They think I have some sort of magic."

The organizers even expressed a certain impatience with the Nouveau Poor, once I introduced the phrase. If there's a symbol for the recession in Los Angeles, Davin Corona of Strategic Actions for a Just Economy said, it's "the policeman facing foreclosure in the suburbs." The already poor, he said—the undocumented immigrants, the sweatshop workers, the janitors, maids and security guards—had all but "disappeared" from both the news media and public policy discussions.

Disappearing with them is what may be the most distinctive and compelling story of this recession. When I got back home, I started calling up experts, like Sharon Parrott, a policy analyst at the Center on Budget and Policy Priorities, who told me, "There's rising unemployment among all demographic groups, but vastly more among the so-called unskilled."

12   How much more? Larry Mishel, the president of the Economic Policy Institute, offers data showing that blue-collar unemployment is increasing three times as fast as white-collar unemployment. The last two recessions—in the early '90s and in 2001—produced mass white-collar layoffs, and while the current one has seen plenty of downsized real-estate agents and financial analysts, the brunt is being borne by the blue-collar working class, which has been sliding downward since deindustrialization began in the '80s.

When I called food banks and homeless shelters around the country, most staff members and directors seemed poised to offer press-pleasing tales of formerly middle-class families brought low. But some, like Toni Muhammad at Gateway Homeless Services in St. Louis, admitted that mostly they see "the long-term poor," who become even poorer when they lose the kind of low-wage jobs that had been so easy for me to find from 1998 to 2000. As Candy Hill, a vice president of Catholic Charities U.S.A., put it, "All the focus is on the middle class—on Wall Street and Main Street—but it's the people on the back streets who are really suffering."

What are the stations between poverty and destitution? Like the Nouveau Poor, the already poor descend through a series of deprivations, though these are less likely to involve forgone vacations than missed meals and medications. The *Times* reported earlier this month that one-third of Americans can no longer afford to comply with their prescriptions.

There are other, less life-threatening, ways to try to make ends meet. The Associated Press has reported that more women from all social classes are resorting to stripping, although "gentlemen's clubs," too, have been hard-hit by the recession. The rural poor are turning increasingly to "food auctions," which offer items that may be past their sell-by dates.

16   And for those who like their meat fresh, there's the option of urban hunting. In Racine, Wis., a 51-year-old laid-off mechanic told me he's supplementing his diet by "shooting squirrels and rabbits and eating them stewed, baked and grilled."

In Detroit, where the wildlife population has mounted as the human population ebbs, a retired truck driver is doing a brisk business in raccoon carcasses, which he recommends marinating with vinegar and spices.

The most common coping strategy, though, is simply to increase the number of paying people per square foot of dwelling space—by doubling up or renting to couch-surfers. It's hard to get firm numbers on overcrowding, because no one likes to acknowledge it to census-takers, journalists or anyone else who might be remotely connected to the authorities. At the legal level, this includes Peg taking in her daughter and two grandchildren in a trailer with barely room for two, or my nephew and his wife preparing to squeeze all four of them into what is essentially a one-bedroom apartment. But stories of Dickensian living arrangements abound.

In Los Angeles, Prof. Peter Dreier, a housing policy expert at Occidental College, says that "people who've lost their jobs, or at least their second jobs, cope by doubling or tripling up in overcrowded apartments, or by paying 50 or 60 or even 70 percent of their incomes in rent." Thelmy Perez, an organizer with Strategic Actions for a Just Economy, is trying to help an elderly couple who could no longer afford the $600 a month rent on their two-bedroom apartment, so they took in six unrelated subtenants and are now facing eviction. According to a community organizer in my own city, Alexandria, Va., the standard apartment in a complex occupied largely by day laborers contains two bedrooms, each housing a family of up to five people, plus an additional person laying claim to the couch.

Overcrowding—rural, suburban and urban—renders the mounting numbers of the poor invisible, especially when the perpetrators have no telltale cars to park on the street. But if this is sometimes a crime against zoning laws, it's not exactly a victimless one. At best, it leads to interrupted sleep and long waits for the bathroom; at worst, to explosions of violence. Catholic Charities is reporting a spike in domestic violence in many parts of the country, which Candy Hill attributes to the combination of unemployment and overcrowding.

20   And doubling up is seldom a stable solution. According to Toni Muhammad, about 70 percent of the people seeking emergency shelter in St. Louis report they had been living with relatives "but the place was too small." When I asked Peg what it was like to share her trailer with her daughter's family, she said bleakly, "I just stay in my bedroom."

The deprivations of the formerly affluent Nouveau Poor are real enough, but the situation of the already poor suggests that they do not necessarily presage a greener, more harmonious future with a flatter distribution of wealth. There are no data yet on the effects of the recession on measures of inequality, but historically the effect of downturns is to increase, not decrease, class polarization.

The recession of the '80s transformed the working class into the working poor, as manufacturing jobs fled to the third world, forcing American workers into the low-paying service and retail sector. The current recession is knocking the working poor down another notch—from low-wage employment and inadequate housing toward erratic employment and no housing at all. Comfortable people have long imagined that American poverty is far more luxurious than the third world variety, but the difference is rapidly narrowing.

Maybe "the economy," as depicted on CNBC, will revive again, restoring the kinds of jobs that sustained the working poor, however inadequately, before the recession. Chances are, though, that they still won't pay enough to live on, at least not at any level of safety and dignity. In fact, hourly wage growth, which had been running at about 4 percent a year, has undergone what the Economic Policy Institute calls a "dramatic collapse" in the last six months alone. In good times and grim ones, the misery at the bottom just keeps piling up, like a bad debt that will eventually come due.

PERSONAL RESPONSE

Write about the degree to which you can identify with the working poor or with those who have had to scale back because of the economy. If you do not identify with either group, write for a few minutes about a job you have had and whether you think you were paid enough for it.

QUESTIONS FOR CLASS OR SMALL-GROUP DISCUSSION

1. Summarize the differences between the "Nouveau Poor" and the working poor, according to Ehrenreich. Do you think her descriptions of these groups of people are accurate? Would you add to or modify what she has said about them?

2. What is Ehrenreich's attitude toward the "Nouveau Poor" and the working poor? Is she more sympathetic toward one group than the other? How can you tell? What is her tone when writing about each of the groups?

3. Explain the title of this essay. Who is "too poor to make the news"? Why?

4. State in your own words what Ehrenreich describes as "the stations between poverty and destitution" (paragraph 14). What coping mechanisms do the working poor use, according to Ehrenreich?

ALL KIDS SHOULD TAKE "POVERTY 101"

DONNA BEEGLE

Donna Beegle has a doctorate in education leadership from Portland State University. She is president and founder of Communication Across Barriers, a consulting firm that works to increase communication across poverty, race, gender and generational barriers, in part with "Poverty 101" workshops. This piece was written for CNN's In America, *a series with the goal of exploring who and what America is, and published on April 18, 2012.*

My dream is that a person will not be able to graduate from college without taking a Poverty 101 course. Poverty hurts all humanity and it's the responsibility of everyone to bond together to eradicate it. Our ignorance about poverty perpetuates it and divides us as a nation.

I didn't always know this. I was born into generational poverty; for many decades, most of my family members were uneducated, unskilled and, like 44 million Americans, illiterate. They survived in temporary, minimum wage jobs that didn't pay in respect, nor provide opportunities for advancement.

My dad worked temporary seasonal jobs, the only ones he could get with limited literacy, no education and no specific job skills. My mom, like her widowed mom, picked cotton. We were highly mobile and survived mostly on migrant labor work in Arizona, California, Oregon and Washington. We followed the fruit season to pick cherries, strawberries, oranges and grapefruits. We picked green beans and dug potatoes. They were workers of the land, never owners. My family worked very hard and worked very long hours, but we were still evicted.

4   In school, I did not know the middle-class life examples teachers used to explain academic subjects. I was unable to understand and speak in their middle-class language; I said "ain't," didn't know whether to use "gone" or "went," didn't know a difference between "seen" or "saw." When told to "go look it up," I dutifully went to the dictionary, only to find five more words I did not know and words no one in my world used. This just reinforced there was something wrong with my family, friends and me. It reinforced that education was not for me.

When I quit school at 15, a teacher said, "Do not quit school, one day, you will want a job." I remember looking at her and saying, "I don't want a job." To me, a job meant you worked really hard and had to leave your family in crisis; that you still got evicted and went hungry. To my teacher, a job meant social honor, security, a roof over her head, insurance, maybe a vacation. She told me I would not go anywhere in life if I wasn't motivated.

If the teacher had been exposed to Poverty 101, she would have the skills needed to find out what motivators made sense to me: My dream in life was to be a mom. Every female I had meaningful interaction with got married and had babies very young. I thought I was put on the planet to be a mom. If my teacher had known my dream, she could have said something like, "Donna you want to be a good mom, don't you? What if one day you have a child that needs your help with some school work? By staying in school, you will be better able to help your child."

In school, I'd grown accustomed to believing that middle-class people, even teachers and principals, didn't care about kids like me. It was much later in my life, when I finally had opportunities to interact with people who study poverty, that I realized it was not that middle-class people did not care.

8   I saw them volunteering for soup kitchens and battered women's shelters and providing Christmas baskets to families. At first, I couldn't figure it out. If they cared, why would they allow poverty to continue to harm fellow human beings? I quickly learned that most held deep stereotypes about people who lived in it. We are segregated in America, spending our time with people who are like us: People in poverty associate with others in poverty, middle-class people spend most of their time with other middle-class people and the wealthy socialize with

the wealthy. They could no more know my life in generational poverty than I could know their lives in the middle class.

If we begin by teaching children about poverty in the K-12 system, everyone would learn about the true causes of poverty and the circumstances that perpetuate it. They would gain empathy and recognition that not everyone has the same chances. More importantly, children in poverty would learn the true causes and be able to externalize the shame taught by their own experiences. It empowers them to understand and change their current context.

The recent recession has proven that none of us are as protected from poverty as we would like to think, that people with incomes from $20,000 to $150,000 identify themselves as middle class, and they can easily be pushed from those levels. Many people who thought they would never be in poverty now need help. Those with college degrees are facing the highest unemployment rates in decades.

Not even people who have lived poverty really understand poverty. For instance, Oprah Winfrey once said that she would rather help children in Africa than children in America; when she asked children in Africa what they wanted, they mostly said they wanted uniforms for school. In America, children said, they wanted iPods and sneakers.

12   But what Oprah and many others fail to understand is the theory of belonging. Paulo Freire, a Brazilian scholar on worldwide poverty, said, "Every society teaches its people what it takes to belong."

In the United States, we are programmed and socialized to believe we need certain things in order to belong. So, when a kid walks into school with a cell phone or the right shoes, she or he will be noticed. They get societal honor, the right to belong—and humans need to belong. We will do anything to belong. That need is right up there with our need to eat. That is why kids join gangs and why people who cannot afford big screen TVs go into debt to get one. To understand poverty and its impacts, we must also understand human needs.

In teaching Poverty 101, we would teach poverty competency like cultural competency—a grounded understanding of poverty and the people who live in it. We would provide a historical perspective that illuminates how our past thinking has shaped our current approaches in addressing poverty, and clear definitions, since most of us know only the word "poverty," whether we're describing generational poverty, working-class poverty, immigrant poverty or situational poverty. We would explore attitudes, beliefs and values about poverty and the people who live in it, and strategies to help people move out of it.

Armed with information, we can challenge some paradigms. Poverty is not a Republican or Democrat issue. It is not a Catholic or Mormon issue. Poverty is a human issue. We are losing so much human potential to poverty. I am convinced that we can do better, but not in ignorance.

PERSONAL RESPONSE

Beegle writes in paragraph 8 that, as a child in poverty, she learned that people have "deep stereotypes about people who lived in [poverty]." Has this been your own observation? Do you and/or the people you know have stereotyped images of those living in poverty?

QUESTIONS FOR CLASS AND SMALL-GROUP DISCUSSION

1. Beegle says that she grew up in "generational poverty." What do you think she means by that?

2. Beegle argues that we live in a segregated America. What kinds of segregation is she referring to? Do you agree with her on this point?

3. Although Beegle does not go into great detail about what she teaches in her "Poverty 101" workshops, she does state what she would like people to learn about poverty. What do you think the goals of that workshop are? She says that all college students should take such a course (paragraph 1). What is your response to that statement?

4. In paragraph 15, Beegle says that poverty is not a political nor a religious issue but "a human issue." Explain what you think she means by that statement. Do you agree with her?

PERSPECTIVES ON POVERTY AND HOMELESSNESS

Suggested Writing Topics

1. Taking into consideration Anna Quindlen's "Our Tired, Our Poor, Our Kids," explore the subject of the effects of poverty on self-esteem or other aspects of the well-being of children.

2. Drawing on at least two of the readings in this chapter, consider the problems associated with meeting the needs of welfare recipients, impoverished families, or homeless people. What possible solutions are there to the problems? Can you propose additional suggestions for reducing the large numbers of people in poverty or without homes?

3. With the readings in this chapter in mind, write your own opinion piece on the subject of poverty and homelessness in America.

4. Write a letter to the editor in response to Kevin Fagan's profile of Mike Dick in "Homeless, Mike Dick Was 51, Looked 66."

5. If you have ever experienced the effects of poverty, too little income, not enough work, or a need to juggle child care with the demands of a job, write an essay describing that experience, how you felt about it, and how you handled it.

6. If you know someone who is homeless, describe that person and the situation he or she is in. Explain the conditions that led to the homelessness, if possible.

7. If you know someone who has lost his or her job because of the economy, write about that person's experiences and the effects of joblessness.

8. Using comments that Donna Beegle makes in her essay "All Kids Should Take 'Poverty 101,'" classify several kinds of poverty by identifying their chief characteristics. How do they differ, and how are they similar?

9. In "All Kids Should Take 'Poverty 101,'" Donna Beegle says that in teaching Poverty 101, they teach "poverty competency" (paragraph 14). Define the term *poverty competency* and give examples to illustrate your definition.

10. Working in small groups and drawing on the essays in this chapter, create a scenario involving one or more of the following people: a welfare recipient or a homeless person, a welfare caseworker or a staff member at a homeless shelter, a police officer, and either or both a wealthy person and a working-class person with a regular income and a home. Provide a situation, create dialogue, and role-play in an effort to understand the varying perspectives of different people on the issue of welfare or homelessness. Then present your scenario to the rest of your classmates. For an individual writing project, do an analysis of the scenario or fully develop the viewpoint of the person whose role you played.

Research Topics

1. Research your state's policy on welfare, including residency requirements, eligibility for payments, monitoring of recipients, and related issues. Then write a paper outlining your opinion of your state's welfare policy, including any recommendations you would make for changing it.

2. Research the effects of poverty on education: how does it affect school performance, school attendance, or study habits?

3. Research the efforts of an American city to eradicate homelessness or meet the needs of the impoverished. Consider how the city assesses the problem, identifies those in need, and creates programs to meet those needs. Include also any successes or failures in those efforts.

4. From time to time, politicians propose establishing orphanages that would house not only orphaned children but also the children of single parents on welfare or parents deemed unfit to raise their children. Research this subject, and then write a paper in which you argue for or against the establishment of such orphanages. Make sure you consider as many perspectives as possible on this complex issue, including the welfare of the child, the rights of the parent or parents, and society's responsibility to protect children.

5. Research the subject of poverty in America. Focus your research on a particular group, such as children, women, two-parent families, or single-parent families, or target a particular aspect of the subject such as the effects of race, parental education, or employment on poverty. Consider starting with one of these classic studies of homelessness and poverty in America and then reading more recent studies: Michael B. Katz's *The Undeserving Poor: From the War on Poverty to the War on Welfare* (1990); Jonathan Kozol's *Rachel and Her Children: Homeless Families in America* (1987); Elliot Liebow's *All Them Who I Am: The Lives of Homeless Women* (1995); or Peter H. Rossi's *Down and Out in America: The Origins of Homelessness* (1991).

6. Research an area of public policy on welfare reform, child welfare, homelessness, public housing, family welfare, food stamps, job training, or any other issue related to any reading in this chapter.

RESPONDING TO VISUALS

Alex Wichman/Getty Images

A homeless man makes the sidewalk his dwelling.

1. What details of the image convey the story, at least superficially, of the person in the picture?
2. Do you think that the photographer expects the image to elicit a particular response in those who see it? If so, what response do you think the photographer expects? What is your response to the photograph?
3. In what ways does the photograph relate to the readings in this chapter?

RESPONDING TO VISUALS

Con Tanasiuk/Design Pics/Jupiter Images

Businessman walking by a homeless person.

1. What does the homeless person's body language say about him?
2. What can you tell about the man walking past the homeless person from the way he is dressed and his facial features? How does the photographer's perspective affect the way viewers see and respond to the situation?
3. What irony do you see in the contrast between the two men?

CHAPTER 14

Gender and Sex Roles

Many people use the word *gender* interchangeably with the word *sex*, but the two have different meanings. Sex is a biological category; a person's sex—whether male or female—is genetically determined. On the other hand, gender refers to the socially constructed set of expectations for behavior based on one's sex. Masculinity and femininity are gender constructs whose definitions vary and change over time and with different cultures or groups within cultures. What is considered appropriate and even desirable behavior for men and women in one culture may be strongly inappropriate in another. Like other cultures, American culture's definitions of masculinity and femininity change with time, shaped by a number of influences, such as parental expectations, peer pressure, and media images. We are born either male or female, and most of us learn to behave in ways consistent with our society's expectations for that sex.

Colleges and universities across the United States (and around the world) have created gender studies programs, offered under different names with different emphases: women's studies, male studies, and lesbian-gay-bisexual (LGB) studies, for instance. Courses within these areas of study are typically interdisciplinary in nature, with instructors from traditional disciplines teaching their specialties from the particular perspective of the program. Thus, a political science instructor teaching in a women's studies program would likely offer a feminist perspective on women in politics. An English instructor might look at selected stories and novels for their portrayal of men in a men's studies course or for their portrayal of homosexuality in an LGB studies program. Gender studies programs may also include courses on sexuality. Whatever the focus of the program, the overarching interest in these courses lies in the ways that one's sex—male or female—or one's gender—masculine or feminine—affects behavior, world view, place in society, role in the home, and other issues associated with being human.

This chapter begins with a review of literature on the debate over what it means to grow up male in America. Thomas Bartlett's "The Puzzle of Boys" looks at a number of recent studies of boys and explains researchers' questions and conclusions about the nature of boyhood. His article gives a general overview of what has become a trend in gender studies toward looking at the difficulties boys face in American culture. This trend marks a shift from decades of studies on girls and women toward more inclusive or balanced efforts to understand both males and females. As you read the essay, consider your feelings about being male or female, recalling especially situations when you were identified on the basis of that characteristic alone.

Next is an article by Deborah Tannen, a professor whose research on the ways that people communicate and interact with one another has had broad appeal to general audiences as well as to academics and students. "Who Does the Talking Here?" touches on a topic that she has studied throughout her career, the differences in communication styles of males and females. In this piece, Tannen responds to an article she had recently read that "claims to lay to rest, once and for all, the stereotype that women talk more than men, by proving—scientifically—that women and men talk equally." As you read her article, think about the ways that the men and women you know talk to one another when they are in a group of their own sex or in mixed-sex gatherings. Do your own observations support or refute those that Tannen makes?

Then, Christina Sommers in "Oh, Come On, Men Aren't Finished" addresses a recent cultural trend supporting the notion that men are in decline and women in ascendency. To the question of why we are debating the decline of men, she answers that "we're living in a society that's enamored with the 'WAW,' or 'Women are Wonderful' phenomenon." She notes that "to violate the spirit of WAW is to invite havoc" and cites examples of books and articles that support that viewpoint. As you read her article, you may find yourself nodding in agreement or shaking your head in dismay. Either way, read it with an open mind and consider whether you agree with Sommers completely, in part, or not at all.

One of the many topics in the broad subject area of gender and sex roles is marriage, both hetero- and homosexual. No doubt the more heated debate has occurred over gay marriage, but the nature of marriage itself often comes up for discussion. The chapter ends with an opinion piece on the subject of marriage, Howard Moody's "Sacred Rite or Civil Right?" Moody asserts that gay marriages show why we need to separate church and state. He gives a historical overview of the roles that both church and state have played in establishing the nature of heterosexual marriage, stressing the differences between the religious definition of marriage and the state's definition. At the heart of his essay is the question of what marriage is, so you may want to think about your own definition of marriage as you read the essay.

THE PUZZLE OF BOYS

THOMAS BARTLETT

Thomas Bartlett, a senior writer for the Chronicle of Higher Education *since 2001, has covered such subjects as teaching, religion, tenure, plagiarism, diploma mills, and other forms of cheating. He has appeared on national radio and television shows such as National Public Radio's* Talk of the Nation *and ABC News's* Nightline. *Bartlett regularly contributes to the* Chronicle's *Off Beat column, which takes a look at funny or unusual trends in higher education. This piece appeared in the* Chronicle of Higher Education *on November 22, 2009.*

My son just turned 3. He loves trains, fire trucks, tools of all kinds, throwing balls, catching balls, spinning until he falls down, chasing cats, tackling dogs, emptying the kitchen drawers of their contents, riding a tricycle, riding a carousel, pretending to be a farmer, pretending to be a cow, dancing, drumming, digging, hiding, seeking, jumping, shouting, and collapsing exhausted into a Thomas the Tank Engine bed wearing Thomas the Tank Engine pajamas after reading a Thomas the Tank Engine book.

That doesn't make him unusual; in fact, in many ways, he couldn't be more typical. Which may be why a relative recently said, "Well, he's definitely all boy." It's a statement that sounds reasonable enough until you think about it. What does "all boy" mean? Masculine? Straight? Something else? Are there partial boys? And is this relative aware of my son's fondness for Hello Kitty and tea sets?

These are the kinds of questions asked by anxious parents and, increasingly, academic researchers. Boyhood studies—virtually unheard of a few years ago—has taken off, with a shelf full of books already published, more on the way, and a new journal devoted to the subject. Much of the focus so far has been on boys falling behind academically, paired with the notion that school is not conducive to the way boys learn. What motivates boys, the argument goes, is different from what motivates girls, and society should adjust accordingly.

4   Not everyone buys the boy talk. Some critics, in particular the American Association of University Women, contend that much of what passes for research about boyhood only reinforces stereotypes and arrives at simplistic conclusions: Boys are competitive! Boys like action! Boys hate books! They argue that this line of thinking miscasts boys as victims and ignores the very real problems faced by girls.

But while this debate is far from settled, the field has expanded to include how marketers target boys, the nature of boys' friendships, and a host of deeper, more philosophical issues, all of which can be boiled down, more or less, to a single question: Just what are boys, anyway?

One of the first so-called boys' books, Michael Gurian's *The Wonder of Boys*, was not immediately embraced by publishers. In fact, it was turned down by 25 houses before finally being purchased by Tarcher/Putnam for a modest sum. This was in the mid-1990s, and everyone was concerned about girls. Girls were drowning in the "sea of Western culture," according to Carol Gilligan. In *Reviving Ophelia*, Mary Pipher bemoaned a "girl-poisoning" culture that emphasized sexiness above all else.

Boys weren't the story. No one wanted to read about them.

8   Or so publishers thought. *The Wonder of Boys* has since sold more than a half-million copies, and Gurian, who has a master's degree in writing and has worked as a family counselor, has become a prominent speaker and consultant on boys' issues. He has written two more books about boys, including *The Purpose of Boys*, published this year, which argues that boys are hard-wired to desire a sense of mission, and that parents and teachers need to understand "boy biology" if they want to help young men succeed.

Drawing on neuroscience research done by others, Gurian argues that boy brains and girl brains are fundamentally dissimilar. In the nature versus nurture debate, Gurian comes down squarely on the side of the former. He catches flak for supposedly over-interpreting neuroscience data to comport with his theories about boys. In *The Trouble with Boys*, a former *Newsweek* reporter, Peg Tyre, takes him to task for arguing that female brains are active even when they're bored, while male brains tend to "shut down" (a conclusion that Ruben Gur, director of the Brain Behavior Laboratory at the University of Pennsylvania, tells Tyre isn't supported by the evidence). Gurian counters that his work has been misrepresented and that the success of his programs backs up his scientific claims.

Close on Gurian's heels was *Real Boys*, by William Pollack. Pollack, an associate clinical professor of psychology at Harvard Medical School and director of the Centers for Men and Young Men, writes that behind their facade of toughness, boys are vulnerable and desperate for emotional connection. Boys, he says, tend to communicate through action. They are more likely to express empathy and affection through an activity, like playing basketball together, than having a heart-to-heart talk. Pollack's view of what makes boys the way they are is less rooted in biology than Gurian's. "What neuroscientists will tell you is that nature and nurture are bonded," says Pollack. "How we nurture from the beginning has an effect." *Real Boys* earned a stamp of approval from Mary Pipher, who writes in the foreword that "our culture is doing a bad job raising boys."

Pollack's book, like Gurian's, was an enormous success. It sold more than 750,000 copies and has been published in 13 countries. Even though it came out a decade ago, Pollack says he still receives e-mail every week from readers. "People were hungry for it," he says.

12   The following year, *Raising Cain,* by Dan Kindlon, an adjunct lecturer in Harvard's School of Public Health, and Michael Thompson, a psychologist in private practice, was published and was later made into a two-hour PBS documentary. Their book ends with seven recommendations for dealing with boys, including "recognize and accept the high activity level of boys and give them safe boy places to express it." The book is partially about interacting with boys on their own terms, but it also encourages adults to help them develop "emotional literacy" and to counter the "culture of cruelty" among older boys. It goes beyond academic performance, dealing with issues like suicide, bullying, and romance.

Perhaps the most provocative book of the bunch is *The War Against Boys: How Misguided Feminism Is Harming Our Young Men,* by Christina Hoff Sommers. As the subtitle suggests, Sommers believes that she's found the villain in this story, making the case that it's boys, not girls, who are being shortchanged and that they need significant help if they're going to close the distance academically. But that does not mean, according to Sommers, that they "need to be rescued from their masculinity."

Those books were best sellers and continue to attract readers and spirited debate. While the authors disagree on the details, they share at least two broad conclusions: (1) Boys are not girls, and (2) Boys are in trouble. Why and how they're different from girls, what's behind their trouble, and what if anything to do about it—all that depends on whom you read.

A backlash was inevitable. In 2008 the American Association of University Women issued a report, "Where the Girls Are: The Facts about Gender Equity in Education," arguing not only that the alleged academic disparity between boys and girls had been exaggerated, but also that the entire crisis was a myth. If anything, the report says, boys are doing better than ever: "The past few decades have seen remarkable gains for girls and boys in education, and no evidence indicates a crisis for boys in particular."

16   So how could the boys-in-trouble crowd have gotten it so wrong? The report has an answer for that: "Many people remain uncomfortable with the educational and professional advances of girls and women, especially when they threaten to outdistance their peers." In other words, it's not genuine concern for boys that's energizing the movement but rather fear of girls surpassing them.

The dispute is, in part, a dispute over data. And like plenty of such squabbles, the outcome hinges on the numbers you decide to use. Boys outperform girls by more than 30 points on the mathematics section of the SAT and a scant four points on the verbal sections (girls best boys by 13 points on the recently added writing section). But many more girls actually take the test. And while it's a fact that boys and girls are both more likely to attend college than they were a generation ago, girls now make up well over half of the student body, and a projection by the Department of Education indicates that the gap will widen considerably over the next decade.

College isn't the only relevant benchmark. Boys are more likely than girls to be diagnosed with attention-deficit disorder, but girls are more likely to be diagnosed with depression. Girls are more likely to report suicide attempts, but boys are more likely to actually kill themselves (according to the Centers for Disease Control and Prevention, 83 percent of suicides between the ages of 10 and 24 are male). Ask a representative of the AAUW about a pitfall that appears to disproportionately affect boys, like attention-deficit disorder, and the representative will counter that the disparity is overplayed or that girls deal with equally troubling issues.

But it's not statistics that have persuaded parents and educators that boys are in desperate straits, according to Sara Mead, a senior research fellow with the New America Foundation, a public-policy institute. Mead wrote a paper in 2006 that argued, much like the later AAUW report, that the boys' crisis was bunk. "What seems to most resonate with teachers and parents is not as much the empirical evidence but this sense of boys being unmoored or purposeless in a vaguely defined way," Mead says in an interview. "That's a really difficult thing to validate more beyond anecdote." She also worries that all this worrying—much of it, she says, from middle-class parents—could have a negative effect on boys, marking them as victims when they're nothing of the sort.

20   Pollack concedes, as Mead and others point out, that poor performance in school is also tied to factors like race and class, but he insists that boys as a group—including white, middle-class boys—are sinking, pointing to studies that suggest they are less likely to do their homework and more likely to drop out of high school. And he has a hunch about why some refuse to acknowledge it: "People look at the adult world and say, 'Men are still in charge.' So they look down at boys and say, 'They are small men, so they must be on the way to success,'" says Pollack. "It's still a man's world. People make the mistake of thinking it's a boy's world."

If the first round of books was focused on the classroom, the second round observes the boy in his natural habitat. The new book *Packaging Boyhood: Saving Our Sons from Superheroes, Slackers, and Other Media Stereotypes* offers an analysis of what boys soak in from TV shows, video games, toys, and other facets of boy-directed pop culture. The news isn't good here, either. According to the book, boys are being taught they have to be tough and cool, athletic and stoic. This starts early with toddler T-shirts emblazoned with "Future All-Star" or "Little Champion." Even once-benign toys like Legos and Nerf have assumed a more hostile profile with Lego Exo-Force Assault Tigers and the Nerf N-Strike Raider Rapid Fire CS-35 Dart Blaster. "That kind of surprised us," says one of the book's three authors, Lyn Mikel Brown, a professor of education and human development at Colby College. "What happened to Nerf? What happened to Lego?"

Brown also co-wrote *Packaging Girlhood*. In that book, the disease was easier to diagnose, what with the Disney princess phenomenon and sexy clothes being marketed to pre-adolescent girls. Everyone was worried about how girls were being portrayed in the mass media and what that was doing to their self-esteem. The messages about boys, however, were easier to miss, in part because they're so ubiquitous. "We expect a certain amount of teasing, bullying, spoofing about being tough enough, even in animated films for the littlest boys," Brown says.

For *Packaging Boyhood,* the authors interviewed more than 600 boys and found that models of manhood were turning up in some unexpected places, like the Discovery Channel's *Man vs. Wild,* in which the star is dropped into the harsh wilderness and forced to forage. They're concerned that such programs, in order to compete against all the stimuli vying for boys' attentions, have become more aggressively in-your-face, more fearlessly risk-taking, manlier than thou. Says Brown: "What really got us was the pumping up of the volume."

24   Brown thinks boys are more complicated, and less single-minded, than adults give them credit for. So does Ken Corbett, whose new book, *Boyhoods: Rethinking Masculinities,* steers clear of generalizations and doesn't try to elucidate the ideal boyhood (thus the plural "masculinities"). Corbett, an assistant professor of psychology at New York University, wants to remind us not how boys are different from girls but how they're different from one another. His background is in clinical psychoanalysis, feminism, and queer studies—in other words, as he points out in the introduction, "not your father's psychoanalysis."

In a chapter titled "Feminine Boys," he writes of counseling the parents of a boy who liked to wear bracelets and perform a princess dance. The father, especially, wasn't sure how to take this, telling Corbett that he wanted a son, not a daughter.

To show how boys can be difficult to define, Corbett tells the story of Hans, a 5-year-old patient of Sigmund Freud, who had a fear of being castrated by, of all things, a horse. Young Hans also fantasizes about having a "widdler," as the boy puts it, as large as his father's. Freud (typically) reads the kid's issues as primarily sexual, and his desire to be more like his father as Oedipal. Corbett, however, doesn't think Hans's interest in his penis is about sex, but rather about becoming bigger, in developing beyond the half-finished sketch of boyhood. "Wishing to be big is wishing to fill in the drawing," Corbett writes.

Corbett disputes the idea that boys as a group are in peril. They have troubles, sure, but so do other people. Treating boys as problems to be solved, rather than subjects to be studied, is a mistake, he says, and much of the writing on boys "doesn't illuminate the experience of being a boy, but it does illuminate the space between a boy and a parent."

28   The experience of being a boy is exactly what Miles Groth wants to capture. Groth, a psychology professor at Wagner College, is editor of *Thymos: Journal of Boyhood Studies,* founded in 2007. An article he wrote in the inaugural issue of the journal, "Has Anyone Seen the Boy? The Fate of the Boy in Becoming a Man," is a sort of call to arms for boyhood-studies scholars. For years, Groth says, academics didn't really discuss boys. They might study a certain subset of boys, but boys per se were off the table. "I think there was some hesitancy for scholars to take up the topic, to show that they're paying attention to guys when we should be paying attention to girls," says Groth. "Now I think there's less of that worry. People don't see it as a reactionary movement."

That has opened the door for scholars like Niobe Way. A professor of applied psychology at New York University, Way recently finished a book, scheduled to be published next year by Harvard University Press, on how boys communicate. She's been interviewing teenage boys about their friendships, and what she's found is remarkable. While it's common wisdom that teenage boys either can't express or don't possess strong feelings about their friends, Way has discovered that boys in their early teens can be downright sentimental when discussing their friendships. When asked what they liked about their best friends, boys frequently said: "They won't laugh at me when I talk about serious things." What has emerged from her research is a portrait of emotionally intelligent boys who care about more than sports and cars. Such an observation might not sound revolutionary, but what boys told her and her fellow researchers during lengthy, probing interviews runs counter to the often one-dimensional portrayal of boys in popular culture. "They were resisting norms of masculinity," she says.

Note the past tense. At some point in high school, that expressiveness vanishes, replaced with a more defensive, closed-off posture, perhaps as boys give in to messages about what it means to be a man. Still, her research undermines the stereotype that boys are somehow incapable of discussing their feelings. "And yet," she says, "this notion of this emotionally illiterate, sex-obsessed, sports-playing boy just keeps getting spit out again and again."

Touchy-feely talk about friendships may seem disconnected from boys' academic woes, but Way insists they're pieces of the same puzzle. "If you don't understand the experience of boyhood," she says, "you'll never understand the achievement gaps."

Books cited in this article:

The Wonder of Boys, by Michael Gurian (Tarcher/Putnam, 1996) *Real Boys*, by William Pollack (Random House, 1998)

Raising Cain, by Dan Kindlon and Michael Thompson (Ballantine Books, 1999)

The War Against Boys, by Christina Hoff Sommers (Simon & Schuster, 2000)

The Trouble with Boys, by Peg Tyre (Crown Publishers, 2008)

Packaging Boyhood, by Lyn Mikel Brown, Sharon Lamb, and Mark Tappan (St. Martin's Press, 2009)

Boyhoods: Rethinking Masculinities, by Ken Corbett (Yale University Press, 2009)

PERSONAL RESPONSE

Select a passage about one of the books that Bartlett reviews and write for a few minutes on your response to the conclusions about boyhood that the author makes.

QUESTIONS FOR CLASS OR SMALL-GROUP DISCUSSION

1. What assumptions about the traditional definitions of sex and gender does Bartlett point out? What do you think it means when a child is described as "all boy" or "all girl"? How do you feel about such labels?

2. Summarize the chief interests of the recent books on boys that Bartlett covers in his article. What are researchers primarily interested in learning about boys? What conclusions have they drawn?

3. State your understanding of the different approaches among researchers in the area of "boyhood studies." On what points do they seem to agree and disagree? How does Bartlett account for the differences?

4. Do you think it is possible for any society, but especially American society, to do away with assigning sex roles? How possible do you think it would be to raise a child not to be conscious of gender? Is such a goal desirable? Explain your answer.

WHO DOES THE TALKING HERE?

DEBORAH TANNEN

Deborah Tannen is a professor of linguistics at Georgetown University. Author of many scholarly articles and books on subjects in her field, she is probably best known for her general-audience books beginning with You Just Don't Understand: Women and Men in Conversation *(1990). Her other books include* Talking from 9 to 5: Women and Men at Work *(1994);* The Argument Culture: Stopping America's War of Words *(1999);* I Only Say This because I Love You: Talking to Your Parents, Partner, Sibs and Kids When You're All Adults *(2002);* You're Wearing That? Understanding Mothers and Daughters in Conversation *(2006); and* You Were Always Mom's Favorite! Sisters in Conversation throughout Their Lives" *(2009). This article appeared in the July 15, 2007, edition of the* Washington Post.

It's no surprise that a one-page article published this month in the journal *Science* inspired innumerable newspaper columns and articles. The study, by Matthias Mehl and four colleagues, claims to lay to rest, once and for all, the stereotype that women talk more than men, by proving—scientifically—that women and men talk equally.

The notion that women talk more was reinforced last year when Louann Brizendine's *The Female Brain* cited the finding that women utter, on average, 20,000 words a day, men 7,000. (Brizendine later disavowed the statistic, as there was no study to back it up.) Mehl and his colleagues outfitted 396 college students with devices that recorded their speech. The female subjects spoke an average of 16,215 words a day, the men 15,669. The difference is insignificant. Case closed.

Or is it? Can we learn who talks more by counting words. No, according to a forthcoming article surveying 70 studies of gender differences in talkativeness. (Imagine—70 studies published in scientific journals, and we're still asking the question.) In their survey, Campbell Leaper and Melanie Ayres found that counting words yielded no consistent differences, though number of words per speaking turn did (Men, on average, used more).

4   This doesn't surprise me. In my own research on gender and language, I quickly surmised that to understand who talks more, you have to ask: What's the situation? What are the speakers using words for?

The following experience conveys the importance of situation. I was address-ing a small group in a suburban Virginia living room. One man stood out because he talked a lot, while his wife, who was sitting beside him, said nothing at all. I described to the group a complaint common among women about men they live with: At the end of a day she tells him what happened, what she thought and how she felt about it. Then she asks, "How was your day?"—and is disappointed when he replies, "Fine," "Nothing much" or "Same old rat race."

The loquacious man spoke up. "You're right," he said. Pointing to his wife, he added, "She's the talker in our family." Everyone laughed. But he explained, "It's true. When we come home, she does all the talking. If she didn't, we'd spend the evening in silence."

The "how was your day?" conversation typifies the kind of talk women tend to do more of: spoken to intimates and focusing on personal experience, your own or others'. I call this "rapport-talk." It contrasts with "report-talk"—giving or exchanging information about impersonal topics, which men tend to do more.

8   Studies that find men talking more are usually carried out in formal experi-ments or public contexts such as meetings. For example, Marjorie Swacker observed an academic conference where women presented 40 percent of the papers and were 42 percent of the audience but asked only 27 percent of the questions; their questions were, on average, also shorter by half than the men's questions. And David and Myra Sadker showed that boys talk more in mixed-sex classrooms—a context common among college students, a factor skewing the results of Mehl's new study.

Many men's comfort with "public talking" explains why a man who tells his wife he has nothing to report about his day might later find a funny story to tell at dinner with two other couples (leaving his wife wondering, "Why didn't he tell me first?").

In addition to situation, you have to consider what speakers are doing with words. Campbell and Ayres note that many studies find women doing more "affiliative speech" such as showing support, agreeing or acknowledging others' comments. Drawing on studies of children at play as well as my own research of adults talking, I often put it this way: For women and girls, talk is the glue that holds a relationship together. Their best friend is the one they tell everything to. Spending an evening at home with a spouse is when this kind of talk comes into its own. Since this situation is uncommon among college students, it's another factor skewing the new study's results.

Women's rapport-talk probably explains why many people think women talk more. A man wants to read the paper, his wife wants to talk; his girlfriend or sister spends hours on the phone with her friend or her mother. He concludes: Women talk more.

12   Yet Leaper and Ayres observed an overall pattern of men speaking more. That's a conclusion women often come to when men hold forth at meetings, in social groups or when delivering one-on-one lectures. All of us—women and men—tend to notice others talking more in situations where we talk less.

Counting may be a start—or a stop along the way—to understanding gender differences. But it's understanding when we tend to talk and what we're doing with words that yields insights we can count on.

PERSONAL RESPONSE

What do your own informal observations reveal about who talks more, males or females?

QUESTIONS FOR CLASS OR SMALL-GROUP DISCUSSION

1. Tannen opens with references to studies on who talks more, men or women. What is her opinion of these works? How might a study of college students skew the results of research into which sex talks more? Why do you think there have been so many studies about women's and men's talkativeness? What is the issue?

2. Explain why Tannen believes that situation is important when considering who talks more, men or women. How effective do you find her personal anecdote in illustrating her point?

3. What do you understand Tannen to mean when she says that studies on gender and language must ask what the speakers are using words for?

4. What is the difference between "rapport talk" and "report talk," according to Tannen? What is "affiliative speech" (paragraph 10)? Do your own observations support or refute her comments on these ways of speaking?

OH, COME ON, MEN AREN'T FINISHED

Christina Sommers

Christina Hoff Sommers was a professor of philosophy at Clark University before becoming a resident scholar at the American Enterprise Institute. Her books include Who Stole Feminism: How Women Have Betrayed Women *(1995);* The War against Boys *(2000); and* The Science on Women in Science *(2009). She has lectured and debated at more than 100 college campuses. This article was posted at* Slate.com *on September 15, 2011.*

For most of human history, men have been the dominant sex because of their capacity to compete, take risks, conceal emotion, and fight for resources. But some claim these masculine traits have become obsolete in the post-industrial, knowledge-based 21st century. Now, it's the empathetic, socially intuitive fairer sex who reign supreme because *those* inbred traits have become integral to the modern economy. Men, we've been told, are passé.

Don't believe this fantasy. Women are joining men as partners in running the world, but they are not replacing men and never will. Yes, women are flourishing in unprecedented and gratifying ways. But men have hardly vanished from the center. After almost 40 years of gender neutral pronouns, it is still men who are more likely than women to run for political office, start businesses, file for patents, tell jokes, write editorials, conduct orchestras, and blow things up. Males succeed and fail more spectacularly than females: More males are Nobel laureates and CEOs. But more males are also in maximum security prisons. Males commit most acts of wanton violence, but it takes other men to stop them.

The male declinists seem to imagine a world of busy, consensus-building women, happily and competently interacting and managing the new economy. They point to the explosion of jobs in the caring, nurturing, and communicating professions: nurses, social workers, veterinarians, website designers, personal coaches, dance therapists, executive producers. Sorry to disturb this idyll, but you cannot sustain a network of nurturers and communicators without someone paying for it. You will still need hard-driven innovators, manufactures, builders, and transporters—not to mention the military.

4   We are told that toughness and assertiveness are obsolete. That is ridiculous—and brings to mind an observation usually attributed to George Orwell: "We sleep peaceably in our beds at night only because rough men stand ready to do violence on our behalf." The world is as dangerous as ever. Think of China with all its millions of unattached young men, or those volatile patriarchal societies where radical Sharia law prevails. Our civilization still depends on the protection of brave men (and some women) who are willing to fight and die to protect us.

Hanna Rosin's *Atlantic* article, "The End of Men," concedes that men are still at the top of the pyramid—but says that "men's hold on power in elite circles is loosening." Loosening, yes, but there is no evidence of a female takeover. Not because women lack the talent—women can be as dazzling as men when they set their mind to it. But fewer women than men *do* set their mind to it. The sexes are equal but exercise that equality in different ways.

Consider science and technology. Women now hold the majority of college degrees and jobs in psychology, biology, and veterinary medicine. Here, they're not just competitive with men, they show signs of overtaking them. But those numbers don't hold in math, physics, computer science and engineering, where men still prevail. In those fields, there's no sign of significant change. According to a recent study from the Commerce Department, men held 70 percent of computer science and math jobs in 2000 and 73 percent in 2009. There are brilliant women who are mathematicians and computer scientists, but all the evidence suggests women prefer to do other things with their talents.

Meanwhile, men continue to file more than 90 percent of patent applications. They drive innovation in technology—and not just with basic hardware. Bill Gates achieved global dominance by designing computers with a friendly, approachable interface. Steve Jobs displaced him by creating elegant, intuitive super-machines that were small enough to fit into an evening bag. A guy named Doug came up with the touchy-feely idea of the mouse. The social network is dominated by women but it was invented by Mark Zuckerberg.

8   Is the technology industry finished? Is engineering finished? Is the military finished? I haven't even mentioned that men hold the lion's share of dangerous, dirty, and necessary jobs that few women seem to want. Men tend to be the truck drivers, builders, oil-rig workers, roofers, loggers, coal miners, taxi drivers, and window washers. Are those jobs passé?

Why, then, are we even having a debate about man's demise? Because we're living in a society that's enamored with the "WAW," or "Women are Wonderful" phenomenon. WAW, a kind of reverse female chauvinism, is everywhere. Magazines, TV shows, newspapers, and even scholarly journals run endless stories and articles claiming women are the better sex. Women, we are told, are superior leaders and communicators. They're also more charitable, empathetic, and noble than men. The rules of the WAW game make it impossible for men to win: If women do something better than men, that is evidence of their superiority. If men outperform women, that's proof of invidious discrimination against the fairer sex.

To violate the spirit of WAW is to invite havoc. Suggest, as Larry Summers did, that men may have some innate advantages in science and math, and prepare to change your job. Write a book or article titled *Are Men Necessary?*, "The End of Men," *Man Down*, or *Women Are from Venus, Men Are from Hell*, and the gods smile.

The idea that men are finished is absurd. But it *is* true that minimally educated men are in serious trouble. Girls do better than boys in school. They get better grades, score higher on reading and writing tests, and are far more likely to go to college. The reasons for girls' educational success are complicated and likely reflect innate differences to some degree: Teenage girls, for example, tend to sit still and pay attention better than teenage boys. But whenever anyone comes up with a plan to help boys in the United States—boy-friendly classrooms, all-male academies, or vocational education tailored to their interests—women's groups such as the American Association of University Women and the National Women's Law Center cry foul and go on the attack.

12   Several years ago, Hasbro Toys tested a furnished playhouse it was considering marketing to both boys and girls. But it soon became clear that that girls and boys did not interact with the structure in the same way. The girls dressed the dolls, kissed them, and played house; the boys catapulted the toy baby carriage from the roof. A Hasbro general manager came up with a brilliant explanation: *Boys and girls are different*. I would add that when they grow up, they complement one another. When parents take a child to a jungle gym at a park, the mother typically says, "Be careful." The father, "Can you get to the top?" Today it's fashionable to claim that we no longer need the catapulters or the "can you get to the top" crowd. But we do.

The cartoonist Nicole Hollander once asked, "Can you imagine a world without men?" Her answer, "No crime and lots of happy fat women." Well, crime would certainly decline, and we'd probably put on a few pounds. But would we be happy? Not most of us. Women, alas, love men, and need them. They are our fathers, husbands, sons, brothers, and friends. Their fate is our fate—this is no zero-sum competition.

Men are not finished because neither men nor women will permit that to happen. After all these years, it turns out women need men much more than a fish needs a bicycle.

PERSONAL RESPONSE

This article received over 125 responses after it appeared online. If you were to post a comment in response to it, what would you say?

QUESTIONS FOR CLASS OR SMALL-GROUP DISCUSSION

1. Describe the tone of this article. How does the title suggest what the tone will be? Is the tone consistent throughout the essay? Select passages that support your assessment.

2. Explain in your own words what Sommers' point is. Where is her thesis or central idea stated? How well do you think she supports her central idea? To what extent do you agree with her? Do you agree with her on all points, some points, or none?

3. Analyze the piece as an argument. Is Sommers logical, reasoned, thorough, and convincing? Explain your answer.

4. The last sentence of the article states that "women need men much more than a fish needs a bicycle." The reference is to a catchphrase that appeared on T-shirts, pinbacks, posters, cartoons, and other pop culture items during the contemporary Women's Movement begun in the late 1960s. Based on what you have read here, how would you describe Sommers' views on feminism? Use evidence from the text to support your conclusion.

SACRED RITE OR CIVIL RIGHT?

HOWARD MOODY

Howard Moody (1921–2012) was a minister at Judson Memorial Church in New York City from 1957 to 1992. Often referred to as the Harriet Tubman of the abortion rights movement, he is best known for his pioneering work for women's rights during the 1960s and 1970s.

Reprinted with permission form the June 5, 2004 issue of *The Nation*. For subscription information, call 1-800-333-8536. Portions of each week's Nation magazine can be accessed at http://www.thenation.com.

Author of several books, including two with Arlene Carmen on abortion rights and prostitution, as well as a collection of essays, The God-Man of Galilee: Studies in Christian Living *(1983), he lectured, preached, and wrote often on issues of ethics and social policy.* "Sacred Rite or Civil Right?" *was first published in the July 5, 2004, issue of the* Nation.

If members of the church that I served for more than three decades were told I would be writing an article in defense of marriage, they wouldn't believe it. My reputation was that when people came to me for counsel about getting married, I tried to talk them out of it. More about that later.

We are now in the midst of a national debate on the nature of marriage, and it promises to be as emotional and polemical as the issues of abortion and homosexuality have been over the past century. What all these debates have in common is that they involved both the laws of the state and the theology of the church. The purpose of this writing is to suggest that the gay-marriage debate is less about the legitimacy of the loving relationship of a same-sex couple than about the relationship of church and state and how they define marriage.

In Western civilization, the faith and beliefs of Christendom played a major role in shaping the laws regarding social relations and moral behavior. Having been nurtured in the Christian faith from childhood and having served a lifetime as an ordained Baptist minister, I feel obligated first to address the religious controversy concerning the nature of marriage. If we look at the history of religious institutions regarding marriage we will find not much unanimity but amazing diversity—it is really a mixed bag. Those who base their position on "tradition" or "what the Bible says" will find anything but clarity. It depends on which "tradition" in what age reading from whose holy scriptures.

4   In the early tradition of the Jewish people, there were multiple wives and not all of them equal. Remember the story of Abraham's wives, Sara and Hagar. Sara couldn't get pregnant, so Hagar presented Abraham with a son. When Sara got angry with Hagar, she forced Abraham to send Hagar and her son Ishmael into the wilderness. In case Christians feel superior about their "tradition" of marriage, I would remind them that their scriptural basis is not as clear about marriage as we might hope. We have Saint Paul's conflicting and condescending words about the institution: "It's better not to marry." Karl Barth called this passage the Magna Carta of the single person. (Maybe we should have taken Saint Paul's advice more seriously. It might have prevented an earlier generation of parents from harassing, cajoling and prodding our young until they were married.) In certain religious branches, the church doesn't recognize the licensed legality of marriage but requires that persons meet certain religious qualifications before the marriage is recognized by the church. For members of the Roman Catholic Church, a "legal divorce" and the right to remarry may not be recognized unless the first marriage has been declared null and void by a decree of the church. It is clear that there is no single religious view of marriage and that history has witnessed some monumental changes in the way "husband and wife" are seen in the relationship of marriage.

In my faith-based understanding, if freedom of choice means anything to individuals (male or female), it means they have several options. They can be single and celibate without being thought of as strange or psychologically unbalanced. They can be single and sexually active without being labeled loose or immoral. Women can be single with child without being thought of as unfit or inadequate. If these choices had been real options, the divorce rate may never have reached nearly 50 percent.

The other, equally significant choice for people to make is that of lifetime commitment to each other and to seal that desire in the vows of a wedding ceremony. That understanding of marriage came out of my community of faith. In my years of ministry I ran a tight ship in regard to the performance of weddings. It wasn't because I didn't believe in marriage (I've been married for sixty years and have two wonderful offspring) but rather my unease about the way marriage was used to force people to marry so they wouldn't be "living in sin."

The failure of the institution can be seen in divorce statistics. I wanted people to know how challenging the promise of those vows was and not to feel this was something they had to do. My first question in premarital counseling was, "Why do you want to get married and spoil a beautiful friendship?" That question often elicited a thoughtful and emotional answer. Though I was miserly in the number of weddings I performed, I always made exceptions when there were couples who had difficulty finding clergy who would officiate. Their difficulty was because they weren't of the same religion, or they had made marital mistakes, or what they couldn't believe. Most of them were "ecclesiastical outlaws," barred from certain sacraments in the church of their choice.

8   The church I served had a number of gay and lesbian couples who had been together for many years, but none of them had asked for public weddings or blessings on their relationship. (There was one commitment ceremony for a gay couple at the end of my tenure.) It was as though they didn't need a piece of paper or a ritual to symbolize their lifelong commitment. They knew if they wanted a religious ceremony, their ministers would officiate and our religious community would joyfully witness.

It was my hope that since the institution of marriage had been used to exclude and demean members of the homosexual community, our church, which was open and affirming, would create with gays and lesbians a new kind of ceremony. It would be an occasion that symbolized, between two people of the same gender, a covenant of intimacy of two people to journey together, breaking new ground in human relationships—an alternative to marriage as we have known it.

However, I can understand why homosexuals want "to be married" in the old fashioned "heterosexual way." After all, most gays and lesbians were born of married parents, raised in a family of siblings; many were nourished in churches and synagogues, taught about a living God before Whom all Her creatures were equally loved. Why wouldn't they conceive their loving relationships in terms of marriage and family and desire that they be confirmed and understood as such? It follows that if these gays and lesbians see their relationship as faith-based, they would want a religious ceremony that seals their intentions to become lifelong partners, lovers and friends, that they would want to be "married."

Even though most religious denominations deny this ceremony to homosexual couples, more and more clergy are, silently and publicly, officiating at religious rituals in which gays and lesbians declare their vows before God and a faith community. One Catholic priest who defied his church's ban said: "We can bless a dog, we can bless a boat, but we can't say a prayer over two people who love each other. You don't have to call it marriage, you can call it a deep and abiding friendship, but you can bless it."

12   We have the right to engage in "religious disobedience" to the regulations of the judicatory that granted us the privilege to officiate at wedding ceremonies, and suffer the consequences. However, when it comes to civil law, it is my contention that the church and its clergy are on much shakier ground in defying the law.

In order to fully understand the conflict that has arisen in this debate over the nature of marriage, it is important to understand the difference between the religious definition of marriage and the state's secular and civil definition. The government's interest is in a legal definition of marriage—a social and voluntary contract between a man and woman in order to protect money, property and children. Marriage is a civil union without benefit of clergy or religious definition. The state is not interested in why two people are "tying the knot," whether it's to gain money, secure a dynasty or raise children. It may be hard for those of us who have a religious or romantic view of marriage to realize that loveless marriages are not that rare. Before the Pill, pregnancy was a frequent motive for getting married. The state doesn't care what the commitment of two people is, whether it's for life or as long as both of you love, whether it's sexually monogamous or an open marriage. There is nothing spiritual, mystical or romantic about the state's license to marry—it's a legal contract.

Thus, George W. Bush is right when he says that "marriage is a sacred institution" when speaking as a Christian, as a member of his Methodist church. But as President of the United States and leader of all Americans, believers and unbelievers, he is wrong. What will surface in this debate as litigation and court decisions multiply is the history of the conflict between the church and the state in defining the nature of marriage. That history will become significant as we move toward a decision on who may be married.

After Christianity became the state religion of the Roman Empire in AD 325, the church maintained absolute control over the regulation of marriage for some 1,000 years. Beginning in the sixteenth century, English kings (especially Henry VIII, who found the inability to get rid of a wife extremely oppressive) and other monarchs in Europe began to wrest control from the church over marital regulations. Ever since, kings, presidents and rulers of all kinds have seen how important the control of marriage is to the regulation of social order. In this nation, the government has always been in charge of marriage.

16   That is why it was not a San Francisco mayor licensing same-sex couples that really threatened the President's religious understanding of marriage but rather the Supreme Judicial Court of Massachusetts; declaring marriage between

same-sex couples a constitutional right, that demanded a call for constitutional amendment. I didn't understand how important that was until I read an op-ed piece in the *Boston Globe* by Peter Gomes, professor of Christian morals and the minister of Memorial Church at Harvard University, that reminds us of a seminal piece of our history:

> The Dutch made civil marriage the law of the land in 1590, and the first marriage in New England, that of Edward Winslow to the widow Susannah White, was performed on May 12, 1621, in Plymouth by Governor William Bradford, in exercise of his office as magistrate.

There would be no clergyman in Plymouth until the arrival of the Rev. Ralph Smith in 1629, but even then marriage would continue to be a civil affair, as these first Puritans opposed the English custom of clerical marriage as unscriptural. Not until 1692, when Plymouth Colony was merged into that of Massachusetts Bay, were the Clergy authorized by the new province to solemnize marriages. To this day in the Commonwealth the clergy, including those of the archdiocese, solemnize marriage legally as agents of the Commonwealth and by its civil authority. Chapter 207 of the General Laws of Massachusetts tells us who may perform such ceremonies.

Now even though it is the civil authority of the state that defines the rights and responsibilities of marriage and therefore who can be married, the state is no more infallible than the church in its judgments. It wasn't until the mid-twentieth century that the Supreme Court declared anti-miscegenation laws unconstitutional. Even after that decision, many mainline churches, where I started my ministry, unofficially discouraged interracial marriages, and many of my colleagues were forbidden to perform such weddings.

The civil law view of marriage has as much historical diversity as the church's own experience because, in part, the church continued to influence the civil law. Although it was the Bible that made "the husband the head of his wife," it was common law that "turned the married pair legally into one person—the husband," as Nancy Cott documents in her book *Public Vows: A History of Marriage and the Nation* (an indispensable resource for anyone seeking to understand the changing nature of marriage in the nation's history). She suggests that "the legal doctrine of marital unity was called coverture . . . [which] meant that the wife could not use legal avenues such as suits or contracts, own assets, or execute legal documents without her husband's collaboration." This view of the wife would not hold water in any court in the land today.

20   As a matter of fact, even in the religious understanding of President Bush and his followers, allowing same-sex couples the right to marry seems a logical conclusion. If marriage is "the most fundamental institution of civilization" and a major contributor to the social order in our society, why would anyone want to shut out homosexuals from the "glorious attributes" of this "sacred institution"? Obviously, the only reason one can discern is that the opponents believe that gay and lesbian people are not worthy of the benefits and spiritual blessings of "marriage."

At the heart of the controversy raging over same-sex marriage is the religious and constitutional principle of the separation of church and state. All of us can probably agree that there was never a solid wall of separation, riddled as it is with breaches. The evidence of that is seen in the ambiguity of tax-free religious institutions, "in God we trust" printed on our money and "under God" in the Pledge of Allegiance to our country. All of us clergy, who are granted permission by the state to officiate at legal marriage ceremonies, have already compromised the "solid wall" by signing the license issued by the state. I would like to believe that my authority to perform religious ceremonies does not come from the state but derives from the vows of ordination and my commitment to God. I refuse to repeat the words, "by the authority invested in me by the State of New York, I pronounce you husband and wife," but by signing the license, I've become the state's "handmaiden."

It seems fitting therefore that we religious folk should now seek to sharpen the difference between ecclesiastical law and civil law as we beseech the state to clarify who can be married by civil law. Further evidence that the issue of church and state is part of the gay-marriage controversy is that two Unitarian ministers have been arrested for solemnizing unions between same-sex couples when no state licenses were involved. Ecclesiastical law may punish those clergy who disobey marital regulations, but the state has no right to invade church practices and criminalize clergy under civil law. There should have been a noisy outcry from all churches, synagogues and mosques at the government's outrageous contravention of the sacred principle of the "free exercise of religion."

I come from a long line of Protestants who believe in "a free church in a free state." In the issue before this nation, the civil law is the determinant of the regulation of marriage, regardless of our religious views, and the Supreme Court will finally decide what the principle of equality means in our Constitution in the third century of our life together as a people. It is likely that the Commonwealth of Massachusetts will probably lead the nation on this matter, as the State of New York led to the Supreme Court decision to allow women reproductive freedom.

24   So what is marriage? It depends on whom you ask, in what era, in what culture. Like all words or institutions, human definitions, whether religious or secular, change with time and history. When our beloved Constitution was written, blacks, Native Americans and, to some extent, women were quasi-human beings with no rights or privileges, but today they are recognized as persons with full citizenship rights. The definition of marriage has been changing over the centuries in this nation, and it will change yet again as homosexuals are seen as ordinary human beings.

In time, and I believe that time is now, we Americans will see that all the fears foisted on us by religious zealots were not real. Heterosexual marriage will still flourish with its statistical failures. The only difference will be that some homosexual couples will join them and probably account for about the same number of failed relationships. And we will discover that it did not matter whether the couples were joined in a religious ceremony or a secular and civil occasion for the statement of their intentions.

PERSONAL RESPONSE

Explain whether you believe that the issue of how marriage is defined by church and state is relevant to the issue of same-sex marriage.

QUESTIONS FOR CLASS OR SMALL-GROUP DISCUSSION

1. Locate Moody's central purpose and discuss whether you are persuaded that his position is valid.
2. What distinctions does Moody draw between the state's definition of marriage and that of the church?
3. To what extent are you convinced that "the state has no right to invade church practices and criminalize clergy under civil law" (paragraph 22)?
4. How would you answer the question, "So what is marriage?" (paragraph 24)?

PERSPECTIVES ON GENDER AND SEX ROLES
Suggested Writing Topics

1. Using Deborah Tannen's "Who Does the Talking Here?" as background information, conduct your own informal research on the conversational patterns of men and women. Do your observations concur or conflict with Tannen's?
2. Read any of the books or articles mentioned by writers in this chapter and write a critique of it.
3. Define "marriage," taking into account Howard Moody's article "Sacred Rite or Civil Right?"
4. Write an essay defining and distinguishing among the terms *sex, gender,* and *sexuality.*
5. Drawing on two or more of the essays in this chapter, write a reflective essay in which you explore your own concepts of masculinity and femininity (and perhaps androgyny) and the way in which that concept has shaped the way you are today. Did your parents or caregivers treat you differently on the basis of your sex? Were you assigned a "gender identity" that you were comfortable with?
6. Write a response to one of the articles in this chapter as if you were going to send it to the publication where the article was first published.
7. Christina Sommers in "Oh, Come On, Men Aren't Finished" writes: "If women do something better than men, that is evidence of their superiority. If men outperform women, that's proof of invidious discrimination against the fairer sex" (paragraph 9). Either support or refute what Sommers says in that passage. Use examples from your own experience or from what you have observed or read to support your position.

8. Examine media images for the ways in which gays and lesbians are portrayed. Focus on a particular medium, such as print advertisements, television situation comedies, or film.

9. Explore ways in which you would like to see definitions of masculinity and femininity changed. How do you think relationships between the sexes would be affected if those changes were made?

10. Write a personal narrative recounting an experience in which you felt you were being treated unfairly or differently from persons of the other sex. What was the situation, how did you feel, and what did you do about it?

11. Explain the degree to which you consider gender issues to be important. Do you think too much is made of gender? Does it matter whether definitions of masculinity and femininity are rigid?

12. Argue the case for or against same-sex marriage to an audience of judges sitting on a state's Supreme Court, trying to decide whether to legalize it.

13. Women have begun to achieve equality with men is such areas as sports and access to professional programs like medicine and the law. Interview at least two people who grew up in the 1950s or 1960s about the sports that girls were allowed to participate in or schools that they were denied access to. Do they have memories of girls and women who were not allowed to play when they wanted to or who were denied access to professional schools because of the quota system? If you have no one to interview, search the Internet or find articles on the subject.

Research Topics

1. Thomas Bartlett in "The Puzzle of Boys" refers to the "nature versus nurture debate" (paragraph 9). Research some aspect of this debate. As with any research topic, you will need to narrow your focus after doing some preliminary reading on the nature and scope of this issue.

2. Deborah Tannen in "Who Does the Talking Here?" refers to some seventy studies published in scientific journals on "gender differences in talkativeness" (paragraph 3). Research the subject by reading some of the studies done on it and arrive at your own conclusions. Include at least one work by Deborah Tannen.

3. Research the history of the contemporary women's movement, the men's movement, or the gay rights movement in America and report on its origins, goals, and influence. You will have to narrow your scope, depending on the time you have for the project and the nature of your purpose.

4. Research the subject of bisexuality, making sure to include differing viewpoints, and then explain your own viewpoint on the topic, supporting your position with relevant source materials.

5. Christina Sommers' "Oh, Come On, Men Aren't Finished" highlights one aspect of gender studies, what many see as the dichotomy between men and women in areas such as profession, characteristics, temperament, and

suitability for certain tasks. She writes: "The sexes are equal but exercise equality in different ways" (paragraph 4). Conduct an investigative analysis of any of the following for their depiction of female and male sex roles: fairy tales, children's stories, advertising images, music videos, television programs, or film. Do you find stereotyped assumptions about masculinity and femininity? In what ways do you think the subject of your analysis reinforces or shapes cultural definitions of masculinity and femininity? Support your findings with research by reading articles or books on the subject.

6. Christina Sommers' "Oh, Come On, Men Aren't Finished" mentions several books and articles that support the "male declinist" view or the "Women are Wonderful" phenomenon. Read some of the sources that she mentions or similar ones that you find in your research and either support or refute Sommers' position that "men aren't finished." You may prefer to take your own position on the subject and defend it with findings from your research.

7. Research the shifting views of both the church and the state on marriage. You may want to begin with Nancy Cott's *Public Vows: A History of Marriage and the Nation* that Howard Moody recommends in "Sacred Rite or Civil Right?"

8. Conduct research on the subject of sex-role stereotyping and its influence on boys and/or girls. You may want to focus just on girls or just on boys or do a comparative analysis. Consider beginning your research by looking at some of the books mentioned by Thomas Bartlett in "The Puzzle of Boys."

9. Research some aspect of women's sports before and after Title IX. Or, to track women's entrance into such professions as law or medicine before and after Title IX. Consider reading the experiences of women who were denied access to medical or law school before the female quota system was abandoned and compare those experiences with what is available to women today.

RESPONDING TO VISUALS

Department of Defense photo by PH2 J. Alan Elliott

A Marine steadies a child playing with the M60 Maremount machine gun mounted atop an M998 High-mobility Multipurpose Wheeled Vehicle (HMMWV). The vehicle is one of the displays on the pier outside the battleship USS IOWA (BB 61) during Navy Appreciation Week.

1. How do the various components of the photograph contribute to its overall impression? For instance, what is the effect of the position of the American flag?
2. What do the looks on the faces of the man and child contribute to the overall effect?
3. Is there any irony in the contrast between the child and the Marine?

RESPONDING TO VISUALS

Axel Lauerer/Getty Images

Woman on a high mountaintop.

1. What emotions do you imagine the woman in the photograph might be having?
2. How does the composition of the photograph convey what this climber has achieved?
3. In what ways might the image be symbolic of what women are capable of achieving? If the person in the photograph were a man, would your response to it change? Could it also be symbolic of what men are capable of achieving?

CHAPTER 15

Race and Ethnicity in America

Racial or ethnic heritage is as important to shaping identity as are sex and social class. One's race or ethnicity can also influence quality of life, educational opportunity, and advancement in employment. American society has a long history of struggling to confront and overcome racism and discrimination on the basis of ethnic heritage. Beginning well before the Civil War, American antislavery groups protested the enslavement of African Americans and worked to abolish slavery in all parts of the country. Other groups besides African Americans have experienced harsh treatment and discrimination solely because of their color or ethnic heritage.

These groups include Chinese men brought to America to help construct a cross-country railroad in the nineteenth century, European immigrants who came to America in large numbers near the end of the nineteenth century in search of better lives than they could expect in their homelands, Japanese men who came in the twentieth century to work at hard labor for money to send home, and Latinos/Latinas and Hispanics migrating north to America. As a result of the heightened awareness of the interplay of race, class, and gender, schools at all levels, from elementary through postgraduate, have incorporated course materials on or created whole courses devoted to those important components of individual identity and history. The readings in this chapter focus on immigrants and minority groups in a country that still struggles with racial inequities and discrimination.

This chapter begins with John J. Savant's "Imagining the Immigrant: Why Legality Must Give Way to Humanity," which addresses the issue of what to do about undocumented illegal immigrants in America. He argues that our common humanity is a prime reason for us to use our imagination, which "speaks to both heart and mind" and will "lead to right action." Consider as you read Savant's article whether you are convinced by his argument.

Next, Mark Krikorian in "The Perpetual Border Battle" examines the issue of illegal immigration from his perspective as executive director of the Center for Immigration Studies, a nonpartisan research organization in Washington, D.C. Establishing the context for his argument by referring to a commonly held belief that the immigration crisis in America has passed [in 2012], he asserts that the crisis is far from resolved. Using statistics from three separate sources, he first acknowledges that there is a lull in the state of illegal immigration and then examines three possible explanations for that lull. Next, having looked at those three, he considers possible future developments. Krikorian then addresses the subject of enforcement of current immigration policies and efforts to reduce the number of illegal immigrants and considers their effectiveness. He ends with his conclusion that the illegal immigration problem in America is far from over. As you read this piece, notice how well organized it is and how Krikorian uses statistics from credible sources to support his generalizations. More importantly, as you consider what he says about the state of illegal immigration in America, think about whether his argument reinforces or counters your own understanding of the immigration issue.

Then, Maryann Cusimano Love points out a number of social problems that indicate that America is far from solving its racial problem. Written when President Obama was still Senator Obama, "Race in America: 'We Would Like to Believe We Are over the Problem'" still makes some relevant observations about race relations in America. Love takes exception to a statement by a Virginia legislator who believes that " 'blacks need to get over' slavery." Think about how you would reply to the legislator and whether you agree with Love's response.

This chapter ends with a memoir by William Melvin Kelley, "Breeds of America: Coming of Age and Coming of Race." A distinguished writer and professor, Kelley recounts his childhood and young adult years growing up as an African-American in New York. The piece touches on racial awareness, racial discrimination, and racial identification that Kelley and his friends experienced during the 1940s and 1950s.

IMAGINING THE IMMIGRANT: WHY LEGALITY MUST GIVE WAY TO HUMANITY

JOHN J. SAVANT

John J. Savant, an emeritus professor of English at Dominican University of California, writes on the issues of philosophy, ethics, and morality. This essay was first published in the October 26, 2009, issue of America *magazine.*

Great detectives, we are told, are able to think like criminals. Similarly, effective therapists learn to enter into the fantasies of their patients. These behaviors are a function of that supreme and godlike faculty we call imagination. Unlike daydream or fancy—a centrifugal spinning away from reality, the mind on holiday— imagination is centripetal, a disciplined contemplation of reality that takes us beneath appearances and into the essence of what we contemplate. Imagination, therefore, can lead to moral clarification. In issues where law and morality seem to clash, as in the current debate over undocumented immigrants, imagination (which speaks to both heart and mind) can lead to right action.

Law and morality are not always commensurate; a law that is just in one context may be inappropriate in another, because laws function more often to allow a workable social order than to represent absolute moral imperatives. We hear it argued, for example, that granting amnesty and a path to citizenship for illegal aliens encourages disrespect for the law—a legitimate concern within the context of normal civic life. What this argument does not address, however, are the social and economic circumstances that significantly alter the normal civic context—for example, the abnormal circumstances that lie at the heart of major migration movements.

Even in very modest circumstances, people prefer their home turf and the comforts of custom to the trauma of dislocation and the uncertainty of the unfamiliar. There will always be adventurers who are at home anywhere in the world, but when populations begin to cross borders in significant numbers, it is almost always out of dire economic necessity or because of severe political persecution. In light of our common humanity—a familial bond with its own intuitions and responsibilities—we cannot make the moral urgings of this bond subservient to the civil proscriptions of law.

Legality versus Starvation

4   Against the compelling urgency of the plight of immigrants, therefore, the claims of legal compliance must give way to the more fundamental claims of our common humanity. If numerous immigrants are here because their families would otherwise live in abject poverty, the issue boils down to legal conformity versus possible starvation. Here is where abstractions must give way to concrete reality.

But as any poet or artist will tell you, the concrete is the realm of the imagination. In attempting to understand what is just, we have to imagine real persons and their concrete situations.

Let's imagine a man named Eusebio. If deported as an illegal alien and thus deprived of an income, he could likely witness the decline of a sickly daughter whose medicines he can no longer purchase, or he might have to face the possibility that her despondent older sister will opt for whatever income prostitution might provide. Ironically, a few miles across the border, some of his countrymen are earning more in a day than he does in a month. He sees his tired wife scrubbing one of her three dresses, his pretty daughter staring glumly at nothing and the streets outside bleak and empty of promise. He does not think, at this moment, of breaking laws. He thinks of his paternal duty and acts not out of greed but out of desperation.

Or imagine a woman named Marta, whose husband has been "disappeared" by a rival faction. Possessing only domestic skills, she tries to support her mother and children by selling gum and postcards to tourists. It is not enough. She leaves her two youngest children and her meager savings with her mother and makes the harrowing journey with her son across the Rio Grande, more desperate than hopeful, driven more by a primal affirmation of life and the panic of love than by any plan. In our concern for "respect for law," can we demote these and many similar tragedies to a category of lesser urgency, considering them the "collateral effects" of market forces?

A Nation of Imagination

America was at one time described as a "City upon a Hill," the "New Zion," a beacon to the world. Many in the mid-19th century would have agreed with the Unitarian minister William Ellery Channing, who proclaimed that our nation represented God's plan for humankind, its freedoms guaranteeing a nobler, more resilient and more just society. He said this, of course, not long before we engaged in one of history's bloodiest civil wars, a war that jarred our self-perception of national innocence and historical exception. Now, with the closing of the frontier and the unparalleled opportunities it made possible for the rugged individual, we have been snatched out of our timeless dream and back into history. The world now watches to see how well our behavior will match our lofty rhetoric.

8   What America has been is largely the product of a historical windfall—the confluence of revolutionary European theory, geographical separation from centers of control, the necessity of (and gradual education in) self-governance and an unimaginable expanse of continent in which to carry out our democratic experiment. What America can become will be the result of the new culture we form in the far more restricted (and realistic) circumstances of a closed frontier. Will we continue to manifest the daring, idealism, generosity and openness to the new and the difficult that marked our frontier forebears at their best? Or will we respond to challenges like the current influx of immigrants with a narrow sense of proprietorship and a very un-American fear of the unknown and the unfamiliar? If we reduce justice to legality and culture to security, we take the first steps toward a

state driven not by enthusiasm but by caution, not by daring but by fear. We will prove that our vaunted magnanimity has been not the natural and characteristic expression of a free and democratic people, but the specious (and transient) product of a magnificent frontier blessed with material plenty.

The American dream has run headlong into a historical crunch time. If we are not to betray the dream, we simply must imagine better. Just as we imagined our dogged pilgrim pioneers and our daring frontier ancestors in creating a heroic mythology and a resourceful and generous self-image, so too does the bond of our common humanity require that we imagine today the blood ties with our immigrant population that render their desperation our own. Historically, humankind finds this a supremely difficult challenge, for our loyalties to family, clan and nation are the schools of our first imaginings in culture, ritual and governance. We tend to resist other ways of living, other cultures, despite the fact that, as cultural historians will affirm, travel, trade and periodic immigrations have ever tended to enrich their host cultures. In the matter of our growing immigrant population, then, can we not imagine better than to build fences and expand border patrols?

The world is rapidly growing smaller, more intimate and more dangerous. Gerald Vann, O.P., in *The Heart of Man*, writes that in true love, "the lover becomes the beloved." Such becoming is truly an act of the imagination. Can we imagine the immigrant in our midst? Can we become the third world citizen whose longings, not unlike our own, still appear so remote? Such becoming can lead to a moral imagination that gives primacy to radical human need over legal compliance. The survival and growth of our own civilization may well depend upon our imagining better.

PERSONAL RESPONSE

Respond to this sentence: "In the matter of our growing immigrant population, then, can we not imagine better than to build fences and expand border patrols?" (paragraph 9).

QUESTIONS FOR CLASS OR SMALL-GROUP DISCUSSION

1. Analyze the structure of Savant's argument. What does he want his audience to do? Where does he acknowledge those opposed to his position and how does he counter them?

2. What appeals does Savant make? (Recall from Chapter 5 that common appeals are to logic, ethics, emotion, and/or shared values.) State specifically where those appeals are made. Do you find them effective?

3. What use does Savant make of the hypothetical examples of Eusebio and Marta? How effective do you find those examples? Do they convince you to agree with Savant?

4. Are you convinced that "legality must give way to humanity"? Why or why not?

THE PERPETUAL BORDER BATTLE

Mark Krikorian

Mark Krikorian has served as executive director of the Center for Immigration Studies (CIS) since 1995. His articles have appeared in numerous national magazines; he has been interviewed on 60 Minutes, Nightline, *and many other news programs; and he is a commentator for* National Review *online. This article appeared in the July–August 2012 issue of* The National Interest, *a publication of the CIS.*

A narrative is taking root among policy makers and opinion leaders that the illegal-immigration problem has been resolved and further concern over the issue is simply unnecessary. A *New York Times* op-ed by University of Southern California professor Dowell Myers exemplified this perspective when it began: "The immigration crisis that has roiled American politics for decades has faded into history."

This idea of complete resolution is highly dubious. There is no doubt that the number of people sneaking across the southern U.S. border has declined significantly, and the total illegal population has dropped somewhat from the record high of several years ago. But there is little reason to conclude this is a permanent development ushering in a new migration paradigm for the United States. More likely, it is merely a pause brought on by the U.S. economic slump and other factors on both sides of the border.

Indeed, it could be argued that the current lull in illegal immigration is just the end of the beginning. The United States has made progress toward the first goal of a sensible immigration policy—namely, developing the means to make an enforcement policy stick. But the country has barely begun the process of crafting a comprehensive immigration policy that has a chance of actually working—or even deciding what such a comprehensive policy should be. Thus, the *New York Times* op-ed had it wrong, and this issue is certain to roil American politics for decades to come.

4   Those on both sides of the issue have valid points in the ongoing debate, and, of course, they also have distinctive policy prescriptions that flow from their conclusions and outlooks. And while it may be too early to tell how long the current lull will last (assuming it hasn't already ended), assessing these policy prescriptions requires us to examine in some detail the state of illegal immigration, the reasons for the current situation and possible future developments.

There's broad agreement that the illegal-immigrant population peaked in 2007 and declined for the next two years. The three main sources of estimates—the Department of Homeland Security, the Pew Hispanic Center and the Center for Immigration Studies—all conclude that in 2007, the illegal population neared or exceeded twelve million (the estimates range from 11.8 to 12.5 million) and

Reprinted by permission from *The National Interest,* July-August 2012.

declined to roughly eleven million (between 10.8 and 11.1 million) by 2009. The decline stopped after 2009, so until new estimates or new facts are developed, it's safe to say that there are currently about eleven million unauthorized residents of the United States. Dramatically higher numbers sometimes bandied about by commentators and politicians—such as a 2005 estimate by Bear Stearns analysts that the illegal population could be as high as twenty million—are almost certainly incorrect. If the number were that high, it would be reflected in birth and death records, since in a modern society such as ours almost no one is born or dies without that fact being administratively recorded, and we have a pretty good idea of the fertility and mortality rates of the illegal population.

It seems clear that illegal crossings at the border, known formally as entries without inspection, are also down. Although illegal entry is not the only source of illegal immigrants—perhaps 40 percent of the illegal population entered legally on some kind of visa and then overstayed—it is the main source, and there's a lot less of it. The only administrative metric available for illegal crossings is the number of apprehensions made by the Border Patrol. This is an imperfect yardstick; a drop in apprehensions could mean there are fewer illegal immigrants available for agents to catch, or it could mean that the Border Patrol is becoming less efficient at finding them. Likewise, the total apprehensions number includes people who attempt to cross multiple times, though such recidivism appears to have declined slightly. It's possible, then, that a drop in apprehensions, coupled with a drop in recidivism, might not indicate a reduction in the actual number of individuals trying to sneak across the border.

But the decrease in the number of arrests at the border is sufficiently steep that the only plausible explanation is that attempted crossings have declined, and the experience of border residents confirms this. Arrests on the Mexican border exceeded one million almost every year since the early 1980s and totaled almost 1.2 million in 2005. In 2007, arrests were under nine hundred thousand. They dropped to a little over half a million in 2009 and 328,000 in 2011. That 2011 number is the lowest seen in the country since the early 1970s.

8   The Pew Hispanic Center has estimated that the total inflow of illegal immigrants, both border jumpers and visa overstayers, declined from 850,000 annually during 2000–2005 to just three hundred thousand annually during 2007–2009. The total number of illegal aliens declined despite a continued inflow of new illegal aliens because, over time, many people stop being illegal aliens. Some return home, some launder their status to become legal immigrants and a few die. Though researchers disagree, both statistical and anecdotal evidence suggests the number of illegal immigrants leaving the United States increased during the recession.

With regard to Mexico in particular, Pew has recently reported that net migration has dropped to zero. This includes all immigrants, both legal and illegal (51 percent of recent Mexican immigrants are illegal). Specifically, Pew compares the 2005–2010 period to 1995–2000 and finds that the number of Mexicans arriving in the United States fell by half and the number returning doubled. From 2005–2010, arrivals and departures were roughly equal, with each figure at about

1.4 million. The number of departures is fudged somewhat, since it includes three hundred thousand U.S.-born (and thus U.S. citizen) children of Mexican immigrants, so even Pew finds continued net Mexican immigration, but the increase in departures (most of them voluntary) and the drop in new arrivals is striking.

There is little doubt that the annual flow of illegal immigrants has slowed and the total illegal population has shrunk somewhat, although eleven million illegal immigrants is still a very large number. While interesting, this fact on its own doesn't tell us much that can be applied to policy. It's necessary to explore the reasons for the decline. Three explanations have been offered: first, the recession; second, increased enforcement; and third, changes in Mexico, the source of roughly 60 percent of the illegal population.

The economy requires the least explanation. Employment is the main magnet drawing illegal immigrants to the United States, so it makes sense that a tighter job market would lead more illegal immigrants to return home and dissuade some prospective illegal immigrants from embarking on the trek north. The recession officially began in December 2007, when the national unemployment rate was 5 percent. A year later, it was 7.3 percent. Another year after that, it reached 9.9 percent. The increase in the unemployment rate was even greater for illegal immigrants. Using young Hispanic immigrants with no more than a high-school education as a proxy for the illegal population (three-quarters of such people are illegal, and they make up two-thirds of the illegal population), we see that their unemployment rate shot up at the start of the recession from around 8 percent to about 15 percent, according to a Center for Immigration Studies analysis. This jump was especially quick and severe because the recession was kicked off by a housing bust, and illegal workers were disproportionately concentrated in construction and extraction jobs. Some 21 percent of these immigrants worked in such occupations, compared with just 5 percent of native-born American workers. This unemployment, combined with tougher times even for those still employed, led to a drop in remittances to Mexico by immigrants in general (both legal and illegal); the total value of remittances sent home dropped 3.6 percent in 2008 and a further 15.7 percent in 2009.

12   As bad as economic conditions were for illegal immigrants, the decline in their numbers began even before the start of the recession, so it seems likely that increased enforcement also has played a role. And that's no surprise, given the buildup in enforcement that has been under way since the Clinton administration. In 1995, there were about five thousand agents in the Border Patrol (most, but not all, working on the Mexican border). That number increased to ten thousand in 2002, hit fifteen thousand five years later and now exceeds twenty-one thousand.

Border fencing is also much more formidable, both in quality and quantity. While there is disagreement about the amount of fencing necessary on the border, there's no dispute that some fencing is essential, particularly in high-traffic areas, to slow and redirect potential illegal crossers.

The little fencing that used to exist consisted of welded-together, corrugated metal sheets acquired by the Border Patrol as army surplus. (They were used in Vietnam as portable landing mats for helicopters.) These were poorly maintained and, since they were solid, prevented agents from seeing what was happening on the other side. What's more, the corrugated ridges sometimes ran horizontally, which turned them into ladders for border jumpers.

Although some of this comically inadequate fencing is still in place, it has been replaced and augmented by modern barriers, first south of San Diego and then along much of the Arizona border and smaller sections in Texas. In compliance with the Secure Fence Act of 2006, there is close to seven hundred miles of fencing now along the two-thousand-mile border with Mexico, supported by technology such as ground sensors, pole-mounted remote cameras and even unmanned drones.

16   Combined with new tactics, the barrier in San Diego, consisting of two rows of fencing separated by a road for Border Patrol vehicles, had a dramatic impact on the flow. While San Diego accounted for more than 40 percent of all apprehensions in 1995, by 2011 it accounted for less than 13 percent of a much smaller total.

The Border Patrol's new tactics were actually pioneered in the mid-1990s in El Paso, the other main crossing point for illegal immigrants at the time, and the decline there has been even more dramatic. In 1993, El Paso accounted for nearly 25 percent of all Border Patrol arrests. By 2011, it accounted for only about 3 percent (again, of a much smaller overall number).

Much of the traffic that originally went through these two locations shifted to Arizona, and the Clinton and Bush administrations were unprepared—or unwilling—to do what was necessary to respond. During much of the first decade of the twenty-first century, Arizona accounted for half of all Border Patrol apprehensions, helping explain the intensity of voter concern over immigration. Most of the Arizona border now has some form of fencing.

There have been significant improvements in enforcement away from the border as well. One of the most important elements of the expansive 1996 immigration law was the 287(g) program, which established a formal mechanism for integrating selected state and local police into federal immigration enforcement. An even broader program known as Secure Communities is on track to connect all police and sheriff's departments in the nation to immigration databases so that every time a suspect is booked, his fingerprints will be checked against both the FBI's records and those of the Department of Homeland Security. The target date for full national coverage is the end of 2013, but two-thirds of the nation's local jurisdictions are already online, including all in the four border states and many others in the West, Midwest and South.

20   One result of these improvements has been an increase in the number of deportations—or "removals," as they are now labeled. (Removals are distinct from "returns," most of which involve Mexicans caught at the border and sent back across by the Border Patrol.) . . . In 1995, about fifty-one thousand people were deported (most of them illegal immigrants, but some legal immigrants who rendered themselves deportable by committing crimes). By 1998, the total had more than tripled to 175,000, and then it more than doubled again by 2008 to 360,000. It has remained close to four hundred thousand for the past several years.

Another vital area in which enforcement has improved is employment. Only in 1986 did it become unlawful for employers to hire illegal immigrants; before then, they were specifically exempted from the definition of "harboring" illegal immigrants by what came to be known as the Texas proviso. But even after 1986, the paper-based enforcement system was easily gamed and had little impact on illegal employment.

That began to change, very slowly, with the enactment of the 1996 law, which required the development of pilot programs to enable employers to electronically verify the information provided by new hires. The current iteration of these programs is called E-Verify, and employers use it to check the name, date of birth and Social Security number of new hires. While still voluntary, the system is having an increasingly large impact. More than three hundred thousand employers currently use it to screen new employees, and last year [2011] about a third of all hires nationwide were run through the system. Although the system is improving daily, it is still possible to fool it with a fully developed stolen identity. But most illegal immigrants don't have the resources for that, and employers in industries with lots of illegal workers are finding that when they inform prospective employees they use E-Verify, many simply leave and look elsewhere.

Other enforcement improvements also merit attention. State driver's license systems (including the nondriver identification cards issued by the state motor-vehicles agencies) are America's national ID system—a decentralized one, to be sure, but a national system nonetheless. The weaknesses of that system became apparent a decade ago when the 9/11 Commission revealed that the nineteen hijackers had between them thirty state-issued pieces of identification, which they used to smoothly navigate American society. The result was the REAL ID Act of 2005, which established minimum standards for state IDs to be accepted for federal purposes, such as boarding airplanes.

24   Although the bill's focus was preventing terrorist access to American society, any weakness can be exploited. Before 9/11, not even half the states checked a license applicant's legal status. Today, only New Mexico and Washington State still issue regular driver's licenses to illegal aliens, while Utah provides a special illegal-alien license. Although the REAL ID Act's deadlines have been repeatedly extended to accommodate state objections, the genuine improvements in identification (including other innovations such as digitized birth records) have made it harder for illegal immigrants to live undetected in the United States.

Finally, states have passed a variety of measures that have contributed to the decline in illegal immigration. These include requirements that landlords verify the legal status of those applying for a lease and making the presence of illegal aliens a state offense. Even where these measures have been held up by the courts, the hyperbolic coverage of them in Spanish-language media outlets effectively persuaded some illegal immigrants to leave and deterred some prospective entrants from making the trip.

One state measure that survived court challenge has been shown to have made a notable difference. In 2007, Arizona passed a law requiring employers in the state to use the federal E-Verify system for hiring as a condition of retaining a business license. It was challenged by the U.S. Chamber of Commerce and various liberal and civil-rights groups, but it was finally upheld by the Supreme Court last year [2011]. Research by the Public Policy Institute of California found that in its first two years, the new law reduced Arizona's illegal population by 17 percent—nearly one hundred thousand persons.

A weak U.S. economy and stronger enforcement are joined by a third possible reason for today's relative lull in illegal immigration: changes within Mexico itself. The key development is the trend toward smaller families, thus slowing population growth and easing pressures for emigration.

28   The UN reports that Mexico's total fertility rate (TFR), the number of children the average woman would have during her lifetime, was 6.7 in the early 1950s; in 1950, the population was about twenty-eight million. Over the next fifty years, that high fertility rate caused Mexico's population to nearly quadruple to one hundred million at the turn of the century and to about 114 million now.

But as Mexico's population exploded, the TFR began to decline. It is now estimated by the UN to be just over 2.2 (the CIA estimates 2.3). This is close to the U.S. rate of about 2.1, which is the "replacement rate" that a country needs for long-term population stability. What's more, the UN projects Mexico's fertility rate will fall to 1.7 by midcentury (about the current rate for Denmark and Finland), at which time Mexico's population is expected to start declining.

Of these three factors—the U.S. economy, an enhanced enforcement regime and Mexico's demographic shifts—the first is obviously the most changeable. The unemployment rate has already begun to decline, dropping from 9.1 percent in August 2011 to 8.2 percent in June of this year. GDP growth resumed in 2010 at an annual rate of 2.8 percent (though the 2011 rate was lower).

What's more, there's evidence that immigrants are capturing a disproportionate share of whatever new jobs are being created. A Center for Immigration Studies report looking specifically at Texas found that, from 2007 through the second quarter of 2011, 81 percent of job growth went to newly arrived immigrants, half of them illegal aliens.

32   The vicissitudes of the economy obviously can't be relied on to limit illegal immigration. So to the degree that the economy is the cause for the current lull, it would seem to be temporary. That raises a question: Even with the return of strong job growth, would the new enforcement measures continue to blunt renewed pressure for illegal immigration?

* * * * * * *

Much needs to be done before the United States has the enforcement arrangements necessary to permanently reduce illegal immigration to a nuisance rather than an ongoing crisis. Start at the border. The increases in the Border Patrol over the past fifteen years have been real, but even at a staff level of twenty-one thousand, the agency—responsible for more than 7,500 miles of our land frontiers—is smaller than the New York City Police Department, which has 34,500 uniformed officers. Furthermore, the improvements in fencing are often exaggerated. Of the nearly seven hundred miles of physical barriers along our southern border, a large portion are Normandy barriers, designed to stop vehicular incursions across the border but of no use in stopping people on foot. What's more, when Congress passed the Secure Fence Act, it imagined double fencing of the kind south of San Diego. In fact, only about 1 percent of the border has a double layer.

This is why the Government Accountability Office reported last year [2011] that only 44 percent of the border is under "operational control," with only 15 percent actually "controlled" (the tightest level of security). That 44 percent figure is triple what it was in 2005, but it's hard to say a task is complete when it's not even half done.

The high level of deportations is likewise deceptive. The administration likes to boast of "record" deportations, but the other half of the story is that the growth in deportations has stopped. The reason annual deportations have been just under four hundred thousand during this administration is that the White House refuses to ask Congress for the funds to increase it further. Like the child on trial for killing his parents who then pleads for mercy as an orphan, the administration has created the very resource constraints it points to as the reason for not increasing deportations further.

36   Beyond that, some key enforcement tools remain unused. The E-Verify system is working well, but its effectiveness is necessarily limited until it is required for all new hires. Regrettably, the president is holding that change hostage in exchange for amnesty for illegal immigrants. In other words, he (and many in both parties who share his perspective) will accept the tool needed to exclude illegal immigrants from the workforce only after amnesty has ensured there are no more illegal aliens left in the workforce.

Another potentially valuable tool that is still not fully functional is a system to track all entries and exits by foreign visitors. As noted above, a large share of the illegal population was admitted legally in some sort of temporary status and never left. But despite a congressional mandate passed in the 1996 immigration-reform bill and reiterated by the 9/11 Commission, we still have no fully functional exit-tracking program and no plans to build one. The lack of such an elementary capability makes a mockery of the claim that our immigration infrastructure is complete.

And then there's the problem of political will. Even the improvements we've put in place over the past fifteen years are of little benefit if they are not used properly. And the current administration has announced that, as a matter of policy, it will seek to arrest and deport only those illegal immigrants who have committed serious, non-immigration offenses. In a series of memos encouraging agents in the field to exercise their "prosecutorial discretion," the administration made clear that it views illegal presence in the United States (and all its ancillary crimes, such as document fraud and identity theft) as a secondary offense, like not buckling your seat belt while driving. In other words, they seek to pursue immigration offenses only in conjunction with other crimes. That means they will deport a rapist after he has completed his U.S. prison sentence, but they are uninterested in ordinary illegal aliens.

While prioritizing limited resources is part of any enforcement regime, this wholesale downgrade of an entire body of law is unprecedented. It's as though the Internal Revenue Service were to announce that ordinary citizens who are not terrorists or money launderers don't need to comply with the tax law because, as a matter of policy, no one would pursue them. The unprecedented and even lawless nature of the administration's approach is perhaps why so many immigration agents in the field have simply refused to obey what they see as an illegal order—one even their labor union said they should resist.

40   Do these things matter if the supply of illegal immigrants is drying up? Unfortunately, lack of sufficient enforcement remains a problem. Lower fertility and declining population are no guarantee that emigration from Mexico will come to an end. Emigration is not analogous to an overflowing cup that stops spilling liquid when the level falls. Migration is based on networks of family, clan and village that can continue to operate long after the conditions that may have sparked the original emigration have disappeared. For example, the states of western-central Mexico—far from the border—that sent farmworkers in the 1940s and 1950s through the so-called bracero program are still disproportionately important sending areas nearly a lifetime after the program began.

Looking at fertility rates in other countries confirms that low birthrates and low emigration are not necessarily connected. Mexico's current TFR is almost identical to that of other countries of emigration—Burma and Indonesia—but also the same as countries of immigration—Saudi Arabia and Argentina. Likewise, South Korea and Russia have some of the lowest TFRs in the world—1.23 and 1.42, respectively. In fact, Russia's population is already declining and is expected to fall about 11 percent by midcentury. And yet both South Korea and Russia are major source countries for immigration to the United States. Though correlation doesn't necessarily imply causation, in both cases the U.S. immigrant populations from those countries have risen just as fertility rates have fallen.

And there's always the rest of the world. Mexicans account for more than half of the current illegal population, but close to another 20 percent comes from Central America, which is even poorer and less developed. And TFRs are still very high in much of Africa and the Middle East. The importance of networks means we get little immigration from, say, Chad, but the U.S. legal-immigration system, especially refugee resettlement and the visa lottery, actually creates new networks for future illegal immigration.

As important as it is to have a functioning immigration-control program, legal immigration is ultimately more consequential. Of the forty million foreign-born people living in the United States, nearly three-quarters of them are legal. Even in 2008–2009, during the two years of the worst recession in living memory, 2.5 million people moved here from abroad, most of them legally. And the problems associated with illegal immigration—burdens on schools, pressure on public services, even wage suppression—have nothing to do with legal status and everything to do with numbers. For example, a fourth of all people in the United States living in poverty are immigrants (legal and illegal) and their young children. Immigrant families account for a third of the uninsured, while 36 percent of immigrant households use at least one federal welfare program.

44   Thus, there is no reason to conclude this big national crisis, or the intense political emotions it generates, will fade from the scene anytime soon. Those who think otherwise are engaging in wishful thinking, likely born of their own favorable view toward the immigration wave of recent decades. The problem is ongoing, as is the civic and political imperative that it be confronted.

PERSONAL RESPONSE

Write about whether Krikorian's argument reinforces or counters your own understanding of the immigration issue. Has your perspective on the issue changed or stayed the same?

QUESTIONS FOR CLASS OR SMALL-GROUP DISCUSSION

1. Krikorian begins with an explanation of why, when the article was written in 2012, there was a "lull in illegal immigration," giving three reasons to account for it. Identify each of those reasons and summarize what he says about them.
2. Having acknowledged the slowdown in the flow of illegal immigrants into the country, Krikorian then looks at reasons for the decline. He identifies three reasons. Locate each one and summarize in your own words what those reasons are.
3. Krikorian says that "much needs to be done before the United States has the enforcement arrangements necessary to permanently reduce illegal immigration to a nuisance rather than an ongoing crisis" (paragraph 33). State in your own words what he feels needs to be done.
4. Krikorian concludes with an explanation of why he thinks the illegal immigration issue is still a problem. What does he have to say on that point? To what extent are you convinced by Krikorian's argument?

RACE IN AMERICA: "WE WOULD LIKE TO BELIEVE WE ARE OVER THE PROBLEM"

Maryann Cusimano Love

Maryann Cusimano Love is an award-winning educator and a New York Times *best-selling author of children's books. An associate professor of international relations in the Politics Department at Catholic University, she has also taught courses in globalization, terrorism, and security at the Pentagon. As a member of the Council on Foreign*

In *America*, February 12, 2007. Copyright © 2007 by America Press, Inc.

Relations, Love has been advising Canadian, Caribbean, and U.S. government and private sector leaders on security issues since 1998. Her books include Beyond Sovereignty: Issues for a Global Agenda *(4th Edition, 2011) and,* Morality Matters: Ethics and the War on Terrorism *(2013). This essay appeared in the February 12, 2007, edition of the Catholic weekly* America.

As Senator Barack Obama explores a presidential bid, media headlines across the country ask, "Is America ready for an African-American president?" Between 50 percent and 62 percent of Americans polled answer yes, that race is no longer a barrier in the United States. But that this is considered a newsworthy headline by all the major media outlets and that around 40 percent of those polled answer no suggests otherwise.

A recent controversy in Virginia echoes the issue. A Virginia state legislator, Delegate Frank D. Hargrove Sr., a Republican from a suburb of Richmond, gave a newspaper interview on Martin Luther King Jr. Day in which he said that "blacks need to get over" slavery. He was stating his opposition to a resolution in the Virginia legislature to apologize for slavery and promote racial reconciliation as part of Virginia's activities marking the 400th anniversary of the English settlement at Jamestown in 1607. Officials tout Jamestown's founding as the birthplace of our nation (predating the pilgrims' landing in Plymouth Rock by 13 years), of representative government, of the rule of law and of American entrepreneurism. (Jamestown was settled by the Virginia Company of London in order to bring profits back to shareholders.) But Jamestown was also the birthplace of slavery in our country. Government time and tax money are being spent on the commemoration. One sponsor of the resolution, state Senator Henry Marsh, notes that while "the whole world's attention is on Virginia" because of the Jamestown anniversary, "Virginia can take a leadership role in promoting racial harmony." Delegate Hargrove disagrees. He argues it is "counterproductive to dwell on it," noting that "not a soul today had anything to do with slavery."

Some of Delegate Hargrove's argument is attractive. It lets us all off the hook for the inequities of the past. My Sicilian and Irish great-grandparents emigrated to the United States in the 1900's. By Hargrove's logic, my family is not responsible for slavery or its aftermath, because we were not here when it happened. On the other hand, my husband's family moved from Scotland and Ireland to the Chesapeake Bay region in the 1600's. We know little of the family history, but the name is common in these parts, on both black and white faces. I laugh in the grocery checkout lane with an African-American over our shared name, Love. Did someone in my family tree own someone in your family tree?

4   The flaw in Hargrove's argument is that the inequities of the past persist today. Noting achievements of African-Americans like Senator Obama, we would like to believe we "are over" the race problem. But the statistics paint a more sobering picture. Dr. David Satcher, the 16th surgeon general of the United States, notes that 85,000 African-Americans died in the year 2000 due to inequality in health care. The infant mortality rate of black babies is double the infant

mortality rate of white babies in the United States. African-Americans have lower life expectancies than white Americans by six or seven years. Twenty-five percent of black Americans live in poverty. One-third of African-American children live in poverty. Black poverty rates are triple those of whites. Tavis Smiley's book, *Covenant with Black America,* explores many other disturbing inequities that persist in the United States today in housing, education and the criminal justice system. The Hatewatch Web site lists cross burnings and activities of white supremacist groups today, and it is possible to track the hate groups currently active in each state. The Harvard online racial bias tests have shown that millions of Americans harbor racial preconceptions. And 16-year-old Kiri Davis repeated the "doll test" used in the 1954 Brown v. Board of Education case with the same infamous results: 4- and 5-year-old black children in Harlem overwhelmingly said that the black dolls were bad and the white dolls were good and pretty. As past inequities continue into the present, we have a moral responsibility to address them.

To "get over" racial problems in America today, we need to understand them and their roots. But we don't. A recent survey conducted by the University of Connecticut found that more than 19 percent of the 14,000 college students in 50 U.S. universities surveyed believed that Martin Luther King Jr.'s "I Have a Dream" speech was advocating the abolition of slavery. I teach a course at Catholic University on the civil rights movement. Our students, most of them graduates of Catholic elementary and high schools, know little of U.S. or Catholic racial history.

The United States is not alone. Such debates are hallmarks of peace-building efforts in post-conflict societies from South Africa to Colombia. We all face these choices, balancing apologies, reconciliation, redress for past wrongs, with attention to present and future problems.

Delegate Hargrove's suggestion that we "get over" the past by not bringing it up can be tempting because it is easy. Senator Obama's vision of a post-racial politics is inviting because it is hopeful. But we are not there yet, and the only way to get there is to work through the present-day ramifications of our persistent past, not only as individuals ("I don't condone racism") but as communities ("What are we doing to end unacceptable racial inequities?").

PERSONAL RESPONSE

What is your response to Delegate Hargrove's statement that " 'blacks need to get over slavery'"?

QUESTIONS FOR CLASS OR SMALL-GROUP DISCUSSION

1. State in your own words why Delegate Hargrove is opposed to a resolution in the Virginia legislature to apologize to blacks for slavery. To what extent do you agree that he has a valid point?
2. Summarize the concessions that Love makes to Hargrove's argument.

3. What does Love offer as proof to support her opposition to Hargrove? Do you find her argument valid?

4. What action does Love propose to help America " 'get over' racial problems" (paragraph 5)? Can you think of ways to "work through the present-day ramifications of [America's] persistent past" (paragraph 7)?

5. How does having elected an African-American president for two terms relate to the question of "getting over" America's racial problem?

BREEDS OF AMERICA: COMING OF AGE, COMING OF RACE

WILLIAM MELVIN KELLEY

William Melvin Kelley is the author of the novels A Different Drummer (1962), A Drop of Patience (1965), and Dem (1967), *among other books. Winner of many awards for his writing, his most recent was the Anisfield–Wolf Book Awards for lifetime achievement. Kelley teaches at Sarah Lawrence College. This memoir was first published in the August 2012 issue of* Harper's.

One day deep in summer in a time when automobiles went away and stayed all day my friends and I sat on the curb and compared skin color. Jackie, a rare kid of German ancestry on the block, had turned red. Guys whose parents came from the boot of Italy had turned tan. But Salvatore, a son of Sicilians, who grew up to become one of New York's Bravest, had turned, as Jackie put it, brown, like Billy. I still remember Sal's embarrassment. Under his brown skin, he blushed. This troubled me. Why should the comparison of his brown skin to my brown skin make him blush?

So did I first meet the concept of race. Before that day, I can't remember anything about it, though my eyes told me that people came in different shades.

I have had to rethink race since the arrival of my grandson, a half Albanian. According to the one-drop rule, his three-sixteenths African blood makes him 100 percent Negro; in today's parlance, a light-skinned black, an obvious absurdity.

4   So how should we list him in the Census? Who divided humanity this way? Nobody comes into the world knowing anything about race. We all have to learn about it. So I've begun to remember how I started becoming Negro.

Contrary to conventional misunderstanding, in my time growing up in New York, Negroes did not talk much about race. Striving Negroes wanted to transcend it. We did not tell our children they would not succeed because of their skin color. We waited until race clobbered hopes, then we'd try to explain the situation: Most Euros did not like us, so we had to overcome by working harder. We had to work twice as hard to get half as far. Accept that fact and don't complain. No one ever explained the economic system of slavery, though we knew about our slave ancestors.

Of course, we also had alternative views. In the 1910s and '20s Marcus Garvey had enlightened us to our position as oppressed people under a worldwide tyranny, and in the 1930s and '40s Elijah Muhammad had begun to see the world through militant Islamic eyes. These views skirted the subversive. My father kept his Garvey and J. A. Rogers high up in his bookcase with his Frank Harris, *My Life and Loves.* He made Dunbar, Hughes, McKay, and Cullen more accessible, on lower shelves.

I grew up in the Northeast Bronx with the children of Italian immigrants, who mostly embraced me. Several things aided me in my acceptance. My Roman Catholic Creole grandmother and mother attended the same churches as my neighbors, St. Mary's and Our Lady of Grace. Besides, I knew and could sing all of Frank Sinatra's songs in a clear boy-soprano voice. Summer evenings I held small groups of boys spellbound. *Put your dreams away for another day and I will take their place in your heart.*

8   My Italo friends much preferred me to most Irish kids. (At that time not everybody considered Italians to be whites.) One day one of a group of Irish kids passing through our block called me a nigger. My Creole mother had armed me against this, without going into it very deeply: anybody who called me a nigger had simultaneously demonstrated his ignorance and his inferiority. I should dismiss the comment as I would dismiss the utterance of a parrot.

So when the Irish kid called me a nigger, I assumed an attitude of superiority and condescension. This did not satisfy my Italo friends. The Irish kid, whom they'd caught while his companions ran away, had insulted me, and they would back me up while I gave the offender a beating. But I demurred, had already lost interest. Why strangle a parrot? But Bobby, Jimmy, Sal, Jerome, and Joey would not have it. They gave the kid a beating and ran him from the block.

I had encountered the word *nigger* before this incident, but coming out of the mouths of Africamericans (united, not hyphenated). One of my father's poker comrades, Mr. Timothy, used it all the time—this nigger this and that nigger that—and my mother and grandmother considered him coarse and rude. My father wanted to leave niggerdom behind in segregated Tennessee, and my gentle mother, who read *Vogue* and the *Ladies' Home Journal,* considered it a curse word. Nobody with any class or breeding would ever use it.

In 1944, I started attending Fieldston, a Euro and predominately Jewish progressive private school. Having repeated first grade, I was older and bigger than my twenty Euro classmates, and my boy-soprano voice made me a star. Over the next twelve years I went wherever my class went, to the Met and MoMA, to Carnegie Hall, to see Scribner make pulp paper for special editions, to the bar mitzvah of a classmate at Temple Emanu-El. I went through the front entrance when I went to visit my friends on Fifth or Park Avenues. Their parents had warned the Irish doormen not to turn me away.

12   At Fieldston Lower, much of the kitchen staff had brown skin. Lila and Bessie, both cooks, treated me especially well. We youngsters had to help with the serving, taking turns going into the kitchen to get a dish of peas or mashed potatoes for the table, where the teacher would spoon it out. Whenever my turn came,

Bessie and Lila made a fuss over me. "Here's our Billy." They gave me extra cake and cookies. Gently and joyfully they let me know that my attending Fieldston made them proud. I represented them.

My mother and my grandmother told me our family history from the unorthodox point of view of Creoles of color. *Creole* comes from the Spanish *criollo*, meaning a native of a country, and denoted persons born in the Americas as distinct from their ancestors in Africa or Europe, but later came also to mean persons of mixed blood, often those who were not visibly so. The African might lurk three or four generations back, forgettable behind Berlioz and good brandy.

According to my mother, Narcissa Agatha Garcia Kelley, and my grandmother Jessie Marin Garcia, before 1900, America acknowledged not three but four races. The word *race* comes to English from Medieval Italian *razzo*, meaning any given breed of horse. Dogs, cattle, and horses had different breeds, the first Portuguese slavers must have mused in 1444, so why should not humans, too, have a *raça*? One breed originated in Europe; another came from Africa; a third, the Indians, inhabited America; and the fourth breed, also from America, developed as a mixture of the first three.

In 1613 the Dutch left ashore on the island of Mannahatta a free man of color named Jan Rodrigues, who established trade with the Indians. A man alone, he pretty quickly got himself an Indian wife. Many others must have followed, because in 1638 the Dutch government outlawed sex with Indians.

16   A four-breed America made sense to my young eyes. (On the radio, the Lone Ranger would put on the berry stain to pass as a half-breed.) Still, I could already discern differences between the swarthy Sicilian Sal and the sunburned German Jackie. Within my own family, though we all answered to the designation Negro (except when we didn't), we came in different shades, ranging from Nana Jessie's white-chocolate color to milk-chocolate- colored me. And my father's friend, the foulmouthed Mr. Timothy, had that disease that made him look like a calico cat.

Yet the world outside our house, excluding American Indians and Asians (another breed), had clearly divided itself into colored and non-colored, to borrow from J. O. Killens. (We had not become black people yet, though some already liked Afro-American.) Any challenge to the two-breed equation met with incomprehension and disbelief. For instance, when Nana Jessie and I went out, people would sometimes come up to her and ask her in Italian or Spanish perché porque she had a piccolo pequeño nero negro ragazzo niño with her. Nana Jessie would answer that she spoke only English, though her dead husband had come from Ponce, Puerto Rico, and she would claim me as her grandson. The Puerto Rican kind of explained my brownness, and the interrogator would drift away.

Neither did my Italo friends accept that Nana Jessie's grandfather Col. F. S. Bartow of Savannah, Georgia, had fought and died for the Confederacy in the Civil War.

"Was he a Negro?"

"No, he was white."

"If he was white," they'd ask, "how could he be related to you?"

"He was white. And very brave. General Beauregard described him as gallant and impetuous."

Bartow died in July 1861 rallying his troops at Manassas, waving a banner, shot through the heart. The Confederates won the battle. So he became a martyr and a hero. Georgia named a county after him. Nana Jessie's mother Josephine (age thirteen) had heard him, her father, make a speech before going off to war, promising to il-lust-rate Georgia and keep the niggers down.

20   Such revelations usually had a chilling effect on pink folks, Italo or otherwise. It slowly dawned on me that people did not want to confront that all this sex, much of it forced, some of it not, had taken place. No wonder my father kept his J. A. Rogers—whose research had unearthed several American presidents with either African or Native blood, and lots of evidence showing how freely the breeds had mixed in America—up on the top shelf with Marcus Garvey and Frank Harris.

Or take Sally Hemings and the confused hypocrite Thomas Jefferson. Everybody makes a big deal out of her breed (Creole in the contemporary context) and her youth (about fourteen when they got started in Paris), but they ignore that mistress Sally and Jefferson's wife had the same father. Jefferson hooked up with his dead wife's half sister.

In sixth grade, in 1950, I started to feel special affection for a girl in my class I'll call Dolly-Jan Issanoff. She had a sweet personality and a shapely blossoming body. We would walk through the halls of school holding hands, until the principal issued an edict forbidding public displays of affection. At the time I did not take this edict personally, but in retrospect I see it as the first in a series of messages designed to enforce an important lesson of Negrohood: Don't mess with Miss Cholly.

Later that year I found myself uninvited from our grade's first couples party, an obvious snub. Everybody knew that Dolly-Jan and I were together. Once again came the lesson: Don't mess with Miss Cholly.

24   Through newspapers and dinner conversation I learned about segregation, that if you wore a brown skin you couldn't get served at certain places in New York. Josephine Baker was snubbed at the Stork Club. I wondered whether they had real storks there. And my parents couldn't tell me about Josephine Baker without telling me about her naughty naked banana dance.

Early on, blessed with an ear for the variations of spoken English, I realized that I lived in four linguistic worlds. In my house we spoke standard, grammatically correct American English, all our *be*'s and *have*'s in the right place. Outside my house on Carpenter Avenue in the Northeast Bronx, where I spent my time when I returned from Fieldston in the West Bronx, the guys spoke working-class New York English tinged with many Italianisms. Like they would say "close delight." At school we spoke standard American English with an emphasis on long French-rooted words and slight Yiddish intonations. On weekends when my father took me to Harlem I found a broad spectrum of speech generally tied to skin color, though dark-skinned men like Paul Robeson or Roland Hayes might speak in an international English, British consonants and American vowels. Ethel Waters rolled her *r*'s. My dentist, Dr. Bessie Delany, spoke Standard with a Southern accent. Sometimes poorly educated light-skinned folks would speak Africamerican vernacular (Ebonics) as well as did dark-brown people. I couldn't speak it then, but I loved listening to it and recognized its expressiveness.

The Negroes who spoke this Africamerican Creole seemed to catch hell. Nobody in my immediate family spoke it, so we didn't catch hell, we just had no money. Only my Aunt Iris, a native of British Guiana, didn't sound American. Nana Jessie and her sister, my great aunt Charlotte (who passed for Euro in her business life and some of her private life), both sounded like the elderly Savannah society women I heard one time on TV. My father had worked hard to eradicate all vestiges of Negroness from his voice. He sounded like a radio announcer and sometimes his brown skin would surprise people who had first encountered him on the phone.

In 1947 they let Jackie Robinson play in the Major League. I had never seen my father more excited about anything. That summer my father took me to Ebbets Field to see Robinson. Along with the many brown-skinned people in the stands, we cheered his every move. Just about every Negro in America became a Dodger fan. Still, having been raised in the Bronx, I remained a Yankee fan even when they met Brooklyn in the World Series.

28   Since I couldn't mess with Miss Cholly, I realized that if I wanted to date I would have to find some brown-skinned girls. My integration into the broader Africamerican society had begun. Southeast of where I lived in the Bronx with my Italo friends, a Negro neighborhood had developed. As a baby I had actually lived in this new 'hood before the end of the Depression drove my father, my mother, and me to Carpenter Avenue, where widowed Nana Jesse lived with her brother Joe, who would sneak off to New Jersey to spend time with his dead wife's Irish relatives.

Though my mother had baptized me Catholic, I decided to attend the Sunday school at St. Luke's Episcopal Church— for the girls. So for the first time in my life, except for trips to Harlem, I found myself surrounded by Negroes.

I did not assimilate into Negro society immediately, and in some ways, though I have lived exclusively with brown-skinned people since November 1968, I have never completely assimilated. The Standard American speech coming out of my brown face made my Africamerican contemporaries uneasy, though their parents liked the way I spoke. After a while I met other private-school Negritos who spoke Standard like me. Not quite the same: their accents sounded more middle-class and Southern than my own, which had a working-class Italo tinge, kind of like Frank Sinatra, whose singing and manner I continued to revere.

Further, I had never learned how to dance properly. At Fieldston I always danced better than my Euro classmates. In any group of Negroes, I danced like an animated man of tin, or like the esteemed President Obama. I confounded the one-drop rule. If one drop made me 100 percent Negro, then why hadn't my seven-sixteenths African blood taught me to dance? (Years later I learned that slave owners had used the one-drop rule to preclude their enslaved sons and daughters from claiming inheritance of property or land. Mr. Cholly gave us race to talk about so we wouldn't talk about the money.)

32   And another thing: I didn't know the music. I hadn't heard "Earth Angel," "One Mint Julep," or "In the Still of the Night." I knew Sinatra, Vic Damone, Frankie Laine, and Bing Crosby. I did know the Ink Spots and a little Armstrong (only as a singer) and some Nat King Cole (as singer and pianist), but no rhythm and blues, and no blues at all. The first time I heard Muddy Waters, his ferocity frightened me. Creoles traditionally did not relate to the blues.

Also, I didn't know the food. Fried chicken, collard greens, black-eyed peas, candied yams with marshmallows, and mulatto rice all seemed exotic to me. Nana Jessie had never learned to cook that well. She usually scorched the rice. Her mother had trained her as a seamstress. After her husband, Narciso Garcia, died, she worked in sweatshops and in freelance as the breadwinner and left the cooking to her mother, Josephine Bartow Marin, who had come north to help her. My mother had learned to cook at Evander Childs High School in a home-economics class, standard American stuff. My father cooked well, but only breakfast food and roasting. As a teenager he had worked on the railroad and greatly admired the Pullman cooks and porters for their cuisine and exquisite manners. He always made perfect pancakes, never scorched, one side just as golden as the other.

In the summer of 1952 my father took me to Tennessee to visit his birthplace and where he had grown up. He never said as much, but I think he wanted me to see the segregated South. However, in planning the trip he used a very informative guidebook produced by the National Urban League that told the brown-skinned traveler exactly where to stop and to stay and so avoid rejection and embarrassment. Thus I saw only the Africamerican South—sandwich shops and motels, colleges and universities, and the spacious houses of my uncles. I loved the South I saw. The brown-skinned girls had fabulous legs because they walked a lot. Their twangy voices made me swoon.

When I encountered my first colored water fountain, on Lookout Mountain, in Georgia, to my private-school mind it seemed absurd, two fountains to dispense the same water. What did Euros want to demonstrate? Did they fear they would contract Negroness? Yet, though nobody watched us, we did not drink from the whites only fountain. Only in southern Illinois did we meet segregation face to face, in the year Adlai Stevenson, governor of Illinois, ran for president. A woman barred us entry to a coffee shop. "I'm sorry, but we don't serve coloreds here." My father sputtered, angry but mostly bewildered. I wondered why she said "I'm sorry." Land of Lincoln.

36   Then in summer 1955 came the murder of Emmett Till. Damn.

His courageous mother made us look at his battered, bloated face. *See what you've done to my boy.* I saw myself in Emmett Till, an outgoing and adventurous fourteen-year-old from Chicago who considered racism and segregation a crazy joke, who was accustomed to talking boldly to anybody, even to some policemen, not realizing the colored and white signs really meant something, complimenting a pretty girl I did not know, like in Chicago and New York. *Hey baby,* Emmett Till said to Miss Carolyn. *Hey baby.*

The murder of light-skinned Emmett Till made me feel like a real Negro. Your skin shade, your manners, your voice didn't matter. Say the wrong thing to the wrong Euro and you'd end up brutalized, beaten, hanged, shot, drowned, killed, dead. Underneath it all, Euros hated us and thought nothing of killing us. I became aware of other indignities—somebody giving Dr. Ralph Bunche some grief, Miles Davis getting beat up by police for standing in front of his workplace, Birdland.

After Emmett Till, living the life of a Negro became a serious business. For the first time, I began to feel an emotion that had probably dogged my father and his father, born in bondage in 1858, the son of his owner, nineteen years old when the federal government betrayed the freedmen and we lost our American Dream of forty acres and a mule and a chance at true economic equality. Dread. Dread came into my life, and futility. *Don't matter what you do and don't matter what you say,/If Mr. Cholly feel he want it, he can take all your shit away.*

40   Dread and the unpredictability of violence. Euros could turn on you in an instant, even after years of kindness and affection. If your friends' parents didn't alert the doorman to your arrival you would have to go around to the service entrance. When it came time to dis-integrate you from the party, you didn't get an invitation and nobody objected. They all went. You stood outside looking in. When some Euro wanted to beat you or even kill you, nobody did anything to stop him. They might arrest somebody for it, but he would get off.

Euros lived in a democracy; Africamericans lived in a police state. But most Euros didn't see the contradiction. By then we had finally studied the Constitution and nobody seemed bothered by the way its high moral rhetoric contrasted with the loopholes some Founding Fathers had created to keep Africans in chains. Euros had accepted and justified slavery among the Greeks and Romans—something about the price of a Great Civilization. Suitably Jeffersonian.

In September 1956 I went away to Harvard, hoping that in the rarefied intellectual atmosphere of Cambridge, Massachusetts, race and racism would evaporate. For the first few months it seemed it had, though a teacher in whose class I did poorly seemed to resent me personally for squandering the great opportunity that the college had bestowed on me.

When it came time for the Harvard–Yale game I got into the spirit of the great event and invited my brown-skinned girlfriend up from New York. Sometime in October I phoned the big hotel up near Radcliffe and made her a reservation for the weekend. The man who took the reservation assured me that I had done all I needed to do to secure it; I didn't have to put down a deposit or anything. "Just show up on Friday night, sir, and you'll find the young lady's room ready for her."

44   My girlfriend came on the train and I went to Back Bay Station to meet her. We stopped in Harvard Yard, where all freshmen lived, and had a drink with my roommates. Around eight o'clock we walked up Mass Ave to the big hotel, finding the lobby jammed with arriving young ladies and their dates. We struggled through the crowd and reached the front desk, told the avuncular desk clerk that we had a reservation under the name of William Kelley for Avis Brown. He went

away for a minute, then returned and, in the politest way, apologized and told us that the hotel had misplaced our reservation and by now all the rooms were gone. Disappointed but accepting the clerk at his word, we left the big hotel. We returned to my room in Holworthy Hall and made phone calls and found my girlfriend a place to stay in a Boston suburb. Of course this disrupted our other plans—it took so long to get to Cambridge and back that we never got to see the Game.

I forgot the incident and for decades never questioned that a mix-up had occurred. Some twenty years later, after I'd made a daring escape to the island nation of Jamaica and lived for several years in a mostly brown-skinned country, I found myself sitting on our small verandah watching my two golden-brown daughters playing with nannybugs in the dirt. My thoughts drifted back to November 1956. The Harvard–Yale Game that I never got to see. Fog dissolving from my memory, I realized, and exclaimed aloud, "Holy spaghetti! On the phone they thought I was Frank Sinatra!"

PERSONAL RESPONSE

Did you learn anything new about race relations in America as you read this memoir? If not, what did the piece reinforce or illustrate that you already knew?

QUESTIONS FOR CLASS OR SMALL-GROUP DISCUSSION

1. Explain the title. What is the significance of "breeds of America"? When did Kelley come of age? What does he mean by "coming of race"?
2. Explain the difference between life inside his house and life outside. How does Kelley distinguish between the two?
3. Summarize the difficulties Kelley had to deal with in trying to "assimilate into Negro society"?
4. Locate passages or specific sentences in this memoir that you find particularly effective or in some way memorable and comment on why you think they are effective or memorable.
5. Kelley mentions a number of people whom you may or may not have heard of before but who inform and enrich his memoir. Identify as many of these references as you can: Marcus Garvey, Elijah Muhammad, J. A. Rogers, Dunbar, Hughes, McKay, and Cullen (paragraph 6); Jan Rodrigues (paragraph 15); J(ohn) O(liver) Killens (paragraph 17); Sally Hemings (paragraph 22); Josephine Baker (paragraph 25); Paul Robeson, Roland Hayes, and Ethel Waters (paragraph 26); Jackie Robinson (paragraph 28); Emmett Till (paragraph 37). There are more that you may want to look up, such as the singers mentioned in paragraph 33 and Ralph Bunche in paragraph 39.

PERSPECTIVES ON RACE AND ETHNICITY IN AMERICA
Suggested Writing Topics

1. Refer to the comments of at least two writers in this chapter in an essay on some aspect of the subject of stereotyping and prejudice. As you plan your essay, consider the following questions: Where do people get prejudices? What aspects of American culture reinforce and/or perpetuate stereotypes? How can you personally work against stereotyping and prejudice?

2. Explore your position on the issue of a "melting pot" (a society in which minorities are assimilated into the dominant culture) versus pluralism (a society in which ethnic and racial groups maintain separate identities, with no dominant culture). Take into consideration the views of two or more authors in this chapter.

3. Explore the subject of the role that labels play in one's identity, self-esteem, and/or self-concept.

4. Narrate a personal experience that changed your own views on the issue of racism.

5. Write a reflective essay on your own cultural heritage, explaining your family's background and how you feel about that heritage.

6. Explain the importance of race or ethnicity to your own self-identity. Is it as important as your sex, your job, your socioeconomic level, or your educational level?

7. Explain your own theory on the conditions that prevent blacks and whites in America from understanding one another's perspectives.

8. Write an essay explaining your viewpoint on illegal immigration, with John J. Savant's "Imagining the Immigrant: Why Legality Must Give Way to Humanity" and Mark Krikorian's "The Perpetual Border Battle" in mind. Explain how immigration is a social problem, what its complexities are, and why the problem is dire.

9. Explore the role of racial and ethnic diversity in your educational experiences in high school and college. Consider these questions: How diverse are the student populations of schools you have attended? How large a component did multiculturalism play in the curricula of courses you have taken? Have you been satisfied with that aspect of your education?

10. Narrate your first experience with prejudice, discrimination, or bigotry, as either a witness or a victim. Describe in detail the incident and how it made you feel.

11. Explain the effects of racial prejudice on a person or a group of people familiar to you.

12. If you are familiar with the difficulties a foreigner has had adjusting to life in your own country, tell about that person's experiences. Or, if you have personally experienced life as a foreigner in a country not your own, describe that experience.

Research Topics

1. Research the subject of a public policy like affirmative action, welfare, or bilingual public education as an effective (or ineffective) way to address racial or ethnic inequities in American society.

2. Research one aspect of the subject of illegal immigration mentioned by John J. Savant in "Imagining the Immigrant: Why Legality Must Give Way to Humanity" and/or Mark Krikorian's "The Perpetual Border Battle." Krikorian's essay mentions many issues that would make excellent topics for research. For instance, his piece was written in 2012. Research "the current state of illegal immigration, reasons for the current situation, and possible future developments" as he does. Consider what has changed since the article was written.

3. Research one of the following topics related to some of the essays in this chapter: Jim Crow; the influx of Chinese immigrants to America in the nineteenth century; the Chinese Exclusion Act of 1882 and its implications for Japanese immigrants; the Japanese religion Shinto; the internment of people of Japanese ancestry in America during World War II; or the economic, political, or historical relationship of the United States with Puerto Rico, Cuba, Central America, or Mexico.

4. Research the subject of multiculturalism in American education by reading differing opinions on the subject.

5. Research the subject of whether America is a classless society. Do certain factors such as culture, ethnicity, demographics, nativity, citizenship, mother tongue, religion, skin color, or race play a role in an individual's prospects for social mobility?

6. Select a topic from any of the suggested writing topics above and expand it to include library research, Internet research, and/or interviews.

7. Select one of the following groups to whom the U.S. federal government has made reparations and research reasons why those reparations were made: Japanese Americans interned in American prisons camp during World War II or the Sioux Indians whose lands were confiscated in 1877.

RESPONDING TO VISUALS

William B. Plowman/Getty Images

A friend comforts the Iraqi-born owner, right, of a restaurant burned by apparently racially motivated arson, Plymouth, Massachusetts, September 19, 2001.

1. What emotions does the photograph evoke in you?
2. The restaurant owner had received threatening telephone calls for days before the fire. How does that knowledge affect your understanding of this photograph?
3. Why did the photographer choose this particular moment to take his picture? What does it convey that a picture of the restaurant ruins alone would not?

RESPONDING TO VISUALS

ROBYN BECK/AFP/Getty Images

Immigrant rights activists march up Broadway in Los Angeles.

1. The full caption for this image is as follows:

   > Immigrant rights activists march up Broadway in the annual
   > May Day rally in downtown Los Angeles on May 1, 2010. An
   > unusually large turnout is expected because of the controversy
   > surrounding a new Arizona law that allows police to check
   > the legal status of people they suspect are illegal migrants.
   > Opponents of the new law contend that it effectively legalizes
   > racial profiling.

   How well does this image capture the essence of a rally? What
   details suggest the mood of the march?

2. According to the caption, the rally is organized by immigrant rights activists. What evidence of activism do you see in the picture?

3. What is your response to the large sign in the upper right-hand side of the
   picture that says, "Please let us be part of your dreams"?

CHAPTER 16

International Relations

In recent years, international relations have become an extremely important branch of political science, the study of politics, and the workings of the government. America's role as a superpower puts it in the position of being closely scrutinized by leaders, journalists, and ordinary citizens around the world. What America does politically is extremely important to other countries because America's actions are likely to affect them either directly or indirectly in many ways, especially economically and politically. The term *global village*, coined a few decades ago to describe the myriad links among the world's nations, is particularly apt when considering international relations and the perception that other countries have of America. Its political events are reported almost instantaneously around the globe by satellite, and magazines and newspapers also play crucial roles in conveying certain images of America and Americans to other nations.

How to deal with terrorism and prevent terrorist activities figures prominently in the making of American foreign policy. America is one of many nations that have experienced terrorism both abroad and at home. For instance, in 1979, militant students in Tehran stormed the U.S. Embassy there and held fifty-two hostages for

444 days. In 1983, a suicide-bomb attack destroyed the U.S. Embassy in Beirut, killing sixty-three. That same year, also in Beirut, Hezbollah suicide bombers claimed responsibility for blowing up U.S. and French military headquarters, killing 241 U.S. and 58 French servicemen. In 1988, Pan Am flight 103, on its way to the United States, exploded over Lockerbie, Scotland, killing 270 people. On American soil, in 1993 a bomb in the underground garage of the World Trade Center killed six and injured more than 1,000 people; in 1995, a truck bomb destroyed a federal building in Oklahoma City, killing 168 and injuring more than 600.

By far the largest acts of terrorism, in terms of lives lost and effects on the economy, the way people live, and American society in countless ways, have been the September 11, 2001, attacks on the World Trade Center in New York City and the Pentagon in Washington, D.C. Those attacks have had profound effects on America and both its allies and foes. Many countries around the world expressed not only their shock and outrage at the terrorism on American soil but also their deep sympathy for the families, friends, and loved ones of those who lost their lives or were injured in the attacks.

The essays in this chapter address some of the issues involved in America's international relations, its foreign policy, and its war on terrorism. First, Paul Johnson in "American Idealism and Realpolitik" comments on America's role as "the reluctant sheriff of a wild world" and the dilemma it finds itself in as it plays that role. As a nation founded on idealism, America is frequently faced with being both a benign champion of weak and oppressed countries while at the same time having to make practical and sometimes Machiavellian decisions about how to deal with the aggressors against the countries it defends. (Note that "realpolitik" refers to politics or diplomacy based primarily on practical considerations, rather than ideological notions.) Johnson raises some intriguing points about this moral dilemma.

Next, Thomas Friedman urges Americans not to let down their guard against terrorists in his essay "Still Not Tired." Citing examples of individual terrorist acts to remind us that the enemy is still active, he calls for vigilance against such acts. Beyond the immediate, though, Friedman believes we must make a long-term commitment to the war on terrorism. Following Friedman's piece, Cathy Young explains in "Lessons from World War II" what we can learn from that war, which she says continues to be a living past with important implications for us today. The war, she contends, reminds us "of the limits of idealism," among other things, and raises the question of how far a nation can allow itself to go in the cause of liberty. Both Friedman and Young make thoughtful observations on the difficult subjects of how we approach the war on terrorism and what we can learn from a devastating world war that occurred more than seventy years ago.

The chapter ends with an optimistic piece by Joseph Nye, Jr., who responds to an article by another respected analyst of America's role in the world, Fareed Zakaria. In "Zakaria's World," Nye counters arguments made in Zakaria's "Are America's Best Days Behind Us?" which appeared in *Time* magazine. As a former dean of Harvard University's Kennedy School of Government and a highly experienced observer of and participant in America's international relations, Nye writes from a position of authority on why Zakaria's outlook on America's future is too pessimistic. As you read his article, think about your own view of America and your feelings about its current strengths and weaknesses as well as its potential for the future.

AMERICAN IDEALISM AND REALPOLITIK

PAUL JOHNSON

> *Paul Johnson, eminent British historian and author, has written col-*
> *umns for decades for such British publications as the* Spectator, *the*
> Daily Mail, *and the* Daily Telegraph. *He also contributes to such*
> *American publications as* National: The Founding Father Review,
> *the* Wall Street Journal, *and the* New York Times. *He has written*
> *over forty books, primarily on history but also on religion and travel.*
> *His most recent are* Napoleon *(2002);* George Washington *(2005);*
> Creators *(2006);* Heroes *(2007); and* Churchill *(2009). In 2006,*
> *Johnson was awarded the Presidential Medal of Freedom. This article*
> *was published in the March 12, 2007, issue of the* Forbes.

America is the reluctant sheriff of a wild world that sometimes seems mired in wrongdoing. The UN has nothing to offer in the way of enforcing laws and dispensing justice, other than spouting pious oratory and initiating feeble missions that usually do more harm than good. NATO plays a limited role, as in Afghanistan, but tends to reflect the timidity (and cowardice) of Continental Europe. Britain and a few other nations such as Australia are willing to follow America's lead but are too weak to act on their own.

That leaves the U.S. to shoulder the responsibility. Otherwise—what? Is brute force to replace the rule of law in the world because there's no one to enforce it? I wish some of those who constantly criticize America's efforts and the judgment of President Bush would ask themselves this simple question: Would you really like to live in a world where the U.S. sits idly by and lets things happen?

Life in such a world would be like the bestial existence described in Thomas Hobbes' great work, *Leviathan.* If people "live without a common power to keep them all in awe, they are in that condition which is called war, and such a war as is of every man against every man." In that lawless state there will be "continual fear and danger of violent death, and the life of man solitary, poor, nasty, brutish and short."

4   In the 350 years since Hobbes wrote his book nothing essential has changed. For proof, look at the poor people of Sudan, in whose struggle the U.S. has not been willing to intervene and whose lives are exactly as Hobbes described. The same is true in Somalia, where the U.S. has been indecisive and vacillating. And this was the case in the former Yugoslavia until the U.S., with great misgiving, finally responded to pressure and sent in its forces.

It's fortunate for the world that in areas in which international law doesn't operate and rogue states do as they please, America will sometimes agree to play Leviathan in order to establish law, at the risk of huge financial expense and its soldiers' lives. It does so because it is a country founded on idealism. A majority of Americans have always believed that a society, under God, must come to the rescue of the poor, weak and oppressed if it has the means to do so. The U.S. has applied this idealism systematically to the world as a whole and in many different ways, from the Marshall Plan, which helped raise Europe from ruin in 1948, to declaring war on international terrorism five years ago.

On the Horns of a Dilemma

America is fundamentally and instinctively idealistic. But following these ideals and acting as the world's policeman raises moral issues. We all agree that the sheriff must be righteous, brave and resolute. But should he also, if the situation demands, be cunning, devious and Machiavellian? In short, should America, along with its idealism, also practice realpolitik? And won't these two forces be in constant practical and moral conflict?

It's difficult to exercise authority in large parts of the world and, to use Hobbes' phrase, "keep them all in awe," without a touch of realpolitik. Britain discovered this in the 19th century, just as the Romans had two millennia before. Moreover, as British statesmen such as Benjamin Disraeli and Robert Cecil, Lord Salisbury, found, imperial realpolitik expressed itself principally in two cynical maxims: "Divide and rule" and "My enemy's enemy is my friend." These two maxims are rearing their heads again in the Middle East, and almost unwittingly—and certainly not from any set purpose—the U.S. finds itself following them.

8   U.S. intervention in Iraq has had the inevitable consequence of fueling the Sunni-Shia feud, which has raged in Islam for 1,000 years at varying degrees of intensity. It's now running hotter than ever, and likely to get worse, as more and more of the Middle East is drawn into it. Of course, with the Sunnis fighting the Shia, they have less time and energy to fight the West, and America finds it easier to rule. But this raises moral dilemmas that the U.S. has so far failed to resolve or publicly recognize.

Another situation where realpolitik could come into play is Iran's nuclear power quest. The moment Iran possesses and can deliver nuclear bombs it will use them against Israel, destroying the entire country and its inhabitants. If this danger becomes imminent, Israel has the means—if suitably assisted—to launch a preemptive strike. Should the U.S. provide such assistance and moral encouragement?

China's progress in advanced military technology, especially Star Wars–like rocket defenses, is also giving American strategists problems: How should the U.S. react? The realpolitik answer would be to assist India, China's natural rival and potential antagonist in east and central Asia, to achieve technological parity. But would it be right to do so?

These kinds of questions can arise almost anywhere but do so especially around ruthless totalitarian regimes that are attempting to acquire more military power than is safe to allow them. North Korea is a case in point. It's one thing for the U.S. to make clear that it will defend its allies, such as South Korea and Japan, from nuclear threats. That is straightforward and honorable. But the realpolitik solution would be to assist and encourage China to deal with the problem of a nuclear-armed and aggressive North Korea, the strategy being based on another old maxim: "Set a thief to catch a thief."

12   I don't envy those in Washington whose duty it is to resolve the dilemma between idealism and realpolitik. But they will not go far wrong if they respect the great tripod on which all geopolitical wisdom rests: the rule of law, the consultation of the people and the certitude that, however strong we may be, we are answerable to a higher power.

PERSONAL RESPONSE

How do you answer Johnson's question in paragraph 2: "Would you really like to live in a world where the United States sits idly by and lets things happen?"

QUESTIONS FOR CLASS OR SMALL-GROUP DISCUSSION

1. Explain the title. In what ways is America idealistic? In what ways must it practice realpolitik, according to Johnson? Do you agree with Johnson on these points?

2. Johnson writes that America's idealism conflicts with its role as "the world's policeman," which "raises moral issues" (paragraph 6)? What do you understand him to mean by that?

3. Johnson mentions several examples of the U.S.'s efforts to help other countries and the "practical and moral conflict" that results. Can you provide other, similar examples to illustrate that point?

4. Comment on the effectiveness of Johnson's conclusion.

STILL NOT TIRED

THOMAS L. FRIEDMAN

Thomas L. Friedman has written for the New York Times *since 1981. In 1995, he became the paper's foreign affairs columnist. Friedman was awarded the 1983 Pulitzer Prize for international reporting (from Lebanon) and the 1988 Pulitzer Prize for international reporting (from Israel). In 2002, he won the Pulitzer Prize for commentary. His book* From Beirut to Jerusalem *(1989) won the National Book Award for nonfiction in 1989. The* Lexus and the

Olive Tree: Understanding Globalization *won the 2000 Overseas Press Club award for best nonfiction book on foreign policy and has been published in twenty languages. He is also author of* Longitudes and Attitudes: Exploring the World after September 11 *(2002);* The World Is Flat: A Brief History of the Twenty-First Century *(2005);* Hot, Flat, and Crowded: Why We Need a Green Revolution—and How It Can Renew America *(2008); and* That Used To Be Us: How America Fell Behind in the World It Invented and How We Can Come Back *(co-written with Michael Mandelbaum 2011). This op-ed column was published in the October 4, 2009, issue of the* New York Times.

He didn't want to wear earplugs. Apparently, he wanted to enjoy the blast.

That is what *The Dallas Morning News* reported about Hosam Maher Husein Smadi, the 19-year-old Jordanian accused of trying to blow up a downtown Dallas skyscraper. He was caught by an F.B.I. sting operation that culminated in his arrest nearly two weeks ago—after Smadi parked a 2001 Ford Explorer Sport Trac, supplied by the F.B.I., in the garage of a Dallas office tower.

"Inside the S.U.V. was a fake bomb, designed to appear similar to one used by Timothy McVeigh in the 1995 Oklahoma City bombing," *The News* wrote. "Authorities say Smadi thought he could detonate it with a cellphone. After parking the vehicle, he got into another vehicle with one of the agents, and they drove several blocks away. An agent offered Smadi earplugs, but he declined, 'indicating that he wanted to hear the blast,' authorities said. He then dialed the phone, thinking it would trigger the bomb. . . . Instead, the agents took him into custody."

4   If that doesn't send a little shiver down your spine, how about this one? BBC.com reported that "it has emerged that an Al Qaeda bomber who died last month while trying to blow up a Saudi prince in Jeddah had hidden the explosives inside his body." He reportedly inserted the bomb and detonator in his rectum to elude metal detectors. My God.

Or how about this? Two weeks ago in Denver, the F.B.I. arrested Najibullah Zazi, a 24-year-old Afghan immigrant, and indicted him on charges of planning to set off a bomb made of the same home-brewed explosives used in the 2005 London transit bombings. He allegedly learned how to do so on a training visit to Pakistan. The *Times* reported that Zazi "had bought some bomb ingredients in beauty supply stores, the authorities said, after viewing instructions on his laptop on how to build such a bomb. When an employee of the Beauty Supply Warehouse asked about the volume of materials he was buying, he remembered Mr. Zazi answering, 'I have a lot of girlfriends.'"

These incidents are worth reflecting on. They tell us some important things. First, we may be tired of this "war on terrorism," but the bad guys are not. They are getting even more "creative."

Second, in this war on terrorism, there is no "good war" or "bad war." There is one war with many fronts, including Europe and our own backyard, requiring many different tactics. It is a war within Islam, between an often too-silent

Muslim mainstream and a violent, motivated, often nihilistic jihadist minority. Theirs is a war over how and whether Islam should embrace modernity. It is a war fueled by humiliation—humiliation particularly among young Muslim males who sense that their faith community has fallen behind others, in terms of both economic opportunity and military clout. This humiliation has spawned various jihadist cults, including Al Qaeda, which believe they have the God-given right to kill infidels, their own secular leaders and less pious Muslims to purify Islam and Islamic lands and thereby restore Muslim grandeur.

8   Third, the newest and maybe most active front in this war is not Afghanistan, but the "virtual Afghanistan"—the loose network of thousands of jihadist Web sites, mosques and prayer groups that recruit, inspire and train young Muslims to kill without any formal orders from Al Qaeda. The young man in Dallas came to F.B.I. attention after espousing war on the U.S. on jihadist Web sites.

Fourth, in the short run, winning this war requires effective police/intelligence action, to kill or capture the jihadists. I call that "the war on terrorists." In the long run, though, winning requires partnering with Arab and Muslim societies to help them build thriving countries, integrated with the world economy, where young people don't grow up in a soil poisoned by religious extremists and choked by petro-dictators so they can never realize their aspirations. I call this "the war on terrorism." It takes a long time.

Our operation in Afghanistan after 9/11 was, for me, only about "the war on terrorists." It was about getting bin Laden. Iraq was "the war on terrorism"—trying to build a decent, pluralistic, consensual government in the heart of the Arab-Muslim world. Despite all we've paid, the outcome in Iraq remains uncertain. But it was at least encouraging to see last week's decision by Prime Minister Nuri Kamal al-Maliki to run in the next election with a nonsectarian, multireligious coalition—a rare thing in the Arab world.

So, what President Obama is actually considering in Afghanistan is shifting from a "war on terrorists" there to a "war on terrorism," including nation-building. I still have serious doubts that we have a real Afghan government partner for that. But if Mr. Obama decides to send more troops, the most important thing is not the number. It is his commitment to see it through. If he seems ambivalent, no one there will stand with us and we'll have no chance. If he seems committed, maybe—maybe—we'll find enough allies. Remember, the bad guys are totally committed—and they are not tired.

PERSONAL RESPONSE

Write about your emotional responses to the news of terrorist attacks. Do you have a vivid memory of the events of September 11, 2001, or of more recent terrorist activities?

QUESTIONS FOR CLASS OR SMALL-GROUP DISCUSSION

1. Explain the title. Who is "still not tired"?
2. Comment on the effectiveness of Friedman's opening paragraph. Why do you think he used those two sentences rather than other details he might have chosen? How does his opening relate to his central point?
3. Discuss the organization of this essay. Why do you think Friedman begins with a series of brief sketches or examples? How do they lead to his central purpose? What is gained or lost by not beginning with his thesis or central point?
4. State in your own words the distinction that Friedman makes between "the war on terrorists" and "the war on terrorism." Do you agree with him that there is a difference? Do you view the two types of war as he does, or do you view them differently?

LESSONS FROM WORLD WAR II

CATHY YOUNG

Cathy Young (Ekaterina Jung) is a journalist and writer. Born in Russia, she immigrated to the United States with her family in 1980 at the age of seventeen and is a graduate of Rutgers University. She writes a monthly column for Reason *magazine and a weekly one for both the* Boston Globe *and* RealClearPolitics.com. *Young is the author of* Growing Up in Moscow: Memories of a Soviet Girlhood *(1989) and* Cease Fire: Why Women and Men Must Join Forces to Achieve True Equality *(1999). This article was published on May 14, 2009, at RealClearPolitics.com.*

This past weekend marked 64 years since the surrender of Nazi Germany and the Allied victory in Europe in World War II (May 8, except in Russia and a few other former Soviet republics where it is commemorated on May 9). In the United States, this date generally receives little notice except on the major anniversaries; in Russia, Victory Day is the most important public holiday, celebrated with much pomp and circumstance. Yet in any country directly affected by World War II, that war holds a unique place in our collective cultural and historical consciousness—a living past that continues to influence the way we see the present.

In modern-day Russia, victory in "the Great Patriotic War" is probably the only major event of the last hundred years that everyone can celebrate, regardless of political beliefs. The war, which took up to 14 million lives in Russia (and as many as 27 million in the entire Soviet Union), and caused untold hardship and suffering to most survivors, is a sacred memory, a source of both grief and rightful pride. For people who saw the collapse of Communism and were suddenly told that the Soviet experiment had not been a glorious struggle for a better future but a 70-year road to nowhere, it means a great deal to know that their country's role in the defeat of Nazism is still a victory they can believe in.

There is, however, a darker side to this legacy. Russian apologists for Communism use the victory in World War II as a validation of the Soviet regime—and sometimes as an excuse for the odious rule of Joseph Stalin, Hitler's rival in butchery. In recent years, the Russian government has exploited the war to promote the image of Russia as a benign power and denigrate the claims of Eastern European countries and former Soviet republics which see themselves as victims not only of Nazi Germany but of Soviet Communism as well.

4   The glorified official Russian view of the war also ignores the extent to which the wartime suffering of the Russian people was inflicted by their own leadership. There is little mention of the fact that untrained, ill-equipped draftees were used as cannon fodder, that regular troops were routinely followed by special units which shot at soldiers who tried to retreat, or Soviet soldiers taken prisoner by the Germans were branded traitors for surrendering and often sent to the gulag prison camps for their homecoming.

But we too have our World War II blind spots—sometimes, ironic mirror images of the Russian ones. Russians commonly downplay the role of American and British allies in defeating the German war machine; Americans, much to the annoyance of Russians, often talk as if we almost single-handedly liberated Europe from Nazism. We, too, remain in thrall to the myth of "The Good War" that often glosses over some of the less noble actions taken on our own side. Even those on the left who denounce the bombing of Hiroshima and the internment of Japanese-Americans rarely mention the firebombing of German cities or the well-documented mistreatment of German civilians and POWs. Little is said about the morality of handing over Eastern Europe to Stalin, or of forcibly repatriating to the USSR Soviet POWs and other Soviet nationals who faced harsh punitive measures and sometimes execution without trial.

The "Good War," like the Good Book, can be put in the service of any agenda. Conservatives invoke it to justify military action: "What about Hitler?" is a devastating, if cliché, rebuttal to the pacifist insistence that there is never a good reason to start a war. It is, to some extent, an unfair argument that much too easily confers the status of Hitler on our enemy of the day. But it also makes a valid and important point: evil does exist (if usually on a smaller scale than Nazism), and to refuse to fight it is to ensure its triumph.

For liberals, particularly in response to the War on Terror and its excesses, World War II is the foremost example of how we were able to defeat a formidable enemy without abandoning our core principles, such as humane treatment of prisoners. But that is not so simple, either. After President Obama's statement attributing the line, "We do not torture," to Sir Winston Churchill, there were revelations that at least one British facility for captive Germans did, in fact, use brutal methods that qualify as torture—though probably without Churchill's knowledge. Besides, are brutal interrogation methods a worse departure from our moral principles than killing civilians in indiscriminate air raids?

8   Despite its darkest moments, World War II remains "the Good War"—not because we were impeccably good, but because we fought an enemy that was as close as one can be to pure evil. It also belies the popular notion that if we cross certain moral lines to achieve our war aims, we will become just as bad as the enemy: the staggering casualties in the firebombing of Dresden notwithstanding, Churchill did not "sink to the level" of the leaders of the Third Reich.

World War II reminds us about the limits of idealism. Looking back, many people wonder if we would have won the war with the level of media openness and respect for human rights that we have today. That's a legitimate question— but its seamy side is a dangerous nostalgia for a "simpler" time when soldiers could do their job without having to think of sissy stuff like rights and legalities.

Perhaps the real lesson of World War II is that a free, civilized society at war will always seek to strike some balance between self-defense and principle. Sometimes, it will err badly. To defend these errors as fully justified is to betray our own values and start on a road that leads to the kind of authoritarian mindset so rampant in Putin's Russia. To condemn them with no understanding of their context is a self-righteous utopian posture that, in the end, does liberal values a disservice.

PERSONAL RESPONSE

Thinking about what you have studied in school or been told about it, write on what World War II means to you.

QUESTIONS FOR CLASS OR SMALL-GROUP DISCUSSION

1. According to Young, how do Russia and the United States differ in the way they commemorate the Allied victory in Europe in World War II? How does that contrast relate to her thesis?
2. What do you understand the phrase "The Good War" to mean? Why does Young call it a "myth" (paragraph 5)?
3. In what ways, according to Young, does World War II remind us of "the limits of idealism" (paragraph 9)? Do you agree with her?
4. What are the "lessons from World War II" (title)?

ZAKARIA'S WORLD

Joseph Nye, Jr.

Joseph Nye, Jr., former dean of the Kennedy School of Government at Harvard University, currently holds the position of Distinguished Service Professor at Harvard. He has worked in three government

Reprinted by permission from Foreign Policy, March 8, 2011.

agencies, received awards for his distinguished service to the government, and appeared on many television news programs. He is a member of the editorial boards of Foreign Policy *and* International Security *magazines, and the author of numerous books and more than a hundred and fifty articles in professional journals. His most recent books are* For the People: Can We Fix Public Service? *(2003);* Soft Power: The Means to Success in World Politics *(2004);* The Powers to Lead *(2008);* The Future of Power *(2011); and* Presidential Leadership and the Creation of the American Era *(2013). This article first appeared in the March 8, 2011, issue of* Foreign Policy.

Fareed Zakaria is one of our most perceptive analysts of America's role in the world, and I generally agree with him. But in the case of his new special essay for *Time*, "Are America's Best Days Behind Us?" I think he paints too gloomy a picture of American decline.

Americans are prone to cycles of belief in decline, and the term itself confuses various dimensions of changing power relations. Some see the American problem as imperial overstretch (though as a percentage of GDP, the United States spends half as much on defense as it did during the Cold War); some see the problem as relative decline caused by the rise of others (though that process could still leave the United States more powerful than any other country); and still others see it as a process of absolute decline or decay such as occurred in the fall of ancient Rome (though Rome was an agrarian society with stagnant economic growth and internecine strife).

Such projections are not new. As Zakaria notes, America's Founding Fathers worried about comparisons to the decline of the Roman Republic. A strand of cultural pessimism is simply very American, extending back to the country's Puritan roots. English novelist Charles Dickens observed a century and a half ago: "[I]f its individual citizens, to a man, are to be believed, [America] always *is* depressed, and always *is* stagnated, and always *is* at an alarming crisis, and never was otherwise."

4   In the last half-century, polls showed Americans believed in their decline after the Soviet Union launched Sputnik in 1957, after Richard Nixon's devaluation of the dollar and the oil shocks in the 1970s, and after the closing of Rust Belt industries and the budget deficits of Ronald Reagan's administration in the 1980s. At the end of that decade, a majority of Americans believed their country was in decline; yet within the next 10 years they believed that America was the sole superpower. And now, after the 2008 financial crisis and recession, polls show a majority believes in decline again. These cycles of declinism tell us more about Americans' collective psychology than underlying shifts in power resources, but as British journalist Gideon Rachman argued in these pages recently [ed. Note: "Think Again: American Decline," *Foreign Policy*, Jan/Feb 2011], maybe this time decline is real. After all, as the Congressional Budget Office warns, on current trends the U.S. national debt will be equal to its GDP in a decade, and that will undermine confidence in the dollar.

Zakaria lists other worrying indicators related to education and infrastructure. According to the OECD [Organization for Economic Co-operation and Development], American 15-year-olds rank 17th in the world in science and 25th in math. The United States is 12th in college graduation rates, 23rd in infrastructure, and 27th in life expectancy. On the other side of the ledger, America ranks first among rich countries in guns, crime, and debt.

All these are very real problems, but one could also note that the United States is still first in total R&D expenditures, first in university rankings, first in Nobel prizes, first on indices of entrepreneurship, and according to the World Economic Forum, the fourth-most competitive economy in the world (behind the small states of Switzerland, Sweden, and Singapore). The United States remains at the forefront of technologies of the future like biotechnology and nanotechnology. This is hardly a picture of absolute economic decay, ancient Rome style. The truth is that one can draw a picture of the United States today that emphasizes either dark or bright colors without being wrong. No one can be sure which shade better portrays the future because the number of potential futures is vast, and which one comes to pass will depend in part on decisions not yet made.

Drawing on the thinking of Mancur Olson, the late great political economist, Zakaria believes that America's very success has made its decision processes sclerotic, like that of industrial Britain. But American culture is far more entrepreneurial and decentralized than that of Britain, where the sons of industrial entrepreneurs sought aristocratic titles and honors in London. If Olson is right, Zakaria says, the solution is to "stay flexible." And despite recurrent historical bouts of concern about it, immigration helps keep America flexible. In 2005, according to *Forbes*, foreign-born immigrants had participated in one of every four technology start-ups in the previous decade. As Singapore's Lee Kuan Yew once put it, China can draw on a talent pool of 1.3 billion people, but the United States not only draws on a talent pool of 7 billion, but can recombine them in a diverse culture that enhances creativity in a way that ethnic Han nationalism cannot.

8   Zakaria also worries about the inefficient American political system. But the Founding Fathers created a system of checks and balances precisely to preserve liberties at the price of efficiency. Moreover, just because we are now going through a period of excessively partisan politics and mistrust of government doesn't mean the American political system is in decline. Some aspects of the current mood are probably cyclical and related to unemployment, while others represent discontent with the bickering and deadlock in today's political process. Compared with the recent past, party politics has indeed become more polarized, but nasty politics is nothing new and goes all the way back to the Founding Fathers. Supporters of John Adams reputedly once called Thomas Jefferson "a mean-spirited, low-lived fellow, the son of a half-breed Indian squaw, sired by a Virginia mulatto father."

Part of the problem of accurate assessment is that faith in government became abnormally high among the generation that survived the Great Depression and won World War II. Over the long view of American history, it was overconfidence in government in the 1950s and early 1960s, not low levels thereafter, that was the anomaly. American government and politics have always had problems, sometimes worse than today's. In assessing political decline, one must beware of the golden glow of the past. It is easy to show decline if one compares the good in the past with the bad in the present.

In addition, we sometimes mistakenly idealize the efficiency of the political process in authoritarian countries like China. When it comes to infrastructure, for example, it is far easier to build high-speed rail lines where there are weak property rights and few lawyers. But if one looks at the important question of how Chinese leaders are struggling to implement their 12th five-year plan—reducing dependence on exports, shifting to internal demand, and reducing regional inequality by moving industry to the west—China is far from efficient. Although central bankers and economic planners know that revaluing the yuan would promote these goals and help head off inflation, a strong coalition of coastal export industries and associated local party bosses seeks to preserve the status quo.

Zakaria notes that one Asian country after another is learning the secrets of Western success, and he is right. In *The Future of Power*, I argue that one of the two great power shifts of this century is the recovery of Asia to what it represented before the Industrial Revolution led to the ascendance of the West: more than half the world's population and its economic production. We should herald Asia's recovery—it has brought millions out of dire poverty—but those with excessive fear of China should remember that Asia is not one entity. In his important book *Rivals*, Bill Emmott reminds us that Japan, India, and others that are concerned about the rise of China welcome an American presence. Can anyone similarly imagine Canada and Mexico seeking a Chinese alliance to balance American power in their neighborhood?

12   Nor is China likely to surpass America anytime soon. Yes, barring political uncertainties, China's size and high rate of economic growth will almost certainly increase its strength relative to that of the United States. Still, China won't necessarily become the world's most powerful country as a result. Even if China suffers no major domestic political setback, many of the current projections based on GDP growth alone are too one-dimensional. They ignore what are likely to be enduring U.S. military and soft-power advantages, as well as China's geopolitical disadvantages in the internal Asian balance of power.

Zakaria is correct that the United States faces serious problems. But issues that preoccupy us today, such as long-term debt, are not insoluble; see for example, the recommendations of the Simpson-Bowles commission, and remember that only a decade ago some people worried about the government *surplus*. Of course, such solutions may forever remain out of reach. But it is worth distinguishing situations for which there are no solutions from those that could, in principle, be solved.

The greatest danger to America is not debt, political paralysis, or China; it is parochialism, turning away from the openness that is the source of its strength and resting on its laurels. As Zakaria says, in the past, worrying about decline has helped avert it. Let us hope that his intelligent though darkly drawn picture will yet again start that healthy process.

PERSONAL RESPONSE

Do you believe that America remains a strong world power, or do you believe it is in decline?

QUESTIONS FOR CLASS OR SMALL-GROUP DISCUSSION

1. What does Nye mean when he says that the term "decline . . . confuses various dimensions of changing power relations" (paragraph 2)?

2. Nye comments that "a strand of cultural pessimism is simply very American" (paragraph 3). State in your own words what you understand him to mean by that statement.

3. Analyze Nye's argument in response to Fareed Zakaria's *Time* magazine article. What is his thesis? What evidence does he use to counter Zakaria? How convincing do you find his argument?

4. How does Nye respond to what many people perceive as serious problems for America? What does he see as the "greatest danger to America"? State what you think he means by that and whether you agree with him.

PERSPECTIVES ON INTERNATIONAL RELATIONS

Suggestions for Writing

1. Respond to Paul Johnson's "American Idealism and Realpolitik," either agreeing or disagreeing with him and using examples to support your position.

2. Support or argue against this statement by Thomas Friedman in "Still Not Tired": "[I]n this war on terrorism, there is no 'good war' or 'bad war.' There is one war with many fronts" (paragraph 7).

3. Expand on, explain, or respond to this statement by Cathy Young in "Lessons from World War II": "[A] free, civilized society at war will always seek to strike some balance between self-defense and principle" (paragraph 10).

4. Joseph Nye, Jr., in "Zakaria's World" affirms his faith in the United States as a strong world leader, countering Fareed Zakaria's warning in his March 3, 2011, *Time* essay "Are America's Best Days Behind Us?" that America is in decline. Read the Zakaria article online or in print and then argue your position on America's future, referring to both Nye and Zakaria. Drawing on Joseph Nye, Jr.'s "Zakaria's World," explain what you think makes America a great country.

5. Explain whether you agree with this statement in Joseph Nye, Jr.'s "Zakaria's World": "The greatest danger to America is not debt, political paralysis, or China; it is parochialism, turning away from the openness that is the source of its strength and resting on its laurels" (paragraph 14).

6. Explain the effect that America's wealth, power, commercialism, or any other aspect of its culture has on the way America is perceived by people in other nations.

7. Explain your position on the question of whether America should be responsible for defending weaker countries from oppression.

8. Select a recent popular film and analyze the image of America that it projects, or, do a close analysis of a person or object from popular culture that you think represents an aspect of American culture.

9. Analyze an American book or story for the image it projects of America. Try to view the book or story objectively, as if you were a foreigner looking for information about America. What impression do you think a foreigner reading the same book or story would get of America?

10. Explain your viewpoint on the issue of how far the state should be allowed to restrict civil liberties for the sake of national security.

11. Write a personal essay explaining your feelings about the September 11, 2001, terrorist attacks and/or how you see them affecting you or your generation in the years to come.

12. Explore the effects on people of a serious event like a terrorist attack, an automobile accident, an encounter with random violence, or a close brush with death. How does such an event affect their sense of security and the way in which they think about their own lives? Use personal experience or observation to write your essay.

Research Topics

1. Research any of the subjects related to America's role in the world that Joseph Nye, Jr., refers to in "Zakaria's World." For instance, in his discussion of American pessimism historically, he mentions the following: the effects of the Russian launch of *Sputnik* in 1957; the effects of the President Nixon's devaluation of the dollar; the decline in oil availability during the 1970s; the closing of Rust Belt industries or budget deficits during the Reagan administration in the 1980s. Select one of those subjects and narrow your focus to a workable research paper topic.

2. Research the subject of America's "soft power" in the period following the September 11, 2001, terrorist attacks on American soil.

3. Research the subject of anti-Americanism in countries other than America, whether it exists and, if so, why it exists and how strong it is.

4. Conduct library research to expand on the views expressed by writers in this chapter on America's foreign policy, America's war on terrorism, or the lessons that a previous war has for us today. You should be able to narrow your focus and determine a central idea for your paper after your preliminary search for sources and early review of the materials.

5. Research the subject of U.S. relations with Japan, China, the Soviet Union, the Middle East, or another foreign country that may figure importantly in the future of the United States. On the basis of your research, assess the importance to the United States of strengthening such relations and the potential effects of allowing relations with that country to deteriorate.

6. Research the conditions surrounding America's involvement in Bosnia, Kuwait, Kosovo, Afghanistan, or other countries where the American military presence was strong. Limit your focus to one aspect of the subject, such as what led to America's involvement, what America's involvement meant to American citizens, or effects on the country of America's intervention. Then argue the extent to which you support that involvement.

7. Research the effects of the September 11, 2001, terrorist attacks in New York and Washington on the American economy, the American image abroad, or America's role in international politics. Other research subjects related to the 9/11/01 terrorist attacks include the impact of the events on Muslim Americans or other ethnic minorities; the creation of the Department of Homeland Security; the role of other nations in coalition-building following the terrorist attacks; and the question of what led to the events of September 11, 2001, or to another large-scale act of terrorism, including what motivated the terrorist attacks. All of these topics are broad, so after selecting one, narrow it down further. For instance, you might begin by asking what the economic effects of the attacks were on the airline industry, investment firms, or the stock exchange, and then further narrow your focus as you begin reading on the subject.

8. Following the terrorist attacks against New York and Washington on September 11, 2001, the North Atlantic Treaty Organization (NATO) invoked article 5 of its mutual defense treaty. Research the purpose of NATO and assess its role in the aftermath of the September 11 attacks.

RESPONDING TO VISUALS

MUNIR UZ ZAMAN/AFP/Getty Image

U.S. Army soldiers pay respects to a fallen comrade who was killed during an insurgent attack.

1. Comment on the perspective from which the picture is taken: what is visually striking about the picture? How might the image be a commentary on war in general?

2. Although you may not be able to see them clearly, the soldiers are kneeling by the boots, guns, caps, and dog-tags of two fallen soldiers. How do those details add to your response to the picture?

3. The memorial ceremony pictured here took place in a military base in Afghanistan. The two men being remembered were killed when attempting to help an old man who turned out to be wearing a suicide vest. How do these details add to the poignancy of the image?

RESPONDING TO VISUALS

Uncle Sam with children from all over the world.

1. What image of America's international relations is conveyed in this drawing?
2. Why do you suppose the artist depicted Uncle Sam dancing with children from around the world? What is gained by having him loom as a tall figure over the little ones? How does the look on Uncle Sam's face add to that impression?
3. Comment on the composition of the drawing. How does the artist convey which countries the children represent? How does color contribute to the overall effect?

PART FOUR

Science and Technology

CHAPTER 17

Social Media

Digital technology is constantly changing, with exciting new, ever-faster programs emerging frequently. Although early researchers recognized the potential of computers, no doubt few of them envisioned the staggering capabilities of what they can do or the extent to which they would be so closely and inextricably linked with people's everyday lives. Increasingly sophisticated computers make child's play of activities that just a few years ago were challenging or impossible tasks. Young children today learn skills—sometimes before they enter school—that many of their grandparents and certainly their great-grandparents will never even try to learn. Indeed, computer technology has advanced at such a rapid rate that its powers seem unlimited, a prospect that fills some with eager anticipation and leaves others feeling intimidated and frightened.

Cyberspace, a word coined by author William Gibson in his sci-fi novel *Neuromancer,* commonly refers to the nonphysical space and sense of community created by Internet users around the world, the virtual "world" that users inhabit when they are online. People can communicate and share files on the Internet through e-mail and at websites; they can conduct research, shop, play games, and do any number of activities that people have been accustomed to do in physical space.

The difference, of course, is that all those activities take place by pressing keys on a keyboard, moving a mouse around, or using a touchpad. Such convenience has changed the way many people conduct their lives, most would say in a positive way. However, the high-tech capabilities of the Internet have also led to problems. The readings in this chapter look at some of those problems as well as the benefits of such technology.

The first reading in the chapter is by Steven Johnson, a writer very much interested in the intersection of technology and the personal, that is, the ways in which the incredible advances in technology affect individual lives. In "Social Connections," Johnson responds to an op-ed piece by Thomas Friedman, in which Friedman suggests that our abilities to communicate instantly because of all the technological devices available to us might actually prevent one-on-one personal communication. Technology, Friedman wrote, actually drives us apart rather than brings us together. Johnson takes exception to this view and explains why he feels just the opposite of Friedman. As you read Johnson's argument, consider whose position you find yourself agreeing with.

The next two essays argue completely different views on social media, originally written for a special feature of the March 2011 issue of *Wired* magazine called "Your Life Torn Open: What the End of Privacy Means for You." In the first, "Sharing Is a Trap," Andrew Keen relies heavily on allusions to art, literature, and social criticism to make his point about the way that the Internet is stripping away privacy. Framing his essay with an allusion to a Vermeer painting of a woman reading a letter, Keen laments the death of privacy. He makes reference to Franz Kafka's *The Trial* and George Orwell's *1984*, draws from John Stuart Mills *On Liberty*, and refers frequently to the ideas of Jeremy Bentham, the 19th-century British philosopher and social reformer. Although his allusions might be challenging, consider the essence of what he says about social media and its pervasiveness in many people's lives. Do you think his fears reasonable or unreasonable?

In contrast to Andrew Keen, Jeff Jarvis embraces social media. In "Get Over It," he praises the "publicness" of social media and gives some very personal examples of how he has benefitted. His fear, he says, is not invasion of privacy but the possibility that the very public nature of social media might be restricted. He does not want any limits placed on what information can be shared online, declaring, "What's public is a public good. Diminish that and it is we, the public, who lose." Thus, Jarvis stands about as far in opposition to Keen as one can get. And as with the Keen article, ask yourself if his hope for the future of social media and its place in our most personal lives is reasonable or unreasonable.

Finally, Jose Antonia Vargas in "Spring Awakening" reviews a book written by an Egyptian who was instrumental in using social media to spark a revolution that eventually led to the ouster of Egypt's president and the dissolution of its ruling power. Vargas's essay demonstrates how a book review can also be an analysis, in this case an analysis of the impact of social media. Wael Ghonim's Revolution 2.0 explains what led to his creation of the "We Are All Khaled Said" Facebook page, its influence in uniting young, educated Egyptians to rally at Tahrir Square in Cairo, and eventually how the movement overthrew the government. As Vargas notes,

"It's a book . . . that serves as a touchstone for future testimonials about a strengthening borderless, digital movement that is set to continually disrupt powerful institutions." Whether you care about social media or not, Vargas's book review is likely to increase your understanding of its potential to effect real social and political change.

SOCIAL CONNECTIONS

STEVEN JOHNSON

Steven Johnson writes for a number of periodicals, including Wired, Discover, *and the* New York Times Magazine. *His books include* Mind Wide Open: Your Brain and the Neuroscience of Everyday Life *(2004);* Everything Bad is Good for You *(2005);* The Ghost Map: The Story of London's Most Terrifying Epidemic and How It Changed Science, Cities, and the Modern World *(2006);* The Invention of Air: A Story of Science, Faith, and the Birth of America *(2008);* Where Good Ideas Come From: The Natural History of Innovation *(2010); and* The Innovator's Cookbook: Essentials for Inventing What is Next *(2011). This article was published in the* New York Times *on November 28, 2006.*

Earlier this month, Thomas Friedman began his column in *The New York Times* with a story about being chauffeured from Paris Charles De Gaulle Airport by a young, French-speaking African driver who chatted on his mobile phone the entire trip, while simultaneously watching a movie on the dashboard. Friedman, for his part, was writing a column on his laptop and listening to Stevie Nicks on the iPod.

Friedman wrote, "There was only one thing we never did: Talk to each other. . . . I relate all this because it illustrates something I've been feeling more and more lately—that technology is dividing us as much as uniting us. Yes, technology can make the far feel near. But it can also make the near feel very far."

This is the lament of iPod Nation: we've built elaborate tools to connect us to our friends—and introduce us to strangers—who are spread across the planet, and at the same time, we've embraced technologies that help us block out the people we share physical space with, technologies that give us the warm cocoon of the personalized soundtrack. We wear white earbuds that announce to the world: whatever you've got to say, I can't hear it.

4   Cities are naturally inclined to suffer disproportionately from these trends, since cities historically have produced public spaces where diverse perspectives can engage with each other—on sidewalks and subways, in bars and, yes, in taxicabs. Thirty years ago, the typical suburban commuter driving solo to work was already listening to his own private soundtrack on the car radio. (If anything, cell

phones have made car-centric communities more social.) But for the classic vision of sidewalk urbanism articulated by Jane Jacobs, the activist and author, the bubble of permanent connectivity poses a real threat. There can be no Speaker's Corner if everyone's listening to his own private podcast.

I take these threats seriously, but let me suggest two reasons I am a bit less worried than Friedman is about the social disconnection of the connected age. One has to do with the past, the other the future.

First, there's a tendency to sentimentalize the public spaces of traditional cities. More than a few commentators have remarked on the ubiquity of the white earbuds on the New York City subways as a sign of urban disconnection. (Steven Levy summarizes and rebuts these objections elegantly in his recent book *The Perfect Thing*.) I rode the subways for almost 15 years before Apple introduced the iPod, and I can say with confidence that the subway system, for all its merits, was not exactly a hotbed of civic discourse even then. On the good days, most everyone was engrossed in their newspaper or their book. (On bad days, we were just trying to steer clear of all the subway vigilantes.) Now at least we have an excuse for not talking to each other.

It's telling that Friedman draws upon that very distinct form of social contact—the cabbie and the fare—since there are few other conventional urban situations that regularly produce substantive political conversation between strangers. The barstool conversation and the public hearing also come to mind, but I'm fairly sure the iPod hasn't infiltrated those zones yet.

8   Then there's the question of where all this technology is taking us. Friedman rightly celebrates "having lots of contacts and easy connectivity." Still, there's an underlying assumption in his piece—appropriate for someone who writes so powerfully about globalization—that connectivity is largely a matter of bringing disparate parts of the planet into closer contact. Yet that is not the whole story. Connectivity—in most instances the specific form of connectivity offered by the Web—has also greatly enhanced and amplified the kinds of conversations that happen in real-world neighborhoods. "Placebloggers" are writing about the micro-news of shared communities: the new playground that's just opened up, or the latest the city council election. The discussion forums at Chowhound are dissecting every change of menu in every hot restaurant in most American cities. Real estate blogs dish about last week's open houses, and trade statistics debating the inevitability of the post-bubble dark ages. (Full disclosure: I have, as James Baker likes to say, a dog in this hunt, in form of a new Web site I helped create called *outside.in*, which tries to organize all those conversations.)

So the idea that the new technology is pushing us away from the people sharing our local spaces is only half true. To be sure, iPods and mobile phones give us fewer opportunities to start conversations with people of different perspectives. But the Web gives us more of those opportunities, and for the most part, I think it gives us *better* opportunities. What it doesn't directly provide is face-to-face connection. So the question becomes: how important is face-to-face? I don't have a full answer to that—clearly it's important, and clearly we lose something in the transition to increasingly virtual interactions.

But just as clearly, we gain. I think of the online debate over the Atlantic Yards project here in Brooklyn—hundreds of voices working through their differences in sometimes excruciating detail. I've made a few volleys in that debate, and while it's true I haven't had face-to-face encounters with the other participants, the intensity and depth of the discussion has been far greater than any conversation on any topic that I've ever had with a stranger on a subway. The conversations unfolding across these sites are, for the most part, marvelous examples of strangers exchanging ideas and values, even without the subtleties of facial expressions and vocal intonation, and the ideas and values they're exchanging all eventually come back to a real-world place. Yes, they can sometimes get contentious. But so can Speaker's Corner. Contentiousness is what it's all about.

PERSONAL RESPONSE

How important to you are such things as a cell phone, laptop, and/or iPod? Would you be lost without them, or would you feel liberated if they were all taken away from you?

QUESTIONS FOR CLASS OR SMALL-GROUP DISCUSSION

1. Explain the controversy about technology that is at the heart of Johnson's opinion piece.
2. Summarize the first point that Johnson makes in his response to critics of the communication technology. Do you agree with him?
3. Summarize the second point in Johnson's response to critics of communication technology. Do you agree with him?
4. What is the "Speaker's Corner" that Johnson mentions in paragraphs 4 and 10? How does his concluding reference to it relate to his central point? What do you think he means by his concluding sentence: "Contentiousness is what it's all about"?

SHARING IS A TRAP

Andrew Keen

Andrew Keen is a British-American Internet entrepreneur, host of "Keen On," a Techcrunch chat show; a columnist for CNN; and a regular commentator for many newspapers, radio, and television programs. He is author of Cult of the Amateur: How the Internet is Killing Our Culture *(2007); and* Digital Vertigo: An Anti-Social Manifesto *(2012). This article was published in the March 2011 issue of* Wired *magazine.*

Reprinted from Wired, March 2011, by permission of the author.

Every so often, when I'm in Amsterdam, I visit the Rijksmuseum to remind my-self about the history of privacy. I go there to gaze at a picture called *The Woman in Blue Reading a Letter*, which was painted by Jan Vermeer in 1663. It is of an unidentified Dutch woman avidly reading a letter. Vermeer's picture, to borrow a phrase from privacy advocates Louis Brandeis and Samuel Warren, is a celebra-tion of the "sacred precincts of private and domestic life". It's as if the artist had kept his distance in order to capture the young woman, cocooned in her private world, at her least socially visible.

Today, as social media continues radically to transform how we communicate and interact, I can't help thinking with a heavy heart about *The Woman in Blue*. You see, in the networking age of Facebook, Twitter and Foursquare, the social invisibility that Vermeer so memorably captured is, to excuse the pun, disappear-ing. That's because, as every Silicon Valley notable, from Eric Schmidt to Mark Zuckerberg, has publicly acknowledged, privacy is dead: a casualty of the cult of the social. Everything and everyone on the internet is becoming collaborative. The future is, in a word, social.

On this future network, we will all know what everyone is doing all the time. It will be the central intelligence agency for 21st century life. As Don Tapscott and Anthony D Williams argue in their 2010 book *Macrowikinomics*, today's "age of network intelligence" represents a "turning point in history" equivalent to the Renaissance. They are, in a sense, right. On today's internet everything we do—from our use of ecommerce, location services and email to online search, adver-tising and entertainment—is increasingly open and transparent. And it is this increasingly ubiquitous social network—fuelled by our billions of confessional tweets and narcissistic updates—that is invading the "sacred precincts" of private and domestic life.

4   Every so often, when I'm in London, I visit University College to remind myself about the future of privacy. I go there to visit the tomb of the utilitarian social reformer Jeremy Bentham, a glass-and-wood mausoleum he dubbed his "AutoIcon", from which the philosopher's waxy corpse has been watching over us for the last 150 years. It was Bentham, you see, who, in 1787, at the dawn of the industrial age, designed what he called a "simple idea in architecture" to im-prove the management of social institutions, from prisons and asylums to work-houses and schools. Bentham imagined a physical network of small rooms in which we would be inspected "every instant of time". He named a tract after his idea, calling it, without irony, *Panopticon; Or, the Inspection House*. Bentham's goal was the elimination of mystery and privacy. Everything, for this utilitarian inven-tor of the greatest-happiness principle, would become shared and thus social. In Bentham's perfectly efficient and transparent world, there would be nowhere for anyone to hide.

Unfortunately, Bentham's panopticon was a dark premonition. The mass me-chanical age of the telegraph, the factory and the motion-picture camera created the physical architecture to transform everyone into exhibits—always observable by our Big Brothers in government, commerce and media. In the industrial age, factories, schools, prisons and, most ominously, entire political systems were built upon this technology of collective surveillance. The last 200 years have indeed been the age of the great exhibition.

Yet nobody in the industrial era actually wanted to become artefacts in this collective exhibition. The great critics of mass society—from John Stuart Mill, Warren and Brandeis to George Orwell, Franz Kafka and Michel Foucault—tried to shield individual privacy from the panopticon's always-on gaze. As Foucault warned, "visibility is a trap." So, from Mill's solitary free thinker in *On Liberty* to Josef K in *The Trial* and Winston Smith in *1984*, the hero of the mass industrial age is the individual who takes pleasure in his own invisibility, who turns his back on the camera, who—in the timeless defense of privacy from Warren and Brandeis—just wants to be "let alone."

Yet now, at the dusk of the industrial and the dawn of the digital age, Bentham's simple idea of architecture has returned. But history never repeats itself, not identically, at least. Today, as the internet evolves from a platform for data into a space for people, the panopticon has reappeared with a chilling twist. What we once saw as a prison is now considered a playground; what was considered pain is today viewed as pleasure. The age of the great exhibition is being replaced by the age of great exhibitionism.

8   Today's "simple architecture" is the internet, that ever-expanding network of networks combining the global web of personal computers, the wireless world of handheld devices and other "smart" social products such as connected televisions and gaming consoles, in which around a quarter of the Earth's population has already taken up residency. With its two billion digitally connected souls and five billion connected devices, the network can house an infinite number of rooms. This is a global building that, more than two centuries after Bentham sketched his design, allows us to be inspected every instant.

This digital world—described by New York University's Clay Shirky as the "connective tissue of society" and by US secretary of state Hillary Clinton as the new "nervous system of the planet"—has been designed to keep us forever on show in our networked crystalline palaces. And today, in an age of transparent online communities such as Twitter, LinkedIn and Facebook, the social has become, in Shirky's words, the "default setting" on the internet, thereby transforming digital technology from a tool of our "second lives" into a central part of real life.

But this real life could have been choreographed by Bentham. As Shirky notes, popular geolocation services such as Foursquare, Gowalla, Google Latitude and Facebook Places, which enable us to "effectively see through walls" and know the exact location of all our friends, are making society more "legible" and allowing us to be read "like a book." No wonder, then, that Jeff Jarvis, one of the leading apostles of what he calls "publicness," promises that social media will make us all immortal.

No wonder, either, that, as the American journalist Katie Roiphe has observed, "Facebook is the novel we are all writing." We are becoming WikiLeakers of our own lives. There has been a massive increase in what Shirky calls "self-produced" legibility. This contemporary mania with self-expression is what two leading American psychologists, Jean Twenge and Keith Campbell, have described as "the narcissism epidemic"—a self-promotional madness driven, they say, by our need to broadcast our uniqueness to the world.

12   While social media, for all its superhuman ability to see through walls, might not quite guarantee immortality, its impact is certainly of immense historical significance, equal, in its own way, to the early industrial revolution. As the venture capitalist John Doerr, a partner at the blue-chip firm Kleiner Perkins, has argued, the "social" represents "the great third wave" of technological innovation, after the invention of the personal computer and the internet. Such is Doerr's confidence in this social revolution that, in October 2010, in partnership with Facebook and the gaming social network Zynga, Kleiner Perkins launched the $250 million sFund dedicated to putting money into social businesses.

Once oriented around the distribution of data, internet innovation is now increasingly focused on social products, services and platforms. Google's data-driven "links" economy is being replaced by Facebook's people-powered "likes." The integration of our personal data—our "social graph"—into online content is becoming the driver of internet innovation. There is now Facebook-powered social search from the Bing and Blekko search engines; social internet browsers such as RockMelt and Firefox; social music from Pandora and the iTunes Ping network; social reading apps on the Kindle and the iPad; social photos from Google's image-sharing platform Picasa; social "location tracking" on Google Maps; socially produced news from *The Washington Post* and *The New York Times*; socially produced information on Quora; a growing infestation of social networks for kids such as the eerily named Togetherville; and, most troublingly of all, medical informational networks such as 23andMe, with the power to transform our DNA records into socially distributed products.

There are services such as Klout that quantify our social influence in this new "reputation" economy and CafeBots, Kleiner's first sFund investment, which provides a Friend Relationship Management (FRM) system for the influencers of this new reputation economy. Then there are multimillion-dollar networks such as Groupon and LivingSocial that transform individual commerce into a social activity; well-backed start-ups such as Miso and Philo that reveal what we are watching on television; and, most bizarrely, quickly growing social-ecommerce web platforms and services such as Blippy and Swipely that publish all our credit-card purchases.

The digital networking of the world is both relentless and inevitable. A report from media-research company Nielsen revealed that in June 2010 Americans spent almost 23 per cent of their online time using social-media networking—up a staggering 43 per cent year on year, with use among 50 to 64-year-olds almost doubling in this period. Facebook, with more than half a billion members investing more than 700 billion of their minutes per month on the network, is expected to hit a billion members within the next 12 months. By the end of 2011, half of all American consumers are expected to own networked smartphones, thereby sweeping them into the social-media maelstrom. Like it or not, Tapscott and

Williams's "age of network intelligence" is imminent—the only question is how intelligent we really all will be in this brave new social world.

16   And all this, I'm afraid, is just the early stages of the social-media revolution. The CEO of Ericsson has predicted that there will be 50 billion connected devices by 2020, making the network more and more invasive and visible. Meanwhile, Mark Zuckerberg, the smiling utilitarian at the heart of this social darkness, has even come up with his own law to imagine the future of the trap he is laying for us all. "I would expect that next year people will share twice as much information as they share this year, and the next year they will be sharing twice as much as they did before," Zuckerberg's Law states.

Zuckerberg's ideas on "sharing" could have been invented by Kafka. Just as Josef K unwittingly shared all his known and unknown information with the authorities, so are we now all sharing our most intimate spiritual, economic and medical information with all the myriad "free" social-media services, products and platforms. And, given that the dominant business model of all this social-media economy is advertising sales, it is inevitable that all this data will end up in the hands of our corporate advertising "friends." That's why Facebook, a six-year-old, barely profitable new-media company with little proprietary technology of its own, was valued recently at about $50 billion. Zuckerberg is taking Bentham's ideas to their ultimate conclusion, and the result is a panopticon in which privacy is relegated like an historical artefact. Facebook even has the audacity, in good Benthamite fashion, to be developing a "Gross Happiness Index" which will supposedly quantify and thus own global sentiment, making the social network the central bank of our new public socio-informational economy. Today's digital social network is a trap. Today's cult of the social, peddled by an unholy alliance of Silicon Valley entrepreneurs and communitarian idealists, is rooted in a misunderstanding of the human condition. The truth is that we aren't naturally social beings. Instead, as Vermeer reminds us in *The Woman in Blue*, human happiness is really about being left alone. *On Liberty*, the 1859 essay by Bentham's godson and former acolyte, John Stuart Mill, remains a classic defence of individual rights in the age of the industrial network and its tyranny of the majority. Today, as we struggle to make sense of the impact of the internet revolution, we need an equivalent On Digital Liberty to protect the right to privacy in the social-media age. Tapscott and Williams believe that the age of networked intelligence will be equal to the Renaissance in its significance. But what if they are wrong? What if the digital revolution, because of its disregard for the right of individual privacy, becomes a new dark ages? And what if all that is left of individual privacy by the end of the 21st century exists in museums alongside Vermeer's *Woman in Blue*? Then what?

PERSONAL RESPONSE

Do you believe that privacy is a right? Are there conditions under which it would be permissible to violate the privacy of others? Have you ever had your own privacy invaded?

QUESTIONS FOR CLASS OR SMALL-GROUP DISCUSSION

1. Explain the use that Keen makes of the Vermeer painting *The Woman in Blue Reading a Letter*. Where in his essay does he refer to it? How effective do you find it as a strategy for advancing his argument?

2. Explain what you understand by Keen's references to Jeremy Bentham. What point does he make by referring to *Panopticon; or the Inspection House*, for instance (paragraph 4)? Identify some of the other allusions and references that Keen makes and explain how they function in his essay. For instance, what is his point with his references to Kafka's Josef K in *The Trial* and Winston Smith in *1984*?

3. What is Keen's fear about social media?

4. How well do you think that Keen argues his point? Are you convinced?

GET OVER IT

JEFF JARVIS

Jeff Jarvis is creator of the weblog BuzzMachine *and co-host of* This Week in Google. *He is author of* What Would Google Do? *(2009) and* Public Parts: How Sharing in the Digital Age Improves the Way We Work and Live *(2011) This article was published in the March 2011 issue of Wired magazine.*

Panic about privacy has often been triggered by technology. When Gutenberg invented his printing press, authors of the day feared having their thoughts and identities recorded permanently and distributed widely. The first serious discussion of a legal right to privacy in the US came in 1890, with the invention of the Kodak camera and the rise of the penny press. Telephones, miniature microphones, video cameras and RFID chips all triggered much fretting. It should come as no surprise, then, that the internet would provoke warnings that privacy is dead, but those alarms will likely lead to more regulation of privacy than ever. We need protection of our privacy and we're getting it.

It's not privacy that concerns me now. It's publicness. I fear our supposed privacy crisis, reputed by the media and abetted by government, could result in our missing many of the opportunities the net affords to connect with each other and with information. In Germany, political and press frenzy on the topic led to 244,000 citizens exercising their *Verpixelungsrecht*, the right to have their buildings pixellated in Google Street View—desecrating the digital landscape and setting a dangerous precedent: if Google can be told not to take pictures of public places, will citizens be censored next?

Germany's privacy chief also decreed that combining geocoding with facial recognition shall be "taboo". Does it make sense to forbid a technology before it is even used? I realize how the notion could sound creepy. But imagine how such a combination could help find missing people (or terrorists).

4   Half a billion people can't be wrong. That's how many of us share friends, photos, videos, activities, locations and romantic interests—our lives—on Facebook, plus much more on Twitter, Flickr, Foursquare, Blippy, blogs and social networks yet to be imagined. "The data suggest that people are self-violating their privacy at a humongous rate," Eric Schmidt told me. "The clear trend is for people to get value out of sharing more and more," Mark Zuckerberg said in an interview.

We are sharing because it brings benefit. We meet people, make friends and stay connected. We spread ideas. We get attention. We gather information. We gain trust through transparency. We collaborate through openness. We are learning how to use our new tools to organize movements. We cross borders. We entertain ourselves. We are served more relevant content and, yes, adverts. We question authority.

That is precisely what the curmudgeons and incumbents of our legacy institutions fear. Publicness shifts control. Secrecy once granted power, now transparency does. Why else would so many governments and corporations be so afraid of Julian Assange? He compels the people's business to be conducted before the people. WikiLeaks forces publicness. Facebook merely enables it. "Our mission," Zuckerberg said, "is to make the world more open and connected."

I live that open life. Not everything I do is or should be public; I especially want to be careful not to drag others into my glasshouse. Yet I have blogged, tweeted, published and broadcast about many experiences, including the most private: my penis and how it no longer functions after surgery for prostate cancer. Can't get much more public than that, now, can I? But good has come of it. I received support and information no doctor's pamphlet could supply. I inspired men to get tested. I helped others through surgery, people who would not have known to reach out to me had I not been public. I could bring attention to a disease that gets too little notice.

8   Publicness disarms stigmas. It provokes generosity. It increases knowledge. I have learned online how much is to be gained from sunlight. The internet is our new tool of publicness. It is vital we protect its openness and its power against censorship born of tyranny or overregulation born of the fear of the new. What's public is a public good. Diminish that and it is we, the public, who lose.

PERSONAL RESPONSE

Jarvis is in favor of our very personal lives being made public. To what extent do you agree with him? Are there limits to what people should share in social media?

QUESTIONS FOR CLASS OR SMALL-GROUP DISCUSSION

1. What do you understand Jarvis to mean when he writes, "It's not privacy that concerns me now. It's publicness" (paragraph 2). What is his fear about social media regulation?

2. In paragraph 4, Jarvis writes: "Half a billion people can't be wrong." Do you agree with him? How strong an argument is that statement?

3. How well do you think Jarvis's argument counters that of Andrew Keen in "Sharing Is a Trap"? If you have not read that essay, analyze Jarvis's as an argument on its own.

4. Explain what you understand Jarvis to mean by the following: "Publicness disarms stigma. It provokes generosity. It increases knowledge" (paragraph 8).

SPRING AWAKENING

JOSE ANTONIO VARGAS

Jose Antonio Vargas is a journalist, multimedia storyteller, and founder of Define American, *a multimedia campaign for immigration reform. He has written for the* Washington Post, *the* Huffington Post *and the* New Yorker. *This review was published online at the New York Times Web site on February 17, 2012 A version of it appeared in print on February 19, 2012, in the* Sunday Book Review.

Revolution 2.0: The Power of the People Is Greater Than the People in Power: A Memoir by Wael Ghonim

In the embryonic, ever evolving era of social media—when milestones come by the day, if not by the second—June 8, 2010, has secured a rightful place in history. That was the day Wael Ghonim, a 29-year-old Google marketing executive, was browsing Facebook in his home in Dubai and found a startling image: a photograph of a bloodied and disfigured face, its jaw broken, a young life taken away. That life, he soon learned, had belonged to Khaled Mohamed Said, a 28-year-old from Alexandria who had been beaten to death by the Egyptian police.

At once angered and animated, the Egyptian-born Ghonim went online and created a Facebook page. "Today they killed Khaled," he wrote. "If I don't act for his sake, tomorrow they will kill me." It took a few moments for Ghonim to settle on a name for the page, one that would fit the character of an increasingly personalized and politically galvanizing Internet. He finally decided on "Kullena Khaled Said"—"We Are All Khaled Said."

4   "Khaled Said was a young man just like me, and what happened to him could have happened to me," Ghonim writes in *Revolution 2.0*, his fast-paced and

engrossing new memoir of political awakening. "All young Egyptians had long been oppressed, enjoying no rights in our own homeland."

Ghonim's memoir is a welcome and cleareyed addition to a growing list of volumes that have aimed (but often failed) to meaningfully analyze social media's impact. It's a book about social media for people who don't think they care about social media. It will also serve as a touchstone for future testimonials about a strengthening borderless digital movement that is set to continually disrupt powerful institutions, be they corporate enterprises or political regimes.

An accidental activist, Ghonim tapped into a shared frustration that became immediately evident online. Two minutes after he started his Facebook page, 300 people had joined it. Three months later, that number had grown to more than 250,000. What bubbled up online inevitably spilled onto the streets, starting with a series of "Silent Stands" that culminated in a massive and historic rally at Tahrir Square in downtown Cairo. "We Are All Khaled Said" helped ignite an uprising that led to the resignation of President Hosni Mubarak and the dissolution of the ruling National Democratic Party. In turn, Ghonim—who was arrested during the height of the protests—reluctantly became one of the leading voices of the Arab Spring.

Ghonim's writing voice is spare and measured, and marked by the same earnest humility he has displayed in media appearances. During the interview he gave on Egyptian television after his release from detention, when he broke down crying as a photo montage of young Egyptians killed in the protests played across the screen, he was quick to point out that "the real heroes" of the revolution were those who had been martyred. He resists being labeled an icon. He insists he represents just one story and says his online activism should be seen only in the context of "hundreds of other pages, Facebook accounts and Twitter profiles" dedicated to covering and organizing the Arab Spring.

8 And he's right. But his individual story resonates on two levels: it epitomizes the coming-of-age of a young Middle Eastern generation that has grown up in the digital era, as well as the transformation of an apolitical man from comfortable executive to prominent activist.

The Middle East is home to roughly 100 million people aged 15 to 29. Many are educated but unemployed. Though only a fraction of Egyptians have Internet access, Ghonim writes, the number of Web users in the country increased to 13.6 million in 2008 from 1.5 million in 2004. Through blogs, Twitter and Facebook, the Web has become a haven for a young, educated class yearning to express its worries and anxieties.

Technology, of course, is not a panacea. Facebook does not a revolution make. In Egypt's case, it was simply a place for venting the outrage resulting from years of repression, economic instability and individual frustration. Ghonim writes that in 2011, out of Egypt's more than 80 million people, some 48 million were poor and 2.5 million lived in extreme poverty. "More than three million young Egyptians are unemployed," he says.

A father of two, Ghonim comes from a relatively prosperous family. Though he places himself in "a small, privileged slice" of Egypt's population, he once shared his countrymen's indifference to politics. "Most of us shied away," he writes, "believing that we could not do anything to change the status quo." Connecting online with other young, educated Egyptians changed his mind.

12   The Internet, Ghonim says, was "instrumental in shaping my experiences as well as my character." Like many who grew up with instant messaging, on-line video games and the here-comes-everybody ethos of sites like Wikipedia, he refers to himself as a "real-life introvert yet an Internet extrovert." He met his wife, Ilka, an American Muslim, online.

Ghonim drew on his considerable skill and knowledge as an online marketer while running the "We Are All Khaled Said" Facebook page. Early on, he de-cided that creating the page, as opposed to a Facebook group, would be a better way to spread information. More important, he knew that maintaining an infor-mal, authentic tone was crucial to amassing allies. People had to see themselves in the page. "Using the pronoun *I* was critical to establishing the fact that the page was not managed by an organization, political party or movement of any kind," he writes. "On the contrary, the writer was an ordinary Egyptian devastated by the brutality inflicted on Khaled Said and motivated to seek justice."

He polled the page's users and sought ideas from others, like how best to publi-cize a rally—through printed fliers and mass text messaging, it turned out. ("Reach-ing working-class Egyptians was not going to happen through the Internet and Facebook," he notes.) He tried to be as inclusive as possible, as when he changed the name of the page's biggest scheduled rally from "Celebrating Egyptian Police Day—January 25" to "January 25: Revolution Against Torture, Poverty, Corruption and Unemployment." "We needed to have everyone join forces: workers, human rights activists, government employees and others who had grown tired of the regime's poli-cies," he writes. "If the invitation to take to the streets had been based solely on hu-man rights, then only a certain segment of Egyptian society would have participated."

As the youth-led Tunisian upheaval further inspired young activists in Egypt, Ghonim was arrested by the secret police. For nearly two weeks, he was held blind-folded and handcuffed, deprived of sleep and subjected to repeated interrogations, as his friends, family and colleagues at Google tried to discover his whereabouts. That he was released as quickly as he was demonstrated the power of Revolution 2.0.

16   A year after Mubarak's ouster, it remains to be seen exactly how and when—or whether—Egypt will transition to a better democracy. What Ghonim's book makes clear, however, is that revolution begins with the self: with what one is willing to stand for online and offline, and what one citizen is willing to risk in the service of his country.

PERSONAL RESPONSE

To what extent have social media affected your life? Have you been moved to action because of something posted on Facebook or Twitter, for instance?

QUESTIONS FOR CLASS OR SMALL-GROUP DISCUSSION

1. This piece is a review of a memoir. How well do you think Vargas balances what the book is about, what the author of the book says, and his own observations?

2. Summarize the effects of Ghonim's creating his Facebook page "We are All Khaled Said."

3. Explain in your own words what Ghonim means when he says that he is "a real-life introvert yet an Internet extrovert" (paragraph 12). What evidence of that statement does Vargas give?

4. The subtitle of Ghonim's book is *The Power of the People is Greater Than the People in Power*. On the basis of what you have read in this article, what do you think that statement means?

PERSPECTIVES ON SOCIAL MEDIA
Suggested Writing Topics

1. In a discussion of whether technology drives us further apart or brings us closer together, Steven Johnson in "Social Connections" admits that "face-to-face" interaction is lost but wonders: "[H]ow important is face-to-face?" (paragraph 9). Write an essay that answers that question. You may want to read Thomas L. Friedman's "The Taxi Driver," which appeared in the *New York Times* on November 1, 2006, and include the views of both Johnson and Friedman in your essay.

2. Explain the usefulness or benefits of a particular social medium, using at least two readings in this chapter.

3. Compare the arguments of Andrew Keen in "Sharing Is a Trap" with Jeff Jarvis's "Get Over It." Which do you think is the more effective argument and why? Are you convinced of the validity of one, both, or neither writer?

4. Explain what Andrew Keen in "Sharing Is a Trap" means when he writes: "Zuckerberg's ideas on 'sharing' could have been invented by Kafka" (paragraph 15). You will have to explain the references to Zuckerberg and Kafka and then why Keen's statement is true (or not).

5. Drawing on Andrew Keen's "Sharing Is a Trap" and Jeff Jarvis's "Get Over It," argue in favor of or against stricter laws governing individual privacy online. What areas would be governed by such legislation? Are individuals themselves responsible for safeguarding their privacy?

6. Write a personal essay on the positive and/or negative aspects of social networks that you are engaged with. Refer to at least one reading in this chapter.

7. Online advertisers argue that they track your shopping and purchasing history online in order to create a profile of you for targeted ads. Argue your position on this issue: are advertisers invading your privacy or making your consumer life more productive, as they might argue? What are the benefits and drawbacks of targeted online advertising? Do the benefits outweigh the drawbacks, or vice versa?

8. Explain the characteristics of a blog that you particularly like to visit, or follow the postings at one blog for a week and do an analysis of the site. Drawing on at least one of the readings in this chapter, explore the impact of digital technology on an aspect of contemporary culture.

9. Read and respond to Steven Levy's *The Perfect Thing*, as mentioned in paragraph 6 of Steven Johnson's "Social Connections."

10. Write a critical analysis of any reading in this chapter, or argue for or against the author's position.

11. Explain what you see as the benefits and/or dangers of the Internet.

12. Explore the direction that you see digital technology going in over the next decade or two.

Research Topics

1. Read several of the references mentioned by Andrew Keen in "Sharing Is a Trap" and take a position on the subject of privacy vs. sharing or another subject suggested by the article. Consider reading Don Tapscott and Anthony D. Williams' *Macrowikinomics*, John Stuart Mills' *On Liberty*, Franz Kafka's *The Trial*, George Orwell's *1984*, and/or any of the other sources that Keen mentions.

2. Read Andrew Keen's Cult *of the Amateur: How the Internet Is Killing Our Culture* and/or *Digital Vertigo: An Anti-Social Manifesto* along with Jeff Jarvis's *What Would Google Do?* and /or *Public Parts: How Sharing in the Digital Age Improves the Way We Work and Live* for a paper on the role of social media in people's lives. Supplement with additional articles or books, form your own position on the subject, and defend your position in paper using the sources you have read.

3. Using Jose Antonio Vargas's "Spring Awakening" as a starting point, research the Arab Spring that began in December 2010 and the role that the Internet played in it. Because there were many uprisings during this period, you may want to give an overview and then focus on one specific revolution. You may want to read Wael Ghonim's *Revolution 2.0* and focus just on the Egyptian uprising, for instance.

4. Research the social impact of networking sites like Facebook or video sharing sites like *YouTube*.

5. Research either the negative or positive effects of social media on behavior. As with any research topic, you will have to do some preliminary research before you can narrow your focus to a manageable topic and workable thesis.

6. Research an area of computer technology that is still in the experimental stages or still being refined.

7. Research the impact of technology in one of the following areas: social networking, medicine, marketing, shopping, entertainment, scholarship/research, American culture, education, or government and politics. You will have to narrow your focus considerably for this subject.

8. Research a problem associated with the Internet such as the availability of pornography for children, the potential dangers of e-mail, the possibility of its use by terrorists, or privacy issues.

RESPONDING TO VISUALS

1. What comment does this cartoon make on the potential negative effects of social media?
2. What sorts of things might the applicant have posted on his Facebook page that would prevent his getting a job?
3. Are there things on your Facebook page that you would not want a potential employer to see?

RESPONDING TO VISUALS

Education Images/Universal Images Group/Getty Images

Huli Wigmen from Papua, New Guinea, use a laptop.

1. What contrasts in the picture does the photographer emphasize?
2. What do you think the men are doing with the laptop? Does it matter that we do not know?
3. What comment does the photograph seem to make about the World Wide Web?

CHAPTER 18

Bioethics

Bioethics has been a growing area of academic interest for several decades. Broadly speaking, it refers to the ethics of biological and health sciences, and its scope encompasses dozens of moral and ethical issues in those areas. Bioethical concerns surround such controversial practices as cloning, cryonics, human genetic engineering, gene therapy, euthanasia, artificial life, chip implants inserted into the brains of humans, and genetically modified foods as well as issues concerning organ donation and transplant, life support, population control, medical research, and the like. Of great interest to bioethicists has been the mapping of the human genome and what to do with the knowledge that resulted.

Research into the complex structure of the human body since James D. Watson and Francis Crick discovered in 1953 that deoxyribonucleic acid (DNA) molecules arrange themselves in a double helix has made enormous advances. The discovery of this pattern in DNA, a substance that transmits the genetic characteristics from one generation to the next, earned Watson and Crick a Nobel Prize in 1962. Their discovery led other scientists to work on such things as recombinant DNA and gene splicing in the 1970s and eventually to the Human Genome Project, whose goal was to map the entire sequence of human DNA. A genome is the complete set of instructions for making a human being. Each nucleus of the 100 trillion cells that make up the human body contains this set of instructions, which is written in the language of DNA. This major undertaking by scientists around the world promises to provide medical doctors with the tools to predict the development of human diseases. When the project began in 1988, scientists thought that it would take fifteen years to complete, but the project progressed faster than first predicted and was finished well ahead of schedule.

Now that the human code has been mapped, scientists can begin to better understand how humans grow, what causes human diseases, and what new drugs would combat those diseases by either preventing or curing them. Scientists already are able to identify variations or defects in the genetic makeup of certain cells in human bodies that may result in diseases with genetic origins. Eventually, they will be able to develop tests of an individual's likelihood of developing one of thousands of inherited diseases such as sickle-cell anemia, cystic fibrosis, or muscular dystrophy, and even heart disease or cancer. Because more than 30,000 genes make up the "instruction manual" for the human body, it will take some time before all of them are codified and their functions known. The Human Genome Project raised a number of difficult ethical questions, however, as two of the essays in this chapter indicate.

In "Patenting Life," Michael Crichton takes up one of the ethical issues that grew out of the success of the Human Genome Project when he explains why genes are allowed to be patented and how that affects everyone's lives, not just those suffering from particular medical problems. He raises objections to the patenting of genes and urges support of a House Bill introduced to stop it. In contrast, John E. Calfee reviews the issue and concludes that there are few major problems with allowing genes to be patented. In "Decoding the Use of Gene Patents," he mentions key objections to patenting genes, such as those that Crichton mentions. He explains the process of getting a patent and the uses that patent holders make of holding the patent to genes. As you read these two essays by writers with opposing viewpoints on this important issue, consider whether you are persuaded by Crichton's arguments that patenting genes is a bad practice or by Calfee's evidence that the practice is far from bad.

The other two essays look at ethical issues raised by the marketing of human organs, specifically kidneys. Miriam Schulman, director of the Markkula Center for Applied Ethics at Santa Clara University, examines the benefits and drawbacks of legalizing kidney sales. In "Kidneys for Sale: A Reconsideration," she asks, "Should such transactions be legalized? What are the ethical questions we should ask about the sale of kidneys?" She then looks closely at the issues and offers suggestions on how such ethical questions can be addressed. Finally, the title of Anthony Gregory's piece, "Why Legalizing Organ Sales Would Help to Save Lives, End Violence," indicates clearly what position he takes on the matter of whether kidney sales should be legalized or not. When reading these essays, pay special attention to the ethical considerations that must be taken into account on the issue of whether kidney sales should be legalized or not. Where do you stand on this issue?

PATENTING LIFE

MICHAEL CRICHTON

*Michael Crichton (1942–2008), was an author, critic, and film pro-
ducer. While earning his degree from Harvard Medical School, he
began writing novels. Among his twenty-five novels are such bestsell-
ers as* The Andromeda Strain *(1969),* The Terminal Man *(1972),*
The Great Train Robbery *(1975),* Sphere *(1987),* Jurassic Park
(1990), Airframe *(1996), and his last,* Pirate Latitudes *(2009). He
was also creator and co-producer of the long-running television drama*
ER. *This essay appeared as an op-ed piece in the February 13, 2007,
edition of the* New York Times.

You, or someone you love, may die because of a gene patent that should never have
been granted in the first place. Sounds far-fetched? Unfortunately, it's only too real.

Gene patents are now used to halt research, prevent medical testing, and
keep vital information from you and your doctor. Gene patents slow the pace of
medical advance on deadly diseases. And they raise costs exorbitantly: a test for
breast cancer that could be done for $1,000 now costs $3,000.

Why? Because the holder of the gene patent can charge whatever he wants,
and does. Couldn't somebody make a cheaper test? Sure, but the patent holder
blocks any competitor's test. He owns the gene. Nobody else can test for it. In
fact, you can't even donate your own breast cancer gene to another scientist without permission. The gene may exist in your body, but it's now private property.

4   This bizarre situation has come to pass because of a mistake by an underfinanced
and understaffed government agency. The United States Patent Office misinter-
preted previous Supreme Court rulings and some years ago began—to the surprise
of everyone, including scientists decoding the genome—to issue patents on genes.

Humans share mostly the same genes. The same genes are found in other
animals as well. Our genetic makeup represents the common heritage of all life on
earth. You can't patent snow, eagles, or gravity, and you shouldn't be able to patent
genes, either. Yet by now one-fifth of the genes in your body are privately owned.

The results have been disastrous. Ordinarily, we imagine patents promote
innovation, but that's because most patents are granted for human inventions.
Genes aren't human inventions, they are features of the natural world. As a result
these patents can be used to block innovation, and hurt patient care.

For example, Canavan disease is an inherited disorder that affects children
starting at 3 months; they cannot crawl or walk, they suffer seizures and eventually become paralyzed and die by adolescence. Formerly there was no test to tell

parents if they were at risk. Families enduring the heartbreak of caring for these children engaged a researcher to identify the gene and produce a test. Canavan families around the world donated tissue and money to help this cause.

8   When the gene was identified in 1993, the families got the commitment of a New York hospital to offer a free test to anyone who wanted it. But the researcher's employer, Miami Children's Hospital Research Institute, patented the gene and refused to allow any health care provider to offer the test without paying a royalty. The parents did not believe genes should be patented and so did not put their names on the patent. Consequently, they had no control over the outcome.

In addition, a gene's owner can in some instances also own the mutations of that gene, and these mutations can be markers for disease. Countries that don't have gene patents actually offer better gene testing than we do, because when multiple labs are allowed to do testing, more mutations are discovered, leading to higher-quality tests.

Apologists for gene patents argue that the issue is a tempest in a teapot, that patent licenses are readily available at minimal cost. That's simply untrue. The owner of the genome for Hepatitis C is paid millions by researchers to study this disease. Not surprisingly, many other researchers choose to study something less expensive.

But forget the costs: why should people or companies own a disease in the first place? They didn't invent it. Yet today, more than 20 human pathogens are privately owned, including haemophilus influenza and Hepatitis C. And we've already mentioned that tests for the BRCA genes for breast cancer cost $3,000. Oh, one more thing: if you undergo the test, the company that owns the patent on the gene can keep your tissue and do research on it without asking your permission. Don't like it? Too bad.

12   The plain truth is that gene patents aren't benign and never will be. When SARS was spreading across the globe, medical researchers hesitated to study it—because of patent concerns. There is no clearer indication that gene patents block innovation, inhibit research, and put us all at risk.

Even your doctor can't get relevant information. An asthma medication only works in certain patients. Yet its manufacturer has squelched efforts by others to develop genetic tests that would determine on whom it will and will not work. Such commercial considerations interfere with a great dream. For years we've been promised the coming era of personalized medicine—medicine suited to our particular body makeup. Gene patents destroy that dream.

Fortunately, two congressmen want to make the full benefit of the decoded genome available to us all. Last Friday, Xavier Becerra, a Democrat of California, and Dave Weldon, a Republican of Florida, sponsored the Genomic Research and Accessibility Act, to ban the practice of patenting genes found in nature. Mr. Becerra has been careful to say the bill does not hamper invention, but rather promotes it. He's right. This bill will fuel innovation, and return our common genetic heritage to us. It deserves our support.

PERSONAL RESPONSE

Crichton believes that "you shouldn't be able to patent genes" (paragraph 5). Do you agree with him? Explain your answer.

QUESTIONS FOR CLASS OR SMALL-GROUP DISCUSSION

1. What are the negative effects of gene patents, according to Crichton?
2. What do supporters of gene patents argue, according to Crichton? Do you think that Crichton effectively addresses those arguments?
3. How well do you think that Crichton argues his position? What argumentative strategies does he use?
4. Do you believe that Crichton has considered all sides of the issue? If not, what do you think he has overlooked?

DECODING THE USE OF GENE PATENTS

JOHN E. CALFEE

John E. Calfee (1941–2011) was a resident scholar at the American Enterprise Institute (AEI) for sixteen years as well as a staff economist and manager in the Bureau of Economics at the Federal Trade Commission. His books include Prices, Markets, and the Pharmaceutical Revolution *(2000) and* Biotechnology and the Patent System *(2007). This article was posted on May 15, 2009, in* American, *the online magazine of the AEI.*

The New York Times ran a story on May 13 about a lawsuit brought by a breast cancer patient and several co-plaintiffs against Myriad Genetics, a biotech firm that owns a patent to a diagnostic test for the BRCA-1 and BRCA-2 genes (not mentioned by name in the story), which are involved in a particularly dangerous form of breast and ovarian cancer. These kinds of cancers rarely respond to targeted biotech treatments such as Herceptin, so the BRCA test can help inform treatment and encourage use of preventive measures. The lawsuit apparently originated from the lead plaintiff's discovery that this rather expensive test (about $3,000) is offered only by Myriad and must be performed on their premises in Salt Lake City, Utah because Myriad owns not only a patent for the test but also for the BRCA genes themselves. The plaintiffs think the U.S. Patent and Trademark Office (PTO) grievously erred when it granted these patents and, in

This article was reprinted with permission from *The American* magazine, a publication of the American Enterprise Institute. Web address: www.american.com.

fact, has erred in granting any gene patents at all. One of the academic researchers and co-plaintiffs was quoted to the effect that gene patents like this one not only increase medical costs but impede academic research.

The *Times* story, which I suspect was better balanced than many of the news stories soon to follow, noted that a 2006 report from the National Academy of Sciences found little evidence that gene patents had adversely affected research. As you might expect, there is more to this story, although the bottom line is consistent with the academy's report rather than with the tenor of the *Times* article as a whole. Human genes can be patented, but not simply by decoding a snippet of DNA and sending a sequence of the letters A, G, C, and T to the PTO. You have to isolate and purify the gene segment in a way that does not occur in nature, and you have to establish some sort of concrete use—"utility" is the standard word—in order to satisfy PTO standards. Gene patents were extremely controversial when the PTO started awarding them (more details are available in a book published by American Enterprise Institute resident scholar Claude Barfield and me). The PTO prevailed against considerable academic and political opposition, however, and eventually the European Union followed suit. A little-appreciated part of this story is that a lot of these patents have been filed not by private firms but by universities on behalf of their researchers. As it happens, some of the BRCA patents are actually co-owned by Myriad's neighbor, the University of Utah.

There are really two complaints about gene patents. One is that when a gene patent gives a seller a monopoly over a product, that product will be sold at monopoly prices, which can be much higher than the competitive price—and moreover, as the plaintiff in the gene patent litigation noticed, that single seller can restrict how a diagnostic is used in addition to how it is priced. Of course, that is what we expect with patented products, and like most economists I support the granting of patents and their consequent pricing power as a tool to foster innovation.

4   There is another possible problem with gene patents, however: they could get in the way of research. As an academic plaintiff noted in the *Times* story, research often involves sifting through all sorts of genetic details including ones that happen to have been patented by someone else. One potentially disastrous scenario is a "patent thicket" in which research is hemmed in by the possibility of bumping into all sorts of patents, such as those the researcher never knew existed. Hundreds or thousands of patent infringement suits could ensue with their legendary costs and delay. In theory, elaborate patent pools could forestall this problem but that would be costly, too, in terms of patent searches and multi-party negotiations.

A number of interested parties including the National Academy of Sciences sought to explore these problems. On the whole, the news is very good. The NAS has twice commissioned surveys led by John Walsh, a well-qualified expert, and both times, little evidence emerged that research laboratories were hemmed in by gene patents (summarized in the same NAS report cited earlier). It turns out that researchers seldom worry about what is patented and what is not. Moreover, litigation has been amazingly rare. That was documented in a 2008 article in *Science* magazine, which found that only six lawsuits had been filed in connection with gene-patented diagnostics and all had been dismissed or settled, apparently with negligible impact on scholarly research. Just two months ago, the journal *Nature*, Britain's version of *Science* (or the other way around, the Brits could justifiably claim), published two articles and an editorial on gene patents. The title of one of those articles, "The Phantom Menace of Gene Patents" is a pretty good summary of the latest findings. The other article concluded that "prices of patented and exclusively licensed tests are not dramatically or consistently higher than those of tests without a monopoly"—a very different scenario from that suggested by the Myriad lawsuit. An accompanying editorial, which emphasized academic gene patenting and was entitled "Property Rights," concluded that "dire predictions that patents will cripple genetics research should be viewed with skepticism on both sides of the Atlantic."

This is not to say there have been no problems at all. But the PTO has resisted parties' over-reaching, such as by attempting to file thousands of gene patents simultaneously with scant attention to "utility." And there is much to be said for broad licensing of gene patents and diagnostics based upon them. On the whole, though, gene patents are turning out to work more or less the way patents are supposed to work and have been working for a couple of centuries and more. The research process, and ultimately patients, are the beneficiaries.

PERSONAL RESPONSE

If you have read the previous essay by Michael Crichton, are you convinced that patenting genes is not only *not* harmful, as Crichton says it is, but beneficial? If you have not read the Crichton piece, explain whether you agree with Calfee.

QUESTIONS FOR CLASS OR SMALL-GROUP DISCUSSION

1. Summarize the nature of the lawsuit that Calfee mentions at the beginning of his essay.
2. State in your own words what the "two complaints about gene patents" are (paragraph 3).
3. What evidence does Calfee use to argue against the complaints about gene patents?
4. Although his essay was not written in response to Michael Crichton's "Patenting Life," Calfee does discuss some of the points that Crichton raises in his essay. How well do you think he counters what Crichton says?

KIDNEYS FOR SALE: A RECONSIDERATION

Miriam Schulman

Miriam Schulman is assistant director of the Markkula Center for Applied Ethics at Santa Clara University, where she manages communication and administrative activities at the Center. She has published articles on various aspects of ethics, including ethical choices that college students face, the ethics of online privacy invasion, the ethics of business practices, and, as here, the ethics of marketing kidneys. This article was published on the Markkula Center Web site in April 2012.

In 1988, the Markkula Center for Applied Ethics published an article, "Kidneys for Sale," which was posted about ten years later on our Web site. It addressed the ethical issues raised by the potential for a market in human body parts.

That article has inspired sporadic emails from people asking for advice about how to sell their organs. In recent years, as the economy has soured, we've noticed an uptick in the number of such messages. Here's a sample:

> I just read your information about how many people need a kidney. I would like more information about it and how I could sell one of my kidneys to your university because I really need money. I want to go to college, but it's really expensive.

These correspondents raise some of the hard questions that are inspiring a reevaluation of the question: Should organ donation remain a completely altruistic "gift of life," or should donors be compensated? The Center's Emerging Issues Group, which meets weekly to discuss ethical issues in the news, addressed these questions at a recent session. This article outlines some of the crucial considerations raised during this discussion.

A Shortage of Donated Organs

4   First, a few facts about the acute shortage of kidneys. As of March 6, the waiting list in the United States for all organs was 113,143, with 91,015 waiting for kidneys. In 2011, there were a total of 15,417 kidney transplants in the United States, 10,185 from deceased donors and 5,232 from living donors.

"Data such as these underscore just how scarce organs are," says Margaret McLean, director of bioethics at the Markkula Center for Applied Ethics. "About 17 people die every day while waiting for a suitable organ. Although numerous strategies have been tried to increase the number of donors—from pink dots on driver's licenses to PR campaigns to donor reciprocal chains to organ swapping—we continue to come up short."

That shortage has led to many violations of both US and international laws against kidney sales. For example, this month the Chinese news agency Xinhua reported that a 17-year-old sold his kidney, which is illegal in China, to get enough money for an iPhone. He is now suffering from renal insufficiency. "Only the truly naïve imagine that organs are not currently being sold on the black market," McLean says. The International Business Times estimates that illegal organ sales constitute a $75 million per year industry.

Should such transactions be legalized? What are the ethical questions we should ask about the sale of kidneys?

The Commodification of Human Life

8   Even if legalizing organ sales might inspire more donations, many ethicists reject this approach because they fear where it may lead: to the commodification of human life. Cynthia Cohen from the Kennedy Institute of Ethics at Georgetown writes, "Human beings ... are of incomparable ethical worth and admit of no equivalent. Each has a value that is beyond the contingencies of supply and demand or of any other relative estimation. They are priceless. Consequently, to sell an integral human body part is to corrupt the very meaning of human dignity."

Despite these concerns, the black market itself has put a value on human organs—about $5,000 according to most reports. Peter Minowitz, professor of political science at SCU, suggests, "The actuality is there's a thriving market for organs, even crossing global boundaries. So even though the sale of organs may, in itself, violate human dignity, that dignity is being violated now on a fairly large scale, especially among the most desperate. Maybe it would be better for them if we legalized the sale and imposed certain standards on it. It's a very complicated series of considerations, mixing moral judgment with what's going on in the real world."

Do No Harm

Undoubtedly, increasing the supply of living donors would be good for organ recipients. According to the Organ Procurement and Transplantation Network, about 90 percent of people who receive a living-donor kidney and 82 percent of those who received a deceased-donor kidney were alive five years after the transplant.

But what happens to the donors? "Usually, in medical ethics, we are looking at harm and good respective to a single patient," says McLean. "Here we are looking at harm and good for two patients where good is going to accrue to one and potential harm to the other."

12   Generally, kidney donation from a living donor is seen as a relatively safe procedure, as the human body functions adequately with only one kidney. The mortality rate for the removal of a kidney (nephrectomy) is between 0.02 and 0.03 percent, major complications affect 1.5 percent of patients, and minor complications affect 8.5 percent. The University of Maryland Transplant Center states:

> The risks of donation are similar to those involved with any major surgery, such as bleeding and infection. Death resulting from kidney donation is extremely rare. Current research indicates that kidney donation does not change life expectancy or increase a person's risks of developing kidney disease or other health problems.

While this picture may accurately reflect the experience of donors in first world countries, those in the developing world report less benign outcomes. Madhav Goyal, Ravindra Mehta, Lawrence Schneiderman, and Ashwini Sehgal studied 305 residents of Chennai, India, who had sold their organs. Participants were asked to rate their health status before and after the operation. Eighty-nine percent of the respondents reported at least some decline in their health. "Fifty percent complained of persistent pain at the nephrectomy site and 33 percent complained of long-term back pain."

McLean points out that society also incurs risks when someone donates a kidney. "Who pays if the donor is harmed or develops renal failure of unrelated etiology 15 years later and needs a transplant?" she asks.

In bioethics, where the first rule is "Do no harm," can the sale of kidneys be judged to conform to this basic principle? Are there better ways to protect donors so that no disproportional harm comes to them?

The Problem of Exploitation and Informed Consent

16   The Indian experience points to another of the key objections that have been raised against the sale of organs: the danger that poor people will be exploited in the transaction. Nicky Santos, S.J., visiting scholar at the Ethics Center and an expert on marketing strategy for impoverished market segments, argues strongly that desperation "drives the poor to make choices which are not really in their best interests." Such lopsided transactions may exacerbate already existing inequities, where the rich have access to excellent health care and the poor do not.

That was the conclusion of the Bellagio Task Force Report to the International Red Cross on "Transplantation, Bodily Integrity, and the International Traffic in Organs":

> Existing social and political inequities are such that commercialization would put powerless and deprived people at still graver risk. The physical well-being of disadvantaged populations, especially in developing countries, is already placed in jeopardy by a variety of causes, including the hazards of inadequate nutrition, substandard housing, unclean water, and parasitic infection. In these circumstances, adding organ sale to this roster would be to subject an already vulnerable group to yet another threat to its physical health and bodily integrity.

On the other hand, some view this attitude as paternalistic. "You could raise the question," says Michael McFarland, S.J. "Are the rich or those in power in a position to tell the poor they are not capable of making a decision? Doesn't that violate their human dignity? It seems to me that a person in desperate circumstances could be making a perfectly rational decision that the sale of a kidney is in his or her best interests."

McFarland, a Center visiting scholar and the former president of College of the Holy Cross, goes on, "You could see the sale of organs as a way for the poor to derive some benefit from donating an organ, which they wouldn't otherwise get.

For example, if a poor person was willing to donate a kidney but couldn't afford to take the time off, wouldn't it be reasonable to allow him or her to be compensated for that time?"

20   More people might be persuaded by this argument if, in fact, kidney sales really did help the poor financially. But in India, donors often did not receive the benefit they expected from the sale of their organs. Ninety-six percent of the people in the study had agreed to the donation to pay off a debt, but six years after the operation, 74 percent of those studied still owed money.

Most of the benefit from organ sales goes to middlemen. Havocscope, which monitors black markets, found last May that the average reported amount paid to kidney donors was $5,000, while the average price paid by recipients was $150,000. "The real injustice to the poor is they are getting so little, while those who are involved in these illegal sales are getting all the money," says Rev. Brendan McGuire, vicar general of the Diocese of San Jose.

Santos believes that the poor cannot really make free decisions to sell their organs because they are so driven by their dire circumstances. McFarland agrees that the issue of consent is the real sticking point for creating a market for organs. "I think what stops us is the concern about being able to count on a genuine free consent on the part of the donor." But he does not believe any moral absolute makes the sale of kidneys unacceptable. "It comes back to the issue of truly informed consent. Do people understand the risks they are taking on? Are those acceptable risks? Are people capable of making free decisions about whether to take those risks?"

Altruism or Justice

Informed consent is, of course, as crucial for organ donation as it would be for organ sale. But donation frames the process as a wholly altruistic act. "For a living donor," says McLean, "it may be a chance to help a family member or friend or even a stranger." For a person signing on to donate organs after death, it may be seen as a way to give back or not to die in vain. And for the family of a deceased donor, it's "a way to have a little bit of someone alive in the world," she continues.

24   Many people value this altruistic aspect of the current system and do not want to see organ donation reduced to a business transaction. But, McFarland asks, "Is it the wisest and most moral policy to run a social system like kidney donation entirely on altruism?" That may be the ideal, he agrees, but since it has not been very effective at meeting the need for organs, it may be better to "strive for justice and not depend totally on altruism."

The idea of justice encompasses concern about the exploitation of the poor, but it raises even broader concerns about fairness. These might be summed up in another email we received at the Ethics Center:

> So what? Is the sale of one's kidney lawful? Morality or ethics has nothing to do with it when you're down and out. Why doesn't someone ask the same of doctors and hospitals when they sell the transplant operation? Why is it when John Q. Public sees a way into the open markets, that he gets hit with the morality/ethical questions?

Is it fair that everyone involved in organ transplantation—doctors, hospital, nurses, recipient—gets something out of the process except the donor or the donor's family?

Also, donors on the black market are rarely paid anything approaching what the kidney is worth. Justice might be better served if donors were paid more. In the Indian study, the average price of an organ in 2001 was $1,410. Nobel Laureate in Economics Gary Becker and his colleague Julio Elias have calculated $45,000 as a fair price. Fairer, still say some ethicists, would be a system that pays the donor a figure closer to the actual cost of maintaining a patient on the waiting list for organs, including the cost of dialysis over many years. Arthur Matas and Mark Schnitzler have calculated that a transplant from a living unrelated donor would save at least $94,579.

28   Alternatively, the donor wouldn't necessarily need to be paid to be compensated. McLean reviews some other proposals to give something back to donors: "One suggestion has been to at least offer to pay funeral expenses for a deceased donor because for many people that's a stumbling block. For live donors—and this could be hugely attractive in the current environment—we might offer to cover their health care for the rest of their lives in exchange for doing this good."

Another cut at fairness has recently been adopted by Israel and is advocated in the United States by the private organization Life Sharers. Top priority on Israel's waiting list goes to candidates who have themselves agreed to be donors. Those who don't sign up as donors get a transplant only if there is an excess of organs.

All proposals to allow the sale of organs raise ethical as well as medical risks. However, as E.A. Friedman and A.L. Friedman argue in Kidney International, Journal of the International Society of Nephrology:

> At least debating the controlled initiation and study of potential regimens that may increase donor kidney supply in the future in a scientifically and ethically responsible manner, is better than doing nothing more productive than complaining about the current system's failure.

PERSONAL RESPONSE

Do you know of anyone who needs or has had an organ transplant? Do you know of anyone who has donated or plans to donate an organ? How do you think you would respond to a friend who says that he or she plans to donate a kidney to a loved one?

QUESTIONS FOR CLASS OR SMALL-GROUP DISCUSSION

1. Schulman asks in paragraph 7 if the sale of kidneys should be legalized. How well does she answer that question?
2. How does the fact that there is a large number of black market sales of organs, especially from third world countries, advance the proposition that kidney sales should be legalized?

3. Schulman sets up a series of questions or issues that need addressing. Summarize the issues, select one that you particularly agree or disagree with, and explain why.

4. Do you think that making organ sales legal and regulating compensations for donors are workable solutions to the problem? What about legalizing other currently illegal trafficking such as prostitution, drugs, or other behaviors that support underground criminal activities? Would making them legal solve the problems?

WHY LEGALIZING ORGAN SALES WOULD HELP TO SAVE LIVES, END VIOLENCE

Anthony Gregory

Anthony Gregory is a research fellow and student programs director at the Independent Institute and is author of The Power of Habeas Corpus in America: From the King's Prerogative to the War on Terror *(2013). He has written hundreds of articles for a wide range of magazines and newspapers. This article was first published in the November 2011 issue of* The Atlantic.

Last month, New Yorker Levy Izhak Rosenbaum pled guilty in federal court to the crime of facilitating illegal kidney transplants. It has been deemed the first proven case of black market organ trafficking in the United States. His lawyers argue that his lawbreaking was benevolent: "The transplants were successful and the donors and recipients are now leading full and healthy lives."

Indeed, why are organ sales illegal? Donors of blood, semen, and eggs, and volunteers for medical trials, are often compensated. Why not apply the same principle to organs?

The very idea of legalization might sound gruesome to most people, but it shouldn't, especially since research shows it would save lives. In the United States, where the 1984 National Organ Transplantation Act prohibits compensation for organ donating, there are only about 20,000 kidneys every year for the approximately 80,000 patients on the waiting list. In 2008, nearly 5,000 died waiting.

4   Many protest that an organ market will lead to unfair advantages for the rich, but this is a characteristic of the current trade.

A global perspective shows how big the problem is. "Millions of people suffer from kidney disease, but in 2007 there were just 64,606 kidney-transplant operations in the entire world," according to George Mason University professor and Independent Institute research director Alexander Tabarrok, writing in the *Wall Street Journal*.

Almost every other country has prohibitions like America's. In Iran, however, selling one's kidney for profit is legal. There are no patients anguishing on the waiting list. The Iranians have solved their kidney shortage by legalizing sales.

Many will protest that an organ market will lead to exploitation and unfair advantages for the rich and powerful. But these are the characteristics of the current illicit organ trade. Moreover, as with drug prohibition today and alcohol prohibition in the 1920s, pushing a market underground is the way to make it rife with violence and criminality.

8   In Japan, for the right price, you can buy livers and kidneys harvested from executed Chinese prisoners. Three years ago in India, police broke up an organ ring that had taken as many as 500 kidneys from poor laborers. The World Health Organization estimates that the black market accounts for 20 percent of kidney transplants worldwide. Everywhere from Latin America to the former Soviet Republics, from the Philippines to South Africa, a huge network has emerged typified by threats, coercion, intimidation, extortion, and shoddy surgeries.

Although not every black market transaction is exploitative—demonstrating that organ sales, in and of themselves, are not the problem—the most unsavory parts of the trade can be attributed to the fact that it is illegal. Witnessing the horror stories, many are calling on governments to crack down even more severely. Unfortunately, prohibition drives up black-market profits, turns the market over to organized crime, and isolates those harmed in the trade from the normal routes of recourse.

Several years ago, transplant surgeon Nadley Hakim at St. Mary's Hospital in London pointed out that "this trade is going on anyway, why not have a controlled trade where if someone wants to donate a kidney for a particular price, that would be acceptable? If it is done safely, the donor will not suffer."

Bringing the market into the open is the best way to ensure the trade's appropriate activity. Since the stakes would be very high, market forces and social pressure would ensure that people are not intimidated or defrauded. In the United States, attitudes are not so casual as to allow gross degeneracy. Enabling a process by which consenting people engage in open transactions would mitigate the exploitation of innocent citizens and underhanded dealing by those seeking to skirt the law.

12   The most fundamental case for legalizing organ sales—an appeal to civil liberty—has proven highly controversial. Liberals like to say, "my body, my choice," and conservatives claim to favor free markets, but true self-ownership would include the right to sell one's body parts, and genuine free enterprise would imply a market in human organs. In any event, studies show that this has become a matter of life and death.

Perhaps the key to progress is more widespread exposure to the facts. In 2008, six experts took on this issue in an Oxford-style debate hosted by National Public Radio. By the end, those in the audience who favored allowing the market climbed from 44 to 60 percent.

Yet, the organ trade continues to operate in the shadows and questionable activities occur in the medical establishment under the color of law. Even today, doctors sometimes legally harvest organ tissue from dead patients without consent. Meanwhile, thousands are perishing and even more are suffering while we wait for the system to change.

The truly decent route would be to allow people to withhold or give their organs freely, especially upon death, even if in exchange for money. Thousands of lives would be saved. Once again, humanitarianism is best served by the respect for civil liberty, and yet we are deprived both, with horribly unfortunate consequences, just to maintain the pretense of state-enforced propriety.

PERSONAL RESPONSE

Would you be willing to donate an organ to a close friend or relative? Write for a few minutes explaining your answer.

QUESTIONS FOR CLASS OR SMALL-GROUP DISCUSSION

1. What explanation does Gregory give for why legalizing organ sales would help save lives and end violence? Are you convinced?
2. In paragraph 4, Gregory writes that people protest that "an organ market will lead to unfair advantages for the rich." What does he have to say to that argument? Do you agree with him?
3. Gregory says that "the most fundamental case for legalizing organ sales [is] an appeal to civil liberty" (paragraph 12). What does he mean by that? To what extent do you agree with him?
4. Assess this article as an argument. What are its strengths and weaknesses? Do you find it logical, with valid evidence and/or convincing proof? If you have read Miriam Schulman's "Kidneys for Sale: A Reconsideration," how do the two arguments compare?

PERSPECTIVES ON BIOETHICS

Suggested Writing Topics

1. Compare the views of Miriam Schulman ("Kidneys for Sale: A Reconsideration") and Anthony Gregory ("Why Legalizing Organs Would Help to Save Lives, End Violence"). Explain where you agree with them, where you disagree, and/or where you have real concerns about what the writers say.
2. Compare the views of Michael Crichton in "Patenting Life" and John E. Calfee in "Decoding the Use of Gene Patents" and explain which one you find more persuasive and why.

3. Argue for or against the right of pharmaceutical companies to hold patents on genes.

4. Argue your position on any of the issues raised in this chapter by responding to the author of the article.

5. Explore one of the ethical, social, or legal problems associated with the patenting of genes or the selling of human organs, referring to at least two of the readings in this chapter. State and defend your own position on the subject.

6. Write an essay on another issue besides the ones identified by the authors of the articles in this chapter that needs to be looked at closely. Consider any of these, which are also listed in the research topics section as possible subjects for lengthier papers that incorporate many sources: increasing incentives for organ donation, access to expensive treatments for self-induced health problems, embryo research, mandatory testing for HIV diseases, compulsory genetic screening for certain risk groups, cryonics, human genetic engineering, artificial life, or genetically modified foods.

7. Interview professionals such as a molecular biologist, an ethics professor, or someone else familiar with genetics research on the ethical, social, and/or legal problems associated with the Human Genome Project or stem cell research. Draw on the views of the professionals whom you interview as you explain your own position on the subject.

Research Topics

1. Michael Crichton in "Patenting Life" says that "gene patents block innovation, inhibit research and put us all at risk," whereas John E. Calfee in "Decoding the Use of Gene Patents" concludes that such patents work the way they are supposed to and "ultimately, the patients are the beneficiaries." Using information cited by both writers as a starting point, research the subject of gene patents and draw your own conclusion about the benefits and drawbacks of patenting genes.

2. Research the National Organ Transplant Act of 1984—what it restricts and allows, what its impact has been on organ transplants, and whether you think it should remain in effect as it is, be amended or revised, or be repealed. Consider the opinions of Miriam Schulman in "Kidneys for Sale: A Reconsideration" and Anthony Gregory in "Why Legalizing Organs Would Help to Save Lives, End Violence" in your research.

3. Research the current state of the controversy over stem cell research, perhaps looking at your own state's laws and federal laws prohibit or allow; then state your own position on the subject, giving its current ethical and legal status.

4. Besides the issues raised in the readings in this chapter, there are numerous other medical issues that raise moral and ethical questions. Research one of the following, explore various viewpoints on the controversy, and

arrive at your own conclusion: increasing incentives for organ donation, universal health care, access to expensive treatments for self-induced health problems, embryo research, mandatory testing for HIV diseases, compulsory genetic screening for certain risk groups or during premarital examinations, the status of genetic disease and genetic therapy, cryonics, human genetic engineering, gene therapy, artificial life, or genetically modified foods. Research the Human Genome Project, and write a paper in which you elaborate on its main objectives, provide representative views on the controversy surrounding it, and explain your own position and why you believe as you do.

5. Research the Genomic Research and Accessibility Act mentioned by Michael Crichton in "Patenting Life." Find out what conditions led to its proposal, what arguments have been made in support of or against it, whether it has passed the House and gone to the Senate, and/or other aspects of the proposed bill.

6. Research the question: Should scientists create human life? Consider pros and cons and arrive at your own conclusion.

7. Select an issue in the area of neurotechnology, such as transcranial magnetic stimulation, implantable brain chips, brain imaging, cochlear implants, lie detection technologies, deep brain stimulators, brain computer interfaces, forensic neuroscience, or neuromarketing. Research the controversy over the issue and arrive at your own conclusion.

8. Research some aspect of the history and/or practice of eugenics, such as the program of Nazi Germany under Hitler or US programs for forced sterilization for mentally ill patients.

RESPONDING TO VISUALS

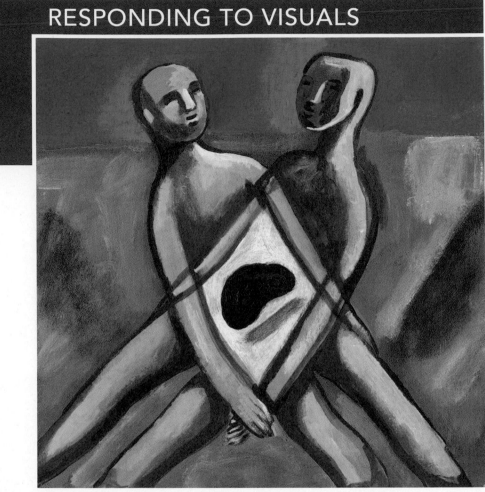

Medical transplantation.

1. What image is created by overlapping the two bodies?
2. Comment on the composition of the image and its use of color. How do those work together to create a striking image?
3. What would you guess is the artist's opinion of organ transplants?

RESPONDING TO VISUALS

JES AZNAR/AFP/Getty Images

Approximately three thousand residents of this slum in Manila have sold their kidneys to escape from poverty.

1. What does this photograph tell you about slum dwellings?
2. What do you imagine it is like to live in a slum like this? Why do you suppose the photographer included children in the picture?
3. Do you think that the image implies a rationale or reason for why three thousand residents of this slum might have sold their kidneys?

CHAPTER 19

Environmental Studies

Environmental issues such as depletion of the ozone layer, global warming, deforestation, and air and water pollution are just a few of the many causes for concern over the health of animal and vegetable life on Earth. Closely connected to these environmental problems is the rapid rate of increase in the world population. As the number of people grows, pressure increases on natural resources. Will Earth provide enough food for everyone? How can water supplies be kept safe for drinking? How does pollution produced by so many humans affect the quality of the air they breathe? How can people stop the ever-widening hole in the ozone layer that protects us from the harmful rays of the sun? How will future generations sustain the rapidly increasing worldwide population? These are just some of the questions confronting scientists, civic leaders, and ordinary people everywhere.

Although most people recognize that humans must keep their environments safe, not everyone agrees on either the nature of the problems or the severity of their consequences. For instance, resource depletion and global warming are the subjects of many debates. Researchers and scientists differ in their beliefs on questions such as Earth's ability to sustain life indefinitely and whether Earth is experiencing global warming and, if so, whether the phenomenon is a cause for alarm.

In the first piece in this chapter, Julia Whitty reports on the widespread invasion of various deadly species in many parts of the world. Explaining how such things as the brown tree snake, the rosy wolfsnail, the red lionfish, the Humboldt squid, and various other creatures have invaded areas where they were previously not found and have devoured, literally, dozens if not hundreds of species, she provides fascinating insight into the devastating effects of biological invasions, which she says are second only to loss of habit as a cause of extinction. Her article is rich with details as she outlines the causal relationship between the introduction of alien species into populations with no defense against them and the subsequent extinction of those defenseless species. Her discussion is framed by a personal account of her visit with an aboriginal couple in Australia, who complain about the invasion of the pond apple native to the Florida Everglades choking out their beloved melaleuca trees. Ironically, Whitty notes, Floridians complain about the melaleuca tree choking out their beloved pond apples. The article touches on many ecological issues, including, briefly, global warming. That subject is taken up by the next author.

In the next reading, Bill McKibben makes an impassioned plea for activism in "Global Warning: Get Up! Stand Up!" Pointing out that previously identified environmental problems were fixable with both changes in behavior as well as legislatively mandated changes, he maintains that Congress has "failed to take on the single greatest challenge human civilization has ever faced." His subtitle, "How to Build a Mass Movement to Halt Climate Change," is a clear indication of the subject of his essay. As you read McKibben's piece, notice his argumentative strategies and ask yourself whether you are persuaded to take action as he so urgently presses his readers to do.

Two more argumentative essays complete the chapter, with each writer seeking to persuade audiences to act. Jeff Corwin in "The Sixth Extinction" gives startling facts about the rapid extinction of species. He points out that somewhere on Earth, "every 20 minutes we lose an animal species." With examples of dying species from several areas of the globe, Corwin hopes to persuade readers to "rise to the cause." Finally, in "Accounting 101 for the 21st Century: A Liberal Arts Education in Carbon," John Petersen urges administrators, instructors, and students on college and university campuses across the nation to respond to the environmental challenge. Using the example of his own institution, Oberlin College, he explains how across the curriculum and across the campus, colleges and universities can act positively to meet the challenges to ensure global environmental health.

WHAT EVERGLADES PYTHONS AND OTHER INVASIVE SPECIES ARE TRYING TO TELL US

JULIA WHITTY

Julia Whitty is the environmental correspondent for Mother Jones *magazine. She is author of a short story collection,* A Tortoise for the Queen

Reprinted from Mother Jones, January/February 2009. © 2009, Foundation for National Progress.

of Tonga *(2002), and the nonfiction books* The Fragile Edge: Diving & Other Adventures in the South Pacific *(2007) and* Deep Blue Home: An Intimate Ecology of Our Wild Ocean *(2010). A former film-maker, Whitty has produced more than seventy nature documentaries for television. She blogs at* The Blue Marble *and* Deep Blue Home. *This article appeared in the January/February 2009 issue of* Mother Jones.

Les Gibson takes me out to teach me how to hunt, which is what he calls fishing. Despite the fact that every public beach in Queensland, Australia, has been periodically closed this season due to blooms of box jellyfish, and despite the fearsome saltwater crocodiles living here, Les strides confidently into the bay with a pair of 10-foot-long bamboo spears and his wooden *woomera*, the multipurpose Aboriginal atlatl, or spear-thrower.

When I ask him if he worries about jellyfish, he tells me Aborigines have a cure for the venom. Do scientists know about this cure? I ask. No, he says, they never ask us anything.

We wade waist deep through water as warm as a bath, Les pointing out schools of mullet, schools of goatfish, a stonefish, a pipefish. I'm wearing polarized sunglasses and have spent much of my life peering through water, yet I can't see what Les sees. Deftly as a striking heron, he loads the woomera and tosses a spear through the surface. It disappears, then jerks up, thrashing with the struggles of an impaled mullet. Clubbing the fish with the woomera, he stuffs it in the back pocket of his shorts, so that now we are wading in waist-deep water in prime crocodile and shark habitat leaking fish blood.

4   In a staccato dance—darting and stopping, tossing the spear, collecting, darting again—Les goes after a blue-spotted lagoon ray and a baby gray reef shark. Somehow he spears the shark intentionally through its pelvic fin, then lifts it to the surface on the tip of one spear and skewers it through the second pelvic fin with his second spear. Thus immobilized, it becomes my combination science-and-culinary lesson, Les pointing out its anatomy while describing favorite recipes. Lesson over, he lets it go, not too much the worse for wear.

He points out a lionfish. That feller is far from home, he says. He gestures offshore, where the sea grows darker and mottled by the Great Barrier Reef. I have just come in from weeks of diving at pinnacles and coral heads loaded with venomous lionfish.

Les is not worried about them either. There's a treatment. Just like there was a treatment for my skin, for a rash of welts and bites garnered in a month of living outdoors and underwater. This morning he cured me. We stood in seawater to our knees, Les rolling between the palms of his hands a mass of *yangga* (green ants) and their leafy nest, stripped off a bush he calls the soapy tree. Crushing ants and leaves, he added a trickle of seawater, rolled some more, repeated, until the whole mass started to foam.

Getta whiff, he said, holding it under my nose. Clears the sinuses. Keeps the bugs away. I slathered the mentholated salve over my skin—like rubbing a magic eraser over my torments.

8   Now Les wants me to try hunting. I throw the spear, but also the woomera, a real idiot move. Eventually I get the hang of it—though I'll never hit anything. No matter how hard I squint, I can't match Les' acuity, even with the milky blue cataracts clouding his 65-year-old eyes.

Les' wife, Marie, shows me how to drag chairs from their beach shack and stack them so I can reach the fruit of the tree she calls *banday*. The berries are as sweet as pineapple. But the one they call white apple, the one they love best, they never see it anymore. And this, she says, cupping another fruit in her hand, this tree came to the beach, and all these fruit hanging here. They're no good.

I recognize the tree and the fruit. It's a pond apple, native of the Florida Everglades. Here it's a weed, one of Australia's worst, an invasive species bullying the marshy ecosystems of Queensland by growing so fast, tall, and thick, it's driving out beloved natives like melaleuca trees. I spent the better part of four years filming in the Everglades, including pond apples and the bullying done to them by invading Australian melaleuca trees growing faster, taller, and thicker than Florida's beloved native pond apples. If there's such a thing as biological irony, this is it.

Les and Marie are Guugu Yimithirr, descendants of Australians Captain James Cook made contact with near here in 1770. Other Europeans followed, along with their symbionts: pigs, cattle, sheep, rabbits, cats. The arrivals proved cataclysmic to all the human cultures inhabiting this island continent, as well as to the native birds, reptiles, mammals, insects, and plants—destroying a hundred millennia of deep ecological dialogue.

12   The problem didn't end there. Nowadays when species obey the commandment to "be fruitful and multiply, to fill the waters in the seas, to let the birds multiply on the Earth," all is decidedly not good. Proliferation on a biblical scale generally signals biological apocalypse, what scientists call invasion—the establishment and spread of introduced species in places they've never lived before. Species have always been on the move. But they've also been held in check by Earth's geographical barriers, like mountains and oceans. Today the rate of invasions has skyrocketed because of our barrier-hopping technology—jets, ships, trains, cars, which transport everything from mammals to microorganisms far beyond their natural ranges. The process is further accelerated by global climate change, that enormous human experiment unwittingly redistricting the natural world.

The results devastate both planetary and human health—most disease organisms, from influenza to malaria, are invaders over most of their range—and few invasions can be stopped once they're successfully established. Biological invasions are now second only to habitat loss as a cause of extinction—the leading cause of the extinction of birds and the second-leading cause of the extinction of fish. Twenty percent of vertebrate species facing extinction are doing so because of pressures from invasive predators or competitors. In a classic example, brown tree snakes arrived in Guam (snakeless but for a worm-sized insectivore) sometime after World War II and systematically ate 15 bird species into extinction while consuming enough small reptiles and mammals to redesign the food web. They also began traveling an expanding network of power lines, electrocuting themselves and causing about 200 power failures annually. In all, invasive species are estimated to cost $1.4 trillion each year.

Islands are critically vulnerable to invasions. The giant African snail, introduced to Hawaii in the 1950s, became a worrisome enough pest that government managers introduced another 15 nonnative snails over six years in an effort to control it. One, the rosy wolfsnail, preferred native Hawaiian snails, consuming 15 of 20 species on Oahu into extinction and leading to an entire genus awarded a listing under the Endangered Species Act. A virtual carbon copy of this disaster took place in Tahiti and the other Society Islands, where the rosy wolfsnail obliterated 56 of 61 native snails.

Pull back far enough, however, and everything is an island. Lakes are islands of water. Mountains are elevational islands. Continents are really big islands. Oceans are vast islands of seawater. In fact, all the landscapes and waterscapes of Earth now shattered by human use are islands afloat in seas of development. These fragments offer none of the benefits of isolation, only the weaknesses. In one measure of just how frighteningly fruitful and multiplicative these incursions have become, the rate of successful invasions in San Francisco Bay rose from about one a year between 1850 and 1970 to one every 14 weeks in the 1990s. Our best hope of addressing this deadly fecundity is to stop it before it starts, and that requires understanding all the strange new ways that species have come to hitchhike on our ride.

16   The red lionfish (*Pterois volitans*) is a creature of indescribable loveliness, a one-foot-long lacy, plume-bearing extravagance of a fish, complete with red, white, and gold stripes along its body, with wispy fins that look like feathers—hence its other common name, the turkey fish. It's a deadly presence on the coral reef, bearing glands at the base of its "feathers," injectable through its "quills," full of potent toxins. Human symptoms of envenomation include intense pain, tingling, blistering, and the possibility of worse—nausea, vomiting, abdominal pain, headache, delirium, seizures, paralysis, respiratory distress, congestive heart failure.

In their native Pacific waters, red lionfish tend to sleep by day, head down under ledges. But at night, they join a cast of nocturnal heavy hitters: sharks on the prowl, barracuda on the hunt, moray eels free swimming in pursuit of prey, sea snakes forgoing their daytime friendliness for serious underwater slithering. Shining my dive torch out into the black, I catch these players sidewinding through the beam like images from an old-time magic-lantern show, vignetted by darkness.

But I don't have to sweep the night for lionfish. They come up close, hovering in midwater, feathers waving hypnotically, staring at me head-on, the stripes on their bodies running right through their independently twirling eyeballs. I begin to think of them as the skunks of the coral reef, perfectly defended, small but invincible, curious, busy, undaunted by size. Few animals live unafraid. Lionfish may be one of them.

They may also be the only animals to use what I call entrancement as a hunting method. Victims seem to fall prey to the fluttering dance of the lionfish's wings as they're unwittingly herded into dead-end corners and narrow alleys.

On moonlit nights with my torch turned off, I've seen lionfish stalking cardinalfish or other plankton pickers, waving their feathery veils to cull one fish from the school, stalking it in mesmerizing slow motion before suddenly and violently extending protrusible jaws, grabbing and suctioning all at once. In filmmaking parlance, it's a jump cut: First there's a little fish, then there isn't, and you never even see the middle part of the action.

20   Lionfish are near-ubiquitous predators on coral reefs of the Indian and Pacific oceans and are part of ancient ecological interactions. Everything from lobsters to soldierfishes knows to give these seductive fan-dancers of the night a wide berth. So what happens when you take coral-reef animals that have never seen lionfish and put them together with lionfish? Aquarists know. It's *War of the Worlds*: aliens with superior technology knocking over the hapless natives and feasting on their remains. It's science fiction. Except now it isn't.

In 1992 a small and intensely powerful Hurricane Andrew roared through south Florida like a 25-mile-wide tornado with gusts of up to 165 miles per hour. The storm was one of only three Category 5 hurricanes to make landfall in the US in the 20th century, striking hard at Biscayne Bay on Florida's east coast. Somewhere along that ravaged shoreline, in some expensive glass-fronted mansion or a humble beach shack, the 17-foot storm surge punched open an aquarium and released a few red lionfish, perhaps only six individuals. Despite formidable conditions in the wake of the hurricane—scouring waves, a month of choking turbidity and ongoing fuel spills from hundreds of damaged boats—the lionfish apparently took hold and multiplied. And multiplied and multiplied.

Three thousand miles from invasion ground zero, Mark Hixon is a professor of marine conservation biology at Oregon State University, a campus 50 miles from the sea, and an unlikely place to find a specialist in coral-reef ecology. He admits it was hard at first, living so far from the ocean. But this school is a hotbed of science and no stranger to environmental controversies, including the spotted owl wars of the 1990s. Hixon has been studying biodiversity on coral reefs since the 1970s. In 2006 he was unwittingly sucked into the hypnotic clutch of the red lionfish when his long-term research sites in the Bahamas were invaded. For a while it appeared this might be a second red lionfish invasion in the Atlantic, perhaps the result of another transport mechanism—ships carrying larval fish in their ballast water. But Hixon highly doubts it, since surveys of exotics off Florida show only popular aquarium fish (emperor angelfish, yellow tang, orbicular batfish) as invaders, not a random sampling of fish from Pacific ports of call, as one would expect if ballast water were the vector. Plus, new genetic research suggests Bahamian lionfish are from the same founder population as Florida lionfish.

For Hixon, the invasion gave his work on protected marine areas new meaning. How to safeguard a protected area from the incursion of an alien? And one spreading like a plague of locusts, he says. Already lionfish have infiltrated Bermuda. They've breached New England. They've occupied Jamaica and the US Virgin Islands. There are unconfirmed reports of lionfish from Puerto Rico, the Yucatán Peninsula, and the Lesser Antilles. So what, you might say. They're pretty, they're reefy, they're just another *fish*, right?

24   Hardly. Hixon and his doctoral student Mark Albins have recorded the lion-fish's disturbing appetites. A single red lionfish on a six-foot-diameter reef ate an average of 79 percent of the resident baby fish during a five-week study period. These tiny juveniles are the stuff of biodiversity, and lionfish are apparently eat-ing four out of five of them, imposing an unsustainable tax on the future. Worse, invasive lionfish have no natural predators, and though there is some evidence that large native groupers in the Atlantic might be learning how to eat them, populations of large native groupers are so severely overfished there simply aren't enough left to do the job.

Here's where it gets really strange. Released from the competitive and preda-tory pressures holding them in check, invaders sometimes become dark super-hero versions of their former selves: bigger, faster, tougher, more populous, and behaviorally different than before. In parts of Guam, brown tree snake popula-tions explode to 13,000 per square mile. Australian spotted jellyfish grow nearly twice as big in invaded Gulf of Mexico waters as at home. Argentine ants fight each other brutally in their native world yet become supremely cooperative when transplanted, joining forces to drive local ants into extinction and threatening important bee pollinators. House mice, hitchhikers on human invasions for the past 8,000 years, are masters of behavioral plasticity. On Gough Island in the South Atlantic, groups of up to 10 mice have learned to attack albatross chicks more than 300 times their own size. Because the chicks have never faced terres-trial predators, they offer no defenses, not even when the mice are eating through their body walls and consuming the food in their bellies. In perhaps the most notorious recent invasion, US wildlife managers are fighting a costly and losing battle against Asian snakeheads, since the fish can live up to four days out of water and can *walk* between ponds and rivers.

Albins and Hixon's research shows lionfish crowding onto reef sites at the rate of 59 per acre—implying they're not only swallowing the future, but starving the present as well, since an average-size adult eats about six pounds of fish and crus-taceans a year, which translates to about 6,000 baby fish. Hixon and Albins have evidence that lionfish behavior may be changing in their new world, that they may be developing into daytime hunters in the Bahamas, whereas they're largely noc-turnal in the Indo-Pacific. This is alarming on two levels. First, lionfish are likely outcompeting native predators (who must also make a living from the same prey populations), and not just coral-reef predators. In the Atlantic, lionfish are expand-ing beyond the tropics. Adults have colonized as far north as North Carolina and juveniles are traveling up to Rhode Island—though they die off each winter. Sec-ond, along these routes, in both tropical and temperate waters, lionfish are encoun-tering naive species with no experience of their venom or entrancement. Hixon and Albins have observed a single lionfish gobbling more than 20 small wrasses in the space of half an hour. It's like shooting fish in a barrel. Far from their native world, the lionfish's impressive tools become weapons of mass destruction.

Hixon mulls the problem constantly—while driving, while walking across campus, eating, socializing. He hopes Bahamian officials can institute a bounty and convince locals that lionfish taste like chicken and are easy to eat once you know how to avoid the spines and cook the fish sufficiently to denature the venom. But until and unless that happens, says Hixon, lionfish may very well become the most devastating marine invasion in human history.

28   Hurricane Andrew's havoc did not end at lionfish. Its killer winds tore up the Everglades' signature sloughs and saw-grass prairies, felling native vegetation and implanting the wracked landscape with tiny seeds of the invasive Australian melaleuca—a lot of seeds, it turns out, since a mature melaleuca can produce more than a million of them per year. Melaleuca were purposely introduced into the Everglades to suck dry "useless" swampland. Unfortunately, by the 1990s, when the swamp had been reimagined as a national treasure, it was too late for the hundreds of thousands of acres desiccated by the invited invaders.

Many successful biological invasions capitalize on mayhem. Both melaleuca and lionfish are what biologists call drivers of ecosystem changes—causing, for instance, changes in biodiversity. But both are also passengers of ecosystem changes, piggybacking on changes already under way: melaleuca on disrupted landscapes, lionfish on overfished reefs. The potential for more powerful hurricanes as a result of global climate change threatens to amplify existing invasions and maybe even foster new ones—a process known as invasional meltdown. Fifty miles to the west of Hixon's lab, in the waters of the North Pacific, a synergy of ecological changes appears to be fueling the invasion of Humboldt squid—aggressive predators reaching nearly seven feet in length (not counting their tentacles) and 110 pounds in weight, and living in schools hundreds or thousands strong. They are known to ecologists as r-strategists: species that live fast, die young, and breed early and profusely. (Humboldt squid produce up to 32 million eggs per female.) R-strategists, like locusts and rats, thrive in unstable environments since their generational turnaround time is short enough for adaptation and evolution to work their miracles.

At the moment, a seriously unstable world beckons the Humboldt squid. Typically confined to the tropics and subtropics, they're now moving northward explosively as waters warm, as their main predators, tuna and billfish such as marlin, are overfished, and as global-warming-induced dead zones appear—Humboldt squid are one of the few animals tolerant of their low oxygen levels. Although the squid have not been accidentally released from a home aquarium or carried across the Panama Canal in the ballast water of a ship or towed around on portable oil drilling platforms (as with Australian spotted jellyfish in the Gulf of Mexico), they are nevertheless invading new realms and are now established as far north as the once-chilly Gulf of Alaska.

Clearly Humboldt squid are passengers on ecosystem changes already under way. But they may be drivers as well. Their move north coincides with the decline of Pacific hake, the West Coast's most important commercial groundfish. Are they gorging on hake as they grow from hatchlings smaller than a grain of rice to seven-foot adults in only a year, maybe two? Whatever they're eating, they're likely to be eating a lot of it, in ways it wasn't eaten before.

32   In Australia, where Florida pond apples are outcompeting native melaleuca, the invasive problem gets really twisted. The pond apple and its seeds are designed to float away for dispersal. But in the wet forests of Queensland, pond apples are

also being dispersed by two fruit-eating species—including feral pigs. Because this is an invasive helping to propagate another invasive, the management directive seems clear: Get rid of them both. But an endangered native species also now eats pond apples—the six-foot-tall flightless bird of the tropical rainforest known as the cassowary. Cassowaries digest pond apples for up to 28 hours before passing the seeds, meaning they're likely planting many new pond apples in the course of their travels. In some parts of their range, cassowaries have come to depend on pond apples. The management directive gets confused.

At Les and Marie Gibson's beach shack on the coast of far north Queensland, Marie tells me about the shy birds—how they talk through the horny crests on their heads (something science is beginning to confirm). She is making a sand painting with some of the 35 colors found in the painted bluffs all around. Her painting tells the story of Yirmbal, the Rainbow Serpent, how, during the uncountable eons before the material world existed, the ancestors dreamt each night of what would come to be and played it out each morning. During this Dreamtime, right here by Les and Marie's beach shack, Yirmbal fought a mighty battle with two enormous hawks that ended when Rainbow Serpent's body burst and all the colors inside her splattered across the world.

Les shows me where. At an enormous red boulder planted on the edge of land and sea. This is Yirmbal, he says, introducing us. Sure enough, squinting, I can see the coiled shape of a great serpent. Stand on those little rocks there, says Les, and look on top of the big rock. Reclining on top, curled in the dappled shade, arrow-shaped head pointed my way, is the unforgettable sight of a death adder.

Long ago, our ancestors left their home world and moved out into the savannas and beyond, getting bigger, smarter, and more invasive along the way.

36   Les leads the way down the beach, melaleuca whispering in the breeze, pond apples bobbing on the waves.

PERSONAL RESPONSE

What did you learn from this article that you did not already know or were not already aware of?

QUESTIONS FOR CLASS AND SMALL GROUP DISCUSSION

1. Whitty says that the arrival of Europeans to Australia "proved cataclysmic" (paragraph 11). What does she mean by that? Whitty goes on to say that the problem has spread all over the earth. How does she account for the skyrocketing rate in the invasion of destructive species?

2. Whitty says that the results of that widespread invasion "devastate[d] both planetary and human health" (paragraph 13). Explain what you understand her to mean by that statement and give examples from her article.

3. Summarize the effects of the spread of red lionfish in areas where it was previously unknown. What role did Hurricane Andrew play in its spread?

4. Whitty writes: "Here's where it gets really strange. . . . [I]nvaders sometimes become dark superhero versions of their former selves" (paragraph 25). Explain what she means by that and cite some of the examples she gives. What are "r-strategists" (paragraph 29)?

GLOBAL WARNING: GET UP! STAND UP!

BILL MCKIBBEN

Bill McKibben, author, educator, and environmentalist, is contributing editor of OnEarth. *His books include* The End of Nature, *the first book for a general audience on global warming (1989);* The Age of Missing Information *(1992);* Hope, Human and Wild: True Stories of Living Lightly on Earth *(1995);* Maybe One: The Case for Smaller Families *(1998);* Long Distance: Testing the Limits of Body and Spirit in a Year of Living Strenuously *(2000);* Enough: Staying Human in an Engineering Age *(2003);* Deep Economy: The Wealth of Communities and the Durable Future *(2007);* EAARTH [sic]: Making a Life on a Tough New Planet *(2008); and* The Global Warming Reader *(2012).* OnEarth, *the quarterly journal of the Natural Resources Defense Council, explores politics, nature, wildlife, culture, science, health, the challenges that confront our planet, and the solutions that promise to heal and protect it. This article appeared in the Spring 2007 issue of* OnEarth.

Here's a short list of the important legislation our federal government has enacted to combat global warming in the years since 1988, when a NASA climatologist, James Hansen, first told Congress that climate change was real:

1.

2.

3.

And what do you know? That bipartisan effort at doing nothing has been highly successful: Our emissions of carbon dioxide have steadily increased over that two-decade span.

Meanwhile, how have the lone superpower's efforts at leading international action to deal with climate change gone? Not too well. We refused to ratify the Kyoto treaty, while the rest of the developed world finally did so. And while we've pressured China over world-shaking issues like DVD piracy, we've happily sold them the parts to help grow their coal-fired electric utility network to a size that matches ours.

Reprinted by permission from *OnEarth*, Spring 2007.

4   In other words, Washington has utterly and completely failed to take on the single greatest challenge human civilization has ever faced.

What's more, Washington, at least so far, couldn't care less about the failure. A flurry of legislation has been introduced in the last couple of months, but scarcely a member of Congress felt compelled to answer in the last election for failing to deal with climate change. A simple "I'm concerned" was more than enough.

Not only that, but scientists revealed last December that a piece of ice the size of 11,000 football fields had broken off an Arctic ice shelf.

So, and here I use a technical term that comes from long study of the intricate science, we're screwed. Unless.

8   If we're going to change any of those nasty facts, we need a movement. A real, broad-based public movement demanding transformation of the way we power our world. A movement as strong, passionate, and willing to sacrifice as the civil rights movement that ended segregation more than a generation ago. This essay is about the possible rise of such a movement—about the role that you might play in making it happen.

It's not the fault of our environmental organizations that such a movement doesn't yet exist. It's the fault of the molecular structure of carbon dioxide.

Modern environmentalism arose in the early 1960s in the wake of *Silent Spring*. That's the moment advocates of "conservation"—the idea that we should protect some areas as refuges amid a benign modernity—began to realize that modernity itself might be a problem, that the bright miracles of our economic life came with shadows. First DDT, but before long phosphates in detergent and sulfur in the smoke stream of coal plants and chlorofluoro-carbons (CFCs) in our air conditioners. And carbon monoxide, carbon with one oxygen atom, the stuff that was helping turn the air above our cities brown.

All were alike in one crucial way: You could take care of the problems they caused with fairly easy technical fixes. Different pesticides that didn't thin eggshells; scrubbers on smokestacks. DuPont ended up making more money on the stuff that replaced CFCs, which had been tearing a hole in the ozone layer. None of these battles was easy: The Natural Resources Defense Council (NRDC) and Greenpeace and Environmental Defense and the Sierra Club and the Union of Concerned Scientists and a thousand Friends of the You-Name-It had to fight like hell to make sure that the fixes got made. But that was the war we armed for: We had the lawyers and the scientists and the regulatory experts and the lobbyists and the fund-raisers. We didn't always win, but the batting average was pretty high: You can swim in more rivers, breathe in more cities. It was a carbon monoxide movement, and the catalytic converter, which washed that chemical from your exhaust, was its emblem. You could drive your car; you just needed the right gear on your tailpipe.

12   But carbon dioxide—carbon with two oxygen atoms—screwed everything up. Carbon dioxide in itself isn't exactly a pollutant. It doesn't hurt you when you breathe it; in fact, for a very long time engineers described a motor as "clean-burning" if it gave off only CO_2 and water vapor. The problem that emerged

into public view in the late 1980s was that its molecular structure trapped heat near the planet that would otherwise radiate back out to space. And, worse, there wasn't a technofix this time—CO_2 was an inevitable by-product of burning fossil fuels. That is to say, the only way to deal with global warming is to move quickly away from fossil fuels.

When you understand that, you understand why Congress has yet to act, and why even big and talented environmental organizations have been largely stymied. Fossil fuel is not like DDT or phosphates or CFCs. It's the absolute center of modern life. An alien scientist arriving on our planet might well conclude that Western human beings are devices for burning coal and gas and oil, since that is what we do from dawn to dusk, and then on into the brightly lit night. When societies get richer, they start reducing other pollutants—even in China some cities have begun to see reductions in sulfur and nitrogen as people demand better pollution controls. But as the Harvard economist Benjamin Friedman conceded in a landmark book in 2005, *The Moral Consequences of Economic Growth*, carbon dioxide is the only pollutant that economic growth doesn't reduce. It is economic growth. It's no accident that the last three centuries, a time of great prosperity, have also been the centuries of coal and oil and gas.

Which means that this is a war that environmentalism as currently constituted simply can't win. Our lobbyists can sit down with congressional staffers and convince them of the need for, say, lower arsenic levels in water supplies; they have enough support to win those kinds of votes. We've managed, brilliantly, to save the Arctic National Wildlife Refuge from drilling. But we lack (by a long shot) the firepower to force, say, a carbon tax that might actually cut fossil fuel use. We've been outgunned by the car companies and the auto unions when it comes to gasoline mileage. We can save the Arctic refuge from oil drilling, but we can't save it from thawing into a northern swamp no caribou would ever wander through. In essence, we have a problem opposite to that of the American military: Well armed for small battles with insurgent polluters, we suddenly find ourselves needing to fight World War II.

What we have now is the superstructure of a movement. We have brilliant scientists, we have superb economists, we have some of the most battle-hardened lawyers and lobbyists you could hope for. The only thing the climate movement lacks is the movement part.

16   Consider this: Last Labor Day weekend, a few of us led a five-day, 50-mile march across our home state of Vermont to demand that our candidates for federal office take stronger stands on climate legislation. We started at Robert Frost's summer writing cabin high in the Green Mountains, happy with the symbolism of choosing a road less taken. As we wandered byways and main roads, we were happy too with the reception we got—crowds waiting to greet us at churches and senior centers and farms, motorists waving and honking even from the largest SUVs. By the time we reached Burlington, the state capital, we had a thousand marchers. (It was more than enough to convince all our candidates, even the conservative Republicans, to endorse strong carbon reductions; they all signed a pledge backing 80 percent cuts in carbon emissions by 2050.) But here's the

not-so-happy thing: The newspapers said that a rally of 1,000 people was the largest that had yet taken place in this nation against global warming. That's pathetic.

But not hopeless. Because that movement is starting to gather, less inside the main environmental organizations than on their fringes.

The student movement, for instance, has come out of nowhere in the last three years. All of a sudden there are hundreds of high schools and college campuses where kids are working for real change in how their dorms and classrooms are heated and lit. And emboldened by their success on campus, they're increasingly involved in state and national and international efforts. Whenever I'm feeling disheartened about how slowly change is coming, I stop by a meeting of the Sunday Night Group at Middlebury College, the campus where I work. A hundred or more students show up for the weekly meetings, and they get right down to business—some on making sure that every light bulb in town is a compact fluorescent, some on making sure that every legislator in the state is a climate convert. On the national level, the group Energy Action has joined 16 student organizations into an effective force. The group's Campus Climate Challenge will soon involve a thousand schools, and its leaders are planning a summer of marches and a platoon of youth to bird-dog presidential candidates.

Or look at the churches and synagogues. Ten years ago there was no religious environmental movement to speak of. Now, "creation care" is an emerging watchword across the spectrum, from Unitarians to evangelicals among the Christian traditions and in Jewish, Buddhist, and Muslim communities as well. And the rhetoric is increasingly matched by action: Groups such as Interfaith Power and Light are organizing congregations to cut energy use, and groups such as Religious Witness for the Earth are organizing people of faith for marches of their own.

20   There's even one very sweet by-product of the roadblock in Washington: In cities and states across the union, big environmental groups and local citizen activists have focused their energy on mayors and governors and learned a good deal in the process. Including this: It's possible to win. If California's Republican governor can decide it's in his interest to embrace strong climate legislation, you know people have done good groundwork. They've worked in public as well as behind the scenes. Activists from the Maryland-based Chesapeake Climate Action Network were arrested last fall for blocking the doors to federal offices to demand more accurate federal science.

The moment is ripe. Hurricane Katrina blew open the door of public opinion, and Al Gore walked valiantly through it with his movie. There are, finally, lots and lots of people who want to know how they can make a difference. Not 51 percent of the people, but we don't need 51 percent. We can do just fine with 15 percent. As long as they're active. As long as they're a movement.

Which brings me, finally, to the point. It's time to unleash as much passion and energy as we can. It's movement time.

What we need is nothing less than a societal transformation. Not a new gizmo, not a few new laws, but a commitment to wean America from fossil fuels in our lifetime and to lead the rest of the world, especially India and China, in the same direction. The shorthand we're using in our April stepitup07.org campaign is the same as it was in our Vermont march: 80 percent cuts by 2050. What we need is big change, starting right now.

24   And that's a message Congress needs to hear. Though the November elections opened new possibilities, they also raised new perils. Instead of James Inhofe, who thought global warming was a hoax, the relevant Senate committee now answers to Barbara Boxer, who understands that it's very real. But the very chance of a deal raises the specter of a bad deal—some small-potatoes around-the-edges kind of action that substitutes the faux realism of Washington politics for the actual physics-and-chemistry realism of our predicament. For instance, when John McCain introduced legislation five years ago that asked for small and more or less voluntary cuts, it was a step forward, and I saluted him on the cover of this magazine. But the current draft of his bill is fairly weak. Even the strongest bills, introduced by Henry Waxman and Bernie Sanders, barely meet the test for what the science demands. And chances are, unless we really do our job on the ground, the measures they're proposing will barely be discussed.

NASA's James Hansen—our premier climatologist—has made it clear we have 10 years to reverse the flow of carbon into the atmosphere. Actually, he made it clear in the fall of 2005, so we have eight and a half years before we cross certain thresholds (Arctic melt, for instance) that commit us to an endless cycle of self-reinforcing feedback loops and, in Hansen's words, a "totally different planet."

That requires transformation, not tinkering. It's not like carbon monoxide or DDT—it's like the women's movement or the civil rights movement, which changed the basic taken-for-granted architecture of our nation. Except it's harder, because this time we don't need the system to accommodate more people; we need the system to change in profound ways.

The only chance is for those of us who see the risk and the opportunity to act—as quickly and as powerfully as ever we can.

PERSONAL RESPONSE

How committed are you to the kind of activism that McKibben calls for?

QUESTIONS FOR CLASS OR SMALL-GROUP DISCUSSION

1. Describe the tone in the opening paragraphs. What is the effect of that tone? Where does the tone change?

2. In paragraph 4, McKibben writes that Washington, DC has failed "to take on the single greatest challenge human civilization has ever faced." What is that challenge? Do you agree that it is the greatest challenge humans have faced? If not, what other challenge(s) are greater?

3. The subtitle of this essay is "How to Build a Mass Movement to Halt Climate Change." Summarize in your own words the actions that McKibben recommends for building a mass movement to halt climate change. Do you agree with him that such a movement will work?

4. How persuasive do you find this article? Are you moved to act?

THE SIXTH EXTINCTION

Jeff Corwin

Jeff Corwin, biologist, Emmy-Award winning producer, and television host of Animal Planet *is the author of* Living on the Edge: Amazing Relationships in the Natural World *(2004) and* 100 Heartbeats: The Race to Save the World's Most Endangered Animal Species *(2009), a book about his experiences tracking the sixth extinction. A companion documentary to the book aired on MSNBC in 2009. This article was published in the* Los Angeles Times *on November 30, 2009.*

There is a holocaust happening. Right now. And it's not confined to one nation or even one region. It is a global crisis.

Species are going extinct en masse.

Every 20 minutes we lose an animal species. If this rate continues, by century's end, 50% of all living species will be gone. It is a phenomenon known as the sixth extinction. The fifth extinction took place 65 million years ago when a meteor smashed into the Earth, killing off the dinosaurs and many other species and opening the door for the rise of mammals. Currently, the sixth extinction is on track to dwarf the fifth.

4   What—or more correctly—who is to blame this time? As Pogo said, "We have met the enemy, and he is us."

The causes of this mass die-off are many: overpopulation, loss of habitat, global warming, species exploitation (the black market for rare animal parts is the third-largest illegal trade in the world, outranked only by weapons and drugs). The list goes on, but it all points to us.

Over the last 15 years, in the course of producing television documentaries and writing about wildlife, I have traveled the globe, and I have witnessed the grim carnage firsthand. I've observed the same story playing out in different locales.

In South Africa, off the coast of Cape Horn, lives one of the most feared predators of all—the great white shark. Yet this awesome creature is powerless before the mindless killing spree that is decimating its species at the jaw-dropping rate of 100 million sharks a year. Many are captured so that their dorsal fins can be chopped off (for shark fin soup). Then, still alive, they are dropped back into the sea, where they die a slow and painful death.

8   Further east, in Indonesia, I witnessed the mass destruction of rain forests to make way for palm oil plantations. Indonesia is now the world's leading producer of palm oil—a product used in many packaged foods and cosmetic goods—and the victims are the Sumatran elephant and orangutan. These beautiful creatures are on the brink of extinction as their habitats go up in smoke, further warming our planet in the process.

One day while swimming off the coast of Indonesia, I came across a river of refuse and raw sewage stretching for miles. These streams and islands of refuse now populate all our oceans; in the middle of the Pacific, there is an island of garbage the size of Texas. This floating pollution serves to choke off and kill sea turtles—driving them closer to extinction. At the same time, the coral reefs where sea turtles get their food supply are dying due to rising sea temperatures from global warming. To top it off, sea turtles are hunted and killed for their meat—considered a delicacy in many Asian countries. It is an ugly but altogether effective one-two-three punch for this unique species.

It's important to understand that this is not just a race to save a handful of charismatic species—animals to which we attach human-inspired values or characteristics. Who wouldn't want to save the sea otter, polar bear, giant panda or gorilla? These striking mammals tug at our heartstrings and often our charitable purse strings. But our actions need to be just as swift and determined when it comes to the valley elderberry longhorn beetle or the distinctly uncuddly, pebbly-skinned Puerto Rican crested toad or the black-footed ferret, whose fate is inextricably intertwined with that of the prairie dog. The reality is that each species, no matter how big, small, friendly or vicious, plays an important and essential role in its ecosystem. And we're in a race to preserve as much of the animal kingdom as possible.

Meanwhile, around the planet there are massive die-offs of amphibians, the canaries in our global coal mine. When frogs and other amphibians, which have existed for hundreds of millions of years, start to vanish, it is a sign that our natural world is in a state of peril. Bat and bee populations are also being decimated. Without bees, there will be no pollination, and without pollination, the predator that is decimating these other species—humankind—will also be headed toward its own extinction. Yes, there is a certain irony there.

12   This was all brought home to me in an intimate way after a recent trip to Panama. My young daughter, Maya, asked if she could accompany me on my next trip there so that she could see one of her favorite animals—the Panamanian golden frog—up close and personal in the jungle. Sadly, I had to tell her no. This small, beautiful frog—the national symbol of Panama—no longer exists in the wild. Only a few live in captivity.

Is there hope? Yes. Because in every place I visited to witness the sixth extinction unfold, I met brave and selfless conservationists, biologists and wildlife scientists working hard to save species.

In Panama, biologist Edgardo Griffith has set up an amphibian rescue center to protect and quarantine rare frogs (including the Panamanian golden frog) before they are all wiped out by the deadly fungus *Chytrid*, which is rapidly killing off frogs on a global scale. In Africa, zoologist Iain Douglas Hamilton is one of many seeking to stop the illegal trade in elephant ivory and rhino horn. In Namibia, zoologist Laurie Marker is making strides to save the cheetah before it goes the way of the saber tooth tiger (or India's Bengal tiger, which is also on the precipice of extinction). In Indonesia, Ian Singleton is raising orphaned orangutans, training them to return to the remaining rain forest—giving them a second chance at living in the wild. In South Africa, Alison Kock is leading a crusade to educate the world about the wholesale destruction of sharks.

Here in the United States, Chris Lucash of the U.S. Fish and Wildlife Service is working to reintroduce the red wolf, now found only in captivity, to the woods of North Carolina. They are just a few of the many who are trying to reverse the species holocaust that threatens the future of our natural world.

16   These committed scientists bring great generosity and devotion to their respective efforts to stop the sixth extinction. But if we don't all rise to the cause and join them in action, they cannot succeed. The hour is near, but it's not too late.

PERSONAL RESPONSE

Write for a few minutes about a detail in this essay that impressed you in some way.

QUESTIONS FOR CLASS OR SMALL-GROUP DISCUSSION

1. Explain what Corwin means by his title, "The Sixth Extinction."
2. Where does Corwin use examples effectively? What do you understand Corwin to mean by the metaphor of canaries in a coal mine (paragraph 11)?
3. What argumentative strategies does Corwin use to persuade his reader to action? Are you persuaded?
4. In his concluding paragraph, Corwin urges readers to "rise to the cause and join them [scientists] in action." How do you think readers can practically join scientists around the globe? What else might individuals do to help stop species extinction?

ACCOUNTING 101 FOR THE 21ST CENTURY: A LIBERAL ARTS EDUCATION IN CARBON

John Petersen

John Petersen is Professor of Environmental Studies and Biology and Director of Oberlin College's Environmental Studies Program. A systems ecologist by training, his research has appeared in the journals Ecology, American Naturalist, *and* BioScience *and in books that he*

Reprinted from *The Chronicle of Higher Education,* June 20, 2008, by permission of the author.

has authored and contributed to. His current research focuses on flows of
energy, cycles of matter, and feedback control mechanisms operating in
the built environment. This article was published in the Chronicle of
Higher Education *on June 20, 2008.*

Recent graduates have a lot to learn about budgeting when they leave college.
Many are financially on their own for the first time, and so rent, grocery bills,
taxes, and, of course, student loans are expenditures they will need to balance
against their incomes. In addition to those personal budgetary challenges, the lives
of our graduates will be profoundly affected by impending national budget crises
associated with the costs of war, a trade imbalance, Social Security, and health care.
And as if those burdens were not enough, the graduates must concern themselves
with a new category of budgeting, one that relates not to money but to carbon.

Today's college graduates confront the first truly worldwide environmental
challenge, that of balancing the carbon budget—the stocks and flow of carbon
through the biosphere—to ameliorate the negative consequences of global climate change. Colleges and universities have an obligation to ensure that we provide our students with the knowledge and experience necessary to accomplish
that challenging task. Many of those essential lessons can take place in classrooms, while an equally educational, parallel curriculum is embodied in the management and development of campus infrastructure, the maintenance of grounds,
and the provisioning of food and transportation for our students.

On college campuses and in our modern industrial economy as a whole, each
bite we eat, each item we discard, each e-mail message we send, and each purchase we make entails a conversion of fossil-fuel carbon to carbon dioxide. Our
growing use of fossil fuels has resulted in a sharp increase in atmospheric carbon
dioxide, and the carbon budget tips farther out of balance each day.

4   Institutions of higher education are poised to play a leading role in developing and executing climate-neutral policies. The good news is that the emergence
of carbon as a universal environmental currency provides a unique and exciting
opportunity to integrate economy, ecology, and culture to solve many vexing environmental and cultural problems. That opportunity, in turn, provides many avenues
for our colleges, students, and graduates to play a role in developing such solutions.

Like an increasing number of our peer institutions, Oberlin College has
adopted a comprehensive environmental policy on energy use, purchasing,
building construction and management, food, transportation, waste, grounds
management, and education. Although not a perfect measure, the transition to
environmental sustainability in every one of these areas can be quantified in terms
of reductions in the college's carbon emissions. Examples of carbon-balancing
policies and projects at Oberlin include:

- A green-energy purchasing agreement with our local utility that
  simultaneously reduces the college's carbon-dioxide emissions by 25 percent
  and generates a "sustainable energy reserve fund" to encourage community-
  based projects that lead to further carbon-dioxide savings. Community projects carried out thus far include research on the feasibility of local wind power
  and a grant that helped open a local gas station that now sells only biofuels.

- A green building policy ensures that all new campus construction achieves a Leadership in Energy and Environmental Design Silver or better rating. The LEED rating system is the nationally accepted benchmark for the design, construction, and operation of buildings that minimize energy use (and encourage other practices that minimize greenhouse-gas emissions) and maximize a range of environmental benefits.

- City Wheels, a car-sharing program, provides access to fuel-efficient automobiles on campuses.

- Our Campus Resource Monitoring System provides students with a minute-by-minute online display of electricity use and associated carbon-dioxide emissions in their residence halls. During a two-week competition, students in residence halls provided with this real-time feedback were able to reduce their electricity use by 56 percent, and the campus as a whole reduced emissions by 148,000 pounds of carbon dioxide.

- Oberlin's Lewis Center for Environmental Studies contains the largest photovoltaic array in Ohio. On an annual basis, the solar cells in the array capture more energy than the total amount that the center uses. The excess emissions-free electricity is sold back to the power company.

- An experimental local "carbon offset" program balances some on-campus greenhouse-gas emissions through projects that reduce emissions in the larger community. For example, in this spring's "Lightbulb Brigade," students provided 10,000 compact fluorescent bulbs to residents in predominantly low-income neighborhoods in exchange for their incandescent bulbs, resulting in savings of about 6,500 tons of carbon dioxide, which could then be credited to Oberlin College.

Many institutions are beginning to recognize such creative campus actions as an imperative. In 2006, Oberlin was the first of its peer institutions to sign the American College and University President's Climate Commitment. By April 2008, the presidents of more than 520 public and private institutions had signed the pledge. Each college commits to develop a budget that will account for all carbon-emissions-associated campus operations, and a long-term plan for balancing that budget to achieve carbon neutrality.

College campuses can serve as laboratories for exploring and developing policies, technologies, attitudes, and behaviors necessary to achieve carbon neutrality. Through class projects, independent research, and student activism, Oberlin students have been key players in all of the environmental initiatives described above. And they have learned a great deal in the process.

8   Institutions across the country are expanding course offerings on the science and policy of climate change. A number of colleges, including Oberlin, Harvard University, the University of Colorado at Boulder, and the University

of California at Berkeley now offer courses in campus sustainability in which students and faculty members engage with administrators and staff members to analyze, explore, and develop strategies to reduce greenhouse-gas emissions at their institutions.

Further, the Disciplinary Associations Network for Sustainability (www .aashe.org/dans) now includes more than 20 national disciplinary associations that have committed to focusing on climate change and environmental sustainability in curricula, research, and professional development. The group includes such diverse organizations as the American Chemical Society, the American Psychological Association, the American Philosophical Association, and the American Academy of Religion. Still needed are mechanisms for easily sharing the creative approaches that instructors and institutions are now developing for teaching climate change across the curriculum.

No one would argue for a monomaniacal focus on carbon or climate in the curriculum, but the fact is that the climate change now under way will touch the personal and professional lives of all of today's students, whether they major in neuroscience, Romance languages, or studio art. Courses that focus directly on climate change are crucial to building expertise, but a systemic approach is necessary to ensure that the entire campus community and the full spectrum of disciplinary perspectives are brought to bear on the challenge before us.

The creativity and critical-thinking skills that emerge from training in the arts and humanities may play a particularly important role in helping students grapple with the meaning of a rapidly changing climate. Literature, religion, sculpture, photography, and language all provide windows for understanding the relationship between humans and their environment.

12   Faculty members need not have expertise in climate science or policy to begin exploring the implications of a changing world with their students. With a bit of creativity, the importance and relevance of climate change can be linked with content of most natural and social-science classes and introduced for discussion without fundamentally altering existing syllabi. What is vital is that students feel empowered to openly discuss their questions, concerns, and ideas so that they are prepared to address personal, professional, and political choices related to climate change as informed citizens.

A key goal of a liberal-arts education in the 21st century must be to equip graduates with a diversity of intellectual tools and learning experiences needed to ensure the health of our planet. The challenge that our students face is daunting, but with the help of supportive institutions and faculty members, they have the opportunity to construct a world and a culture that are vast improvements on the ones they inherit.

PERSONAL RESPONSE

Explain your position on the subject of individual responsibility for environmental health and/or reducing your carbon footprint.

QUESTIONS FOR CLASS OR SMALL-GROUP DISCUSSION

1. Explain Peterson's opening analogy of college graduates needing to budget. Do you find it an effective lead-in to his main focus?

2. Discuss the steps that Peterson's own college has taken to reduce carbon emissions and enhance environmental sustainability. How does your campus compare?

3. What actions does Peterson call on college administrators, faculty, and students to take? Do you think that such actions are possible?

4. Peterson's final paragraph begins with this statement: "A key goal of a liberal-arts education in the 21st century must be to equip graduates with . . . tools and learning experiences . . . to ensure the health of our planet." Do you agree with him? Explain your answer.

PERSPECTIVES ON ENVIRONMENTAL STUDIES

Suggested Writing Topics

1. Write about Julia Whitty's "What Everglades Pythons and Other Invasive Species Are Trying to Tell Us" by explaining what it is that those species *are* trying to tell us.

2. Explain the extent to which you think humans are responsible for any of the biological invasions mentioned in Julia Whitty's "What Everglades Pythons and Other Invasive Species Are Trying to Tell Us."

3. If you have witnessed firsthand any of the invasions mentioned in Julia Whitty's "What Everglades Pythons and Other Invasive Species Are Trying to Tell Us," narrate your experience.

4. If you are committed to the kind of activism that Bill McKibben urges in "Global Warning: Get Up! Stand Up!" explain the nature of your activism and analyze its effectiveness for you personally.

5. Jeff Corwin in "The Sixth Extinction" urges us all "to rise to the cause and join them [scientists] in action." Explain what you can do personally to respond to Corwin's call for action.

6. Propose practical conservation steps that students on your campus or the campus as a whole can take, as John Petersen in "Accounting 101 for the 21st Century: A Liberal Arts Education in Carbon" says that his campus does. If your campus is already "green," explain what it does and what you think it accomplishes.

7. Explain your own position on the issue of global warming or any of the environmental issues mentioned in the readings in this chapter.

8. Write an essay that offers possible solutions to one of the major environmental issues confronting people today.

9. Write an essay in response to issues raised by the author of any of the essays in this chapter.

10. Argue the extent to which you think pressure from lobbyists should influence the thinking of legislators considering measures that would tighten regulations on environmental issues.

11. Write a letter to the editor of your campus or community newspaper in which you urge students on your campus and citizens in the community to take actions to reverse the current abuse of natural resources.

12. Write a letter to the president of a corporation that you know abuses the environment urging him or her to make changes in the way the company produces its product. If you refuse to buy the product because of its production methods, say so.

13. Although the writers in this chapter address a wide range of environmental issues, these selections do not provide exhaustive coverage. Select an environmental issue that is not addressed in these essays, explain the problem in detail, and if possible, offer solutions.

Research Topics

1. Research the effects of global climate changes on the invasion of a particular species, such as any of those mentioned in Julia Whitty's "What Everglades Pythons and Other Invasive Species Are Trying to Tell Us."

2. Julia Whitty's "What Everglades Pythons and Other Invasive Species Are Trying to Tell Us" mentions many subjects that are potential research projects. Select one of those and research it in depth, explaining its impact in a way similar to what Whitty does in her article. For instance, read more about the invasions of the red lionfish, the Humboldt squid, the brown tree snake, or the rosy wolfsnail. Research the invasion of the pond apple in Australia or the melaleuca in Florida. Read more about "invasional meltdown" or the impact of "r-strategists" on biodiversity.

3. Research the biological impact of Europeans arriving in Australia in the 18th century.

4. Find out more about the sixth extinction and focus on one specific aspect of it to research.

5. Conduct library research on the impact of socioeconomic inequities on environmental issues and argue your position on the subject. Consider including interviews of environmentalists, sociologists, and/or economists from your campus in your research.

6. Research the Kyoto Treaty, explain the controversy that surrounds the treaty, and explain your own viewpoint on it.

7. Research the work of scientists like Baron Alexander von Humboldt, Charles Darwin, or Thomas Malthus and write a paper arguing the relevance of their ideas to today's environmental issues.

8. Select any of the environmental issues mentioned in this chapter as a research subject. Make sure that you fairly present both sides of the issue as you explain your own position.

RESPONDING TO VISUALS

Rick McKee/Augusta Chronicle

Editorial cartoon.

1. Explain the joke in the cartoon bubbles.
2. What issue is the subject of the cartoon?
3. This cartoon appeared on the editorial page of the *Augusta Chronicle* in January 2011. What position do you think the editorial take on that issue?

RESPONDING TO VISUALS

Mark Ruchlewicz/SuperStock

Man blocking the flow of toxic waste in the river with smoke emitting from handgun.

1. What do the smokestacks in the shape of guns represent?
2. What does the man in the river represent?
3. How effective do you find this image as a statement on environmentalism?

PART **FIVE**

Business and Economics

CHAPTER 20

Marketing and the American Consumer

In their characteristic consumption and materialism, Americans are both the envy of people in other nations and the objects of their criticism. America has long been regarded as the "land of plenty," with a plethora of products to buy and a standard of living that allows most citizens to buy them. Yet such plenitude can lead to overconsumption, creating a need to buy for the sake of buying that can become a kind of obsession. Some people seek psychological counseling for this compulsion, whereas others seek financial counseling to manage the debts they have built up as a result of their need to buy things.

Indeed, shopping is so central to the lives of Americans that malls have become more than places to find virtually any product people want and need; they have become social centers, where people gather to meet friends, eat, hang out, exercise, and be entertained. Some regard this penchant for spending money and acquiring goods as a symptom of some inner emptiness, with malls, shopping strips, and discount stores replacing the spiritual centers that once held primary importance in people's lives. Others, especially manufacturers of products and the people who sell them, regard consumerism as a hearty indicator of the nation's economic health.

Smart phones and other hand-held devices have made shopping from any-where a breeze, as electronic technology has essentially transformed the way that people shop. Social media has become a gold mine for advertisers, as merchants track consumers' browsing and purchasing online and then populate websites with ads targeted specifically for them. Now it is not only "Black Friday," the day after Thanksgiving when Christmas shopping kicks off with a zest as shoppers flock to stores with prices deeply discounted for that day, but also "Cyber Monday," when retailers offer deep discounts on online purchases. The Internet may well be replac-ing the shopping malls and traditional store fronts of Main Street.

In the first selection in this chapter, Gary Ruskin and Juliet Schor discuss the negative effects of the pervasive spread of commercialism throughout far too many aspects of American life. "Every Nook and Cranny: The Dangerous Spread of Commercialized Culture" cites numerous examples of the commercialization of gov-ernment and culture and argues that the effects are almost all negative. Noting that advertising has only recently "been recognized as having political and social merit," Ruskin and Schor complain that it now invades "nearly every nook and cranny of life." You may find yourself nodding in agreement as they mention many ways in which advertising has invaded everyday life. Whether you agree with them that such pervasiveness is dangerous is something you will have to decide for yourself.

Then, Michael J. Sandel in "What Isn't for Sale?" looks at marketing in a new light, explaining how markets and market values have gradually come to govern our lives. He comments on the decades before the financial crisis of 2008 as a period of ever-strengthening faith in the market as a "primary means for achieving the pub-lic good," a view that he calls "market triumphalism." He contends that our faith in market values is now being questioned and identifies and discusses reasons why. Finally, he argues for a national debate on "the role and reach of markets." Sandel raises some intriguing points about American society's movement toward believing that almost anything can be sold and why we should be worried about it. After read-ing his essay, consider whether you agree with him or if you think he is overstating the risks of living in a society that thinks it is all right to sell anything.

The next reading, "Marketing to the Millennials," by Suzy Menkes, explains the new approaches to marketing that upscale luxury and fashion brands are taking. She asks, "If the exclusivity inherent in traditional luxury is an obsolete factor, how do you market to the Millennials?" Part of the explanation lies in the differences in consumer habits among Millennials, Generation X members, and Baby Boomers. No matter what category of consumer you fit into, you will likely be interested in what she has to say about how advertisers profile these groups and shape their strategies as a result.

Finally, Anna Quindlen in "Stuff Is Not Salvation" comments on Americans' inclination to buy things that they don't need. Writing just before Christmas, she asks: "[W]hy in the world did we buy all this junk in the first place?" As you read what Quindlen has to say about "addiction to consumption," ask yourself about your own buying habits. Do you see yourself in Quindlen's description of the behavior of shoppers? Do you like to buy for the sake of buying, whether you need a product or not?

EVERY NOOK AND CRANNY: THE DANGEROUS SPREAD OF COMMERCIALIZED CULTURE

GARY RUSKIN AND JULIET SCHOR

Gary Ruskin is executive director of Commercial Alert, a nonprofit organization whose mission is "to keep the commercial culture within its proper sphere, and to prevent it from exploiting children and subverting the higher values of family, community, environmental integrity and democracy" (http://www.commercialalert.org/about/). Juliet Schor is a professor of sociology at Boston College and author of The Overworked American: The Unexpected Decline of Leisure *(1991);* The Overspent American: Upscaling, Downshifting and the New Consumer *(1998); and* Born to Buy: The Commercialized Child and the New Consumer Culture *(2004). She serves on the board of directors of Commercial Alert. This article was first published in the January/ February 2005 issue of* Multinational Monitor, *a publication that tracks activity in the corporate world, especially in third world countries.*

In December, many people in Washington, D.C., paused to absorb the meaning in the lighting of the National Christmas Tree, at the White House Ellipse. At that event, President George W. Bush reflected that the "love and gifts" of Christmas were "signs and symbols of even a greater love and gift that came on a holy night."

But these signs weren't the only ones on display. Perhaps it was not surprising that the illumination was sponsored by MCI, which, as MCI WorldCom, committed one of the largest corporate frauds in history. Such public displays of commercialism have become commonplace in the United States.

The rise of commercialism is an artifact of the growth of corporate power. It began as part of a political and ideological response by corporations to wage pressures, rising social expenditures, and the successes of the environmental and consumer movements in the late 1960s and early 1970s. Corporations fostered the anti-tax movement and support for corporate welfare, which helped create funding crises in state and local governments and schools, and made them more willing to carry commercial advertising. They promoted "free market" ideology, privatization and consumerism, while denigrating the public sphere. In the late 1970s, Mobil Oil began its decades-long advertising on the *New York Times* op-ed page, one example of a larger corporate effort to reverse a precipitous decline in public approval of corporations. They also became adept at manipulating the campaign finance system, and weaknesses in the federal bribery statute, to procure influence in governments at all levels.

4   Perhaps most importantly, the commercialization of government and culture and the growing importance of material acquisition and consumer lifestyles were hastened by the co-optation of potentially countervailing institutions, such as churches (papal visits have been sponsored by Pepsi, Federal Express, and Mercedes-Benz), governments, schools, universities, and nongovernmental organizations.

     While advertising has long been an element in the circus of U.S. life, not until recently has it been recognized as having political or social merit. For nearly two centuries, advertising (lawyers call it commercial speech) was not protected by the U.S. Constitution. The U.S. Supreme Court ruled in 1942 that states could regulate commercial speech at will. But in 1976, the Court granted constitutional protection to commercial speech. Corporations have used this new right of speech to proliferate advertising into nearly every nook and cranny of life.

Entering the Schoolhouse

During most of the twentieth century, there was little advertising in schools. That changed in 1989, when Chris Whittle's Channel One enticed schools to accept advertising, by offering to loan TV sets to classrooms. Each school day, Channel One features at least two minutes of ads, and 10 minutes of news, fluff, banter, and quizzes. The program is shown to about 8 million children in 12,000 schools.

     Soda, candy and fast food companies soon learned Channel One's lesson of using financial incentives to gain access to schoolchildren. By 2000, 94 percent of high schools allowed the sale of soda, and 72 percent allowed sale of chocolate candy. Energy, candy, personal care products, even automobile manufacturers have entered the classroom with "sponsored educational materials"—that is, ads in the guise of free "curricula."

8   Until recently, corporate incursion in schools has mainly gone under the radar. However, the rise of childhood obesity has engendered stiff political opposition to junk food marketing, and in the last three years, coalitions of progressives, conservatives and public health groups have made headway. The State of California has banned the sale of soda in elementary, middle and junior high schools. In Maine, soda and candy suppliers have removed their products from vending machines in all schools. Arkansas banned candy and soda vending machines in elementary schools. Los Angeles, Chicago and New York have city-wide bans on the sale of soda in schools. Channel One was expelled from the Nashville public schools in the 2002–2003 school year, and will be removed from Seattle in early 2005. Thanks to activist pressure, a company called ZapMe!, which placed computers in thousands of schools to advertise and extract data from students, was removed from all schools across the country.

Ad Creep and Spam Culture

Advertisers have long relied on 30-second TV spots to deliver messages to mass audiences. During the 1990s, the impact of these ads began to drop off, in part because viewers simply clicked to different programs during ads. In response, many advertisers began to place ads elsewhere, leading to "ad creep"—the spread of ads throughout social space and cultural institutions. Whole new marketing sub-specialties developed, such as "place-based" advertising, which coerces captive viewers to watch video ads. Examples include ads before movies, ads on buses and trains in cities (Chicago, Milwaukee and Orlando), and CNN's Airport channel. Video ads are also now common on ATMs, gas pumps, in convenience stores and doctors' offices.

Another form of ad creep is "product placement," in which advertisers pay to have their product included in movies, TV shows, museum exhibits, or other forms of media and culture. Product placement is thought to be more effective than the traditional 30-second ad because it sneaks by the viewer's critical faculties. Product placement has recently occurred in novels, and children's books. Some U.S. TV programs (*American Idol, The Restaurant, The Apprentice*) and movies (*Minority Report, Cellular*) are so full of product placement that they resemble infomercials. By contrast, many European nations, such as Austria, Germany, Norway and the United Kingdom, ban or sharply restrict product placement on television.

Commercial use of the Internet was forbidden as recently as the early 1990s, and the first spam wasn't sent until 1994. But the marketing industry quickly penetrated this sphere as well, and now 70 percent of all e-mail is spam, according to the spam filter firm Postini Inc. Pop-ups, pop-unders and ad-ware have become major annoyances for Internet users. Telemarketing became so unpopular that the corporate-friendly Federal Trade Commission established a National Do Not Call Registry, which has brought relief from telemarketing calls to 64 million households.

12   Even major cultural institutions have been harnessed by the advertising industry. During 2001–2002, the Smithsonian Institution, perhaps the most important U.S. cultural institution, established the General Motors Hall of Transportation and the Lockheed Martin Imax Theater. Following public opposition and Congressional action, the commercialization of the Smithsonian has largely been halted. In 2000, the Library of Congress hosted a giant celebration for Coca-Cola, essentially converting the nation's most important library into a prop to sell soda pop.

Targeting Kids

For a time, institutions of childhood were relatively uncommercialized, as adults subscribed to the notion of childhood innocence, and the need to keep children from the "profane" commercial world. But what was once a trickle of advertising to children has become a flood. Corporations spend about $15 billion marketing to children in the United States each year, and by the mid-1990s, the average child was exposed to 40,000 TV ads annually.

Children have few legal protections from corporate marketers in the United States. This contrasts strongly to the European Union, which has enacted restrictions. Norway and Sweden have banned television advertising to children under

12 years of age; in Italy, advertising during TV cartoons is illegal, and toy advertising is illegal in Greece between 7 AM and 11 PM. Advertising before and after children's programs is banned in Austria.

Government Brought to You by . . .

As fiscal crises have descended upon local governments, they have turned to advertisers as a revenue source. This trend began inauspiciously in Buffalo, New York, in 1995 when Pratt & Lambert, a local paint company, purchased the right to call itself the city's official paint. The next year the company was bought by Sherwin-Williams, which closed the local factory and eliminated its 200 jobs.

16   In 1997, Ocean City, Maryland, signed an exclusive marketing deal to make Coca-Cola the city's official drink, and other cities have followed with similar deals with Coke or Pepsi. Even mighty New York City has succumbed, signing a $166 million exclusive marketing deal with Snapple, after which some critics dubbed it the "Big Snapple."

At the United Nations, UNICEF made a stir in 2002 when it announced that it would "team up" with McDonald's, the world's largest fast food company, to promote "McDonald's World Children's Day" in celebration of the anniversary of the United Nations adoption of the Convention on the Rights of the Child. Public health and children's advocates across the globe protested, prompting UNICEF to decline participation in later years.

Another victory for the anti-commercialism forces, perhaps the most significant, came in 2004, when the World Health Organization's Framework Convention on Tobacco Control became legally binding. The treaty commits nations to prohibit tobacco advertising to the extent their constitutions allow it.

Impacts

Because the phenomenon of commercialism has become so ubiquitous, it is not surprising that its effects are as well. Perhaps most alarming has been the epidemic of marketing-related diseases afflicting people in the United States, and especially children, such as obesity, type 2 diabetes and smoking-related illnesses. Each day, about 2,000 U.S. children begin to smoke, and about one-third of them will die from tobacco-related illnesses. Children are inundated with advertising for high calorie junk food and fast food, and, predictably, 15 percent of U.S. children aged 6 to 19 are now overweight.

20   Excessive commercialism is also creating a more materialistic populace. In 2003, the annual UCLA survey of incoming college freshmen found that the number of students who said it was a very important or essential life goal to "develop a meaningful philosophy of life" fell to an all-time low of 39 percent, while succeeding financially has increased to a 13-year high, at 74 percent. High involvement in consumer culture has been shown (by Schor) to be a significant cause of depression, anxiety, low self-esteem and psychosomatic complaints in

children, findings which parallel similar studies of materialism among teens and adults. Other impacts are more intangible. A 2004 poll by Yankelovich Partners, found that 61 percent of the U.S. public "feel that the amount of marketing and advertising is out of control," and 65 percent "feel constantly bombarded with too much advertising and marketing." Is advertising diminishing our sense of general well-being? Perhaps.

The purpose of most commercial advertising is to increase demand for a product. As John Kenneth Galbraith noted 40 years ago, the macro effect of advertising is to artificially boost the demand for private goods, thereby reducing the "demand" or support for unadvertised, public goods. The predictable result has been the backlash to taxes, and reduced provision of public goods and services.

This imbalance also affects the natural environment. The additional consumption created by the estimated \$265 billion that the advertising industry will spend in 2004 will also yield more pollution, natural resource destruction, carbon dioxide emissions and global warming.

Finally, advertising has also contributed to a narrowing of the public discourse, as advertising-driven media grow ever more timid. Sometimes it seems as if we live in an echo chamber, a place where corporations speak and everyone else listens.

24   Governments at all levels have failed to address these impacts. That may be because the most insidious effect of commercialism is to undermine government integrity. As governments adopt commercial values, and are integrated into corporate marketing, they develop conflicts of interest that make them less likely to take stands against commercialism.

Disgust among Yourselves

As corporations consolidate their control over governments and culture, we don't expect an outright reversal of commercialization in the near future.

That's true despite considerable public sentiment for more limits and regulations on advertising and marketing. However, as commercialism grows more intrusive, public distaste for it will likely increase, as will political support for restricting it. In the long run, we believe this hopeful trend will gather strength.

In the not-too-distant future, the significance of the lighting of the National Christmas Tree may no longer be overshadowed by public relations efforts to create goodwill for corporate wrongdoers.

PERSONAL RESPONSE

Ruskin and Schor ask in paragraph 20: "Is advertising diminishing our sense of general well-being?" Look at the examples they give in that and the previous paragraph and then answer the question by examining whether your own general well-being has been affected by advertising.

QUESTIONS FOR CLASS OR SMALL-GROUP DISCUSSION

1. Ruskin and Schor mention ways in which commercialism has entered the schoolroom (paragraphs 6–8). Were any of the examples they cite part of your own school experience? Can you give other examples of the invasion of commercialism into schools?

2. What other examples of "ad creep" (paragraph 9) can you give besides the ones that Ruskin and Schor mention? Discuss whether you believe that such advertising should be banned or restricted in the United States, as it is in other countries.

3. Summarize the effects cited by Ruskin and Schor of the "ubiquitous" nature of commercialization (paragraph 19). Do you think that they provide enough evidence to support their contention?

4. Are you convinced by Ruskin and Schor's argument that the spread of commercialism is "dangerous"? Explain your answer.

WHAT ISN'T FOR SALE?

MICHAEL J. SANDEL

Michael J. Sandel is a professor of government at Harvard University. For more than twenty years he has taught a popular course called Justice, which has been filmed and offered online and made into a multi-part series in both the United States and the United Kingdom. His books include Public Philosophy: Essays on Morality in Politics *(2006);* The Case against Perfection: Ethics in the Age of Genetic Engineering *(2007);* Justice: A Reader *(2007);* Justice: What's the Right Thing to Do? *(2009); and* What Money Can't Buy: The Moral Limits of Markets *(2012). This essay was first published in the* Atlantic *in April 2012.*

There are some things money can't buy—but these days, not many. Almost everything is up for sale. For example:

- *A prison-cell upgrade: $90 a night.* In Santa Ana, California, and some other cities, nonviolent offenders can pay for a clean, quiet jail cell, without any non-paying prisoners to disturb them.

- *Access to the carpool lane while driving solo: $8.* Minneapolis, San Diego, Houston, Seattle, and other cities have sought to ease traffic congestion by letting solo drivers pay to drive in carpool lanes, at rates that vary according to traffic.

- *The services of an Indian surrogate mother: $8,000.* Western couples seeking surrogates increasingly outsource the job to India, and the price is less than one-third the going rate in the United States.
- *The right to shoot an endangered black rhino: $250,000.* South Africa has begun letting some ranchers sell hunters the right to kill a limited number of rhinos, to give the ranchers an incentive to raise and protect the endangered species.
- *Your doctor's cellphone number: $1,500 and up per year.* A growing number of "concierge" doctors offer cellphone access and same-day appointments for patients willing to pay annual fees ranging from $1,500 to $25,000.
- *The right to emit a metric ton of carbon dioxide into the atmosphere: $10.50.* The European Union runs a carbon-dioxide-emissions market that enables companies to buy and sell the right to pollute.
- *The right to immigrate to the United States: $500,000.* Foreigners who invest $500,000 and create at least 10 full-time jobs in an area of high unemployment are eligible for a green card that entitles them to permanent residency.

Not everyone can afford to buy these things. But today there are lots of new ways to make money. If you need to earn some extra cash, here are some novel possibilities:

- *Sell space on your forehead to display commercial advertising: $10,000.* A single mother in Utah who needed money for her son's education was paid $10,000 by an online casino to install a permanent tattoo of the casino's Web address on her forehead. Temporary tattoo ads earn less.
- *Serve as a human guinea pig in a drug-safety trial for a pharmaceutical company: $7,500.* The pay can be higher or lower, depending on the invasiveness of the procedure used to test the drug's effect and the discomfort involved.
- *Fight in Somalia or Afghanistan for a private military contractor: up to $1,000 a day.* The pay varies according to qualifications, experience, and nationality.
- *Stand in line overnight on Capitol Hill to hold a place for a lobbyist who wants to attend a congressional hearing: $15–$20 an hour.* Lobbyists pay line-standing companies, who hire homeless people and others to queue up.
- *If you are a second-grader in an underachieving Dallas school, read a book: $2.* To encourage reading, schools pay kids for each book they read.

We live in a time when almost everything can be bought and sold. Over the past three decades, markets—and market values—have come to govern our lives as never before. We did not arrive at this condition through any deliberate choice. It is almost as if it came upon us.

4   As the Cold War ended, markets and market thinking enjoyed unrivaled prestige, and understandably so. No other mechanism for organizing the production and distribution of goods had proved as successful at generating affluence and prosperity. And yet even as growing numbers of countries around the world embraced market mechanisms in the operation of their economies, something else was happening. Market values were coming to play a greater and greater role in social life.

Economics was becoming an imperial domain. Today, the logic of buying and selling no longer applies to material goods alone. It increasingly governs the whole of life.

The years leading up to the financial crisis of 2008 were a heady time of market faith and deregulation—an era of market triumphalism. The era began in the early 1980s, when Ronald Reagan and Margaret Thatcher proclaimed their conviction that markets, not government, held the key to prosperity and freedom. And it continued into the 1990s with the market-friendly liberalism of Bill Clinton and Tony Blair, who moderated but consolidated the faith that markets are the primary means for achieving the public good.

Today, that faith is in question. The financial crisis did more than cast doubt on the ability of markets to allocate risk efficiently. It also prompted a widespread sense that markets have become detached from morals, and that we need to somehow reconnect the two. But it's not obvious what this would mean, or how we should go about it.

Some say the moral failing at the heart of market triumphalism was greed, which led to irresponsible risk-taking. The solution, according to this view, is to rein in greed, insist on greater integrity and responsibility among bankers and Wall Street executives, and enact sensible regulations to prevent a similar crisis from happening again.

8   This is, at best, a partial diagnosis. While it is certainly true that greed played a role in the financial crisis, something bigger was and is at stake. The most fateful change that unfolded during the past three decades was not an increase in greed. It was the reach of markets, and of market values, into spheres of life traditionally governed by nonmarket norms. To contend with this condition, we need to do more than inveigh against greed; we need to have a public debate about where markets belong—and where they don't.

Consider, for example, the proliferation of for-profit schools, hospitals, and prisons, and the outsourcing of war to private military contractors. (In Iraq and Afghanistan, private contractors have actually outnumbered U.S. military troops.) Consider the eclipse of public police forces by private security firms—especially in the U.S. and the U.K., where the number of private guards is almost twice the number of public police officers.

Or consider the pharmaceutical companies' aggressive marketing of prescription drugs directly to consumers, a practice now prevalent in the U.S. but prohibited in most other countries. (If you've ever seen the television commercials on the evening news, you could be forgiven for thinking that the greatest health crisis in the world is not malaria or river blindness or sleeping sickness but an epidemic of erectile dysfunction.)

Consider too the reach of commercial advertising into public schools, from buses to corridors to cafeterias; the sale of "naming rights" to parks and civic spaces; the blurred boundaries, within journalism, between news and advertising, likely to blur further as newspapers and magazines struggle to survive; the marketing of "designer" eggs and sperm for assisted reproduction; the buying and selling, by companies and countries, of the right to pollute; a system of campaign finance in the U.S. that comes close to permitting the buying and selling of elections.

12   These uses of markets to allocate health, education, public safety, national security, criminal justice, environmental protection, recreation, procreation, and other social goods were for the most part unheard-of 30 years ago. Today, we take them largely for granted.

Why worry that we are moving toward a society in which everything is up for sale?

For two reasons. One is about inequality, the other about corruption. First, consider inequality. In a society where everything is for sale, life is harder for those of modest means. The more money can buy, the more affluence—or the lack of it—matters. If the only advantage of affluence were the ability to afford yachts, sports cars, and fancy vacations, inequalities of income and wealth would matter less than they do today. But as money comes to buy more and more, the distribution of income and wealth looms larger.

The second reason we should hesitate to put everything up for sale is more difficult to describe. It is not about inequality and fairness but about the corrosive tendency of markets. Putting a price on the good things in life can corrupt them. That's because markets don't only allocate goods; they express and promote certain attitudes toward the goods being exchanged. Paying kids to read books might get them to read more, but might also teach them to regard reading as a chore rather than a source of intrinsic satisfaction. Hiring foreign mercenaries to fight our wars might spare the lives of our citizens, but might also corrupt the meaning of citizenship.

16   Economists often assume that markets are inert, that they do not affect the goods being exchanged. But this is untrue. Markets leave their mark. Sometimes, market values crowd out nonmarket values worth caring about.

When we decide that certain goods may be bought and sold, we decide, at least implicitly, that it is appropriate to treat them as commodities, as instruments of profit and use. But not all goods are properly valued in this way. The most obvious example is human beings. Slavery was appalling because it treated human beings as a commodity, to be bought and sold at auction. Such treatment fails to value human beings as persons, worthy of dignity and respect; it sees them as instruments of gain and objects of use.

Something similar can be said of other cherished goods and practices. We don't allow children to be bought and sold, no matter how difficult the process of adoption can be or how willing impatient prospective parents might be. Even if the prospective buyers would treat the child responsibly, we worry that a market in children would express and promote the wrong way of valuing them. Children are properly regarded not as consumer goods but as beings worthy of love and care. Or consider the rights and obligations of citizenship. If you are called to jury duty, you can't hire a substitute to take your place. Nor do we allow citizens to sell their votes, even though others might be eager to buy them. Why not? Because we believe that civic duties are not private property but public responsibilities. To outsource them is to demean them, to value them in the wrong way.

These examples illustrate a broader point: some of the good things in life are degraded if turned into commodities. So to decide where the market belongs, and where it should be kept at a distance, we have to decide how to value the goods in question—health, education, family life, nature, art, civic duties, and so on. These are moral and political questions, not merely economic ones. To resolve them, we have to debate, case by case, the moral meaning of these goods, and the proper way of valuing them.

20   This is a debate we didn't have during the era of market triumphalism. As a result, without quite realizing it—without ever deciding to do so—we drifted from having a market economy to being a market society.

The difference is this: A market economy is a tool—a valuable and effective tool—for organizing productive activity. A market society is a way of life in which market values seep into every aspect of human endeavor. It's a place where social relations are made over in the image of the market.

The great missing debate in contemporary politics is about the role and reach of markets. Do we want a market economy, or a market society? What role should markets play in public life and personal relations? How can we decide which goods should be bought and sold, and which should be governed by non-market values? Where should money's writ not run?

Even if you agree that we need to grapple with big questions about the morality of markets, you might doubt that our public discourse is up to the task. It's a legitimate worry. At a time when political argument consists mainly of shouting matches on cable television, partisan vitriol on talk radio, and ideological food fights on the floor of Congress, it's hard to imagine a reasoned public debate about such controversial moral questions as the right way to value procreation, children, education, health, the environment, citizenship, and other goods. I believe such a debate is possible, but only if we are willing to broaden the terms of our public discourse and grapple more explicitly with competing notions of the good life.

24   In hopes of avoiding sectarian strife, we often insist that citizens leave their moral and spiritual convictions behind when they enter the public square. But the reluctance to admit arguments about the good life into politics has had an unanticipated consequence. It has helped prepare the way for market triumphalism, and for the continuing hold of market reasoning.

In its own way, market reasoning also empties public life of moral argument. Part of the appeal of markets is that they don't pass judgment on the preferences they satisfy. They don't ask whether some ways of valuing goods are higher, or worthier, than others. If someone is willing to pay for sex, or a kidney, and a consenting adult is willing to sell, the only question the economist asks is "How much?" Markets don't wag fingers. They don't discriminate between worthy preferences and unworthy ones. Each party to a deal decides for him- or herself what value to place on the things being exchanged.

This nonjudgmental stance toward values lies at the heart of market reasoning, and explains much of its appeal. But our reluctance to engage in moral and spiritual argument, together with our embrace of markets, has exacted a heavy price: it has drained public discourse of moral and civic energy, and contributed to the technocratic, managerial politics afflicting many societies today.

A debate about the moral limits of markets would enable us to decide, as a society, where markets serve the public good and where they do not belong. Thinking through the appropriate place of markets requires that we reason together, in public, about the right way to value the social goods we prize. It would be folly to expect that a more morally robust public discourse, even at its best, would lead to agreement on every contested question. But it would make for a healthier public life. And it would make us more aware of the price we pay for living in a society where everything is up for sale.

PERSONAL RESPONSE

Select one item from the list of bulleted items that one can buy (paragraph 1) and write a response to it, stating whether you think such a thing is all right or whether you think it goes too far, and why. Do the same for the list of ways that people can make money (paragraph 2).

QUESTIONS FOR CLASS OR SMALL-GROUP DISCUSSION

1. What is Sandel's central purpose? What relationship do his opening paragraphs have with his central purpose?
2. What does Sandel mean by the term "market triumphalism"? He asserts that faith in markets is now in question. How does he account for that loss of faith? Do you agree with him on this point?
3. What does Sandel have to say about morality in the market place? Where did it lapse, according to him, and how can it be re-established? What do you think of his analysis of this point?
4. How does Sandel answer this question: "Why worry that we are moving toward a society in which everything is up for sale" (paragraph 13)? To what extent do you agree with him?

MARKETING TO THE MILLENNIALS

Suzy Menkes

Suzy Menkes is a British journalist and head fashion editor of the International Herald Tribune. *She travels the world covering international designer collections. She is also an expert on jewelry and the British royal family and has written the following books:* The Royal Jewels *(1985),* The Windsor Style *(1987), and* Queen and Country *(1992). Menkes was named an officer of the Order of the British*

Empire for her services to journalism and also named a chevalier of the Legion of Honor by President Jacques Chirac of France. This article was published on March 2, 2010, in the New York Times.

The model Lily Donaldson's hair coils, floats and springs across the screen, creating arresting images in slow motion. As the last strand fades, you brace yourself for the hair spray advertisement that will batter away the emotion and kill the dream.

But it doesn't happen. Nor at the close of a video of a Rodarte woman—all distressed glamour in a techno-thriller of hallucinatory tension. Not even when you give your personal verdict by clicking on the love/don't love buttons. There are no distractions, just an intriguing feeling of an experience without blandishments and no e-commerce in sight.

Nowness.com, the Web site unveiled by LVMH Moët Hennessy Louis Vuitton last week, is as different as could be imagined from the group's defunct eluxury.com, which it replaces. Instead of urgent offers to buy, each video clip, artistic image and cultural commentary creates a mood and suggests that you have entered an exclusive world where you can absorb and be informed. The pleasure is measured by the time you choose to spend in this enfolding world of art laced with the fashionable.

4   If you search for the LVMH name or any indication that the site is underwritten by the world's biggest luxury group, the nearest you get is a fleeting reference to Fendi or another brand that the cognoscenti would recognize as part of the group.

Behind the concept of this interactive platform to create a luxury experience online is Kamel Ouadi, the digital vice president of Nowness. He describes the site as a subtle, discreet and elegant way to offer original, interesting and ever-changing content to intelligent and aspirational people—and those who are already embedded in the digital culture.

"It is not a commercial platform, although we hope that when we have raised the traffic, we can have partnerships with others as well as give animated and customized information," says Mr. Ouadi, explaining how a visitor's viewing choices will be streamlined into a personal portfolio.

Finding a way to reach a generation that is eager to be entertained and informed, yet resistant to the familiar, in-your-face 20th-century approach, is the focus of every smart luxury and fashion brand. As the fourth and final round of the international collections opens in Paris on Wednesday, the buzz is more around live-streaming shows and 3-D technology than about seasonal trends.

8   The target is the Millennials, defined as those born in the 1980s who came of age with the new century and are now between 18 and 28. The fact that they have grown up wired—linked as soon as they start to socialize via cellphones, computers and video games—is not the only defining characteristic. They have a different mind-set, making former methods of approach obsolete. This is the generation of free downloads, easy access to everything—what the American psychologist Nathan Brody calls "the entitled generation."

If the exclusivity inherent in traditional luxury is an obsolete factor, how do you market to the Millennials?

"We think a lot about the mind-set of the consumers—what are the youngsters doing, does it differ country by country, region by region—we need a deep understanding because that is crucial for the future," says Robert Polet, president and chief executive of Gucci Group.

Like other executives, Mr. Polet refers to the definitive report by the Pew Research Center, a U.S.-based nonprofit public opinion research group, that explored the behaviors, values and opinions of the teens and 20-somethings that make up the Millennial Generation.

12   One of the most evident changes is social networking, which is embraced by 75 percent of the Millennials, compared with 50 percent of the Generation X members (ages 30 to 45) and just 30 percent of Baby Boomers (aged 46 to 64).

"These unique factors make them very savvy consumers, who pay great attention to the value of what they buy and require a different way to interact with brands," says Mr. Polet. "At Gucci Group, we recognize their transformative power in the way they engage with luxury brands. We are embracing different ways of creating dialogue through social media. Some of our brands have launched Facebook and Twitter pages and iPhone applications."

The executive was referring particularly to products, playlists and videos introduced by Gucci, with the active involvement of Frida Giannini, its 38-year-old creative director.

Angela Ahrendts, chief executive of Burberry, sees Christopher Bailey, the brand's 38-year-old chief creative officer, as "a bridge into the Millennial consumer." Their joint embrace of new technology is already legendary within the fashion world.

16   It encompasses the wired interiors of the London and New York headquarters, the embrace of videos, Skype-ing between design team and factory, as well as the more outwardly visible live-streaming and 3-D filming of recent shows and the "Art of the Trench," the Web site set up specifically to promote the iconic Burberry trench coat with the photo blogger Scott Schuman, known as the Sartorialist.

"Attracting the Millennial customer to luxury started two years ago—I said that we can either get crushed or ride the greatest wave of our life," says Ms. Ahrendts. "We brought people on the team who were Millennials. I knew it was not my mother tongue—and I don't have time to learn it."

One savvy move was to make Emma Watson, born in 1990 and who famously plays Hermione in the Harry Potter movie series, the new face of Burberry.

"She was 19. She is a Millennial. And it is all about attitude," says Ms. Ahrendts. She also explained that the idea of global Internet reach was particularly important for countries like India and South America, where the young population is burgeoning and where Burberry has not yet opened brick-and-mortar stores.

20   Although youth is always cited as the key to the Millennial generation, the digital state of mind encompasses a broader reach than might be

expected. If Generation X is, as Pew's research claims, 50 percent techno-savvy enough to be involved in social media, those members could be well-paid consumers who are much more important to fashion retailers than the younger Millennials.

Mr. Ouadi says that LVMH's Nowness Web site is aimed at 35 to 40 year olds. It seems to reach out to a cross-culture generation more aware of art as an interesting and pleasurable experience than the clubbing/music/movies pursuits detailed on Twitter and Facebook.

So age is not necessarily the only guarantee of belonging to the wired world.

Giorgio Armani, 75, is not actively involved with the Internet, and yet he has been adamant that his company must reach out to the new generation, via Facebook, YouTube and more.

24   "Our goal is always to create a seamless brand experience, especially with our younger lines, communicating the brand wherever the customer wants to touch it—on their mobile devices, via a social network, on blogs, in store, in print and outdoor media," says John Hooks, deputy chairman of the Armani company.

The executive referred to the mobile phone applications that were follow-ups to the introduction of the Emporio Armani e-commerce site in 2007. Emporio customers can buy by phone, browse information and view backstage videos of runway shows. Similarly, there is an Emporio YouTube channel.

And the A/X Armani brand, aimed at young customers, has focused on "m-commerce," or mobile phone shopping, which includes the A/X music label. Lady Gaga's recent appearance in a space age Armani creation seems to have revved up the brand's Facebook site, with 50,000 of its 268,000 "friends" joining in the last month.

What about designers themselves? Are they all deeply involved on the technology as well as the creative side? Paradoxically, they often say that they try to stay clear of techno-babble, seeing it as a distraction or an overload of information.

28   Raf Simons, 42, had street smarts when he started his career, even basing a men's collection on the backpacking generation. But, even though his clothes are modernist, even futuristic, he admits he is now out of the loop.

"I feel like an oldie—when I started there was no computer and no mobile phones—I can't follow the kids these days," says Mr. Simons. "Do I miss something?"

"I am very old school," he adds. "Not that I regret it."

The designer, who also works for the Jil Sander label, says he does not believe that the fashion world has changed so radically in recent years, except in certain respects.

32   "The only thing that has changed a lot is that we were always defined as elite—and everybody is going to have access to everything at any time," he says. "It can kill the actual experience in its own time."

Traditionally, magazines have been the conduit that filtered fashion and delivered it to the consumer. Now those same publications are acutely aware that there are other ways to deliver fashion directly, not least by the brands themselves.

Significantly, the LVMH site debuted publicly on the same day as Vogue.it, the new Web site of Italian Vogue. That Condé Nast site was introduced at an event that projected images from the magazine on the façade of a Milan palazzo and drew an overwhelming number of fashion influentials to see its pages spring to life on screen.

Forward-looking magazines are hyper-aware of the need for a digital experience. Terry Jones started the hip British magazine i-D with his wife, Tricia, 30 years ago and has kept its youthful, edgy quality. He sees dramatic change in the medium—but not necessarily in the soul of the Millennial generation.

36   "Fundamentally, I think human nature is the same—but the condition of the generation of today is different," says Mr. Jones, "The idea is to have easy access to everything, compared to when everything in fashion was kept under corporate control."

As Nowness.com shows, it is the smart minds in the corporate luxury world who are trying to get back control from the chaotic cacophony that is the Internet. Only this time, the idea is to listen to consumers, instead of talking at them—especially if they are 20-something Millennials who are set to take over a digitalized world.

PERSONAL RESPONSE

Do advertisements influence you to buy products? Whether you can afford luxury items or not, how appealing do you find advertisements for such products?

QUESTIONS FOR CLASS OR SMALL-GROUP DISCUSSION

1. State in your own words the approach that venders of luxury and fashion items are taking to market their products to Millennials.

2. Menkes characterizes traditional approaches to advertising as "batter[ing] away the emotion and kill[ing] the drama" (paragraph 1) and as "in-your-face" (paragraph 7). Do you agree with her on this point? Can you give examples that either support or refute her statements?

3. Menkes quotes John Hooks, deputy chairmain of Armani, as saying "our goal is always to create a seamless brand experience" (paragraph 24). What do you understand him to mean by that? What is a "seamless brand experience"?

4. Menkes reports that designer Raf Simons feels that he is "out of the loop" because when he started, "there was no computer and no mobile phones." He asks, "Do I miss something?" How would you answer his question? What is he missing, if anything, by being "out of the loop"?

STUFF IS NOT SALVATION

Anna Quindlen

Anna Quindlen is a novelist, social critic, and journalist. In 1986, she began her syndicated column "Life in the Thirties" in the New York Times, *and a few years later "Public and Private," for which she won a Pulitzer Prize in 1992. She contributed to* Newsweek's *prestigious back-page column, "The Last Word," every other week until she retired in 2009. Her columns are collected in* Living Out Loud *(1988);* Thinking Out Loud *(1992); and* Loud and Clear *(2004). She has written the following novels:* Object Lessons *(1991);* One True Thing *(1994);* Black and Blue *(1998);* Blessings *(2003); and* Being Perfect *(2004). Among her nonfiction books are* How Reading Changed My Life *(1998);* A Short Guide to a Happy Life *(2000); and* Imagining London: A Tour of the World's Greatest Fictional City *(2004). This essay appeared in the December 22, 2008, issue of* Newsweek.

As the boom times fade, an important holiday question surfaces: why in the world did we buy all this junk in the first place?

What passes for the holiday season began before dawn the day after Thanksgiving, when a worker at a Wal-Mart in Valley Stream, N.Y., was trampled to death by a mob of bargain hunters. Afterward, there were reports that some people, mesmerized by cheap consumer electronics and discounted toys, kept shopping even after announcements to clear the store.

These are dark days in the United States: the cataclysmic stock-market declines, the industries edging up on bankruptcy, the home foreclosures and the waves of layoffs. But the prospect of an end to plenty has uncovered what may ultimately be a more pernicious problem, an addiction to consumption so out of control that it qualifies as a sickness. The suffocation of a store employee by a stampede of shoppers was horrifying, but it wasn't entirely surprising.

4   Americans have been on an acquisition binge for decades. I suspect television advertising, which made me want a Chatty Cathy doll so much as a kid that when I saw her under the tree my head almost exploded. By contrast, my father will be happy to tell you about the excitement of getting an orange in his stocking during the Depression. The depression before this one.

A critical difference between then and now is credit. The orange had to be paid for. The rite of passage for a child when I was young was a solemn visit to the local bank, there to exchange birthday money for a savings passbook. Every once in a while, like magic, a bit of extra money would appear. Interest. Yippee.

The passbook was replaced by plastic, so that today Americans are overwhelmed by debt and the national savings rate is calculated, like an algebra equation, in negatives. By 2010 Americans will be a trillion dollars in the hole on credit-card debt alone.

But let's look, not at the numbers, but the atmospherics. Appliances, toys, clothes, gadgets. Junk. There's the sad truth. Wall Street executives may have made investments that lost their value, but, in a much smaller way, so did the rest of us. "I looked into my closet the other day and thought, why did I buy all this stuff?" one friend said recently. A person in the United States replaces a cell phone every 16 months, not because the cell phone is old, but because it is oldish. My mother used to complain that the Christmas toys were grubby and forgotten by Easter. (I didn't even really like dolls, especially dolls who introduced themselves to you over and over again when you pulled the ring in their necks.) Now much of the country is made up of people with the acquisition habits of a 7-year-old, desire untethered from need, or the ability to pay. The result is a booming business in those free-standing storage facilities, where junk goes to linger in a persistent vegetative state, somewhere between eBay and the dump.

8   Oh, there is still plenty of need. But it is for real things, things that matter: college tuition, prescription drugs, rent. Food pantries and soup kitchens all over the country have seen demand for their services soar. Homelessness, which had fallen in recent years, may rebound as people lose their jobs and their houses. For the first time this month, the number of people on food stamps will exceed the 30 million mark.

Hard times offer the opportunity to ask hard questions, and one of them is the one my friend asked, staring at sweaters and shoes: why did we buy all this stuff? Did anyone really need a flat-screen in the bedroom, or a designer handbag, or three cars? If the mall is our temple, then Marc Jacobs is God. There's a scary thought.

The drumbeat that accompanied Black Friday this year was that the numbers had to redeem us, that if enough money was spent by shoppers it would indicate that things were not so bad after all. But what the economy required was at odds with a necessary epiphany. Because things are dire, many people have become hesitant to spend money on trifles. And in the process they began to realize that it's all trifles.

Here I go, stating the obvious: stuff does not bring salvation. But if it's so obvious, how come for so long people have not realized it? The happiest families I know aren't the ones with the most square footage, living in one of those cavernous houses with enough garage space to start a homeless shelter. (There's a holiday suggestion right there.) And of course they are not people who are in real want. Just because consumption is bankrupt doesn't mean that poverty is ennobling.

12   But somewhere in between there is a family like one I know in rural Pennsylvania, raising bees for honey (and for the science, and the fun, of it), digging a pond out of the downhill flow of the stream, with three kids who somehow, incredibly, don't spend six months of the year whining for the toy du jour.

(The youngest once demurred when someone offered him another box on his birthday; "I already have a present," he said.) The mother of the household says having less means her family appreciates possessions more. "I can give you a story about every item, really," she says of what they own. In other words, what they have has meaning. And meaning, real meaning, is what we are always trying to possess. Ask people what they'd grab if their house were on fire, the way our national house is on fire right now. No one ever says it's the tricked-up microwave they got at Wal-Mart.

PERSONAL RESPONSE

What would you grab if your house or apartment were on fire (paragraph 12)? Why?

QUESTIONS FOR CLASS OR SMALL-GROUP DISCUSSION

1. What is Quindlen's thesis or central idea? Do you agree with her that "stuff is not salvation"?

2. Quindlen writes: "Now much of the country is made up of people with the acquisition habits of a 7-year-old . . . ." (paragraph 7). What does she mean? Do your observations support or contradict her statement?

3. What contrast does Quindlen draw between real need and a need for "junk" (paragraph 7). To what extent do you agree with her?

4. How effective do you find Quindlen's conclusion?

PERSPECTIVES ON MARKETING AND THE AMERICAN CONSUMER

Suggested Writing Topics

1. Argue against or in support of the contention of Gary Ruskin and Juliet Schor in "Every Nook and Cranny" that commercialism is "dangerous" to the public.

2. Illustrate this statement in Michael J. Sandel's "What Isn't for Sale?" with examples from your personal observations: "We live in a time when almost everything can be bought and sold" (paragraph 3).

3. Explain the distinction that Michael J. Sandel makes between "a market economy" and "a market society" in "What Isn't for Sale?" and then answer the question, "Do we want a market economy or a market society?" (paragraph 22).

4. Use examples to illustrate this statement from Michael J. Sandel's "What Isn't for Sale?": "Some of the good things in life are degraded if turned into commodities" (paragraph 20).

5. Argue for or against the proposition that the United States should "ban or sharply restrict product placement on television" (Gary Ruskin and Juliet Schor, "Every Nook and Cranny," paragraph 10).

6. Classify consumers' shopping and buying habits on the basis of what generation they belong to, using Millennials, Generation X members, and Baby Boomers as your three groups.

7. Write an essay in response to the statement in Anna Quindlen's "Stuff Is Not Salvation" that Americans have "an addiction to consumption so out of control that it qualifies as a sickness" (paragraph 3).

8. Drawing on any of the readings in the chapter, write an essay on the importance of young consumers to the American economy.

9. Drawing on readings in this chapter, explain the pressures you think America's high-consumption society puts on young people and the effects of those pressures.

10. Write an essay on the image you think that American consumerism presents to the rest of the world and whether you think that image is good or a bad.

11. Imagine that you are marketing a product that has traditionally been sold to one particular segment of the market, such as white, middle-class males. Now you want to increase your sales by targeting other groups. Select a particular group and create a sales campaign aimed at that group.

12. Explain the effects on you or someone you know of a change in income, suddenly coming into money, or acquiring some coveted material possession.

13. Analyze the positive and negative effects of America's emphasis on consumerism on one particular group of people, such as young people, the elderly, working-class people, the wealthy, or those living in poverty.

14. Explain what you think shopping malls, discount stores, and overstocked supermarkets suggest about Americans' values. For instance, what impression do you think that foreign visitors get of America when they see the sizes of and selections in those marketplaces?

Research Topics

1. Research one of the many subjects raised by Gary Ruskin and Juliet Schor in "Every Nook and Cranny," such as their assertion (paragraph 4) that "the commercialization of government and culture and the growing importance of material acquisition and consumer lifestyles was hastened by the co-optation of potentially countervailing institutions, such as churches . . . , governments, schools, universities, and nongovernmental organizations."

2. Using Michael J. Sandel's "What Isn't for Sale?" as a starting point, argue in support of or against Sandel's contention that America has become a market society.

3. Research for an answer to this question in Michael J. Sandel's "What Isn't for Sale?": "How can we decide which goods should be bought and sold, and which should be governed by nonmarket values?" (paragraph 23).

4. Research the marketing strategies of a major business, perhaps one mentioned in this chapter. Assess what you see as its successes and/or failures in promoting its products.

5. Select a particular product (such as automobiles, cosmetics, clothing, or beer) or a particular target population (such as children, overweight women, or the elderly) and research the market strategies used by major companies for that particular product or group.

6. Research the recent advertising campaign of a major corporation whose product poses a threat to the environment or to human health and well-being.

7. Research the subject of American consumerism and arrive at your own conclusion about its effects on Americans and American values. This is a broad subject, so look for ways to narrow your focus as quickly as you can.

8. Research the impact of suburban malls on city-center or small mom-and-pop neighborhood businesses.

9. Research the impact that the Internet has had on suburban malls and neighborhood businesses.

RESPONDING TO VISUALS

JOHN MACDOUGALL/AFP/GettyImages

Woman walks by a fashion ad on a street in Berlin.

1. The caption tells us that this is a "fashion ad," but what product is being advertised? How can you tell?

2. What details of the advertisement do you find persuasive? Would you be inclined to consider buying the product because of this advertisement?

3. Comment on the composition of this photograph: what is the effect of the woman walking past the ad being dominated by the woman jumping in the advertisement? How do the two figures contrast?

RESPONDING TO VISUALS

Tetra Images

Barcode of American flag.

1. What do the most obvious components of this picture—the dollar signs instead of stars and the bars instead of stars and stripes—represent?
2. What does the word 'SALE" add to the impact of the image?
3. What comment on American commercialism does this image make or imply?

CHAPTER 21

The Workplace

The workplace can have enormous influence on people's lives. Most Americans work outside the home, either full-time or part-time, spending significant portions of their lives on the job. The physical atmosphere of the workplace, the friendliness of coworkers, wages and benefits, and the attitudes of supervisors or bosses play pivotal roles not only in the way workers perform but also in the way they feel about themselves. Tension, anxiety, and stress in the workplace can lower production for the company and produce actual illnesses in workers, whereas a pleasant atmosphere, good benefits, and relatively low stress can boost production and make employees look forward to going to work. Research has demonstrated that the quality of life in the workplace has a direct effect on the quality of work employees do and on their general well-being.

If, like most college students, you have had a job or are currently working, think about your own experiences as a worker. Do you feel a sense of community in your workplace? Is your work fun? Tedious? Challenging? How would you characterize the relationship between management and employees where you work (or have worked)? Is what you earn adequate enough to meet your financial needs? Do you have benefits with your job? These questions all relate to the quality of your work experience, and how you answer them reveals a great deal about your workplace.

The readings in this chapter address both the job market and the workplace atmosphere. The first two address the subject of the job market, one from the perspective of companies looking for workers and the other from the perspective of a job seeker looking for work. Peter Cappelli's "Why Companies Aren't Getting the Employees They Need," looks at the job market from the perspective of the employer. A number of large companies complain that there are not enough qualified, skilled workers to fill vacant positions. Cappelli notes that these companies blame schools and the government, but he argues that the fault is theirs, explains why they are at fault, and offers some practical solutions to the problem. From a different perspective, Peter Weinberg in "Escape from the Job Jungle," describes his months-long search for work. Using humor to explain his search methods and their lack of success, he represents the age group of newly graduated twenty- to twenty-four-year-olds who begin the job search with great optimism, only to discover that it takes work and persistence to find the right job for their qualifications.

The other two readings focus on the workplace environment. Meghan Casserly in "Workplace Snitching: If You See Something, Should You Say Something?" explores the subject of whistle blowing and its counterpart, retaliation. Noting that "retaliation or retribution for calling out bad deeds in the office is on the rise," she provides data to support that statement and offers an explanation that links whistle blowing and retaliation to the state of the economy. Then, Jeff Jacoby's "Oh, Brother" takes a look at the subject of employees' rights in the workplace by siding with the employer in a case before a Superior Court in Massachusetts. As you no doubt know, "Big Brother" is a reference to the fictional director of Oceania in the George Orwell novel *1984*. Oceania is a totalitarian state where citizens are always under surveillance and are constantly being reminded that "Big Brother is watching you." As you read his piece, consider whether you agree with Jacoby's position on the case or whether you take the opposite position on it.

WHY COMPANIES AREN'T GETTING THE EMPLOYEES THEY NEED

Peter Cappelli

Peter Cappelli is the George W. Taylor professor of management at the University of Pennsylvania's Wharton School and director of Wharton's Center for Human Resources. He is also a research associate at the National Bureau of Economic Research, served as senior advisor to the Kingdom of Bahrain for Employment Policy from 2003–2005, and is a Distinguished Scholar of the Ministry of Manpower for Singapore. His books include Talent Management: Managing Talent in an Age of Uncertainty *(2008);* Managing the Older Worker *(with Bill Novelli) (2010); and* Why Good People Can't Get Jobs *(2012). This article was published in the* Wall Street Journal *on October 24, 2011.*

Everybody's heard the complaints about recruiting lately. Even with unemployment hovering around 9%, companies are grousing that they can't find skilled workers, and filling a job can take months of hunting. Employers are quick to lay blame. Schools aren't giving kids the right kind of training. The government isn't letting in enough high-skill immigrants. The list goes on and on. But I believe that the real culprits are the employers themselves.

With an abundance of workers to choose from, employers are demanding more of job candidates than ever before. They want prospective workers to be able to fill a role right away, without any training or ramp-up time.

Bad for Companies, Bad for Economy

In other words, to get a job, you have to have that job already. It's a Catch-22 situation for workers—and it's hurting companies and the economy.

4   To get America's job engine revving again, companies need to stop pinning so much of the blame on our nation's education system. They need to drop the idea of finding perfect candidates and look for people who could do the job with a bit of training and practice. There are plenty of ways to get workers up to speed without investing too much time and money, such as putting new employees on extended probationary periods and relying more on internal hires, who know the ropes better than outsiders would. It's a fundamental change from business as usual. But the way we're doing things now just isn't working.

The Big Myths

The perceptions about a lack of skilled workers are pervasive. The staffing company ManpowerGroup, for instance, reports that 52% of U.S. employers surveyed say they have difficulty filling positions because of talent shortages. But the problem is an illusion. Some of the complaints about skill shortages boil down to the fact that employers can't get candidates to accept jobs at the wages offered. That's an affordability problem, not a skill shortage. A real shortage means not being able to find appropriate candidates at market-clearing wages. We wouldn't say there is a shortage of diamonds when they are incredibly expensive; we can buy all we want at the prevailing prices.

The real problem, then, is more appropriately an inflexibility problem. Finding candidates to fit jobs is not like finding pistons to fit engines, where the requirements are precise and can't be varied. Jobs can be organized in many different ways so that candidates who have very different credentials can do them successfully. Only about 10% of the people in IT jobs during the Silicon Valley tech boom of the 1990s, for example, had IT-related degrees. While it might be great to have a Ph.D. graduate read your electrical meter, almost anyone with a little training could do the job pretty well.

A Training Shortage

And make no mistake: There are plenty of people out there who could step into jobs with just a bit of training—even recent graduates who don't have much job experience. Despite employers' complaints about the education system, college students are pursuing more vocationally oriented course work than ever before, with degrees in highly specialized fields like pharmaceutical marketing and retail logistics.

8   Unfortunately, American companies don't seem to do training anymore. Data are hard to come by, but we know that apprenticeship programs have largely disappeared, along with management-training programs. And the amount of training that the average new hire gets in the first year or so could be measured in hours and counted on the fingers of one hand. Much of that includes what vendors do when they bring in new equipment: "Here's how to work this copier." The shortage of opportunities to learn on the job helps explain the phenomenon of people queueing up for unpaid internships, in some cases even paying to get access to a situation where they can work free to get access to valuable on-the-job experience.

Companies in other countries do things differently. In Europe, for instance, training is often mandated, and apprenticeships and other programs that help provide work experience are part of the infrastructure. The result: European countries aren't having skill-shortage complaints at the same level as in the U.S., and the nations that have the most established apprenticeship programs—the Scandinavian nations, Germany and Switzerland—have low unemployment.

Employers here at home rightly point to a significant constraint that they face in training workers: They train them and make the investment, but then someone else offers them more money and hires them away.

The Way Forward

That is a real problem. What's the answer? We aren't going to get European-style apprenticeships in the U.S. They require too much cooperation among employers and bigger investments in infrastructure than any government entity is willing to provide. We're also not going to go back to the lifetime-employment models that made years-long training programs possible.

12   But I'm also convinced that some of the problem we're up against is simply a failure of imagination. Here are three ways in which employees can get the skills they need without the employer having to invest in a lot of upfront training.

Work with Education Providers: If job candidates don't have the skills you need, make them go to school before you hire them.

Community colleges in many states, especially North Carolina, have proved to be good partners with employers by tailoring very applied course work to the specific needs of the employer. Candidates qualify to be hired once they complete the courses—which they pay for themselves, at least in part. For instance, a manufacturer might require that prospective job candidates first pass a course on quality control or using certain machine tools.

Going back to school isn't just for new hires, either; it also works for internal candidates. In this setup, the employer pays the tuition costs through tuition

Where Jobs Go Wanting

Percentage of employers reporting difficulty filling positions by country, 2010 vs. 2011

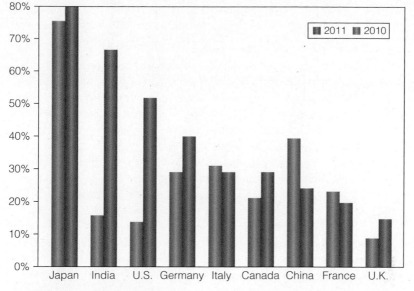

The Help That's Most Wanted

Hardest jobs for U.S. employers to fill

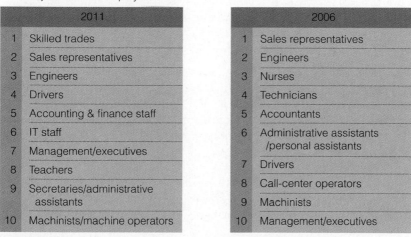

	2011		2006
1	Skilled trades	1	Sales representatives
2	Sales representatives	2	Engineers
3	Engineers	3	Nurses
4	Drivers	4	Technicians
5	Accounting & finance staff	5	Accountants
6	IT staff	6	Administrative assistants /personal assistants
7	Management/executives	7	Drivers
8	Teachers	8	Call-center operators
9	Secretaries/administrative assistants	9	Machinists
10	Machinists/machine operators	10	Management/executives

Source: ManpowerGroup

reimbursement. But the employees make the bigger investment by spending their own time, almost always off work, learning the material.

16 **Bring Back Aspects of Apprenticeship:** In this arrangement, apprentices are paid less while they are mastering their craft—so employers aren't paying for training and a big salary at the same time. Accounting firms, law firms and professional-services firms have long operated this way, and have made lots of money off their young associates.

Of course, a full apprenticeship model—with testing and credentials associated with different stages of experience—wouldn't work in all industries. But a simpler setup would: Companies could give their new workers a longer probationary period—with lower pay—until they get up to speed on the requirements of the job.

Promote from Within: Employees have useful knowledge that no outsider could have and should make great candidates for filling jobs higher up. In recent years, however, an incredible two-thirds of all vacancies, even in large companies, have been filled by hiring from the outside, according to data from Taleo Corp., a talent-management company. That figure has dropped somewhat lately because of market conditions. But a generation ago, the number was close to 10%, as internal promotions and transfers were used to fill virtually all positions.

These days, many companies simply don't believe their own workers have the necessary skills to take on new roles. But, once again, many workers could step into those jobs with a bit of training. And there's one on-the-job education strategy that doesn't cost companies a dime: Organize work so that employees are given projects that help them learn new skills. For example, a marketing manager may not know how to compute the return on marketing programs but might learn that skill while working on a team project with colleagues from the finance department.

20   Pursuing options like these vastly expands the supply of talent that employers can tap, making it both cheaper and easier to fill jobs. Of course, it's also much better for society. It helps build the supply of human capital in the economy, as well as opening the pathway for more people to get jobs. It's an important instance where company self-interest and societal interest just happen to coincide.

PERSONAL RESPONSE

If you were ever turned down for a job because you did not have the skills to perform it, describe that experience. If that has not been your experience and you have been hired for a job, describe that experience.

QUESTIONS FOR CLASS OR SMALL-GROUP DISCUSSION

1. According to Cappelli, who do companies blame for their not being able to recruit qualified people? Who does Cappelli blame?

2. How does Cappelli answer the question posed by his title?

3. State in your own words what the "big myths" are, as explained in the section with that subheading, and then state what the reality is, according to Cappelli.

4. Summarize the recommendations that Cappelli makes to help companies get the people they need for skilled jobs. What do you think of his recommendations? Do you think they are practical?

ESCAPE FROM THE JOB JUNGLE

Peter Weinberg

Peter Weinberg is a recent college graduate who is now working and living in New York. This piece was posted on the Huffington Post *website on March 19, 2012.*

At first, I was sure I'd find a job. I graduated Phi Beta Kappa from a well-branded college, I did hard time in the internship trenches for four consecutive summers, and according to Indeed.com, there were hundreds of job openings in New York City. All I had to do was pick one with the words "assistant" "junior" or "associate" in the title, upload my resume, and go back to watching *Curb Your Enthusiasm.* A few days later, employers would swamp my inbox, promising me big stacks of money and a swivel chair of my very own. That's how the Internet works: you click what you want and you get it.

I applied to 53 jobs in July, according to the tally marks I carved into my parents' dining room table while playing the harmonica. But the big sack I bought to hold all my salary never filled up, and I began to suspect something just wasn't right.

I googled "economy," and found all sorts of disconcerting information.

4   Especially this one: the unemployment rate among recent college graduates was 9.6%. Also, according to a recent study from the Buzz Kill Institute, the longer it took me to find a job, the more scarred I'd be for the rest of my life. Then I stumbled upon an article by Thomas Friedman, who insisted that nowadays, people have to invent their own jobs. So I invented NemAssist.com. It's like Match.com, but instead of finding true love, you find an archenemy. It's a speed hating service that helps you find loathe at first sight.

It was a brilliant invention, but none of my friends in finance wanted to invest, and NemAssist never started up (thanks for nothing, Tom). Back at square one, I decided to write up a list of Four Strategies for Finding Work. I crossed out "Online Applications" and "Entrepreneurship" and moved on to Strategy 3: "Loco-Motion."

Loco-Motion is when doing something completely insane moves you forward in life. You hear the success stories all the time: "I hired a plane to skywrite my resume above the beach in South Hampton. Two days later I started at Morgan Stanley." So I called the Drug Policy Alliance and asked for the e-mail address of the director. Then I sent him a long rambling e-mail about my history thesis on Reagan's war on drugs. The next day, I had my first interview.

I didn't get the job, but I started to believe in the power of Loco-Motion. So I tried it again, except this time I called Google and asked to speak to Larry Page. The sound of the phone hanging up is still ringing in my ears.

8   I wrote "50/50 odds" next to Loco-Motion, and moved on to Strategy 4: Networking. For the whole month of September, I spun an intricate networking

web, like some kind of exotic Jewish spider. I talked to 28 strangers. Friends of friends of friends. They worked at HBO and ABC, Time Inc. and the Daily Beast, BBDO and Dentsu, Penguin and Simon & Shuster, and more. Assistants steered me through cubicle labyrinths and deposited me on plush couches in big offices. No one had any jobs to offer, but everyone had advice, which I jotted down diligently in a legal pad. On the way out, I'd look around at all the lucky workers, entranced, like a little boy at an aquarium, his face flush against the glass.

I liked networking, but it didn't seem to work. By September, it still hadn't landed me one single interview. I did pick up two part time gigs as a writing tutor and a manager for a small theater company, both procured through Strategy 1, which actually had 2/55 odds in the end.

On September 8th, a switch flipped on inside me. My mood plummeted from "cautious optimism" to "nihilistic despair." On that day, for 20 of my 23 years, I'd been sitting in a classroom. Now I was sitting in a La-Z-Boy in a bathrobe. What really pushed me over the edge that day was an article in *The Atlantic*, which claimed that I belonged to a "Lost Generation." At first I assumed this referred to young adults who were severely disappointed by the season finale of *Lost*. It didn't, but that was the idea that stuck with me. Maybe life is just like *Lost*: you invest so much time and energy throughout so many seasons, and it all adds up to nothing.

And then, a fly landed in my networking web. I hurried over to inspect the body—it was a full-time freelancing gig at an ad agency. Could I come in for an interview on Thursday? I checked my schedule. Thursday was free (and so was every day after Thursday).

12   As I sat and waited in an awfully swank lobby, I started flipping through that legal pad I'd spent my summer filling up. As the snippets of wisdom fluttered by, I realized how well networking had prepared me for an interview. Four ad execs had poured their brains out to me. I had prepared answers for any possible question, even those horrible HR-type ones like "what is your greatest weakness?" ("You mean besides being a perfectionist? Kryptonite.") That's the thing about networking—it's the only job-getting strategy that actually makes you more employable.

Flash forward to December 9th, and I'm in a swivel chair, spinning round and round in the sickly white light of an office. After three months of freelancing, my boss, Jack, had just offered me a job.

Lucky. Unbelievably lucky. That's how I felt as I swiveled. Also, a little dizzy. Also, a little guilty.

I started thinking about all the other 20- to 24-year-olds out there, still stuck in the search, bleeding out in the job jungle, their ankles shackled by debt with miles and miles to go till the next interview. Can they all network their way out of there? Will Indeed.com throw them a vine? Can they find a part-time path to prosperity? Will Lady Luck bail them out?

16   I'd hate to play the odds on that one.

PERSONAL RESPONSE

Write about any failure or success you have had in trying to find work. If you have never applied for a job, write about the experience of someone you know.

QUESTIONS FOR CLASS OR SMALL-GROUP DISCUSSION

1. Why do you think that Weinberg describes his job search as a "jungle" (title)?
2. What misconceptions about how easy it would be to get a job after graduation does Weinberg dispel?
3. Despite his humor, does Weinberg make any serious recommendations on how to get a job? What do you think of his advice?
4. Is Weinberg pessimistic or optimistic about job prospects for young people? He specifically mentions the 20–24 age group because that is the group he fits into. Do you think his observations about searching for a job apply to any age group?

WORKPLACE SNITCHING: IF YOU SEE SOMETHING, SHOULD YOU SAY SOMETHING?

Meghan Casserly

Meghan Casserly is a Forbes *magazine staff writer and previously worked as a reporter for* Philadelphia CityPaper. *As a writer for* Forbes, *which features articles on business and financial news, Casserly looks at startup businesses from her perspective as a woman and is especially interested in promoting women in business. In 2012, she was responsible for placing women on the covers of two issues of the magazine. This article was published in the January 2012 edition of* Forbes.

When Corina Allen was dismissed from her job by Radio One, which owns two local stations in Texas, in 2007, she knew she had a discrimination claim on her hands. While Texas is an "at will" state, meaning employees can be terminated without reason, something felt amiss. She filed complaint with the Equal Employment Opportunity Commission and didn't look back, accepting a position with CBS before ultimately opening her own advertising and media placement agency. When she knocked on the door of Radio One in 2009, hoping to launch a campaign for a client on KBXX-FM, Allen was welcomed by former colleagues eager to do business with a familiar face. All seemed well, but soon the request was passed higher and higher up the ladder until Allen was told in no uncertain terms by Vice President Doug Abernathy that because of her previous complaint, the company would not do business with her or her clients.

Sound fair? Sound legal?

Sounds like retaliation, which, when it comes to business is anything but. Lucky for Allen, her conversation with Abernathy was recorded and in May 2011 a judge awarded her over $700,000 [the case is in appeal] in punitive damages. Retaliation against employees for whistle-blowing, it seems, is no joke in the eyes of the law.

4   Unfortunately for employees though, retaliation or retribution for calling out bad deeds in the office is on the rise. According to new research from the Ethics Resource Center, one in five employees who has reported an ethical breach or misconduct of a colleague has faced some ugly payback, ranging from the benign—exclusion from a work activity by management—to cases like Allen's where loss of business can occur, to much more extreme incidences of harassment and physical harm. All told, more than 8.8 million people experienced retaliation for blowing the whistle from 2009–2011.

"I've definitely found retaliation to be on the rise," says Thomas Padgett, a civil rights attorney on Corina Allen's case whose stories make Allen's incidences of retribution seem like a cake walk: one open case features a woman who reported sexual harassment and was shoved into a bathroom wall by a male colleague who then threatened to toss her over a railing. As someone with his finger to the pulse of reprehensible workplace behavior, Padgett says it all comes down to two things. First off, a general lack of civility in the world today. "Bosses have become much more willing to treat people poorly because of the fact that civil discourse in our society has become so prevalent," he says. "That translates into the way we treat each other at work."

After taking aim at the state of the world's code of conduct Padgett says another factor is at play in the rise of workplace retaliation: "Fear." Fear of losing their jobs can drive a person to do some crazy things, he says. In incidences where you've violated a company code or—worse—a law, and someone is in a position to threaten your job by reporting it, well, you might be tempted to do whatever's in your power to make them pay. "The quickest way to get out of a tough situation is to squash whatever, or whoever, is threatening you," he says.

Ouch. The rules on snitching have been nebulous since the playground. But in a year when a decent number of high level University employees saw serious repercussions for *not* tattling on a colleague, it's become more apparent than ever that when your career's on the line, doing the "right thing" generally means calling out the bad guys. In fact, new provisions from the Securities and Exchange Commission will go into effect this summer that will actually reward whistle-blowers for their tattle-talery.

8   Still it's more than a little troubling to know that physical violence can be a repercussion to doing the "right thing." The vast majority of companies have what are known as "open door" policies and strict "non-retaliation" guidelines to protect employees from bad behavior, but signs from both the ERC study and from attorneys like Padgett indicate it's actually commonplace.

Patricia Harned, Ph.D., the president of the Ethics Resource Center, says that while ethical misconduct—which runs the gamut from discrimination to insider trading–is down, reporting of this kind of behavior (that is, the number who said something as opposed to just seeing it) is at a record high of 65%. And that, she says, is a good thing. "There's really a chain reaction happening in the wake of the recession," Harned says. "A down economy drives management and leaders to instill a sense of 'we're all in this together' to their employees." Employees hear this message as "integrity matters" and that strengthens their commitment to the company. As a result, she says, they're more mindful of the behavior of their peers and more likely to report violations they perceive as a threat to the success of the group.

But as the economy begins to slowly recover, Harned says employees are seeing their managers turn away from the "integrity matters" approach and back to business as usual. "The focus is returning to the bottom line, to making as much money as possible," she says, which is historically a time when ethical standards start to slip. "As retaliation is directly linked to management behavior, it's not surprising to see that it is also on the rise."

In fact, when we asked the ERC to dig down deeper into the numbers on retaliation, they revealed exclusively to *Forbes* that not only do the majority of employees who make complaints or report violations do so to their manager or direct supervisor, but that first-line supervisors and managers are, in fact, the employees that say they experience the most retaliation for finger pointing. The results, which show 27% of first-line managers reporting retaliation for reporting ethical violations, Harned says indicate an even bigger drop in reporting to come. "Once an employee feels threatened by retaliation, the likelihood he or his employees will continue to report violations drops precipitously," she says. "Be sure that if a quarter of employees say they've experienced retaliation for do-gooding, the other 75% know about it."

12   But it's not all boo-hooing. The silver lining of this bad behavior is that employees increasingly have the right to do something about it, particularly if they have the gumption to go outside of the company with their complaint in the first place. "There's a difference between people who complained about something to their manager and were treated poorly afterwards," says Lori Adelson, labor and employment attorney with the law firm Arnstein & Lehr, where she represents employers in retaliation suits. Filing a complaint with the EEOC, however, and alleging discrimination, or reporting a violation of Sarbanes-Oxley [a 2002 Act mandating reform to enhance corporate responsibility and combat corporate and accounting fraud], have provisions that protect whistle-blowers from retaliation.

From Adelson's perch, representing the employers' perspective, the legal system has made it too easy for employees to file claims of discrimination or wrongdoing—to the point where she says the power is being abused. "Employees have too much ammunition," she says, and says the tough economy is making the situation even worse. "As indicator, an unprecedented amount of claims against employers are being filed in Florida. It's one of the most depressed economies in the country and over two thirds of claims nationwide are being filed there."

But whether the repressed economy creates a workplace environment rife with abusive behavior and retaliation or rather the perfect setting for abusing the system with baseless lawsuits is open for debate. ERC data shows that more employees are calling out colleagues for bad behavior, only to see damage to their careers, harassment or physical harm as a result. Does it make you think twice about saying something? Understandably so. But Padgett would have you know one thing about your rights: "If the truth is on your side, with the right evidence, these [cases] are among the easiest to win."

PERSONAL RESPONSE

What do you think you would do if you saw a co-worker doing something that was against company rules? What if you knew that you would be harassed by your co-workers for blowing the whistle? Would that make a difference?

QUESTIONS FOR CLASS OR SMALL-GROUP DISCUSSION

1. How does the example of Corina Allen in the initial paragraphs introduce Casserly's subject?
2. According to Casserly and the people she interviewed, what accounts for the rise in the number of "people experienc[ing] retaliation for blowing the whistle from 2009 [to] 2011" (paragraph 4)?
3. Summarize what Casserly has to say about the relationship of the incidence of whistle-blowing and retaliation to the state of the economy.
4. How does Casserly answer the question in her title? How would you answer it?

OH, BROTHER

JEFF JACOBY

Jeff Jacoby was chief editorial writer for the Boston Herald *from 1987 until becoming an op-ed columnist for the* Boston Globe *in 1994. Trained as a lawyer, he has been a political commentator for Boston's National Public Radio affiliate and was host of* Talk of New England, *a weekly television program, for several years. In 1999, Jacoby became the first recipient of the Breindel Award for Excellence in Opinion Journalism. In December 2009, he was presented by the Zionist Organization of America with its Ben Hecht Award for Outstanding Journalism on the Middle East. This opinion piece was first published in the* Boston Globe *on December 10, 2006.*

BIG BROTHER has been busy.

New York City's board of health voted last week to ban the use of trans fats in restaurants, a step that will force many of the Big Apple's 26,000 eating establishments to radically alter the way they prepare food. The prohibition is being called a model for other cities, such as Chicago, where similar bans have been proposed.

Is it a good idea to avoid food made with trans fats? That depends on what you consider good. Trans fats raise the risk of heart disease by increasing levels of LDL ("bad") cholesterol. They also contribute to the appealing taste of many baked and fried foods, and provide an economical alternative to saturated fats. As with most things in life, trans fats carry both risks and benefits. Do the long-term health concerns outweigh the short-term pleasures? That's a question of values— one that scientists and regulators aren't competent to answer.

4   Different people have different priorities. They make different choices about the fats in their diet, just as they make different choices about whether to drive a Toyota, drink their coffee black, or get a tattoo. In a free society, men and women decide such things for themselves. In New York, men and women are now a little less free. And since a loss of liberty anywhere is a threat to liberty everywhere, the rest of us are now a little less free as well.

But that doesn't trouble the lifestyle bullies. They are quite sure that they have the right to dictate people's eating habits. "It's basically a slow form of poison," sniffs David Katz of the Yale Prevention Research Center. "I applaud New York City, and frankly, I think there should be a nationwide ban."

Yes, why go through the trouble of making your own decision about trans fats or anything else when officious bureaucrats are willing to make it for you? It's so much easier to prohibit something—smoking in bars, say, or cycling without a helmet, or using marijuana, or gambling, or working a job for less than some "minimum" wage—than to allow adults the freedom to choose.

But Big Brother doesn't always appear as a hectoring nanny. Indeed, sometimes he comes disguised as a victim of the bullies.

8   Consider the plight of Scott Rodrigues, who lost his job with the Scotts lawn-care corporation when a drug test showed that he had violated a company rule against smoking at any time—on or off the job. Scotts no longer hires tobacco users, since they drive up the cost of medical insurance, and Rodrigues, a former pack-a-day smoker, knew about the policy and was trying to kick his habit. He was down to about six cigarettes daily when he was fired.

Now he claims that Scotts violated his privacy and civil rights, and is suing his ex-employer in Superior Court.

"How employees want to lead their private lives is their own business," his lawyer told the *Boston Globe*. "Next they're going to say, 'you don't get enough exercise'.... I don't think anybody ought to be smoking cigarettes, but as long as it's legal, it's none of the employer's business as long as it doesn't impact the workplace."

It's hard not to feel a measure of sympathy for Rodrigues. Many activities endanger health and can drive up the cost of health insurance, from drag-racing to overeating to promiscuous sex, yet none of them appears to be grounds for termination at Scotts. It seems capricious to treat smokers so harshly.

12   But capricious or not, Scotts is entitled to condition its employment on any criteria it wishes. (With the exception of the "protected categories"—race, religion, etc.—itemized in civil rights statutes) Rodrigues has not been cheated. Scotts is a private firm, and if it chooses not to employ smokers—or skiers, or Socialists, or "Seinfeld" fans—its decision should stand. Rodrigues is free to vent

his disappointment, to criticize Scotts, even to organize a boycott. But forcing the company to defend itself against a groundless lawsuit goes too far. It is an abuse of governmental power—an assault on the liberty of employers to operate freely in the market. It is a different kind of bullying than the ban on trans fats, but it's an act of bullying nonetheless.

The price of liberty, Thomas Jefferson warned, is eternal vigilance. But too few of us have been vigilant, and the bullies keep gaining ground.

PERSONAL RESPONSE

Write about an experience in which you felt that being prevented from doing something—or being told not to do it—was unfair.

QUESTIONS FOR CLASS OR SMALL-GROUP DISCUSSION

1. How is the allusion to George Orwell's novel *1984* relevant to Jacoby's essay?
2. Why do you think Jacoby begins with a discussion of New York City's ban on trans fats in restaurants? How is that subject related to his discussion of the lawsuit that Scott Rodrigues filed against the Scotts lawn care company?
3. Jacoby believes that "Scotts is entitled to condition its employment on any criteria it wishes. . . . Rodrigues has not been cheated" (paragraph 12). To what extent do you agree with him?
4. Why does Jacoby call Rodrigues a bully (paragraph 12)? Do you agree with Jacoby on this point?

PERSPECTIVES ON THE WORKPLACE

Suggested Writing Topics

1. Argue whether you agree with the suggestions that Peter Cappelli makes in "Why Companies Aren't Getting the Employees They Need" for how companies can get the recruits they want.
2. Write about your own experience searching for a job, as Peter Weinberg does in "Escape from the Job Jungle."
3. Explain your answer to the question in Meghan Casserly's title "Workplace Snitching: If You See Something, Should You Say Something?"
4. Write an editorial in reply to Jeff Jacoby's opinion piece "Oh, Brother." Explain whether you agree with the law that lets private employers determine any criteria they want as a condition of employment.
5. Explain what you value most in a job and why. Is it having fun, making lots of money, meeting challenges, or some other aspect of it? Or conduct your own informal interview on the subject of expectations for a job and report your results.

6. Drawing on at least one of the essays in this chapter, describe what you see as the ideal job or ideal working conditions.

7. Describe your work experiences and the extent to which self-satisfaction or self-motivation contributes to your performance.

8. Argue in support of or against the contention made by many workers and implied by a couple of the authors in this chapter that employers unfairly violate the basic rights of workers.

9. Argue in support of or against drug testing in the workplace.

Research Topics

1. Starting with Peter Cappelli's "Why Companies Aren't Getting the Employees They Need," research the subject of jobs that go unfilled, as noted in his graph "The Help That's Most Wanted." Cappelli compares the hardest jobs for companies to fill in 2011 versus those that were hardest to fill in 2006. Update the information in the graph and research explanations to account for which jobs are going unfilled. An alternative is to do the same for the other graph showing the percentage of employers who report difficulty in filling positions, by country.

2. Using Meghan Casserly's article "Workplace Snitching: If You See Something, Should You Say Something?" as a starting point, research the subject of whistle blowing and workplace retaliation. For instance, she writes that "more than 8.8 million people experienced retaliation for blowing the whistle from 2009-2011." Is that number still accurate, on the rise, or decreasing? How is such data gathered?

3. Meghan Casserly in "Workplace Snitching: If You See Something, Should You Say Something?" reports that in 2012, the Securities and Exchange Commission placed into effect new provisions "that will actually reward whistle-blowers for their tattle-talery." Research those provisions and their effect on whistle-blowing in the workplace.

4. Research the European regulations outlawing wage and benefit discrimination against part-time workers and argue whether you think the United States ought to have such a goal and, if so, whether it could realistically attain it.

5. Research the topic of the differences between women's and men's managerial styles.

6. Research the topic of the effect of workplace environment on employee productivity and morale.

7. Research the subject of the right to free speech or the right to privacy in the work place.

8. Research workers' perceptions of their workplaces. If possible, interview people who work full-time about their work place experiences and combine the results of your interview(s) with your other sources.

RESPONDING TO VISUALS

1. What makes this cartoon funny?
2. What play on words is at work in the heading "Santa's Workshop"?
3. What serious subject related to the workplace does the cartoon comment on?

RESPONDING TO VISUALS

Julie Toy/Getty Images

Working mother on the way to work, holding her daughter.

1. What image of working and parenting does the photograph convey?
2. What do the looks on the faces of both mother and child suggest about how each felt at the moment the photograph was taken?
3. What details of the photograph convey the tensions between being simultaneously a parent and a worker?

CHAPTER 22

American Business in the Global Marketplace

If we live in a global village, we also buy and sell in a global marketplace. Manufacturers that once exported goods to other nations now build plants and sell goods directly in those countries. American businesses that once limited themselves to the domestic market are now expanding operations beyond the United States as they compete in foreign markets. Indeed, most trade analysts predict that the twenty-first century will see enormous growth in global prosperity as businesses compete for foreign trade and increase their expansion in the global marketplace. Certainly, the ease of international travel makes the process of conducting business with other countries not much more difficult than travel from state to state was in former days, and Internet capabilities have had enormous impact on business communication.

Combine those factors with the rise in market economies in previously communist countries, and you have some compelling reasons to account for optimistic forecasts for the global economy in the twenty-first century.

It is not just sales to other countries that contribute to the globalization of the marketplace but production as well. Throughout the twentieth century, American wholesalers and retailers imported goods that were made abroad. American consumers were used to seeing the words "made in China" or "made in Taiwan," for instance, on the products that they purchased. Then, it became popular for American manufacturers to either outsource the labor to make their products in a foreign country or physically to move abroad. Workers in other countries could be hired to make parts and/or assemble products at wages considerably less than what manufacturers would have to pay workers in the United States, and many American manufacturers found it just as cost-effective to relocate their factories. Central and South America were particularly appealing for such moves because transportation of the products into the United States was fairly easy.

Now, with the development of high-tech telecommunications and the globalization of the economy, many businesses are outsourcing their work to countries all over the world, or they are offshoring completely. Now not only Central and South America, but also India, China, Eastern Europe, North and South Africa, Asia Pacific, and New Zealand have all become outsourcing centers for American businesses.

The readings in this chapter look at issues related to doing business abroad, starting with matters related to working conditions in countries that supply goods to American businesses. The first reading, "Secrets, Lies, and Sweatshops" by Dexter Roberts and Pete Engardio, examines the issue of unfair labor practices in foreign factories. These issues center on wages, working conditions, and number of hours worked. While many American companies practice routine and frequent audits of the foreign manufacturers who supply their goods, the foreign companies find a variety of ways to pass those audits while not complying with labor codes. They argue that the American companies they sell to demand low prices on the goods, making it nearly impossible for them to pay the wages, schedule work hours, and comply with other fair labor practices. This reading spotlights a real dilemma facing foreign manufacturers in a way that may have you seeing the issue in a new light.

Then, Benjamin Powell's "In Defense of 'Sweatshops,'" takes what some may consider an unusual approach to the subject of sweatshop labor. We hear much from activists protesting sweatshops in third world countries, but Powell, an economist who has researched wages, benefits, and alternatives available to workers in those countries, believes there should be more, not fewer, sweatshops. His defense of sweatshops may surprise you, but read his piece with an open mind and consider his evidence. His approach, he tells us, does not rely on anecdotal evidence but rather on a systematic quantification of data.

The next two pieces feature issues related to American companies trying to sell their products abroad. Thus, John Boudreau's "Dominant Elsewhere, Google Struggles in China" looks at how well an Internet giant, Google, is doing as a competitor in the global Internet market. His article reports on the successes and failures of Google in China and the implications that Google's story has for other international giants attempting to gain a large share of the market there. Then, Jamie Anderson, Martin Kupp, and Ronan Moaligou report on approaches to meeting challenges in difficult markets, focusing primarily on how telecommunication companies have had successes in developing countries. These countries, with large-city slums, far-flung rural areas, and "lawless regions and battle zones" pose special problems for companies wanting to market and sell their products. The authors identify the challenges facing companies and use the examples of Celtel and Vodafone, both mobile telecommunications companies, which made great progress in Nigeria and India in sales of their products.

SECRETS, LIES, AND SWEATSHOPS

Dexter Roberts and Pete Engardio

Dexter Roberts is the Asia News editor and China bureau chief for Bloomberg Businessweek. *Pete Engardio is a senior writer for* BusinessWeek *and co-author of* Meltdown: Asia's Boom, Bust, and Beyond *(1999). This article was a* BusinessWeek *magazine cover story podcast on November 26, 2006, and was written with Aaron Bernstein in Washington, Stanley Holmes in Seattle, and Xiang Ji in Beijing.*

Tang Yinghong was caught in an impossible squeeze. For years, his employer, Ningbo Beifa Group, had prospered as a top supplier of pens, mechanical pencils, and highlighters to Wal-Mart Stores (WMT) and other major retailers. But late last year, Tang learned that auditors from Wal-Mart, Beifa's biggest customer, were about to inspect labor conditions at the factory in the Chinese coastal city of Ningbo where he worked as an administrator. Wal-Mart had already on three occasions caught Beifa paying its 3,000 workers less than China's minimum wage and violating overtime rules, Tang says. Under the U.S. chain's labor rules, a fourth offense would end the relationship.

Help arrived suddenly in the form of an unexpected phone call from a man calling himself Lai Mingwei. The caller said he was with Shanghai Corporate Responsibility Management & Consulting Co., and for a $5,000 fee, he'd take care of Tang's Wal-Mart problem. "He promised us he could definitely get us a pass for the audit," Tang says.

Lai provided advice on how to create fake but authentic-looking records and suggested that Beifa hustle any workers with grievances out of the factory on the day of the audit, Tang recounts. The consultant also coached Beifa managers on what questions they could expect from Wal-Mart's inspectors, says Tang. After following much of Lai's advice, the Beifa factory in Ningbo passed the audit earlier this year, Tang says, even though the company didn't change any of its practices.

4   For more than a decade, major American retailers and name brands have answered accusations that they exploit "sweatshop" labor with elaborate codes of conduct and on-site monitoring. But in China many factories have just gotten better at concealing abuses. Internal industry documents reviewed by *Business-Week* reveal that numerous Chinese factories keep double sets of books to fool auditors and distribute scripts for employees to recite if they are questioned. And a new breed of Chinese consultant has sprung up to assist companies like Beifa in evading audits. "Tutoring and helping factories deal with audits has become an industry in China," says Tang, 34, who recently left Beifa of his own volition to start a Web site for workers.

A lawyer for Beifa, Zhou Jie, confirms that the company employed the Shanghai consulting firm but denies any dishonesty related to wages, hours, or outside monitoring. Past audits had "disclosed some problems, and we took necessary measures correspondingly," he explains in a letter responding to questions. The lawyer adds that Beifa has "become the target of accusations" by former employees "whose unreasonable demands have not been satisfied." Reached by cell phone, a man identifying himself as Lai says that the Shanghai consulting firm helps suppliers pass audits, but he declines to comment on his work for Beifa.

Wal-Mart spokeswoman Amy Wyatt says the giant retailer will investigate the allegations about Beifa brought to its attention by *BusinessWeek*. Wal-Mart has stepped up factory inspections, she adds, but it acknowledges that some suppliers are trying to undermine monitoring: "We recognize there is a problem. There are always improvements that need to be made, but we are confident that new procedures are improving conditions."

Chinese export manufacturing is rife with tales of deception. The largest single source of American imports, China's factories this year are expected to ship goods to the U.S. worth $280 billion. American companies continually demand lower prices from their Chinese suppliers, allowing American consumers to enjoy inexpensive clothes, sneakers, and electronics. But factory managers in China complain in interviews that U.S. price pressure creates a powerful incentive to cheat on labor standards that American companies promote as a badge of responsible capitalism. These standards generally incorporate the official minimum wage, which is set by local or provincial governments and ranges from $45 to $101 a month. American companies also typically say they hew to the government-mandated workweek of 40 to 44 hours, beyond which higher overtime pay is required. These figures can be misleading, however, as the Beijing government has had only limited success in pushing local authorities to enforce Chinese labor laws. That's another reason abuses persist and factory oversight frequently fails.

8   Some American companies now concede that the cheating is far more pervasive than they had imagined. "We've come to realize that, while monitoring is crucial to measuring the performance of our suppliers, it doesn't per se lead to sustainable improvements," says Hannah Jones, Nike Inc.'s (NKE) vice-president for corporate responsibility. "We still have the same core problems."

This raises disturbing questions. Guarantees by multi-nationals that offshore suppliers are meeting widely accepted codes of conduct have been important to maintaining political support in the U.S. for growing trade ties with China, especially in the wake of protests by unions and anti-globalization activists. "For many retailers, audits are a way of covering themselves," says Auret van Heerden, chief executive of the Fair Labor Assn., a coalition of 20 apparel and sporting goods makers and retailers, including Nike, Adidas Group, Eddie Bauer, and Nordstrom (JWN). But can corporations successfully impose Western labor standards on a nation that lacks real unions and a meaningful rule of law?

Historically associated with sweatshop abuses but now trying to reform its suppliers, Nike says that one factory it caught falsifying records several years ago is the Zhi Qiao Garments Co. The dingy concrete-walled facility set near mango groves and rice paddies in the steamy southern city of Panyu employs 600 workers, most in their early 20s. They wear blue smocks and lean over stitching machines and large steam-blasting irons. Today the factory complies with labor-law requirements, Nike says, but Zhi Qiao's general manager, Peter Wang, says it's not easy. "Before, we all played the cat-and-mouse game," but that has ended, he claims. "Any improvement you make costs more money." Providing for overtime wages is his biggest challenge, he says. By law, he is supposed to provide time-and-a-half pay after eight hours on weekdays and between double and triple pay for Saturdays, Sundays, and holidays. "The price [Nike pays] never increases one penny," Wang complains, "but compliance with labor codes definitely raises costs."

A Nike spokesman says in a written statement that the company, based in Beaverton, Ore., "believes wages are best set by the local marketplace in which a contract factory competes for its workforce." One way Nike and several other companies are seeking to improve labor conditions is teaching their suppliers more efficient production methods that reduce the need for overtime.

12   The problems in China aren't limited to garment factories, where labor activists have documented sweatshop conditions since the early 1990s. Widespread violations of Chinese labor laws are also surfacing in factories supplying everything from furniture and household appliances to electronics and computers. Hewlett-Packard (HPQ), Dell (DELL), and other companies that rely heavily on contractors in China to supply notebook PCs, digital cameras, and handheld devices have formed an industry alliance to combat the abuses.

A compliance manager for a major multinational company who has overseen many factory audits says that the percentage of Chinese suppliers caught submitting false payroll records has risen from 46% to 75% in the past four years. This manager, who requested anonymity, estimates that only 20% of Chinese suppliers comply with wage rules, while just 5% obey hour limitations. A recent visit by the compliance manager to a toy manufacturer in Shenzhen illustrated the crude ways that some suppliers conceal mistreatment. The manager recalls smelling strong paint fumes in the poorly ventilated and aging factory building. Young women employees were hunched over die-injection molds, using spray guns to paint storybook figurines. The compliance manager discovered a second workshop behind a locked door that a factory official initially refused to open but eventually did. In the back room, a young woman, who appeared to be under the legal working age of 16, tried to hide behind her co-workers on the production line, the visiting compliance manager says. The Chinese factory official admitted he was violating various work rules.

The situation in China is hard to keep in perspective. For all the shortcomings in factory conditions and oversight, even some critics say that workers' circumstances are improving overall. However compromised, pressure from multinationals has curbed some of the most egregious abuses by outside suppliers. Factories owned directly by such corporations as Motorola Inc. (MOT) and General Electric Co. (GE) generally haven't been accused of mistreating their employees. And a booming economy and tightening labor supply in China have emboldened workers in some areas to demand better wages, frequently with success. Even so, many Chinese laborers, especially migrants from poor rural regions, still seek to work as many hours as possible, regardless of whether they are properly paid.

In this shifting, often murky environment, labor auditing has mushroomed into a multimillion-dollar industry. Internal corporate investigators and such global auditing agencies as Cal Safety Compliance of Switzerland, and Bureau Veritas of France operate a convoluted and uncoordinated oversight system. They follow varying corporate codes of conduct, resulting in some big Chinese factories having to post seven or eight different sets of rules. Some factories receive almost daily visits from inspection teams demanding payroll and production records, facility tours, and interviews with managers and workers. "McDonald's (MCD), Walt Disney (DIS), and Wal-Mart are doing thousands of audits a year that are not harmonized," says van Heerden of Fair Labor. Among factory managers, "audit fatigue sets in," he says.

16   Some companies that thought they were making dramatic progress are discovering otherwise. A study commissioned by Nike last year covered 569 factories it uses in China and around the world that employ more than 300,000 workers. It found labor-code violations in every single one. Some factories "hide their work practices by maintaining two or even three sets of books," by coaching workers to "mislead auditors about their work hours, and by sending portions of production to unauthorized contractors where we have no oversight," the Nike study found.

The Fair Labor Assn. released its own study last November based on unannounced audits of 88 of its members' supplier factories in 18 countries. It found an average of 18 violations per factory, including excessive hours, underpayment of wages, health and safety problems, and worker harassment. The actual violation rate is probably higher, the FLA said, because "factory personnel have become sophisticated in concealing noncompliance related to wages. They often hide original documents and show monitors falsified books."

While recently auditing an apparel manufacturer in Dongguan that supplies American importers, the corporate compliance manager says he discussed wage levels with the factory's Hong Kong-based owner. The 2,000 employees who operate sewing and stitching machines in the multi-story complex often put in overtime but earn an average of only $125 a month, an amount the owner grudgingly acknowledged to the compliance manager doesn't meet Chinese overtime-pay requirements or corporate labor codes. "These goals are a fantasy," the owner said. "Maybe in two or three decades we can meet them."

Pinning down what Chinese production workers are paid can be tricky. Based on Chinese government figures, the average manufacturing wage in China is 64 cents an hour, according to the U.S. Bureau of Labor Statistics and demographer Judith Banister of Javelin Investments, a consulting firm in Beijing. That rate assumes a 40-hour week. In fact, 60- to 100-hour weeks are common in China, meaning that the real manufacturing wage is far less. Based on his own calculations from plant inspections, the veteran compliance manager estimates that employees at garment, electronics, and other export factories typically work more than 80 hours a week and make only 42 cents an hour. *BusinessWeek* reviewed summaries of 28 recent industry audits of Chinese factories serving U.S. customers. A few factories supplying Black & Decker (BDK), Williams-Sonoma, and other well-known brands turned up clean, the summaries show. But these facilities were the exceptions.

20   At most of the factories, auditors discovered records apparently meant to falsify payrolls and time sheets. One typical report concerns Zhongshan Tat Shing Toys Factory, which employs 650 people in the southern city of Zhongshan. The factory's main customers are Wal-Mart and Target (TGT). When an American-sponsored inspection team showed up this spring, factory managers produced time sheets showing each worker put in eight hours a day, Monday through Friday, and was paid double the local minimum wage of 43 cents per hour for eight hours on Saturday, according to an audit report.

But when auditors interviewed workers in one section, some said that they were paid less than the minimum wage and that most of them were obliged to work an extra three to five hours a day, without overtime pay, the report shows. Most toiled an entire month without a day off. Workers told auditors that the factory had a different set of records showing actual overtime hours, the report says. Factory officials claimed that some of the papers had been destroyed by fire.

Wal-Mart's Wyatt doesn't dispute the discrepancies but stresses that the company is getting more aggressive overall in its monitoring. Wal-Mart says it does more audits than any other company—13,600 reviews of 7,200 factories last year alone—and permanently banned 141 factories in 2005 as a result of serious infractions, such as using child labor. In a written statement, Target doesn't respond to the allegations but says that it "takes very seriously" the fair treatment of factory workers. It adds that it "is committed to taking corrective action—up to and including termination of the relationship for vendors" that violate local labor law or Target's code of conduct. The Zhongshan factory didn't respond to repeated requests for comment.

An audit late last year of Young Sun Lighting Co., a maker of lamps for Home Depot (HD), Sears (SHLD), and other retailers, highlighted similar inconsistencies. Every employee was on the job five days a week from 8 a.m. to 5:30 p.m., with a lunch break and no overtime hours, according to interviews with managers, as well as time sheets and payroll records provided by the 300-worker factory in Dongguan, an industrial city in Guangdong Province. But other records auditors found at the site and elsewhere—backed up by auditor interviews with workers—revealed that laborers worked an extra three to five hours a day with only one or two days a month off during peak production periods. Workers said they received overtime pay, but the "auditor strongly felt that these workers were coached," the audit report states.

24   Young Sun denies ever violating the rules set by its Western customers. In written answers to questions, the lighting manufacturer says that it doesn't coach employees on how to respond to auditors and that "at present, there are no" workers who are putting in three to five extra hours a day and getting only one or two days off each month. Young Sun says that it follows all local Chinese overtime rules.

Home Depot doesn't contest the inconsistencies in the audit reports about Young Sun and three other factories in China. "There is no perfect factory, I can guarantee you," a company spokeswoman says. Instead of cutting off wayward suppliers, Home Depot says that it works with factories on corrective actions. If the retailer becomes aware of severe offenses, such as the use of child labor, it terminates the supplier. A Sears spokesman declined to comment.

Coaching of workers and midlevel managers to mislead auditors is widespread, the auditing reports and *BusinessWeek* interviews show. A document obtained last year during an inspection at one Chinese fabric export factory in the southern city of Guangzhou instructed administrators to take these actions when faced with a surprise audit: "First notify underage trainees, underage full-time workers, and workers without identification to leave the manufacturing workshop through the back door. Order them not to loiter near the dormitory area. Secondly, immediately order the receptionist to gather all relevant documents and papers." Other pointers include instructing all workers to put on necessary protective equipment such as earplugs and face masks.

Some U.S. retailers say this evidence isn't representative and that their auditing efforts are working. *BusinessWeek* asked J.C. Penney Co. (JCP) about audit reports included among those the magazine reviewed that appear to show falsification of records to hide overtime and pay violations at two factories serving the large retailer. Penney spokeswoman Darcie M. Brossart says the company immediately investigated the factories, and its "auditors observed no evidence of any legal compliance issues."

28   In any case, the two factories are too small to be seen as typical, Penney executives argue. The chain has been consolidating its China supply base and says that 80% of its imports now come from factories with several thousand workers apiece, which are managed by large Hong Kong trading companies that employ

their own auditors. Quality inspectors for Penney and other buyers are at their supplier sites constantly, so overtime violations are hard to hide, Brossart says.

Chinese factory officials say, however, that just because infractions are difficult to discern doesn't mean they're not occurring. "It's a challenge for us to meet these codes of conduct," says Ron Chang, the Taiwanese general manager of Nike supplier Shoetown Footwear Co., which employs 15,000 workers in Qingyuan, Guangdong. Given the fierce competition in China for foreign production work, "we can't ask Nike to increase our price," he says, so "how can we afford to pay the higher salary?" By reducing profit margins from 30% to 5% over the past 18 years, Shoetown has managed to stay in business and obey Nike's rules, he says.

But squeezing margins doesn't solve the larger social issue. Chang says he regularly loses skilled employees to rival factories that break the rules because many workers are eager to put in longer hours than he offers, regardless of whether they get paid overtime rates. Ultimately, the economics of global outsourcing may trump any system of oversight that Western companies attempt. And these harsh economic realities could make it exceedingly difficult to achieve both the low prices and the humane working conditions that U.S. consumers have been promised.

PERSONAL RESPONSE

Explain whether you would be willing to pay more for products like electronics, shoes, and clothes so that workers in the foreign countries who make those items can have fair wages and healthy working conditions.

QUESTIONS FOR CLASS OR SMALL-GROUP DISCUSSION

1. State in your own words how the title reflects the content of the article. Whose secrets and lies? What conditions constitute "sweatshops"? What is the dilemma facing foreign manufacturers, such as the Chinese managers that the authors quote?

2. How does the way that Chinese and other foreign manufacturing companies get around compliance with fair labor practices raise "disturbing questions" (paragraph 9)? What do American multinationals have to say about the lack of compliance? What are they doing to help their offshore providers comply with labor codes?

3. Dexter and Engardio state: "The situation in China is hard to keep in perspective" (paragraph 14). State in your own words what they mean by that statement.

4. Dexter and Engardio refer to "the larger social issues" in their concluding paragraph. What are those issues? What do you think both American multinational companies and foreign manufacturers should or can do to resolve the dilemma described in this article?

IN DEFENSE OF "SWEATSHOPS"

Benjamin Powell

Benjamin Powell teaches at the Rawls College of Business and is director of the Free Market Institute at Texas Tech University. He also serves as senior fellow with the Independent Institute and North American Editor of the Review of Austrian Economics. *Powell is editor of* Making Poor Nations Rich: Entrepreneurship and the Process of Development *(2007) and coeditor (with Randall Holcombe) of* Housing America: Building Out of a Crisis *(2009). This article was published in the Library of Economics and Liberty on June 2, 2008.*

I do not want to work in a third world "sweatshop." If you are reading this on a computer, chances are you don't either. Sweatshops have deplorable working conditions and extremely low pay—compared to the alternative employment available to me and probably you. That is why we choose not to work in sweatshops. All too often the fact that we have better alternatives leads first world activists to conclude that there must be better alternatives for third world workers too.

Economists across the political spectrum have pointed out that for many sweatshop workers the alternatives are much, much worse.[1] In one famous 1993 case U.S. senator Tom Harkin proposed banning imports from countries that employed children in sweatshops. In response a factory in Bangladesh laid off 50,000 children. What was their next best alternative? According to the British charity Oxfam a large number of them became prostitutes.[2]

The national media spotlight focused on sweatshops in 1996 after Charles Kernaghan, of the National Labor Committee, accused Kathy Lee Gifford of exploiting children in Honduran sweatshops. He flew a 15 year old worker, Wendy Diaz, to the United States to meet Kathy Lee. Kathy Lee exploded into tears and apologized on the air, promising to pay higher wages.

4   Should Kathy Lee have cried? Her Honduran workers earned 31 cents per hour. At 10 hours per day, which is not uncommon in a sweatshop, a worker would earn $3.10. Yet nearly a quarter of Hondurans earn less than $1 per day and nearly half earn less than $2 per day.

Wendy Diaz's message should have been, "Don't cry for me, Kathy Lee. Cry for the Hondurans not fortunate enough to work for you." Instead the U.S. media compared $3.10 per day to U.S. alternatives, not Honduran alternatives. But U.S. alternatives are irrelevant. No one is offering these workers green cards.

What Are the Alternatives to Sweatshops?

Economists have often pointed to anecdotal evidence that alternatives to sweatshops are much worse. But until David Skarbek and I published a study

From "Sweatshop Wages and Third World Living Standards" by Bejamin Powell and David Skarbek. From *The Journal of Labor Research*, Spring 2006, Vol. 27, No. 2. Reprinted with permission from Springer Publishing Company.

in the 2006 *Journal of Labor Research*, nobody had systematically quantified the alternatives[3]. We searched U.S. popular news sources for claims of sweatshop exploitation in the third world and found 43 specific accusations of exploitation in 11 countries in Latin America and Asia. We found that sweatshop workers typically earn much more than the average in these countries. Here are the facts:

We obtained apparel industry hourly wage data for 10 of the countries accused of using sweatshop labor. We compared the apparel industry wages to average living standards in the country where the factories were located. Figure 1 summarizes our findings.[4]

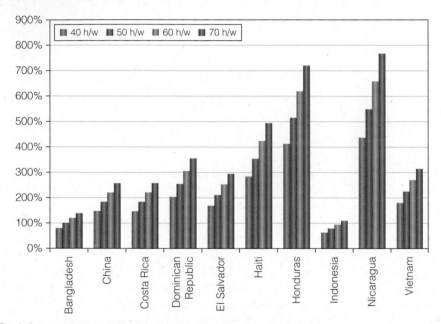

Fig. 1. Apparel Industry Wages as a Percent of Average National Income.

Source: Reprinted from "Sweatshop Wages and Third World Living Standards," by Benjamin Powell and David Skarbek, *The Journal of Labor Research,* Spring 2006, 27:2, with kind permission of Springer Science+Business Media B.V.

8   Working in the apparel industry in any one of these countries results in earning more than the average income in that country. In half of the countries it results in earning more than three times the national average.[5]

Next we investigated the specific sweatshop wages cited in U.S. news sources. We averaged the sweatshop wages reported in each of the 11 countries and again compared them to average living standards. Figure 2 summarizes our findings.

Even in specific cases where a company was allegedly exploiting sweatshop labor we found the jobs were usually better than average. In 9 of the 11 countries we surveyed, the average reported sweatshop wage, based on a 70-hour work week, equaled or exceeded average incomes. In Cambodia, Haiti, Nicaragua, and Honduras, the average wage paid by a firm accused of being a sweatshop is more

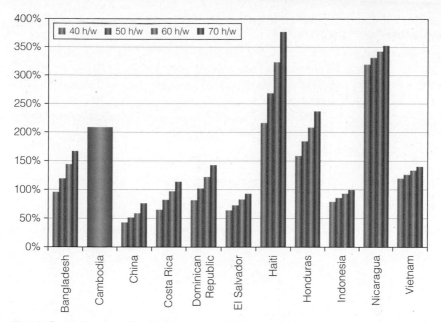

Note: In Cambodia only weekly sweatshop wage data were available.

Fig. 2. Average Protested Sweatshop Wages as a Percent of Average National Income.

Source: Reprinted from "Sweatshop Wages and Third World Living Standards," by Benjamin Powell and David Skarbek, *The Journal of Labor Research,* Spring 2006, 27:2, with kind permission of Springer Science+Business Media B.V.

than double the average income in that country. The Kathy Lee Gifford factory in Honduras was not an outlier—it was the norm.

Because sweatshops are better than the available alternatives, any reforms aimed at improving the lives of workers in sweatshops must not jeopardize the jobs that they already have. To analyze a reform we must understand what determines worker compensation.

What Determines Wages and Compensation?

12 If a Nicaraguan sweatshop worker creates $2.50 per hour worth of revenue (net of non-labor costs) for a firm then $2.50 per hour is the absolute most a firm would be willing to pay the worker. If the firm paid him $2.51 per hour, the firm would lose one cent per hour he worked. A profit maximizing firm, therefore, would lay the worker off.

Of course a firm would want to pay this worker less than $2.50 per hour in order to earn greater profits. Ideally the firm would like to pay the worker nothing and capture the entire $2.50 of value he creates per hour as profit. Why doesn't a firm do that? The reason is that a firm must persuade the worker to accept the job. To do that, the firm must offer him more than his next best available alternative.[6]

The amount a worker is paid is less than or equal to the amount he contributes to a firm's net revenue and more than or equal to the value of the worker's

538 CHAPTER 22 American Business in the Global Marketplace

next best alternative. In any particular situation the actual compensation falls somewhere between those two bounds.

Wages are low in the third world because worker productivity is low (upper bound) and workers' alternatives are lousy (lower bound). To get sustained improvements in overall compensation, policies must raise worker productivity and/or increase alternatives available to workers. Policies that try to raise compensation but fail to move these two bounds risk raising compensation above a worker's upper bound resulting in his losing his job and moving to a less-desirable alternative.

16   What about non-monetary compensation? Sweatshops often have long hours, few bathroom breaks, and poor health and safety conditions. How are these determined?

Compensation can be paid in wages or in benefits, which may include health, safety, comfort, longer breaks, and fewer working hours. In some cases, improved health or safety can increase worker productivity and firm profits. In these cases firms will provide these benefits out of their own self-interest. However, often these benefits do not directly increase profits and so the firm regards such benefits to workers as costs to itself, in which case these costs are like wages.

A profit-maximizing firm is indifferent between compensating workers with wages or compensating them with health, safety, and leisure benefits of the same value when doing so does not affect overall productivity. What the firm really cares about is the overall cost of the total compensation package.

Workers, on the other hand, do care about the mix of compensation they receive. Few of us would be willing to work for no money wage and instead take our entire pay in benefits. We want some of each. Furthermore, when our overall compensation goes up, we tend to desire more non-monetary benefits.

20   For most people, comfort and safety are what economists call "normal goods," that is, goods that we demand more of as our income rises. Factory workers in third world countries are no different. Unfortunately, many of them have low productivity, and so their overall compensation level is low. Therefore, they want most of their compensation in wages and little in health or safety improvements.

Evaluating Anti-Sweatshop Proposals

The anti-sweatshop movement consists of unions, student groups, politicians, celebrities, and religious groups.[7] Each group has its own favored "cures" for sweatshop conditions. These groups claim that their proposals would help third world workers.

Some of these proposals would prohibit people in the United States from importing any goods made in sweatshops. What determines whether the good is made in a sweatshop is whether it is made in any way that violates labor standards. Such standards typically include minimum ages for employment, minimum wages, standards of occupational safety and health, and hours of work.[8]

Such standards do nothing to make workers more productive. The upper bound of their compensation is unchanged. Such mandates risk raising compensation above laborers' productivity and throwing them into worse alternatives by eliminating or reducing the U.S. demand for their products. Employers will meet health and safety mandates by either laying off workers or by improving health and safety while lowering wages against workers' wishes. In either case, the standards would make workers worse off.

24   The aforementioned Charles Kernaghan testified before Congress on one of these pieces of legislation, claiming:

Once passed, this legislation will reward decent U.S. companies which are striving to adhere to the law. Worker rights standards in China, Bangladesh and other countries across the world will be raised, improving conditions for tens of millions of working people. Your legislation will for the first time also create a level playing field for American workers to compete fairly in the global economy.[9]

Contrary to his assertion, anti-sweatshop laws would make third world workers worse off by lowering the demand for their labor. As his testimony alludes to though, such laws would make some American workers better off because they would no longer have to compete with third world labor: U.S. consumers would be, to some extent, a captive market. Although Kernaghan and some other opponents of sweatshops claim that they are attempting to help third world workers, their true motives are revealed by the language of one of these pieces of legislation: "Businesses have a right to be free from competition with companies that use sweatshop labor." A more-honest statement would be, "U.S. workers have a right not to face competition from poor third world workers and by outlawing competition from the third world we can enhance union wages at the expense of poorer people who work in sweatshops."

Kernaghan and other first world union members pretend to take up the cause of poor workers but the policies they advocate would actually make those very workers worse off. As economist David Henderson said, "[s]omeone who intentionally gets you fired is not your friend."[10] Charles Kernaghan is no friend to third world workers.

Conclusion

28   Not only are sweatshops better than current worker alternatives, but they are also part of the process of development that ultimately raises living standards. That process took about 150 years in Britain and the United States but closer to 30 years in the Japan, South Korea, Hong Kong, and Taiwan.

When companies open sweatshops they bring technology and physical capital with them. Better technology and more capital raise worker productivity. Over time this raises their wages. As more sweatshops open, more alternatives are available to workers raising the amount a firm must bid to hire them.

The good news for sweatshop workers today is that the world has better technology and more capital than ever before. Development in these countries can happen even faster than it did in the East Asian tigers. If activists in the United States do not undermine the process of development by eliminating these countries' ability to attract sweatshops, then third world countries that adopt market friendly institutions will grow rapidly and sweatshop pay and working conditions will improve even faster than they did in the United States or East Asia. Meanwhile, what the third world so badly needs is more "sweatshop jobs," not fewer.

Endnotes

1. Walter Williams, "Sweatshop Exploitation." January 27, 2004. Paul Krugman, "In Praise of Cheap Labor, Bad Jobs at Bad Wages Are Better Than No Jobs at All." *Slate*, March 21, 1997.

2. Paul Krugman, *the New York Times*. April 22, 2001.

3. Benjamin Powell and David Skarbek, "Sweatshop Wages and Third World Living Standards: Are the Jobs Worth the Sweat?" *Journal of Labor Research*. Vol. 27, No. 2. Spring 2006.

4. All figures are reproduced from our *Journal of Labor Research* article. See the original article for notes on data sources and quantification methods.

5. Data on actual hours worked were not available. Therefore, we provided earnings estimates based on various numbers of hours worked. Since one characteristic of sweatshops is long working hours, we believe the estimates based on 70 hours per week are the most accurate.

6. I am excluding from my analysis any situation where a firm or government uses the threat of violence to coerce the worker into accepting the job. In those situations, the job is not better than the next best alternative because otherwise a firm wouldn't need to use force to get the worker to take the job.

7. It is a classic mix of "bootleggers and Baptists." Bootleggers in the case of sweatshops are the U.S. unions who stand to gain when their lower priced substitute, third world workers, is eliminated from the market. The "Baptists" are the true but misguided believers.

8. These minimums are determined by laws and regulations of the country of origin. For a discussion of why these laws should not be followed see Benjamin Powell, "In Reply to Sweatshop Sophistries." *Human Rights Quarterly*. Vol. 28. No. 4. Nov. 2006.

9. Testimonies at the Senate Subcommittee on Interstate Commerce, Trade and Tourism Hearing. Statement of Charles Kernaghan. February 14, 2007.

10. David Henderson, "The Case for Sweatshops." *Weekly Standard*, February 7, 2000.

PERSONAL RESPONSE

With whom do you find yourself siding: those like Powell, who believes that third world sweatshop labor is good for workers in those countries, or those like Charles Kernaghan of the National Labor Committee, who believes that sweatshops are bad for workers?

QUESTIONS FOR CLASS OR SMALL-GROUP DISCUSSION

1. How does Powell define "sweatshop"?
2. Explain in your own words how the two graphs included in the article support Powell's position.
3. Analyze the structure of Powell's argument. Where does he state his thesis? Where does he acknowledge the opposition? What proof does he offer to support his position? What conclusions does he draw from his evidence?
4. Are you convinced by Powell's defense of sweatshops? Explain your answer.

DOMINANT ELSEWHERE, GOOGLE STRUGGLES IN CHINA

JOHN BOUDREAU

John Boudreau is a staff writer covering global business and technology for the San Jose Mercury News. *This article was published in the October 8, 2009, issue of the* Mercury News.

In China Google means underdog. While the Mountain View company dominates the search market in the United States, it is not part of the pop lexicon on the other side of the Pacific. In its nine years in China, which now has the world's largest Internet audience, Google has struggled.

It has seen its services temporarily shut down by the government, and has been accused of purveying porn. Google China has also been out maneuvered by a nimble rival, Baidu.com, the look-alike site that claims more than 60 percent of the market in China.

"It's a constant struggle," said Yuke, a Google employee who goes by one name. He was Google's lead product manager in China before managing the social responsibility department. "Sometimes we move ahead; sometimes we lose ground. It's a tough fight."

4   In many ways, Google's experience in China is typical of what international companies face when trying to tap into the emerging wealth of this vast nation of 1.3 billion. They learn, often at great cost, that their China enterprises need "a lot of hand-holding," said Mark Natkin, managing director of Beijing-based Marbridge Consulting.

Google's China business represented just a sliver of its 2008 revenue of $21.8 billion, "a rounding error" of not more than $300 million, according to RBC Capital Markets analyst Ross Sandler.

Other Silicon Valley global giants have been humbled here, as well. In 2005, Yahoo handed over operations of Yahoo China to Alibaba after the Sunnyvale, Calif., company took a $1 billion, 40 percent stake in its erstwhile Chinese competitor. Five years ago, eBay appeared untouchable in China after acquiring EachNet, China's then-leading online auctioneer. Now, though, eBay ranks far behind Taobao, which controls about 80 percent of the online retail market.

"I call it the Pacific Ocean gap," said Victor Koo, chief executive of Youku. com, a Beijing-based online video site. "If you have to wait for a conference call across the Pacific (before making a decision), it can take days. You can't compete. We make decisions faster and we understand the market better."

8   Though Google launched a Chinese version of its search engine in 2000, before Baidu showed up, it wasn't until 2005 that the Mountain View, Calif., company dispatched an on-the-ground team led by the charismatic Kai-Fu Lee, who just left the company to start a venture fund. Under his leadership, Google nearly doubled its share of the market to 31 percent.

But Baidu dominates China's online culture and has trumpeted its Chinese roots in commercials appealing to nationalism.

"In China, everybody uses Baidu," said Meya Hsu, a 20-year-old college student sitting in a cafe with her MacBook laptop. She uses Google only as a last resort, such as to look up information about American pop stars.

Until recently, Google has done next to no marketing, said Kaiser Kuo, a Beijing writer and China Internet expert. Most people can't even spell Google and are unaware that there's a simpler URL, g.cn.

12   Google's ramp-up is an acknowledgment of a rapidly growing market: China's 700 million mobile phone subscribers and 338 million Internet users dwarf those of any other country.

Google's 500 employees in China share a 10-story complex in Tsinghua Science Park in Beijing's high-tech Haidian district. The company has transported its valley culture here—workers curl up on brightly colored couches with laptops, play pingpong, take belly dancing lessons and nibble throughout the day on free snacks and meals prepared by a chef. Teams of engineers devise China-specific products, including a free music service that features lyrics for karaoke-loving Chinese.

Google now is "putting up a fight. They have made good progress," said Youku.com's Koo.

But Google may always face special scrutiny from the government, which is wary of foreign Internet companies. It not only has shut down Google on occasions but also has redirected Internet traffic to Baidu.

16   Google has been careful not to provide products—such as blog services— that require it to gather personal data on users for fear of being forced to turn over information to the government, a decision that hurts it in the market, analysts say. Google runs its Gmail service on servers located outside China, making it more secure from government eyes.

"They are haunted by the ghost of Tom Lantos," said Kuo, referring to the late San Mateo, Calif., congressman who berated Yahoo executives during congressional hearings after the company handed over e-mail records of journalist

Shi Tao, who was accused by the Chinese authorities of leaking state secrets abroad and sentenced in 2007 to 10 years in prison.

This summer, online activists relied on Google's Gmail to successfully campaign against the government's efforts to require PC makers to install Internet filtering software on all new machines. "We always tell Chinese people to use non-China-based services," said a Shanghai-based researcher who goes by the name Isaac Mao.

While sometimes running afoul of the Chinese government, Google has been hammered by human rights organizations for cooperating with the government's efforts to block politically sensitive search results. Google searches in China filter out findings objectionable to the government, but users are told they are not getting access to all information because of government restrictions.

20   "I think Google has tried to strike a balance between protecting access to as much information as possible and to expand that while at the same time not being purer than the pope so people don't get access to information in China," said Susan Shirk, a former deputy assistant secretary of state in the Clinton administration responsible for U.S. relations with China. Google, she added, is playing an important role in China's online civil society.

"Any foreign company that does content online is in for a rough period," said Rebecca MacKinnon, an expert on the Internet in China at the University of Hong Kong. "If you want to beat the Chinese competitors, you have to really lower your ethical standards in terms of how you are going to treat your users. I don't see any other way to do it."

China-based Googlers, however, believe time is on their side. As China's telecom giants invest an estimated $59 billion in 3G infrastructure in 200 cities during the next three years, Google hopes to capture leadership in mobile search. Its partnership with China Mobile, the country's largest mobile carrier, will deploy Google's Android operating system on handsets.

"From a pure technology point of view, it's very hard to compete with Google," said Feng Hong, the company's product manager of music search. "There is a long, long way for Google to go.

PERSONAL RESPONSE

Write for a few minutes in response to the information that international giants such as Google, eBay, and Yahoo are not doing well in the Chinese market. Are you surprised?

QUESTIONS FOR CLASS OR SMALL-GROUP DISCUSSION

1. Comment on the effectiveness of the opening paragraph. This is a newspaper article, which means that the reporter has been trained to make the first paragraph an attention grabber and also a succinct statement of what the entire article is about. How successfully do you think Boudreau has been at capturing reader attention?

2. State in your own words why Baidu is doing better in China than Google.

3. What has Google done to improve its business in China?

4. In what ways might Google's struggle to dominate in China be representative of the competition of all international businesses to dominate in the global marketplace?

LESSONS FROM THE DEVELOPING WORLD

JAMIE ANDERSON, MARTIN KUPP, AND RONAN MOALIGOU

Jamie Anderson is an adjunct professor in strategic management at the TiasNimbas Business School in Tilburg, the Netherlands. Martin Kupp is a member of the academic faculty at the European School of Management and Technology in Berlin. Ronan Moaligou is a senior manager at consulting firm Globalpraxis Group in Barcelona. This article was published in the Wall Street Journal *on June 15, 2012.*

The developing world is home to some of the most challenging markets for any business: Urban slums. Rural backwaters. Lawless regions and battle zones. But hundreds of millions of potential customers live in these places, and a few pioneering companies are thriving there. Their success offers lessons on how to tap these complex environments for profits and growth.

All of these markets share certain challenges. They often lack functioning legal systems, so contracts are rarely enforceable. Theft, vandalism and physical violence are common. Skilled workers are hard to find.

The widespread poverty in these areas makes it difficult for many people to afford whatever a company is selling. Marketing is challenging because conventional advertising media like television and radio don't reach many of the people in these environments, and more-direct approaches can be dangerous. And winning the acceptance of the people living in these communities, for companies and their products, is tricky because these societies are often a patchwork of religious, linguistic and cultural diversity.

4   Little wonder, then, that to succeed in the face of such challenges, companies first must recognize that traditional business strategies won't work. Instead, companies need to find local partners familiar with the terrain, and rely on those partners to help guide their operations and develop strategies unique to each market. And to sustain a business in these environments, companies need to assert their value to their employees, partners and the broader community by supporting their development.

"It has to be a win-win for the company and for local people," says Lars Stork, formerly chief operating officer of Celtel Nigeria, one of several telecommunications companies that have been at the forefront of expansion into these areas. "If not, any results will be short term."

Here's a look at how Mr. Stork and others learned those lessons.

The Locals Know

In mid-2007, Celtel Nigeria was the second-largest mobile-telecommunications company in the Nigerian market, with a 28% market share and about eight million subscribers. The company—now known as Zain Nigeria after becoming part of Zain Group, which is owned by Kuwait's Mobile Telecommunications Co.—had done well serving Nigeria's cities and larger towns, but had only recently shifted its attention to poorer consumers in rural areas.

8   Although roughly half of Nigeria's population lives in rural regions, the challenge of reaching them was daunting. For starters, village-level chiefs and religious leaders held significant power in many regions of Nigeria. Even after national authorities approved Celtel's plans for expanding its network, the company needed to win the approval of tribal leaders to install signal transmitters and other equipment and to send its employees to tribal areas to maintain the network.

Many areas of Nigeria weren't reached by television or radio signals, making the promotion of products and services particularly challenging. Some other traditional marketing approaches were also difficult: Billboards were quickly stolen and recycled for building materials or fencing, and it was dangerous in some regions for Celtel staff to travel for direct-marketing activities at markets and other rural gatherings.

Two-Way Street
Tips on how companies can succeed in the developing world

■ **Identify** local partners who understand local customers and culture.

■ **Don't rely** on existing partners from developed markets to have the skills necessary to succeed here.

■ **Identify** local entrepreneurs with basic business acumen and a willingness to commit to long-term relationships.

■ **Build** own insights, and learn from business partners.

■ **Take** a ground-up approach, and be willing to experiment with new business processes.

■ **Don't enter** into complex agreements with prescribed solutions.

■ **Provide** relevant skills and capabilities to empower local partners for improved performance.

■ **Strive** to build loyalty and trust through sustainable win-win partnerships.

■ **Internalize** skills learned from local partners, and look for opportunities to use those lessons in new markets.

■ **Strive** to achieve both economic and social good.

source: Jamie Anderson, Martin Kupp and Ronan Mcalgou

Security at base stations was a major concern. Vandalism and theft of equipment was common, even after Celtel posted armed guards, recruited from the community and elsewhere.

Mr. Stork realized that he was fighting a losing battle and needed to enlist the help of people in the communities Celtel aimed to serve. "Working with local people is the only way to succeed in rural Nigeria," he says. "They understand the local dynamics and know how to survive in what can be an extremely challenging environment."

12 Celtel initiated a franchising program, recruiting small-business owners to act as its exclusive representatives in their communities. The entrepreneurs are responsible for marketing and distributing Celtel products and services, and for basic maintenance and security at the base stations. Celtel recognized that its partners didn't need experience in the mobile-telecommunications industry. More important was basic commercial acumen, entrepreneurial spirit and a deep understanding of how to manage the local environment.

By the end of 2008, the Celtel network had grown to some 650 franchisees in the deep rural regions of Nigeria, and the average franchised site produced a 160% return on original investment within a year of launch. Sales by franchisees of recharge vouchers—a form of prepaid air time—exceeded the company's initial forecasts by more than 120%. Vandalism and theft have all but disappeared in regions with high levels of franchisee site supervision.

Other companies have discovered the importance of local partners in slums and conflict zones.

Vodafone Essar Ltd., an Indian unit of the U.K.'s Vodafone Group, serves the slums of Mumbai, some of the most populous shantytowns in the world, with partners chosen from among the local businesspeople.

16 "The people we work with know the slum," says Naveen Chopra, Vodafone Essar's chief executive of Mumbai Circle. "They might be tailors or fancy-good shop owners or outlets selling day-to-day consumables. We cannot simply walk into the slum as Vodafone and start doing business, given the intricacies. But these local businesspeople already run businesses in this market, and we wanted to benefit from their wisdom."

Growing Together

Companies that have succeeded in these environments also realized that local partners were crucial not only in establishing their operations but also to building their business.

In Nigeria, the 25 entrepreneurs who became Celtel franchisees in the first phase of that program helped define the responsibilities of franchise holders and suggested ways they could fulfill their roles more effectively. For instance, at the suggestion of one pilot franchisee, Celtel provides four or five motorcycles to each franchised site to help franchisees deliver more-efficient servicing of surrounding villages. Many franchisees have also started to offer installment financing and barter deals for cellphones, an extension of established local commercial practices.

In Mumbai, Vodafone's partners helped Mr. Chopra solve a fundamental problem: the difficulty of beaming cellular signals into the inner reaches of the city's sprawling slums. The density of housing in the slums makes it impossible to erect the same sort of network of transmission towers used to serve other areas.

20   The company first tried beaming its service into the slums from surrounding buildings, but that failed to achieve coverage deep inside the slums. Then a large retailer interviewed as a possible distributor suggested a new approach: recruit large retail outlets around the slum to sell the company's products and services—and also to hoist mini-transmitters above their shops. The retailers would be responsible for the security and basic maintenance of the transmitters.

The strategy was crucial to Vodafone's success in the Mumbai slums, where revenue has far exceeded the company's initial expectations. And not just because of the improved network coverage. The mini-transmitters brought the partnership between Vodafone and the retailers to a new level. Each retailer "becomes your ear to the ground to the local community," Mr. Chopra says. The retailer "tells you what opportunities there are, where you need to launch a particular tariff plan" to cater to the many different communities within the slum. "So he becomes a very integral part of the way you do the business."

Something for Everyone

Companies in these environments also have discovered the importance of establishing relationships that benefit their employees and business partners and the communities they work in.

"Once the economics are right, once you have a win-win" for the company and its partners, says Mr. Chopra, "you have a relationship that is resilient. It is about respecting the fact that your associate in the slum may do only a small turnover, but for that person a small turnover is a big amount, and you call him for the same meetings that you call your other urban distributors. He gets recognition and respect, and in turn this builds trust and loyalty."

24   Trust and loyalty can also be built by helping employees and business partners develop business skills. Celtel set up three-day workshops at regional company offices to train new franchisees in sales and marketing techniques, accounting and financial management, retail operations, basic maintenance of base stations, site security and human-resources management. And once in business, franchisees are provided with regular training events organized at the regional level.

In the chaos of Iraq after the fall of Saddam Hussein's regime, a newly formed Iraqi unit of Zain sent local engineers abroad for training in building and operating a mobile network, in effect becoming a corporate university that provided the education and skills required to run its business. The company also has provided training in other aspects of the business, including marketing and communications, distribution and customer care.

Companies also reached out beyond partners and employees, to weave themselves into the communities where they operate. Celtel shared a percentage of its franchise revenues with local communities, allocating the funds in cooperation with franchisees, village authority figures and sometimes non-governmental organizations.

Zain has helped many Iraqis find medical attention, both inside and outside the country; supported local sporting activities, the Iraqi national soccer team and the country's Olympic athletes; and helped reassemble the Iraqi symphony orchestra.

28   "Our message has been that we are part of Iraqi society, and we are dynamically tied to Iraq and its people," says Ali Al Dhawi, chief executive officer of Zain's Iraqi unit. "We suffer what Iraq suffers, and we enjoy what Iraq enjoys."

PERSONAL RESPONSE

The article identifies some creative solutions to what seemed like insurmountable obstacles. Write about an obstacle that you overcame.

QUESTIONS FOR CLASS OR SMALL-GROUP DISCUSSION

1. What are the challenges in developing countries facing companies who want to access those markets?
2. State in your own words what Celtel did in Nigeria. Why do you think that approach worked?
3. How do companies like Celtel and Vodafone help franchisees build their businesses?
4. What lessons from the developing world did American businesses learn (title)?

PERSPECTIVES ON AMERICAN BUSINESS IN THE GLOBAL MARKETPLACE

Suggested Writing Topics

1. Write an essay in response to Benjamin Powell's defense of sweatshops.
2. Write a synthesis using Benjamin Powell's "In Defense of 'Sweatshops'" and Dexter Roberts and Pete Engardio's "Secrets, Lies, and Sweatshops" to analyze the dilemma posed by trying to maintain fair labor practices in companies who struggle to meet low prices demanded by the businesses they sell to.

3. Describe your own buying habits in terms of whether you are socially conscious or not. Do you consciously buy only "fair trade" products, for instance? Do you boycott products of companies that employ sweatshop labor?

4. Select a statement from any of the essays in this chapter that you would like to respond to, elaborate on, or argue for or against.

5. Compare and contrast the benefits of offshore outsourcing.

6. If you know someone who has lost a job because the company moved offshore, narrate that person's experience.

7. Discuss the implications for both American consumers and American businesses of the rapid expansion of the global marketplace.

8. Explain how you see changes in the global economy affecting you personally, both as a consumer and as a (perhaps future) member of the workforce.

9. Assess the impact of foreign products on a typical day in your life. Which imported items are important to your daily life?

10. Write an essay from the point of view of a market researcher for a new corporation looking for rapid growth through global marketing. Make up a product and a corporation name; then prepare a report for the board of directors of your company in which you recommend expanding efforts in one of the world's newest market areas.

Research Topics

1. Using Benjamin Powell's "In Defense of 'Sweatshops'" as a starting point, research some aspect of the issues surrounding sweatshop labor.

2. Using "Secrets, Lies, and Sweatshops" by Dexter Roberts and Pete Engardio as a starting point, research the subject of the growth of both companies that help foreign manufacturers evade or pass labor code audits and companies that conduct audits on foreign manufacturers.

3. Research the subject of outsourcing and draw your own conclusions about the extent to which outsourcing should be cause for concern.

4. Research Celtel's or Vodafone's business practices in developing countries that make it a model of success.

5. Using John Boudreau's "Dominant Elsewhere, Google Struggles in China" as a starting point, research Google's struggle to gain a stronghold in China, or select another international giant such as Yahoo or eBay and research its success or failure to dominate in the Chinese market.

6. Research the economic impact of outsourcing by focusing on one particular type of business.

7. Research the subject of the non-economic benefits or drawbacks to out-sourcing. For instance, some researchers say that outsourcing has resulted in creating allies in the war on terrorism. Can you confirm or refute that claim?

8. Research the effects of the North American Free Trade Agreement (NAFTA) on the American economy and workers.

9. Research the subject of trade protectionism and state your conclusions on its positive or negative effects.

10. Research the economic changes in the past decade in any of these geographic areas: Asia, Asia Pacific, Latin America, Eastern Europe, or sub-Saharan Africa. Read about developments in the area and projections for the future, and then report your findings and conclusions.

11. Research the global investment strategies of any major American corporation. Draw some conclusions about the effectiveness of such strategies in your paper.

12. Analyze the connections between the information revolution and the global spread of market economies. How do they affect or influence one another?

13. Select an area such as politics, technology, or economics. Then conduct library research to determine both the positive and negative implications of the enormous global changes in that area, including a prediction of the effects of these changes on the American economy in the next decade.

RESPONDING TO VISUALS

Cristian Baitg/Getty Images

China and United States shaking hands.

1. What comment on the business world does this image make?
2. What are the implications of the hands being those of the United States and China?
3. What details extend the implication of the image to include the global marketplace?

RESPONDING TO VISUALS

Kuni Takahashi/Getty Images

Young boys working in a textile factory in India

1. Comment on the perspective from which the photograph was taken. What is emphasized? What do the somewhat blurred images of the other boys in the background add to the picture?

2. What image of the boys' work does the photograph convey? If the caption had not told you that they are working in a factory, would you have said that they looked unhappy?

3. If you have read the articles on sweatshop labor in this chapter or already knew about sweatshops, how does this image fit with your mental picture or view of sweatshop labor?

GLOSSARY OF TERMS

abstract. A summary of the essential points of a text. It is usually quite short, no more than a paragraph.

ad hominem **arguments.** Attacking the character of the arguer rather than the argument itself.

analogy. A comparison of two things to show their similarity.

analysis. Dividing a subject into its separate parts for individual study.

appeal. A rhetorical strategy used in argumentation to be persuasive; a persuasive technique that goes beyond fact or logic to engage audience's sympathy, sense of higher power or authority, or reasoning. Classic persuasion relies on a combination of **ethical**, **logical**, and **emotional appeals** to sway an audience.

argument/persuasion. An argument is an attempt to prove the validity of a position by offering supporting proof. Persuasion takes argument one step further by convincing an audience to adopt a viewpoint or take action.

Aristotelian logic. Formal, classic argumentation that typically follows one of two common lines of reasoning, **deductive** and **inductive** reasoning.

attributive tag. A short identifying phrase or clause that identifies ("attributes") the source of a quotation or paraphrase: *Mugabane explains . . . ; According to Sissela Bok, . . . ; Singer, a Princeton University professor who publishes widely on bioethics issues, recommends. . . .*

audience. The readers of a piece of writing, the individual or group for whom a writer writes.

backing. According to the Toulmin model of reasoning, the support or evidence for a warrant.

begging the question (circular reasoning). Making a claim that simply rephrases another claim in other words.

blog. A personal website which the owner uses for whatever purpose he or she likes, such as a daily record of thoughts or experiences or links to other sites. The term derives from the phrase "web log."

body of an essay. The paragraphs between the introduction and conclusion of an essay that develop, support, explain, or illustrate the thesis or central idea of a paper.

book review. A report that summarizes only the main ideas of a book and provides critical commentary on it. Usually in a book review, you will also be asked to give your personal response to the book, including both your opinion of the ideas it presents and an evaluation of its worth or credibility.

brainstorming. Writing for a short, set period of time everything related to a general subject in order to generate a workable topic for a paper.

Cause-effect analysis. An expository mode explaining why something happened or showing what happened as a result of something—or perhaps both.

citation. A reference that provides supporting illustrations or examples for your own ideas; the authority or source of that information is identified.

claim. In the Toulman model of reasoning, the proposition, a debatable or controversial assertion, drawn from the data or grounds, based on the **warrant** (the underlying assumption). The point your paper is making, your thesis or arguable position statement.

classification/division. The process of sorting information and ideas into categories or groups (classification); the act of breaking information, ideas, or concepts into parts in order to better understand them (division).

comparison/contrast. Showing a strong similarity or a strong dissimilarity between two things. Comparing or contrasting usually promotes one of two purposes: to show each of two subjects distinctly by considering both side by side, or to evaluate or judge two things.

concession. Agreement with an opponent on certain points or acknowledging that an opposing argument cannot be refuted.

conclusion. In an essay, the final paragraph(s) that bring the paper to a satisfying close.

conditions of rebuttal. Weaknesses in the opposing argument that provide ways to counter the argument, usually by showing flaws in logic or weakness of supporting evidence.

connotation. The emotional associations of a word, as distinct from **denotation**, the literal meaning. Connotative meaning applies to images and things as well.

context. The circumstances, setting, or surrounding of a word, an image, or an event.

critique. An evaluation of a work's logic, rhetorical soundness, and overall effectiveness.

data or **grounds.** In the Toulmin model of reasoning, the evidence that support a claim. They constitute proof and demonstrate that the claim is true.

debate. A discussion involving opposing points in an argument. In formal debate, opposing teams defend and attack a specific proposition.

deductive reasoning. In argumentation, the movement from a general principle or shared premise to a conclusion about a specific instance.

definition. The process of making clear a precise meaning or significance. In definition, a writer conveys the essential characteristics of something by distinguishing it from all other things in its class.

description. A conveyance through words of the essential nature of a person, place, or thing by appealing to the senses, that is, by evoking through words certain sights, smells, sounds, or tactile sensations. The purpose of description may be objective—to convey information without bias—or it may be subjective—to express feelings, impressions, or attitudes about a person, place, or thing.

diction. A writer's word choice and level of usage, which varies in informal and formal language; slang, regional, nonstandard, and colloquial language; and jargon.

dropped quotation. A quotation that appears without an introduction, as if it had just been dropped into a paper.

editing. Re-examining written work for errors in grammar, mechanics, and punctuation.

either/or reasoning. Admitting only two sides to an issue and asserting that the writer's is the only possible correct one.

ellipsis points. Used in quoting source material, three spaced periods indicate that words have been omitted.

emotional appeal. A rhetorical strategy that attempts to move an audience on an affective or emotional level with startling, disturbing, or touching examples.

ethical appeal. A rhetorical strategy that calls upon authority or the credibility of sources to persuade.

expository writing. Writing with the goal of informing or presenting an objective explanation on a subject. Types of expository writing include cause-effect analysis, classification-division, comparison or contrast, and definition.

expressive writing. Emphasizes the writer's feelings and subjective view of the world.

evaluation. A judgment about worth, quality, or credibility.

exemplification. Showing by example; using specific details or instances to illustrate, support, or make specific.

fallacies or common flaws. Components of argument that are false or misleading, thus making the reasoning illogical and the argument essentially invalid.

false analogy. Falsely claiming that, because something resembles something else in one way, it resembles it in all ways.

forum. An open discussion or exchange of ideas among many people.

freewriting. The act of writing down every idea that occurs to you about your topic without stopping to examine what you are writing.

grammar. Refers to sentence construction, especially avoiding fragments and run-ons; subject-verb and pronoun-antecedent agreement; correct use of case for nouns and pronouns; and using adjectives and adverbs correctly,

hasty or faulty generalization. The drawing of a broad conclusion on the basis of very little evidence.

hypothesis. A tentative explanation to account for some phenomenon or set of facts. It is in essence a theory or an assumption that can be tested by further investigation and is assumed to be true for the purpose of argument or investigation.

illustration. An explanation or clarification, usually using example or comparison.

inductive reasoning. In argumentation, the movement from a number of specific instances to a general principle.

introduction. The opening words, sentences, or paragraphs that begin a piece of writing.

invention. Generating ideas for writing.

journal. A personal record of experiences, thoughts, or responses to something, usually kept separate from other writings, as in a diary or notebook.

listserv. An e-mail based discussion group of a specific topic.

loaded words (emotionally charged language). Language guaranteed to appeal to audiences on an emotional rather than an intellectual level. A loaded word has highly charged emotional overtones or connotations that evoke a strong response, either positive or negative, that goes beyond the denotation or specific definition given in a dictionary. Often the meaning or emotional association of the words varies from person to person or group to group.

logical appeal. A rhetorical strategy that applies sound reasoning in order to persuade.

mechanics. In writing, refers to spelling words correctly, including correct hyphenation; correct use of italics; and use of capital letters, numbers, and abbreviations.

narration. The re-creation of an experience for a specific purpose, such as to illustrate a point, report information, entertain, or persuade. A narrative may be a brief anecdote, a story, or a case history.

non sequitur. Drawing inferences or conclusions that do not follow logically from available evidence.

oversimplification. Offering a solution or an explanation that is too simple for the problem or issue being argued.

paraphrase. A restatement of a passage in your own words. A paraphrase is somewhat shorter than the original but retains its essential meaning.

persuasive writing. Seeks to convince readers of the validity of an author's position on an issue and sometimes even to move them to action.

point of view. The perspective from which a piece is written: first person (I, we), second person (you), or third person (he/she/it/one, they).

position paper. A detailed report that explains, justifies, or recommends a particular course of action.

post hoc, ergo propter hoc **reasoning.** Assuming that something happened simply because it followed something else without evidence of a causal relationship.

précis. A concise summary of the highlights of a written text.

premise. An assumption or a proposition on which an argument is based or from which a conclusion is drawn.

prewriting. The first stage of the writing process, when writers determine their purpose, identify their audience, discover their subject, narrow their focus, and plan their writing strategy.

proposition. A statement of a position on a subject, a course of action, or a topic for discussion or debate.

punctuation. Refers to the use of commas, colons, semicolons, apostrophes, and quotation marks.

qualifiers. Words or phrases that, when added to a word or phrase, modify its meaning by limiting (she is partially correct) or enhancing (he is completely correct) it. In argumentation, such words allow the writer to make concessions to the opposition.

reading critically. The process of making a careful, thoughtful, and thorough consideration of a piece of writing by looking at its different parts.

rebuttal. Response addressed to opposing arguments, such as demonstrating a flaw in logic or reasoning or exposing faulty or weak supporting evidence.

red herring. Diverting the audience's attention from the main issue at hand to an irrelevant issue.

revision. Re-examination of written work. **Global revision** examines the whole essay or entire paragraphs and addresses the issues of purpose, audience, organization, and content as well as style and clarity. **Sentence revision** looks at individual sentences for clarifying or refining.

rhetoric. The art or study of using written or spoken language effectively.

rhetorical analysis. The process of making a careful, thoughtful, and thorough consideration of a piece of writing by looking at its different parts.

rhetorical fallacy. A flaw or error in reasoning that renders an argument invalid or weakens it considerably.

rhetorical mode. A strategy used to organize and develop ideas in a writing assignment. Broadly, there are four traditional modes: exposition, argumentation, narration, and description.

Rogerian argument. Based on the work of the American psychologist Carl R. Rogers, an approach to argumentation that adopts the stance of listening to opposing arguments with an open mind, making concessions, and attempting to find a common ground.

slanted word. A word whose connotation (suggestive meaning as opposed to actual meaning) is used to advance an argument for its emotional association.

social networking sites. Online service or platform whose function is to provide a forum for messages, pictures, weblinks, and other means of establishing connections among people.

stereotyping. A form of generalization or oversimplification in which an entire group is narrowly labeled or perceived on the basis of a few in the group.

strategy. A plan of action to achieve a specific goal; the way that an assignment is organized and developed.

subject. A general or broad area of interest.

summary. A concise presentation of the main points or highlights of a text.

syllogism. Traditional form of deductive reasoning that has two premises and a conclusion.

syntax. The arrangement of words or phrases to create sentences.

synthesis. Combining the ideas of two or more authors and integrating those ideas into your own discussion.

thesis statement. A statement of the specific purpose of a paper. A thesis is essentially a one-sentence summary of what you will argue, explain, illustrate, define, describe, or otherwise develop in the rest of the paper. It usually comes very early in a paper.

tone. A writer's attitude toward subject and audience, conveyed through word choice and diction.

topic. A specific, focused, and clearly defined area of interest. A topic is a narrow aspect of a subject.

topic sentence. Sentence stating the focus or central idea of a paragraph.

Toulmin model of reasoning. A model of informal argumentation, or practical reasoning, described by Stephen Toulmin, a twentieth-century philosopher, mathematician, and physicist.

transition. A linking of ideas, thoughts, or points; making the connection between clauses, sentences, and/or paragraphs clear.

transitional words. Words that show the connection between ideas, clauses, sentences, and paragraphs.

warrant. According to the Toulmin model of reasoning, the underlying assumptions or inferences that are taken for granted and that connect the claim to the data.

workshop. Similar in intent to a forum, a workshop is characterized by exchanges of information, ideas, and opinions, usually among a small group of people. Both workshops and forums involve interaction and exchange of ideas more than panel discussions, which typically allot more time to panel members than to audience participants.

INDEX